Lecture Notes in Computer Science 4714

Commenced Publication in 1973
Founding and Former Series Editors:
Gerhard Goos, Juris Hartmanis, and Jan van Leeuwen

Gustavo Alonso   Peter Dadam
Michael Rosemann (Eds.)

Business Process Management

5th International Conference, BPM 2007
Brisbane, Australia, September 24-28, 2007
Proceedings

 Springer

Volume Editors

Gustavo Alonso
ETH Zürich, Department of Computer Science
8092 Zürich, Switzerland,
E-mail: alonso@inf.ethz.ch

Peter Dadam
Universität Ulm
Institut für Datenbanken und Informationssysteme
89069 Ulm, Germany
E-mail: peter.dadam@uni-ulm.de

Michael Rosemann
Queensland University of Technology
BPM Group, Faculty of Information Technology
126 Margaret Street, Brisbane Qld 4000, Australia
E-mail: m.rosemann@qut.edu.au

Library of Congress Control Number: 2007935136

CR Subject Classification (1998): H.3.5, H.4.1, H.5.3, K.4.3, K.4.4, K.6, J.1

LNCS Sublibrary: SL 3 – Information Systems and Application, incl. Internet/Web
and HCI

ISSN   0302-9743
ISBN-10   3-540-75182-3 Springer Berlin Heidelberg New York
ISBN-13   978-3-540-75182-3 Springer Berlin Heidelberg New York

Springer is a part of Springer Science+Business Media

springer.com

© Springer-Verlag Berlin Heidelberg 2007

Typesetting: Camera-ready by author, data conversion by Scientific Publishing Services, Chennai, India
Printed on acid-free paper   SPIN: 12163038   06/3180   5 4 3 2 1 0

Preface

The 5th International Conference on Business Process Management (BPM 2007) was held in Brisbane, Australia, on September 25-27, 2007, and organized by the BPM Research Group, Faculty of Information Technology, Queensland University of Technology. The present volume includes the papers accepted for presentation at the main conference. The quantity and quality of paper submissions was again very strong. The papers came from authors located in 41 different countries and were geographically well distributed: 75 papers originated from Europe, 37 from Asia, 17 from the Americas, 18 from Australia, and 5 from Africa.

All papers were reviewed by at least three reviewers and the selection process was extremely competitive. In total, 152 papers have been submitted of which we selected 21 as full research papers and one as an industry paper leading to an acceptance rate of 14.5%. Furthermore, 8 papers have been selected as short papers. In addition to these papers, invited keynote presentations were delivered by Simon Dale, Senior Vice President and Chief Technology Officer, SAP Asia Pacific Japan, Steve Tieman, Vice President Estée Lauder Companies, USA, John Deeb from Oracle Australia and Shawn Bowers from the Genome Center at University of California, Davis, USA. We are very grateful for the contributions of our invited speakers and for the support of the sponsors that facilitated these keynotes.

In particular, we are very appreciative of the tremendous efforts of the members of the carefully selected Program Committee and the additional reviewers. It is only through a thorough review process that the high scientific quality of this conference could be guaranteed. Furthermore, we like to thank the members of the BPM Conference Steering Committee for the valuable guidance along the entire process of organizing this event.

As a preamble to the main conference, a total of six workshops were held. These workshops were selected out of a pool of 20 workshop proposals. The proceedings with all papers of these workshops will be published in a separate volume of Springer's *Lecture Notes in Computer Science* series.

A conference like BPM 2007 can not be organized without the significant support of a number of people. In particular, we like to thank Marlon Dumas for his outstanding contributions as the Organizing Chair of BPM 2007. We also like to thank Helen Paik who was responsible for consolidating these proceedings. Finally, we like to thank Alistair Barros and Justin O'Sullivan (Industrial Co-Chairs), Arthur ter Hofstede and Boulaem Bentallah (Workshop Co-Chairs), Michael Adams and Shazia Sadiq (Demo Co-Chairs), David Edmond (Tutorial Chair), and Michael zur Muehlen and Chengfei Liu (Publicity Co-Chairs) and the many other people who helped with the local organization.

We hope that BPM 2007 provides comprehensive and detailed insights into the current state of the art, sets directions for future research initiatives and can contribute to the transfer of academic knowledge into practical applications.

July 2007
                                                                Gustavo Alonso
                                                                  Peter Dadam
                                                            Michael Rosemann

Organization

The 5th International Conference on Business Process Management (BPM 2007) was organized by the BPM Research Group, Faculty of Information Technology, Queensland University of Technology, Brisbane, Australia.

Executive Committee

General Chair	Michael Rosemann
	(Queensland University of Technology, Australia)
Program Co-Chairs	Gutavo Alonso (ETH Zürich Switzerland)
	Peter Dadam (University Ulm, Germany)
	Michael Rosemann
	(Queensland University of Technology, Australia)
Organization Chair	Marlon Dumas
	(Queensland University of Technology, Australia)
Industrial Co-Chairs	Alistair Barros (SAP Research, Australia)
	Justin O'Sullivan (Suncorp, Australia)
Workshop Co-Chairs	Arthur ter Hofstede
	(Queensland University of Technology, Australia)
	Boualem Bentallah
	(University of New South Wales, Australia)
Demo Co-Chairs	Michael Adams
	(Queensland University of Technology, Australia)
	Shazia Sadiq (University of Queensland, Australia)
Tutorial Chair	David Edmond
	(Queensland University of Technology, Australia)
Publicity Co-Chairs	Michael zur Muehlen
	(Stevens Institute of Technology, USA)
	Chengfei Liu
	(Swinburne University of Technology, Australia)
Proceedings Chair	Hye-young Helen Paik
	(University of New South Wales, Australia)

Program Committee

Wil van der Aalst (The Netherlands)
Karim Baina (Morocco)
Steve Battle (UK)
Jörg Becker (Germany)
Boualem Benatallah (Australia)

Djamal Benslimane (France)
Daniela Berardi (Italy)
M. Brian Blake (USA)
Jorge Cardoso (Portugal)
Malu Castellanos (USA)

Sanjay Chaudhary (India)
Leonid Churilov (Australia)
Francisco Curbera (USA)
Tom Davenport (USA)
Joerg Desel (Germany)
Asuman Dogac (Turkey)
Marlon Dumas (Australia)
Johann Eder (Austria)
Dimitrios Georgakopoulos (USA)
Claude Godart (France)
Peter Green (Australia)
Paul Grefen (The Netherlands)
Kees van Hee (The Netherlands)
Arthur ter Hofstede (Australia)
Rick Hull (USA)
Stefan Jablonski (Germany)
Gerti Kappel (Austria)
Dimitris Karagiannis (Austria)
Haim Kilov (USA)
Frank Leymann (Germany)
Heiko Ludwig (USA)
Zongwei Luo (Hongkong)
Kwang-Hoon Kim (Korea)
Akhil Kumar (USA)
Peri Loucopoulos (UK)
Axel Martens (USA)

Lars Mathiassen (USA)
Mike Papazoglou (The Netherlands)
Cesare Pautasso (Switzerland)
Barbara Pernici (Italy)
Olivier Perrin (France)
Calton Pu (USA)
Frank Puhlmann (Germany)
Udhai Reddy (India)
Manfred Reichert (The Netherlands)
Hajo Reijers (The Netherlands)
Wolfgang Reisig (Germany)
Stefanie Rinderle (Germany)
Shazia Sadiq (Australia)
Wasim Sadiq (Australia)
Heiko Schuldt (Austria)
Sia Siew Kien (Singapore)
Jianwen Su (USA)
Stefan Tai (USA)
Farouk Toumani (France)
Vijay Vaishnavi (USA)
Franck van Breugel (Canada)
Kunal Verma (USA)
Mathias Weske (Germany)
Michal Zaremba (Ireland)
Michael zur Muehlen (USA)

Referees

Said Achchab
Samuil Angelov
Winfried Appl
Danilo Ardagna
Arun (Naga) Ayachitula
Salah Baina
Donald Baker
Taiseera Al Balushi
Wasana Bandara
Robin Bergenthum
Kamal Bhattacharya
Sami Bhiri
Ralph Bobrik
Carmen Bratosin
Jan Bretschneider
Ross Brown

Cinzia Cappiello
Andrzej Cichocki
Gloria Cravo
Gero Decker
Remco Dijkman
Rachid ElMeziane
Derar Eleyan
Rik Eshuis
Dirk Fahland
Joao Ferreira
Hans-Georg Fill
Mariagrazia Fugini
Manolo Garcia-Solaco
Joy Garfield
Andreas Glausch
Thomas Gschwind

Ozgur Gulderen
Christian W. Günther
Hakim Hacid
Danny T. Ho
Janez Hrastnik
Christian Huemer
Peter Höfferer
Yildiray Kabak
Gerrit Kamp
Dimka Karastoyanova
Oliver Kopp
Birgit Korherr
Jochen Kuester
Gokce Banu Laleci
Christoph Langguth
Marek Lehmann
Rong Liu
Niels Lohmann
Robert Lorenz
Linh Thao Ly
Zhilei Ma
Simon Malkowski
Jürgen Mangler
Chris Manning
Peter Massuthe
Sebastian Mauser
Ralph Mietzner
Stefano Modafferi
Thorsten Moeller
Marion Murzek
Enrico Mussi
Bela Mutschler
Dominic Müller
Shin Nakajima
Tuncay Namli
Martin Nemetz
Mariska Netjes
Hamid Reza Motahari Nezhad
Marian Nodine
Paul O'Brien
Alper Okcan
Mehmet Olduz

Umut Orhan
Chun Ouyang
Jarungjit Parnjai
Horst Pichler
Julien Ponge
Michael Predeschly
Jan Recker
Guy Redding
Al Robb
Marcello La Rosa
Terry Rowlands
Nick Russell
Thorsten Scheibler
Helen Schonenberg
Martina Seidl
Alexander Serebrenik
Zhe Shan
Larisa Shwartz
Natalia Sidorova
Jeremy Sproston
Christian Stahl
Tobias Unger
Irene Vanderfeesten
Eric Verbeek
Hagen Voelzer
Laura Voicu
Jochem Vonk
Marc Voorhoeve
Ting Wang
Jinpeng Wei
Edgar Weippl
Jan Martijn van der Werf
Branimir Wetzstein
Matthias Wieland
Manuel Wimmer
Darrell Woelk
Qinyi Wu
Moe Wynn
DongMing Xu
Mustafa Yuksel
Feras Abou Moghdeb

Sponsoring and Endorsing Institutions

 SAP

 QUT

 Suncorp

 IDS Scheer

 Hewlett Packard

 Oracle

 EII ARC Research Network

 Australian Computer Society

 Super EU Project

 EMISA

 WfMC

 Object Management Group

ABPMP

Table of Contents

Compliance and Change

Process Configuration and Execution

Formal Foundations of BPM

Business Process Mining

Semantic Issues in BPM

The Process-Oriented Organisation:
A Holistic View
Developing a Framework for Business Process Orientation Maturity

Peter Willaert, Joachim Van den Bergh, Jurgen Willems,
and Dirk Deschoolmeester

Vlerick Leuven Gent Management School
Reep 1, 9000 Gent, Belgium
{peter.willaert,joachim.vandenbergh,jurgen.willems,
dirk.deschoolmeester}@vlerick.be
www.vlerick.be/bpm

Abstract. Processes are the core of organisations. Business Process Management (BPM) argues organisations can gain competitive advantage by improving and innovating their processes through a holistic process-oriented view. An organisation can be more or less process-oriented depending on their experience in applying process thinking for better results. The aim of this paper is to define a framework for identifying characteristics of Business Process Orientation and to provide a valid tool for measuring the degree of Business Process Orientation (BPO) of an organisation based on empirical research in 30 international organisations. A holistic view on integrated process management and change is taken as a starting point.

Keywords: Business Process Orientation, BPM Success Factors and Measures, BPM Maturity, BPM Governance.

1 Introduction

Processes are at the centre of today's and tomorrow's competition. Organisations have come to the conclusion that efficiency as well as quality and service are to be available in processes. Due to this tendency Business Process Management (BPM) came to light as an attractive management solution for a variety of organisational problems. But what does it really mean to be process-oriented? As organisations accumulate efforts in process improvements they gain experience and develop a process-oriented view. So some organisations will be more mature in such a process view than others. How can an organisation identify whether it is process-oriented or not? Until today only a few models and frameworks exist to describe and measure.

Business Process Orientation. This paper aims to develop a holistic framework for measuring the degree of BPO within an organisation, based on research. In the first section the relevance of Business Process Orientation (BPO) is highlighted. Subsequently a holistic view on BPO is elaborated. In the last section the construct is tested by empirical research, followed by conclusions and avenues for further research.

G. Alonso, P. Dadam, and M. Rosemann (Eds.): BPM 2007, LNCS 4714, pp. 1–15, 2007.

2 Business Process Orientation

2.1 Why Business Process Orientation (BPO)?

Cost reduction is commonly the primary concern for organisations willing to create a sustainable competitive advantage. Still a major attention for bottom line continues to exist but currently customer demands and environmental issues put growing pressure on this classic view on the organisational model [1]. Organisations have to face the fact of changing environments and process management has become an important way to handle this [2]. Therefore agility is a very important success factor for modern organisations. Having an overview of a process allows to easily modify it and proactively look for possible solutions for problems due to deficiencies in the process. So being process-oriented means a more pronounced view on processes but also greater agility for the organisation [3]. The challenge is now to have a flexible and efficient value chain at the same time [1]. Therein lays the relevance of being process-oriented for organisations.

Secondly the ultimate aim of a core business process is to deliver value to the customer. Managing these processes critically improves customer satisfaction whereas functional structures form barriers to customer satisfaction [4].

Thirdly more and more evidence is found showing the strategic value of processes. McCormack and Johnson [5] investigated on Business Process Orientation and found that companies with strong signs of BPO also performed better. The study shows that the development of BPO in an organisation will lead to positive outcomes, both from an internal perspective and a resultant perspective. Business Process Orientation has been shown to reduce inter-functional conflict and increase interdepartmental connectedness and integration, both of which impact long and short-term performance. Moreover the hypothesis stating there is a direct positive impact on self-evaluated business performance is validated in his study as well as the positive relationship of BPO to the long-term health of an organisation. Building BPO into an organisation appears to have significant positive impacts, so it is believed to be worth the investment [5]. The authors also explain that the e-society is a major driver for BPO. E-business and e-collaboration have provoked changes in the organisational landscape especially with regards to cross-organisational cooperation. There are fewer barriers to hamper potential competitors [5]. The study described in this paper has found inspiration in McCormack's research amongst others. Whereas most studies focused on the impact of Business Process Orientation on organisational performance, this paper aims at:

-   elaborating the BPO concept by determining which characteristics and its underlying factors influence the process orientedness of an organisation
-   Validating a scale for assessing a company's process orientation maturity

2.2 BPO Principles

Literature review learns there are several general definitions of BPO. The most extended version was delivered by McCormack and Johnson. "Business Process Orientation of an organisation is the level at which an organisation pays attention to its relevant (core) processes" (end-to-end view across the borders of departments, organisations, countries, etc.) [7] The definition implies that people in the organisation develop a process-driven mindset. According to these authors there are three dimensions to process orientation assessment: Process Management and Measurement, Process Jobs and Process View [5].

1. Process Management and Measurement (PM): There are measures in place that include process aspects such as output quality, cycle time, process cost and variability.
2. Process Jobs (PJ): Process related tasks and roles are defined. E.g. a product development process owner rather than a research manager.
3. Process view (PV): Thorough documentation and understanding from top to bottom and beginning to end of a process exists in the organisation.

In another approach BPMGroup developed the 8 Omega framework as a tool to facilitate the implementation of Business Process Management linking 4 high level dimensions: Strategy, People, Process and Systems to 8 activities in the implementation process [6]. What does it mean to be more or less mature considering BPO? An organisation that has a high maturity is believed to have a more structured approach on Business Process Management. Both 'hard and soft' characteristics of Business Process Orientation are in place. Less mature organisations tend to approach Business Process Management more in an ad hoc way [7]. Finally, another maturity model was developed by Rosemann, de Bruin and Power. In this model 6 factors having an impact on the BPO maturity are defined: Strategic Alignment, Culture, People, Methods,, Governance and IS/IT [8]. A rigorous methodology is applied in this work. The dimensions they used confirm the relevance of a holistic view, although they differ from the dimensions described in this paper.

2.3 Holistic View

It is obvious that changing an organisation's more pervasive habits of functional management into BPO will demand knowledge and skills in several domains. A lot of management disciplines are involved in Business Process Management. This is often referred to as a holistic view on BPM. It embraces parts of Change management, IT management, Project management and deals with a lot of stakeholders such as suppliers, customers, employees and shareholders. According to Burlton the multidisciplinary character as described above is a strength rather than a weakness to BPM [2].

Applying BPO in your organisation requires a holistic approach to the implementation and application of Business Process Management [9]. Fig. 1. A holistic view on BPM' gives an overview of what such a holistic view entails. The central aspect is a continuous improvement cycle or methodology to analyse, redesign and measure processes in order to improve process performance. When applying this methodology, one has to be aware to broaden his view and take into account the company's environment, strategy, values & beliefs, information technology and finally the resistance to change from personnel working in the organisation.

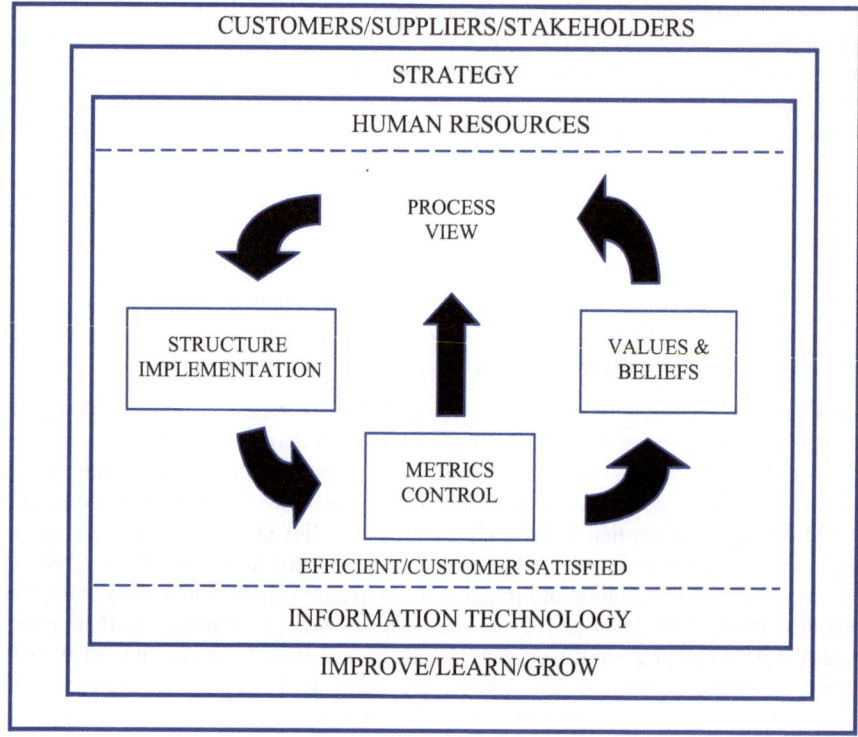

Fig. 1. A holistic view on BPM

The organisation's business processes need to support the overall strategy. In order to do so, introducing a "process" performance measurement system might be helpful (e.g. balanced scorecard, strategy map) in order to align the organisation's activities, and more specific the organisation's processes on the strategy. The most important driver is to make sure that people are being evaluated and rewarded based on 'Key Performance Indicators' (KPI) that contribute to the bottom-line strategy. Both internal efficiency and customer satisfaction must be reflected in the KPIs. Based on KPI measurements, management can find information to redesign and improve processes. Moreover there is not only the need to set up a strategic measuring system, but also a strategic control system that aligns departmental and personal objectives with the strategy on a continuous basis. It is clear that applying BPM has a considerable impact on the people in the organisation. Making a company process-oriented will not only influence logical relationships of the business processes, but on the long run employees also need to take responsibility for their process outcomes. New and different roles will therefore be assigned to the employees.

This shift in responsibilities also has its impact on the organisational structure. A process-oriented organisation tries to organise responsibilities as much as possible horizontally, in addition to the more traditional vertical, hierarchical structure. Task- or process responsibilities that originally belonged to different managers are now being rearranged in a new role or function (sometimes called process owner).

Implementing a process-oriented organisational structure will have no effect if people's mentality does not change accordingly. A more process-centred mindset with people is reflected in the fact that they more often work together with people in other departments in a proactive way. Sharing information and learning more with cross-functional knowledge and teamwork are also characteristics of such a mindset. Evading behaviour with regard to task responsibilities and other dysfunctional habits (which are typical failures in functionally specialised organisations) need to be avoided and make place for a culture of cooperation and strongly imposed customer orientation.

This can only be attained on condition that people are involved and trained in methods for business process improvement. Resistance to change from people is often found to be a barrier for a successful implementation. Therefore effective management of human resources is part of any process improvement initiative. Increasing involvement can only be achieved by communicating a mission and organisational strategy which is meaningful and inspiring, and also by setting up objectives which are not only clear, but also feasible. A management information system which can produce the relevant, actual and useful information, can improve the involvement of employees. Documenting and communicating the business processes is also a means for improving communication across the organisation. The biggest challenge however is to keep this information up-to-date and accessible for everyone who is involved. Strong internal communication on the methodology and achieved results is the key to overall success.

In summary business processes need to be continuously evaluated, improved and implemented in the organisational structure within a supportive framework of human resources and process-oriented information systems. Corporate strategy is the guideline in this model, inspiring a process-minded culture of continuous learning and improvement. The above described holistic view on Business Process Management already contains a lot of characteristics of a process-oriented organisation. In the following paragraphs a model for Business Process Orientation, by means of 8 dimensions and their respective characteristics, is developed and elaborated based on the above proposed holistic view.

3 Research Design

3.1 Business Process Orientation as a Theoretical Construct

Based on the holistic view a theoretical construct for Business Process Orientation was developed. Business Process Orientation (as measured by the respondent's perception) is represented by characteristics grouped in 8 dimensions. These dimensions are produced as a result of literature review, expert interviews, academic visions and case studies within several organisations. The more of these characteristics an organisation shows, the more it will be considered business process-oriented. It is then assumed that being more business process-oriented has a positive effect on organisational performance. However this assumption is not examined in this paper. In the following sections the 8 dimensions will be defined. The following hypotheses were tested:

H1: The degree of customer-orientation is positively related to the degree of BPO.

H2: The degree of process view in an organisation is positively related to the degree of BPO.

H3: The degree of organisational integration characteristics is positively related to the degree of BPO.

H4: The degree of process performance characteristics in an organisation positively related to the degree of BPO.

H5: The degree to which culture, values and beliefs are process-minded is positively related to the degree of BPO.

H6: The degree of people management characteristics in an organisation is positively related to the degree of BPO.

H7: The presence of process supportive information technology in an organisation is positively related to the degree of BPO.

H8: The degree to which an organisation is supplier-oriented is positively related to the degree of BPO.

3.2 Detailed Overview and Description of Components

3.2.1 Customer Orientation (CO)

Customers are the reason of existence for every organisation and will serve as the foundation of BPO. Being process-oriented starts by looking further than the organisational boundaries. Knowing the customers is the starting point, because becoming process-oriented requires a company to adapt its (internal) processes to the different customers and their wishes [10], [11]. This dimension investigates the organisation's ability to understand and assess customer's requirements, and maintain customer relationships. A first discussion that arises is who to consider as a customer. The customer is an entity downstream of the process. Customers can be either internal or external, but eventually the value delivered to the external customer should be optimised [12].

Furthermore customers are valuable information sources for process improvement. An organisation should carefully identify its customers for each process [2, 10, 13, 14 and 15]. In addition Tonchia and Tramontano describe the 'visibility of the final customer' as the greatest achievement of process management. To their views anyone active in a process must be aware of the final aim of the specific process: customer satisfaction [15]. Customer requirements have a dynamic character. Therefore customer oriented organisations have the need for flexible processes, which can be adapted to changing customer expectations [12]. Understanding the customers' expectations allows an organisation to proactively search for improvements in processes to stay ahead of competition. Moreover customer satisfaction has to be measured in a correct way on a regular basis. It can deliver crucial input for process improvements [10, 14]. BPO requires from an organisation to look further than the next department, since process orientation promotes a cross-departmental view on organisations. In many cases intermediate organisations are active in between the next department and the real end-consumer or customer. These can be subsidiaries; a sales office network or any other partner organisation. Considering the fact that these intermediate organisations are the first external customer in the value chain before the consumer, they are the target group looking at customer orientation [14].

3.2.2 Process View (PV)

Adapting the processes to the customer's requirements and wishes requires that everyone in the organisation has a clear view and understanding of the company's processes. This means any employee involved in the process is familiar with process specific terms and has at least notion of the concept 'process orientation'. Good and thorough process documentation is the basis for process performance measurement, analysis and improvement. A process-oriented view requires the presence of sufficient process documentation, the use of this documentation and the company's view and thinking about business processes and process management. McCormack argues that a process view facilitates innovative process improvement initiatives and the implementation of a process-oriented structure [16]. In their study McCormack and Johnson identified process view as a category to assess an organisation's process orientation [5].

It is critical that processes are well identified, defined and mapped in order to select and improve the right process to improve customer value [20]. Therefore process modelling is an important step in the BPM cycle. Preferably processes are visualised in some sort of 'modelling language'. The visualisation of processes in itself can provide organisations with new insights in the complexity of their processes and it is often the first step in a BPM implementation [18].

3.2.3 Organisational Structure (OS)

In order to make process documentation, KPIs and people management useful organisations have to adapt their structure to this process view. Measuring process outcome is not sufficient if no one is held responsible for it. Cross-functional integration efforts need to be formalised in official functions. A vertically oriented company can take actions or initiatives to break through departmental boundaries to become more process-oriented. Typically multidisciplinary teams are assigned to integrate functional structures [16, 19]. Depending on the needs and complexity of the organisation an integration mechanism, such as multidisciplinary teams, can be arranged ad hoc or on a regular basis [20]. In practice very often a role is created to take up responsibility for the horizontal overview of a process. A role which is sometimes referred to as process owner. The process owner or equivalent needs to be given certain decision autonomy and responsibilities with regards to the process. The process owner is accountable and responsible for the outcome of the process, which has direct impact on the customer. The process owner role can be allocated to someone in the hierarchical structure, so it is not necessarily resulting in new managerial functions. Sometimes organisations decide to start up a centre of excellence regarding business processes. This centre is very often referred to as Business Process Office. The Business Process Office or equivalent has the specific skills and knowledge required to set up and manage business process improvement initiatives. This office is often centrally installed on a high level. The process-support organisation was researched and linked to the BPO maturity concept by Willems et al. [21].

The heart of BPM governance is how the company organises its managers to assure that its processes meet its expectations. An organisation that relies entirely on a traditional departmental organisation chart cannot support a process-centric organisational view. There is a natural tension between a departmental approach to structuring an organisation and a process focused approach. A process-oriented organisation is an organisation in which the organisational structure (the organisation chart) is adapted to its processes. This does not mean that a company should be structured completely horizontally, since this would be in conflict with the driving principle of specialisation, which has to be considered as well [16]. Most organisations that are process focused are applying some kind of matrix management model, combining horizontal with vertical, with varying success. Some managers continue to be responsible for departmental or functional groups, like sales, marketing, manufacturing, and new product development however, other managers are responsible for value chains or large scale processes, which creates inevitably confusion and tensions. The perfect balance is yet to be found [10]. How the process and the departmental managers relate to one another varies from one company to another. In some companies specific individuals occupy multiple managerial roles. Thus, one individual might be both the manager of manufacturing and the manager of the end-to-end process.

Also a process-oriented organisation has the need to establish hierarchical structures and process architectures. High level processes are the responsibility of a high level (executive) process owner. A high-level process is then divided into major business processes. These business processes are divided into sub-processes, that all need to be managed by a hierarchical infrastructure of process managers.

3.2.4 Process Performance (PP)

Describing the processes is a large step in becoming process-oriented. However business process improvement requires that the processes are continuously measured and analysed, i.e. defining and implementing performance measures and KPIs that allow executives to monitor processes. One has to be aware that KPIs do not necessarily support the processes, because they are mostly derived from the company's strategy and translated into "departmental" objectives with related KPIs. Such measures usually focus on financial performance or sales volumes, which are typically departmental measures. These are useful measures but they have little information to offer regarding processes. A horizontal process-oriented view on the company also requires related KPIs that also measure cross-departmental process inputs, outputs and outcomes, the so-called process performance measures. Outcome indicators indicate whether the customer is satisfied and profit has been generated whereas output indicators measure the output as it is (e.g. X units per hour) [12].

In order to be able to make sound analysis and take the right process improvement initiatives, a company needs to have a good idea about the performance of its end-to-end business processes. Identifying the right KPIs, measuring them on a regular basis and analysing the data in a correct way forms a basis for taking the right decisions and knowing where the problems in the processes occur. Performance measurement involves defining the concept, selecting components and deciding on how to measure them. Process performance measurement can be a vital tool for strategy execution by signalling what is really important, providing ways to measure what is important, fixing accountability for behaviour and results, and helping to improve performance [22].

3.2.5 Culture, Values and Beliefs (CVB)

The lack of a change supportive culture is often blamed when process improvement actions fail [12]. There is a strong link between work culture and organisational performance [23]. Therefore process orientation has to be part of the organisational culture. Aspects of process orientation, like customer orientation should be reflected in the beliefs, values, and principles that the organisation has publicly committed to. In this section, the mindset for process management and processes in general is assessed. This relates to teamwork, innovative culture, awareness of mission and values of your company, etc. [10].

An important aspect of process orientation with cultural implications is inspiring leadership and executive support. It is the top management's responsibility to direct the organisation towards process orientation. Stimulating interdepartmental and proactive behaviour is key to introducing process orientation [12, 14].

3.2.6 People Management (PM)

People are a company's most important asset. Human capital is a basis for improvement and innovation in processes. Marr *et al.* define: "Human Capital contains knowledge assets provided by employees in forms of skills, competence, commitment, motivation and loyalty as well as in form of advice or tips." [24] Balzarova *et al.* [25] identified 'Training and Learning by doing' and 'Managing resistance to change' as key success factors of implementing process-based management. These are clearly characteristics of people management. In terms of people the big challenge for both line managers and senior managers is to know how changes to a process affect employees. Process orientation implies the development of new skills for the employees. In a process-oriented organisation, people will be identified, evaluated and rewarded based on their competences in understanding and improving processes. Therefore it is required that people are trained and informed to improve processes and to think in terms of processes. Also the ability and willingness to be team players and contributors is very important. People need to have clear goals and incentives to reach these goals [24].

3.2.7 Information Technology (IT)

IT forms a core component of the performance improvement programs of companies. Most processes are enabled by a combination of IT, information and organisational/human resource change. IT is both an enabler and implementer of process change. Attaran [26] considers IT and process management as natural partners. In this dimension it is investigated whether your company has IT systems in place that function as an enabler of your business processes and whether they give the right support for process improvement initiatives. IT systems should be flexible to facilitate process improvements. A process-oriented IT system supports information exchange across departments [9, 10].

More and more IT software vendors provide BPM tools. These tools form a platform for several applications. The integration of applications is very important for process-oriented organisations since the diversity of applications could hamper the integration efforts between departments. Some BPM suites provide a modelling and simulation function which is helpful in the process mapping phase. Other tasks for IT are setting and controlling strategic KPIs. Therefore IT will be even more indispensable in a process-centric organisation. In the end business process management is ultimately a matter of human resources where IT can play an important facilitating role.

3.2.8 Supplier Perspective (SP)

Although there is more pressure on suppliers to anticipate needs, respond to them, and perform better than in the past, there are also pressures on customers to treat their suppliers consistently well and to cooperate in order to smoothen the processes. In this section, orientation towards the suppliers of your organisation is assessed.

Processes clearly extend the organisational borders in today's economy. As technology evolves, boundaries fade and suppliers become partners. Sharing information and knowledge with suppliers is a characteristic of process orientation [15]. Partnerships are arising everywhere on the global business community. The fast deployment of the internet has induced e-business and e-collaboration. Online platforms are shared with suppliers in order to manage processes in a much more efficient and faster way. Consider organisations as part of a larger system. This 'system view' delivers insight in the interactions with both customers and suppliers and other involved stakeholders. Lee et al. argue that process models should encompass these interactions within the value chain. Also information sharing with suppliers is considered important for effective process management [27]. The 'Extended Enterprise' concept is one example of dissolving organisational borders. It says that organisations are not limited to their employees and managers but that they include partners, customers, suppliers and other potential stakeholders. The supplier is often neglected, although good relations with suppliers add value to the processes. Streamlining a process includes good supplier management as they deliver crucial resources or inputs for processes [14].

4 Validation of the BPO Construct

4.1 Data Collection and Cleaning

Data were gathered in two consecutive rounds respectively in June 2006 and between October and December 2006. Participating companies were selected on an ad hoc basis. The sample consists of a balanced set of both small and large companies. Organisations from different sectors were asked to participate. As a result a set of 30 companies was developed. The respondents for each company had to be management level and from different departmental backgrounds. The survey ended up with a total of 725 unfiltered responses. The first step was to clean the gathered data in order to prepare them for analysis. After elimination 595 valid individual results were left for statistical analysis.

4.2 Scale Development

The authors developed a questionnaire assessing the indicators of process orientation based on the 8 dimensions in the proposed holistic BPO model. The items were created as a result of profound literature research, the authors' experience and information obtained from interviews with experts and practitioners. In total the questionnaire consisted of 72 questions. This number also includes additional questions to measure the participant's perception of the level of process orientation in his/her organisation and to assess the impact of BPM projects in the present and the future. Ultimately, specifications on the characteristics of the participant's organisation and function were asked. All questions assessing the level of BPO were measured using a 7 point Likert-scale (1 being "strongly disagree", 4 being "Neither agree nor disagree", 7 being "strongly agree"). The perception of the BPO level was measured using a 10 point scale.

4.3 Statistical Data Analysis

Reliability analysis and Correlation analysis
The reliability of each dimension was statistically tested using Cronbach's alpha[1]. Alpha showed values higher than 0,7 on all dimensions which means all dimensions have consistent items.

Table 1. Reliability analysis for the BPO model dimensions

	Cronbach's alpha	N
CO	0,769	10
PV	0,837	9
OS	0,806	8
PP	0,899	11
CVB	0,815	10
PM	0,812	7
IT	0,811	6
SP	0,891	7

Alpha increases to 0,829 for the OS dimension when item OS8 is removed. This means that question OS8 varies differently from the other questions in the organisational structure dimension. Therefore this item does not fit in the OS dimension. OS8 refers to business process outsourcing. All items/questions within each dimension should be correlated in order to have a consistent set of questions in the dimensions. Analysis of the inter-item correlations revealed low correlation between OS8 and the other OS items. Apart from OS all dimensions showed strong inter-item correlations.

Factor analysis
Having defined the 8 dimensions of the BPO model factor analysis was executed to test the relevance of the dimensions proposed and possibly detect other underlying factors with a significant influence on organisational BPO maturity. The aim is to develop the model and questionnaire into a complete and trustworthy process orientation assessment tool. The use of factor analysis on this survey needs to be explored by executing the 'Bartlett test of sphericity' and the 'Kaiser-Meyer-Olkin

---

[1] Cronbach's alpha: "Alpha is defined as the proportion of a scale's total variance that is attributable to a common source, presumably the true score of a latent variable underlying the items." [28] Preferably alpha should be higher than 0,7. Alpha is a value between 0 and 1.

measure of sampling adequacy'[2]. The KMO-index is higher than 0,7 for all dimensions. It is decided that it is appropriate to apply factor analysis. The method for factor analysis chosen was the Principal component method. The resulting factor loading matrix was Varimax (Variance of square loadings Maximalised) rotated. The criterion to decide on the number of factors was eigenvalue > 1,000. SPSS analysis led to 14 significant factors to be explained. These 14 factors cumulatively explained 59,607 % of total variance. The latent variable or underlying construct of the survey is the perceived BPO score, measured in question 14 of the questionnaire. The 8 dimensions and their respective subsets of questions are the variables presumably influencing the BPO score.

Regression analysis
Predicting power of the questionnaire is revealed by Linear Regression analysis. The hypothesis to be tested here is whether one of the coefficients is zero. The b-coefficients represent the influence each dimension has on the model. Significance has to be below the 0,05 level. General perception, scored by each participant, was taken as dependent variable. The average scores on the 8 dimensions of the model were inserted as independent variables. The model can be formulated as follows:

Employee General Perception of BPO $= b_0 + b_1 AVG(CO) + b_2 AVG(PV) + b_3 AVG(OS) + b_4 AVG(PP) + b_5 AVG(CVB) + b_6 AVG(PM) + b_7 AVG(IT) + b_8 AVG(SP) + \varepsilon$ (ε represents the residual)

Table 2. Regression analysis, SPSS Output

		Unstandardized Coefficients		Standardized Coefficients	T	Sig.
		B	Std. Error	Beta		
1	(Constant)	-1,350	0,352		-3,840	0,000
	AverageCO	0,108	0,077	0,050	1,405	0,161
	AveragePV	0,288	0,071	0,166	4,086	0,000
	AverageOS	0,191	0,071	0,108	2,679	0,008
	AveragePP	0,367	0,072	0,225	5,079	0,000
	AverageCVB	0,143	0,079	0,062	1,814	0,070
	AveragePM	0,160	0,066	0,092	2,427	0,016
	AverageIT	0,296	0,056	0,183	5,282	0,000
	AverageSP	0,154	0,060	0,088	2,556	0,011

a Dependent Variable: General Perception.

As a result of the ANOVA (Analysis of Variance) test, the hypothesis can be rejected with a significance level of 0,000 . So at least one of the coefficients is

---

[2] The significance of the Bartlett test needs to be less than 0,05 in order to reject the hypothesis, which means factor analysis can be executed. The KMO measure is a value between 0 and 1 and needs to be higher than 0,5 and preferably higher than 0,7.

different from zero. Therefore analysis by dimension is executed. It is observed in table 2 that the CO dimension has a significance level slightly higher than 0,05. This means that the CO dimension has low, insignificant predicting power for the model. The CVB dimension also has a significance level higher than 0,05. Again this means this dimension has insignificant predicting power concerning the dependent variable.

R Square is calculated as 0.557 which means the model as a whole has a predicting power of 55,7% as shown in table 3. In other words a total of 55,7% of the variation in the dependent variable General BPO perception is explained by the variation in the independent variables of the model. Adjusted R Square, which includes a correction of R Square for the number of independent variables, still shows 55% predicting power. Thus hypotheses 2,3,4,6,7 and 8 are supported by the regression analysis. There is no statistical support for hypotheses 1 and 5.

Table 3. SPSS Output Linear Regression Analysis

Model	R	R Square	Adjusted R Square	Std. Error of the Estimate
1	0,746(a)	0,557	0,551	1,184

a Predictors: (Constant), AverageSP, AveragePV, AverageCVB, AverageIT, AverageCO, AveragePM, AverageOS, AveragePP.

5 Conclusions and Avenues for Future Research

In the attempt to construct a model for Business Process Orientation a few interesting conclusions came to light. Statistical analysis validated the predicting power of the PV, OS, PP, PM, IT and SP dimensions that were believed to define the indicators of Business Process Orientation. Therefore this research contributes to a better understanding of the different aspects involved in being process-oriented. BPO requires a broader perspective than quality or IT for instance. Being process-oriented is in other words a matter of mastering a whole range of techniques and principles in order to improve business processes and organisational performance. It is the authors' believe that an integrated effort to improve these domains leads to increased BPO in an organisation.

Correlation analysis and Cronbach's alpha showed that all dimensions have internal consistency. There is no statistical evidence for the influence of the CO and CVB dimensions. Several explanations are possible. Therefore it is suggested to revise and restructure both dimensions and proceed to a new data collection round. It is important to keep in mind that this study has a static character and does not exclude the influence of dynamic factors nor the influence of personal opinions.

It is suggested that process outsourcing could be treated as a dimension apart from the OS dimension or excluded from the survey. Factor analysis revealed 14 factors significantly influencing the degree of BPO. To a certain extent these factors overlap with the dimensions defined in this paper. The presence of some other factors can be explained. An important observation is that factor analysis revealed the distinction between a customer complaints factor, a customer satisfaction and requirements factor, and a factor probing for process-related communication with the customer. In future research the presumed positive relation between BPO and organisational performance has to be tested in order to complete the model. Another topic for future research based on the survey could be a study on the influence of company-specific characteristics such as size and sector on the degree of BPO.

This study shows that BPO as a concept should be considered from a holistic, multidisciplinary perspective. The degree to which an organisation is process-oriented is influenced by aspects of several domains described in this paper. The practical value of this research lays in its relevance for organisations wanting to assess their process-orientedness. Furthermore the framework helps to understand the dynamics of process improvement.The proposed holistic approach has proven to be valuable and allows for identifying domains on which to focus when prioritising BPM initiatives.

References

1. Buciuman-Coman, V., Sahlean, A.G.: The dynamically stable enterprise: engineered for change, BPMGroup. In: search of BPM Excellence: Straight from the thought leaders, Meghan-Kiffer Press, Tampa (2005)
2. Burlton, R.T.: Business Process Management: Profiting from process, SAMS, Indianapolis (2001)
3. Smith, H., Fingar, P.: Business Process Management: The third wave. Meghan-Kiffer Press, Tampa (2003)
4. Zairi, M.: Business Process Management: a boundaryless approach to modern competitiveness. Business Process Management Journal 3(1), 64–80 (1997)
5. McCormack, K.P., Johnson, W.C.: Business Process Orientation: Gaining the e-business competitive advantage. CRC Press, Boca Raton (2001)
6. Towers, S., Lyneham-Brown, D., Schurter, T., McGregor, M.: 8 Omega, BPMGroup. In: search of BPM Excellence: Straight from the thought leaders, Meghan-Kiffer Press, Tampa (2005)
7. Harmon, P.: Evaluating an Organization's Business Process Maturity. Business Process Trends 2(3), 1–11 (2004), online available on: http://www.caciasl.com/pdf/BPtrendLevelEval1to5.pdf
8. Rosemann, M., de Bruin, T., Power, B.: BPM Maturity. In: Jeston, J., Nelis, J. (eds.) Business Process Management: Practical Guidelines for Successful Implementations, Elsevier, Oxford (2006)
9. Hung, R.Y.: Business Process Management as Competitive Advantage: a review and empirical study. Total Quality Management 17(1), 21–40 (2006)
10. Davenport, T.H.: Process Innovation: Reengineering Work Through Information Technology. Ernst & Young. Harvard Business School Press, Boston (1993)
11. Harmon, P.: Business process change: a manager's guide to improving, redesigning and automating processes. Morgan Kaufmann, San Francisco (2003)
12. Tenner, A.R., DeToro, I.J.: Process Redesign: the implementation guide for managers. Prentice Hall, New Jersey (2000)
13. Hammer, M.: Beyond Reengineering: How the Process-Centered Organization is Changing Our Lives. HarperBusiness, New York (1996)
14. Harrington, H.J.: Business Process Improvement: the breakthrough strategy for total quality, productivity and competitiveness. McGraw-Hill, USA (1991)

15. Tonchia, S., Tramontano, A.: Process Management for the extended enterprise: Organisational and ICT Networks. Springer, Berlin (2004)
16. McCormack, K.P., Johnson, W.C., Walker, W.T.: Supply Chain networks and business process orientation. CRC Press, Boca Raton (2003)
17. Rummler, G.A., Ramias, A.J., Rummler, R.A.: Potential Pitfalls on the Road to a Process Managed Organization (PMO), Business Process Trends 2(3) (2006)
18. DeToro, I., McCabe, T.: How to stay flexible and elude fads. Quality Progress 30(3), 55–60 (1997)
19. Byrne, J.A.: The horizontal corporation Business Week, 76–81 (1993)
20. Galbraith, J.R.: Designing Organizations, an executive briefing on strategy, structure, and process. Jossey-Bass Publishers, San Francisco (1995)
21. Willems, J., Willaert, P., Deschoolmeester, D.: Setting up a business process-support organisation: the role of a business process office. In: Information Resources Management Association, International Conference (2007) (forthcoming)
22. Willaert, P., Willems, J., Deschoolmeester, D., Viaene, S.: Process Performance Measurement: Identifying KPI's that link process performance to company strategy. In: Paper presented at the International Resources Management Association (IRMA) Conference 2006 held in Washington, D.C. (May 21-24, 2006)
23. Kotter, J.P., Heskett, J.L.: Corporate culture and performance. The Free Press, New York (2003)
24. Marr, B., Schiuma, G.: Business performance measurement - past, present and future. Management Decision 41(8), 680–687 (2003)
25. Balzarova, M.A., Bamber, C.J., McCambridge, S., Sharp, J.M.: Key success factors in implementation of process-based management: A UK housing association experience. Business Process Management Journal 10(4), 387–399 (2004)
26. Attaran, M.: Information technology and business-process redesign. Business Process Management Journal 9(4), 440–458 (2003)
27. Lee, S.M., Olson, D.L., Trimi, S., Rosacker, K.M.: An integrated method to evaluate business process alternatives. Business Process Management Journal 11(2), 198–212 (2005)
28. DeVellis, R.F.: Scale Development: theory and applications. Sage Publications, Newbury Park (1991)

Challenges in Business Performance Measurement: The Case of a Corporate IT Function

Stephen Corea[1] and Andy Watters[2]

[1] Information Systems Group, Warwick Business School, University of Warwick, Coventry, CV4 7AL, United Kingdom
steve.corea@wbs.ac.uk
[2] SAP, Feltham, Middlesex, TW14 8HD United Kingdom
andy.watters@sap.com

Abstract. Contemporary organisations are increasingly adopting performance measurement activity to assess their level of achievement of strategic objectives and delivery of stakeholder value. This qualitative research sought to increase understanding of the challenges involved in this area. An in-depth case study of the corporate IT services unit of a global company highlighted key challenges pertaining to: (i) deriving value from performance measurement practices; (ii) establishing appropriate and useful performance measures; (iii) implementing effective information collation and dashboard practices. The need to transform performance measurement from a tool for simply monitoring/reporting to one of learning what factors drive results (so as to be able to influence these factors) is suggested as a way to increase the value derived from such practices. This is seen to imply a need to rethink major notions of balance and strategic relevance that have been advanced hitherto as leading design principles.

Keywords: Performance measurement, dashboards, IT evaluation, strategy.

1 Introduction

Business performance measurement refers to practices of collecting and presenting relevant information to a company's management staff, as a means of assessing the firm's progress towards achieving its strategic aims (Kennerley & Neely, 2003). Information technology software known as executive information systems (EIS) are often the mechanism used for capturing and delivering appropriately formatted data to inform such evaluation and decision-making (Watson & Frolick, 1993). Typically, the performance information is presented on 'dashboard' screens. Dashboards are visual interfaces on which easy-to-read textual or graphical representations of measurement data is displayed to management staff. These software interfaces usually allow staff to drill down data i.e. to move from higher levels of summarised information to lower levels of more detailed, finely granulated data (Frolick & Ariyachandra, 2006).

Adopting formal performance measurement systems around the use of dashboards has become increasingly commonplace among contemporary organisations. Given the heightened competitive pressures they face, and the need for improved responsiveness

G. Alonso, P. Dadam, and M. Rosemann (Eds.): BPM 2007, LNCS 4714, pp. 16–31, 2007.

to customers, it is imperative for firms to be able to monitor and assess their level of advancement towards strategic objectives and delivery of stakeholder value (Johnson, 1983; Kennerley & Neely, 2003). Recent theoretical developments in this IS research area have produced several sophisticated performance measurement frameworks, such as the balanced scorecard approach (Kaplan & Norton, 1992), aimed at helping firms to tackle this important requirement.

It may be perceived, however, that much of these recent theoretical developments have tended to be prescriptive or normative in nature, referring to idealised models of performance measurement. Correspondingly, there appears to have been insufficient research studies geared towards illuminating the difficulties or problems companies face *in situ*, in their attempts to mount such practices under operational conditions and constraints. This inadequacy needs to be redressed, as many organisations appear to face major challenges in implementing dashboard based performance measurement systems. McCunn (1998) suggests up to 70% of performance management initiatives in companies fail to take root or adequately deliver anticipated benefits.

This exploratory study thus sought to increase current understanding of critical challenges that can arise when organisations apply measurement practices around the use of dashboard systems. In particular, while many past studies have tended to adopt a top-down perspective on such practices by emphasising their derivation from the standpoint of overarching formal measurement frameworks (Kaplan & Norton, 1992; Neely et al., 2001), this research adopted a bottom-up perspective by looking at the challenges affecting the design/use of the dashboards themselves, and the implications which they raise regarding the over-arching measurement principles they embody. An in-depth case study inquiry was made of dashboard based performance measurement practices within the corporate IT unit of a large multi-national organisation. The main difficulties and shortcomings characterising this unit's efforts were seen to illustrate key issues in this arena, and are critically discussed to suggest concerns and questions that future studies may investigate further as a basis of theoretical development.

2 Literature Review

This section undertakes a brief review of key aspects of the nature of performance measurement and use of management dashboards, that past studies have emphasised. This includes coverage of the design of performance measures/metrics, which is seen to be fundamental to an effective system.

2.1 Performance Measurement

Traditional methods of assessing organisational performance have predominantly stressed the use of financial measures such as return on investment (Johnson, 1983). During the 1980s, however, realisation grew that such traditional methods were no longer sufficient for organisations competing in highly competitive, dynamic markets (Johnson & Kaplan, 1987). The limitations of traditional approaches to performance measurement were exposed by numerous studies, which suggested that such efforts: lacked strategic focus and were inadequate for strategic decision-making (Skinner, 1974; Kaplan & Norton, 1992); provided scant information on root causes (Ittner & Larcker, 1998); offered only historical backward-looking views of performance, while lacking predictive ability to explain future performance (Ittner & Larcker, 1998); failed to link non-financial metrics to financial numbers (Kaplan & Norton, 1992); were unable to account for intangible assets (Bukowitz & Petrash, 1997); measured created value ineffectively (Lehn & Makhija, 1996); merely reported functional, not cross functional, processes (Ittner & Larcker, 1998); and, tended to have too many financial measures that did not aggregate well from the operational to the strategic level (Kaplan & Norton, 1992).

The main recognition which emerged was that a robust performance measurement system should take a 'balanced' approach (i.e. taking into account both financial and non-financial factors), and enable the presentation of holistic, relevant information for reviewing performance and identifying areas of improvement. This principle was well embodied within the Balanced Scorecard Approach (Kaplan & Norton, 1992), which underscored the need to take into account non-financial dimensions of organisational functioning such as the customer perspective, or the ability of a firm to develop its human assets through staff learning or knowledge management. Other contemporary frameworks that aim at this principle are the Performance Prism (Neely et al., 2001), and the Integrated Performance Measurement Framework (Medori & Steeple, 2000).

A key area of consideration in implementing such frameworks is the identification of performance measures or metrics (also known in business parlance as KPIs, key performance indicators). The efficacy of measurement systems ultimately rest on the quality of the measures used, which should be regularly evaluated to ensure ongoing validity. However organisations often struggle to identify such metrics that accurately capture progress toward goal attainment (Neely et al., 1997). Numerous researchers have discussed this challenge of definition. Lea and Parker (1989) assert that metrics must be transparent and visible to all, simple to understand, have visual impact, and focus on improvements rather than variance. With regard specifically to measures for IT performance evaluation, Stanwick and Stanwick (2005) suggested a spread across three different categories: (i) efficiency i.e. how effectively IT reduces overall costs of operations; (ii) effectiveness i.e. ability of IT to increase overall value to customers and suppliers; and (iii) productivity i.e. ability to increase the level of work output per employee. Neely et al (1997) summarised diverse studies in this area and identified the twenty-two most cited considerations when designing a performance measure.

A strong injunction made by many researchers (e.g. Kaplan & Norton, 1992; Cross & Lynch, 1990, De Toni & Tanchia, 2001) is that performance measurement should be grounded in strategy: a clear organisational strategy, and associated objectives or targets, must be determined before any measurement activities begun. The strategic aims must then translate into specific measures and indicators that directly address the performance area in question. Without clearly specified objectives providing clarity on what constitutes success in relation to a certain strategy, practices of performance measurement are seen to be of little value to management.

Reflecting a requirement raised by several researchers that some measures should be predictive, Eckerson (2006) proposed the need for any performance measurement system to incorporate a high proportion of 'leading indicators', which refer to drivers and predictors of traditional business targets termed in turn as 'lagging indicators'. The concepts of leading and lagging indicators can be challenging to grasp and apply. Lagging indicators denote past activity. Conventional organisational measures/KPIs are usually lag indicators: action is taken, then the target is reached (i.e. lags behind);

hence past activity is being measured. In contrast, leading indictors represent factors *driving* the move towards the target, thus predicting future performance. For example, within a typical sales environment, monitoring yearly sales targets is a key practice, and most firms report on their monthly progress towards their annual target. Such a metric (i.e. monthly sales) exemplifies a classic lagging indicator: the measured result follows (or lags behind) other prior activities, such as telephone calls to prospective clients, meetings with clients, and quotes issued. Such activities, if measured (i.e. no. of calls, meetings, quotes), would thus constitute the leading indicators (or predictors) of the monthly or yearly sales targets (i.e. more telephone calls equates to more client meetings; more meetings equates to more opportunities to issue quotes for products; more quotes equates to more sales; more sales mean targets are met).

2.2 Dashboard Design and Use

Performance measurement systems must have visual impact (Lea & Parker, 1989). The term dashboard has been coined to denote the interface or mechanism enabling graphical representation of a performance measurement system. Few (2005) defines a dashboard as a visual display of the most important pieces of information needed to achieve one or more objectives, that have been consolidated and arranged on a single screen so they can be monitored at a glance. Dashboards are aimed at aiding decision makers in managing behaviour and setting expectations, and thus their design needs to be given proper consideration. Measures should be presented in a hierarchical manner to ensure the right information gets to the right organisational level, and information should be in a concise easy to digest format. Few (2005) recommends dashboards should encompass the following features: simple graphics for ease of digestion; key emphasis on summaries and exceptions; information finely customised for the task; presentation of measures in different states and a time-series form to highlight trends; drill-down capabilities, enabling consumers to observe root causes and underlying factors of change in performance (or progress to targets).

3 Methodology

This exploratory study aimed at deriving greater understanding of key challenges and critical management issues surrounding the delivery of performance measurement practices in companies. The interpretive case study method (Klein & Myers, 1999; Walsham, 1995), which is suitable for eliciting an in-depth understanding regarding how challenges arise in a contemporary real-life setting, was adopted as the research strategy. The corporation in which this research was conducted, called Multicorp (a pseudonym), is a large multi-national manufacturer of cigarettes and other tobacco-based products, with factories in over fifty countries. This research focussed solely on the operations and performance measurement activity of one major business unit in Multicorp's operations: namely, its centralised corporate IT function, known as GITS (Group IT Services). GITS had been recently formed in 2004. It is made up of over 500 staff in eight departments.

Semi-structured interviews, focussed on the nature and challenges of performance measurement in GITS, constituted the main basis of inquiry. Twenty-seven interviews (backed by informal conversations) were held with a significant range of management staff and stakeholders over a three-month period from June to August 2006. These interviews typically lasted around forty-five minutes to an hour, and were aided by a set of open-ended questions and probes which addressed a range of aspects, including the nature and use of the performance measurement system, the definition and utility of measures/metrics, the design and presentation of dashboards, and their population and maintenance. In addition, company documentation was also consulted for further corroboration. Data from interviews and fieldnotes was inductively analysed using the constant comparative method (Glaser & Strauss, 1967): subjected to repeated scrutiny to identify patterned regularities in the form of common themes, issues or dilemmas. In the following account of the case findings, some figures of financial performance data (e.g. amount of cost savings) have been omitted to preserve anonymity.

4 Case Analysis and Findings

This section begins with a background description of the structure and operations of GITS (Group IT Services) and its parent firm Multicorp, followed by an analysis of the dashboards and performance measurement practices at GITS. Key challenges and shortcomings characterising these practices are identified.

4.1 Operational Background and Strategy

Multicorp is a major manufacturer of cigarettes and other tobacco-based products, with a portfolio of over 300 brands sold in 180 'end-markets' (i.e. country-specific regions), and factories in fifty-four countries. The geographic makeup of the industry is shifting: the volume of cigarettes smoked in Western countries is declining, while Eastern European and Asian markets are growing. On the whole however, this mature industry remains stable: the number of smokers worldwide is not expected to change significantly in the next fifteen years. With static volumes and predicted revenues, the challenge of providing continuous value to shareholders is therefore strongly seen as one of achieving greater efficiency. This gave rise to the present corporate strategy in Multicorp, aimed at delivering significant cost savings across the business, especially in support activities. As a result, several cost-saving initiatives have been initiated.

One key initiative involves a move away from traditional IT services provision, in which operating entities around the globe carry local responsibility for all aspects of IT, to a centralised, 'shared services' model, intended to lever substantial cost savings via economies of scale. Accordingly, Group Information Technology Services (GITS) was formed in 2004 as the unit responsible for global IT delivery. Its role is to migrate Multicorp from its present geographically-led, end-market IT units to a functionally-led and centralised IT supply side operation by 2009. Cost savings of £100 million are expected from the move. Since its inception GITS has therefore been assimilating and rationalising IT provision from Multicorp's business units worldwide.

GITS is structured in terms of three main client-facing units (Application Services, Technical Services and Customer Services) underpinned by several support functions. It is led by a 10-member management team, made up of the general manager and the subordinate managers of functional departments, who assume overall responsibility for GITS strategy and functioning, and report ultimately to Multicorp's CIO. GITS' business vision of delivering 'Irresistible Value' is underpinned by a strategy focussed on the following aspects: (i) the planned transfer of all end-market IT services over to GITS management by 2009 (i.e. so delivering the volume of services by which cost savings can be achieved); (ii) the improvement of existing service quality processes in order to meet a customer service score of at least 4.5 out of 5; (iii) cost savings, via centralisation and the move to an outsourced IT service model; and (iv) the ongoing development of talent appropriate for being a leading shared services organisation (an annual survey of staff skills and morale, known as the 'Staff Development Survey', is used to assess this).

4.2 Dashboard and Measurement Practices

The dynamic nature of operations at GITS, which is rapidly expanding in terms of headcount, geographic spread and scope of services, has meant that monitoring of its performance against ambitious strategic targets has become increasingly critical. One manager noted: "Two years ago GITS had less than 100 staff, the management team could sit in a room and discuss in detail operational issues throughout the department. Now we're more than 500 strong, and are doing far more things. We haven't a clue what is going on out there, and don't know what operational things we should be looking at." However, there has been limited systemisation hitherto in terms of the performance measurement practices at GITS. No formal comprehensive measurement framework or method has been adopted for informing the definition, monitoring and reporting of performance. Although clear departmental targets have been set, there is little sense in most of the departments of performance measurement as being a formal process or system: there is a lack of policy or procedure for reporting progress against targets on a monthly basis, and no reference to the term 'performance measurement' in operational documents. Only two departments, Application Services and Technical Services, have each set up a dashboard as a reporting mechanism. In the management team the use of a dashboard, the Leadership dashboard, has only recently emerged.

An evaluation of these dashboards (as they were at the time of this study in mid-2006) is undertaken next, beginning in each case with a brief account of their design and maintenance, and followed by an evaluation of their utility and features.

GITS Leadership Dashboard
The GITS Leadership dashboard is the newest of the three, having first appeared in May 2006. It is a Microsoft PowerPoint presentation of about 15 slides with graphical displays of performance data. It was developed in the spring of 2006 at the behest of the general manager, who identified the need for using it to inform management team meetings, and to demonstrate progress towards departmental targets to staff members. Responsibility for the Leadership dashboard's creation and population was delegated to an administrative assistant in the finance department: for whom no guidance was given regarding its content, and no formal procedure instituted for regular updating, review or dissemination. This administrator explained its construction as a matter of expediency, rather than one of clear planning: "I put together the dashboard based on GITS targets and what I thought the leadership team needed to see ... I put together the dashboard once a month, but there isn't a specific date for me to complete it by."

Its population was viewed as a cumbersome, time-consuming activity. While most of the required data is readily available, information owners are spread across functional units across the globe. With no top-down mandate requiring them to supply the data, the administrator struggles to obtain updates in a timely manner: "I don't think they take it seriously. It can take two or three days to get even a simple piece of info."

The summary screen of the dashboard (the first of the PowerPoint slides) is shown in Figure 1. Given its recent construction and prolonged data refreshment process, the dashboard had only seen sparing use at management meetings in the summer of 2006. In fact, a few team members were unaware of its existence at the time of study: "I was not aware that there was a leadership dashboard...and looking at it now, to be honest it is of little use to me." Feedback from interviews with management team members evinced that on the whole its value as a tool was notably restricted. Seventy percent of them expressed doubts as to the accuracy and timeliness of the data. The limitation of the dashboard's utility was also perceived to stem from two other key factors: (i) the lack of predictive data; and (ii) inadequacies of performance measures.

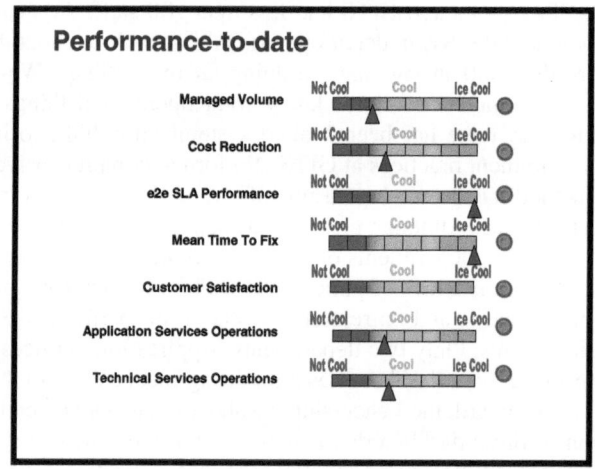

Fig. 1. Summary screen of GITS Leadership dashboard[1]

The Leadership dashboard focuses on the reporting of progress against the annual strategic targets at GITS. The only performance measures reported in this dashboard are those indicating how far GITS has moved towards a given target in this period. This reflects the focus of the managed team on achieving the specified targets, which are clearly linked to personal objectives and bonus payments: "We need to know how we're doing against the targets – that is what we are bonused on." No provision had been made, however, for data having predictive ability or indicating recent trends. Almost all the measures displayed on the Leadership dashboard are 'lagging' rather

---

[1] In this summary screen (Figure 1), performance data is seen a graphically scale that is indicative of 'cool targets' (GITS' specified targets for the year) and 'ice cool targets' (specified stretch targets i.e. targets set in the hope, rather than expectation, they will be reached: a bonus usually follows achievement).

than 'leading' indicators. This was seen by several managers to preclude their ability to clearly understand the factors shaping performance in these areas: (i) "I've no idea what drives the numbers .... I'm not sure if anyone has"; (ii) "The main drivers of the targets?....you tell me!"

A separate shortcoming is that many of the graphs and charts, intended to show progress against targets, were not clearly labelled to indicate what the targets were, on the assumption that managers already knew this information. However, this was seen by some staff to presume too much on their ability to retain and recall all such targets.

Another area of apparent difficulty concerned the choice of performance measures for assessing progress towards strategic targets. The strategic objectives set for GITS in 2006, grouped under three areas, were as follows: (i) *Financial targets*: additional sum of revenue from the transfer of end-market services to centralised GITS control; amount of cost savings from economies of scale enabled by this transfer; (ii) *Quality targets*: a customer satisfaction score (CSS) of 3.6 in the year-end CSS survey; an average 99.75% (worldwide) availability on key systems through the year; an average worldwide Mean Time to Fix (MTTF) for key systems of less than 9 hours; training 2 Six Sigma 'black belts' and 10 'green belts' by end of the year; (iii) *People targets*: a 'Staff Development Survey' score of more than 22 in the year-end survey; the training of line managers in client facing areas to Six Sigma 'green belt' status.

There was evidence of lack of clarity and standardisation on the definition of some of these measures. For example, the financial target measuring the achievement of full GITS control over services seemed straightforward, being based on identifying how much additional volume has been transferred to GITS the previous month. However, the definition of what constitutes a transfer of volume was unclear, with two differing versions in currency among the managers: (i) "We count managed volume against our target only when services have been transferred to GITS, and the first invoice sent to the end-market"; versus (ii) "Managed volume is just that: services which we (GITS) manage. It doesn't matter if we haven't billed the customer yet."

Another example concerns cost savings (the second financial target) which refers to the amount of money GITS commits to save its customers (the end- markets) in the next financial year. This is measured on the basis of how much GITS has progressed to its target, for next year's savings, in a given period. There are two types of cost saving: (i) Savings related to a service which GITS is currently providing, and which it commits to providing at lower cost to its customers in the next financial year; and (ii) A service not currently provided to an end-market by GITS, but which will be provided from 1st January, at a cost less than that currently paid by the end-market. While these definitions of cost savings are uniformly agreed, the method for assessing progress to this target is not standardised, with two differing versions offered: (i) "We claim that we have achieved a cost saving when we sign a contract with an outsource provider to provide the service at a cost lower next year than our current deal."; (ii) "Cost savings are claimed when we release next years' price list to the end markets: in May, with confirmation in early December."

Some of the measures incorporated in the dashboard also did not appear to be the most appropriate candidates to reflect performance. For example, the financial targets result in the reporting of volume of services provided in terms of revenue size, as well as cost reductions for the users of those service. However they are not an indication of the actual profit or loss incurred by GITS, and so provide a misleading or incomplete picture of financial status. These measures can be augmented: "Service line profit and loss: yes, we have that data, but it isn't included in the current dashboard." Another instance of inadequacy concerns the Quality target of getting a customer satisfaction score of 3.6 by year-end. Progress towards this target is only measured in a year-end survey: there are no interim measures of satisfaction. GITS recently begun a project to develop such an interim assessment process, however at present it is not possible to track progress towards this target within a given period.

The array of measures currently represented on the Leadership dashboard also left some key areas of performance untracked. For example, there was no performance data relating to Six Sigma training objectives being reported in the dashboard, despite it being available and singularly owned by the Service Improvement department: the administrator who created the dashboard had decided it was not worth showing to the management team. There were also no measurement data on the Staff Development Survey score. An opportunity to introduce 'leading indicators' for that target was also perceived to exist here, in terms of specific skill development initiatives undertaken to address areas of concern raised by staff in the 2005 staff survey. The progress of such initiatives was suggested by one manager as a suitable predictor for performance in the current year's survey.

This need for capturing more performance measurement data also included a need for identifying leading indicators for key measures. Two precise, objective Quality-related measures, 'Percentage Availability of Systems' and 'MTTF', were seen to be useful leading indicators of year-end CSS (customer satisfaction score). However, as with most other performance measures reported to the management team, there were no predictive, leading indictors in place for either of these, despite their importance to GITS' Service Improvement department: "MTTF and Availability are key targets for us, they represent the most visible aspects of our services. Being able to control and drive improvements here is critical."

The dashboards used internally by two of the eight functional groupings at GITS, the Application Services and Technical Services departments, are jointly treated next.

Application Services and Technical Services Dashboards
The Application Services dashboard had been in operation for over a year (at the time of the study), as a mechanism for reporting progress on targets specific to the Application Services department (the targets that this department observes consist of a mix: some specified for them by the GITS management, and several others introduced by departmental management). The Application Services dashboard is often consulted during discussions among supervisory staff in the department, in addition to its use in a reporting role at departmental meetings. The dashboard, created in Microsoft Excel, displays all performance measurement information on a single worksheet displayed in Figure 2. Drill down ability is limited to a second worksheet holding a large amount of financial data. The dashboard lacks any graphics and the small font size (chosen to enable all data to be presented on one screen) renders information difficult to digest at a glance. The status of efforts relative to different departmental objectives are shown through colour shading of cells displaying results. No trend analysis is incorporated, but there is a column of forecasted year-end results.

Legend: On Target / Within 10% of Target / More than 10% Below Target	Responsible	Unit	2004 Actual	2005 Year End Budget	Current Period Actual	Current Period Budget	2005 Year To Date Actual	2005 Year To Date Budget	Current Year End Forecast
Financial									
Managed Volume- Ongoing	Tim	£'Ms	18.2	14		0.9	2.4	10.1	14.0
Cost Reduction	Tim	£'Ms	7.2	7		2.3	4.1	4.4	7.6
Cost Avoidance	Tim	£'Ms	3.5	4		0.3		1.7	4.0
Overhead Rate	Tim	%	10	8		8.0%	9.5%	8.0%	8.0
Service Metrics									
E2E SLA Performance	David	%	N/A	99.5%	100.0%	98.5%	99.7%	98.5%	99.5%
Timeliness of First Response	David	Hours	N/A	1.90	0.6	1.9	2.3	1.9	1.9
Problem Resolution	David	Days	N/A	1.00	0.1	1.0	0.9	1.0	1.0
Customer Perception									
Project Evaluation	David	/5	N/A	3.50	4.0	3.5	4.0	3.5	3.5
Customer Satisfaction Survey	Simon	/5	3.5	3.50	3.3	3.5	3.4	3.5	3.3
Improvement Evaluation	David	/5	N/A	3.50		3.5		3.5	3.5
Operational Efficiency									
Coverage Level Within Agreed Response Time	Dan	%	N/A	80.0%	95%	80%	97%	80%	80%
Incident Evaluation	David	#	N/A	3.50	4.0	3.5	3.7	3.5	3.5
Service Office Response Time	David	%	N/A	95.0%	100.0%	95.0%	90.8%	95.0%	95.0%
EAS/ES Demand Fulfilment	Thorsten	%	N/A	90.0%	98%	95%	95%	90%	90%
Resource Utilisation	Thorsten	%	100	100.0%	113%	100%	93%	100%	100%
Permanent Headcount	Mike	#	184	220	206	206	206	206	220
Staff Development Rating	Mike	/32	20	22	22	22	22	22	22
Prince 2 Accreditation	Mike	%	62.0%	80.0%	99%	75%	97%	75%	80%
Leading Through Change Participation	Simon	%	N/A	95.0%	98%	100%	98%	100%	98%

Row groupings (left margin labels): "Driving for Results" (Financial, Service Metrics, Customer Perception, Operational Efficiency); "Global Building"; "P&O"

Fig. 2. GITS Application Services dashboard

A clearly defined program of data collection is in place to populate the dashboard on a monthly basis. Each of the performance measures has been allocated an owner, who is responsible for tracking and reporting respective data in an agreed timeframe. These data owners email their scores, by a given monthly deadline, to the second-in-command of the department's management staff, who takes personal responsibility for the task of collation and updating. However, while this assistant manager has little difficulty obtaining required data in a timely manner, the effort involved in keying in and updating numerous bits of data on the spreadsheet sometimes stretches beyond his time and ability, given the need to perform all his other normal job duties. Thus, there are instances when pieces of dashboard data are not entirely current or missing. Nevertheless, this dashboard is seen as a useful monitoring tool by the Application Services manager: "It's fairly detailed … there is a lot of tekkie stuff to report on, and the dashboard pretty much covers it all. We use it to inform senior staff how we're getting on. It forms a major element of our management team meetings."

The Technical Services dashboard (like the Application Services described above) also serves as a tool for reporting progress on departmental targets i.e. specific to the Application Services function. It has been in use for eight months. Built in Microsoft Excel, it consists of a main front-page summary screen displaying key measures, seen in Figure 3, that is linked to several other spreadsheets with data tables for drill-down functionality. There is a distinct lack of graphical representation. The dashboard relies on texts and colour coding to indicate progress against targets, and does not offer any trend or projection data.

Efforts are made to update this dashboard on a monthly basis, with a number of management staff within the department having responsibility for obtaining data from units across diverse global sites. However, the refreshing process is often impeded by delays in acquiring the data, resulting in specific data sets being omitted from report. The dashboard is generally seen to be of limited value, being regarded nominally as a reporting tool for the purpose of Technical Services management meetings. It is used

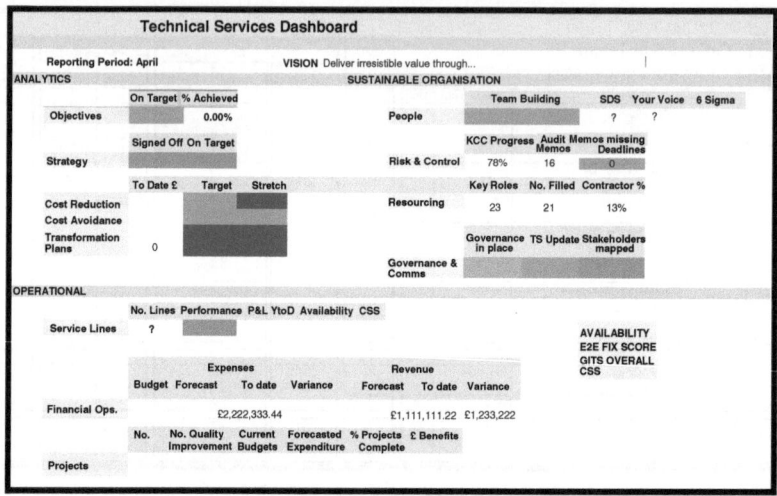

Fig. 3. Summary screen of GITS Technical Services dashboard

sparingly in the department; in fact the Technical Services manager prefers to consult a 'surrogate' version at his office, in the form of a whiteboard. He viewed the current version of the dashboard as a start-up effort: "The dashboard is okay, there are some useful items in it, but it was our first effort at monitoring performance; its better than nothing." Its lack of perceived value had nevertheless recently motivated the manager to set a management trainee the task of redeveloping it.

Both the Application and Technical Services dashboards, given their departmental focus, differ from the management team's Leadership dashboard in terms of the scope of measures they track. Both dashboards are used by departmental staff to follow not only the progress of departmental targets specified by GITS management (i.e. derived from GITS strategic objectives), but also to track self-chosen measures seen as useful to the respective department management teams. For instance, only about half of the performance measures displayed on the Application Services dashboard are directly related to the strategic targets specified for the department by the GITS management. Remaining measures, like 'Resource Utilisation', 'Permanent Headcount', 'Prince2 Accreditation' or 'Leading Through Change', had been introduced independently by departmental staff. In the Technical Services dashboard only three of eleven measures being tracked are targets that GITS management had allocated to the department.

There appeared to be two reasons for this. One of this was that the 'extra' (i.e. non-strategy derived) measures were seen by managers as useful or "nice to know" aspects for assessing how well their department are functioning operationally, as explained by the Technical Services manager: "There are quite a few measures which don't directly relate to strategy or targets, but we think it is worthwhile to keep track of them. It helps to know the operational health of the business." The other reason has to do with what may be termed 'signalling': demonstrating value or social status to stakeholders. For example, both the Application and Technical Services groups keep track of 'Cost Avoidance' on the dashboards. This measure is not tied to departmental targets or the GITS strategy but is justified on grounds of 'political' expediency, as the Application

Services manager explained: "We benchmark the charge rates of our project managers against external consultancy providers; we're less expensive, and the difference is classed as Cost Avoidance. It helps us demonstrate our value to the business."

Certain shortcomings in these two departmental dashboards mirrored those of the Leadership dashboard noted earlier (i.e. lack of predictive data, inadequate measures). In both the Application and Technical Services dashboards, almost all measures were of the lagging type, with rare exceptions (e.g. 'Timeliness of First Response' was seen as a leading indicator for 'Mean Time to Failure'). There was a common recognition among key users that the utility of both dashboards is significantly limited by the lack of 'actionable' information being presented (i.e. information that could suggest a need for proactive action to improve results, or turn around a worsening situation), and that more predictive data is needed, as averred by the Application Services manager: "It's more of a reporting tool than a driving tool, when I get some time I'll look into adding some more measures to it."

There was also evidence of inadequacies in the scope of measurement, and lack of clarity or commonly agreed definitions regarding certain measures. As with the GITS Leadership dashboard, the financial measures actually represented volume of services managed, and savings to end customers, rather than financial performance of the unit itself (this was to be expected given that these departments simply measure their own slice of the overall strategic targets). The Technical services dashboard, which seemed much less used and valued than the Application Services dashboard, also had certain targets whose measures appeared problematic. For example, the 'Objectives' measure had been introduced to represent a qualitative assessment of overall progress towards achievement of all the Technical Services targets (i.e. an average of the percentage achievement of all objectives). This improper 'measure of all measures' contravenes key principles of measurement design: the need to be objective, or related to a specific target (Neely et al., 1997). Another instance is the 'Strategy' measure, said to assess how many policy documents relating to corporate strategic aims had been 'signed off' by the departmental management. However, the Technical Services management staff were unclear of its value as a marker of performance. One manager noted: "I'm not sure what that one looks at, I don't know if it has ever been discussed." There are also a few defunct, unused measures on the dashboard: like one named 'Risk and Control', which was explained by the Technical Services manager: "When we put together the dashboard, someone suggested monitoring risk management. I made space in the dashboard for it, but then we never agreed what we were going to measure."

4.3 Summary

Thus, in summary, the performance measurement activities at GITS may be seen as a whole to be significantly limited in the value they offer for improving organisational effectiveness. This was partly due to technical reasons of inadequacy in information collection mechanisms and quality of dashboard design quality. It was also due to the lack of a top-down mandate and systematic programme (e.g. a formal measurement framework) that was driving and guiding the implementation of these practices: the absence of that has resulted in ad-hoc, disconnected efforts to date, and little more than vanilla reporting of progress.

While these challenges that have been seen to beset the performance measurement practices at GITS may not necessarily be empirically generalisable to those of other organisations (that operate under other unique contexts, and with different resources at their disposal), they nevertheless illuminate a subset of the key difficulties that may impede dashboard-based performance measurement efforts. Thus the context-specific circumstances of the above case study may be taken here to serve as a basis for theory development or 'theoretical generalisation' (Walsham, 1995), insofar as they illustrate or challenge existing theoretical perspectives. In particular, it may be argued that the above case analyses support/exemplify previous theorising and research regarding the design and use of dashboards, while, on the other hand, appearing to suggest a need to challenge certain principle tenets hitherto advocated as central to the formulation of effective performance measurement systems. These aspects are discussed next.

5   Discussion

The preceding case study evaluations highlighted several challenges that might be encountered when mounting dashboard based performance measurement practices in the corporate IT unit of a globally distributed organisation. Such challenges raise key implications with regard to supporting or challenging existing theory on such aspects as: (i) establishing appropriate and useful performance measures; (ii) implementing effective information collation and dashboard practices; and (iii) deriving value from business performance measurement practices.

5.1   Challenges of Dashboard Design/Use

The challenges illuminated in the preceding case study are consistent with previous studies in this arena. A principle challenge has been seen to lie in the establishment of appropriate performance measures that are relevant and deliver useful insights to the management teams. A key dimension of this is the difficulty of identifying leading indicators, as highlighted in past studies. Neely et al (2000) asserted that managers are often not aware of the factors that impact on their results, and correspondingly, the type of measures to report on. Eckerson (2006) observed that the main difficulty in defining performance measures is in identifying the most suitable leading indicators. This was borne out at GITS, where the drivers of progress towards strategic goals did not appear to be obvious to the managers who had set these targets.

It may be argued thus that with regard to GITS (or other organisations with similar systems) a useful step would thus be to re-orientate the fundamental aim underpinning these practices. The current practices and tools used at GITS seem to have been set up simply as a way to monitor progress towards target attainment, rather than providing an effective way to understand the salient factors or conditions shaping performance (and thus enable staff to influence such factors and achieve improved outcomes). This limited underlying orientation at GITS is reflected in the over-riding predominance of lagging over leading indicators among the measures tracked on the unit's dashboards, which restricts the ability of management staff to exercise control or make proactive interventions on the back of such information.

The significant problems in the quality and timeliness of dashboard data seen in the case of GITS underscores a challenge identified in past studies (Dixon et al., 1990; Medori & Steeple, 2000) of setting up well-organised procedures or mechanisms for collecting information, and of implementing well-designed interfaces for presentation (especially when data is to be obtained from diverse sources in a globally-distributed firm like Multicorp). A significant amount of process rationalisation, mobilisation of committed staff action, as well as investment in information technologies, has to be orchestrated in the background for dashboard displays of performance measurement to be an effective basis of organisational enhancement (Bourne et. al, 2003). A related challenge, seen in the case, lies in achieving common understanding and definitions of particular measures and the indicators used to represent them (Neely et al., 1997).

5.2 Performance Measurement Principles

The challenges illustrated by the case analyses indicate the complexity involved in mounting effective dashboard-based performance measurement practices. They also suggest a need to look more deeply at, and perhaps redefine, certain basic principles (or tenets) of performance measurement that characterise existing theory, as follows.

A primary recognition which emerged in this field over the last two areas was that a robust business performance measurement system needs to incorporate a 'balanced' perspective, by taking into account both financial and non-financial aspects to enable the presentation of holistic, relevant information for reviewing performance (Lynch & Cross, 1991; Kaplan & Norton, 1992; Medori & Steeple, 2000). The notion of balance however, is viewed primarily in the light of a distribution between financial and non-financial performance indicators. This financial vs. non-financial 'lever' is certainly useful, especially if the underlying principle or aim of a performance measurement system is seen as that of a tool for monitoring performance, and holistically reflecting both quantitative and qualitative dimensions. However, a key contemporary challenge illustrated by the preceding case analysis lies in increasing the value of performance measurement practices to be 'actionable': based on factors or quantities which can be influenced or controlled (Neeley et al. 1997). Such a key transformation in the role of a performance measurement a system, from a tool for monitoring/reporting to a tool of learning, requires the introduction of a significant amount of leading indicators and predictive data, to balance or complement existing lagging indicators. Thus the notion of equilibrium to be aimed at implies a new lever (i.e. lagging vs. leading indicators), in addition to the financial vs. non-financial lever, as the basis of design.

Another key principle that has been strongly emphasised in past theorising in this area, is that performance measurement should be clearly grounded in strategy (Cross & Lynch, 1990, Dixon et al. 1990). Neely et al. (1997), who reviewed diverse studies to identify the twenty-two most cited considerations when designing a performance measure, placed the need for the measure to be 'derived from strategy' as first on this list. However, this key design consideration appears problematic for several reasons. Firstly, it denies recognition of the need for lower-level organisational units to track various operational aspects of their performance that may not be linked specifically (or even indirectly) to a particular corporate strategy, as seen in the case example of the measures used by the Application and Technical Services departments.

Secondly, the nature of the strategy has to be taken into account when applying this design tenet. In the preceding case, the corporate strategy of Multicorp was essentially efficiency-focussed, aimed at cost-cutting and economising initiatives i.e. centralising IT services through GITS. Such a cost-reduction strategy can be seen to encourage heavy use of financial indicators and discourage incorporation of non-financial ones, thus impeding balanced assessment (some managers at GITS tended to focus only on financial aspects i.e. "I don't bother reporting non-financial benefits of projects; I'm not sure how to capture this data"). Thus, there appear to be grounds for suggesting a need to decouple strategy from measurement design, in cases where strategy does not lend itself to a balanced approach. The critical challenge of including more leadings indicators in performance measurement systems may also be tackled more effectively, if greater emphasis is placed within organisations on identifying the factors that shape or influence operations as the basis of measurement design, rather than the monitoring of adherence to strategic goals as the all encompassing principle.

6 Conclusion

This study contributes toward current theoretical understanding of the challenges faced in undertaking dashboard-based business performance measurement. While past studies have tended to adopt a top-down perspective on such practices by emphasising their derivation from the standpoint of overarching measurement frameworks, this research adopted a bottom-up perspective by taking an indepth look at the challenges affecting the design/use of dashboards in a particular case organisation, and the key theoretical implications they raised regarding over-arching measurement principles.

The difficulties illustrated by the case study highlight the degree of commitment and investment of resources that organisations must muster in order to undertake such activities effectively. The complexity surrounding business performance measurement is seen here to suggest a need for rethinking some of the fundamental design tenets that have hitherto been advanced. Future research is needed to shed further light on any contingencies or exceptions governing the application of such principles. There is also a need for further research to clarify the derivation of leading indicators, so that firms may know how to augment the predictive, actionable aspect of these practices.

References

1. Bourne, M., Franco, M., Wilkes, J.: Corporate Performance Management. Measuring Business Excellence 7, 15–21 (2003)
2. Bukowitz, W.R., Petrash, G.P.: Visualising, measuring, and managing knowledge. Research and Technology Management 40, 24–31 (1997)
3. Cross, K.F., Lynch, R.L.: The SMART way to define and sustain success. National Productivity Review 9, 23–33 (1990)
4. De Toni, A., Tonchia, S.: Performance measurement systems - models, characteristics and measures. International Journal of Productions and Operations Management 1, 347–354 (2001)
5. Dixon, J.R., Nanni, A.J., Vollmann, T.E.: The new performance challenge: Measuring operations for world-class competition, Homewood, IL, Dow Jones-Irwin (1990)

6. Eckerson, W.: Performance Dashboards: Measuring Monitoring and Managing Your Business. John Wiley & Sons, New Jersey (2006)
7. Few, S.: Dashboard Design: Beyond Meters, Gauges, ad Traffic Lights. Business Intelligence Journal 10, 18–24 (2005)
8. Frolick, M.N., Ariyachandra, T.R.: Business Performance Management: One Truth. Information Systems Management 23(1), 41 (2006)
9. Glaser, B., Strauss, A.: The discovery of grounded theory, Aldine, Chicago (1967)
10. Ittner, C.D., Larcker, D.F.: Innovations in performance measurement: trends and research implications. Journal of Management Accounting Research 10, 205–238 (1998)
11. Johnson, H.T.: The search for gain in markets and firms: a review of the historical emergence of management accounting systems. Accounting, Organisations and Society 16, 63–80 (1983)
12. Kaplan, R.S., Norton, D.P.: The balanced scorecard - measures that drive performance. Harvard Business Review 70, 71–79 (1992)
13. Kennerley, M., Neely, A.: Measuring performance in a changing business environment. International Journal of Operations and Production Management 23(2), 213–229 (2003)
14. Klein, H., Myers, M.: A set of principles for conducting and evaluating interpretive field studies in Information Systems. MIS Quarterly 23(1), 67–94 (1999)
15. Lea, R., Parker, B.: The JIT Spiral of Continuous Improvement. IMDS 4, 10–13 (1989)
16. Lehn, K., Makhija, A.K.: EVA and MVA as performance measures and signals for strategic change. Strategy and Leadership 24, 34–38 (1996)
17. McCunn, P.: The Balanced Scorecard: the eleventh commandment. Management Accounting, pp. 34–36 (1998)
18. Medori, D., Steeple, D.: A framework for auditing and enhancing performance measurement systems. International Journal of Operations and Production Management 20, 520–533 (2000)
19. Neely, A., Adams, C., Crowe, P.: The performance prism in practice. Measuring Business Excellence 5(2), 6 (2001)
20. Neely, A., Mills, J., Platts, K., Richards, H., Bourne, M.: Performance measurement system design: developing and testing a process-based approach. International Journal of Operations and Production Management 20 (2000)
21. Neely, A., Richards, H., Mills, J., Platts, K., Bourne, M.: Designing performance measures: a structured approach. International Journal of Operations & Production Management 17, 1131–1152 (1997)
22. Skinner, W.: The decline, fall and renewal of manufacturing. Industrial Engineering, pp. 32–38 (1974)
23. Stanwick, P., Stanwick, S.: IT Performance: How Do You Measure a Moving Target? The Journal of Corporate Accounting and Finance 13, 19–24 (2005)
24. Walsham, G.: Interpretive case studies in IS research: nature and method. European Journal of Information Systems 4(2), 74–81 (1995)
25. Watson, H., Frolick, M.: Determining Information Requirements for an EIS. MIS Quarterly 17, 52–67 (1993)

On the Performance of Workflow Processes with Distributed Actors: Does Place Matter?

Hajo A. Reijers[1], Minseok Song[1], and Byungduk Jeong[1,2]

[1] Department of Technology Management, Eindhoven University of Technology,
P.O.Box 513, NL-5600 MB, Eindhoven, The Netherlands
{h.a.reijers,m.s.song}@tue.nl
[2] Department of Industrial Engineering, Korea Advanced Institute of Science and
Technology, South Korea
tauruseo@kaist.ac.kr

Abstract. Current workflow technology offers rich features to manage and enact business processes. In principle, the technology enables actors to cooperate in the execution of business processes regardless of their geographical location. Furthermore, the technology is considered as an efficient means to reduce processing times. In this paper, we evaluate the effects on the performance of a workflow process in an organizational setting where actors are geographically distributed. The studied process is exceptional, because equivalent tasks can be performed at different locations. We have analyzed a large workflow process log with state-of-the art mining tools associated with the ProM framework. Our analysis leads to the conclusion that there is a positive effect on process performance when workflow actors are geographically close.

Keywords: Workflow management, performance evaluation, process mining, case study.

1 Introduction

Since the mid 1990s, Workflow Management Systems (WfMSs) have received wide attention as a research subject in the IS community. Recent interest for Process-aware Information Systems [11] breathes new life into WfMS's fundamental concept, the distribution of work to people and systems on the basis of a pre-defined process model [1]. The industrial success of WfMS's can be clearly seen in, for example, the Netherlands and South-Korea, where every bank, insurance company, ministry, and most municipalities have adopted this technology.

Nonetheless, little is known about the extent to which workflow technology helps organizations to execute their business processes more efficiently and effectively. Market analysts and software vendors boast success stories, but they hardly play an impartial role in this discussion. To fill this white space, a research project was initiated in 2001 by Eindhoven University of Technology and Deloitte Consultancy. The purpose of the project was to involve as large a number of Dutch organizations as possible to closely monitor their experiences with implementing and using WfMSs to support their business processes over a period of time. For an overview of the preliminary results, the reader is referred

G. Alonso, P. Dadam, and M. Rosemann (Eds.): BPM 2007, LNCS 4714, pp. 32–47, 2007.

to [22]. This project, in which 10 organizations are involved and over 20 business processes, is currently nearing its completion.

One of the organizations that participated in the mentioned project is a Dutch municipality, which started the implementation of the WfMS Staffware for their invoice handling process in 2003. In the second half of 2004, they went "live". The research project we mentioned gave us access to the WfMS's process log which contained the registered events for 2005's production, covering over 12,000 completed cases (invoices) in total. The interesting thing is that there are tasks which can be executed at 10 different locations all across the city. After all, an invoice in this setting can pertain to almost anything (e.g., pencils, pc's, or furniture) and it must be checked by the responsible civil servant who issued it. Such a civil servant may be working at the city's fire brigade, swimming pool, theater, or any of the other locations. So, this implementation site provided a rare opportunity to evaluate whether it matters for process performance when actors are geographically distributed.

In this paper, we focus on processing time and transfer time as performance measures to investigate whether a relation exists between geographical location and process performance. As far as we know, this has not been investigated before in the setting of an actual WfMS implementation on the basis of real data. But insight into this relation - if it exists - may be valuable to manage and influence the performance of future workflow implementations.

In the next section we will start with an overview of related work. In Section 3 we will describe our research design, in particular the hypotheses we set out to investigate. Then, we will describe the case study in more detail and report our analysis and findings in in Section 4. The paper ends with a discussion and some concluding remarks.

2   Related Work

2.1   Workflow and Geography

By having a WfMS in place for the logistic management of a business process, such processes can theoretically be executed faster and more efficiently [19]. WfMS vendors claim that these advantages materialize in practice. In academic papers, various single case studies of workflow implementations are described and a small number of studies that involve multiple implementations [15,18,21]. Most of the studies that explicitly consider performance established a positive effect of workflow technology, in particular in [21]. However, none of these studies examined whether the geographical distribution of actors played any part in such performance improvement. (Note that the *architectural* issues that relate to distributed workflow processing have been widely studied, e.g. in [12,13,20]).

It was established in the seminal work by Thomas Allen at MIT [4] that geographical distances between actors may matter. In the late 1970s, Allen undertook a project to determine how the distance between engineers' offices coincided with the level of regular technical communication between them. The results of that research, now known as the *Allen Curve*, revealed that when there is more distance between people they will communicate less frequently.

However, it is believed that due to the massive utilization of information and communication technologies (ICTs) the precise physical location of individual participants will become irrelevant to their interactions [7,8]. ICTs are a key enabler for the emergence and sustained popularity of so-called virtual teams, i.e. groups of geographically and organizationally dispersed coworkers that are assembled using a combination of telecommunications and information technologies to accomplish an organizational task [25]. WfMSs too enable the fast communication and collaboration between geographically dispersed users and can therefore be expected to contribute to improved interaction between them [6,23,24]. In particular, in [1] it is stated that "The introduction of a WfMS lowers the physical barriers between the various sections of an organisation". It continues that a WfMS can, for example, be used to more evenly distribute work among geographically scattered resources. Therefore, we may assume from existing literature that it is less relevant where people reside physically for the performance of a process that is managed by a WfMS.

2.2   Process Mining

In this paper, we use process mining techniques to analyze business process execution results. Process mining allows the discovery of knowledge based on a process log [3]. The process log, which is provided by most process aware information systems, records the execution of tasks in some business processes. Process mining can deal with several perspectives, such as the process perspective, organizational perspective, performance perspective, etc. To support process mining, several tools have been developed [14,16,2,10]. The ProM framework has been developed to support various process mining algorithms such as these. It was designed to easily add new algorithms and techniques into it by means of plug-ins[10]. A plug-in is basically the implementation of an algorithm that is of use in the process mining area.

Figure 1 shows an overview of the ProM framework. ProM reads log files in the XML format through the Log filter component. This component can handle large data sets and sort the events within a case according to their time stamps. Through the Import plug-ins a wide variety of models can be loaded, ranging from Petri nets to logical formulae. The Mining plug-ins perform the actual process mining. The Analysis plug-ins take a mining result and perform an analysis. The ProM framework provides several analysis techniques such as Petrinet analysis, social network analysis, performance analysis, etc. The Conversion plug-ins can convert a mining result into another format, e.g., from an EPC into a Petri net.

3   Research Design

This section explains our research questions and describes the research method with which they are addressed. The objective of this study is to determine how

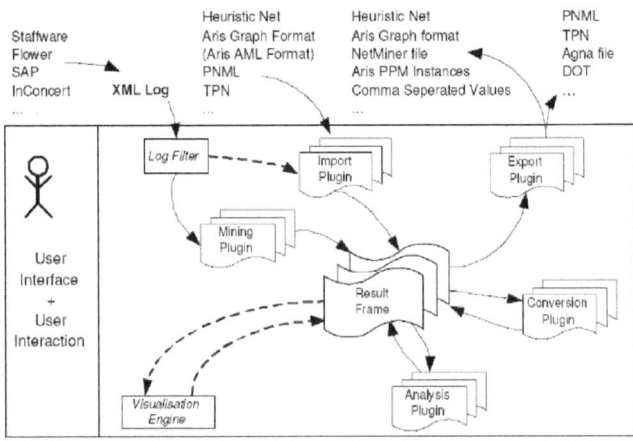

Fig. 1. Overview of the ProM framework [10]

the performance of a business processes is affected by the use of a WfMS in a geographically distributed setting. Before explaining our research questions, the two process performance indicators selected to investigate are defined as follows:

- *Processing time:* the time between the start of a task and its completion,
- *Transfer time:* the time between the completion of a task and the start of a subsequently executed latter task

Applying a WfMS could result in a reduction of processing times, because it delivers the right work to the right person at the right time. When a WfMS takes care of assigning work to actors, it is perhaps less relevant where these actors are located geographically. When companies introduce WfMSs, they normally perform business process re-engineering projects. During the projects, they carry out as-is analyses and try to remove the geographical influences in the execution of business processes by standardizing the tasks in the business processes. After that, they design new business processes and implement them with WfMSs. In WfMSs, when a task is completed, the task is immediately assigned to a proper actor (the worklist of the actor) in spite of his/her geographical location. Next, it is handled by the actor. Thus, it seems that the introduction of workflow technology takes away any geographical influences. To evaluate this argument, we established a research procedure as shown in Figure 2. Under this procedure, we examine whether processing and transfer times are affected by workflow technology in terms of the geographical location of its involved actors.

The first step is generating our hypotheses. Our research questions led to the formulation of two hypotheses:

- *Hypothesis 1:* The processing time of equivalent tasks is equally distributed, despite the geographical locations in which the tasks are performed.

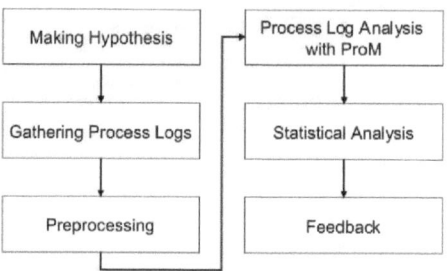

Fig. 2. The research procedure

- *Hypothesis 2:* The transfer time between tasks within the same geographical location is equally distributed as the transfer time between tasks across geographical locations.

Hypothesis 1 deals with the first research question. For the hypothesis, we considered tasks that can be performed in several geographical locations. We calculated processing times of tasks within each location and compared them. *Hypothesis 2* addresses the second question. In this case, we took into account the pairs of tasks that can be successively executed in the same geographical location or across different geographical locations. Note that geographical separation may also lead to time differences between locations. However, in this paper, this is not the case.

After generating the hypotheses, we gathered process logs from the involved organization, which operates Staffware as its WfMS. Since the process logs gathered were stored in a proprietary format, we had to preprocess the process logs. They were converted into a standard MXML format [10]. After the conversion, we analyzed them with the ProM framework and its associated tools. We removed irrelevant tasks and calculated relevant processing and transfer times. After that, we performed various statistical tests to examine our hypotheses. Since the ProM framework does not support statistical analysis, we generated the data for statistical analysis from ProM and used Statgraphics Centurion XV for the tests. The analysis results from ProM and the statistical test results were reported to the organization that provided the logs. Finally, we gathered their feedback.

4 Case Study

4.1 Context

The context of our case study is the Urban Management Service of a municipality of 90,000 citizens, situated in the northern part of the Netherlands. The municipality is one of the organizations that is involved in our longitudinal study into the effectiveness of workflow management technology [22]. In 2000, the board of the municipality decided to implement a WfMS throughout the organization, which encompasses some 300 people. Mainly because of restricted budgets and some technical setbacks, it lasted until 2004 before the first two business processes were supported with this technology. One of these two processes involves the handling of invoices, which is the focus of our analysis.

On a yearly basis, the municipality deals with some 20,000 invoices that pertain to everything that the municipality purchases. The overall process consists of 26 tasks and may involve almost every employee of the Urban Management Service. After all, an important check is whether the invoice is 'legitimate' in the sense that it corresponds with an authorized purchase by some employee, to be checked by that employee himself/herself. The general procedure is that an invoice is scanned and subsequently sent by the WfMS to the central financial department. A clerk registers the invoice after which it is sent to the proper local financial office. These local financial offices are distributed over all the geographical locations of the municipality (e.g. the mayor's office, the city's swimming pool, the fire brigade, etc.). Depending on the kind of invoice, there are various checks that need to take place: the person responsible for the budget that is used for the purchase must approve (the budget keeper); the fit between the purchase with the supplier's contract (if any) must be established; various managers may be required to authorize the invoice depending on the amount of the money involved; etc. Eventually, a purchase may be paid by the central financial office.

4.2   Analysis Procedure

In the case study under consideration, a process log is automatically generated by the WfMS executing the invoice handling process. A process log consists of several *instances* or *cases*, each of which may comprise several audit trail entries. An *audit trail entry* corresponds to an atomic *event* such as schedule, start, or completion of a task. Each audit trail entry records task name, event type, actor and time stamp. Figure 3 shows the example of translated process logs. In the figure, the names of actors are replaced by artificial IDs to ensure confidentiality and privacy. The process log starts with the *WorkflowLog* element that contains *Source*, and *Process* elements. The *Source* element refers to the information about the software or the system that was used to record the log. In our case study, the log comes from a "Staffware" system. The *Process* element represents the process to which the process log belongs. *ProcessInstance* elements correspond to cases. The *AuditTrailEntry* element represents a log line. It contains *WorkflowModelElement*, *EventType*, *Timestamp*, and *Originator* elements. The *WorkflowModelElement* refers to the activity the event corresponds to. The *EventType* specifies the type of the event, e.g., *schedule* (i.e., a task becomes enabled for a specific instance), *start* (the beginning of a task instance), and *complete* (the completion of a task instance), etc. The *Timestamp* refers to the time when the event occurred and the *Originator* corresponds to the originator who initiates the event.

The process log we analyzed covered slightly more than 12,000 instances (completely handled invoices), as processed by the municipality in the first half of 2005. This pertained to a huge amount of data: It has more than 200,000 events

```
<?xml version="1.0" encoding="UTF-8"?>
<WorkflowLog xmlns:xsi="http://www.w3.org/2001/XMLSchema-instance"
 xsi:noNamespaceSchemaLocation="http://www.is.tm.tue.nl/research/processmining/
                                WorkflowLog.xsd">
    <Source program="Staffware"/>
      <Process id="Facturen" description="none">
            <ProcessInstance id="4-21334" description="none">
            <AuditTrailEntry>
            <WorkflowModelElement>PREREG</WorkflowModelElement>
                <EventType>schedule</EventType>
                <Originator>actor1</Originator>
                <Timestamp>2005-07-13T13:55:00+01:00</Timestamp>
            </AuditTrailEntry>
            <AuditTrailEntry>
            <WorkflowModelElement>CODFCTBF</WorkflowModelElement>
                <EventType>start</EventType>
                <Originator>actor2</Originator>
                <Timestamp>2005-07-13T13:58:00+01:00</Timestamp>
            </AuditTrailEntry>
            <AuditTrailEntry>
            <WorkflowModelElement>CODFCTBF</WorkflowModelElement>
                <EventType>complete</EventType>
                <Originator>actor2</Originator>
                <Timestamp>2005-07-13T14:01:00+01:00</Timestamp>
            </AuditTrailEntry>
            ...
```

Fig. 3. An example log

and about 350 actors are involved in the process. We investigated the whole process log and decided to focus our attention to two specific elements. First of all, we decided to analyze the processing times of five specific *tasks*, being the most important checks as prioritized by the financial management. The five tasks are CODFCTBF, CONTRUIF, ROUTEFEZ, CONTRCOD, and FBCONCOD. Note that the five tasks can be performed in several geographical locations. We left out administrative tasks like scanning, keying in data, categorizing, archiving, etc. Secondly, we considered four *pairs* of tasks where we could establish that at times they were subsequently performed within the same geographical unit and at other times across different units. They are ROUTEFEZ-CODFCTBF, CODFCTBF-CONTRUIF, CODFCTBF-CONTRCOD, and CONTRCOD-BEO ORDSR.

We calculated the processing time of each task and the transfer time of each pair. Before the actual mining starts, the process data was filtered to focus on a specific task or pair. The ProM framework provides several filters that enable the removal of irrelevant information from process logs. For example, the *event log filter* is used to extract the events in which we are interested. If we apply the filter to the log in Figure 3 and filter out the 'PREREG' activity, we obtain the log in Figure 4 where the 'PREREG' activity is removed. Besides the *event log filter*, we also applied several filters to preprocess the log and improve its analyzability.

After applying the filters, we used the performance sequence diagram analysis plug-in. This plug-in makes a sequence diagram from process logs and shows performance measures such as average throughput time, transfer time, time spent in a task, etc. A sequence diagram has vertical and horizontal dimensions. The

```
<?xml version="1.0" encoding="UTF-8"?>
<WorkflowLog xmlns:xsi="http://www.w3.org/2001/XMLSchema-instance"
 xsi:noNamespaceSchemaLocation="http://www.is.tm.tue.nl/research/processmining/
                               WorkflowLog.xsd">
    <Source program="Staffware"/>
        <Process id="Facturen" description="none">
            <ProcessInstance id="4-21334" description="none">
            <AuditTrailEntry>
            <WorkflowModelElement>CODFCTBF</WorkflowModelElement>
                <EventType>start</EventType>
                <Originator>actor2</Originator>
                <Timestamp>2005-07-13T13:58:00+01:00</Timestamp>
            </AuditTrailEntry>
            <AuditTrailEntry>
            <WorkflowModelElement>CODFCTBF</WorkflowModelElement>
                <EventType>complete</EventType>
                <Originator>actor2</Originator>
                <Timestamp>2005-07-13T14:01:00+01:00</Timestamp>
            </AuditTrailEntry>
            ...
```

Fig. 4. The filtered log

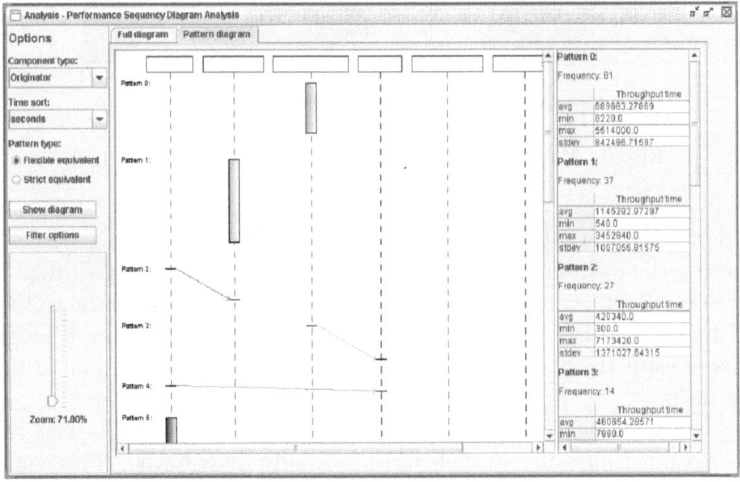

Fig. 5. ProM screenshot showing sequence diagram (pattern view)

vertical dimension is a time dimension and the horizontal dimension shows clas-
sifier roles that represent geographical locations.

Figure 5 shows the sequence diagram of transfer time for the ROUTEFEZ-
CODFCTBF pair. In the figure, there are two kinds of patterns, such as boxes
and arrows. When a transfer happens within a geographical location, it is represented as a box. If it happens across different geographical locations, an arrow
between them is drawn. As shown in the figure, the transfer times also vary
according to the various geographical locations.

With the ProM framework, we can calculate performance indicators (i.e. average time, minimum time, maximum time, and standard deviation) of both

processing and transfer times. We exported the analysis result of the ProM framework to Statgraphics and performed statistical analysis.

4.3   Analysis and Findings

Processing time. For our analysis, we determined the average processing times of all five tasks under consideration. The results for the CODFCTBF task, which covers the largest number of different geographical locations, is shown in Figure 6. The task involves the check on the legitimacy of the invoice by the responsible budget keeper.

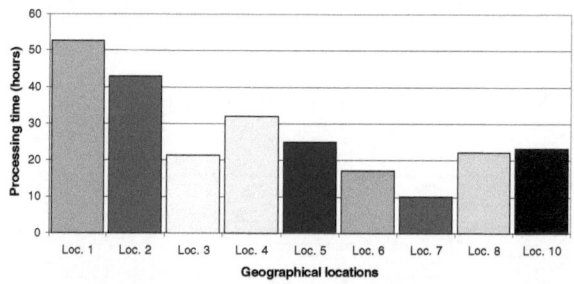

Fig. 6. Average processing time of the CODFCTBF task

The figure shows that the average processing times for the CODFCTBF task differ across the various geographical locations. These averages range between the extremes of approximately 10 hours and 53 hours. Although the CONTRUIF, ROUTEFEZ, CONTRCOD and FBCONCOD tasks involve fewer geographical locations – respectively only 3, 7, 6 and 2 – the variation is similar to the CODFCTBF task.

Using the Kolmogorov-Smirnov test, we could reject with a 95% reliability that processing times of any task were normally distributed. This violates the assumptions for most standard parametric tests to determine statistical differences (e.g. ANOVA), which explains our use of the distribution-free Kruskal-Wallis test that compares medians. For all tasks under consideration, this test leads with a 95% confidence to the outcome that there is a *significant difference between the processing times across various locations*. Because of the existence of outliers, we also applied Mood's median test, which is less powerful but more robust in this respect: It leads to the same result.

To illustrate the relative difference within the processing times for a single task, we present a Box-and-Whisker plot (also known as *boxplot*) for the CODFCTBF task in Figure 7. In the plot, the medians are shown as notches between the lower and upper quartiles. The plot suggests differences between, for example, the medians of locations 1 and 3, locations 2 and 4, etc.

To investigate whether the found differences in processing times across the geographical locations persist over time or are rather of a transient nature, we

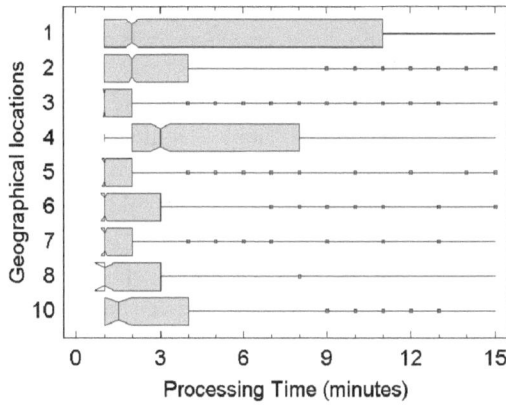

Fig. 7. Box-and-Whisker plot for the CODFCTBF task

split up the overall log in 6 chronologically subsequent smaller logs of equal size and analyzed these as well. As additional analyses confirmed the non-normality of the processing times within all sublogs, we again used the Kruskal-Wallis test. The result is shown in Table 1. Note that the columns from the second to the seventh represent each sublog.

Table 1. The Kruskal-Wallis test result (processing time), significant differences at a 95% confidence interval indicated with '*'

task	1	2	3	4	5	6
CODFCTBF	*	*	*	*	*	*
CONTRUIF	–	*	*	–	–	–
ROUTEFEZ	*	*	*	*	*	*
CONTRCOD	*	*	*	*	*	*
FBCONCOD	*	*	*	*	*	*

What can be seen is that for all but the CONTRUIF task the processing times across the locations vary significantly at a 95% confidence level for *all* its sublogs. (For the CONTRUIF task, this difference is only significant for the 2nd and 3rd sublog and is therefore considered as being of a transient nature.) So, we reject our first hypothesis. Processing times tend to differ significantly across the geographical locations where they are performed and do so for successive periods of time.

Transfer time. For analyzing the transfer time, we focus on the four pairs of tasks we mentioned earlier. The transfer points were selected because on the basis of a content analysis of the tasks it can be imagined that the involved tasks either take place entirely within the same geographical location or that each task is carried out in a different location. In the first case, we speak of an *intra transfer*, as the work is transferred between executors within the same location; in the second case, an *inter transfer*, as the executors are at different locations.

An analysis of the process log indicated that only for two of the pairs where intra and inter transfers take place there is sufficient data to compare these transfers in a meaningful way. For the other two, there are at most 50 observations of inter transfers versus thousands of observed cases for inter transfers. Therefore, we focus on the following two pairs:

1. *from ROUTEFEZ to CODFCTBF:* the initial check by a local financial clerk whether an invoice is intended for the sector that the clerk is attached to, and if so, the subsequent check on the legitimacy of the invoice by a budget keeper;

2. *from CODFCTBF to CONTRCOD:* the legitimacy check by a budget keeper followed by the check of a local financial clerk whether the control code as filled out by the budget keeper is correct;

For these pairs, there are respectively 2125 and 1764 inter transfers and approximately three times as many intra transfers within each category.

Application of the Kolmogorov-Smirnov test points out that with a 95% confidence the idea can be rejected that transfer times for either pair are normally distributed. This makes a test that focuses on the comparison of medians of the transfer times more suitable. Figure 8 shows that for both transfer types, the median of the inter transfer time exceeds that of the intra transfer time, although this difference is larger in the case of transfers from ROUTEFEZ to CODFCTBF.

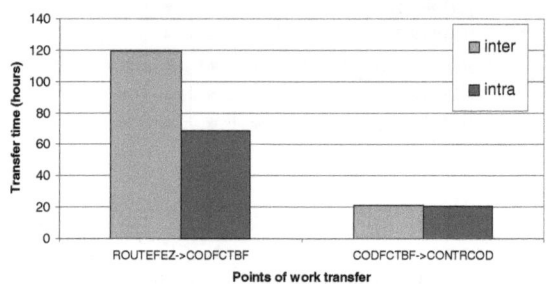

Fig. 8. Median transfer times at transfer points

Similar as for the analysis of the processing times, the Kruskal-Wallis test was selected to test the equality of medians between intra and inter transfers. In the presence of outliers, Mood's median test was applied as a more robust yet less powerful, additional test. For *both* transfer types, the Kruskal-Wallis test shows significant differences between intra and inter transfers at a 95% confidence interval. At the same confidence level, Mood's median test only shows a significant difference for the transfer of work from ROUTEFEZ to CODFCTBF.

For both transfer types, box-and-whisker plots that show the area between the lower quartile and upper quartile of the data values with the median in the middle, are given in Figures 9. Small markers (plus signs) indicate the means for intra and inter transfer times.

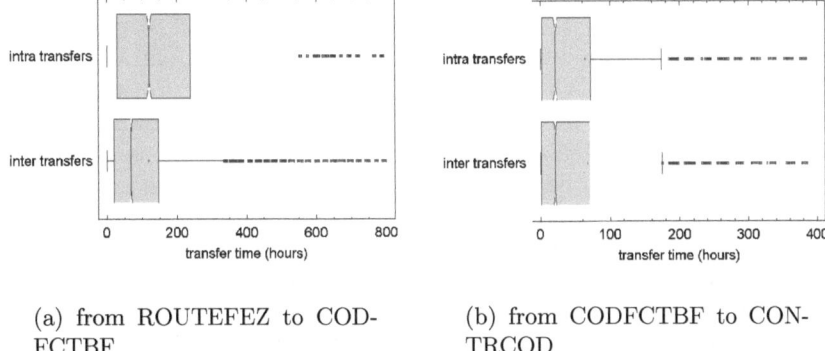

(a) from ROUTEFEZ to CODFCTBF

(b) from CODFCTBF to CONTRCOD

Fig. 9. Detail Box-and-Whisker plots for the transfer of work

So, both statistical tests point at a *significant difference* between the intra and inter transfer times for the transfer of work from ROUTEFEZ to CODFCTBF, where inter transfers clearly exceed intra transfer times. The approximate confidence intervals for the medians, indicated by the notches in the quartile bodies in the Box-and-Whisker plot, confirm this result as they are wide apart and do not overlap. The difference is not so apparent for work being transferred from CODFCTBF to CONTRCOD.

Finally, to determine whether the differences between the intra and inter transfer times persist over time, the complete log is split up in 6 subsequent smaller logs of equal size. The procedure is similar as in the case of the analysis of processing times, as described earlier in this section. As Kolmogorov-Smirnov tests confirmed the non-normality of the transfer times times within all sublogs, we again used the Kruskal-Wallis test. The result is shown in Table 2.

Table 2. the Kruskal-Wallis test result (transfer time), significant differences at a 95% confidence interval indicated with '*'

task pair	1	2	3	4	5	6
From ROUTEFEZ to CODFCTBF	*	*	*	*	*	*
From CODFCTBF to CONTRCOD	-	*	*	-	*	*

For the pair ROUTEFEZ-CODFCTBF the significant difference between intra and inter transfers is present in *all* sublogs. Therefore, we reject our second hypothesis. After all, for this pair at least we see that intra and inter transfer times vary significantly over a long period of time.

4.4   Discussion

Summary of findings. We rejected our hypotheses that suppose that work-flow technology takes away geographical barriers (Hypotheses 1 and 2). With respect to the first part, our analysis shows significant differences between processing times of equivalent tasks across different geographical locations; similarly significant differences between intra and inter transfer times are found.

Evaluation. We gathered feedback on the found results from a team of the involved municipality, which included the financial manager, functional administrator of the workflow system, a systems integrator responsible for technical modifications, and a budget-keeper/executor. We had a one-and-a-half hour meeting with them in the city town-hall, where we presented and discussed the results, followed-up by several e-mail contacts and phone conversations.

No satisfactory explanation could be found for the surprising differences in processing times (Hypothesis 1), as the team members once more confirmed that the tasks are strictly equivalent across the various locations. Differences in local skills and perhaps informal norms may contribute to the difference. This is in line with research in the tradition of "social ecology" [5]. It positions that different social settings, such as offices and meeting rooms, are associated with different behavioral norms, mental schemas, and even scripts that sharply affect the way people act and the expectations they have of others.

After considerable deliberation, a possible explanation was found for the difference in transfer times (Hypothesis 2). Within the municipality, local financial clerks are provided with reports on "open" invoices. These can be used to urge budget keepers to check the invoices that are with them for some time. The team from the municipality suspects that this encouragement is done more frequently and more persuasively in settings where the clerks and budget keepers are in the same location, which may well explain the distinctive difference between transfer times from ROUTEFEZ and CODFCTBF.

But even if the encounters between financial clerks and budget keepers are not planned, the effect of spontaneous communication between them should not be underestimated. It seems logical that spontaneous encounters will take place more frequently when people reside in the same building. With spontaneous casual communication, people can learn, informally, how one anothers work is going, anticipate each others strengths and failings, monitor group progress, coordinate their actions, do favors for one another, and come to the rescue at the last minute when things go wrong [9]. But physical separation drastically reduces the likelihood of voluntary work collaboration [17].

Limitations. Clearly, this study is carried out within the setting of a single organization, so the usual limitations apply with respect to generalizing its results.

A more specific concern could be raised on the validity of reasoning over process performance, as we strongly focused on the analysis of an automatically generated process log. Obviously, process logs are by no means a full representation of what is going on in an organization. However, for the reported case it seems likely that the recorded events follow actual work execution quite closely, as confirmed by the team of the municipality. In another part of the larger research project we are involved in (see [22]), we have seen an implementation where people worked around the workflow system on a wide scale, e.g. using the workflow system in batch mode to check out work that was completed manually much earlier. In such a case, it would be much more dubious to draw conclusions of the kind we did. The patterns in the process logs that hinted at such anomalous behavior, i.e. (1) extremely short processing times and (2) many "bursts" of task completions followed by relatively long periods of inactivity, were not present in the situation of the municipality.

A final limitation that needs to be mentioned is that only a restricted period (half a year) was used as a time window for the evaluation of the invoice handling's process performance. We attempted to counter this issue with carrying out our analyses on the level of sub-logs as well, but we cannot rule out entirely that we have witnessed a temporary effect.

Implications for practical use. The most important implication from our work for practice is that workflow technology should not be assumed to level all geographical barriers between people just by itself. High expectations on workflow technology need to be re-adjusted, for example, when they are considered as infrastructure for worldwide operating enterprises that "follow the sun". Explicit efforts must be taken to create equal circumstances for all involved workers if equal performance is desired. In addition, geographical proximity of workers favors their interaction, as was already suggested by the work of Allen [4]. Organizations must explicitly look for and implement procedures, tools, and housing opportunities to stimulate interaction patterns among actors or should expect differences in performance to occur.

5 Conclusions

WfMSs are supposed to efficiently and effectively support actors in the execution of business processes they are involved in, regardless of their geographical location. In this paper, we critically evaluated this assumption through a study into the performance of a WfMS in an organizational context. We analyzed a large workflow process logs with the ProM framework and associated tools. We found that the geographical location and distance between actors was a major distinguishing factor in process performance. The feedback from the organization brought a partial explanation for the phenomenon, i.e. that people are more inclined to urge others to complete their work when they are geographically close to them. Also, the positive effects of spontaneous interactions between collocated workers may be at work here.

Our paper contributes to a better understanding of the organizational effectiveness of workflow technology, which is an important but not so widely researched topic. Furthermore, the paper clearly demonstrates the feasibility of process mining techniques in evaluating current situations or answering managerial questions related to process enactment. Since only logs from a single organization were used, our results are clearly open to discussion.

In future work, we plan to repeat our analysis with logs from other organizations, taking into account other potential factors affecting performance (e.g. organizational hierarchy). It would be highly desirable to find organizations with highly distributed actors for reasons of comparison.

Acknowledgement

This research is supported by the Technology Foundation STW, applied science division of NWO and the technology programme of the Dutch Ministry of Economic Affairs. Byungduk Jeong is visiting the Department of Technology Management at Eindhoven University of Technology, supported by the Korea Research Foundation Grant founded by the Korean Government (KRF-2006-612-D00098). Moreover, we would like to thank the many people involved in the development of ProM.

References

1. van der Aalst, W.M.P., van Hee, K.M.: Workflow Management: Models, Methods, and Systems. MIT Press, Cambridge, MA (2002)
2. van der Aalst, W.M.P., Reijers, H.A., Song, M.: Discovering social networks from event logs. Computer Supported Cooperative Work 14(6), 549–593 (2005)
3. van der Aalst, W.M.P., Weijters, A.J.M.M., Maruster, L.: Workflow Mining: Discovering Process Models from Event Logs. IEEE Transactions on Knowledge and Data Engineering 16(9), 1128–1142 (2004)
4. Allen, T.: Managing the Flow of Technology: Technology Transfer and the Dissemination of Technological Information within the R&D Organisation. MIT Press, Cambridge, MA (1977)
5. Barker, R.G.: Ecological psychology. Stanford University Press, Stanford, Calif (1968)
6. Becker, J., Vossen, G.: Geschaftsprozesmodellierung und Workflow-Management: Eine Einfuhring, chapter Geschaftsprozesmodellierung und Workflow-Management. Modelle, Methoden, Werkzeuge, Albany, pp. 17–26 (1996)
7. Boutellier, R., Gassmann, O., Macho, H., Roux, M.: Management of Dispersed R&D Teams. R&D Management 28(1), 13–25 (1998)
8. Carmel, E., Agarwal, R.: Tactical approaches for alleviating distance in global software development. Software, IEEE 18(2), 22–29 (2001)
9. Davenport, T.H.: Process innovation. Harvard Business School Press, Boston, Mass (1994)
10. van Dongen, B.F., de Medeiros, A.K.A., Verbeek, H.M.W., Weijters, A.J.M.M., van der Aalst, W.M.P.: The ProM framework: A new era in process mining tool support. In: Ciardo, G., Darondeau, P. (eds.) ICATPN 2005. LNCS, vol. 3536, pp. 444–454. Springer, Heidelberg (2005)
11. Dumas, M., van der Aalst, W.M.P., ter Hofstede, A.H.: Process-aware information systems: bridging people and software through process technology (2005)
12. Georgakopoulos, D., Hornick, M., Sheth, A.: An overview of workflow management: From process modeling to workflow automation infrastructure. Distributed and Parallel Databases 3(2), 119–153 (1995)

13. Grefen, P., Pernici, B., Sánchez, G.: Database Support for Workflow Management: The Wide Project. Kluwer Academic Pub., Dordrecht (1999)
14. Herbst, J., Karagiannis, D.: Workflow mining with InWoLvE. Computers in Industry 53(3), 245–264 (2004)
15. Herrmann, T., Hoffmann, M.: The Metamorphoses of Workflow Projects in their Early Stages. Computer Supported Cooperative Work (CSCW) 14(5), 399–432 (2005)
16. IDS Scheer. ARIS Process Performance Manager (ARIS PPM) (2002), http://www.ids-scheer.com
17. Kraut, R.E., Fussell, S.R., Brennan, S.E., Siegel, J.: Understanding effects of proximity on collaboration: Implications for technologies to support remote collaborative work. Distributed work, pp. 137–162 (2002)
18. Kueng, P.: The effects of workflow systems on organizations: A qualitative study. In: Van der Aalst, W.M.P., Desel, J., Oberweis, A. (eds.) Business process management: Models, techniques, and empirical studies, pp. 301–316. Springer, Berlin (2000)
19. Lawrence, P. (ed): Workflow Handbook 1997, Workflow Management Coalition. John Wiley and Sons, New York (1997)
20. Mohan, C., Alonso, G., Gunthor, R., Kamath, M.: Exotica: A Research Perspective on Workflow Management Systems. Data Engineering Bulletin 18(1), 19–26 (1995)
21. Oba, M., Onada, S., Komoda, N.: Evaluating the quantitative effects of workflow systems based on real cases. In: Proceedings of the 33rd Hawaii international conference on system sciences, vol. 6, p. 6031. IEEE, Washington, DC (2000)
22. Reijers, H.A., van der Aalst, W.M.P.: The Effectivenes of Workflow Management Systems: Predictions and Lessons Learned. International Journal of Information Management 56(5), 457–471 (2005)
23. Sengupta, K., Zhao, J.L.: Improving the communicational effectiveness of virtual organizations through workflow automation. International Journal of Electronic Commerce 3(1), 49–69 (1998)
24. Steinfield, C., Jang, C.Y., Pfaff, B.: Supporting virtual team collaboration: the TeamSCOPE system. In: Proceedings of the international ACM SIGGROUP conference on Supporting group work, pp. 81–90 (1999)
25. Townsend, A.M., DeMarie, S.M., Hendrickson, A.R.: Virtual teams: Technology and the workplace of the future. IEEE Engineering Management Review 28(2), 69–80 (2000)

What Makes Process Models Understandable?

Jan Mendling[1], Hajo A. Reijers[2], and Jorge Cardoso[3]

[1] Vienna University of Economics and Business Administration
Augasse 2-6, 1090 Vienna, Austria
jan.mendling@wu-wien.ac.at
[2] Eindhoven University of Technology
P.O. Box 513, 5600 MB Eindhoven, The Netherlands
h.a.reijers@tue.nl
[3] University of Madeira
9000-390 Funchal, Portugal
jcardoso@uma.pt

Abstract. Despite that formal and informal quality aspects are of significant importance to business process modeling, there is only little empirical work reported on process model quality and its impact factors. In this paper we investigate understandability as a proxy for quality of process models and focus on its relations with personal and model characteristics. We used a questionnaire in classes at three European universities and generated several novel hypotheses from an exploratory data analysis. Furthermore, we interviewed practitioners to validate our findings. The results reveal that participants tend to exaggerate the differences in model understandability, that self-assessment of modeling competence appears to be invalid, and that the number of arcs in models has an important influence on understandability.

1   Introduction

Even though workflow and process modeling have been used extensively over the past 30 years, we know surprisingly little about the act of modeling and which factors contribute to a "good" process model in terms of human understandability. This observation contrasts with the large body of knowledge that is available for the formal analysis and verification of desirable properties, in particular for Petri nets. To guarantee a certain degree of design quality of the model artifact in a wider sense, several authors propose guidelines for the act of modeling (e.g. [1,2]) but yet with little impact on modeling practice. Clearly, an empirical research agenda is required for acquiring new insights into quality (cf. [3]) and usage aspects (cf. [4]) of process modeling.

Following this line of argumentation, a recent empirical study provides evidence that larger, real-world process models tend to have more formal flaws (such as e.g. deadlocks) than smaller models [5,6]. One obvious hypothesis related to this phenomenon would be that human modelers loose track of the interrelations of large and complex models due to their limited cognitive capabilities (cf. [7]), and then introduce errors that they would not insert in a small model. There

G. Alonso, P. Dadam, and M. Rosemann (Eds.): BPM 2007, LNCS 4714, pp. 48–63, 2007.

are further factors such as the degrees of sequentiality, concurrency, or structuredness that presumably affect the understandability of a process model [8]. Validating such hypothetical relationships empirically would not only represent a major step forward towards understanding quality of process models beyond verification, but also provide a sound theoretical basis for defining guidelines for process modeling in general.

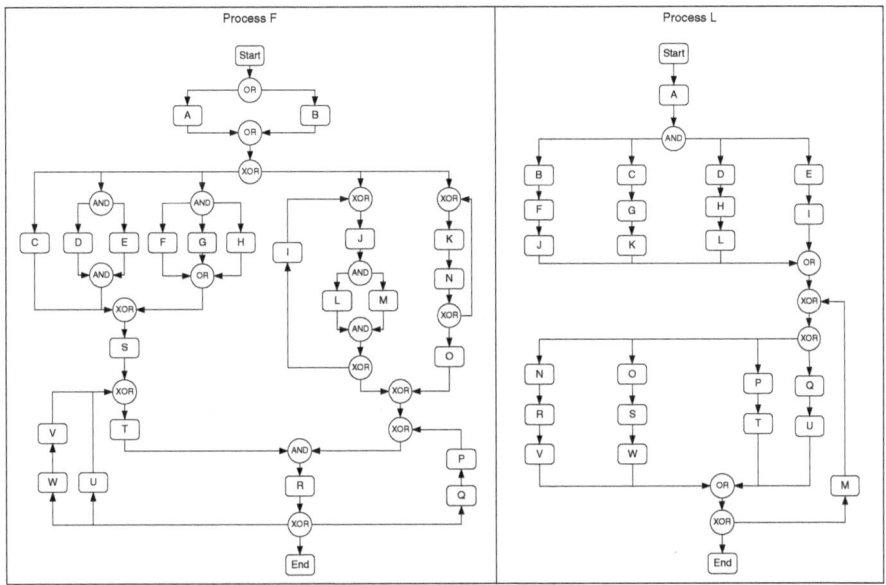

Fig. 1. Proces model F and process model L from the questionnaire

Since only little research has been conducted on quality aspects of process models so far [3], we approach this area with an experimental design focusing on the understandability of process models (*not* of process modeling languages). By having a questionnaire filled out by 73 students who followed courses on process modeling at the Eindhoven University of Technology, the University of Madeira, and the Vienna University of Economics and Business Administration, we aim to gain insight into empirical connections between personal and model characteristics and the ability of a person to understand a process model properly. Figure 1 shows two process models that were included in the questionnaire. Furthermore, we conducted interviews in order to contrast the findings of the questionnaire with expert opinions. In this context, our contribution is twofold. First, we provide an operationalization of understandability as well as of personal and model related factors that may influence process model understandability. Second, we contribute new findings to the still meagre body of empirical knowledge on process modeling. Against this background, the remainder of the paper is structured as follows. In Section 2 we discuss related work and identify a lack of empirically validated insight on the understandability of process models. Then, Section 3 introduces the research design, i.e. in particular, the conceptualization of the questionnaire, the statistical analysis that can be applied on the acquired data, and the role of the expert interviews. In Section 4 we present the results of the analysis and the interviews. Section 5 concludes the paper, discusses limitations of the findings, and identifies open questions that need to be addressed by future research.

2   Related Work

There are basically three streams of research related to our work in the conceptual modeling area: top-down quality frameworks, bottom-up metrics related to quality aspects, and empirical surveys related to modeling techniques.

One prominent *top-down quality framework* is the SEQUAL framework [9,10]. It builds on semiotic theory and defines several quality aspects based on relationships between a model, a body of knowledge, a domain, a modeling language, and the activities of learning, taking action, and modeling. In essence, syntactic quality relates to model and modeling language; semantic quality to model, domain, and knowledge; and pragmatic quality relates to model and modeling and its ability to enable learning and action. Although the framework does not provide an operational definition of how to determine the various degrees of quality, it has been found useful for business process modeling in experiments [11]. The Guidelines of Modeling (GoM) [2] define an alternative quality framework that is inspired by general accounting principles. The guidelines include the six principles of correctness, clarity, relevance, comparability, economic efficiency, and systematic design. This framework was operationalized for EPCs and also tested in experiments [2]. Furthermore, there are authors (e.g. [3]) advocating a specification of a quality framework for conceptual modeling in compliance with the ISO 9126 standard [12] for software quality. A respective adaptation to business process modeling is reported in [13]. Our experiments addresses partial aspects for these frameworks. In particular, we focus on understandability of process models as an enabler of pragmatic quality (SEQUAL) and clarity (GoM). This requires us not only to ask about understandability, but also check whether models are interpreted correctly. This is in line with research of Gemino and Wand [14] who experimented on conclusions that people can draw from models.

There is several work on *bottom-up metrics related to quality aspects* of process models, stemming from different research and partially isolated from each other (see [15,16,17,18,19,20,21,22,23] or for an overview [8]). Several of these contributions are theoretic without empirical validation. Most authors doing experiments focus on the relationship between metrics and quality aspects: *Canfora et al.* study the connection mainly between count metrics – for example, the number of tasks or splits – and maintainability of software process models [21]; *Cardoso* validates the correlation between control flow complexity and perceived complexity [24]; and *Mendling et al.* use metrics to predict control flow errors such as deadlocks in process models [6,8]. The results reveal that an increase in size of a model appears to have a negative impact on quality. This finding has an impact on the design of our questionnaire. To gain insights that are independent of process size, we keep the number of tasks constant and study which other factors might have an impact on understandability.

Finally, there are some *empirical surveys* related to modeling techniques. In [25] the authors study how business process modeling languages have matured over time. While this is valuable research it does not reveal insights on single, concrete process models. The same holds for [26] who study the usability of UML. In [27] the authors also approach understandability, not of individual process models, but on the level of the modeling language. They find out that EPCs seem to be more understandable than Petri nets. Inspired by this survey we decided to use an EPC-like notation in our questionnaire to minimize the impact of the notation on understandability.

To summarize, there is essentially one relation that seems to be confirmed by related research, and that is that larger models tend to be negatively connected with quality. The aim of our questionnaire is to enhance this rather limited body of knowledge.

3   Research Design

Only little research has been conducted on quality aspects of process models so far [3]. In particular, we identify the following six research questions related to the factors that might influence understandability of process models (cf. [27,8,28,10]):

1. What *personal* factors (beyond general psychological and intellectual factors) have an influence?
2. Which *model* characteristics (e.g. number and type of splits) contribute to a good understandability?
3. How does the modeling *purpose* (e.g. documentation versus enactment) relate to understandability?
4. How is understandability related to knowledge about the *domain* that is described in the model?
5. Which differences in understandability exist when observing semantically equivalent models described in different *modeling languages*?
6. What is the impact of different *visual layout* strategies or graph drawing algorithms on understandability?

We approach these questions with an experimental design focusing on personal and model characteristics (question 1 and 2). Furthermore, we strive to neutralize the influence of the other factors: related to question 3, we gathered a set of process models from practice that were all created for documentation purposes. To eliminate the influence of domain knowledge (question 4), we recoded the task labels to capital letters A to W. Based on the observation by [27] that EPCs appear to be easier to understand than Petri nets, we chose for an EPC-like notation without events. The participants received a short informal description of the semantics similar to [29, p.25] (question 5). Finally, we drew all models in the same top-to-bottom style with the start element at the top and end element at the bottom (question 6).

3.1 Phases of the Experiment

The experiment was conducted in three phases. First, we collected a set of eight process models from practice with an equivalent number of tasks (25) and constructed two additional variants for each of them by changing the type of some routing elements (e.g. a particular XOR-split in a AND-split). For these 24 process models we built a questionnaire that measured the following variables:

- THEORY: Students made a self-assessment of theoretical knowledge in business process modeling on a five point ordinal scale,
- PRACTICE: Students made a self-assessment of practical experience in business process modeling on a four point ordinal scale,
- PERCEIVED: For each model, students made an assessment of the perceived difficulty of the model,
- SCORE: For each model, students answered a set of eight closed questions about order, concurrency, exclusiveness, or repetition of tasks in the model and one open question where respondents were free to identify a model problem (if they felt there was any); from the answers we calculated SCORE as the sum of correct answers to serve as an operationalization of understandability; i.e. SCORE measures in how far the semantics of the model are interpreted correctly by the participant.
- RANKING: For all variants of the same model, students ranked these regarding their relative perceived understandability. For example, students were asked if process A was more difficult to understand than process B.

The correct answers for the questions relating to SCORE were determined with the EPC analysis tools introduced in [30]. While the closed answers were evaluated automatically, the open answers had to be interpreted and matched with the errors detected by the tools. The same EPC analysis tools were also used to calculate the set of METRICS (cf. next section). For this first version of the questionnaire, we conducted a pre-test which led to a reduction of the model set to 12 process models, i.e. four models in three variants each, and a reformulation of some questions. We basically dropped the more simple models for preventing fatigue. Second, we created six versions of the questionnaire with different randomized order of models and variants for eliminating learning effects throughout the answering. The questionnaire was filled out in class settings at the various universities by 73 students in total. It led to a total of 847 complete model evaluations. At the time of the experiment, students were following or completing courses on process modeling at the Eindhoven University of Technology, the University of Madeira, and the Vienna University of Economics and Business Administration. Participation was voluntarily. The motivation for the students was the fact that they felt to be in a competitive situation with the other universities, and that we informed them that the questionnaire would be a good exam preparation. The answers were coded and analyzed using the statistics software packages SPSS and Statgraphics. Third, we conducted interviews with experts in business process modeling to contrast our findings with insights from practitioners. This validation is of particular importance considering the insecure external validity of student experiments in information systems research (see [3]).

3.2 Hypothetical Relations Between Factors and Understandability

This section discusses the hypothetical relation between the various factors and understandability. Table 1 gives an overview. In particular, we expect that the perceived difficulty of a process model (PERCEIVED) would be negatively connected with the SCORE as an operationalization of actual understandability. The same positive connection is assumed with THEORY and PRACTICE while the count metrics #NODE, etc., and the DIAMETER of the process model (i.e. the longest path) should be related to a lower understandability. The precise formulae for calculating these and the following metrics are presented in [8]. The SEQUENTIALITY, i.e. the degree to which the model is constructed of task sequences, is expected to be positively connected with understandability. The same is expected for SEPARABILITY, which relates to the degree of articulation points in a model (i.e. nodes whose deletion separates the process model into multiple components), and STRUCTUREDNESS, which relates to how far a process model is built by nesting blocks of matching join and split routing elements. Both CONNECTIVITY and DENSITY relate arcs to nodes: the former by dividing #arcs by #nodes, the latter by dividing #arcs to the maximally possible number of arcs. The TOKEN SPLIT metric captures how many new tokens can be introduced by AND- and OR-splits. It should be negatively connected with understandability. The AVERAGE and MAXIMUM CONNECTOR DEGREE refer to the number of input and output arcs of a routing element, which are expected to be negatively connected with SCORE. The same expectation is there for potential routing elements' MISMATCH, also calculated on the basis of their degree and summed up per routing element; for DEPTH related to the nesting of structured blocks; for the CONTROL FLOW COMPLEXITY metric as the number of choices that can be made at splits in the model; and for CONNECTOR HETEROGENEITY as the degree to which routing elements of different types appear in a model. In the subsequent section we contrast these hypothetical connections with the results of the questionnaire.

4   Results

This section presents the results of the questionnaire and interviews. We first analyze the distribution of SCORE in Section 4.1 and discuss its connection with PERCEIVED difficulty in Section 4.2. Then, we analyze personal factors and their connection with SCORE in Section 4.3. In Section 4.4 we consider the connection of model-related factors operationalized by the set of metrics. The final part of this section is devoted to our interviews with modeling experts.

Table 1. Hypothetical relation between factors and understandability

factor	SCORE	factor	SCORE
PERCEIVED	+	CONNECTIVITY	−
THEORY	+	DENSITY	−
PRACTICE	+	TOKEN SPLITS	−
#NODES	−	AV. CONNECTOR DEGREE	−
#ARCS	−	MAX. CONNECTOR DEGREE	−
#TASKS	−	MISMATCH	−
#CONNECTOR	−	SEPARABILITY	+
#AND (JOIN, SPLIT)	−	DEPTH	−
#XOR (JOIN, SPLIT)	−	STRUCTUREDNESS	+
#OR (JOIN, SPLIT)	−	CONTROL FLOW COMPLEXITY	−
DIAMETER	−	CONNECTOR HETEROGENEITY	−
SEQUENTIALITY	+		

4.1   Distribution of Score

If we apply a standard grading scheme with 10% intervals[1] there would have been 8 students having an A, 27 having a B, 21 with a C, 8 with a D, and 9 with an E. Beyond that, the mean SCORE for all but one of the models ranges between 6.8 and 7.4 with 9 being the maximum, while one model has only a mean SCORE of 5.5. To further examine the distribution of SCORE across the models we applied both Kruskal-Wallis and Mood's median tests at 95% confidence levels [31]. Both non-parametric tests focus on medians to determine differences between distributions, which is appropriate here because SCORE displays significant deviations from a normal distribution. Interestingly, both test results point to the model with the low mean SCORE being different from the other models (P-values $\ll$ 0.05). It is model L, which was already shown in Figure 1. When all models are compared with these tests *excluding* model L, no significant differences between the models can be observed with respect to SCORE (P-values > 0.25).

If we take a closer look at model L, it seems a little odd that this model has such a low SCORE value. As we described in Section 3.1, the questionnaire includes four sets of models and each of these sets includes three slightly different models. Models in the same group differ only with respect to the type of routing elements. But each model in the group that L belongs to has only six routing elements, while the models in other groups contain two or three times this number. Also, the number of arcs in the L model group (37) is lower than that of the other groups (48, 57, and 59). So, L seems to come from a group of models that appears to be relatively easy to see through. Now the question rises why the other models in the same group as L do not show such a comparably low SCORE value. In Figure 2 we display all three models. Note that only model fragments are displayed for ease of visualization. Observed from the top down, it is the type of the second logical routing element that actually distinguishes the

---

[1] A's for 90% score or better, B's for 80%-90%, etc.; E's for less than 60%.

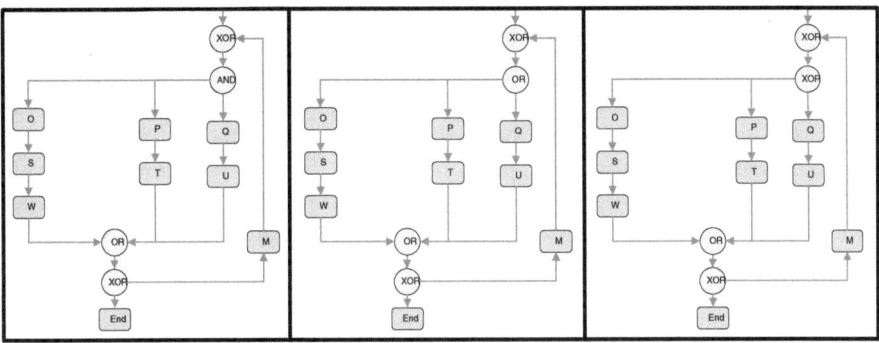

Fig. 2. Fragments of model variants J, K, and L (from left to right)

three models from each other. For model L this is an XOR-split routing element, for the other models an AND-split and OR-split respectively.

When considering the answers of the respondents on a detail level, two questions stand out as they received few correct answers for model L ($\ll$ 20) and many correct answers ($>$ 20) for the other two models. These questions are:

- "If T is executed for a case, can U be executed for the same case?", and
- "Can T, M, and O all be executed for the same case?"

It is clear to see that the distinguishing connectors in the two leftmost models, i.e. the AND-split and OR-split respectively, directly allow for the interleaved execution of T and U. But even for L – the rightmost model in Figure 2 – it is possible that T and U will be executed for the same case. However, this can only happen after a cycle through M. This is presumably overlooked by many respondents. Similarly with respect to the second question, many respondents failed to see that T, M, and O can be executed in the rightmost model (just as this is possible in the other two models of course). So, in general, there is no significant difference in SCORE across the various models; the notable exception is model L which generated a low SCORE value because of the subtle interplay between connector and model structure elements.

4.2   Relation Between Perceived and Score

In addition to SCORE we also analyzed the distribution of PERCEIVED. In particular, we used Kendall's coefficient of agreement u [32,31] to determine whether a ranking can be established by the perception of all participants. Interestingly, for each of the four groups of variants a *total* ordering emerges from the respondents' answers that is significant at a 95% confidence level. This result is confirmed by another part of our questionnaire in which we explicitly asked the respondents to rate the relative differences in understandability between three models from *different* groups. So, despite the fact that it was allowed to rate models as equally difficult to understand, respondents do see distinct differences in the understandability of models within each set and even across the sets.

By now, we see different patterns emerging from the distributions of PER-CEIVED and SCORE. While models are perceived as distinctly different from each other, the actual numbers of correct answers they generate do not differ significantly. There is the notable exception of model L, with a very low SCORE value and, indeed, model L is also perceived as the most difficult model to understand within its group. To investigate the (absence of the) relation between PERCEIVED and SCORE closer, we determined the Pearson correlation coefficient between the variables for all complete 847 model evaluations we gathered. The correlation coefficient equals 0.234 with a P-value $\ll 0.05$, which indicates a significant but relatively weak correlation at a 95% confidence interval.

The insight that we derive from this part of our analysis is that there is a rather loose relation between PERCEIVED and SCORE. Despite a significant statistical relation, respondents tend to *exaggerate* the differences in model understandability for models for which they do not produce significantly different numbers of correct answers. The variations in SCORE also gives us two additional insights. First of all, as all models have the same number of tasks, the lack of significant differences in SCORE across most models potentially points to the fact that model size is the primary factor that impacts model understandability. If so, it would be reasonable that models with equal numbers of tasks appear equally difficult to understand. For the remainder of the analysis we assume that the other factors under investigation (see Section 3.2) are indeed to be considered as of secondary importance. Secondly, it follows from our detailed analysis of model L that a single change in a model element *can* have a significant impact on a model's understandability. So, despite the potentially dominant impact of size, the search for the additional impact factors is indeed relevant.

4.3   Personal Factors and Score

Before we undertook our experiment, we had no reason to expect differences in SCORE between respondents with different university backgrounds. All respondents had received at least a basic training in the use of process modeling techniques at the time they took the questionnaire. Also, the exposure to process modeling in practice would be negligible for all involved respondents. To test the absence of such a difference, we computed the total SCORE over the 12 models. For each respondent, this figure lies between 0 and 108, the latter being the theoretical maximum in case of answering all 9 questions for each of the 12 models correctly. For our respondents, total SCORE ranges between 11 and 103 with an average value of 81.2. In Figure 3, total SCORE is shown for all students in ascending order.

If no difference would exist between the three distributions of total SCORE, students can be assumed to perform similarly across the three universities. To test this, we again applied the non-parametric Kruskal-Wallis test, because application of the Shapiro-Wilk W test indicates that with a 95% confidence total SCORE is not normally distributed for any university.

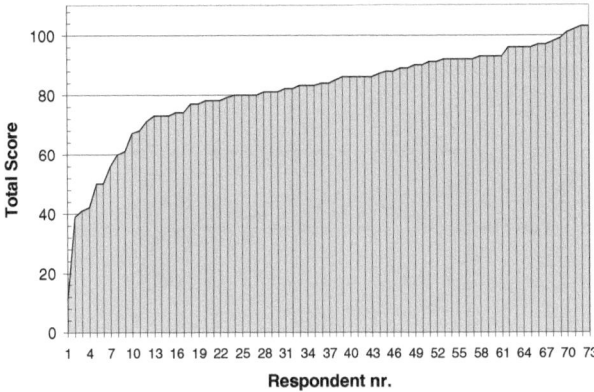

Fig. 3. Total SCORE for respondents

Contrary to expectations, the application of the Kruskal-Wallis test does indicate that there is a statistically significant difference among the medians at a 95% confidence level (P-value ≪ 0.05). In other words, differences exist in the ability of respondents to answer questions correctly *across* the three universities. Additional pairwise Mann-Whitney tests [31] indicate that respondents from Eindhoven perform significantly better than respondents from each of the other two universities (P-values ≪ 0.05), although the difference between the respondents from the universities of Vienna and Madeira is not significant (P-value = 0.061). In Figure 4, box plots are shown for TUe and non-TUe students.

A retrospective analysis of the courses offered at the various universities revealed that the hours spent on actual modeling is the highest in Eindhoven, which may explain the noted difference. In particular, Eindhoven students have been explicitly and thoroughly taught about 'soundness' [33], a general correctness criterion for workflow nets. An alternative explanation is that Eindhoven students are graduate students where the students from Madeira and Vienna are still in their 3rd year of undergraduate studies. Interestingly, across the different universities different modeling techniques are taught. The Eindhoven students were trained in workflow nets (based on the Petri net formalism), the Vienna students in EPCs, and the Madeira students had knowledge of both the Petri net formalism and EPCs. So, the choice of our EPC-like notation does not obviously favor students who are familiar with EPCs.

A search for other differences within the respondent population did not reveal any convincing factors. In particular, both the variables THEORY (0.203) and PRACTICE (0.070) do correlate weakly with total SCORE, but these correlations are not significant at the 95% confidence level. The variables are neither very useful in the identification of clusters with differing total SCORE performances. For example, the clearest identification of two different clusters that resulted from the application of various agglomerative clustering algorithms (e.g. nearest neighbor, media, Ward's method) is shown in Figure 5. Here, the group average distance between clusters is used. It can be seen that most clusters extend across almost the entire range of THEORY and PRACTICE. So, these values have little relation with SCORE. It suggests that, in the context of this study, students' *self-assessments are not valid.*

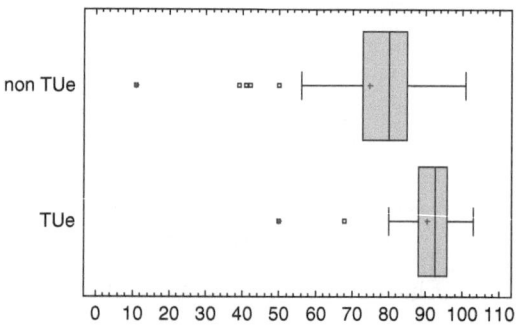

Fig. 4. Total score for TUe and non-TUe respondents

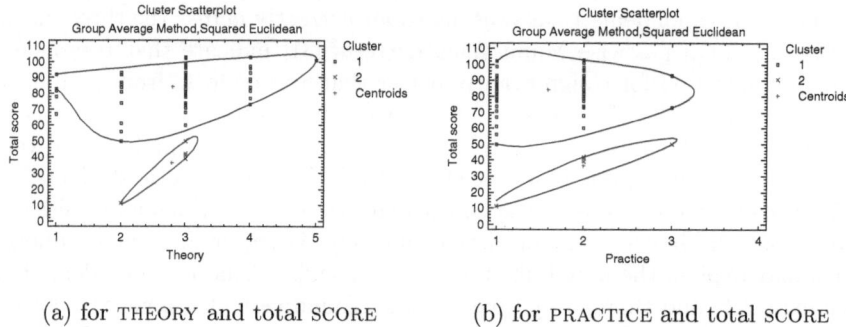

(a) for THEORY and total SCORE   (b) for PRACTICE and total SCORE

Fig. 5. Cluster scatterplots

4.4   Metrics and Score

In this section, the search for secondary factors that have an impact on the understandability of process models is described. As explained in Section 3.2, we take a wide range of potential factors into consideration. To determine their power to explain variations in model understandability, we established for each model its average SCORE (computed over the 73 respondents) and determined Pearson correlation coefficients with all potential factors.

From the correlation coefficients, only the signs of #OR JOINS, DENSITY, AVERAGE CONNECTOR DEGREE, MISMATCH, and CONNECTOR HETEROGENITY correspond with the hypothesized influences as given in Table 1. However, only the correlation coefficients of DENSITY and AVERAGE CONNECTOR DEGREE are significant at a 95% confidence level (see Table 2).

Table 2. Factors with expected impact on understandability

factor	corr.coeff.	P-value
#OR JOINS	-0.330	0.295
DENSITY	-0.618	0.032*
AV. CONNECTOR DEGREE	-0.674	0.016*
MISMATCH	-0.438	0.154
CONNECTOR HETEROGENITY	-0.312	0.323

*significant at 95% confidence level.

To deeper examine the value of the distinguished factors in explaining differences in SCORE, we developed various linear regression models – even though it should be noted that the number of 12 different model observations is quite low for this purpose. We compared all 31 ($= 2^5 - 1$) linear regression models that take a non-empty subset into account of the factors shown in Table 2. To differentiate between the regression models, we used the adjusted R^2 statistic that measures how the variability in the SCORE is explained by each model. Within this setting, no multivariate regression model had acceptable t-values.

The best adjusted R^2 statistic equals 45% and belongs to the regression model that uses AVERAGE CONNECTOR DEGREE – one of the factors that correlates significantly with average SCORE. For this regression model, the Durbin-Watson statistic value indicates that there is no serial autocorrelation in the residuals at the 95% confidence level. In Figure 6 a plot is shown of the fitted model values using this regression model. Note that the outlying model L can be clearly identified at the bottom right corner.

As stated, the number of models is too small to make any strong claims. Still, from the factors considered we see that the two factors which most

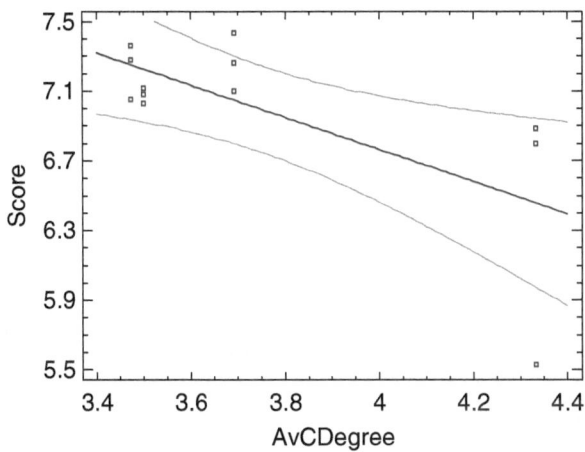

Fig. 6. Linear regression model (including 95% confidence levels)

convincingly relate to model understandability *both* concern the number of arcs in a process model. The AVERAGE CONNECTOR DEGREE measures the model's average of incoming/outcoming arcs per routing element, while DENSITY gives the ratio of existing arcs to the maximal number of arcs between the nodes in the model (i.e. when it would be completely connected). Both factors point to the negative effect of a relatively high number of arcs on a model's understandability.

4.5   Expert Interviews

To validate our results, we interviewed 12 professional process modellers on the insights gained from our questionnaire. On average this group possessed over 10 years of expertise in developing process models, mainly for documentation purposes, but most had experience with enactment models as well. The professionals are employed in 7 different companies, four of which being consultancy firms, two financials, and one utilities company.

With respect to *personal factors*, the experts emphasized the value of subjects' analytical skills and visual perceptiveness to understand process models. Aside from these mental faculties, both modeling experience and familiarity with the modeling technique at hand were mentioned often as being of positive influence. While the former aspect is explicitly confirmed by the findings from our questionnaire, we have no direct support for the second aspect.

Next, we asked the experts whether users are capable of *assessing their own ability to understand process models*. Half of the experts predominantly thought so, while the others predominantly thought the opposite. In the former group, modeling experience and familiarity with the modeling technique were mentioned by almost all as important conditional factors. One of the experts from the latter group indicated that "people tend to overestimate themselves, particularly men". Interestingly, one respondent indicated that people in general will be able to understand what a model intends to communicate, but that it is hard to determine whether a model is completely correct. The image emerges that proper self-assessment with respect to model understandability is problematic to say the least, which is consistent with our findings.

Finally, experts indicated a decreasing relevance of (a) model-related factors, (b) person-related factors, and (c) domain knowledge for the understanding of process models. The model-related factors that were mentioned most as positively influencing model understandability: unambiguity (7 times), simplicity (4 times), structuredness (4 times) and modularity (4 times). From the less-mentioned factors, the supposed positive effects of textual support is interesting to mention, i.e. well-chosen textual descriptions of model elements (3 times) and textual context information on the model in general (3 times). Part of the factors mentioned seem to overlap with the factors considered in this study (e.g. simplicity and structuredness), while others are food for further research (e.g. modularity and textual support).

5 Conclusions

We set out with this research to develop a better insight into the factors that make process models understandable for humans. From the six research questions in Section 3, we focused on the relations between personal and model characteristics (questions 1 and 2). Our findings suggest that *personal factors* indeed influence the ability to understand process models. In particular, it seems that the amount of theoretical modeling knowledge of the subjects may play a role here. At the same time, our respondents were not capable of a proper self-assessment with respect to their modeling proficiency. With respect to the *model characteristics*, our findings from the questionnaire seem to underline the insight that model size is of dominant importance on model understandability. Yet, small variations between models *can* lead to significant differences in their comprehensibility. This means that secondary explanatory factors are still missing from the picture. From our analysis of a wide set of candidate factors, the AVERAGE CONNECTOR DEGREE is the most convincing factor that relates to model understandability, followed by a model's DENSITY. Both factors point at the negative effect of a relatively high number of arcs on a model's understandability.

To counter the potentially limited validity of an experiment involving students, we *interviewed* a number of experienced process modelers. Their opinions generally supported our findings, while the interviews also generated further factors to investigate. Our research is characterized by other *limitations*, in particular the small set of models being considered and the limited set of participants. With larger sets in future replications of the experiment, we can investigate the impact of secondary factors in greater detail. The other directions for *future research* follow logically from the research questions we did not address yet. While we tried to neutralize the influences of the modeling purpose, knowledge of the domain, modeling language, and layout strategy, these are all issues that need further exploration.

References

1. Hoppenbrouwers, S., Proper, H., van der Weide, T.: A Fundamental View on the Process of Conceptual Modeling. In: Delcambre, L.M.L., Kop, C., Mayr, H.C., Mylopoulos, J., Pastor, Ó. (eds.) ER 2005. LNCS, vol. 3716, pp. 128–143. Springer, Heidelberg (2005)
2. Becker, J., Rosemann, M., Uthmann, C.: Guidelines of Business Process Modeling. In: van der Aalst, W., Desel, J., Oberweis, A. (eds.) Business Process Management. Models, Techniques, and Empirical Studies, pp. 30–49. Springer, Berlin (2000)
3. Moody, D.: Theoretical and practical issues in evaluating the quality of conceptual models: current state and future directions. Data & Knowledge Engineering 55, 243–276 (2005)
4. Davies, I., Green, P., Rosemann, M., Indulska, M., Gallo, S.: How do practitioners use conceptual modeling in practice? Data & Knowledge Engineering 58, 358–380 (2006)
5. Mendling, J., Moser, M., Neumann, G., Verbeek, H., Dongen, B., Aalst, W.: Faulty EPCs in the SAP Reference Model. In: Dustdar, S., Fiadeiro, J.L., Sheth, A. (eds.) BPM 2006. LNCS, vol. 4102, pp. 451–457. Springer, Heidelberg (2006)

6. Mendling, J., Moser, M., Neumann, G., Verbeek, H., Dongen, B., Aalst, W.: A Quantitative Analysis of Faulty EPCs in the SAP Reference Model. BPM Center Report BPM-06-08, BPMCenter.org (2006)

7. Simon, H.: Sciences of the Artificial, 3rd edn. MIT Press, Cambridge (1996)

8. Mendling, J.: Detection and Prediction of Errors in EPC Business Process Models. PhD thesis, Vienna University of Economics and Business Administration (2007)

9. Lindland, O.I., Sindre, G., Sølvberg, A.: Understanding quality in conceptual modeling. IEEE Software 11(2), 42–49 (1994)

10. Krogstie, J., Sindre, G., Jørgensen, H.D.: Process models representing knowledge for action: a revised quality framework. European Journal of Information Systems 15, 91–102 (2006)

11. Moody, D., Sindre, G., Brasethvik, T., Sølvberg, A.: Evaluating the quality of process models: Empirical testing of a quality framework. In: Spaccapietra, S., March, S.T., Kambayashi, Y. (eds.) ER 2002. LNCS, vol. 2503, pp. 380–396. Springer, Heidelberg (2002)

12. Int. Standards Org (ISO): Information technology - software product evaluation - quality characteristics and guide lines for their use. ISO/IEC IS 9126 (1991)

13. Güceglioglu, A.S., Demirörs, O.: Using software quality characteristics to measure business process quality. In: van der Aalst, W.M.P., Benatallah, B., Casati, F., Curbera, F. (eds.) BPM 2005. LNCS, vol. 3649, pp. 374–379. Springer, Heidelberg (2005)

14. Gemino, A., Wand, Y.: Evaluating modeling techniques based on models of learning. Commun. ACM 46, 79–84 (2003)

15. Lee, G., Yoon, J.M.: An empirical study on the complexity metrics of petri nets. Microelectronics and Reliability 32, 323–329 (1992)

16. Nissen, M.E.: Redesigning reengineering through measurement-driven inference. MIS Quarterly 22, 509–534 (1998)

17. Morasca, S.: Measuring attributes of concurrent software specifications in petri nets. In: METRICS '99: Proceedings of the 6th International Symposium on Software Metrics, Washington, DC, USA, pp. 100–110. IEEE Computer Society, Los Alamitos (1999)

18. Reijers, H., Vanderfeesten, I.: Cohesion and coupling metrics for workflow process design. In: Desel, J., Pernici, B., Weske, M. (eds.) BPM 2004. LNCS, vol. 3080, pp. 290–305. Springer, Heidelberg (2004)

19. Cardoso, J.: Evaluating Workflows and Web Process Complexity. In: Workflow Handbook, Future Strategies, Inc., Lighthouse Point, USA pp. 284–290 (2005)

20. Balasubramanian, S., Gupta, M.: Structural metrics for goal based business process design and evaluation. Business Process Management Journal 11, 680–694 (2005)

21. Canfora, G., García, F., Piattini, M., Ruiz, F., Visaggio, C.: A family of experiments to validate metrics for software process models. Journal of Systems and Software 77, 113–129 (2005)

22. Aguilar, E.R., Ruiz, F., García, F., Piattini, M.: Towards a Suite of Metrics for Business Process Models in BPMN. In: Manolopoulos, Y., Filipe, J., Constantopoulos, P., Cordeiro, J. (eds.) ICEIS 2006 - Proceedings of the Eighth International Conference on Enterprise Information Systems (III), pp. 440–443 (2006)

23. Laue, R., Gruhn, V.: Complexity metrics for business process models. In: Abramowicz, W., Mayr, H.C. (eds.) 9th International Conference on Business Information Systems (BIS 2006). Lecture Notes in Informatics, vol. 85, pp. 1–12 (2006)

24. Cardoso, J.: Process control-flow complexity metric: An empirical validation. In: Proceedings of IEEE International Conference on Services Computing (IEEE SCC 06), Chicago, USA, September 18-22, pp. 167–173. IEEE Computer Society, Los Alamitos (2006)
25. Rosemann, M., Recker, J., Indulska, M., Green, P.: A study of the evolution of the representational capabilities of process modeling grammars. In: Dubois, E., Pohl, K. (eds.) CAiSE 2006. LNCS, vol. 4001, pp. 447–461. Springer, Heidelberg (2006)
26. Agarwal, R., Sinha, A.P.: Object-oriented modeling with uml: a study of developers' perceptions. Commun. ACM 46, 248–256 (2003)
27. Sarshar, K., Loos, P.: Comparing the control-flow of epc and petri net from the end-user perspective. In: van der Aalst, W.M.P., Benatallah, B., Casati, F., Curbera, F. (eds.) BPM 2005. LNCS, vol. 3649, pp. 434–439. Springer, Heidelberg (2005)
28. Lange, C., Chaudron, M.: Effects of defects in uml models: an experimental investigation. In: Osterweil, L.J., Rombach, H.D., Soffa, M.L. (eds.) 28th International Conference on Software Engineering (ICSE 2006), Shanghai, China, May 20-28, 2006, pp. 401–411. ACM Press, New York (2006)
29. Mendling, J., Aalst, W.: Towards EPC Semantics based on State and Context. In: Nüttgens, M., Rump, F.J., Mendling, J. (eds.) Proceedings of the 5th GI Workshop on Business Process Management with Event-Driven Process Chains (EPK, Vienna, Austria, German Informatics Society pp.25–48 (2006)
30. Mendling, J., Aalst, W.: Formalization and Verification of EPCs with OR-Joins Based on State and Context. In: Krogstie, J., Opdahl, A.L., Sindre, G. (eds.) CAiSE 2007. LNCS, vol. 4495, Springer, Heidelberg (2007)
31. Siegel, S., Castellan, N.J.: Nonparametric Statistics for the Behavorial Sciences, 2nd edn. McGraw-Hill, New York (1988)
32. Kendall, M.G.: Rank Correlation Methods, 4th edn. Griffin, London (1970)
33. Aalst, W.: Workflow Verification: Finding Control-Flow Errors Using Petri-Net-Based Techniques. In: van der Aalst, W.M.P., Desel, J., Oberweis, A. (eds.) Business Process Management. LNCS, vol. 1806, pp. 161–183. Springer, Heidelberg (2000)

Modeling of Task-Based Authorization Constraints in BPMN

Christian Wolter and Andreas Schaad

SAP Research
Vincenz-Priessnitz-Str. 1, 76131 Karlsruhe, Germany
{christian.wolter,andreas.schaad}@sap.com

Abstract. Workflows model and control the execution of business processes in an organisation by defining a set of tasks to be done. The specification of workflows is well-elaborated and heavily tool supported. Task-based access control is tailored to specify authorization constraints for task allocation in workflows. Existing workflow modeling notations do not support the description of authorization constraints for task allocation commonly referred to as resource allocation patterns.

In this paper we propose an extension for the Business Process Modeling Notation (BPMN) to express such authorizations within the workflow model, enabling the support of resource allocation pattern, such as Separation of Duty, Role-Based Allocation, Case Handling, or History-Based Allocation in BPMN. These pattern allow to specify authorization constraints, for instance role-task assignments, separation of duty, and binding of duty constraints. Based on a formal approach we develop an authorization constraint artifact for BPMN to describe such constraints.

As a pragmatic demonstration of the feasibility of our proposed extension we model authorization constraints inspired by a real world banking workflow scenario. In the course of this paper we identify several aspects of future work related to verification and consistency analysis of modeled authorization constraints, tool-supported and pattern-driven authorization constraint description, and automatic derivation of authorization policies, such as defined by the eXtensible Access Control Markup Language (XACML).

Keywords: Security in business processes, Business process modeling and analysis.

1 Introduction

Process-aware information systems, such as workflow management systems, enterprise resource planning applications, and customer relationship management systems are used to control and monitor business activities [1]. In the application area of business activity or workflow specification, modeling patterns have emerged assigned to different business and organizational perspectives. The control flow perspective focuses on the aspect of process control such as process flow, routing, synchronization, and merging. Patterns related to the data perspective address issues, such as data visibility, data interaction, data transfer, and data-based routing. A recent perspective is that of resource

G. Alonso, P. Dadam, and M. Rosemann (Eds.): BPM 2007, LNCS 4714, pp. 64–79, 2007.

allocation patterns. It focuses on the manner in which work is distributed and managed by human resources associated with a workflow [2].

"The resource perspective centers on the modeling of resources and their interaction with a process-aware information system" [1]. Resources can be differentiated into human and non-human resources. Resource patterns were investigated with respect to levering the interaction of humans with the information system beyond the assignment and execution of tasks in an user's task list. Especially, so called creation patterns deal with the specification of task advertisement and allocation restrictions (i.e. who may claim and execute a task) [2].

Control of work allocation and execution is a recognized fundamental principle of human interaction in computer security originating from organisational theory enforced by authorization constraints [3]. One of the earliest authorization constraints for human work allocation control is the four-eyes principle and first appeared in Saltzer and Schroeder [4]. Later the term separation of duty was introduced in [5] as a principle for integrity and a mechanism for error control and preventing fraud. In human-centric workflows this is done by limiting an user's work allocation statically and dynamically [6]. In the former an user's work allocation is limited a priori for instance by assigning a role with a fixed set of tasks. In the latter an user's work allocation is constrained depending on the tasks the user recently performed. In [7], Botha gives a taxonomy for different kinds of static and dynamic separation of duty and describes the conflicting entities paradigm for tasks implying that the risk of fraud increases if the associations with those tasks are not carefully controlled and monitored.

1.1 Problem Statement

Recent work has shown that existing modeling notations, such as BPMN, UML 2.0 AD, or ORACLE BPEL provide poor support for most resource allocation pattern [1,2]. The Separation of Duty, History-Based, Case Handling, and Role-Based resource allocation pattern address the aspect of defining authorization constraints, such as it is well known in the application domain of task-based security administration for workflows. Task-based authorization constraints express who is allowed or must perform a certain task under specific circumstances in the context of a workflow, but most resource allocation pattern are not supported by well elaborated modeling notations as stated in [2]. Therefore, it should be explored if the domain of business process modeling, resource allocation patterns, and the specification of authorization constraints for workflows can be united.

A possible approach would be to create a new workflow modeling notation with a focus on task-based authorization specification or to extend an existing graphical policy specification language, such as LaSCO [8], with control flow elements. In [2], Aalst *et al.* claim to enhance existing process modeling notations to support the resource allocation perspective, rather then creating new notations that overlap with existing ones along the control flow perspective. From the domain of security engineering Crampton stated "[..] that existing approaches to the specification of authorization constraints are unnecessarily complicated" [9] and not directly specified within the workflow model itself. This might lead to inconsistency issues in the case of model changes, when the related authorization constraints are not changed as well. Recent extensions to existing process execution languages such as RBAC-WS-BPEL [10] and BPEL4People [11] indicate that the fusion of business process definition and related authorization specification for manual tasks is at hand. One possible next step would be to leverage the definition of authorization constraints into the process of workflow modeling.

Therefore, in this paper we propose a refinement of the Business Process Modeling Notation to enable a description of authorization constraints, without affecting the control flow semantics of BPMN as desired in [12] and avoiding an overly complex specification language. The extended notation allows the specification of task-based authorization constraints and enhance the support of resource allocation patterns by BPMN, such as the Separation of Duty pattern [1,2]. The extension enables the description of role hierarchies, separation of duty, and binding of duty constraints within the BPMN model. We choose BPMN because of its capabilities to be mapped onto BPEL [13,14] an emerging standard in workflow specification. On the other hand BPMN has an appealing graphical notation. The basic flow elements of BPMN are extremely easy to understand and grasp. Even security specialists who are not very familiar with the details of BPMN are able to understand these diagrams.

In essence, the contributions of this paper are as follows,

- it is a formal definition of authorization constraints in the context of workflow models.
- it provides example workflow constraints derived from the banking domain and their formal representation.
- it is an evaluation of BPMN's capabilities to express task-based authorization constraints in the context of resource allocation and defines a BPMN extension for the specification of appropriate authorization constraints.
- it applies the proposed BPMN extension to a real world banking scenario to evaluate its applicability.

The rest of the paper is organized as follows. In Section 2 we discuss a formal definition of authorization constraints for workflow environments and provide some preliminary examples. A banking workflow is presented in Section 3 and several real world authorization constraints for this example process are given along with their formal representation. In the subsequent section we propose a BPMN extension based on our formal definition to visualize the discussed authorization constraints. We apply our notation to the example banking workflow in order to demonstrate the feasibility of our proposal. In Section 4 we proceed with an overview of related work in the area of authorization constraint modeling and specification. In Section 5 we discuss and conclude our approach and outline some suggestions of future work, such as model consistency and verification analysis.

2   Authorization Constraints for Workflows

The definition of organisational roles is a suitable concept for expressing elaborate and fine-grained authorization control. Thus, it is not surprising that defining authorization constraints received particular attention with the progress made in role-based access control [15]. The definition of authorizations that should not be owned by the same user in order to make fraudulent acts more difficult to commit evolved into the principle of conflict of interest. Conflict of interest in workflows can be expressed by defining conflicting tasks in the context of task-based access control [16]. In [7], conflicting tasks are characterized by an increased risk for potential misuse and fraud if a single user is authorized to perform them all. Therefore, the authorization to allocate and perform conflicting tasks has to be constrained carefully.

In [9], Crampton identified and formalized different authorization constraint types for conflicting tasks in workflows. Namely, entailment constraints for defining authorizations depending on already performed tasks and additional cardinality constraints to express separation of duty and binding of duty requirements for workflow tasks and tasks instances. He defined an entailment constraint as: "If the execution of a task t_2 is constrained by the execution of another task t_1, where $t_1 < t_2$, then we say that t_2 is an entailed task of t_1" [9]. Here "$<$" denotes a temporal dependence between the execution of task t_1 and t_2, meaning t_1 was executed prior to t_2. According to his definition entailment constraints are related to exactly two tasks. In [10], he identified this restriction and outlined future work to extend the definition of entailment constraints. In what follows we develop a formalized authorization constraint that builds on previous work of Crampton, but overcomes the existing limitations. Therefore, our proposed authorization constraint specification can be applied to an arbitrary set of conflicting workflow tasks and task instances, across role boundaries, and beyond simple task sequences.

2.1 Formalization of Authorization Constraints

To provide a formalized definition we will begin with defining user-role assignments and task-role assignments. Further, we define conflicting tasks and present a general definition of an authorization constraint. We consider a task assignment as the determination of a set of potential users allowed to perform a task. An allocation is the actual claim to perform an assigned task by an user.

Task-Role Assignment
Tasks assigned to roles are a first approach to restrict task authorization according to user roles. If there exists a set of tasks that imply a potential risk of fraud or misuse when performed by the same user, such task authorizations can be distributed among different roles at design time of the workflow. Therefore, a task-based assignment of tasks according to an user's role enforces separation of duty security requirements as long as an user is restricted to a single role within a workflow instance. This is commonly referred to as static separation of duty [3].

We define T as the set of tasks $\{t_1, t_2, ..., t_l\}$ and R as a set of roles $\{r_1, r_2, ..., r_m\}$. We assume the existence of a partially ordered set of relations between roles $\langle R, \leq \rangle$ that can be visualized as a role hierarchy. If $r_1, r_2 \in R$ and $r_1 < r_2$, then we say r_2 dominates r_1 with respect to organisational role superiority (e.g., $r_{Clerk} < r_{Manager}$). Further, we define U as the set of users $\{u_1, u_2, ..., u_n\}$. Let $TR \subseteq (T \times R)$ be a many-to-many task-role assignment relation and let $UR \subseteq (U \times R)$ be a many-to-many user-role assignment relation. This means, users are associated with roles using the user-role assignment relation and tasks are associated with roles using the task-role assignment relation. Further, we will assume that a task is an atomic action within the context of a workflow. According to [9] we define:

$$R(t) = \{r_m \in R : \exists (t_l, r_m) \in TR(t)\}$$
$$U(t) = \{u_n \in U : \exists (u_n, r_m) \in UR, r_m \in R(t)\}.$$

In other words $R(t)$ is the set of roles authorized to allocate a task t_l. Thus, $U(t)$ is the set of users authorized to allocate and perform the task t_l.

Conflicting Tasks

In some cases conflicting tasks cannot be assigned to different roles without segmenting the existing roles in such a way that they become unmanageable with respect to the referred organisational role model. In addition, role hierarchies can be used to act in two previously separated roles and thus regaining the authorization to allocate conflicting tasks, e.g. a manager may act as a clerk and as his own supervisor. Hence, we have to define additional constraints between tasks that do not depend on potential task-role assignments.

For this reason we define a workflow model N as a *tuple* (T, c_i, c_o, F). A workflow consists of a set of tasks T. Let c_i be the start condition and c_o the end condition of the workflow. The control flow relation (i.e., task sequence, splits, and joins) of all tasks in T is defined by the relation $F \subseteq (c_i \times T) \cup (T \times c_o) \cup (T \times T)$. That means every task in the workflow (T, F) is on a directed path from c_i to c_o.

We define a set of conflicting tasks of a workflow N as $T_c \subseteq T$. According to [9] the set T_c contains tasks whose allocation depends on the allocation of previously performed tasks of T_c. Such dependencies are described as an entailment between the tasks of T_c [9]. We define $t_n \in T_c$ as an entailed task of $t_m \in T_c$, when the allocation of t_n is constrained by the allocation of task t_m, where $t_m < t_n$ (i.e. on a direct path from c_i to c_o, t_m is performed before t_n).

Task Authorization Constraint

With the definition of sets of conflicting tasks and the general understanding that the authorization of an user to perform further conflicting tasks of the same set depends on his and other users previous actions in a workflow we can define a task authorization constraint c for a set of conflicting tasks as:

$$c = (T_c, n_u, m_{th}), \text{ with } n_u, m_{th} \in \mathbb{N}.$$

The value n_u defines the minimal number of different users that have to allocate a task $t_k \in T_c$. Let t_{k_i} be an instance of the task t_k. We define m_{th} as the threshold value of the sum of task instances $t_{k_i}, \forall t \in T_c$ an user u_n is allowed to allocate:

$$m_{th}(u_n) = \sum (t_{k_i}(u_n)), \forall t \in T_c,$$
$$m_{th}(u_n) \leq m_{th}, \forall u \in U.$$

It should be mentioned that m_{th} sums up the task instances of all tasks in T_c, while n_u dictates the number of different users that have to allocate at least one tasks instance of tasks $\in T_c$. The following Table 1 gives some example constraints based on common task allocation requirements.

Table 1. Example Constraints

c_n	Workflow	Separation of Duty Requirement	Formal Constraint (T_c, n_u, m_{th})
c_1	t1 → t2	Task t_1 and t_2 must be performed by different users.	$c_1 = (\{t_1, t_2\}, 2, 1)$
c_2	t1 → t2	Task t_1 and t_2 must be performed by the same user.	$c_1 = (\{t_1, t_2\}, 1, 2)$
c_3	t1 → t2; t4 ← t3	Two users must be involved in performing t_1, t_2, t_3, and t_4.	$c_1 = (\{t_1, t_2, t_3, t_4\}, 2, 3)$ Here, the maximum value of m_{th} is implicitly dictated by n_u.
c_4	t1 → t2; t4 ← t3	Two users must be involved and each user may only perform two out of four tasks.	$c_1 = (\{t_1, t_2, t_3, t_4\}, 2, 2)$ Unlike c_3, $m_{th} = 2$, otherwise the 2-out-of-4 requirement can not be expressed as a constraint.
c_5	t1 → t2	The same task can only be performed twice by the same user and t_1 and t_2 must be performed by different users.	$c_1 = (\{t_1, t_2\}, 2, 2)$

Our definition of authorization constraints allows to specify constrained workflow models that may encounter a deadlock situation due to shortage of different users or inconsistencies between nested constraints at run time. In [9], an algorithm is presented that is able to determine inconsistent workflow authorization constraints. This algorithm is based on a simulation-based approach by exhaustively searching possible execution paths of a constrained workflow without an occurring deadlock situation due to authorization constraints. This approach is limited to constraints defined on a pair of tasks and has to be expanded to an arbitrary set of tasks per constraint. We are aware of this important consistency issue and are planning to apply the algorithm to our BPMN models at design time, but refer to Section 5 and consider this topic as future work.

2.2 Conflicting Tasks in a Banking Workflow

In this section we present an example workflow inspired and in parts derived from the banking application workflow that is given in [3]. We discuss several conflicting tasks and their related task allocation constraints for this example workflow. For each constraint we provide a formal description based on the authorization constraint definition of the last subsection. We keep the example workflow as simple and intuitive as possible without losing ourself in routing, messaging, and exception details, but with the idea in mind that our approach can be applied to a real world scenario.

The process describes the necessary steps for opening an account for a customer. Therefore, the customer's personal data is acquired. The customer is identified and the customer's credit worthiness is checked by an external institution. Afterwards, one of several product bundles is chosen. A form is printed for the selected bundle that is signed by the customer and the bank. The described process is illustrated in Figure 1.

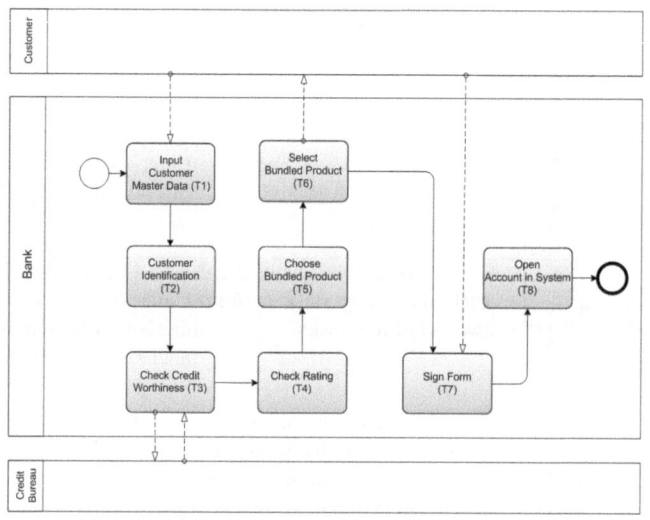

Fig. 1. Example Banking Workflow

The following set of task assignment constraints is a subset of properties that were discussed in [3] with SAP Banking solution architects:

1. *A Clerk must interact with the customer*
   This constraint describes the role definition of a clerk according to task-role and user-task assignment. There exists a direct relationship to the Role-Based Allocation discussed in [1]. This requirement can be expressed with the role definition:

$$TR_{clerk} = \{t_1, t_2, t_3, t_4, t_5, t_6, t_8\} \ (Role\text{-}Based)$$

2. *A bank manager must sign the form as a clerk's supervisor and can act as a clerk regarding any other task*
   This is another role definition related to the Role-Based Allocation. Here, the role manager inherits the set of task authorizations of the role clerk and extends the set with task t_7. This requirement can be expressed with the role definition of a manager:

$$TR_{manager} = \{TR_{clerk} \cup t_7\} \ (Role\text{-}Based)$$

3. *An user must not check the credit worthiness and rating for the same customer.*
A separation of duty requirement that is related to the Separation of Duty resource allocation pattern describing that the same user must not perform two conflicting tasks [1]. In this example the resulting authorization constraint would be:

$$c_3 = (\{t_3, t_4\}, 2, 1) \textit{ (Separation of Duty, Role-Based, History-Based)}$$

4. *A bank manager may act as a clerk, but must not sign his own form.*
This requirement is similar to the previous constraint, but this time the set of conflicting tasks spans two different roles (e.g. the role clerk and the role manager). Thus, the same user capable of acting in two different roles for the same workflow instance would still violate this requirement. For example, an user acts in the role of a clerk and later changes to the manager role in order to sign his own form. Therefore, the resulting authorization constraint preventing the exploitation of the role hierarchy would be:

$$c_4 = (\{t_7, t_8\}, 2, 1) \textit{ (Separation of Duty, Role-Based, History-Based)}$$

5. *An user acquiring the customer data must identify the customer's account.*
This requirement is related to the binding of duty principle discussed in [9]. This means the same user performing a previous task is automatically assigned to all other tasks of the same set. In [1], additional patterns are discussed, such as Case Handling, History-based Allocation, and Retain Familiar patterns. They are based on the idea that further allocation is done automatically due to some previous activities. Hence, binding of duty requirements are related to those resource allocation pattern. The resulting constraint is:

$$c_5 = (\{t_1, t_2\}, 1, 2) \textit{ (Case Handling, Role-Based, History-Based, Retain Familiar)}$$

6. *For a single customer an user must not perform more than five tasks.*
This is a dynamic separation of duty constraint allowing a clerk to allocate any tasks as long as he does not allocate more than five tasks for the same workflow. This constraint is more flexible than the previous separation of duty constraints, because it cannot be determined in advance which tasks an user will allocate, depending on his allocation behaviour his authorized tasks vary for each workflow instance. The according authorization constraint would be:

$$c_6 = (TR_{clerk}, 2, 5) \textit{ (History-Based)}$$

3   Modeling of Authorization Constraints

Several authorization specification languages and modeling approaches can be found in the literature [3,4,7,9,17,18,19]. None of these languages and approaches was applied in the context of workflow modeling itself, but rather done in a separate specification and modeling environment, sometimes even without access to the related workflow model making the whole process error prone and inconsistent with the related workflow, when it changes. In this section we address this problem by integrating the notation of an authorization constraint into a strong visual and commonly used workflow modeling notation, such as BPMN.

3.1   Extension of BPMN

The Business Process Modeling Notation (BPMN) has a general look-and-feel that makes it easy to be understood by diagram modelers and any viewer of the diagram. Besides its strong visual expressiveness, another important aspect of BPMN is its extensibility capabilities as stated by the creators of BPMN [12]. When extending BPMN it is important to neither change the general footprint of any existing flow element, such as events, activities and gateways. Nor should any new flow element be added, because no specification will be available describing how it will be connected to existing flow elements. Therefore, BPMN provides the concept of artifacts to extend the expressiveness of BPMN without affecting the basic sequence or message flow of a process model or the mapping to execution languages, such as BPEL. The artifacts are designed to be open to allow annotations and makers to convey specialized information [12].

To model task allocation constraints within the workflow model, according to our formal definition, we need to express manual tasks and their assigned roles. It must be possible to define a partial role order with respect to role hierarchies. Further, we need the possibility to define groups of manual tasks we can apply constrains to. As a last step, it is necessary to express the authorization constraint we discussed in the last section. Most of the requirements can be already fulfilled in BPMN with an existing graphical element and we need to extend its semantic. In the case of the authorization constraint itself we derive a new artifact from the textual annotation element.

The entity relationship diagram depicted in Figure 2 shows an extract of the BPMN metamodel [20] and highlights the entities, named according to the BPMN specification, necessary to express authorization constraints within BPMN.

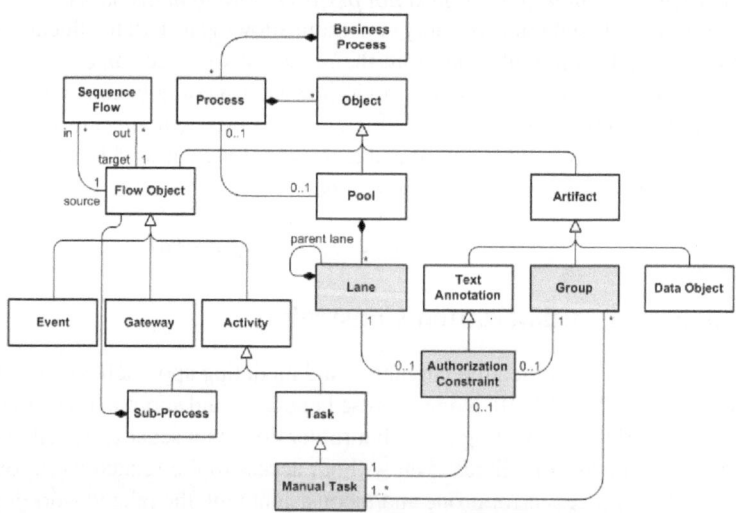

Fig. 2. Extract of the extended BPMN Metamodel

Manual Tasks and Roles

An activity is a generic term for a task that someone performs. A task can be atomic or non-atomic (here we restrict ourself to atomic tasks). Pools or lanes may contain tasks. Each task in BPMN comes with a boolean attribute *Manual Task* that can be used to specify a task as manual, i.e. it must be performed by an user. Lanes are used to assign tasks to organisational roles of a rights management system and refer to the classical role-task authorization. Nested lanes are used to represent the role-based task authorization inheritance and role hierarchy. For example in Figure 3 the Manager role inherits the task authorizations for task $t1$ and $t3$ from the nested role Clerk. Note that we consider the Pool entity a functional unit, such as a department or an institution, rather than an organisational role.

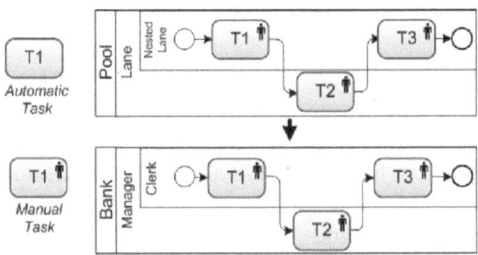

Fig. 3. Manual Tasks and Roles in BPMN

Grouping of Tasks

Grouping of activities does not affect the sequence flow. Groups can be used for documentation or analysis purposes. They can be defined by using the group artifact, lanes, or multiple and looped tasks. Unlike lanes, groups do not map to roles or groups in the context of rights management systems, but are used to define a group of activities and assign a dedicated authorization constraint to this group. We consider multiple instance tasks and looped tasks as a group with exactly one task, but an arbitrary number of task instances. Therefore, the following Figure 4 shows BPMN elements that we consider as a mechanism to define groups of tasks:

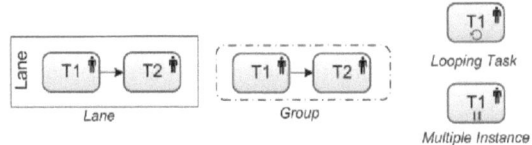

Fig. 4. Task Groups in BPMN

Authorization Constraint Artifact

Without an authorization constraint a group of tasks has no semantic in the sense of conflicting tasks associated with it. In the context of conflicting tasks definition we derive the authorization constraint from the textual annotation as a new entity. Text annotations are a mechanism for a modeler to provide additional information for the reader of a BPMN diagram. The authorization constraints contains the two values of our formal authorization constraint definition, namely n_u and m_{th}:

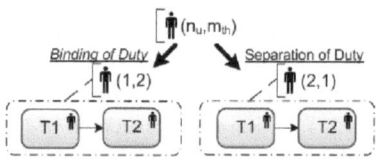

Fig. 5. Allocation Constraint Artifact

A single allocation constraint can be associated with a group artifact defining a set of (manual) tasks, a lane (i.e., a special kind of task group), and as a third option, an allocation constraint can be added to a single manual task. This is necessary in the case of multiple instances or loops. Because an organisational role is defined by a lane, the complete set of authorization constraints for each lane is based on the assigned constraints for this lane, nested lanes, and all constraints assigned to groups and single manual tasks embedded within the corresponding lane.

3.2 Revisited Banking Constraints

To demonstrate the applicability of our approach we apply our proposed BPMN extension to the example banking workflow and model the discussed authorization constraints. The constrained workflow model is illustrated in Figure 6.

The role-based authorization constraint c_1 is expressed by assigning the set of tasks $\{t_1, t_2, t_3, t_4, t_5, t_6, t_8\}$ to the role clerk. The second role-based authorization constraint c_2 is expressed by combining the tasks of the role clerk with the task t_7. The nesting of the lane *clerk* within the lane *manager* expresses the role hierarchy requirement and task authorization inheritance postulated in c_2 and c_4.

The separation of duty requirements c_3 and c_4 are visualized by defining a set of conflicting tasks $\{t_3, t_4\}$ and $\{t_7, t_8\}$ and by adding the related authorization constraint for both groups. In the same way we expressed the binding of duty constraint c_5. The separation of duty constraint c_6, limiting the executive power of a single clerk over the whole workflow to five tasks, is directly assigned to the clerk lane.

4   Related Work

In the area of security constraint and requirement modeling most work concentrates on the expression of application security and access control for their exposed services. There exists little related work in the domain of specifying task-based authorization constraints within the context of workflow models. This observation is supported by research done by Aalst *et al.* in [1,2] outlining that existing modeling notations only

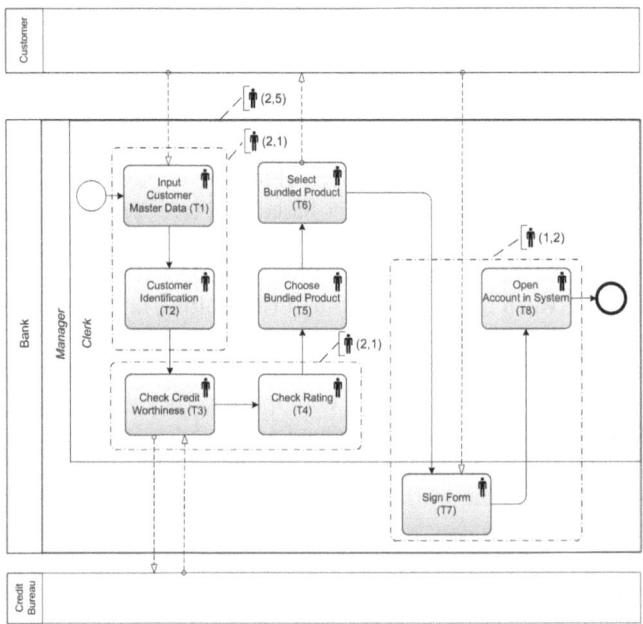

Fig. 6. Constrained Banking Workflow

sparsely support the resource perspective, especially the Separation of Duty pattern that is directly related to the expression of task-based authorization constraints within process and workflow models. Therefore, most related work in the area of security modeling can be found in the extension of UML-based notations:

Jürjens presented in [21] the UMLSec extension for UML to express security relevant information within a system specification diagram. The focus of UMLSec lies primarily on the modeling of communication-based security requirements for software rather than on the modeling of authorization constraints for task-based access control in workflow environments.

Dobmeier and Pernul defined an UML-based model for modeling attribute-based authorization constraints. They provided an expressive fine-grained access control model for accessing services in open systems, such as Web Services. Because their model lack the specification of dependencies between service calls, it is not possible to express entailment constraints for workflows, such as we follow in our task-based approach with a direct relation to workflow tasks and their flow relation.

Basin *et al.* proposed SecureUML a model-driven security approach for process-oriented system in [22]. They characterized a process by its possible states and specify authorization constraints for allowed state transitions. Their security constraints are not directly defined within a process model, but rather on potential states. Within their UML constraint model a process is included as an abstract stereotype and the security specialist has to know all potential process states, while we provide an intuitive perspective on the model and define authorization constraints in the model itself.

Chang *et al.* [23] proposed VTBAC, a visual business centric task-based security specification language to express authorization constraints for hyperlink paradigm based e-Business workflows. While VTBAC could be used to express authorization constraints within the workflow model itself, it is not possible to express entailment constraints, such as separation of duty or binding of duty.

In [24], Huang and Atluri presented SecureFlow, an implementation of their Work-flow Authorization Model with a browser-based interface. Authorizations can be defined for users, roles, and workflow tasks. In contrast to our worfklow model approach they do not use a graph notation. Instead, tasks are selected from a list of tasks, thus the flow relation between the tasks is getting lost resulting in a less intuitive approach compared to ours.

Knorr and Stromer presented in [18] an approach for modeling separation of duty constraints for Petri-Net-based workflow descriptions. They developed a modeling environment for defining an organisational model with roles and users, a workflow description as a Petri Net, and authorization constraints. Unlike our proposed approach, the organisational model, the workflow model and the constraints were defined separately in three different perspectives at the cost of transparency of dependencies between the different models. In addition, their Petri-Net notation is rudimentary and has a weak visual expression.

One aspect of the European research project Serenity [25] is the definition of security patterns for workflows and the development of security tools. The provision of a graphical interface for security analysis and design, the use of formal verification methods, and the ability to handle complex workflows are desired properties. Unlike our approach, their current focus lies on the specification of security pattern and constraints for automatic business processes. In contrast, it seems the description of authorization constraints for manual tasks is not a primary concern in Serenity.

Hoagland *et al.* developed LaSCO [8] a graph-based specification language of security policies. In LaSCO, a security policy is stated by specifying that if a system is in a certain state, a specific access constraint must hold for that system. LaSCO policies are specified as expressions in logic and as directed graphs, giving a visual view of the policy. A LaSCO specification can be automatically translated into executable code that checks an invocation of a Java application with respect to a policy. LaSCO can be used to define task authorizations in a graph-based notation. Nevertheless, the application domain of the graphical notation is restricted to the specification of authorization controls without considering any control flow related modeling aspects for workflows.

There exist a broad area of business rules languages that define the behaviour of processes within a company. Such rules can be divided into dispositive rules affecting the design of processes, for instance according to compliance regulations, and operative rules describing and steering the process flow itself. Nevertheless, business rules are mainly applied in the context of automated business processes [26]. Their practicability in the context of human-centric workflows needs some further investigation.

5 Conclusion

In this paper we presented a novel approach to describe authorization constraints for manual tasks within the Business Process Modeling Notation. Our primary concern is to find an user-centric approach to specify task-based authorization constraints within the context of the related workflow model. Therefore, we propose a method to define authorization constraints, such as role-task assignments, role hierarchies, separation of duty and binding of duty constraints with a strong graphical notation language. By starting with a formalized description of expressing such constraints, we added security relevant semantics to the group and lane elements of BPMN and derived a new textual artifact from the textual annotation element. We used example constraints from a banking workflow as a pragmatic approach to demonstrate the feasibility of our proposed graphical extension. There exists several areas of potential future work, such as BPMN model checking for consistency of authorization constraints, automatic generation of access control policies, and modeling patterns for authorization constraints with tool support.

5.1 Future Work

We consider this paper as a primer for future related work in three different areas:

As stated in Section 3 the verification of consistent authorization constraints is not in the scope of this paper. As shown in our banking example authorization constraints can be nested (cf. c_3 and c_5) potentially resulting in contradicting policies and deadlock situation when these constraint are evaluated and applied to the task assignment at runtime. In [9], Crampton already proposed an algorithm to conduct consistency checks and reveal potential deadlock situations. We plan to further investigate this problem and are going to propose an extended algorithm that can be applied to our definition of conflicting tasks and plan to use model checking languages such as Alloy [3] to provide constraint verification and consistency at design time.

From the modeling perspective it is possible to develop a collection of task-based authorization constraint patterns, such as they are commonly used for the control flow perspective. Further we may apply our approach to sub-processes and more complex workflows, e.g workflow with complex gateways, compensation, and cancellation activities. It is also interesting to investigate to what degree delegation, revocation and supervision constraints can be modeled within the workflow [27]. We also intend to apply authorization constraints to other workflow modeling notations, such as XPDL [28] and BPEL4People, to regain model exchangeability. From an usability perspective we plan to apply a user-centric design approach based on prototype iteration to further enhance the proposed notation extension by empirical studies considering end-user feedback.

A third direction of future work would be to develop a prototype implementation based on a model-driven approach [29] to derive machine readable authorization policies. Therefore, we suggest to develop a model transformation from our BPMN extension to XACML [30] or RBAC-WS-BPEL [10] to automatically derive task authorization policy sets that can be deployed in an enterprise environment.

References

1. Russell, N., van der Aalst, W.M.P., ter Hofstede, A.H.M., Edmond, D.: Workflow Resource Patterns: Identification, Representation and Tool Support. In: Pastor, Ó., Falcão e Cunha, J. (eds.) CAiSE 2005. LNCS, vol. 3520, Springer, Heidelberg (2005)
2. Wohed, P., van der Aalst, W.M.P., Dumas, M., ter Hofstede, A.H.M., Russell, N.: On the Suitability of BPMN for Business Process Modelling. In: Proceedings of the 4th International Conference on Business Process Management (BPM) (2006)
3. Schaad, A., Lotz, V., Sohr, K.: A Model-checking Approach to Analysing Organisational Controls in a Loan Origination Process. In: SACMAT '06: Proceedings of the eleventh ACM symposium on Access control models and technologies
4. Saltzer, J.H., Schroeder, M.D.: The Protection of Information in Computer Systems. In: 4th ACM Symposium on Operating System Principles (1975)
5. Clark, D., Wilson, D.: A Comparison of Commercial and Military Security Policies. In: IEEE Symposium on Security and Privacy (1987)
6. Nash, M., Poland, K.: Some Conundrums Concerning Separation of Duty. In: IEEE Symposium on Security and Privacy, Oakland, CA pp. 201-209 (1990)
7. Botha, R.A., Eloff, J.H.P.: Separation of duties for access control enforcement in workflow environments (2001)
8. Hoagland, J.A., Pandey, R., Levitt, K.N.: Security Policy Specification Using a Graphical Approach. Technical Report (1998)
9. Tan, K., Crampton, J., Gunter, C.: The consistency of task-based authorization constraints in workflow systems. In: CSFW '04: Proceedings of the 17th IEEE workshop on Computer Security Foundations (2004)
10. Bertino, E., Crampton, J., Paci, F.: Access control and authorization constraints for WS-BPEL. In: Proceedings of IEEE International Conference on Web Services (2006)
11. Kloppmann, M., Koenig, D., Leymann, F., Pfau, G., Rickayzen, A., von Riegen, C., Schmidt, P., Trickovic, I.: WS-BPEL Extension for People - BPEL4People (2005)
12. Object Management Group: Business Process Modeling Notation Specification (2006), http://www.bpmn.org
13. Stephen, A.: White. Using BPMN to Model a BPEL Process. BPTrends (2005)
14. Recker, J., Mendling, J.: On the translation between bpmn and bpel: Conceptual mismatch between process modeling languages
15. Ahn, G., Sandhu, R.: Role-based authorization constraints specification. ACM Trans. Inf. Syst. Secur. 3(4), 207–226 (2000)
16. Thomas, R.K., Sandhu, R.S.: Task-Based Authorization Controls (TBAC): A Family of Models for Active and Enterprise-Oriented Autorization Management. In: IFIP Workshop on Database Security, pp. 166–181 (1997)
17. Bertino, E., Ferrari, E., Atluri, V.: The Specification and Enforcement of Authorization Constraints in Workflow Management Systems. ACM Transactions on Information and System Security 2, 65–104 (1999)
18. Knorr, K., Stromer, H.: Modeling and Analyzing Separation of Duties in Workflow Environments. In: Sec '01: Proceedings of the 16th international conference on Information security: Trusted information, pp. 199–212 (2001)
19. Dobmeier, W., Pernuk, G.: Modellierung von Zugiffsrichtlinien für offene Systeme. In: Tagungsband Fachgruppentreffen Entwicklungsmethoden für Informationssysteme und deren Anwendung (EMISA '06) (2006)
20. Kalnins, A., Vitolins, V.: Use of UML and Model Transformations for Workflow Process Definitions. TECHNIKA 3 (2006)

21. Jürjens, J.: UMLsec: Extending UML for Secure Systems Development. In: UML '02: Proceedings of the 5th International Conference on The Unified Modeling Language, pp. 412–425 (2002)
22. Basin, D., Doser, J., Lodderstedt, T.: Model Driven Security for Process-Oriented Systems. In: SACMAT '03: Proceedings of the eighth ACM symposium on Access control models and technologies, pp. 100–109 (2003)
23. Chang, S.K., Polese, G., Cibelli, M., Thomas, R.: Visual Authorization Modeling in E-commerce Applications. IEEE MultiMedia 10(1), 44–54 (2003)
24. Huang, W.-K., Atluri, V.: SecureFlow: A Secure Web-enabled Work ow Management System. In: Proceedings of the fourth ACM workshop on Role-based access control (1999)
25. Kostaki, P., Kokolakis, S., Pandolfo, C.: Serenity - System Engineering for Security & Dependability WP A2.D4.1 (2006), http://www.serenity-project.org
26. Iwaihara, M.: Access Control of XML Documents and Business Rule Processing for Advanced Information Exchange. In: Second International Conference on Informatics Research for Development of Knowledge Society Infrastructure (ICKS'07), pp. 177–184 (2007)
27. Schaad, A.: An Extended Analysis of Delegating Obligations (2004)
28. Shapiro, R., Marin, R.N.M.: XML Process Definition Language Version 2.0. Workflow Management Coalition (2005)
29. Kleppe, A., Warmer, J., Bast, W.: MDA Explained: The Model Driven Architecture: Practice and Promise. Addison Wesley, Reading (2003)
30. Moses, T.: eXtensible Access Control Markup Language Version 2.0. OASIS Standard (2005)

BPMN: How Much Does It Cost?
An Incremental Approach*

Matteo Magnani[1] and Danilo Montesi[2]

[1] University of Bologna, Italy
matteo.magnani@cs.unibo.it
[2] University of Bologna, Italy
danilo.montesi@unibo.it

Abstract. In this paper we propose some extensions of the business process modeling notation (BPMN) to be able to evaluate the overall cost of business process diagrams. The BPMN is very expressive, and a general treatment of this problem is very complex. Therefore, it seems reasonable to define classes of business process diagrams capturing real processes and to develop efficient analysis methods for these classes. In the paper we define some relevant subsets of the BPMN, extend them with the concept of cost, and provide computational models for each class, in most cases reducing them to existing problems for which efficient solutions already exist.

1 Introduction

The Business Process Modeling Notation (BPMN) is a standard set of visual constructs to draw Business Process Diagrams (BPDs) [1]. BPDs make it possible to design critical processes that will be executed inside large enterprises without needing strong technical knowledge, which is otherwise required to configure complex ERP systems. In addition, BPDs allow a fine-grained control over existing processes during all their life cycle, with the aim of improving their functionality. In particular, from a BPD we expect to be able to know how a specific activity is performed and how much it costs. The specification and computation of the cost associated to BPDs written using the BPMN is the object of this paper. As BPDs are intended to model real company processes, the concept of (monetary) *cost* discussed in this paper is different from the concept of (software) performance, as we will clarify later.

While the BPMN is very powerful with respect to the representation of activities and their cooperation, it does not natively support the concept of cost, that would enable process re-engineering and analysis. The BPMN includes the possibility of adding textual properties to each visual construct. Therefore, we may think of specifying the cost of each element as a property, like in Figure 1(a),

---

* This work has been supported by projects Prin 2005 "Middleware basato su Java per la fornitura di servizi interattivi di TV digitale" and CIPE 4/2004 "Innovazione e centri di ricerca nelle Marche".

G. Alonso, P. Dadam, and M. Rosemann (Eds.): BPM 2007, LNCS 4714, pp. 80–87, 2007.

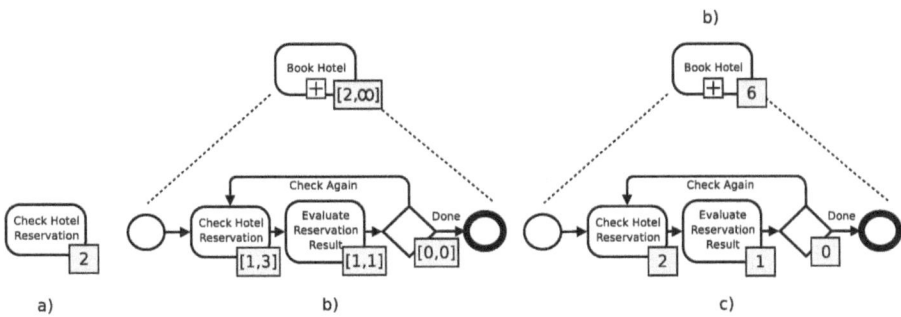

Fig. 1. Extending BPMN basic constructs: simple costs (a) cannot be applied to sub-processes. Two options are cost intervals (c) and average costs (d).

where we have represented a task (`Check Hotel Reservation`) and its cost (2). However, as soon as we introduce other constructs this simple extension can no longer be used. In fact, while it may be reasonable to define the cost of a task (atomic activity), it makes no sense to indicate the cost of a sub-process. For example, consider a `Book Hotel` sub-process and its expansion, which consists in checking the hotel reservation, evaluating its result, and if it is not satisfying checking it again until we succeed. The cost of the `Book Hotel` sub-process depends on the branch of the gateway we follow and consequently it is not fixed. For example, it will be 3 if we go straight to the end of the process, 6 if we go back once, 9 if we go back twice, and so on. Two options to define a homogeneous cost model are to use cost intervals, as in Figure 1(b), and average costs (Figure 1(c)). In both cases these extensions can be applied also to sub-processes.

While the computation of these metrics for aggregate constructs (like sub-processes) is straightforward in Figure 1(b), and may be intuitive in Figure 1(c), their computation can be very difficult in general. In this paper we show how to extend several subsets of the BPMN with these metrics, and how to aggregate them efficiently. Notice that a concept that must not be confused with the *cost* of a process is its execution *time*, which is sometimes used as a synonym of *performance*: the cost of performing any two activities is the sum of the costs to perform each of them, even if they are performed in parallel. However, cost and time are often dependent on each other: the cost of many activities is proportional to the time needed to perform it, which may vary because of the synchronization with other activities. In the literature time performance has been studied extensively [2,3] and will not be addressed in this paper.

With regard to additive costs, to the best of our knowledge there are no other proposals to extend the BPMN in the literature. However, this topic has already been studied in the fields of business process management and software engineering. The main approach adopted to evaluate the cost of a process or of a system makes use of Petri Nets, and has already been applied to business process management before the definition of the BPMN [4]. In particular, this approach is based on *simulation*: business processes are translated into place/transition nets, and a set of random runs is used to estimate the overall cost. In general, the number of different runs is exponential on the number of transitions, making the number of runs to be used to achieve good estimates possibly very high. The state explosion is evident in [5], where a specific application of cost estimation is described.

Simulation has been used to face the complexity of the BPMN and other business process notations. However, this complexity is often not necessary to represent relevant processes. As it is mentioned in the BPMN specification, we must consider that *the free-form nature of BPMN can create modeling situations that cannot be executed or will behave in a manner that is not expected by the modeler* [1]. Saying it with other words, the expressive power of BPMN does not correspond to the set of business processes we are interested to model. Therefore, we must be careful not to adopt very complex analysis tools just because of features of the notation that are not necessary, or potentially lead to wrong diagrams. On the contrary, we can identify subsets of the BPMN, or classes of diagrams, and develop efficient analysis methods for them. Then, given a diagram we can classify it and apply the most appropriate technique to compute its cost. In particular, we will show that for some of these classes the analysis of BPDs can be reduced to well known problems for which efficient solutions already exist. Using the same approach, other classes of diagrams that we have not treated in this paper may be isolated as well, to cover incrementally richer features of the BPMN.

2   Single-Token Independent Processes

The first and simplest class of processes that we consider makes use of the following constructs: 1 start event, 0–N tasks, 0–N exclusive data-based gateways, 0–N sequence flows, with exactly one flow exiting from each task and one flow entering each gateway, 1–N end events. In addition, we assume that the cost of each task does not depend on time and on the tasks previously executed.

The name of this class indicates that we may think that a single conceptual token is created at the start event and traverses the diagram until it reaches an end event. Each time it touches an element of the diagram we pay its associated cost. Therefore, to evaluate the overall cost of a diagram we must estimate the minimum-cost, maximum-cost and average-cost trips of the token. These diagrams can be treated as having a single end event, modeling each end event with a task and connecting them to a new end event.

2.1   Cost Intervals

The analysis of these diagrams extended with cost intervals is very simple. All the aforementioned constructs are extended with an interval [min_cost,max_cost], that must be explicitly specified for all constructs — if they are not known, symbolic values can be used without affecting the approach. Another variation that does not change our discussion is to omit costs on sequence flows, events or gateways — in the following we will represent costs on activities, events and gateways, but the approach would be the same with more or less extensions. These constructs can be immediately mapped to a directed graph, with each node annotated with its minimun and maximum cost.

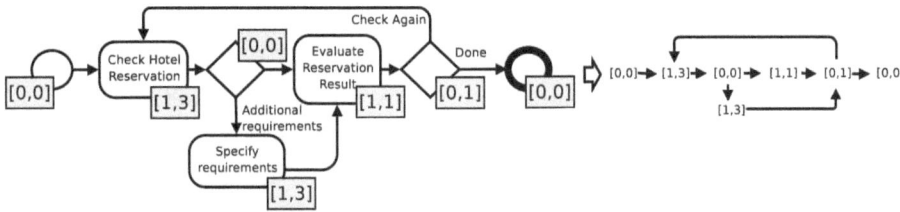

Fig. 2. A single-token independent process extended with cost intervals and its graphical representation

After having translated the diagram into a directed graph, the computation of the minimum and maximum costs of the whole process is trivial, and corresponds to the minimum-cost (shortest) path from the start node to the end node. This can be computed using Dijkstra's algorithm in time $O(n \log n)$, where n is the number of tasks, gateways, events and sequence flows. Similarly, we can compute the longest path to find the maximum cost of the process, which can be done in linear time for directed acyclic graphs, plus the time needed to check if the graph contains a cycle, in which case the maximum cost diverges.

In Figure 2 we have represented an example of a single-token independent process. In this case, the cost of the whole process belongs to the interval $[2, +\infty]$. The cost of the same process without the second gateway, i.e., without the cycle,would be comprised between 2 and 7.

2.2   Average Cost

Intervals may be sufficient in many cases. However, the risk with intervals is that they can rapidly diverge, as in the case illustrated in Figure 2. If we look at the figure, we can easily see that we cannot limit the number of activities performed before terminating the process. However, we can also see that the process will terminate most of the times after a few loops. The average time depends on the probability that the evaluation of the reservation result succeeds.

The extension to manage average costs consists in adding a cost to each of the available constructs, and probabilities to all alternative branches representing the likelihood to follow that branch conditioned on the fact that we arrived at the gateway (we will thus require that the probabilities sum to one for each gateway). Probabilities (that in this case are simple frequencies) can be guessed during the design phase, and we may play with them to see how different behaviors influence the cost of the process. Alternatively, they can be estimated empirically, or we

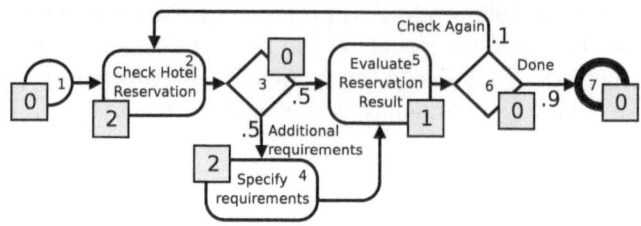

Fig. 3. A single-token independent process extended with average costs

may assign equal probabilities to all branches if we do not know and cannot estimate them. We have illustrated an extended diagram in Figure 3.

From an extended diagram, we can express for each node the average cost of a token to start from it and reach the end event. We notate this cost $\text{avg}(i)$, where i is the construct from which the token starts its journey — we have annotated all the tasks of Figure 3 with indexes. The average cost is defined recursively: if our token is on the `Specify requirements` task of Figure 3, the average cost to reach the end of the process is the cost of the task (2) plus the cost to reach the end of the process from the subsequent `Evaluate Reservation Result` task ($\text{avg}(4) = 2 + \text{avg}(5)$). On gateways, the average of the alternative branches is taken. If we write down all the equations, we can see that the average cost to reach the end of the process from each place can be expressed as a non homogeneous linear equation system. From this, we can evaluate the average cost of the whole process, which corresponds to $\text{avg}(1)$, and in this case is $\frac{40}{9} \simeq 4.5$.

Basically, we have reduced the problem of evaluating the average cost of the process (and from every place) to the resolution of a linear system of n equations and n unknowns. This allows us to apply all the mathematical theory developed on this general problem — for a collection of results on this topic consult [6]. Among the interesting properties of our matrices, we have that if the graph is acyclic the coefficient matrix is triangular (decreasing the complexity of its evaluation), and if the probability of reaching any node from any other in *exactly* k steps tends to 0 when $k \to \infty$ we know that the system has exactly one solution.

3   Single-Token Nested Independent Processes

This class is a simple extension of the previous, and uses the following constructs: 1 start event, 0–N tasks, 0–N exclusive data-based gateways, 0–N sequence flows, with exactly one flow across each task and one flow entering each gateway, **0–N sub-processes**, 1–N end events. In addition, we assume that the cost of each task does not depend on time and on the tasks previously executed.

The extension of the previous class with sub-processes is straightforward. In fact, the cost of each sub-process can be evaluated independently of its siblings. When its cost has been evaluated, we can treat it as a simple task and apply the methods defined for the previous class. In case of other levels of nesting, i.e., sub-processes that contain other sub-processes, the evaluation is performed recursively. As the sub-process relationship is not cyclic, we are sure that the computation will stop, and the time complexity of the evaluation does not change with regard to the previous class.

As an example, consider Figure 4. To compute the average cost of the upper diagram we first compute the cost of the `Book hotel` sub-process, using the previous approaches, then we compute the cost of the upper diagram as if it were a single-token independent process. The same procedure can be applied to interval cost diagrams.

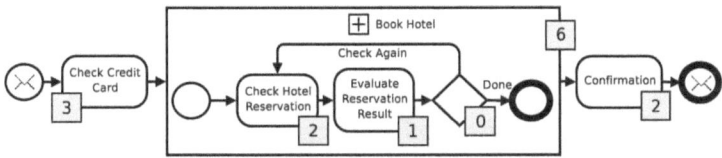

Fig. 4. A single-token nested independent process extended with average costs

Before switching our attention to more complex diagrams, we should notice that single-token processes can be extended using other constructs of the BPMN, like intermediate events or some special start and end events — for space reasons, we do not provide a complete treatment of all the constructs that would fall in this class. See Figure 5 for an example with an exception event.

4   Multi-token Multiple-End Nested Processes

Processes in this class are composed of a set of single-token (nested) independent processes, where the end event can be substituted by an inclusive gateway, and terminating with: 0–N end events, or 0–N inclusive gateways (split-join), or 0–N inclusive gateways (merge-join), shared by different single-token processes. In addition, we require that cycles are allowed only inside each single token (nested) independent process.

This class adds parallelism to business process diagrams, allowing the existence of many tokens inside the same diagram. However, we assume to be able to split it so that each token has its own independent traveling space. This property has been indicated in Figure 5 using dotted squares to separate different single-token portions of the diagram. This behavior is obtained through token producers (start events, split joins and merge joins) and token consumers (end events, split joins and merge joins). Between a token producer and the token consumers reachable by that token[1], we can use the same evaluation approaches of the previous classes. Then, each single-token portion of the diagram can be represented as a node in a graph, of which we know how to compute the cost.

---

[1] Remember that sets of end events may be considered as a single end event, i.e., a single consumer.

However, we cannot guarantee that all single-token portions will be activated. Consider again Figure 5. The first token is produced at the start event, and may die at the lower end event, if an exception occurs, or after the `Check Credit Card` task, where there is an implicit split join. Similarly, one of the three tokens created at the same split join can die before reaching the merge join preceding the `Confirmation` task. Basically, each token can terminate its associated process in different ways. We will conclude the paper discussing the evaluation of average costs on this kind of graphs.

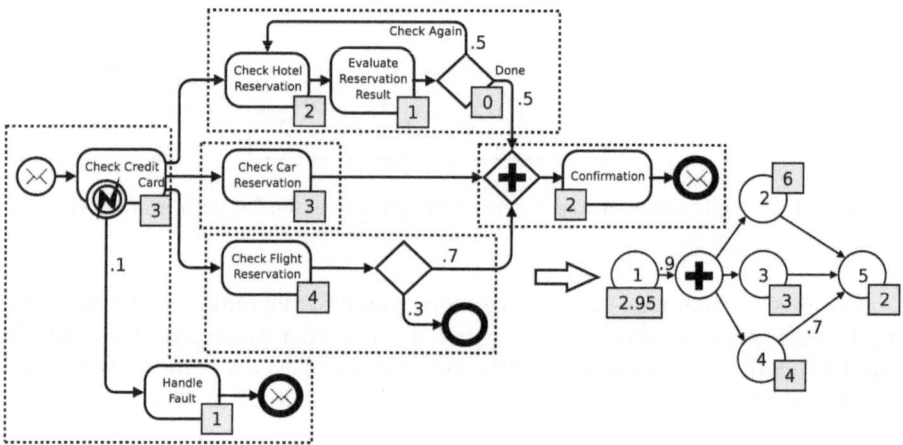

Fig. 5. A multi-token multiple-end nested process extended with average costs

Let us consider a super-graph structure that models our processes, separating single-token processes and representing each one with a node. For each node, the contribution of its local average cost (computed as usual) to the total cost of the diagram will be conditioned on its *activation*, and thus multiplied by the probability of being activated, which recursively depends on the probability of reaching its predecessors. If we go back to the example of Figure 5 we obtain the following system: $p_a(1) = 1, p_a(+) = p_a(1) \cdot .9, p_a(2) = p_a(+), p_a(3) = p_a(+), p_a(4) = p_a(+), p_a(5) = p_a(2) + p_a(3|2) + p_a(4|3,2) \cdot .7$. The only particularity of this system is the presence of conditional probabilities. However, they are not difficult to manage: the only possible dependency may happen at split-joins, where the fact that a node has been activated in the sub-graph rooted at it implies that it has been activated as well. Therefore, in our example we can state that $p_a(+|2 \cup 3 \cup 4 \cup 5) = 1$, and in general for all split-joins + we have that $p_a(+|\bigcup_{s \in SG(+)} s) = 1$, where $SG(+)$ is the set of nodes reachable by the node +. In our example, as we can now directly compute from the graph on the bottom of Figure 5, the overall average cost of the process is therefore: $2.95 + .9 \cdot 6 + .9 \cdot 3 + .9 \cdot 4 + .9 \cdot .7 \cdot 2 = 15.91$.

5 Conclusion

Managing costs inside BPMN diagrams may be very useful but also very complex. However, in this paper we have shown that we may define classes of diagrams for which the management of costs can be reduced to existing and well studied problems. In particular, we have defined the following main classes: single-token independent processes, single-token nested independent processes, and multi-token multiple-end nested processes. These classes of diagrams have been extended both with cost intervals and average costs, except the last class, for which we have presented only the average case. In this way, we have captured many significant business processes and provided a way to evaluate their overall cost. This has been done reducing cost evaluation to existing and more general problems.

The ideas presented in this work can be further developed following several directions. First, probabilistic cost distributions and probability intervals could be used instead of intervals and average costs, with many advantages that we cannot discuss here for space reasons. Second, additional classes of diagrams can be defined and studied, both to include constructs of the BPMN that we have not treated for space reasons and to tackle diagrams that cannot be managed using the methods applied in this paper. Then, it would be useful to compare these classes with the basic workflow patterns described in [7]. Finally, the same ideas described in our work should be applied to the concept of time and compared with the large literature on this topic, with the final aim of producing joint models dealing both with cost and time.

References

1. OMG: Business process modeling notation specification (2006)
2. Donatelli, S., Ribaudo, M., Hillston, J.: A comparison of performance evaluation process algebra and generalized stochastic petri nets. In: International Workshop on Petri Nets and Performance Models (1995)
3. Marsan, M.A., Bobbio, A., Donatelli, S.: Petri nets in performance analysis: An introduction. In: Lectures on Petri Nets I: Basic Models, Advances in Petri Nets, pp. 211–256. Springer, London (1998)
4. Desel, J., Erwin, T.: Modeling, simulation and analysis of business processes. In: Business Process Management, pp.129–141 (2000)
5. Kiritsis, D., Neuendorf, K.P., Xirouchakis, P.: Petri net techniques for process planning cost estimation. Adv. Eng. Softw. 30(6), 375–387 (1999)
6. Seneta, E.: Non-negative Matrices and Markov Chains. Springer, Heidelberg (2006)
7. van Der Aalst, W.M.P., Hofstede, A.H.M., Kiepuszewski, B., Barros, A.P.: Workflow patterns. Distributed and Parallel Databases (2003)

View-Based Process Visualization[*]

Ralph Bobrik[1], Manfred Reichert[2], and Thomas Bauer[3]

[1] Institute of Databases and Information Systems, Ulm University, Germany
ralph.bobrik@uni-ulm.de
[2] Information Systems Group, University of Twente, The Netherlands
m.u.reichert@cs.utwente.nl
[3] DaimlerChrysler Group Research & Adv. Engineering, GR/EPD, Ulm, Germany
thomas.tb.bauer@daimlerchrysler.com

Abstract. In large organizations different users or user roles have distinguished perspectives over business processes and related data. Personalized views of the managed processes are needed. Existing BPM tools, however, do not provide adequate mechanisms for building and visualizing such views. Very often processes are displayed to users in the same way as drawn by the process designer. To tackle this inflexibility this paper presents a visualization approach, which allows to create personalized process views based on well-defined, parameterizable operations. Respective view operations can be flexibly composed in order to reduce or aggregate process information in the desired way. This allows us to consider the specific needs of the respective applications (e.g., process monitoring tools or process editors). Altogether, the realized view concept enables advanced support for process visualization.

1   Introduction

To streamline their way of doing business, companies have to deal with a large number of processes involving different domains, organizations, and tasks. Often, these business processes are long-running, comprise a large quantity of activities, and involve a multitude of user groups. Each of these user groups or roles needs a different view on the process with an adapted visualization and a customized granularity of information [1]. For example, managers usually prefer an abstract overview of the process, whereas process participants need a more detailed view on the process parts they are involved in. In such scenarios, personalized process visualization is a much needed functionality. Despite its practical importance, current BPM tools do not offer adequate visualization support. Very often, processes are displayed to the user in more or less the same way as drawn by the designer. There are some tools which allow to alter the graphical appearance of a process and to hide selected process aspects (e.g., data flow). Sophisticated concepts for building and managing process views, however, are missing.

In Proviado we are developing an advanced approach for visualizing large processes consisting of hundreds up to thousands of activities. To elaborate basic visualization requirements we conducted several case studies [2]. This has led

---

[*] This work has been funded by *DaimlerChrysler Group Research.*

G. Alonso, P. Dadam, and M. Rosemann (Eds.): BPM 2007, LNCS 4714, pp. 88–95, 2007.
© Springer-Verlag Berlin Heidelberg 2007

us to three dimensions needed for process visualization [3]. First, it must be possible to reduce complexity by discarding or aggregating process information not relevant in the given context. Second, the notation and graphical appearance of process elements (e.g., activities, data objects, control connectors) must be customizable. Third, different presentation forms (e.g., process graph, swim lane, calendar, table) should be supported.

This paper focuses on the first dimension, i.e., the provision of a flexible component for building process views. Such a view component must cover a variety of use cases. For example, it must be possible to create process views which only contain activities the current user is involved in or which only show non-completed process parts. Often, process models contain "technical" activities (e.g., data transformation steps) which shall be excluded from visualization. Finally, selected process elements may have to be hidden or aggregated to meet confidentiality constraints. To enable such use cases, the Proviado approach allows to create process views based on well-defined, parameterizable view operations. Basically, we distinguish between two kinds of view operations either based on graph reduction or graph aggregation techniques. While the former can be used to remove elements from a process graph, the latter are applied to abstract process information (e.g., by aggregating a set of activities to an abstract one).

Section 2 gives background information needed for understanding this paper. In Section 3 we sketch basics of the Proviado view building mechanism. Section 4 gives insights into practical issues and presents a more complex example for defining and creating process views. Section 5 discusses related work. The paper concludes with a summary in Section 6.

2 Backgrounds

In a process-aware information system each business process is represented by a process scheme P; i.e., a process graph which consists of (atomic) activities and control dependencies between them (cf. Fig. 1). For control flow modeling we use control edges as well as structural activities (e.g., ANDsplit, XORsplit).

Definition 1. *A process scheme is a tuple $P = (N, E, EC, NT)$ where*

- *N is a set of activities;*
- *$E \subset N \times N$ is a precedence relation (notation: $e = (n_{src}, n_{dest}) \in E$)*
- *$EC : E \rightarrow Conds \cup \{\text{TRUE}\}$ assigns transition conditions to control edges.*
- *$NT : N \rightarrow \{Activity, ANDsplit, ANDjoin, ORsplit, ORjoin, XORsplit, XORjoin\}$ assigns to each node $n \in N$ a node type $NT(n)$*

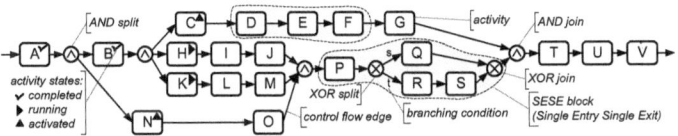

Fig. 1. Example for a process instance

Definition 1 only covers the control flow perspective; though loop backs are supported we exclude them here. The same applies to other process aspects (e.g., data elements, data flow) which can be handled by the Proviado view operations. Furthermore, process schemes have to meet several constraints: first, we assume that a process scheme has one start and one end node. Second, each process scheme has to be connected; i.e., each activity can be reached from the start node and from each activity the end node is reachable. Third, branchings may be arbitrarily nested. Fourth, a particular path in a branching must be merged with an eligible join node (e.g., a branch following an XORsplit must not merge with an ANDjoin). Finally, view operations sketched in the following make use of the concept of SESE graphs (also known as Hammock graphs).

Definition 2 (SESE). *Let $P = (N, E, EC, NT)$ be a process scheme and let $X \subseteq N$ be a set of activity nodes. The subgraph P' induced by X is called SESE (Single Entry Single Exit) iff P' is connected and has exactly one incoming edge and one outgoing edge connecting it with P.*

At run-time new process instances can be created and executed based on a process scheme P. Regarding the process instance from Fig. 1, for example, activities A and B are completed, activities C and N are activated (i.e., offered in worklists), and activities H and K are running.

3   View Fundamentals

We introduce basic view operations and summarize properties of resulting process views. As a first example consider the process instance from Fig. 2a. Assume that each of the activity sets $\{B, C, H, K\}$, $\{J, L\}$, and $\{T, U, V\}$ shall be aggregated, i.e., each of them shall be replaced by one abstract node. Assume further that activity sets $\{E, F, G\}$ and $\{R, S\}$ shall be "removed" from this process instance. A possible view resulting from respective aggregations and reductions is depicted in Fig. 2b. Generally, process views exhibit an information loss when compared to the original process. As an important requirement view operations should have a precise semantics and be applicable to both process schemes and process instances. Furthermore, it must be possible to remove process elements (*reduction*) or to replace them by abstracted elements (*aggregation*). When building process views it is also very important to preserve the structure of non-affected process parts. Finally, view building operations must be highly parameterizable in order to meet application requirements best and to be able to control the degree of desirable or tolerable information loss.

We first give a simplified definition of *process view*. The concrete properties of such a view depend on the applied view operations and their parameterization.

Definition 3 (Process View). *Let $P = (N, E, EC, NT)$ be a process scheme with activity set $A \subseteq N$. Then: A process view on P is a process scheme $V(P) = (N', E', EC', NT')$ whose activity set $A' \subseteq N'$ has been derived from P by reducing and/or aggregating activities from $A \subseteq N$.*

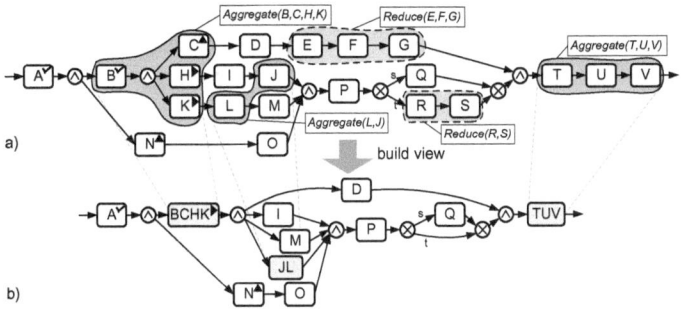

Fig. 2. Example for a process view

A process view is created by composing a set of view building operations: $V(P) = Op_n \circ \ldots \circ Op_1(P)$. The semantics of the generated view is determined by these operations. Proviado uses a multi-layered operational approach (cf. Section 4). There are elementary view operations of which each is describing how a given set of activities has to be processed (e.g., reduce or aggregate) considering a particular process structure (e.g., sequence of activities, branching). On top of this, single-aspect view operations are provided which analyze the structure of the activity set and then decide which elementary operations have to be applied.

3.1 Views Based on Graph Reduction

One basic requirement for a view component constitutes its ability to remove process elements (e.g., activities) if desired. For this purpose, Proviado provides a set of elementary reduction operations as depicted in Fig. 3. Based on these elementary operations, higher-level reduction operations (e.g., for removing an arbitrary set of activities) can be realized. Usually, reduction is applied if irrelevant information has to be removed from a process scheme or confidential process details shall be hidden from a particular user group.

View operations can be characterized based on different properties. Reduction of activities always comes along with a loss of information while preserving the overall structure of the remaining activities (i.e., the activities being present in both the original process scheme and the view scheme). The latter property can be expressed taking the notion of *order preservation*. This property reflects the natural requirement that the order of two activities in a process scheme must not be reversed when building a corresponding view. Obviously, the elementary

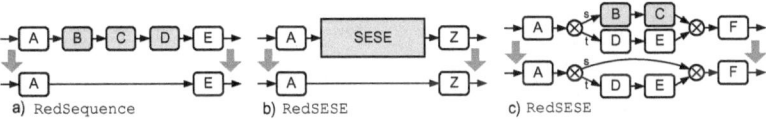

Fig. 3. Different elementary reduction operations

reduction operations depicted in Fig. 3 are order preserving. More generally, this property is basic for the integrity of process schemes and corresponding views.

We first look at elementary reduction operations (cf. Fig. 3). The reduction of an activity sequence (RedSequence) is realized by removing the respective activities from the process scheme and by adding a new control edge instead. Reduction of a SESE (cf. Fig. 3b) is performed similarly to RedSequence. Since there are only two edges connecting the SESE with its surrounding, the SESE is completely removed and a new edge between its predecessor and successor is added. To reduce not connected activity sets the single-aspect view operation REDUCECF is provided. Reduction is performed stepwise. First, the activities to be reduced are divided into subsets, such that each sub-graph induced by a respective subset is a SESE. Second, to each sub-graph, the operation RedSESE is applied; i.e., REDUCECF is based on the reduction of connected components using the elementary operation RedSESE.

The algorithms we apply in this context are generic, and can therefore result in unnecessary process elements, e.g., non-needed structure nodes, empty paths in a parallel branching, etc. Respective elements are removed in Proviado afterwards by applying well-defined graph simplification rules to the created view scheme (see Fig.4 for examples). Note that this is not always straightforward. For example, when reducing a complete branch of a parallel branching, the resulting control edge can be removed as well. As opposed to this, in case of an XOR- or OR-branching the empty path (i.e., control edge) must be preserved. Otherwise an inconsistent process scheme would result (cf. Fig. 3c). Similarly, when applying simplification rules to XOR- or OR-branchings the respective conditions EC must be recalculated as depicted in Fig. 4.

3.2 Views Based on Graph Aggregation

As opposed to reduction-based views, aggregation aims at summarizing several activities into one abstracted activity. Depending on the concrete structure of the sub-graph induced by the set of activities to be aggregated, different graph transformations have to be applied. In particular the aggregation of not connected activity sets necessitates a more complex restructuring of the process graph. Fig. 5a shows the standard case for activity aggregation. For more complex scenarios Proviado offers a set of aggregation operations that allow building arbitrary aggregations.

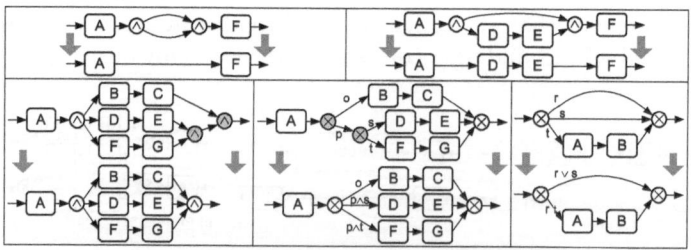

Fig. 4. Examples of Process Graph Simplification Rules

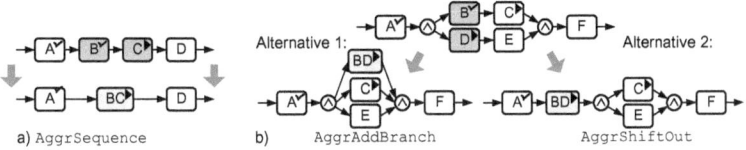

Fig. 5. Different elementary aggregation operations

As Fig. 5b indicates, in a given context, there may exist more than one possible form of aggregation resulting in view schemes with different properties. In this example, two subsequent activities are in state *Activated*, what constitutes an inconsistency in most workflow systems. Opposed to this, for process visualization such inconsistencies are tolerable in most cases. Similarly, aggregating J and L in Fig. 2 removes the dependency between (I, J) and (L, M). This form of aggregation may be considered as imprecise in certain cases, but is usually considered as sufficiently detailed for process visualization. For details see [4].

4   View Application

So far, we have presented a set of elementary and single-aspect operations for building process views. In practice, users need high-level operations hiding as much complexity from them as possible when creating process views. The sketched single-aspect view operations – in this paper we have focussed on the control flow aspect – take as parameter a set of activities to be reduced or aggregated, and then determine the appropriate elementary operations to be applied. Additionally, we need view operations allowing for the predicate-based specification of the relevant set of activities, or even more advanced operations like "show only activities of a particular user". To meet these requirements Proviado organizes view building operations in four layers: *elementary operations*, *single-aspect operations*, *multi-aspect operations* and *high-level operations*. In this layered approach, operations at more elevated layers may access operations from all underlying levels. Consequently, for defining a process view the user or application can make use of all operations provided in the different layers. Finally, Proviado provides additional operations at the different levels for dealing with data flow as well and for calculating attribute values of aggregated activities.

Fig. 6 depicts an example of a process view based on a high-level operation including a predicate. The view shall generate a reduced process scheme that contains only activities the current user is involved in. For this purpose a high-level operation *ShowMyActivities* generates a predicate for a given user name. This predicate identifies all activities executed without participation of the user; note that this constitutes the negation of the aforementioned set (Step 1). Step 2 invokes the multi-aspect operation Reduce that calculates the set of relevant activities S. The single-aspect operation REDUCECF then subdivides S into SESE components S_i (Step 3). These connected components are processed by the elementary operation RedSESE (Step 4). Applying the appropriate simplification rules yields the compactified process scheme (Step 5).

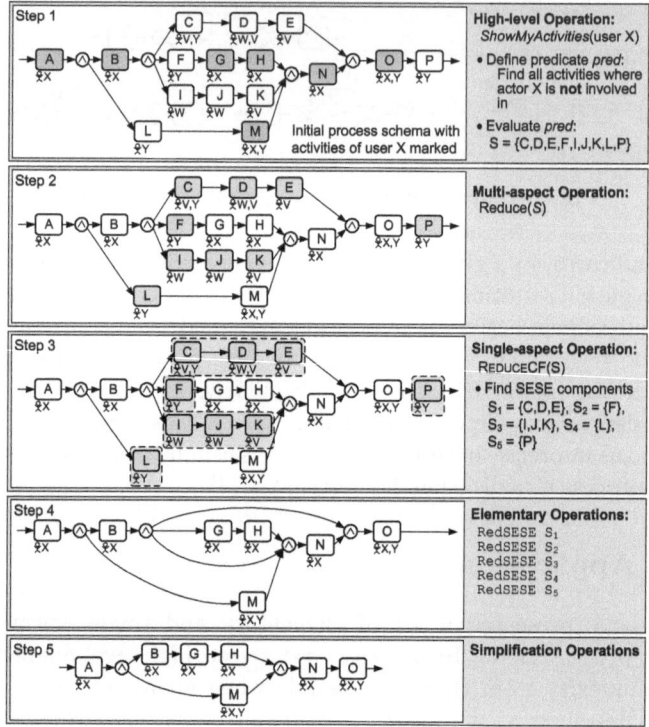

Fig. 6. Performing a complex view-operation

5 Related Work

Process views have been an emerging topic in research for several years. Most approaches focus on inter-organizational processes and use process views to build an abstracted version (public process) of an internal process (private process) in order to hide implementation details [5,6,7]. In [8] a top-down approach is used. Starting with a global process describing the interactions between partners, each participant details his part of the process by inserting activities. In this context, so-called *inheritance-preserving* transformation rules are applied. All these approaches stay at an conceptual level and do not follow an operational approach, i.e. the process view is foreseen to be modeled by the process designer. Regarding user-specific views, [9] provide techniques to extract the subgraph induced by the activities conducted by the user. We have presented a high-level operation that accomplishes this task as well based on graph reduction operations. Only few papers propose operations similar to reduction and aggregation. [10] uses graph reduction to verify structural correctness of process schemes. Control flow structures are removed stepwise following certain rules. View generation by aggregation is described in [11] where 'virtual' processes are built by aggregating connected sets of activities. – Altogether, all approaches have in common that the view building mechanisms are very strict regarding the execution equivalence of the original process model and the corresponding view. In Proviado small inconsistencies are tolerated in favor of a more adequate visualization [4].

6 Summary

For personalized visualizations of large business processes respective process schemes must be customizable retaining only the information relevant for the current user. We have sketched some basic concepts of the Proviado view mechanism which allows to adapt process schemes to specific user groups. While reduction provides techniques to hide irrelevant parts of the process, aggregation allows for abstracting process details by summarizing arbitrary sets of activities in one abstract node. We have implemented the presented view mechanism and realized large parts of the Proviado visualization framework. This framework allows for flexible and user-specific visualization of business processes [3] and shall be transferred to industrial practice to support business process monitoring.

References

1. Streit, A., Pham, B., Brown, R.: Visualization support for managing large business process specifications. In: van der Aalst, W.M.P., Benatallah, B., Casati, F., Curbera, F. (eds.) BPM 2005. LNCS, vol. 3649, pp. 205–219. Springer, Heidelberg (2005)
2. Bobrik, R., Reichert, M., Bauer, T.: Requirements for the visualization of system-spanning business processes. In: Andersen, K.V., Debenham, J., Wagner, R. (eds.) DEXA 2005. LNCS, vol. 3588, pp. 948–954. Springer, Heidelberg (2005)
3. Bobrik, R., Bauer, T., Reichert, M.: Proviado - personalized and configurable visualizations of business processes. In: Bauknecht, K., Pröll, B., Werthner, H. (eds.) EC-Web 2006. LNCS, vol. 4082, Springer, Heidelberg (2006)
4. Bobrik, R., Reichert, M., Bauer, T.: Parameterizable views for process visualization. Tech. Report TR-CTIT-07-37, CTIT, University of Twente (2007)
5. Chebbi, I., Dustdar, S., Tataa, S.: The view-based approach to dynamic inter-organizational workflow cooperation. Data Knowl. Engin. 56, 139–173 (2006)
6. Chiu, D.K.W., Cheung, S.C., Till, S., Karlapalem, K., Li, Q., Kafeza, E.: Workflow view driven cross-organizational interoperability in a web service environment. Information Technology and Management 5, 221–250 (2004)
7. Schulz, K.A., Orlowska, M.E.: Facilitating cross-organisational workflows with a workflow view approach. Data Knowledge Engineering 51, 109–147 (2004)
8. Aalst, W.v: Inheritance of interorganizational workflows: How to agree to disagree without loosing control? Inf. Techn. and Mgmt Journal 2, 195–231 (2002)
9. Shen, M., Liu, D.R.: Discovering role-relevant process-views for recommending workflow information. In: Mařík, V., Štěpánková, O., Retschitzegger, W. (eds.) DEXA 2003. LNCS, vol. 2736, pp. 836–845. Springer, Heidelberg (2003)
10. Sadiq, W., Orlowska, M.E.: Analyzing process models using graph reduction techniques. Information Systems 25, 117–134 (2000)
11. Liu, D.R., Shen, M.: Workflow modeling for virtual processes: an order-preserving process-view approach. Information Systems 28, 505–532 (2003)

BPM on Top of SOA: Experiences from the Financial Industry

Steen Brahe

Danske Bank and IT University of Copenhagen, Denmark
stbr@danskebank.dk

Abstract. Service Oriented Architecture (SOA) forms an ideal infrastructure for Business Process Management as applications are invoked using standard interfaces and protocols. Automatic services can be composed together with human tasks into complex business processes that cross departmental borders and integrate customer and partner processes. Despite the current hype around SOA and BPM, reports on industrial experiences are still very limited. This paper presents results from empirical studies on adopting BPM and SOA throughout the last 4 years in the IT organization of Danske Bank, one of the largest financial institutions in northern Europe and a pioneer in adopting SOA. The study shows the benefit from automating a traditional business process using BPM and SOA, but it also reveals several challenges, technical and organizational, of converting traditional development into service- and process-oriented development.

1 Introduction

Service Oriented Architecture (SOA) [1] and Business Process Management (BPM) [2] are claimed to be two important topics for making an enterprise responsive to a changing market. By service-enabling its existing legacy systems and using service-oriented development techniques for new application development, the enterprise should be able to create loosely coupled and reusable services that can be composed and orchestrated into complex business processes which integrate human tasks and systems across departmental silos. The concepts of SOA and BPM are getting much attention from both academia and industry, and there seems to be an agreement on the importance and the benefits for an enterprise to adopt these.

Although BPM has its roots in Workflow Management (WFM) [3], a topic of research since the 70'es [4], BPM based on SOA and SOA itself have been around for only a few years. As with WFM, BPM has not yet got an industrial break through and there are only limited documented experiences about adopting BPM and SOA. Experience reports mostly describe the benefits seen from the business perspective. Not much is said about challenges in adopting the concepts, methods and technologies as seen from the IT development and the organizational perspective.

G. Alonso, P. Dadam, and M. Rosemann (Eds.): BPM 2007, LNCS 4714, pp. 96–111, 2007.

This paper presents empirical research carried out in the IT organization of Danske Bank, one of the pioneering companies in adopting BPM and SOA.

The author, who previous was a part of the development team responsible for the BPM infrastructure, has through interviews, workshops and document studies, examined two large and independent projects both implementing cross departmental processes. The *customer package* project implements the business process for creating financial products such as credit cards, bank accounts and internet bank access. This process integrates services from more that 10 different systems. The *Account settlement* project implements the business process to finish a customer's engagement in the group, e.g. closing accounts. This process integrates services from around 15 different systems. Both projects consist of around 30 separate processes and integration to 50 different service operations in total, and include several human tasks. There are large similarities between the two projects; they were developed shortly after the adoption of SOA and were the first business processes to be automated using workflow techniques. All people involved had no previous experience with BPM and SOA.

Throughout the paper, the customer package project is used as the main case to describe the experiences. First, the history of the customer package process is described from the business perspective. This shows the business value of using BPM and SOA to support an existing business process. Second, the same story is described as seen by the IT organization. This reveals another side of the story as several challenges were faced by the development team.

The rest of the paper is organized as follows. Section 2 presents some background information and introduces Danske Bank. In section 3 the history of the customer package process is described from the business perspective including the benefits gained from automating the traditional work practice. Challenges experienced by the development team responsible for implementing the process are described in section 4. Section 5 describes lessons learned based on the experiences. Section 6 describes related work, and section 7 gives a summary.

2   Background Information

This section introduces Service Oriented Architecture and Danske Bank, the enterprise in which this study has been carried out. The following concepts related to the term "process" are used throughout the paper:

- Process / Business process. A coordinated set of tasks for handling a business event. For example the work practice of handling loan applications.
- As-is / to-be process. High level conceptual (business) models of the business process.
- Solution model. A detailed model of the business process. Is a logical specification of how to implement the business process.
- Workflow: A program that is able to coordinate and control the different tasks that make up the business process. It is an implementation of the solution model.

- Process instance: An instance of a workflow, e.g. a loan application for customer A.
- Development process: The software development practice followed by a development team to define a solution model and implement it as a workflow.

2.1 Service Oriented Architecture

Service Oriented Architecture is an enterprise architecture that advocates loosely coupled and reusable systems. It has evolved from component-based development and distributed internet architectures as a new abstraction layer that allows internal and external systems to interact using common standards and protocols. SOA makes it possible for an enterprise to open up its legacy systems to other systems and services. As SOA provides an enterprise *architecture* for building systems, service orientation represents a new paradigm of software *development* that seeks to bridge the gap between business and IT. Business analysts and architects define requirements and solutions in terms of services. When developers implement the solution, these services are either located in the local service repository or developed from scratch. The business and technical people have got a common language for their work.

2.2 Danske Bank

The financial group, Danske Bank, dates back to 1871 where it was founded in Copenhagen as "The Danish Farmer Bank". Since then, it has grown to become the largest financial group in Denmark - and one of the largest in northern Europe. It comprises a variety of financial services such as banking, mortgage credit, insurance, pension, capital management, leasing and real estate agency.

Danske Bank has grown through acquisitions, mainly due to its successful IT strategy - one group, one system. This strategy focuses on using the same systems throughout all products, distribution channels, brands and markets. When acquiring a new company, its current products, processes and data are converted to the Danske Bank platform, while existing systems are dismissed.

To support and fulfill its IT strategy, Danske Bank has adopted a Service Oriented Architecture at which all new application development is targeted and where existing legacy systems are service enabled. Applications and services developed for one part of the group, can through a central service library and repository be located and used by other parts of the group. As Danske Bank started out implementing SOA before the web services standard was defined, it has developed its own proprietary standard for service specifications. Currently, the enterprise has several thousand different service operations.

Support for automating business processes is achieved through a BPM system from IBM, but is extended in areas where business requirements were not fulfilled. Business processes are implemented using BPEL [5]. Fig. 1 illustrates BPM on top of SOA; how a business process implemented as a workflow through SOA is able to bind together people and applications across departmental borders.

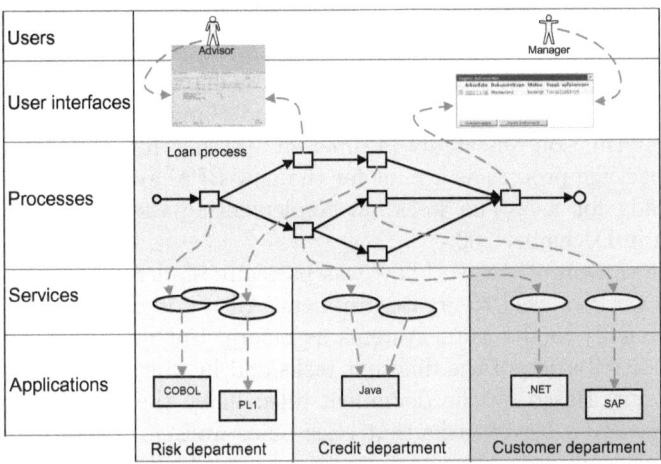

Fig. 1. Business processes as a composition of services and human tasks

For business and IT development, Danske Bank has defined its own service-oriented development process that is based on models; in fact most requirements and design decisions are captured by models. In the analysis phase, a business analyst together with the process participants define current and future work processes in high level terms as two models called the *as-is* and the *to-be* process. Further, a solution architect defines a solution model, which describes all automatic and all human tasks that make up the business process. In the specification phase, the solution model is further detailed with references to existing and new services, user interfaces, etc.

The solution model, related documents and related models, as e.g. models for service specifications, describe the solution in detail and are the specification used by a process developer to implement the business process as a workflow.

Analysts and architects define business process models as flowcharts using an enterprise specific modeling notation. Until late 2006, an outdated modeling tool called CoolBiz was used for modeling. Today, CoolBiz is replaced by Websphere Business Modeler from IBM.

3 Experiences – From the Business Perspective

In June 2003 Danske Bank introduced a new sales concept called *Customer Packages* which bundled a number of financial products, e.g. a credit card and an account. When a customer visited a branch he or she could sign up for a customer package containing e.g. an account, a credit card and an internet bank account. A Word document was printed, filled in and signed. When the customer had left the branch, the customer adviser would send the document by mail to a back office department, where a group of people were responsible for reading through the received documents and creating the different products in different legacy systems.

The customer package creation process handled by back office was highly predictable and production-like and involved systems from several departments throughout the group. A workflow for this cross departmental process would be able to link the different systems together and eliminate the need for entering the same information repeatedly in different systems. It was decided to use the customer package process as a pilot for the new BPM system that had recently become ready for use. The workflow implementing the process was put into production in December 2003.

The first version of the workflow was basically implemented precisely as the back office workers used to create products. All products except one were still created manually in the same systems as before. But now, the workflow automated the distribution of the different tasks and in which sequence they should be carried out. Based on the document filled in by the customer adviser, the workflow created a list of tasks that back office workers should handle. A back office worker would log onto a task system, where the list of tasks - or products to be created - was listed. When accepting a task, the worker was automatically transferred to the system for creating the given product, and available data were present, delivered by the workflow. The workflow hereby became the glue that bound the different systems together, see Fig. 2.

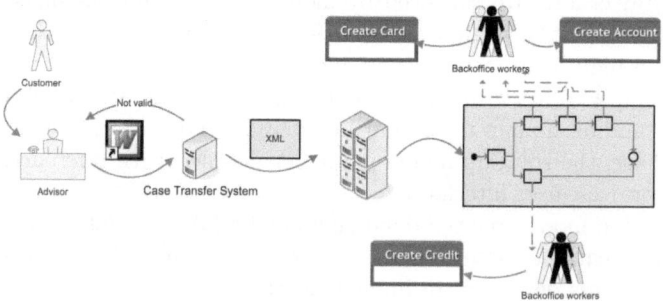

Fig. 2. Workflow enabled back office process with workers creating the products

The workflow-enabled process was an improvement of the previous product creation process because the system made the relevant information available to the back office workers, and guided them directly to the relevant systems from the task list.

Now, having implemented the business process as a workflow, the business department began to look for optimization possibilities. The obvious optimization of a workflow-enabled process is to automate the manual tasks in the process, i.e. to perform the worker's tasks through automatic services. The business department started to contact the departments responsible for the product systems and requested automatic product creation services. Unfortunately, most of the departments did not have the resources for developing the required services. However, one important product that always had to be created for a customer package was an account. The Account department agreed to develop an automatic account service. It was incorporated into a new version of the customer package workflow. Now, the back office workers did not have to create accounts anymore; it was handled automatically by the workflow and the new account service. This was an eye opener for the business department; "Are we able to automate the creation of accounts, then we will also through systematic work be able to automate much more of the product creations".

For about two years, the process has systematically been improved and optimized by looking for the most expensive and time consuming tasks. In the first version of the process, all tasks were handled manually. Today, the process is running in version 6 and 80% of all the products are created automatically. The back office workers have saved much time, which today is used for other activities.

3.1 Current Status and Future Development

The customer package process will be optimized further. It may not be possible to automate the process completely, but it should be possible to automate more than 80%. It requires system owners to develop automatic services and this has been experienced to be a bottleneck because of lack of resources, as other departments have other tasks to handle with higher priorities.

The business process consists of one main controlling workflow, a product creation workflow and workflows for each product creation. In total, it consists of about 30 workflows and 200 service invocations or human tasks.

Back in 2003 when the customer agreement department was established, about 200 customer packages were handled each day. Today, that number is about 1800, of which about 80% is handled by BPM. The other half is handled manually due to complex settings or errors in input data, cases too complex or expensive to include in the workflow.

The history of customer packages shows how a successful business idea has gradually been optimized by use of workflow technology. The use of BPM first automated the coordination of tasks. Next, it allowed the continuously optimization of the process by automating manual tasks in the process. The efficiency of customer advisers and back office workers has improved significantly, and the use of BPM has proved to be of real business value.

4   Experiences – From the IT Development Perspective

After having described experiences from the business perspective, let's look inside the IT development organization and evaluate their experiences. First, we shall look at the challenges of getting from a business model of current work practices to an implementation, and second, we shall categorize the problems into organizational and technical issues.

Problems related to test, deployment, operation of the process instances, and change management have also been observed but will not be described here. For further information about these challenges the reader is referred to [6].

4.1   From Business Model to Implementation

Two business analysts and the back office workers analyzed the current work situation and defined a model of current work practice. This model illustrated the different process steps and dependencies between them; which products should be created and in which sequence. To keep the transition from manual to automatic process control as simple as possible, it was decided to implement the existing work practice directly instead of a reengineered work process. A solution model was defined in cooperation with a solution architect. For the developer, this model described what the implementation should contain. The initial solution model contained 12 activities, mainly manual creation of different financial products. It was approved by both the users and the business analysts as a valid solution.

Solution not Complete: Only Main Road. The solution model and related information were given to the developer, who started to construct the implementation. Soon, during the initial unit test of the workflow, it turned out that the solution model only considered the "main" road of the process, the process of handling a customer package when everything was as expected. Many exceptions and special cases were not covered. After confrontation with the analyst and the users, they recognized many scenarios that they had not taken into consideration; different card types had to be created, the customer might have required a special leather bag, what should happen if the user forgot to sign the document, etc. Such exceptions are crucial to describe to ensure that the automatic process control executes in the same way as current work practice. Several times during the implementation phase, the developer had to talk to the analyst and to the users to understand the business scenario and to update the solution model. After several iterations, the solution model was complete and the workflow implemented. The first version of the workflow that was deployed contained 36 activities, three times the amount of the initial solution. The solution model had through the entire project been used by the developer as the contract to communicate to the business analysts and users what was to be implemented. The solution had clearly grown much compared to the initial design. It was a large surprise to the analyst and the users how much they had missed in the initial solution. They had not previously tried to describe work processes in such detail and were not used to get a solution that exactly matched their description. Only through good will and hard work by the developer, the business got the solution they needed.

Missing or Imprecise Information. Imprecise or missing information in the solution model was another challenge faced by the developer. Each time the developer discovered imprecise definitions or missing information about data, decisions or presentations, he had to stop developing and contact the analyst and architect to discuss what to do. Roughly, these challenges can be divided into three types:

Activities not Broken Down. As an example, an activity was described as "create all cards". When the developer should implement such an activity, he had to consider if a new service should be developed to create a bunch of cards, if an existing service for creating one card should be called several times in a loop structure, and what should be done in case of failures when creating the cards? Such decisions are not implementation issues; it is decisions that should have been modeled in details in the solution model. The activity should have been broken down into smaller pieces in an earlier phase of the development process.

Sequence of Dependent Activities. Activities in a process may depend on each other. For instance, an account must be created before creating a card. Such dependencies were not always described explicitly and the developer had to figure out how to organize the control flow. These dependencies should have been described in the solution model.

Missing Information. Some important information was neither defined by the analyst, nor by the architect. The architect had not considered which data to use when defining service invocations or user interface based activities. Both activity types may require data that is not present and that has to be retrieved from somewhere else. The developer discovered missing data definitions when it was not possible to invoke a service, because that data was missing e.g. an account number for creating a card. When defining a human task, the architect had to decide how to present such a task to the back office workers, e.g. what text labels and data to show in the task list that is presented to the worker. Often, these data were not described either. When defining decision points in the process, the architect often described in plain text what the decision was about, but he did not describe which data to use.

Common to the above challenges is that the implementation process cannot continue until the developer gets more information from the analyst or architect. Such extra iterations causes a longer development time.

Using SOA. In addition to challenges in getting a consistent solution model, the developer also faced challenges regarding system integration because the workflow was integrating systems from different departments. All new software components must be developed and exposed as services in order to be accessible from other systems. The following three challenges were faced:

Service Location and Documentation. Thousands of service operations exist in the enterprise, but it has been experienced as difficult to locate a required service. Further, it is rarely documented well. All services can be found in a service library where also documentation, input/output descriptions as well as examples should be present. However, the service library is a new feature in the group and only a few service operations have been documented. The two examined projects use a total of about 50 different service operations from several business units, and of these only four have been documented. Because of the lack of documentation, in all cases except one the process developer had to contact the developer responsible for a given service to understand how to invoke it and how to handle response values. Some services require up to 100 input parameters without any documentation, which makes it very difficult for anyone to invoke the service.

Service Standards. Most of the services integrated into the workflow have been implemented using naming conventions and other rules defined by the service provider. Instead of naming services according to their functionality, they are often named according to their system name. A CreateCustomer service operation may e.g. be named KNI001, which makes it impossible for anyone to find and understand it. Most services are implemented on a mainframe using COBOL, and often they return codes describing different states of the service execution or possible exceptions. As no enterprise standards have been used for return codes, exception handling must be implemented differently for each service invocation.

Service Granularity and Reusability. Services to be invoked from the workflow have in several cases been too general or too specific to be useful. For instance, a credit service operation covered many different situations of creating credits for a customer, but it also required information that were not available from within the workflow. This granularity challenge was solved by requesting the responsible department for a new service operation responsible for creating the credit needed for the customer package workflow. This new (composite) service operation then collected required information and subsequently invoked the general credit service. Such a service has to be developed by the responsible department and in several cases, departments did not have resources for developing required services for the customer package workflow.

Repeated Manual Implementation Work. The idea of Model Driven Development (MDD) [7] is to transform models directly into code, but the commercial development tools in these projects do not provide flexibility to allow customization of the transformations. When implementing the solution model as a workflow, the developer therefore manually reads, interprets, and transforms the model into code. This is a repetitive and time consuming process with great risk of mistakes. First, when the developer starts implementing the solution model, he maps each task in the model to an implementation. Often, one task corresponds to a service invocation, a manual human task or a human task executed using a user interface, but it may also refer to an enterprise specific type such as a bundle. A bundle is a concept used by the architects in Danske Bank to describe a service invocation that must be executed a number of times and the process may only continue when all invocations have finished. This concept is similar to the workflow pattern "Multiple instances with a priori runtime knowledge" [8]. The WFM system did not support implementation of this pattern for the first versions of the customer package workflow. Hence, the enterprise extended the commercial WFM system to allow implementation of such a construct directly in the workflow language. Second, the enterprise has defined standards for implementing workflows with regard to logging and exception handling. Throughout the workflow, a specific logging mechanism used by all systems in the enterprise is used to log status information about the execution. For each service invocation or human task, different mechanisms are implemented to handle possible system and business failures. When implementing a service invocation, a human task or a more complex task such as a bundle, the developer has to do the same job again and again. It is the same patterns, the same code and the same type of information that must be created. This is trivial, time consuming, and error prone. Further, there is a risk that developers do not follow standards, which results in low-quality implementations.

Fault Handling. As in traditional programming, BPEL processes need to take fault handling into consideration. Workflows are executed by a process engine and when errors occur during execution, they have to be handled by the BPEL program. Here, faults fall into two categories, business faults and technical faults.

First, business faults are errors returned from invoked services. Such errors typically occur when services are invoked with incorrect data, some preconditions that not met, or some other internal conditions inside the services cannot execute correctly. Business errors are recognized in the process based on special return codes from the invoked service. These return codes must be known by the developer to make the correct error handling. As described earlier, such return codes are seldom documented and the information must be obtained orally from the service developer.

Second, technical faults may occur several places in the process. For instance, when mapping data from one variable to another, which is done before all service invocations, values have to be retrieved from the underlying database. Although this is handled by the process engine, the database connection may be missing due to system breakdown which means that an exception is thrown and has to be handled by the process. If this is not considered by the developer, there is a risk of process instances getting into invalid states.

Error handling turned out to be one of the most time consuming activities during development of a BPEL process. Further, it has shown to be of utter importance to avoid process instances getting into invalid states.

Model Synchronicity. During the first versions of the customer package work-flow, the developer and the architect manually synchronized the solution model and the code. Much information about the solution had to be defined in both places. At some point, changes began to be implemented directly in the code without updating the solution model and some technical documentation was made in plain text. The original solution model diverged more and more from the actual implementation and hence it became useless as a design and documentation artifact.

Many of the challenges described above are common for software development in general. For instance, missing and imprecise information in solution models are related to not following the development process, and careful fault handling has always been difficult. Specific to BPM and SOA are challenges related to service granularity and reusability. Services must be developed for reusability across the entire enterprise which requires right level of granularity, documentation and use of standards.

4.2   Organizational Challenges

Several of the challenges described above are due to organizational issues. All involved parties in both projects were new to service-oriented and model-driven development, and as the project was the first of its kind in using BPM, there were no in-house experiences. As stated in section 2.2 the enterprise has defined its own service-oriented development process. To some degree it is similar to the service-oriented analysis and design steps described by Erl [1].

Had the projects followed the prescribed development process probably many of the experienced challenges would have been avoided. However, the challenges of locating existing services, getting the right service granularity, and missing documentation would not be solved by following an appropriate development process as the challenges are caused by other project teams.

Three things were missing regarding the development process; *Education, best practice examples* and *architectural governance*. Both model-driven and service-oriented development are new ways of developing software and requires changes in the mindset of developers, architects and analysts. Such changes are hard to implement and requires much effort from the organization and people.

People involved in the two projects were not educated in model-driven and service-oriented development. Further, the development process was hard to understand, and it was difficult to find out where to get support. In particular, there were no best practice examples available to learn from. Therefore, people worked as they used to. The architect responsible for the first version of the customer package workflow, though, used the development process to document design decisions in the solution model and used it as a contract for what to be implemented. The users and the analysts were not used to this, they worked as they used to and therefore they missed to describe large part of the solution. Following the development process, they would probably have recognized the missing and contradiction parts during initial tests. Today neither of the examined projects have any valid solution models, mainly due to not following the development process.

Developers responsible for services in other departments were probably not educated sufficiently either. Their services were developed as traditional mainframe systems with a new service interface on top which indicated that they neither had been service-orientated when developing. This is obvious for service enabling of existing legacy systems, but it also appeared for newly developed systems. This directly caused challenges for both of the examined projects as it became harder to integrate the services into the workflows. Had the service developers been service-oriented, they would probably have created more well-defined and loosely coupled services which were easier to integrate.

An architectural governance instance would be able to stop the projects early on and guide them on correct use of the development process. If the first version of the solution model for the customer package business process had been through an initial test before implementation, much of the missing activities would probably have been found. Such a governance instance would also be able to guide service developers to develop reusable and documented services, meaning easier integration for other projects.

4.3   Technological Challenges

Further from organizational challenges, several challenges are related to technology as follows.

Complexity. It requires knowledge of many technologies to develop workflows. The developer must understand technologies such as WSDL, XML, BPEL, Java and XPath. Furthermore, complex concepts as transaction control and compensation handling must be understood and how to be used in the workflows. Fault handling, event logging and common enterprise specific patterns and standard must be known, understood and followed.

Technology Evolution. Technologies to support SOA and BPM are still under strong evolution. For instance, the area of BPM is characterized by rapid change in technology. Two radical changes in the basic language in about three years indicate an immature technology. First, the proprietary FDML language was used, which was based on the WSFL standard, a predecessor to BPEL. It was then replaced by BPEL in version 1, and now it is BPEL version 2. Each change has been without backward compatibility meaning much work of converting existing workflows.

Tool Support. There is a significant gap between a solution model of a business process and the actual implementation as a workflow. The commercial tools used are not able to bridge from the solution model to an implementation as they are not extensible to support enterprise specific standards. The developer must interpret a solution model and make the transformation manually based on achieved domain knowledge. Therefore, the same implementation patterns must repeatedly be implemented. When changing the solution, changes have to be applied manually in two places; in the solution model and in the implementation. Effective model-driven tool support should address at least four issues; 1. Allow enterprise specific modeling standards and transformations. 2. Ensure that required information is present in models and that these are valid. 3. Consistency between model and code. 4. Allow smaller changes to be made in generated code. Brahe [9] describes an approach that uses Domain Specific Languages (DSLs) and customized pattern-based transformations for business process modeling and implementation. The approach addresses many of the observed challenges and solves the first three issues above; Using DSLs, enterprise standards are directly available in the modeling tools and it can be ensured that required information is present in a model. Customized transformations make it possible to retrieve the implementation directly from the model as enterprise specific patterns and standards are captured by the transformations. Hence, changes are made only to the model and they can be synchronized to the implementation. Furthermore, repetitive manual implementation work is eliminated. Unfortunately, the tools used, i.e. CoolBiz and Websphere Business Modeler does not support such an approach. A trend among software vendors seems to be that a business process modeled in e.g. BPMN is able to be directly mapped to BPEL using standardized transformations. This approach does not fulfill the four issues and has not been sufficient for Danske Bank.

5   Lessons Learned

Based on past experiences, the enterprise has gained much knowledge to be used for future projects. This is described in the following sections.

5.1   Development Process

As stated above many of the experienced challenges would probably have been met if the project had followed the prescribed development process. As the organizational challenges illustrate, it is important that projects follow a service-oriented and model-driven development process to ensure that services are developed for reusability and that defined solutions are complete. It is not easy to shift from traditional software development to service orientation, therefore it is necessary with sufficient education in using the service-oriented paradigm. Best practice examples are important as examples are one of the easiest way to learn from. As people tend to work in such ways that they achieve short term goals fast, a strong architectural governance function is important to ensure that all projects work in the same direction to also achieve long time goals by developing services that are reusable across departments. The group has learned from the early experiences that goes back about 3 years, and today focuses much on organizational implementation. Project teams are offered education in the development process, improved tool support and guidance by enterprise architects. Further, architectural governance has been improved by having checkpoints throughout the complete development process, where projects are expected to deliver certain development artifacts and participate in events as e.g. static tests of solution models.

Further from not following the prescribed development process, many of the experienced challenges in the two examined projects can be attributed to inexperience. Therefore, having people experienced in SOA and BPM on a project is crucial. At least one person, an architect or a developer needs to master the technology as well as having an understanding of the business scenario. Such a person is able to communicate directly with users and translate requirements to technology and hereby bridge the gap between business and IT. The customer package project has shown that direct cooperation between users and developers is beneficial as much misunderstanding is eliminated when the user can explain directly to the developer about current work practice and the developer understands how to implement it. Many exception conditions were surveyed in this communication. The developer directly understood how the work practice was carried out, and new ideas came up for the solution.

Business Process Reengineering (BPR)[10] is an approach that seeks to re-engineer and optimize a business process at the same time as new IT support is developed for the process. This approach has not been used. Actually, the stepwise optimization of the customer package business process seems to be very successful. By implementing the manual business process as it was, where only the coordination of work was automated, made the transition easier for the participating workers. Gradually, the process has been optimized and it has been easy for the back office workers to adopt to the changes. While the BPR approach may be able to provide higher return on investment, the stepwise optimization gives the possibility to gradually learn from execution statistics, to locate bottlenecks and to introduce changes to the back office workers in a controlled matter.

5.2 Tool Support

While a mature development process is crucial for successful adoption of BPM and SOA, support for the development process by efficient tools is crucial for adoption of the development process. Otherwise, developers will circumvent the process. Tools and technologies related to SOA, BPM and model-driven development are still evolving rapidly. As described previously, manual synchronization of changes between models and code is not an efficient development practice. Tools should provide a high degree of flexibility to allow an enterprise to define and utilize its own modeling concepts and write its own transformations from model to implementation. Such flexibility would allow architects and developers to create precise models based on enterprise-specific standards which by the tools can be transformed to an implementation. As commercial tools have been insufficient to support the development process efficiently, the enterprise has developed several coding standards and tooling extensions to make developers more efficient and the resulting implementation less error prone. This includes a unit-test and simulation framework for testing services and workflows, a validation engine to check a workflow against enterprise-specific coding styles and automatic error fixes, a pattern generator to generate parts of a workflow from a specification and a graphical presentation of process instances used for monitoring during test and operation of workflows. These tool extensions have shown to be very valuable although commercial tool support were preferable.

6 Related Work

Not much experience has been described about challenges in adopting BPM and SOA. A few papers have been describing experiences and challenges on adopting SOA, but none of these have been including BPM. For instance, Mahajan et. al. [11] present lessons learned from 3 years of SOA implementation in a large US city government but do not describe any experienced challenges. Archarya et al. [12] make a more detailed presentation by describing experiences in building an enterprise business application based on SOA. They mention the right level of granularity of services as a key issue. Further, they also point out weaknesses in current tools for building SOA based applications and request for tools that simplifies the complete development process by utilizing higher level tools that are fundamentally aware of SOA. Both issues are in line with what have been observed in this paper. Lewis et. al. [13] discusses common misconceptions about SOA. The intent is to provide a more differentiated picture of SOA and to caution about important issues while creating a SOA strategy. A key point of the paper is, that even if SOA may be the best approach available to achieve interoperability, agility and reuse goals, building and managing large scale IT systems is still difficult. To the author's knowledge, the only paper describing challenges regarding both BPM and SOA is Woodley et. al. [14] who discus challenges regarding service granularity, transactions, and error and exception handling, though this paper is not based on real experiences.

7   Summary

This paper has described results from an empirical study on early experiences in adopting SOA and BPM in a large organization. The examinations cover both business experiences as well as experiences from within the IT organization.

From a birds eye view, the study has shown business value of using BPM and SOA to integrate systems across different departments and platforms and to automate manual work procedures. By automating the traditional work practice of handling product creations for a customer package it has been possible continuously and stepwise to optimize and automate expensive manual tasks of the process with the result that today only 20% of all products are created manually compared to previous practice. Further, data is automatically carried around between different systems making the work for the back office workers easier and more efficient.

Going from the birds eye view to look inside the development organization and follow the team responsible for implementing the business processes reveals another picture. It shows the complexity and difficulties of adopting BPM and SOA. Many challenges known from traditional programming languages are still present when developing workflows in BPEL. This includes fault and exception handling, lack of documentation of integrated services and synchronicity between solution model and implementation. Business processes implemented as workflows rely heavily on SOA. Therefore it is crucial for easy integration of different services that these have been developed for reusability and are documented properly.

The empirical study shows that although BPM and SOA provide value to the business, they are concepts, methods and techniques that are not easy to adopt. It requires organizational implementation which includes educational efforts, best practice examples and architectural governance to ensure that projects follow the development process and service-oriented guidelines. Further, commercial standards and tools have not yet been found mature to support a model-driven and service-oriented development process efficiently.

References

1. Erl, T.: Service Oriented Architecture: Concepts, Technology and Design. Prentice-Hall, Englewood Cliffs (2005)
2. van der Aalst, W.M.P., Hofstede, A.H.M., Weske, M.: Business Process Management: A Survey. In: van der Aalst, W.M.P., ter Hofstede, A.H.M., Weske, M. (eds.) BPM 2003. LNCS, vol. 2678, pp. 1–12. Springer, Heidelberg (2003)

3. Leymann, F., Roller, D.: Production Workflow: Concepts and Techniques. Prentice-Hall, Englewood Cliffs (2000)
4. Zisman, M.D.: Representation, Specification and Automation of Office Procedures. PhD thesis, University of Pennsylvania, Wharton School of Business (1977)
5. Andrews, T., et al.: Business Process Execution Language for Web Services (BPEL4WS). Version 1.1 (2003),
   http://www-128.ibm.com/developerworks/library/
6. Brahe, S.: Early Experiences on Adopting BPM and SOA: An Empirical Study. Technical Report TR-2007-96, IT University of Copenhagen (2007)
7. Stahl, T., Völter, M., Bettin, J., Haase, A., Helsen, S.: Model-Driven Software Development: Technology, Engineering, Management. Wiley, Chichester (2006)
8. van der Aalst, W.M.P., Hofstede, A.H.M., Kiepuszewski, B., Barros, A.P.: Workflow Patterns. Distributed and Parallel Databases 14, 5–51 (2003)
9. Brahe, S., Bordbar, B.: A Pattern-based Approach to Business Process Modeling and Implementation in Web Services. In: Georgakopoulos, D., et al. (eds.) ICSOC 2006. LNCS, vol. 4294, pp. 161–172. Springer, Heidelberg (2006)
10. Davenport, T.H.: Process Innovation: Reengineering Work Through Information Technology. Harvard Business School Press, Boston, Mass (1993)
11. Mahajan, R.: SOA and the Enterprise – Lessons from the City. In: IEEE International Conference on Web Services (ICWS'06), pp. 939–944. IEEE Computer Society, Los Alamitos (2006)
12. Acharya, M., Kulkarni, A., Kuppili, R., Mani, R., More, N., Narayanan, S., Patel, P., Schuelke, K.W., Subramanian, S.N.: SOA in the Real World - Experiences. In: Benatallah, B., Casati, F., Traverso, P. (eds.) ICSOC 2005. LNCS, vol. 3826, pp. 437–449. Springer, Heidelberg (2005)
13. Lewis, G.A., Morris, E., Simanta, S., Wrage, L.: Common Misconceptions about Service-Oriented Architecture. In: Sixth International IEEE Conference on Commercial-off-the-Shelf (COTS)-Based Software Systems (ICCBSS'07), pp. 123–130. IEEE Computer Society, Los Alamitos (2007)
14. Woodley, T., Gagnon, S.: BPM and SOA: Synergies and Challenges. In: Ngu, A.H.H., Kitsuregawa, M., Neuhold, E.J., Chung, J.-Y., Sheng, Q.Z. (eds.) WISE 2005. LNCS, vol. 3806, pp. 679–688. Springer, Heidelberg (2005)

Matching Customer Processes with Business Processes of Banks: The Example of Small and Medium-Sized Enterprises as Bank Customers

Diana Heckl and Jürgen Moormann

Frankfurt School of Finance & Management, Sonnemannstr. 9-11,
60314 Frankfurt, Germany
{d.heckl,j.moormann}@frankfurt-school.de

Abstract. Even though, financial services providers claim to offer customer-orientated services, they still focus on delivering products instead of providing solutions to their customers' issues. Especially, small and medium-sized enterprises only get offered products which solve isolated problems, e.g. liquidity, financing, and investment services. However, these services do not reflect the intrinsic requirements of business clients such as procurement, sales and marketing, order fulfillment. Hence, customers' perception of banking services is often far from satisfaction. Therefore, the consistent alignment of financial services to customer processes becomes increasingly important to enhance competitiveness of banks. To provide such a continuous support of customer needs this paper examines the identification of customer processes and requirements and proposes a process model which closely ties up to customer processes. This approach expands current notion of banking. The authors present their approach by using an example of small and medium-sized enterprises as clients of commercial banks.

Keywords: Banking industry, business process modeling, customer centricity, customer orientation, customer process.

1 Introduction

In most countries, small and medium-sized enterprises (SMEs) play a vital role in contribution to the respective GDP.[1] To accomplish their business goals they have an enormous need for financial products. This is what makes this customer segment most attractive to banks.

To be successful in the SME segment banks have to offer a high level of customization. Customization requires the consequent alignment of all company activities towards the customer's requirements, expectations, and wishes [1],[2],[3]. In most banks today, this alignment only includes serving the customer fast and courteously as well as being at the customer's disposal in the case of questions and problems with certain products and services [5]. But customization should not be limited to support

---

[1] E.g., in Germany SMEs contribute more than 53 per cent to the country's GDP [4].

G. Alonso, P. Dadam, and M. Rosemann (Eds.): BPM 2007, LNCS 4714, pp. 112–124, 2007.

the customer in arranging the financial products which are sought after. In order to achieve true customization, a clear focus on the customer's preferences and expectations is absolutely essential [6],[7]. The processes of the clients have to be understood thoroughly. Product-oriented thinking has to be transformed into customer-centric and process-driven thinking, turning the processes of a client into the starting point of all business activities of the company.

An appropriate instrument for a holistic identification of the customer requirements can be seen in the idea of customer processes. A customer process can be characterized as the entire procedure customers pass through to meet a desire or to solve a problem. Such a process comprises every single step until a specific wish has been fulfilled or the solution for a problem has been found [8].

Business processes which are strictly focused on identifying and meeting the needs of customers are called customer-centric business processes [9],[10]. Piller and Moeslein [11] describe the approach as "integrating the customer into value creation". Gustafsson, Ekdahl, and Edvardsson [12] apply the idea of a rigorous customer focused service development to the airline industry. Alt and Puschmann [13] demonstrate the usage of customer processes in the case of the pharmaceutical industry. Kahmer and Moormann [14] analyze the alignment of Web sites of banks to customer processes. Also, an approach for creating value-adding services at the example of the customer process "Death and Inheritance" has been developed [15].

Literature on the design of bank-related business processes based on customer processes is still scarce. A helpful approach has been provided by Heinrich [16] for retail banking. He argues that the processes and the resulting requirements and expectations of customers should be the beginning of the conceptual design of a process model. Heinrich proposes that all basic requirements of the customers should be specified. With the customer processes in mind, the bank should determine which parts of a process should be covered by the bank to accomplish the real needs of the customer. Then the decision has to be made, which activities should be carried out in-house or external and which role co-operating partners should play.

In this paper the design of a customer-centric business process model will be presented. The model allows a bank to align its business processes closely to the processes of their customers (SMEs). The result will be high level of customization and a new spectrum of services which provide added value to the customers.

In the following section the basic requirements of SME clients will be specified and structured. It might be difficult for business clients to formulate exactly their basic requirements. Therefore, these requirements have to be derived from the structure of the client's business which is reflected in the client's processes (i.e., the customer processes). For this purpose the SME's core processes, support processes, and management processes have to be identified. Also, all customer processes which can be reasonably supported by banks have to be selected. The generic derivation of the customer's basic requirements provides the opportunity to develop new services for demands that have not yet been recognized as potential value-added services.

The third section of this paper includes an exploration of the current customer process orientation of banks within the SME segment. By interviewing experts, the authors analyze the customer orientation while looking at the actual business processes of commercial banks. Within Section 4 a specific customer process will be described and analyzed in regard to support this process with appropriate services and products of a bank. On this basis the authors establish a process vision as well as the design of a process model to support the SMEs' business. In Section 5 the model will be discussed, and the last section offers a conclusion.

2   Identification of Customer Processes

In the case of the SME segment customer processes are those processes which an enterprise passes through in order to get its needs satisfied. Within its diverse processes a SME client needs a multitude of information, services, and products. These can be obtained by various suppliers – among them there are banks, advocates, delivery services, and many other institutions.

Since literature does not provide a process model of SME clients as it was required for our research, a survey has been conducted. The survey comprised enterprises of different industries (excluding service companies) with a revenue-range from €2.5 m to €200 m. From the database of a large German bank (DZ Bank AG) 450 companies have been randomly selected. The questionnaires have been mailed to the companies in 2005, with the request to reply within a period of four weeks. 91 questionnaires have been sent back which is equal to a rate of return of 20.2 per cent. This rate corresponds with similar studies (e.g., Appiah-Adu and Singh [17]). In the following those results will be described which are relevant for the design of our model.

Figure 1 shows the result concerning the question which processes should be considered as established business processes of SMEs. These processes are very differently to those supported by banks nowadays (see Section 3). The core processes

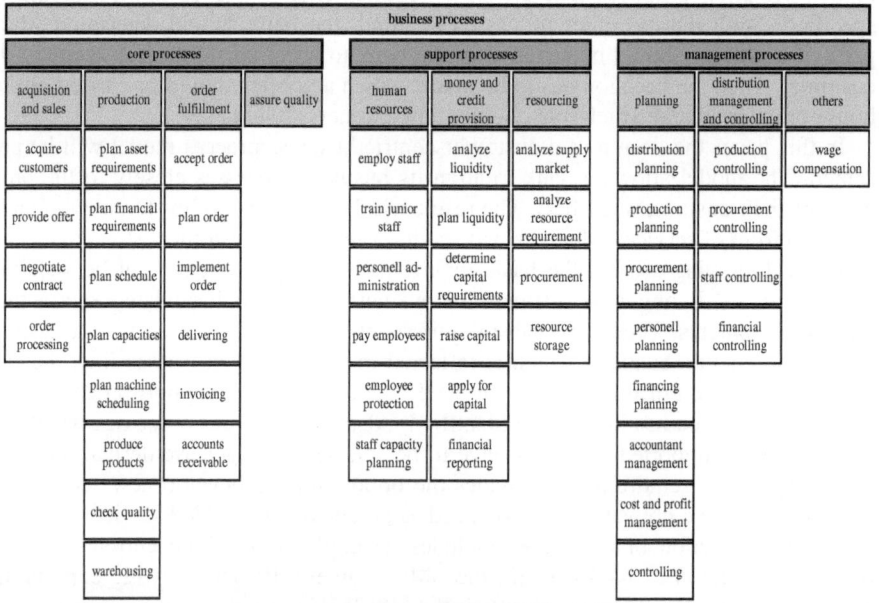

Fig. 1. Business processes of SME clients

planning (39.7%), *distribution management and controlling* (38.1%) as well as *acquisition and sales* (30.2%) were regarded from the respondents as those processes which receive insufficient attention within the current product and services spectrum of banks.

The results of the survey also show that the respondents wish an explicit support through banks for the core process *acquisition and sales* (23.5%). Besides, they regard the banks' support in a number of sub processes as very important.

Finally, the results clearly point out that SMEs desire process support via their bank – but only for those processes, they expect the banks to possess adequate competence.

3   Assessment of the Current Customer Process Orientation in Banks

Business processes consist of a comprehensive chain of value creating activities which generate specific outputs required by customers and whose results have strategic importance for the enterprise [18],[19]. The total of all business processes provides the fulfillment of a superior company mission – namely the achievement of sufficient profits. But to which extent have banks implemented a customer-centric process structure? And to what extent do processes of SME clients build the starting point for the process design in banks? To gain some insight into these questions experts have been interviewed using a semi-structural format. The interviewees have been chosen from the five largest banks in Germany (Deutsche Bank AG, Dresdner Bank AG, Commerzbank AG, DZ Bank AG, and LBBW). Five in-depth interviews have been conducted with managers who are responsible for the process design for the SME business of their bank.

All interviewees described the SME clients as a "strategic business segment" within their bank because of the expected profits with these clients. All five banks regarded the importance of business with SMEs as very high and put customers' needs and expectations into the focus of their customer care. The ambition of their customer counseling is a comprehensive advice according to the requirements of the customer. However, the support of certain customer processes is barely taken into account. The interviews showed that up to now a rather general support for SME clients is offered. To be precise the current support is limited to the process *money and credit provision* and some sub processes in terms of information providing. Processes like acquisition and sales are not explicitly considered within the banks' customer care. Therefore, the authors can certify neither a comprehensive analysis of the customer needs and problems nor the development of adequate and innovative products and services. The experts of the banks identified problems in being too far away from their clients' processes and problems.

Summarizing the interviews it can be concluded that banks still work very product-oriented. Like in the past they follow an inside-out-perspective. Customer orientation is only understood as the satisfaction and fulfillment of directly observable customer requirements. An advanced consideration of the underlying customer processes and the resulting customer needs – i.e., an outside-in-perspective – is currently not implemented.

Given the large number of SME clients and the enormous potential of this market segment, banks should change their perspective. Instead of following the inside-out-approach they should identify new business opportunities along the value chain of their customers [20]. In the following section the authors present a model which aims to directly match SME processes with the business processes of banks.

4   Design of a Customer-Centric Business Process Model

The basis for the development of a customer-centric business process model is the identification of sub processes for the specific customer process. Then each sub process has to be checked for possible products and services which could be provided in order to support the respective customer sub process. In a next step the bank would analyze whether the specific customer sub process should be supported by the bank itself or by a co-operating partner. Finally, detailed product and service packages as well as sales and communication channels have to be defined. This definition has to refer to the in-house products and services as well as to the products and services of the co-operating partners. Thus, the bank's business process will be fully based on the business needs of its SME clients.

In the following we describe the design of a customer-centric business process model for the *acquisition and sales process*. For this purpose, it is necessary to notice that the *acquisition and sales process* of the selling enterprise corresponds to the *resourcing process* (which includes procurement) of the buying enterprise. To use synergies during the process modeling procedure both processes will be included into our model.

4.1   Steps of the Acquisition and Sales Process

The process *acquisition and sales* is probably the most important one for SME clients. Therefore, the bank has to understand every step to identify opportunities for support.

Within this process a SME uses market analyses to examine the current and future market situation and the surrounding environment in which the enterprise is acting (sub process *analyze sales market*). On the basis of the attained information, potential customers will be identified and acquired (*acquire customers*). Strategies, e.g. concerning product and product line policy, will be formulated. In the next sub process (*analyze customer requirements*) individual products have to be developed according to the customers' specifications. Also, the production costs have to be calculated. The SME also has to deliver advice (*give product advice*) and will make an offer to the customer (*provide offer*). In a next step the *contract* will be *negotiated*. At the order's maturity date the products for the customer have to be compiled and sent out (*order processing*). Simultaneously, the issuing and posting of an invoice as well as the accounts receivable are carried out. If the payment does not happen in time, the commercial and – where necessary – legal dunning proceeding starts.

After having identified the sub processes of the SMEs' *acquisition and sales process*, each sub process has to be analyzed for possible products and services. Within the sales market analysis, comprehensive market data could be offered to the enterprise, e.g. detailed information about potential customers and the targeted market as well as market prospects and competition analyses. Generally, publications, road shows, advertisement as well as sales promotions (e.g. calculating of discounts, design of payment options, provision of turnover credits and other additional services) could be helpful for acquiring customers. Information about competitors (e.g. prices, delivery time, quality measures) can help the SME client to prepare a competitive offer. Additionally, the enterprise could create financial opportunities (e.g. loans, subsidies) to definitely convince the potential customer. Credit rating concerning the buyer can be used to estimate the solvency of the contract partner. If the result is a comprehensive contract (e.g. in the case of selling a plant and/or delivering into certain countries), legal consultancy will be necessary. Also fulfilling guarantees or document transactions in the export business (e.g. letters of credit) can be covenanted as contract assurance. For transportation of goods logistic companies like shipping firms or specialized mail-order firms have to be involved. That is why transport insurances might be desirable. Support during the suspension of payments or insolvency of the SMEs' clients might be necessary as well.

Analogous to the *acquisition and sales process* the diverse sub processes can be also identified for the *resourcing process*. In the same way as shown above the identified sub processes have to be checked for suitable products and services.

4.2 Structure of the Business Process Model

As we have shown the *acquisition and sales process* as well as the *resourcing process* can substantially be supported by value-adding products and services of banks. But a bank should not necessarily produce and deliver all mentioned services on its own. The core competencies of a bank (e.g. provision of liquidity) would fall into the background and additional products and services could probably not be offered at competitive prices. However, products and services which support the customer processes can be offered by co-operating partners (e.g. insurance companies, leasing partners, mortgage banks, market research companies, consultancies, agencies for business news, patent offices). Co-operations between a bank as a service integrator and partners as services providers appear to be a favorable approach.

The vision of the customer-centric process model depicted in Figure 2 is based on the generic business architecture model of Winter [21]. Winter describes how companies respectively business units can cooperate in a value creation network as service integrators, shared services providers, exclusive services providers, and public services providers using a business collaboration infrastructure. The customer processes are the conceptual basis of this model. The bank as a service integrator holistically supports certain customer processes and integrates the service components of shared services providers (e.g., banks specialized in back office transactions), exclusive services providers (e.g., affiliates of a bank or an association) as well as public services providers (e.g., Web services providers). The integration of these partners can be realized via a shared, open collaboration infrastructure (e.g., a customer portal).

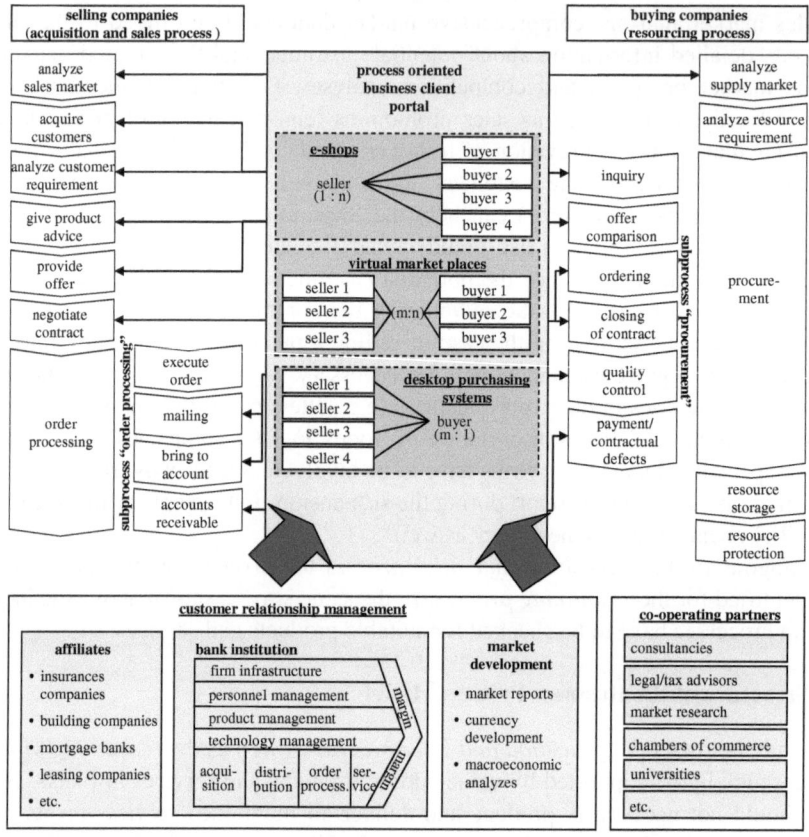

Fig. 2. Customer-centric business process model

The starting point of the proposed process model is represented by the SME clients' *acquisition and sales process* and the *resourcing process*. Both processes are closely aligned to each other because the selling company passes through the *acquisition and sales process*, while at the same time the buying company passes through the *resourcing process*. In order to support both processes the bank as a service integrator has to provide a collaboration platform (e.g., a business customer portal). This platform should include information, interaction and transaction functions. The involved enterprises must have the opportunity to collect information about potential buying and selling companies, to communicate, and to deal with them [22]. The customer buying cycle, which constitutes the interface between the buying and the selling companies, has to be completely supported by the collaboration platform. Therefore, the integration of e-procurement systems (e.g., via Web services providers) within the business customer portal can be very helpful. Systems for e-procurement enable the provision of products, the negotiation of prices as well as the conclusion of sales contracts. There are three basic systems to be distinguished: E-shops (1 seller to n buyers; 1:n relation), desktop purchasing systems (m sellers to 1 buyer; m:1 relation) and virtual marketplaces (m sellers to n buyers; m:n relation) [23].

The bank – in its role of a service integrator – provides the access to the e-procurement systems through the business customer portal. The Web services providers support the sub processes *provide offer* and *negotiate contract* of the selling companies as well as the sub processes *ordering* and *closing of contract* of the buying companies. Further support is provided by the bank's own services, services of affiliates, or services of other co-operating partners. The integration of all partners is implemented within the business customer portal.

4.3   Details of the Sub Process "Provide Offer"

In order to implement the concept of the customer-oriented business process model as shown above, each sub process has to be detailed. We will demonstrate the concept exemplarily on the sub process *provide offer* which is a part of the *acquisition and sales process* of the selling SMEs (Fig. 3). Within this sub process the offer for the product recipient has to be specified.

The selling enterprise gets in contact with the e-procurement providers (public service) using the business customer portal of the bank (service integrator) in order to present its range of products. At the same time the seller has to specify conditions like price, quality, payment, and delivery conditions. During these steps the enterprise will be supported by services of the business customer portal.

Concerning pricing the selling SME can get support in the form of market surveys, industry reports, and reference prices of other selling enterprises (public services providers). The variety of different offers in virtual market places can be helpful for defining competitive prices. Regarding the selection of an appropriate vendor, the most important argument in addition to the price is the product quality. In this context promotional activities like positive customer ratings, quality studies, or external quality inspectors (public service) can help. Moreover, bank guarantees or specific payment conditions can be arranged (bank as a service integrator).

In most cases the delivery conditions are determined by in-house information about the fleet and the packaging costs. That is why fleet and transport insurances are provided (shared services providers or exclusive services providers). If the company does not run an in-house fleet, the search for an appropriate carrier has to be supported (public service). Concerning export the company can find information about documents against acceptance/payment options. Furthermore, the selling company has the possibility to propose financing alternatives to the buying company in order to facilitate the transaction (service integrator or exclusive services provider).

Regarding financial services the entire customer buying cycle (CBC) will be supported by the portal. The CBC comprises the animation phase (problem and demand analysis), the evaluation phase (personal advice, transparent offer), the acquisition phase (easy and fast closing), and the after sales phase (e.g. problem solution).

After putting all parts of the offer together, it will be proposed in the e-procurement system respectively sent to the inquiring customer. If both sides are interested, the partners will proceed to the sub process *negotiate contract*.

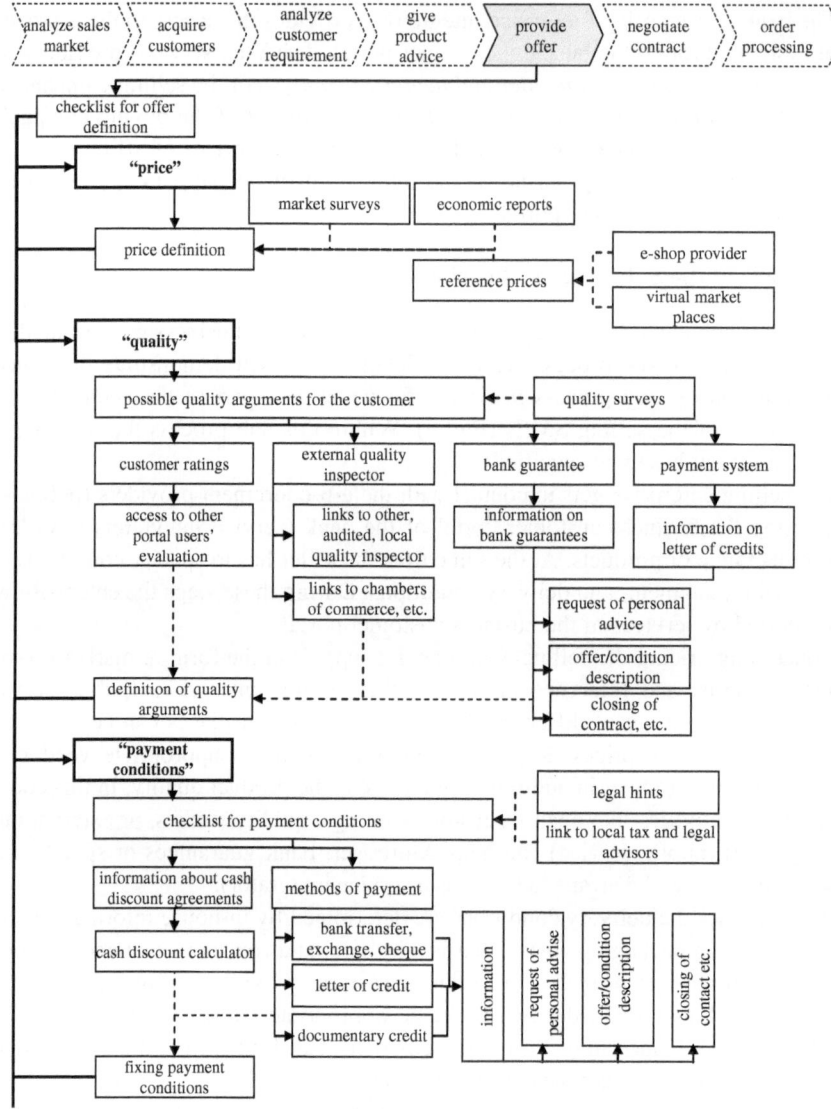

Fig. 3. Activities of the sub process *"Provide offer"(partial view)*

5 Discussion

The business process model described above aims to support the customer processes *acquisition and sales* and *resourcing* of SMEs. In this model the clients' requirements have been derived from their own underlying processes and will be satisfied by products and services which are directly linked to the customer processes. This approach goes far beyond the current status in banking and offers substantial advantages. But it has its weak points, too.

For instance, the concept bears the risk that clients deny the bank's competence for producing and delivering the offered value-added services. Also, insufficient services of co-operating partners may have a negative influence on the bank's image. Another critical point might be that a customer only receives information which is delivered for a particular process step. Thus, the customer obtains information depending on the bank. The client's requirements can only be met, if the bank identifies all possible needs of the customer, anticipates all sub processes and single activities and if the bank integrates them into the portal. In this case the SME clients have the chance to follow their individual procedure within their own process structure.

On the other hand, a customer-centric business process model provides a high level of comfort to SMEs due to temporally and locally unlimited access to information, the direct access to markets, and the provision of individual custom-made services. The main attraction of the model lies in the close link of the customer process with the organizational units of the bank through the business customer portal. Now the bank's processes are truly aligned with the customer processes of SMEs. In addition, the high transparency, the reduced transaction costs as well as the direct access to needed products and services contribute to an increasing customer satisfaction and customer loyalty. The effects for the bank and the co-operating partners will be reflected in increasing revenues and profits (through cross selling, commission fees, etc.). Certainly, the choice of acting as a service integrator depends on the strategic positioning of the respective bank.

The idea of customer process oriented support has already been propagated by scientists and consultants for years. In non-financial areas, first examples are available. Pfizer set up a comprehensive process for clinical tests including doctors who register at Pfizer Portal, and several banks who deliver a number of services like payment processing, treasury services, liquidity services, and financial reporting (Eleanor project). The Swiss chocolate company Lindt & Spruengli analyzed a number of customer processes. Now they act as an integrator in order to support the customer process "Making a Gift" – involving a logistic company, a financial services provider and a company providing consignment sales and storage services.

The application in banks is still missing. Interviews show that customer orientation plays a major role in banking, but the interpretation of customer orientation is still limited to solving and satisfying immediately apparent customer demands. In the case of SMEs a closer consideration of customer processes is neglected because SME clients are often regarded as too divergent. On the contrary, banks need standardized business processes for customer service of small and medium-sized clients in order to decrease operation costs [24].

A number of large banks, in particular, have built corporate client portals offering financial products and services as well as financial market information to their clients. When looking at these banks we have to state that these types of portals already reflect parts of the customer process, but they are still strictly product driven. As the examples of large US banks show (Figure 4), the client has exactly to know which product and services it requires. The structure of the portal should be transferred from a product-oriented to a customer process-oriented structure.

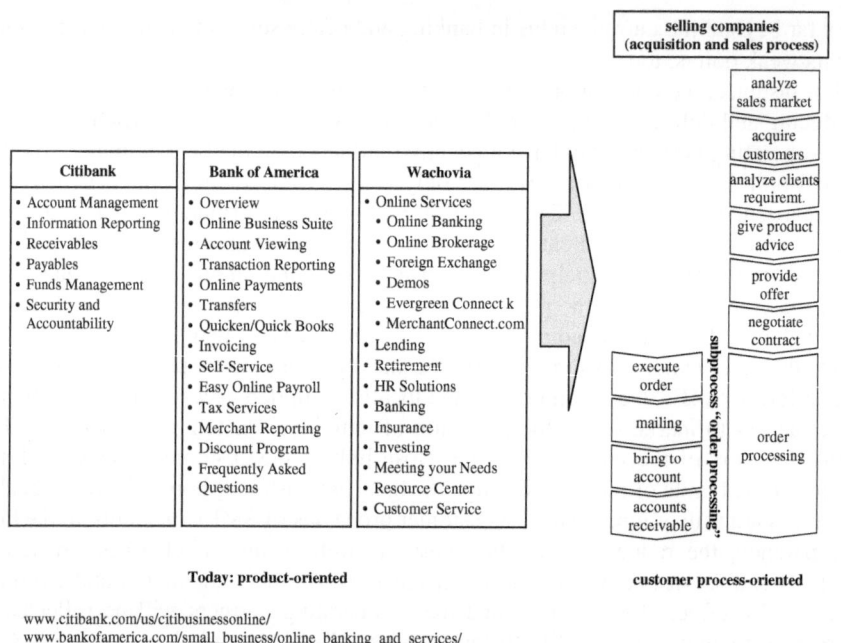

Citibank	Bank of America	Wachovia
• Account Management • Information Reporting • Receivables • Payables • Funds Management • Security and Accountability	• Overview • Online Business Suite • Account Viewing • Transaction Reporting • Online Payments • Transfers • Quicken/Quick Books • Invoicing • Self-Service • Easy Online Payroll • Tax Services • Merchant Reporting • Discount Program • Frequently Asked Questions	• Online Services • Online Banking • Online Brokerage • Foreign Exchange • Demos • Evergreen Connect k • MerchantConnect.com • Lending • Retirement • HR Solutions • Banking • Insurance • Investing • Meeting your Needs • Resource Center • Customer Service

Today: product-oriented

customer process-oriented

www.citibank.com/us/citibusinessonline/
www.bankofamerica.com/small_business/online_banking_and_services/
www.wachovia.com/small_biz/

Fig. 4. Transformation of banks towards customer-centric enterprises

Continually it has been demanded that banks orientate themselves much closer at customer needs and produce innovative services which create added value for their clients [25]. The presented process model for banks and their SME clients offers the methodological basis for developing an efficient support of customer processes and for improving customer orientation. The model allows the banks to integrate themselves into the processes of their customers.

The proposed model helps to bridge the gap between efficiency on the one side and service on the other side [26]. The only way to break the trade-off is to build networks and to integrate the partners into the banks' and the clients' processes. The customers enter specific data which can be processed automatically in the customer relationship management system of the bank. The integration reduces operation costs and moreover puts the bank in a position to generate innovative services for the customer. Garczorz and Schwenke [27] emphasize the opportunity of drawing conclusions from these digital contacts to gain information about product utilization behavior and to generate sales activities automatically. Also, the integration of co-operating partners might generate additional profits in terms of commission fees.

There are many steps to go. The required products and services of the respective sub process as well as the related prices need to be analyzed explicitly within a requirements, acceptance, and pricing study. Moreover, customer needs have to be analyzed and the desired process support has to be defined in detail. Finally, technical requirements and legal restrictions of the model have to be verified.

6 Conclusion

In recent years massive cost reduction programs have been conducted in the banking industry. But a long-term success cannot be achieved without the development of new business ideas, innovative products and services, and intensive customer retention. To be successful in the area of small and medium-sized enterprises, banks have to provide products and services which effectively satisfy the needs of their SME clients. Problem solving, however, can only be successful if the true customer processes are identified.

In this paper we presented the design of a customer-centric business process model. The model allows a bank to align its business processes closely to the processes of their customers (SMEs). On this basis the banks' own processes can be developed. Together with co-operating partners the bank is able to cover and support the entire customer process and to develop a new spectrum of services which provide added value to their customers. The matching of customer and business processes leads to a new level of co-operation between SME clients and their banks. Furthermore, this approach helps banks to transit from product-oriented institutions into process-driven and customer-centric organizations.

References

1. Tseng, M.M., Piller, F.T.: The Customer Centric Enterprise. In: Tseng, M.M., Pillar, F.T. (eds.) The Customer Centric Enterprise. Advances in Mass Customization and Personalization, pp. 3–16. Springer, Heidelberg (2003)
2. Hammer, M.: The Agenda: What Every Business Must Do to Dominate the Decade. Crown Business, New York (2002)
3. Lampel, J., Mintzberg, H.: Customizing Customization. Sloan Management Review 37(1), 21–30 (1996)
4. Bundesministerium der Finanzen (ed.): Fortentwicklung der Unternehmensbesteuerung: Steuerentlastungen und Abbau unnoetiger Steuerbuerokratie, 6.5.2005, Berlin (2005)
5. Caselli, S.: Corporate Banking Strategies: Products, Markets and Channels. In: De Laurentis, G. (ed.) Strategy and Organization of Corporate Banking, pp. 37–62. Springer, Berlin (2005)
6. Vandermerwe, S.: How Increasing Value to Customers Improve Business Results. MIT Sloan Management Review 42(1), 27–37 (2000)
7. Edvardsson, B.: Quality in New Service Development: Key Concepts and a Frame of Reference. International Journal of Production Economics 52(1-2), 31–46 (1997)
8. Behara, R.S., Fontenot, G.F., Gresham, A.B.: Customer Process Approach to Building Loyalty. Total Quality Management 13(5), 603–611 (2002)
9. Bolton, M.: Customer Centric Business Processing. International Journal of Productivity and Performance Management 53(1), 44–51 (2004)
10. Chen, I.J., Popovich, K.: Understanding Customer Relationship Management (CRM). People, Process and Technology. Business Process Management Journal 9(5), 672–688 (2003)
11. Piller, F.T., Moeslein, K.: From Economies of Scale towards Economies of Customer Integration. Working Paper No. 31, Department of General and Industrial Management, Technical University Munich (2002)

12. Gustafsson, A., Ekdahl, F., Edvardsson, B.: Customer Focused Service Development in Practice. A Case Study at Scandinavian Airlines System (SAS). International Journal of Service Industry Management 10(4), 344–358 (1999)
13. Alt, R., Puschmann, T.: Developing Customer Process Orientation: The Case of Pharma Corp. Business Process Management Journal 11(4), 297–315 (2005)
14. Kahmer, N., Moormann, J.: Alignment of Web Sites to Customer Processes: A Study in the Banking Industry. In: Proceedings of the 7th International Conference on Enterprise Information Systems (ICEIS, 25.-28.5.2005) Miami/FL Vol. 4, pp.32–39 (2005)
15. Moormann, J.: Creating Value-Added Services for Bank Customers Using Intelligent Documents. Banks and Bank Systems 1(2), 58–68 (2006)
16. Heinrich, B.: Die konzeptionelle Gestaltung des Multichannel-Vertriebs anhand von Kundenbeduerfnissen. In: Leist, S., Winter, R. (eds.) Retail Banking im Informationszeitalter, pp. 73–91. Springer, Heidelberg (2002)
17. Appiah-Adu, K., Singh, S.: Customer Orientation and Performance: A Study of SMEs. Management Decision 36(6), 385–394 (1998)
18. Davenport, T.: Process Innovation. Reengineering Work through Information Technology. Harvard Business School Press, Boston (1993)
19. Hammer, M., Champy, J.: Reengineering the Corporation: A Manifesto for Business Revolution. Harper Business, New York (1993)
20. Binder, R.F., Behnstedt, R.: Firmenkundengeschäft: Corporate Treasury – die neue Perspektive. Die Bank (8), 44–46 (2005)
21. Winter, R.: Modelle, Techniken und Werkzeuge im Business Engineering. In: Oesterle, H., Winter, R. (eds.) Business Engineering. Auf dem Weg zum Unternehmen des Informationszeitalters. 2nd edn, pp. 87–118. Springer, Heidelberg (2003)
22. Davydov, M.M: Corporate Portals and e-Business Integration. McGraw-Hill, New York (2001)
23. Archer, N., Gebauer, J.: Managing in the Context of the New Electronic Marketplace. Working Paper No. 447, DeGroote School of Business McMaster University, Hamilton, Ontario, Canada (2000)
24. Freiberger, T.: Strukturwandel im Firmenkundengeschaeft der Banken in Deutschland. In: Duttenhoefer, S., Keller, B. (eds.) Handbuch Vertriebsmanagement Finanzdienstleistungen, Knapp, Frankfurt (2004)
25. Spath, D., Engstler, M., Vocke, C.: Bank & Zukunft 2005 – Trendstudie. Fraunhofer-IRB, Stuttgart (2005)
26. Frei, F.X: Breaking the Trade-Off between Efficiency and Service. Harvard Business Review 84(11), 92–101 (2006)
27. Garczorz, I., Schwenke, M.: Internetstrategien für Firmenkunden –Firmenkundenportale in der Sackgasse? In: Petzel, E. (ed.): E-Finance. Gabler, Wiesbaden, pp. 707-729 (2005)

Workflow Management Systems + Swarm Intelligence = Dynamic Task Assignment for Emergency Management Applications

Hajo A. Reijers[1], Monique H. Jansen-Vullers[1], Michael zur Muehlen[2], and Winfried Appl[2]

[1] Eindhoven University of Technology, Department of Management Technology, Den Dolech 2, 5600 MB, Eindhoven, The Netherlands
{h.a.reijers,m.h.jansen-vullers}@tue.nl
[2] Stevens Institute of Technology, Howe School of Technology Management, Castle Point on Hudson, Hoboken, NJ 07030, USA
{michael.zurmuehlen,winfried.appl}@stevens.edu

Abstract. The assignment of tasks to human performers is a critical component in people-centric business process management systems. Workflow management systems typically assign work items using strategies that only consider qualified resources. There are, however, situations, where this approach falls short. For instance, in emergency response situations, tasks need to be carried out by resources that are available immediately, even if they do not match all skill requirements. This paper compares the performance of a set of six task assignment mechanisms for workflow applications using a scenario from the emergency management domain. In particular, we develop and simulate assignment strategies inspired by stimulus/response models derived from swarm intelligence, and benchmark these strategies against conventional task assignment strategies. Our findings show that swarm intelligence-based approaches outperform the traditional assignment of tasks in ad-hoc organizations, and that workflow-based emergency management systems could benefit significantly from these novel task assignment strategies.

Keywords: Business Process Management, Workflow, Task Assignment, Swarm Intelligence.

1 Introduction

Workflow Management Systems (WfMS) coordinate tasks, resources and data according to the formal representation of the process logic, the workflow model [1]. The assignment of work items to human performers is a critical component in people-centric business process management scenarios. Excessive task automation and poor design of work assignment strategies are critical issues that can jeopardize the success of workflow projects [2].

During the *build time* of a workflow application, the workflow application designer has to describe both the structure of the business process to be automated, and the

G. Alonso, P. Dadam, and M. Rosemann (Eds.): BPM 2007, LNCS 4714, pp. 125–140, 2007.

resources that carry out the process. At *run time*, work items are assigned to resources based on assignment policies that determine the strategy for how process work should be allocated. Upon the instantiation of a workflow task, the workflow enactment service places work items on the work lists of qualified performers who are determined using a process of *role resolution*. For the assignment of pending work items different strategies can be implemented, such as first-come-first-served, market-based allocation mechanisms or hierarchical distribution algorithms. These strategies have an impact on how the workflow enactment service prioritizes activities and notifies candidate performers.

Many commercial WfMSs focus on process routing, while (1) oversimplifying resource and task attributes [3] and (2) providing limited facilities to represent dynamic changes in the actual organizational structure of their environment [4]. The factors used to determine the optimal set of resources to be charged with a pending activity is currently workflow-driven: qualifications of resources are treated as *static* values. The amount of dynamics employed in current WfMSs goes no further than linking the allocation mechanism to certain properties of the process instance at hand, e.g. its priority.

In this paper we focus on the domain of Emergency Management Services, where the shortcomings of traditional workflow-based task assignment mechanisms become very apparent. Emergency Management Services are concerned with improving public safety, and share the common objective of responding to citizen calls for assistance as quickly as possible to reduce loss of life and injury [5]. Examples of these services are those delivered by police and fire departments and emergency medical services of hospitals. Characteristic for emergency settings is that after a work item has been available for some time, it should rather be performed by a less qualified resource, than not performed at all (e.g., first response in case of injuries).

As a source of inspiration to extend workflow assignment policies, we turn to Swarm Intelligence [6]. This is a term dubbed for the collective behavior that emerges from groups of social insects. Social insects, such as ants or wasps, divide labor amongst the resources in such a way that the ratios of workers performing different tasks can vary (i.e., workers switch tasks) in response to internal perturbations or external challenges. Algorithms that mimic this behavior have been successfully applied to reduce set up times and throughput times for production scheduling in industrial settings (e.g. [7] and [8]).

The paper is organized as follows. In the next section, we introduce the sub-area of Swarm Intelligence relevant to our study, the stimulus/response model by Bonabeau et al. [9], and discuss the specific requirements of the emergency management domain. Section 3 outlines our research design: We use discrete event simulation to evaluate the effectiveness of various task assignment strategies in a realistic emergency management scenario. The results are presented in Section 4, which is followed by an overview of related work (Section 5). We conclude the paper with a discussion of our findings, limitations, and an outlook on future work (Section 6).

2 Background

2.1 Swarm Intelligence

For years, scientists have been studying ants, bees and wasps because of the amazing efficiency of social insects in finding the shortest path to a food source, spreading alarm in a colony, or dividing labor [6]. Building on many empirical experiments and observations, various models for labor division of social insects were developed (e.g. [10]). These so-called *threshold models* consist of two components. First, a *threshold* exists for each resource towards each task type, which indicates how responsive a resource is towards a certain task type. The lower this threshold is, the more responsive a resource becomes to perform a task of this type. The second component involves the *stimulus*, which is available for each pending task. The more important a task becomes, the higher its stimulus will be. Eventually, even resources with a high threshold towards a certain task type will respond to a work item of this type, given that it has a high stimulus.

In this paper, threshold models are modified to show behavior similar to bidding mechanisms for task assignment. The setting is a workflow environment where pending work items are approached similar to a job market with job seekers of different activity levels. Job seekers with a low task threshold will make a relatively high bid and the highest bidder will be given the pending task, while job seekers with high threshold levels will not become active until the stimulus reaches the threshold (compare [9]). The threshold for each job seeker to perform a certain task at a particular time scales with the contribution that a job seeker adds to the global performance. For example, the threshold may relate to the shortest distance for a wasp to pick up food [10,11], so that the global optimum is a minimum function, i.e. the overall time that is required to pick up all food should be minimal.

Threshold models can be extended with a learning mechanism. This mechanism ensures that the threshold towards a certain task type decreases when a resource is working on that task type (i.e., the resource learns to perform it well) and increases for all other resources that are not performing that particular task type (i.e., they forget how to perform the task). The threshold models that include the learning mechanism are referred to as *learning threshold models*, in contrast to the *fixed threshold models*. One advantage of a learning threshold model over a fixed threshold model is in the area of robustness, which various biological studies point out as an essential element of colonies [12,13].

In this study, we consider three different threshold models, which we introduce more formally now. We denote a threshold with $\pi_{r,i}$, which represents the threshold for resource r towards task i at a certain time. The stimulus S_i describes the demand to perform task i at a particular time. The stimulus that is used for our task assignment studies is updated after each discrete time step with a constant δ. This way, the stimulus S_i is used to improve the probability of completion for task i, which becomes more important over time [14]. The fixed threshold model for ants (F-ANT), as proposed by [15], lets resource r bid for task i with the following bid:

$$\frac{S_i^2}{S_i^2 + (\pi_{r,i}^2)^{\chi}},$$

where $\chi \in [1,\infty)$ is a moderating coefficient that determines the impact of the threshold on the level of the bid. If two resources both place the highest bid, the task is allocated randomly between these two resources.

A specific case of the F-ANT model is the fixed threshold model for wasps, as described in [10]. Here, $\chi=1$. We refer to this model as F-WASP.

We also consider a learning threshold model, which can be seen as a refinement of the F-WASP model. An additional threshold $\theta_{r,i}$ is introduced, which exists for resource r towards task i and which evolves over time. Using ξ and φ as respectively the learning and forgetting coefficients, $\theta_{r,i}$ is lowered at each discrete time step with ξ when a resource works on a task of type i and increased with φ if not. In the learning threshold model for wasps (L-WASP), resource r bids for task i with the bid:

$$\frac{S_i^2}{S_i^2 + \alpha\theta_{r,i}^2 + \beta\pi_{r,i}^2},$$

where α and β are positive coefficients that determine the relative importance of the thresholds and θ is usually restricted to a certain positive domain.

The F-ANT, F-WASP, and L-WASP models can be considered as the basic threshold models in the Swarm Intelligence domain and they were chosen based on their known value in industrial optimization problems (e.g. [7] and [8]).

2.2 Emergency Management Domain

The performance of typical business processes, such as those found in governmental agencies, banks, insurance companies, etc., is measured in a variety of ways. This variety stems from the different stakeholders involved that may pursue different interests. However, in the Emergency Management Domain the primary concern is to reduce loss of life, injury and damage to property. Therefore, *timeliness of execution* is the most dominant performance evaluation criteria in this domain [5]. Other considerations such as efficiency and costs are often irrelevant, neglected, or can be seen as variations of the time criteria. In this study we focus on two different ways of making this criteria operational:

1. *Throughput Time* (TPT), which measures the time between an incoming Emergency Call and the moment that the incident is resolved, and
2. *Response Time* (RT), which is the time between the incoming Emergency Call and the moment that the emergency response begins at the location of the incident.

While an incident's TPT includes its RT, favoring one criteria over the other may lead to different decisions. Consider, e.g., the dilemma to send out an available unit to assist at a large incident X (to which a single unit has already responded) or to respond to a small incident Y that has just occurred. The first option will lower the TPT of X, the second will lower the RT to Y. While minimizing TPT reduces the negative consequences of incidents, such as loss of life, injury and damage to property, a large RT has its own set of negative consequences [16,17]. Just as described in [16], we consider TPT and RT as equally important.

Furthermore, even though reducing the average TPT and RT is of the utmost importance, emergency responders must take into account the principle of *equity* [5], which states that similar incoming emergency calls must be treated equally. In particular, incidents that occur further away from an emergency center must not be structurally neglected in favor of nearby incidents.

Typical business processes differ from emergency services in that resources in the latter environment are generally trained and equipped to perform all kinds of tasks besides their specialization, while this is not necessarily so in non-emergency settings. The advantage of this generalist approach is that non-specialists can perform tasks when specialists are unavailable. The disadvantage of this approach is that the processing times for tasks performed by non-specialists are typically greater. For example, a fire-fighting unit with a small aerial ladder is capable to perform high angle rescues using ropes and manual ladders. Characteristically, this takes longer than a rescue attempt by a team using a vehicle with a longer and flexible aerial ladder [16]. As we will demonstrate, a supply of heterogeneous resources is an important ingredient to the emergency response scenario that we use to benchmark different task assignment strategies.

3 Methodology

In this section we benchmark the task assignment mechanisms that originate from the swarm intelligence concepts with three conventional task assignment mechanisms, using an example scenario from the emergency management domain. First we describe the three conventional assignment mechanisms used for benchmarking. We then introduce the simulation scenario, followed by the simulation model, the simulation approach and the design of the experiments.

3.1 Conventional Task Assignment Mechanisms

To better understand the performance and the behavior of the threshold models introduced above, we evaluate them against three conventional task assignment mechanisms: First-in, First-out (FiFo), a Greedy dispatch rule and the Dynamic Model.

The FiFo mechanism assigns tasks in the sequence of arrival of new cases. FiFo queuing is a simple and robust allocation rule [18] and widely used in commercial WfMSs [4]. Tasks are dispatched based on a best-available basis. If no qualified performer can be found in the system, the assignment of a task will be deferred until a qualified resource becomes available. Most WfMSs buffer this gap by using work lists as local queues for individual resources. The FiFo mechanism will then place arriving tasks on the work list of (one or more) suitably qualified resources. The actual allocation of work (i.e., the decision, which of multiple resources performs the task) can be implemented using a similar First-Come-First-Served mechanism, or through auction or other bidding protocols.

The Greedy mechanism assigns tasks to resources that can complete the task in the shortest time possible. This heuristic has been applied to several task assignment problems [8,19,20]. In a WfMS the Greedy mechanism resembles the Shortest Processing Time (SPT) rule, which can be used as a dispatch rule in WfMSs [18]. The SPT rule optimizes the assignment of pending tasks based on the assumption of resource-independent processing times of the task. The Greedy rule ensures that a pending task is assigned to the resource that guarantees the shortest processing time. Since in practice task-processing times depend on the capabilities of individual resources, a Greedy mechanism needs to compute the expected completion time for all task-resource combinations that qualify for the assignment.

The third model used as a benchmark for the threshold approach is a task assignment model proposed by Kumar et al. [3]. This model includes the parameters *suitability* and *urgency*. Suitability is the inherent qualification of a resource to perform a specific task. This may include qualifications, authorizations, and permissions. In addition, each work item is assigned a time-dependent urgency value. Each of the resources (r) bids for a work item (i) using an assignment function taking into account *suitability (r,i)* and *urgency(i)*. The work item is then assigned to the resource with the highest computed bid. Note that the other two parameters in Kumar's model are not considered in this study, as they add little value in the scenario under consideration (see Section 3.2). In particular, there are no constraints, which makes the *conformance* parameter obsolete, and resources work in shifts, so that the *availability* parameter is not adding much value. While each of the three benchmark mechanisms represents a dynamic assignment mechanism, we denote Kumar's model as the Dynamic Model, just as it is referenced in the original work.

3.2 Emergency Response Scenario

To benchmark all proposed task assignment mechanisms we performed a simulation study using a fictional emergency response scenario. This scenario contains a Local Fire Station (LFS), which responds to relatively small incidents in its district, i.e. Emergency Calls (ECs). Such emergencies never require more than three fire fighting units. The process descriptions, resources and processing times for this scenario are based on data from the Austin Fire Department [16].

In this scenario, we defined a limited set of twelve EC types that have equal priority and a set of heterogeneous resources with different specializations (i.e., varying levels of task suitability). An EC of type 'water rescue' requires a specialized rescue team with diving skills. Should this team be unavailable, a less suitable resource can (and should) respond to the incident, e.g., one fire fighter with a boat may respond. If a non-perfect resource responds, the processing times of incident-related tasks will increase. The resources work in shifts of 24 hours. Within these 24 hours all personnel is available for work. After 24 hours the shift personnel is replaced by a new set of resources. There are always enough resources available to fill a shift, i.e. we do not account for absences or vacation times [16]. When maintenance is performed, a spare vehicle with exact the same specification is available.

Processing times are based on a defined minimal processing time, which may be different for each type of tasks. If a task is assigned to a less suitable resource, this minimal processing time is multiplied by a penalty factor that accounts for the degree of unsuitability.

A Location Model defines the operating area of the LFS. This Model is used to compute the travel distance of units to incidents within the LFS district. The distance between the responders and the incident is an input parameter for the task assignment mechanisms. The calculation of distances is done using Euclidean or Manhattan distance grids [21]. The Location Model is a square shaped territory (grid) that indicates a part of a city. At the north side of the territory a river runs from east to west. The LFS is located at the center of the territory.

3.3 Model Building and Validation

All models used for the experiments share the same structure and were built using CPN tools. This simulation language is based on the logic of Colored Petri Nets and is suitable for discrete event simulation [22].

All models share a six module structure as shown in Fig. 1. The *environment module* represents the environment of the LFS. This module creates the ECs and defines their associated characteristics. Newly arriving ECs are routed through the model and are handled in the *process module*. When resources have finished working on the tasks for a particular EC, they will still be located at the incident site. The *drive back module* manages their return to the LFS. Each time a work item is made available by the process module it is managed by the *task module*. This module queues the task until the task is assigned and completed. After the task has been completed, the task module allows the process module to access the task again. The task module consists of two other modules, i.e. the *failure module* and *allocation module*. The allocation module is unique for each proposed mechanism.

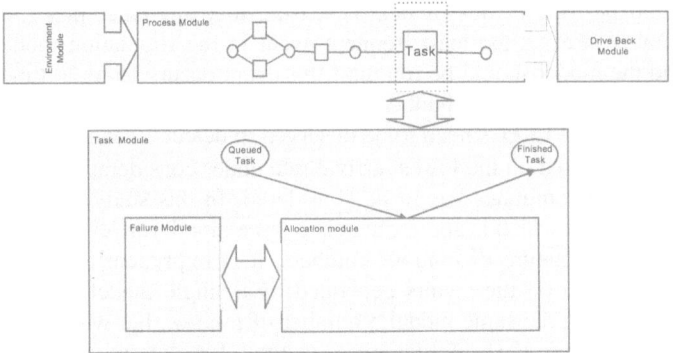

Fig. 1. General model structure

The CPN models are used to collect data, and to analyze the performance of the different assignment mechanisms in the sample scenario with regard to TPT and RT. Data is collected for each EC type individually. We are interested to learn whether mechanisms that seem to perform well on overall TPT and RT treat individual EC types different from other mechanisms. The average utilization of each resource is measured for all experiments performed in this study.

Verification of the model consists of checking the code, inspecting output reports and verifying that the modeled elements correctly represent the real world equivalents [23]. Making use of the state space tool, it is possible to check the model on home, liveness and fairness properties [22]. In addition, we verified the model by simulating EC distributions and routing. The expected counts were within a 99% confidence interval of the observed CPN model counts, hence, we considered the CPN model to be qualified. Since the model is based on a fictional case it is not possible to validate the model against real life data or historical data. The use of mathematical queuing models is not feasible in this situation, because processing times heavily depend on the resource that performs a task. For this reason a simulation study is essential.

3.4 Simulation Approach

Prior to starting the actual experimentation stage, a number of issues need to be addressed, i.e., the warm-up period, run length and the number of replications. Also, a number of parameters must be set in order to optimally use the mechanisms.

The length of the warm-up period needs to be evaluated, if the state of the model at starting time does not represent the steady state of the actual system. The warm-up period is the amount of (simulated) time that a model needs to run before the statistical data collection begins [23]. In this research, the warm-up period is evaluated based on the moving average of the TPT. It appeared that all experiments that are concerned with non-learning assignment mechanisms, i.e., FiFo, Greedy, the Dynamic Model and F-WASP, evolve in the same way, and reach a steady state at $t = 25000$ minutes. For the L-WASP mechanism the steady state is observed from $t = 36000$.

Once the model has warmed up, the run length of the model has to be decided. One method for deciding this is inspecting the random numbers sampled. As a rule of thumb, a minimum of 15 to 20 random numbers for each type of random number stream should be used in this model. To ensure that this takes place for all of the random number streams the least frequent event in the simulation model should be selected and the model should be run until this event occurs 15 to 20 times [23]. This event is the occasion of a chemical structural fire with a probability of 0.011. Therefore, at least 1818 ECs need to be observed to detect 20 chemical structure fires of this category. Based on the lowest arrival rate under consideration, i.e., $\lambda = 11000$, a period of $t = 86867$ minutes has to be considered. In this study a run length of $t = 125000$ was applied, which is approximately a three month run length.

Due to the very nature of random numbers, it is imprudent to draw conclusions from a model based on the results generated by a single model run. Replication is defined as executing the same model a number of times n, but with different random numbers in each run [23]. A statistical method for determining the number of replications is described by [24]. Applying this procedure led to a satisfying accuracy level at 20 replications for all mechanisms at low and high arrival rate, i.e., the deviation of a replication never exceeded 5% of the average.

In addition to the general simulation settings, some parameters need to be tuned for the Dynamic Model and the threshold models. For the Dynamic Model two parameters have to be tuned: urgency (u) and suitability (S), which are both in the interval [0.0-1.0]. The Dynamic Model originally uses an urgency level of interval [0.9-1.0] with parameter $u = 0.1$ when a work item is queued for a period t. This rigid approach is refined in this study. A larger interval is chosen, i.e. [0.5-1.0] and $u = 0.05$: The urgency level starts at 0.5 and increases each discrete time step with a constant 0.05. The suitability parameter S is also in the interval [0.5-1.0]: The least capable resources to perform a task type have a suitability rating of 0.5, the best one for that same task type has a suitability rating of 1.0. The rest of the capable resources scale in between this interval.

The settings of the threshold models are based on the literature and a sensitivity analysis. The stimulus (S) represents the number of time steps an EC is in the WfMS, in this study we use $S=1$ [14]. The parameter tuning for the learning mechanism can be based on a genetic algorithm [25], a simple hand tuning technique [26], or a sensitivity analysis that first sets the most important parameter followed by the parameter with the second highest impact, and so on [27]. Based on the latter approach, we derived the threshold values as well as the learning importance α and the task duration component β. The exact values have been tuned based on a sensitivity analysis. For L-WASP this resulted in $\alpha=0.02$ and $\beta=1$; for F-ANT in $\chi=1.1$. The learning coefficient ξ and forgetting coefficient φ have an insignificant or moderate influence and tuning is not necessary. To set these parameters in a sensible manner in this study, the values from the social insect behavior are taken: $\xi=10$ and $\varphi=1$ [10].

3.5 Design of the Experiments

In this study, we compare six different mechanisms for task assignment. We want to answer three distinct questions. How do the mechanisms perform regarding the TPT and RT:

1. At increasing arrival rates?
2. When the fire station is located further away from the river (both at low and high resource utilization levels)?
3. At an increasing failure rate (both at low and high resource utilization levels)?

To answer the first question we used six different scenarios. The arrival rate is denoted by λ and represents the average arrival of ECs each year. We chose arrival rates that correspond to an average resource utilization of the mobile resources of respectively 0.34, 0.43, 0.53, 0.62, 0.71, and 0.80. The six alternative mechanisms are tested for these six different arrival rates. This results in 36 experiments.

To answer the second question we set two parameters to derive the different scenarios. For each of the two settings two different *river locations* are chosen, thus influencing the traveling time. In this alternative, also two different *arrival rates* are considered, i.e. for a low and high resource utilization. The two settings of the two parameters result in four scenarios.

To answer the third question, we again set two parameters to derive the different scenarios. For each of the two settings two *failure probabilities* are proposed: 0.02 and 0.05. Again, two different *arrival rates* are considered. The two key parameters with two settings results in four scenarios.

In total over a hundred experiments were performed to address the objectives of this simulation study. The complex CPN models require a lot of computing power. Experiments that require models with high arrival rate settings (23000 arrivals a year), take approximately 15-30 hours to finish all 20 replications on a Pentium 4 with 5GB RAM. Five such systems were required for a period of three weeks to perform all experiments. The output of all these experiments were collected, analyzed and documented according to the structured procedures as described in the next section.

3.6 Procedure for Mechanism Comparison

The performance of each mechanism during a particular experiment depends on RT and TPT that are measured for all ECs and for each EC type individually. To compare different alternatives the procedure mentioned below was followed.

For each experiment, a summary of all 20 runs for each performance was provided in one overall CPN report, including the average and the standard deviation of all 20 runs. To assess the performance for all mechanisms, the overall RT and TPT were plotted in a graph for the increasing arrival rates. To test whether the differences between mechanisms are significant a pair wise comparison was made. It is not safe to assume equal variances, therefore we applied the Welch test and not a pooled variance test 24]. When comparing more than two alternatives and making several confidence interval statements simultaneously, the individual confidence levels of the separate comparisons have to be adjusted upwards to reduce the number of type 1 errors (rejecting the null hypothesis when it is true). Therefore, we applied the Bonferroni correction to all measurements [24,28]. To test whether a specific mechanism respects the equity property (similar incoming emergency calls are treated equally), a Kolmogorov-Smirnov test was applied to determine whether the emergency incidents that exceeded the response time limit were uniformly distributed over the Location Model.

4 Results

4.1 Ranking

On the basis of the simulation study, the various allocation mechanisms can be ranked with respect to their performance in minimizing TPT and RT. For each of these criteria, a mechanism is ranked higher if its average value as aggregated over all ECs is significantly lower. If two mechanisms do not differ in this respect, the mechanism that significantly outperforms the other for *most* of the 12 EC types is considered to be better. The latter procedure was explicitly necessary to distinguish between the performance of the F-ANT and F-WASP mechanisms. For all comparisons, a confidence level of 95% is applied.

In Fig. 2, mechanism rankings are shown for low and high levels of utilization, i.e., aggregated over the lowest and highest three levels of resource utilization.

Our analysis provides various insights, of which the most important ones are as follows:

- At both utilization levels, the Greedy mechanism delivers the best performance with respect to RT. However, it is the only mechanism that violates the equity property (this is indicated by the shading in Fig. 2). The Greedy mechanism leads to a favorable handling of incidents that are closest to the LFS, since it prefers the use of idle resources for performing tasks with a short task duration which *includes* the travel time. Clearly, this is unacceptable for society (e.g. cats are saved from nearby trees while the chemical factory further away is burning).

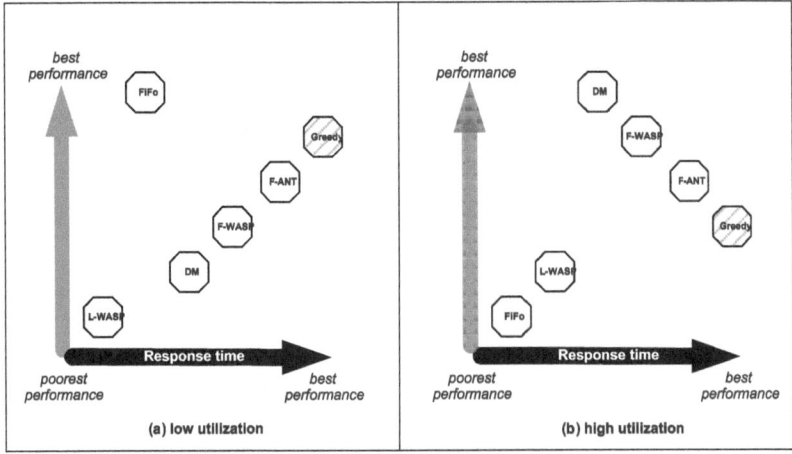

Fig. 2. Ranking of allocation mechanisms

- In contrary to the good performance of the L-WASP mechanism in studies like [8], [9] and [29] it performs markedly poor in this study. The reason for this is that its learning property has a negative impact in the context of the heterogeneous fire-fighting units. The incidental assignment of EC types to less suitable resources (e.g. when more suitable resources are occupied) leads to a structural preference for using such resources over time.

- The FiFo mechanism performs well with respect to TPT when resource utilization is low, but it is the worst performing mechanism overall at high utilization levels. Because it strictly focuses on the arrival pattern, it completely fails to exploit the different resource capabilities.

- The Dynamic Model is almost the mirror image of the FiFo mechanism. Its performance is poor at low levels of utilization, but it is the best performer on TPT at high utilization levels. The reason for the latter is its subtle balancing of the incident urgency and a resource's suitability, while ignoring the task duration. We found that the Dynamic Model commits particularly fast to EC types that multiple resources can work on, while other mechanisms (e.g. Greedy, F-WASP and F-ANT) prefer work items that they can finish fast (at least initially). Because the Dynamic Model does not consider the task durations, it is outperformed with respect to response time at high utilizations by the F-ANT and F-WASP mechanisms.

- The F-ANT and F-WASP mechanisms provide the best trade-offs in minimizing both TPT and RT. When not considering the Greedy algorithm (violating the equity property) they are only outperformed at TPT. At a high utilization level it depends on the relative value of minimizing either TPT or RT which of the two mechanisms is preferable. Note that the absolute differences in TPT and RT between the two are generally smaller than for other mechanisms.

- The *absolute* differences in TPT and RPT between the various mechanisms tend to increase when the utilization increases. Clearly, this is not captured by our ranking of the models in Figure 2, as the axes reflect ordinal scales. There is no satisfactory, way to summarize the absolute differences within the limitations of this paper because of the great variations of these differences over EC types and the statistical subtleties that result from aggregating these differences. The most important insight here is that at higher utilization levels the choice of assignment mechanism is all the more important, as differences become more apparent. In other words, with an excess of resources everything will turn out well anyway.

4.2 Robustness

To test the robustness of the rankings as presented in the previous section, we examined two additional scenarios (see Section 3.5). In the first scenario, the river is relocated from the northern side of the grid to the center, close to the LFS. We expected this to generate a general advantage with regard to RT and TPT for this EC type (e.g. river rescues) of 3.068 minutes. Oddly, the gap between the L-WASP mechanism and the other mechanisms turned out to be larger after the relocation, perhaps because of the poor allocation decisions it makes anyway. In addition, FiFo and the Dynamic Model improve their performance after relocation, which conforms precisely with the expected gain. This makes sense: Both mechanisms do no consider travel time in their decision-making. For Greedy, F-ANT and F-WASP mechanisms, their favorable position increases towards the other mechanism for the river rescues. But only for the Greedy mechanism this increase is significantly larger than expected. This once more illustrates that this mechanism structurally favors incidents that are close to the LFS.

In the second scenario, the impact of an increasing (mechanical) failure rate of firefighting units was examined. From the evaluation of this scenario we conclude that the difference between the Dynamic Model on the one hand and F-WASP and F-ANT on the other decreases as the failure rate increases. Also, the L-WASP mechanism performs even poorer when the failure rate increases. The overall ranking of the mechanisms, however, is not affected. In summary, the evaluation of both scenarios suggests that the ranking incorporates a certain level of robustness.

5 Related Work

Decentralized resource allocation is of particular interest to various scientific domains. An impressive amount of studies has exposed different aspects of the problem and respective algorithms for solving it. We will subsequently point out only a small excerpt of these approaches which are most relevant to our research.

In the workflow management domain, numerous authors tried to tackle the problem from an implementation perspective [30,31]. They predominantly focus either on modeling organizational structures with process elements linking to them, e.g. [4,31,32] or on the definition of criteria for assignment mechanisms, e.g. [33,34]. Research in the area of resource management in workflow applications is centered around access control mechanisms and policies that permit or restrict the ability of individual resources to perform tasks [35,36]. Dynamic resource allocation is of considerable importance to the fields of distributed (grid) computing [37], robotics [38] and multi-agent systems [39]. These domains draw heavily on market-based algorithms, as well as on reinforcement learning techniques. Shen proposed to extend current task assignment mechanisms beyond the static role-concept by including criteria such as the social proximity of workflow participants, or the compatibility of tasks with the existing content of work lists [34]. Allocation mechanisms inspired by economic principles, such as auctions and games, have been studied by Tan and Harker [40], as well as Alt et al. [41]. Auction protocols for the scheduling of decentralized resources have been discussed in other domains as well [42].

Despite the considerable amount of related work, we are unaware of research that specifically deals with dynamic algorithms for distributed task assignment in the business process management domain. There are two notable exceptions, however: the model by Kumar et al [3] takes into account the tradeoff between flexibility and efficiency (see Section 3.1). For the example case described therein, we were able to produce similar results with our stimulus/response model (these results are not included in this paper because of page restrictions). This indicates a high similarity in the effectiveness of both approaches. However, in this paper we show that Kumar's model is less robust in dealing with different time criteria.

The other exception is the work in [43]. This approach is based on the estimation of execution times and possible routes that cases will follow. When a new case arrives, a snapshot of the system is taken and a static scheduling problem based on this snapshot and the estimations is being solved. The resulting preliminary schedule is implemented and the whole procedure is repeated as soon as the next job arrives. The capability of this algorithm to minimize late jobs depends on the accuracy of the estimations and the solution quality of the scheduling instance. An important insight from this paper coinciding with ours is that when utilization rates are greater than or equal to 65%, almost every other technique than the FiFo rule is advantageous.

6 Discussion and Conclusion

Our studies show a favorable performance of fixed stimulus/response-models as a basis for workflow task assignment in emergency response situations. In particular, these models provide a balanced trade-off between the performance criteria that are important in this domain.

Among the most important limitations of our study, it must be noted that in our simulation model the execution of tasks cannot be interrupted: ACID properties are strictly enforced [18]. In real world fire fighting situations, tasks can be interrupted (e.g., a fire fighter will stop saving a cat from a tree if called to extinguish a chemical fire elsewhere). Also, we do not consider false alarms, which sometimes amount to 50% of all fire incidents [16]. Finally, the higher utilization levels we studied are beyond what is normal for emergency response situations (there, utilization levels are typically between 35% and 45% [44]). These limitations restrict general statements on the effectiveness of workflow technology in the emergency management domain. At the same time, various developments point at the increasing importance and use of workflow technology in this domain, as illustrated by the RESCUE [45], CITI [46], and AMIRA projects [47]. In addition, the emergency management domain itself may undergo changes, e.g., in the form of increasing resource utilization at local fire stations and by assigning larger incidents to regional fire stations. The implementation of swarm intelligence-based algorithms could contribute to robust process performance both at low and high resource utilization levels.

The main insight from our study is that stimulus/response-based task assignment mechanisms are appropriate in environments where timeliness of call resolution is critical. In particular, as most WfMSs dispatch work items to their performers on a FiFo basis, the latter strategy should be reconsidered in situations where timeliness is critical and resources are scarce. Models inspired by swarm intelligence could serve as a template for mechanisms that are more sensitive to (a) the impact of the elapsed time on the urgency of cases and (b) variations in the suitability of cross-trained resources. Since the environment in which businesses operate is increasingly complex, it can be expected that Business Process Management will have to provide capabilities similar to those of emergency management systems in order to continually provide valuable competitive advantage.

Acknowledgments. This research is supported by the Technology Foundation STW, applied science division of NWO and the technology programme of the Dutch Ministry of Economic Affairs. Preparatory work was supported by the US ARMY TACOM/ARDEC. We wish to acknowledge the contributions by Thomas Steinbusch (Eindhoven University of Technology) in carrying out the simulation study, members from the Austin Fire Department in the creation of the emergency scenario, and Andrea Freßmann (University of Trier) for her overall assistance and advice.

References

1. WfMC Terminology and Glossary, 3rd edn. Workflow Management Coalition, Winchester (ID) (1999)
2. Moore, C.: Common Mistakes in Workflow Implementations. Giga Information Group, Cambridge, MA (2002)
3. Kumar, A., van der Aalst, W.M.P., Verbeek, H.M.W.: Dynamic Work Distributio. In: Workflow Management Systems: How to Balance Quality and Performance, Journal of Management Information Systems 18(3) (2002)
4. Zur Mühlen, M.: Organizational Management in Workflow Applications – Issues and Perspectives. Information Technology and Management 5, 271–291 (2004)
5. Swersey, A.J.: The Deployment of Police, Fire and Emergency Medical Units. In: Pollock, S.M., et al. (eds.) Handbooks in OR&MS, vol. 6, Elsevier Science, Amsterdam (1994)
6. Beni, G., Wang, J.: Swarm intelligence in cellular robotic systems. In: Proc. NATO Advanced Workshop on Robotics and Biological Systems, Il Ciocco, Tuscany, Italy (1989)
7. Meyer, C., Bonabeau, E.: Swarm Intelligence: A Whole New Way to Think About Business, Harvard Business Review, May 2001, pp. 106–117 (2001)
8. Ghizzioli, R., Nouyan, S., Birattari, M., Dorigo, M.: An Ant-Based Algorithm for the Dynamic Task assignment Problem, TR/IRIDIA (2004)
9. Bonabeau, E., Dorigo, M., Theraulaz, G.: Swarm Intelligence: From Natural to Artificial Systems, Santa Fe Institute Studies in the Sciences of Complexity. Oxford University Press, Oxford (1999)

10. Bonabeau, E., Sobkowski, A., Theraulaz, G., Deneubourg, J.L.: Adaptive task allocation inspired by a model of division of labor in social insects; Biocomputation and Emergent Computing. World Scientific, Singapore (1997)
11. Price, R., Tino, P.: Evaluation Of Adaptive Nature Inspired Task Allocation Against Alternate Decentralized Multi-agent Strategies. In: Yao, X., Burke, E.K., Lozano, J.A., Smith, J., Merelo-Guervós, J.J., Bullinaria, J.A., Rowe, J.E., Tiňo, P., Kabán, A., Schwefel, H.-P. (eds.) Parallel Problem Solving from Nature - PPSN VIII. LNCS, vol. 3242, pp. 982–990. Springer, Heidelberg (2004)
12. Robinson, G.: Regulation of the division of labor in insect societies. Annual review, Entomol 37, 637–665 (1992)
13. Wilson, E.: The sociogenisis of insect colonies. Science 228, 1489–1495 (1985)
14. Theraulaz, G., Bonabeau, E., Deneubourg, J.: Response threshold reinforcement division of labour in insects societies. In: Proceedings Royal Societies, London (1998)
15. Campos, M., Bonabeau, E., Theraulaz, G., Deneubourg, J.: Dynamic Scheduling and Division of Labor in Social Insects. Adaptive behaviour 8, 83–92 (2001)
16. Austin Fire Department: Austin Fire Department, Austin City Connections (2006), http://www.ci.austin.tx.us/fire/default.htm
17. Centraal Bureau voor de Statistiek, Brandweerstatistiek 2004; Voorburg/Heerlen (2004)
18. van der Aalst, W.M.P., van Hee, K.: Workflow Management: Models, Methods and Systems. The MIT Press, Cambridge, Massachusetts (2002)
19. Gerkey, B., Mataric, M.: Multi-Robot Task assignment: Analyzing the Complexity and Optimality of Key Architectures. In: Proceedings of the 2003 IEEE International Conference on Robotics and Automation, Taipei, Taiwan (2003)
20. Gottlieb, J., Puchta, A., Solnon, C.: A Study of Greedy, Local Search, and Ant Colony Optimization Approaches for Car Sequencing Problems. In: Raidl, G.R., Cagnoni, S., Cardalda, J.J.R., Corne, D.W., Gottlieb, J., Guillot, A., Hart, E., Johnson, C.G., Marchiori, E., Meyer, J.-A., Middendorf, M. (eds.) EvoIASP 2003, EvoWorkshops 2003, EvoSTIM 2003, EvoROB/EvoRobot 2003, EvoCOP 2003, EvoBIO 2003, and EvoMUSART 2003. LNCS, vol. 2611, Springer, Heidelberg (2003)
21. Rushton, G.: Applications of Location Models, Annual of Operations Research 18 (1989)
22. Jensen, K.: Coloured Petri Nets, Basic Concepts, Analysis Methods and Practical Use, 2nd edn., vol. 1. Springer, Heidelberg (1997)
23. Mehta, A.: Smart Modeling – Basic Methodology and Advanced Tools. In: Proceedings of the 2000 Winter Simulation Conference (2000)
24. Law, A.M., Kelton, W.D.: Simulation Modeling and Analysis, 3rd edn. MCgraw Hill International Series (2000)
25. Goldberg, D.: Genetic Algorithms in Search, Optimization and Machine Learning. Addison-Wesley, Reading, MA (1989)
26. Cicirello, V., Smith, S.: Wasp-like Agents for Distributed Factory Coordination. Autonomous Agents and Multi-Agents Systems 8, 237–266 (2004)
27. Kittithreerapronchai, O., Anderson, C.: Do ants paint trucks better than chickens? Markets versus response thresholds for distributed dynamic scheduling. In: Proceedings of the 2003 IEEE Congress on Evolutionary Computation, IEEE Press, Los Alamitos (2003)
28. Hays, W.: Statistics, 5th edn., USA, Orlando Florida (1994)
29. Cicirello, V., Smith, S.: Wasp-like Agents for Distributed Factory Coordination. Autonomous Agents and Multi-Agents Systems 8, 237–266 (2004)
30. Bussler, C.: Analysis of the Organization Modeling Capability of Workflow-Management-Systems. In: Amoroso, D.L. (ed.) Conference of the Pacific Research Institute for Information Systems and Management (PRIISM '96), Maui, HI, USA (1996)

31. Rupietta, W.: Organizational Models for Cooperative Office Applications. In: Karagiannis, D. (ed.) DEXA 1994. LNCS, vol. 856, Springer, Heidelberg (1994)
32. van der Aalst, W.M.P., Kumar, A., Verbeek, H.M.W.: Organizational Modeling in UML and XML in the context of Workflow Systems. In: Matsui, M., Zuccherato, R.J. (eds.) SAC 2003. LNCS, vol. 3006, Springer, Heidelberg (2004)
33. Momotko, M., Subieta, K.: Dynamic Changes in Workflow Participant Assignment. In: Manolopoulos, Y., Návrat, P. (eds.) ADBIS 2002. LNCS, vol. 2435, Springer, Heidelberg (2002)
34. Shen, M., Tzen, G.-H., Lio, D.-R.: Multi-Criteria Task Assignment in Workflow Management Systems. In: Sprague, R.J. (ed.) 36th HICSS, IEEE, Waikoloa, HI (2003)
35. Huang, Y.-N., Shan, M.-C.: Policy-Based Resource Management. In: Jarke, M., Oberweis, A. (eds.) CAiSE 1999. LNCS, vol. 1626, Springer, Heidelberg (1999)
36. Bussler, C., Jablonski, S.: Policy Resolution for Workflow Management. In: Sprague, R.J. (ed.) 28th Hawaii International Conference on Systems Sciences (HICSS 1995), IEEE, Hawaii (1995)
37. Gomoluch, J., Schroeder, M.: Market-Based Resource Allocation for Grid Computing: A Model and Simulation. In: Proc. 1st. Int'l. Workshop on Middleware for Grid Computing (MGC) (2003)
38. Krieger, M.J.B., Billeter, J.-B., et al.: Ant-like task allocation and recruitment in cooperative robots. Nature 406(31), 992–995 (2000)
39. Shehory, O., Kraus, S.: Methods for task allocation via agent coalition formation. Artificial Intelligence Journal 101(1-2), 165–200 (1998)
40. Tan, J.C., Harker, P.T.: Designing Workflow Coordination: Centralized Versus Market-Based Mechanisms. Information Systems Research 10, 328–342 (1999)
41. Alt, R., Klein, S., Kuhn, C.: Service Task Allocation as an Internal Market. In: Baets, W.R.J. (ed.) Second European Conference on Information Systems (ECIS 1994). Nijenrode University Press, Netherlands, pp. 424–432 (1994)
42. Wellman, M.P., Walsh, W.E., Wurman, P.R., MacKie-Mason, J.K.: Auction protocols for decentralized scheduling. Games and Economic Behavior 35, 271–303 (2001)
43. Baggio, G., Wainer, J., Ellis, C.: Applying scheduling techniques to minimize the number of late jobs in workflow systems. In: Handschuh, H., Hasan, M.A. (eds.) SAC 2004. LNCS, vol. 3357, pp. 1396–1403. Springer, Heidelberg (2004)
44. Bonin, G.: Final Report, Assessment of Fire and EMS Services Branchburg Township, New Jersey; Tridata, A Division of Sustem Planning Corporation (2005)
45. Mehrotra, S., Butts, C., Kalashnikov, N.: Project Rescue: Challenges in Responding to the Unexpected. SPIE 5304, 179–192 (2004)
46. Amer, A., Brustoloni, J., Chrysanthis, P.K., Hauskrecht, M., Labrinidis, A., Melhem, R., Mosse, D., Pruhs, K., Comfort, L.: Secure-CITI: A Secure Critical Information Technology Infrastructure for Disaster Management, Hazard Reduction and Response in Metropolitan Regions (2003)
47. Freßmann, A.: Adaptive Workflow Support for Search Processes within Fire Service Organisations, University of Trier (2006)

Evaluating Peer-to-Peer for Loosely Coupled Business Collaboration: A Case Study

Fabian Stäber[1] and Jörg P. Müller[2]

[1] Siemens AG, Corporate Technology, Information and Communications
Otto-Hahn-Ring 6, Munich, 81739, Germany
[2] Clausthal University of Technology,
Julius-Albert-Str. 4, Clausthal-Zellerfeld, 38678, Germany

Abstract. Built-in support for self-organization, reliability, and decentralized management makes peer-to-peer an inherently suitable paradigm for loosely coupled business collaboration applications. However, current raw peer-to-peer algorithms are not sufficient to fulfill the requirements of distributed business process management. In this paper, we make the case for a generic service layer between peer-to-peer overlay and business application; we identify a number of important service layer components, and we evaluate these components with respect to requirements gathered from an industrial case study: automotive collaborative product development (CPD).

1 Introduction

Over the past few years, the peer-to-peer paradigm has been receiving broad attention in research and industry alike. Within the ATHENA IP[1], we have investigated the applicability of peer-to-peer protocols and architectures for a number of *collaborative business processes*, one of them being automotive collaborative product development (CPD, [1]). We have gathered further experience by building a peer-to-peer based Business Resource Management Framework (BRMF, [2]), and by applying BRMF to the automotive application. Studying business integration in the automotive industry, we learned that second tier suppliers join and leave the supplier network very dynamically. Handling the fluctuation of suppliers is a great challenge for business collaboration. A software platform enabling business integration among suppliers must support this churn.

Considering the capability of peer-to-peer systems to support easy to use plug-and-play networks in combination with resilience, reliability, decentralized management, and loosely coupled control, it seems that peer-to-peer technologies fit perfectly as a basis for implementing the type of dynamic collaboration processes as mentioned above. However, while the use of peer-to-peer technologies for business integration has been proposed in several research papers (e.g., [2,3]), peer-to-peer has not yet become a significant technology on the business applications market.

---

[1] http://www.athena-ip.org

G. Alonso, P. Dadam, and M. Rosemann (Eds.): BPM 2007, LNCS 4714, pp. 141–148, 2007.

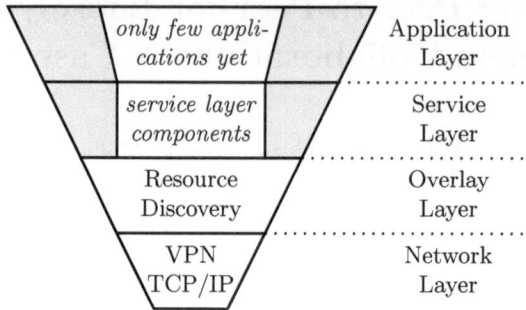

Fig. 1. Layers for Peer-to-Peer Based Applications

The reason for this becomes clear when decomposing peer-to-peer applications into different layers, as illustrated in Figure 1. The raw peer-to-peer overlay does not match the requirements of real-world business collaboration scenarios. Therefore, a service layer needs to be introduced, providing the functionality required by the application. However, although the overlay layer has been a research topic for several years, to our knowledge there is no significant related work addressing service layer components as independent building blocks that can be composed to meet the application requirements. Pushing this research forward is the key towards enabling collaborative business process management to benefit from peer-to-peer computing.

This paper is organized as follows. In the next section, we give the problem statement. In Section 3, we introduce the use case and present the required background in peer-to-peer computing. Section 4 identifies the requirements of the use case regarding the peer-to-peer service layer, and Section 5 presents the service layer components that can be used to meet the requirements. Finally, we summarize the interdependencies of the service layer components.

2   Problem Statement

The reason for the gap between the application requirements and the service layer is not that there are too few service layer components available. Rather, the problem is that current peer-to-peer projects provide monolithic, domain specific solutions, and do not distinguish generic service layer components. This makes it hard to benefit from peer-to-peer in new domains, like peer-to-peer based CPD applications.

In this paper, we analyze the requirements of a CPD scenario in the automotive industry and review the concepts behind current peer-to-peer projects with similar requirements. We extract generic, domain independent service layer components needed to implement our scenario, and analyze the interdependencies between these components.

Based on the analysis, we evaluate the feasibility of applying peer-to-peer technologies in CPD. The goal is to enable business collaboration to benefit

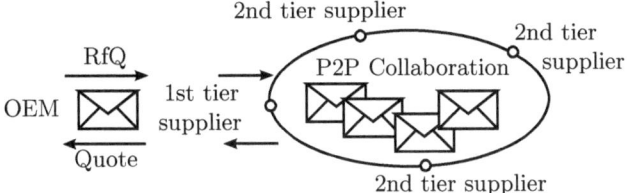

Fig. 2. P2P-Based CPD Scenario

from the self-organization and resilience offered by peer-to-peer systems. Our goal is to provide a novel view of peer-to-peer based applications, with a service layer as an independent layer, and to investigate interrelations between different generic service layer components are analyzed.

3   Background

In this section we briefly introduce the background necessary to identify the gap between the requirements of the CPD application and the services offered by the overlay layer. We first introduce the CPD scenario, and then briefly give an overview of peer-to-peer technologies.

3.1   Use Case Scenario

Figure 2 shows a Collaborative Product Development (CPD) scenario in the automotive industry, that was developed as part of the ATHENA project. A car manufacturer (OEM, Original Equipment Manufacturer) issues Requests for Quotations (RfQs) to its first tier suppliers. The engineers on the supplier side analyze the technical specifications in the RfQ and discuss them with the second tier suppliers. After this, the first tier supplier generates a proposal for alternative technical specifications and returns this proposal to the OEM. In turn, the OEM revises and updates its RfQ, and issues a new version. This negotiation cycle repeats until all parties agree on a feasible specification.

We learned that second tier suppliers join and leave the environment very dynamically. In this paper, we address the requirements on a business collaboration platform that is able to support the churn on the supplier side. The collaboration platform has two tasks. First, it must serve as a messaging platform, allowing the business partners to notify each other about new documents in a fluctuating environment. Second, the platform must serve as a data store, keeping the published technical specifications available in the face of churn.

3.2   Peer-to-Peer Technologies

In this section we will briefly introduce peer-to-peer background, and motivate why we focus on Distributed Hash Tables (DHTs) for the rest of this paper.

From an abstract point of view, a peer-to-peer overlay can be seen as a distributed routing protocol, mapping *keywords* to *peers* being responsible for the given keywords. The most common use of peer-to-peer overlays is to build data sharing applications on top of them. A piece of data to be shared in a peer-to-peer application is called a *resource*. Each resource must be associated with one or more keywords that can be used to find the peers being responsible for the resource. In the simplest case, a keyword could be the filename of the resource.

In the CPD scenario presented above, the resources to be shared are business documents, like RfQs or Quotes. It is necessary to provide the recipients of these documents guaranteed access to the resources being available. The type of peer-to-peer overlays being able to provide guaranteed access is known as *Distributed Hash Tables* (DHTs). There are several DHT implementations, but conceptually all of them provide the same functionality. Some DHTs provide a unique one-to-one mapping between a single keyword and a unique peer being responsible for the keyword, and some of them provide a generic n-to-m mapping, yielding a set of responsible peers for a set of keywords.

In the rest of this paper, we will view the DHT as an abstract layer being able to look up peers for a given set of keywords. In Section 5 we show how to compose service layer components providing rich features on top of the raw peer-to-peer layer.

4   Application Requirements

Analyzing the CPD scenario, we identified eight requirements to be considered when evaluating the service layer components in Section 5. The choice of these requirements is based on the following considerations: First, we only consider requirements regarding the underlying service layer. More requirements can be found on the application layer, but these do not directly correspond to service layer components. Second, we only choose requirements of a generic nature, which means that these requirements can also be found in other application scenarios in a similar way. That way, we can benefit from ideas that are found in other peer-to-peer based applications.

Messaging. As shown in Section 3, the collaboration platform must not only serve as a data store for business documents, but also notify the respective business partners if documents are added, updated or removed. Doing so requires some messaging functionality.

Traffic Load Balancing. The peers in the peer-to-peer infrastructure are all operated by the participating business partners. Each peer acts as a router for other peers. The network traffic should be equally distributed among all peers. It must be avoided that a single peer is flooded with all the traffic.

Data Load Balancing. Each peer should store roughly the same amount of data.

Data Consistency. Due to the decentralized nature of peer-to-peer systems, there is no central instance defining which version of a document is the current one. Therefore, it is required that the collaboration infrastructure provides means for maintaining a consistent view of the versions of all resources.

Security. Business partners may be both, collaborators and competitors at the same time. Therefore, secure communication must be guaranteed, which means that the communication must be confidential, reliable and authenticated. Additionally, data stored in the network must be encrypted and resistant to malicious modifications or removal.

Resilience. We observe that in the use case business partners join and leave the supplier network very dynamically. The underlying infrastructure must catch up with this churn.

Rich Queries. There must be a way for business partners to describe documents they are interested in. The underlying collaboration platform must offer some rich query language for formulating complex queries.

Low Network Load. All the requirements above could be easily implemented if we had infinitely low delay and unbounded throughput. However, small suppliers often have limited bandwidth connections. Deploying the system in these environments must be feasible.

5   Evaluation of Service Layer Components

In this section, we evaluate service layer components clustered by their functionality. The choice of the service layer components is derived from the requirements we analyzed regarding the CPD scenario. As this is only a short paper, we restrict ourselves to giving a very brief survey of existing service layer solutions, and to providing an evaluation matrix giving an idea of how a methodology for evaluating the interrelationships between these service layer components should look like.

Subscriptions are used to notify business partners if documents of interest are added, updated, or removed. This is essential if the application does not only require a data store, but also messaging functionality. A survey of multicast solutions including references to related work can be found in [4]. Besides adding messaging functionality, subscriptions also reduce network traffic, as polling can be avoided. On the downside, certain security challenges are introduced, as the peer being responsible for a certain keyword learns who of its competitors is subscribed for that keyword.

Replication means that backup copies of the documents are stored on different peers in the peer-to-peer overlay. If the peer being responsible for a document fails, a backup peer can take over the responsibility, and the document remains available. Apart from increasing reliability, replication also fosters traffic load balancing, as there are more than one peers that can be queried for each document.

There are simple replication strategies, copying each resource to a fixed number of neighboring peers, and there are more sophisticated replication strategies, adapting on the popularity of the documents. A survey and evaluation of different strategies can be found in [5].

Fuzzy Hashing is a way to avoid *hotspots* in terms of data load, i.e. to relieve peers suffering from too much data to be stored. This is achieved by replacing the strict mapping of resources to keywords with an adaptable, fuzzy mapping [6,7]. Apart from fostering load balancing, fuzzy hashing also has a positive effect on security, because with fuzzy hashing no peer has the full control of all resources with a certain keyword.

Consensus Protocols must be combined with replication strategies in order to avoid concurrent modifications. If a document is replicated in the peer-to-peer overlay, it cannot be guaranteed that all modifications to the document will be consistent among all the copies of the document. Using consensus protocols, atomic transactions can be implemented [8,9,10].

Additionally, the use of consensus protocols has a positive impact on security, because a single peer can be kept from tampering with documents.

Confidential Communication is essential in the CPD scenario, as the suppliers may be both, cooperators and competitors at the same time. Confidential communication must fulfill three properties: Sender authentication, content encryption, and anonymous communication paths, securing that intermediate peers on the communication path cannot learn who is communicating with whom.

Implementing confidential communication on the service layer requires that the peer-to-peer overlay is built on top of a *virtual private network*, (VPN), providing a *public key infrastructure* (PKI). The unique PKI certificates can be used to prevent Sybil attacks [11], and the public key encryption can be used to implement Onion Routing [12], providing anonymous communication paths.

Redundant Paths are used to prevent attacks on the DHT's routing mechanism. The confidential communication introduced above a secure environment for the CPD scenario, but it relies on the overlay's lookup algorithm to work correctly. The reliability of the lookup mechanism can be increased using redundant lookup paths [13]. Additionally, redundant lookup paths have a positive impact on traffic load balancing, as there is no single lookup paths being a potential bottleneck.

Search Indexes are used to implement rich queries on top of the peer-to-peer overlay's trivial keyword lookup mechanism. We identified four major technologies to implement high level queries: Ontologies, as applied in the Edutella project [14], SQL, as implemented in the PIER project [15], XPath, as in the Active XML project [16], and index servers providing full text search, as with Lucene [17]. Although the related work on distributed ontologies, SQL, and XPath looks promising, one must always keep in mind that queries that affect a large number of peers do not scale. Therefore, distributed query languages will always be restricted to a subset of their non-distributed counterparts.

6   Conclusions and Outlook

Figure 3 shows an evaluation matrix of the components introduced in Section 5. The + and − signs stand for positive or negative impact on the corresponding requirement area. The results are the following:

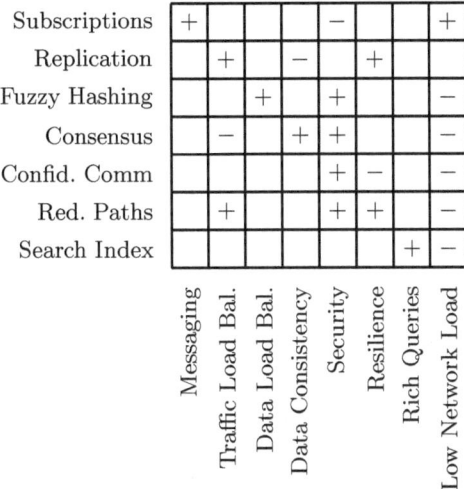

	Messaging	Traffic Load Bal.	Data Load Bal.	Data Consistency	Security	Resilience	Rich Queries	Low Network Load
Subscriptions	+				−			+
Replication		+		−		+		
Fuzzy Hashing			+	+				−
Consensus		−		+	+			−
Confid. Comm					+	−		−
Red. Paths		+			+	+		−
Search Index							+	−

Fig. 3. Benefits and Conflicts of Service Layer Components with Requirements

1. All the requirements we identified in the CPD scenario are supported by one or more service layer components.
2. There is no one-to-one mapping of service layer components and requirements. Most service layer components have impact on several requirements.
3. All service layer components have positive and negative impacts. While some requirements are fulfilled using these components, other requirements are corrupted. That means that applying any of these service layer components is always a trade-off.

The evaluation framework presented in this paper provides one step towards enabling collaborative business processes to benefit from the self-organization and resilience of decentralized peer-to-peer systems. Our next steps are to apply our view of the service layer to other scenarios and other requirements. The comparison of the results will result in an evaluation of what interrelations on the service layer are triggered by specific use case requirements, and what interrelations are more universal.

References

1. Stäber, F., Sobrito, G., Müller, J.P., Bartlang, U., Friese, T.: Interoperability challenges and solutions in automotive collaborative product development. In: Proc. of the 3rd International Conference on Interoperability for Enterprise Software and Applications, Enterprise Interoperability, vol. 2, pp. 709–720. Springer, London (2007)
2. Friese, T., Müller, J.P., Smith, M., Freisleben, B.: A robust business resource management framework based on a peer-to-peer infrastructure. In: CEC '05: Proc. of the 7th International IEEE Conference on E-Commerce Technology, pp. 215–222. IEEE Press, Los Alamitos (2005)

3. Androutsellis-Theotokis, S., Spinellis, D., Karakoidas, V.: Performing peer-to-peer e-business transactions: A requirements analysis and preliminary design proposal. In: Karmakar, N., Isaías, P. (eds.) Proc. of the IADIS International e-Commerce 2004 Conference, IADIS Press, pp. 399–404 (2004)

4. Abad, C.L., Yurcik, W., Campbell, R.H.: A survey and comparison of end-system overlay multicast solutions suitable for network-centric warfare. In: Suresh, R. (ed.) Battlespace Digitization and Network-Centric Systems IV. SPIE, vol. 5441, pp. 215–226 (2004)

5. Leslie, M., Davies, J., Huffman, T.: Replication strategies for reliable decentralised storage. In: ARES '06: Proc. of the First International Conference on Availability, Reliability and Security, pp. 740–747 (2006)

6. Mitzenmacher, M.: The power of two choices in randomized load balancing. IEEE Transactions on Parallel and Distributed Systems 12(10), 1094–1104 (2001)

7. Rieche, S., Petrak, L., Wehrle, K.: A thermal-dissipation-based approach for balancing data load in distributed hash tables. In: LCN '04: Proc. of the 29th Annual IEEE International Conference on Local Computer Networks, pp. 15–23. IEEE Computer Society Press, Los Alamitos (2004)

8. Lamport, L., Shostak, R., Pease, M.: The byzantine generals problem. TOPLAS: ACM Transactions on Programming Languages and Systems 4(3), 382–401 (1982)

9. Lamport, L.: Paxos made simple. SIGACT News 32(4), 18–25 (2001)

10. Muthitacharoen, A., Gilbert, S., Morris, R.: Etna: a fault-tolerant algorithm for atomic mutable dht data. Technical Report MIT-LCS-TR-993, MIT Computer Science and Artificial Intelligence Laboratory (2005)

11. Douceur, J.R.: The sybil attack. In: Druschel, P., Kaashoek, M.F., Rowstron, A. (eds.) IPTPS 2002. LNCS, vol. 2429, pp. 251–260. Springer, Heidelberg (2002)

12. Stäber, F., Bartlang, U., Müller, J.P.: Using onion routing to secure peer-to-peer supported business collaboration. In: Proc. of eChallenges 2006, Exploiting the Knowledge Economy: Issues, Applications and Case Studies, vol. 3, pp. 181–188. IOS Press, Amsterdam (2006)

13. Srivatsa, M., Liu, L.: Vulnerabilities and security threats in structured overlay networks: a quantitative analysis. In: ACSAC 2004, pp. 252–261. IEEE Press, Los Alamitos (2004)

14. Nejdl, W., Wolf, B., Qu, C., Decker, S., Sintek, M., Naeve, A., Nilsson, M., Palmér, M., Risch, T.: Edutella: A p2p networking infrastructure based on RDF. In: WWW '02: Proc. of the 11th Int. World Wide Web Conference, pp. 604–615 (2002)

15. Huebsch, R., Chun, B., Hellerstein, J., Loo, B.T., Maniatis, P., Roscoe, T., Shenker, S., Stoica, I., Yumerefendi, A.R.: The architecture of PIER: an internet-scale query processor. In: CIDR '05: Proc. of the 2nd Conference on Innovative Data Systems Research, pp. 28–43 (2005)

16. Abiteboul, S., Benjelloun, O., Milo, T.: The active xml project: an overview. Technical Report 331, Gemo, INRIA-Futurs (10, 2005)

17. Gospodnetić, O., Hatcher, E.: Lucene in Action. Manning Publications Co., Greenwich, CT (2005)

Modeling Control Objectives for Business Process Compliance

Shazia Sadiq[1], Guido Governatori[1], and Kioumars Namiri[2]

[1] School of Information Technology and Electrical Engineering,
The University of Queensland, St Lucia QLD 4072.
Brisbane, Australia
[2] SAP Research Centre CEC Karlsruhe, SAP AG, Vincenz-Prießnitz-Str.1
76131 Karlsruhe, Germany
{shazia, guido}@itee.uq.edu.au, kioumars.namiri@sap.com

Abstract. Business process design is primarily driven by process improvement objectives. However, the role of control objectives stemming from regulations and standards is becoming increasingly important for businesses in light of recent events that led to some of the largest scandals in corporate history. As organizations strive to meet compliance agendas, there is an evident need to provide systematic approaches that assist in the understanding of the interplay between (often conflicting) business and control objectives during business process design. In this paper, our objective is twofold. We will firstly present a research agenda in the space of business process compliance, identifying major technical and organizational challenges. We then tackle a part of the overall problem space, which deals with the effective modeling of control objectives and subsequently their propagation onto business process models. Control objective modeling is proposed through a specialized modal logic based on normative systems theory, and the visualization of control objectives on business process models is achieved procedurally. The proposed approach is demonstrated in the context of a purchase-to-pay scenario.

Keywords: Compliance, Risk, Internal Controls, Business Process Design.

1 Introduction

The importance of compliance has dramatically increased over the last few years for businesses in several industry sectors. Essentially, compliance is ensuring that business processes, operations and practice are in accordance with a prescribed and/or agreed set of norms. Compliance requirements may stem from legislature and regulatory bodies (e.g. Sarbanes-Oxley, Basel II, HIPAA), standards and codes of practice (e.g. SCOR, ISO9000) and also business partner contracts. Compliance related software and services is expected to reach a market value of over $27billion this year [17]. The boost in business investment is primarily a consequence of regulatory mandates that emerged as a result of recent events that led to some of the largest scandals in corporate history such as Enron (USA) and HIH (Australia). In

G. Alonso, P. Dadam, and M. Rosemann (Eds.): BPM 2007, LNCS 4714, pp. 149–164, 2007.

spite of mandated deadlines there is evidence that many organizations are still struggling with their compliance initiatives. A recent report [4] identifies the gap between management focus on compliance related issues and IT's lack of ability to implement the critical policies and procedures.

A number of compliance service/solution providers are currently available. Traditionally these are large consulting firms such as PriceWaterhouseCoppers, Deliotte etc. However software vendors are also emerging ranging from large corporations with products such as IBM Lotus workplace for Business Controls & Reporting, Microsoft Office Solutions Accelerator for Sarbanes-Oxley, SAP GRC (Governance, Risk and Compliance) Solution, as well as niche vendors such as OpenPages, Paisley Consulting, Qumas Inc and several others.

Compliance is predominantly viewed as a burden, although there are indications that businesses have started to see the regulations as an opportunity to improve their business processes and operations. Industry reports [17] indicate that up to 80% of companies said they expected to reap business benefits from improving their compliance regimens. This has opened a new but complex set of challenges for enterprise software vendors.

Currently there are two main approaches towards achieving compliance. First is *retrospective reporting*, wherein traditional audits are conducted for "after-the-fact" detection, often through manual checks by expensive consultants. A second and more recent approach is to provide some level of automation through *automated detection*. The bulk of existing software solutions for compliance follow this approach. The proposed solutions hook into variety of enterprise system components (e.g. SAP HR, LDAP Directory, Groupware etc.) and generate audit reports against hard-coded checks performed on the requisite system. These solutions often specialize in certain class of checks, for example the widely supported checks that relate to Segregation of Duty violations in role management systems. However, this approach still resides in the space of "after-the-fact" detection. Although, the assessment time is reduced, and correspondingly the time to remediation and/or mitigation of control deficiencies is also improved. This improvement is much sought after as is evident from the heavy investment in compliance software during the last few years.

A major issue with the above approaches (in varying degrees of impact) is the lack of sustainability. Even with automated detection facility, the hard coded check repositories can quickly grow out of control making it extremely difficult to evolve and maintain them for changing legislatures and compliance requirements. In addition to external pressures, there is often a company internal push towards quality of service initiatives for process improvement which have similar requirements. The complexity of the situation is exasperated by the presence of dynamically changing collaborative processes shared with business partners. The diversity, scale and complexity of compliance requirements warrant a highly systematic and well-grounded approach.

We believe that a sustainable approach for achieving compliance should fundamentally have a preventative focus. As such, we envisage an approach that provides the capability to capture compliance requirements through a generic requirements modeling framework, and subsequently facilitate the propagation of these requirements into business process models and enterprise applications, thus achieving *compliance by design*.

In light of the heavy socio, economic and environmental costs of non-compliance, a priori embedding of requisite checks and triggers into the enterprise applications is clearly desirable but also extremely difficult given that the technology landscape of today's organizations is disparate, and distributed. This is further complicated by several factors, legacy systems, distributed operations, outsourcing, and imperfect work practices to name a few.

Business process models may seem the most natural venue for the modeling of compliance related controls. However, our study indicates that an attempt to prematurely load business process models with compliance controls will be highly problematic from a practical standpoint. This is the basic premise of our approach.

In this paper, our objective is two fold. We will firstly present in section 2, a detailed discussion on the problem space of business process compliance, identifying major technical and organizational challenges. The scale of the problem space is beyond the scope of one paper, however, in this paper we tackle a part of the overall space, which deals with the effective modeling of control objectives (in section 3), and subsequently its interplay with business process models (in section 4). We present a review of current literature in section 5, followed by an outlook on future challenges in section 6.

2   The Problem Space

Business process management is well recognized as a means to enforce corporate policy. Regulatory mandates also provide policies and guidelines for business practice. One may argue why a separate requirements modeling facility is required to capture compliance requirements for business processes. We identify the following reasons against this argument:

Firstly, the source of these two objectives will be distinct both from an ownership and governance perspective, as well as from a timeline perspective. Where as businesses can be expected to have some form of business objectives, control objectives will be dictated by mostly external sources and at different times.

Secondly, the two have differing concerns, namely business objectives and control objectives. Thus the use of business process languages to model control objectives may not provide a conceptually faithful representation. Compliance is in essence a normative notion, and thus control objectives are fundamentally descriptive, i.e. indicating *what* needs to be done (in order to comply). Business process specifications are fundamentally prescriptive in nature, i.e. detailing *how* business activity should take place. There is evidence of some developments towards descriptive approaches for BPM, but these works were predominantly focused on achieving flexibility in business process execution (see e.g. [18], [20]).

Thirdly, there is likelihood of conflicts, inconsistencies and redundancies within the two specifications. The intersection of the two needs to be carefully studied.

In summary we present in Figure 1, the interconnect between Process Management and Controls Management. The two are formulated by different stakeholders and have different lifecycles. The design of controls will impact on the way a business process is executed. On the other hand, a (re)design of a business process causes an update of the risk assessment, which may lead to a new/updated set of controls. Additionally, business process monitoring will assess the design of internal controls and serve as an input to internal controls certification.

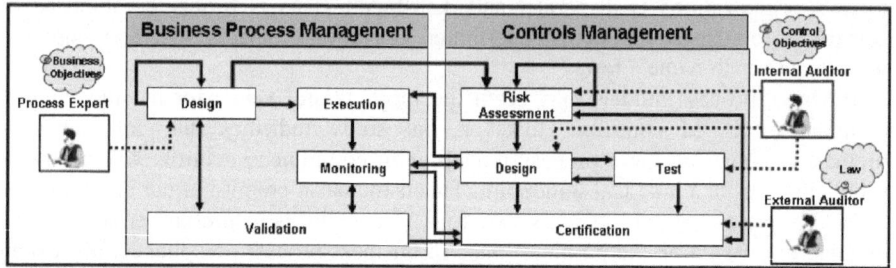

Fig. 1. Interconnect of Process Management and Controls Management

Given the scale and diversity of compliance requirements and additionally the fact that these requirements may frequently change, business process compliance is indeed a large and complex problem area with several challenges. Following our initial premise that business and control objectives are (or should be) designed separately, but must converge at some point, we present below a list of essential methods and techniques that need to be developed to tackle this overall problem.

2.1 Control Directory Management

Regulations and other compliance directives are complex, vague and require interpretation. Often in legalese, these mandates need to be translated by experts. For example the COSO framework [6] is recognized by regulatory bodies as a defacto standard for realizing controls for financial reporting. A company-specific interpretation results in the following (textual) information being created:

<control objective, risk, internal control [1]>

For example:

Control objective:	*prevent unauthorized use of purchase order process*
Risk:	*unauthorized creation of purchase orders and payments to non-existing suppliers*
Internal control:	*The creation and approval of purchase orders must be undertaken by two separate purchase officers*

The above example is typical of the well known segregation of duty constraint (one individual does not participate in more than one key trading or operational function) mandated by Sarbanes-Oxley 404.

---

[1] "Internal control is broadly defined as a process, effected by an entity's board of directors, management and other personnel designed to provide reasonable assurance regarding the achievement of objectives in the following categories: Effectiveness and efficiency of operations; Reliability of financial reporting; and Compliance with applicable laws and regulations." [6].

However, business will typically deal with a number of regulations/standards at one time. Thus there is a need to provide a structured means of managing the various interpretations within regional, industry sector and organizational contexts. We identify this as a need for a *controls directory*. Control directory management could be supported by database technology, and/or could present some interesting content management challenges, but will be an essential component in the overall solution. There is some evidence in industry reports [e.g. SAP GRC Repository] that large solution vendors are producing repositories of control objectives (and associated parameters) against the major regulations.

2.2 Ontological Alignment

Interpretation of regulations from legal /financial experts comes in the form of textual descriptions (see example in section above). Establishing an agreement on terms and usage between these descriptions and the business processes and constituent activities/transactions is a difficult but essential aspect of the overall methodology.

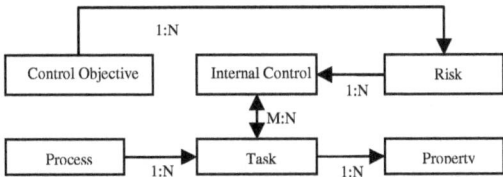

Fig. 2. Relationships between Process Modeling and Control Modeling Concepts

In the Fig 2, we present the relationships between the basic process modeling and control modeling concepts. Clearly the relationship between process task and internal controls is much deeper than shown as it would require alignment between embedded concepts e.g. task identification, particular data items, roles and performers etc. However, it is evident that several controls may be applicable on a task, and one control may impact on multiple tasks as well. What tools and techniques are utilized to provide an effective alignment between the two conceptual spaces is not the focus of this paper, but none the less an important question at hand.

2.3 Modeling Control Objectives

The motivation to model control objectives is multifaceted: Firstly, a generic requirements modeling framework for compliance by design will provide a substantial improvement over current after-the-fact detection approaches. Secondly, it will allow for an analysis of compliance rules thus providing the ability to discover hidden dependencies, and view in holistic context, while maintaining a comprehensible working space. Thirdly, a precise and unambiguous (formal) specification will facilitate the systematic enrichment of business processes with control objectives.

A fundamental question in this regard is the *appropriate formalism* to undertake the task. In the next section we will deliberate further on this question, and also provide a discussion of complementary approaches in the section on related work.

2.4 Process Model Enrichment

In this context, we use the term process model enrichment as the ability to enhance enterprise models (business processes) with compliance requirements. This is essentially provided as *process annotation* (see section 4). The resultant visualization of control objectives on the process model, facilitates a better understanding of the interaction between the two specifications for both stakeholders (process owners as well as compliance officers).

However, the visualization is only a first step. The new checks introduced within the process model, can in turn be used to analyse the model for measures such as *compliance distance* that can provide a quantification of the effort required to achieve a compliant process model. Eventually, process models may need to be modified to include the compliance requirements.

2.5 Event Monitoring

The support provided in the design of compliant processes through process annotation and analysis and resultant process changes, will eventually lead to a *model driven enforcement of compliance controls* (where process management systems are in place). However, it is naïve to assume that all organizations have the complete implementation of the BPM lifecycle, and hence the process models and underlying applications may be disconnected. In this case, it is important to provide support for compliance through run time monitoring. This has been the agenda for several vendors in this space targeting the so called *automated detection,* described earlier. In general event monitoring is a well studied research topic [see e.g. www.complexevents.com], and although has not been widely/explictly associated with the compliance issue (notably excepting [10]), its usage in fraud detection and security is closely related.

Although, our work is primarily targeted at achieving *compliance by design* by adopting a preventative approach facilitated by business process models, the work on formal modeling of control objectives has taken into account the violations and resultant reparation policies that may surface at runtime (see next section).

3   Modeling Control Objectives

Our observation is that a compliance requirement (or its translation into a control objective and subsequently internal controls) can be reduced to the identification of what obligations an enterprise has to fulfill to be deemed as compliant. Initial work in this area [12] in the context of business contracts (a special case of compliance) has already provided the basic concepts leading to the adoption of formal models of normative systems as a candidate representation for control objectives.

In general a formal model of a normative system provides a precise and unambiguous account of the obligations, permissions, prohibitions as well as other normative positions an entity is subject to in the context where the normative system applies. To formalize normative systems one has to capture the logical properties of the notions of the normative concepts (e.g., obligations, prohibitions, permissions, violations, ...) and how these relate to the entities in an organization and to the activities to be performed. Deontic logic is the branch of logic that studies normative concepts such as obligations, permissions, prohibitions and related notions. Over the years many different deontic logics have been proposed to capture the intuitions behind these notions. Standard Deontic Logic (SDL) offers a very idealized and abstract conceptual representation of the basic normative notions [5], but at the same time it suffers from several drawbacks given its high level of abstraction. One of the main limitations in this context is its inability to reason with violations, and the obligations arising in response to violations [19].

We propose FCL-Formal Contract Language [15] as formalism to express normative specifications. FCL is a combination of an efficient non-monotonic formalism (defeasible logic) and a deontic logic of violations [14] offering the right trade off between expressive power and computational complexity. The key idea of the logic of violations, backed-up by current views of legal theory, is that a normative document consists of a set of (normative) clauses regulating the intended behaviour of a system, and given the non-monotonic nature of normative systems (i.e., normative concepts admit exceptions), it is not possible to consider the clauses of the normative document in isolation, but the normative documents must be conceived as a whole (often clauses in apparently unrelated sections of the document can have mutual effects on each other).

In addition the document specifies only explicit behaviors. The basic mechanism of the logic of violations [14] takes a modular approach to the problem and it recursively deduces new clauses from the existing clauses in a module and combines clauses related to violations and obligations generated in response to violations. Then it recursively merges the clauses in different modules and computes new clauses resulting from the interaction among modules. The modularity of the mechanism used by FCL is of particular relevance for compliance since the architecture of modern enterprise systems is based on the composition of diverse components. In this way it is possible to revise the specifications of a component of a business process or a section in the normative specifications without being forced to perform a complete revision of the representation of the business process or of the normative document as it is often the case with hard-coded solutions.

Furthermore, the reasoning mechanism of defeasible logic is based on constructive proofs, thus for any conclusions it is possible to have a trace of the derivation, which then can be used to provide an explanation of the reasons why the conclusion has been obtained. This property is very important for compliance and auditing, since we are not only interested that a process is not compliant but we want the reasons why it does not comply.

In the following sections, we will provide an illustration on the use of FCL through a purchase-to-pay scenario which is often impacted by several regulations and best practice standards depending on the industry sector, region and organizational setup. A representative list of possible control objectives for the scenario is also provided. The FCL encoding is intended to demonstrate the natural fit of the proposed formalism for control objectives, and in turn provide the basis for business process model enrichment and analysis, which will be discussed in section 4.

3.1 Purchase-to-Pay (P2P) Scenario

Purchase-to-Pay is a well known process within procurement applications. A simplified version of the process is given in Figure 2. The assumption is that the design of this process was governed primarily by business (improvement) objectives. Figure 2 provides the supplier perspective as well (in the lower half) for completeness.

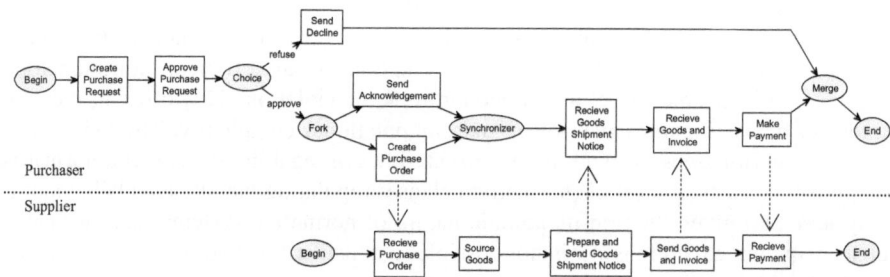

Fig. 3. Purchase-to-Pay Scenario

The generic P2P process may be subject to a number of control objectives emerging from compliance requirements (regional regulations, commercial standards, partner obligations etc.). In the table below we present a selected set of control objectives. Each of these objectives will have a corresponding risk statement, as well as a translation to an internal control indicating *effective* implementation [6] of the control objective.

Table 1. Control Objectives for Purchase-to-Pay Scenario

Control Objective	Risk	Internal Control
Prevent unauthorized use of purchase order process	Unauthorized creation of purchase orders and payments to non-existing suppliers	The creation and approval of purchase requests must be undertaken by two separate purchase officers
	Misappropriation of goods	Every Invoice must contain a valid Purchase Order Number
Ensure adequate supply of materials	Production delays due to lack of resources/ materials	Supplier can be charged a penalty if goods not received within k days of receipt of goods shipment notice
Timely and efficient P2P Process	Production delays due to lack of resources/ materials	Purchase requests not closed (declined or converted to Purchase Orders) within k days should raise an alert to purchasing manager

3.2 FCL Basics

In this section we outline the basic elements of FCL in order to illustrate how to use this formalism to represent and reason about "normative" specifications relative to a business process. For detailed presentation of the formalism we refer to [15], [12].

A rule in FCL is an expression of the form $r{:}A_1,..., A_n{\Rightarrow} B$, where r is the name of the rule (unique for each rule), $A_1,..., A_n$ are the premises, (propositions in the logic), and B is the conclusion of the rule (again B is a proposition of the logic).

The propositions of the logic are built from a finite set of atomic propositions, and the following operators: ¬(negation), O(obligation), P(permission), ⊗(violation/reparation). The formation rules are as follows:

- every atomic proposition is a proposition;
- if p is an atomic proposition, then ¬ p, is a proposition;
- if p is a proposition then Op is an obligation proposition and Pp is a permission proposition; obligation propositions and permission propositions are deontic propositions
- if $p_1,...,p_n$ are obligation propositions and q is a deontic proposition, then $p_1\otimes$ ... $\otimes p_n\otimes q$ is a reparation chain;

A simple proposition corresponds to a factual statement. The deontic operators are then indexed by the subject of the normative position corresponding to the operator. Thus $O_sSendInvoice$ means that the supplier s has the obligation to send the invoice to the purchaser, and $P_pChargePenalty$ means that the purchaser p is entitled (permitted) to charge a penalty to the supplier. A reparation chain, for example

$$O_sProvideGoodsTimely\otimes O_sOfferDiscout\otimes P_pChargePenalty$$

captures obligations and normative positions arising in response to violations of obligation. Thus the expression above means that the supplier has the obligation to send the goods in a timely manner, but in case she does not comply with this (i.e., she violates the obligation do so) then she has the "secondary" obligation to offer a discount for the merchandise, and in case that she fails to fulfill this obligation (i.e., we have a violation of the possible reparation of the "primary" obligation), then, finally, the purchaser can charge the supplier with the penalty.

As usual in normative reasoning we have two types of rules: definitional rules and normative rules. A definitional rule gives us the conditions that assert a factual statement, while a normative rule allows us to conclude a normative positions (i.e., an obligation, a permission or a prohibition, where a prohibition is O¬ or equivalently ¬ P). According to the above distinction in definitional rules the conclusion is a proposition, and in normative rules the conclusion is either a deontic proposition or a reparation chain. In both cases the premises are propositions and deontic propositions, but not reparation chains.

FCL offers two reasoning modules: (1) a normaliser to make explicit rules that can be derived from explicitly given rules by merging their normative conclusions, to remove redundancy and identify conflicts rules; and (2) an inference engine to derive conclusions given some propositions as input.

Finally to incorporate the temporal dimension we timestamp all propositions in the language, and we adopt the persistence mechanism devised in [16] to deal with temporalised normative positions. Essentially if we can assert the conclusion $p:t_0$, i.e., p holds at time t_0, then we can continue to assert p for all $t'>t_0$, until we have an event such that we can terminate the validity of p.

3.3 Encoding

Below we provide FCL encoding for the internal controls specified in Table 1.

The creation and approval of purchase requests must be undertaken by two separate purchase officers

$c1: CreatePR(x,y):t, PurchaseOfficer(y):t, PurchaseOfficer(z):t', y \neq z:t' \Rightarrow O_p ApprovedPR(x,z):t'$

The predicate $CreatedPR(x,y):t$ means that at time t, y has created a Purchase Request whose Id is x; the meaning of $ApprovedPR$ is similar. The predicate $PurchaseOfficer(x)$ states that at the time of the timestap t, x plays the role of purchase officer.

Every Invoice must contain a valid Purchase Order Number.

$$c2: Invoice(x,y):t, PurchaseOrderNumber(x,z):t \Rightarrow O_s Include(y,z):t$$

This internal control gives rise to two rules in FCL. The meaning of the predicates is as follows: $Invoice(x,y):t$ means at time t, the object with Id y is the invoice for some purchase order x"; $PurchaseOrderNumber(x,z):t$ means at time t, z is the purchase order number for order x"; $Include(y,z):t$ means the object z is included in the object z.

Supplier can be charged a penalty if goods not received within k days of receipt of goods shipment notice

$$c3: GoodShipmentNotice(x,y):t \Rightarrow O_s SendGood(x):t+k \otimes P_p ChargePenalty$$

Notice that this internal control presupposes the existence of a primary obligation to provide the goods within k days (*SendGood*). In case this provision in violated then the purchaser is entitled to charge the supplier with the established penalty.

Purchase requests not closed (declined or converted to Purchase Orders) within k days should raise an alert to purchasing manager

$$c4.1: CreatePR(x,y):t \Rightarrow O_p ClosePR(x):t+k \otimes O_p AlertPurchaseManager:t+k$$

Here $ClosePR(x):t+k$ gives the deadline to change the status of a purchase request from open ($\neg ClosePR(x)$) to closed. Beside the normative provision give by rule $c4.1$, this internal control gives conditions under which we can change the status of a request from open to close.

$$c4.2: ApprovePR(x,y):t' \Rightarrow ClosePR(x):t'$$
$$c4.3: Decline(x):t' \Rightarrow ClosePR(x):t'$$

Notice that the last two rules are definitional rules and not normative rules. However an additional rule is needed to set the status of a purchase request as open when it is created. Thus we introduce the rule

$$c4.4: CreatePR(x,y):t' \Rightarrow \neg ClosePR(x):t'$$

In this case we make use of the persistence condition discussed at the end of the previous section to maintain the state of the request as open until we can close as result of firing either $c4.2$ or $c4.3$. If this does not happened before $t+k$ we have a violation of the primary obligation of rule $c4.1$, and thus we fire the obligation to alert the purchase manager as response of this violation.

4 Process Model Enrichment

The example presented in Fig. 3 follows a simple language which can be mapped to several commercial/standard (e.g. BPMN) and formal (e.g. Petri-nets) languages. We use the notation only for its graphic simplicity. The following basic concepts provide basics for the language.

The **process model** $P = <N, F>$ is a directed graph where N is a finite set of nodes, F is a flow relation $F \subseteq N \times N$. Flows show the control flow of the process. Nodes are classified into tasks (T) and coordinators (C), where $N = C \cup T$ and $C \cap T = \phi$. For each node $n \in N$, following basic attributes are defined:

$nodeType[n] \in \{$ TASK, COORDINATOR $\}$ represents type of n.
$coordinatorType[n] \in \{$ begin, end, choice, merge, fork, synchronizer $\}$

A task $t \in T$ is not a mere node in the process graph, but has rich semantics which are defined through its properties, such as process relevant application data, temporal constraints, resources requirements etc.

Given these basic and well known concepts, the task ahead is to introduce the concepts relating to control objectives into the process while still maintaining a clear separation of concerns. To achieve this, we introduce a new concept of *control tags*.

4.1 Control Tags

We identify four types of control tags. Each tag will represent a control objective, and (one of) its corresponding internal control.

- **Flow Tag:** A flow tag represents a control objective that would impact on (the flow of) the business activities, e.g. approval of leave must occur before payment for travel.
- **Data Tag:** A data tag identifies the data retention and lineage requirements, e.g. a medical practice must retain the time of commencement of pathology tests.
- **Resource Tag:** A resource tag represents controls relating to access, role management and authorization, e.g. persons performing cash application and bank reconciliation must be different as it allows differences between cash deposited and cash collections posted to be covered up.
- **Time Tag:** A time tag identifies controls for meeting time constraints such as deadlines and maximum durations, e.g. a water leakage complaint must be investigated within 12 hours of lodging.

Control tags are constructed through parsing[2] of FCL expressions, representing normative rules. Each control tag is thereby represented by the schema shown in Table 2. The propositions related to checking of conditions are listed under *state* and represent new checks that may need to be incorporated into the process. The *operation* relates to the deontic operations in the expressions and identify new actions that may have to be undertaken within the process. As the final step in the control modeling phase, the operations in the control tags are type linked, resulting in the values listed under the *type* column in Table 2.

Table 2. Control Tags for Purchase-to-Pay Scenario

Rule	State	Task		Operation	Type	Task
c1	CreatePR(x,y):t, PurchaseOfficer(y):t, PurchaseOfficer(z):t', y≠z:t'	Create Purchase Request		O_pApprove PR(x,z):t'	Resource	Approve Purchase Request
c2	Invoice(x,y):t, PurchaseOrderNumber(x,z):t	Send Goods and Invoice		O_sInclude(y, z):t	Data	Send Goods and Invoice
c3	GoodShipmentNotice(x,y):t	Send Goods Shipment Notice		O_sSendGood(x):t+k	Time	Send Goods and Invoice
				P_pChargePenalty	Flow	Make Payment
c4.1	CreatePR(x,y):t	Create Purchase Request		O_pClosePR (x):t+k	Time	Create Purchase Request
				O_pAlertPurchaseManager:t+k	Flow	Create Purchase Request

Lastly, an alignment of the terms used within the two specifications, namely process model (P) and control model (FCL expressions) is required. As discussed previously, it is unrealistic that the two specifications will always be constructed in synch, simply because of their disparate lifecycles, stakeholder groups and purpose within the organization. However, the overall approach presented in this paper (section 2), proposes a systematic way to converge the two. Table 2 provides an illustration of such an alignment in the context of the Purchase-to-Pay scenario. For each control tag, the effected process *tasks* are identified.

It is trivial to observe that the above alignment may be implicitly undertaken at the time of FCL encoding through appropriate tools (as discussed in section 2.2) that allow writing of FCL propositions to use naming consistent to process model task (and task property) names.

4.2 Process Annotation

Given Table 2, the annotation of the process model with control tags, can be done programmatically leading to automatic visualization of the control tags on business process models. Fig 4 shows a subset of the control tags given in Table 2. The

---

[2] FCL encodings can be mapped to RuleML, and consequently provide an automated means of processing. For details on RuleML mapping see [13].

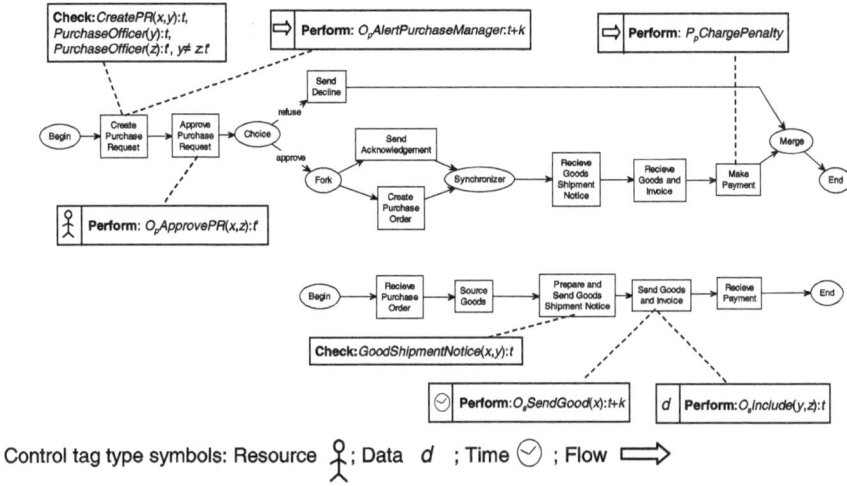

Fig. 4. Visualization of Control Tags

annotation distinguishes two aspects of control tags: All propositions related to *state* are annotated as "check" and all deontic operations are annotated as "perform". Furthermore, the *type* of the control tag is visualized through a representative symbol.

Checks as well as perform actions of type resource, data and time represent possible modification of the effected tasks (i.e. their underlying properties). However perform actions of type flow represent possible changes to the task set and/or order of execution.

Process annotation allows the process designers to import and visualize control objectives within the process modeling space. In addition to the support provided to process designers through the above, we also propose the use of analysis tools. These can provide e.g. support for identifying conflicts and redundancies between the two specifications. Similarly, they can provide an evaluation of the measure of compliance. To this effect, we introduce the notion of *compliance distance*. Compliance distance is basically a quantitative measure of *how much* a process model may have to be changed in response to a given set of control objectives. This design time analysis can be undertaken based on FCL encoding and its alignment with process tasks as given in Table 2. We base our notion of compliance distance on the two aspects of control tags: Namely the checks (*state* related propositions) and perform actions (deontic *operations*) as derived from the FCL expressions. An FCL rule is of the form $r:c_1,..., c_n \Rightarrow p_1 \otimes ... \otimes p_m$, where C represents the set of checks and P represents the set of perform actions. Given r rules against a given set of control objectives, a simplistic compliance distance can be computed as a sum of the number of elements in C and P. For example, for the Purchase-to-Pay scenario, the compliance distance is computed as 13 (7 checks and 6 performs).

The notion of compliance distance can be also used at run time to measure how much a particular instance deviates from the expected behavior. For example this can be done by simply counting the number of recoverable violations (i.e., unfulfilled obligations not in the last position of a reparation chain) that occurred in the process instance. However, this method considers all potential violation at the same level, thus a more realistic way would be to associate to each potential violation a cost, and then the compliance distance of a process instance from the expected ideal behavior is the sum of the cost of all actual violations in the process.

In summary, the purpose of the annotation and analysis is to provide design time support to process owners to create compliant business processes. The proposed methods provide a structured and systematic approach to undertaking changes in the process model in response to compliance requirements. Fig. 5 summarizes the overall methodology.

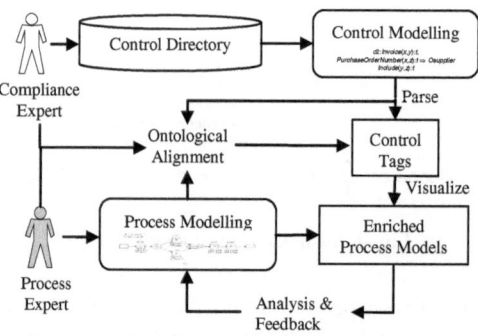

Fig. 5. Summary of Overall Methodology

5 Related Work

Both process modeling as well as modeling of normative requirements are well studied fields independently, but until recently the interactions between the two have been largely ignored [7], [21]. Some notable exceptions are the relationships between the execution (performance) of business contract based on their formal representation [9]. Research on closely related issues has also been carried out in the field of autonomous agents [8], [2].

A plethora of proposals exist both in the research community on formal modelling of rules, as well as in the commercial arena through business rule management systems (see e.g. ilog.com). It is obvious that the modelling of control objectives will be undertaken as rules, although the question of appropriate formalism is still under studied. We have proposed FCL as a candidate which has proved effective due to its ability to reason with violations, but we acknowledge that further empirical study is necessary to effectively evaluate the appropriateness of FCL.

Another closely related area is process monitoring. This is a widely studied area, which has several commercial solutions (business activity monitoring, business intelligence etc). Noteworthy in research literature is the synergy with process mining techniques [1] which provide the capability to discover runtime process behavior (and deviations) and can thereby assist in detection of compliance violations.

There have been recently some efforts towards support for business process modelling against compliance requirements. In particular the work of [22] provides an appealing method for integrating risks in business processes. The proposed technique for "risk-aware" business process models is developed for EPCs (Event Process

Chains) using an extended notation. Similarly [11] present a logical language PENELOPE, that provides the ability to verify temporal constraints arising from compliance requirements on effected business processes. Distinct from the above works, the contribution of this paper has been on firstly providing an overall methodology for a model driven approach to business process compliance, and secondly on a structured technique for process model enrichment based on formal modelling of control objectives.

Lastly, significant research exists on the modelling of control flow in business processes, particularly in the use of patterns to identify commonly used constructs [www.workflowpatterns.com]. On a similar note, [10] provide temporal rule patterns for regulatory policies, although the objective of this work is to facilitate event monitoring rather than the usage of the patterns for support of design time activities.

6 Conclusions and Outlook

Process and control modeling represent two distinct but mutually dependent specifications in current enterprise systems. In this paper, we take the view that the two specifications, will be created somewhat independently, at different times, and by different stakeholders, using their respective conceptually faithful representation schemes. However the convergence of the two must be supported in order to achieve business practices that our compliant with control objectives stemming from various regulatory, standard and contractual concerns. This convergence should be supported with a systematic and well structured approach.

We have proposed such an approach. The approach allows a formal representation of control objectives in FCL, a language suitable to capture the declarative nature of compliance requirements. In turn we have introduced the concept of control tags that can be derived from FCL, and used to visually annotate and analyze typical graph based process models. We argue that such process enrichment and associated analysis capability will be instrumental in the (re) design of compliant business processes.

Next steps in our work entail the development of demonstrable methods to parse FCL to derive control tags and provide improved process annotation and analysis. The notion of compliance distance for process analysis also poses interesting research questions. We also plan to pursue the evaluation of the suability of FCL from various angles which includes an empirical study to assess the usability FCL, further theoretical analysis of its expressiveness and processing scalability, and investigation of FCL rules as an instrument for identification of runtime control violations.

References

1. van der Aalst, W.M.P., van Dongen, B.F., Herbst, J., Maruster, L., Schimm, G., Weijters, A.J.M.M.: Workflow Mining: A Survey of Issues and Approaches. Data & Knowledge Engineering 47, 237–267 (2003)
2. Alberti, M., Chesani, F., Gavanelli, M., Lamma, E., Mello, P., Torroni, P.: Compliance verification of agent interaction: A logic based tool. Applied Artificial Intelligence 20(2-4), 133–157 (2006)
3. Antoniou, G., Billington, D., Governatori, G., Maher, M.J.: Representation results for defeasible logic. ACM Transactions on Computational Logic 2(2), 255–287 (2001)

4. BPM Forum CEE: The Future. Building the Compliance Enabled Enterprise. Report produced by GlobalFluency in partnership with: AXS-One, Chief Executive Magazine and IT Compliance Institute (2006)
5. Carmo, J., Jones, A.J.I.: Deontic Logic and Contrary-to-Duties. In: Handbook of Philosophical Logic, 2nd edn., vol. 8, pp. 265–344. Kluwer, Dordrecht (2002)
6. COSO - The Committee of Sponsoring Organizations of the Treadway Commission Internal Control – Integrated Framework (May 1994)
7. Desai, N., Mallya, A.U., Chopra, A.K., Singh, M.P.: Interaction Protocols as Design Abstractions for Business Processes. IEEE Transaction on Software Engineering 31(12), 1015–1027 (2005)
8. Dignum, V., Vázquez-Salceda, J., Dignum, F.: OMNI: Introducing Social Structure, Norms and Ontologies into Agent Organizations. In: Bordini, R.H., Dastani, M., Dix, J., Seghrouchni, A.E.F. (eds.) Programming Multi-Agent Systems. LNCS (LNAI), vol. 3346, pp. 181–198. Springer, Heidelberg (2005)
9. Farrell, D.H., Sergot, M.J., Sallé, M., Bartolini, C.: Using the event calculus for tracking the normative state in contracts. International Journal of Cooperative Information Systems 14(2-3), 99–129 (2005)
10. Giblin, C., Muller, S., Pfitzmann, B.: From regulatory policies to event monitoring rules: Towards model driven compliance automation. IBM Research Report. Zurich Research Laboratory (October 2006)
11. Goedertier, S., Vanthienen, J.: Designing Compliant Business Processes with Obligations and Permissions. In: Eder, J., Dustdar, S. (eds.) Business Process Management Workshops. LNCS, vol. 4103, pp. 5–14. Springer, Heidelberg (2006)
12. Governatori, G., Milosevic, Z., Sadiq, S.: Compliance checking between business processes and business contracts. In: Proceedings of the 10th IEEE Conference on Enterprise Distributed Object Computing, Hong Kong, October 16-20, 2006, pp. 16–20. IEEE Computer Society Press, Los Alamitos (2006)
13. Governatori, G.: Representing Business Contracts in RuleML. International Journal of Cooperative Information Systems 14(2-3), 181–216 (2005)
14. Governatori, G., Rotolo, A.: Logic of Violations: A Gentzen System for Reasoning on Contrary-To-Duty Obligations. Australasian Journal of Logic 4, 193–215 (2006)
15. Governatori, G., Milosevic, Z.: A Formal Analysis of a Business Contract Language. International Journal of Cooperative Information Systems 15(4), 659–685 (2006)
16. Governatori, G., Rotolo, A., Sartor, G.: Temporalised normative positions in defeasible logic. In: Gardner, A. (ed.) Procedings of the 10th International Conference on Artificial Intelligence and Law, pp. 25–34. ACM Press, New York (2005)
17. Hagerty, J.: SOX Spending for 2006. AMR Research, Boston USA. (November 29, 2007)
18. Pesic, M., van der Aalst, W.M.P.: A Declarative Approach for Flexible Business Processes. In: Eder, J., Dustdar, S. (eds.) Business Process Management Workshops. LNCS, vol. 4103, pp. 169–180. Springer, Heidelberg (2006)
19. Sartor, G.: Legal Reasoning: A Cognitive Approach to the Law. Springer, Heidelberg (2005)
20. Sadiq, S., Sadiq, W., Orlowska, M.: A Framework for Constraint Specification and Validation in Flexible Workflows. Information Systems 30(5), 349–378 (2005)
21. Padmanabhan, V., Governatori, G., Sadiq, S., Colomb, R., Rotolo, A.: Process Modeling: The Deontic Way. In: Stumptner, M., Hartmann, S., Kiyoki, Y. (eds.) Australia-Pacific Conference on Conceptual Modeling 2006, CRPIT, vol. 53, pp. 75–84 (2006)
22. zur Muehlen, M., Rosemann, M.: Integrating Risks in Business Process Models. In: 16th Australasian Conference on Information Systems. November 29 – December 2, Sydney, Australia (2005)

Generation of Business Process Models for Object Life Cycle Compliance

Jochen M. Küster[1], Ksenia Ryndina[1,2], and Harald Gall[2]

[1] IBM Zurich Research Laboratory, Säumerstr. 4
8803 Rüschlikon, Switzerland
{jku,ryn}@zurich.ibm.com
[2] Department of Informatics, University of Zurich, Binzmühlestr. 14
8050 Zurich, Switzerland
gall@ifi.unizh.ch

Abstract. Business process models usually capture data exchanged between tasks in terms of objects. These objects are commonly standardized using reference data models that prescribe, among other things, allowed object states. Allowed state transitions can be modeled as object life cycles that require compliance of business processes. In this paper, we first establish a notion of compliance of a business process model with an object life cycle. We then propose a technique for generating a compliant business process model from a set of given reference object life cycles.

1 Introduction

Business process models are nowadays a well-established means for representing business processes in terms of tasks that need to be performed to achieve a certain business goal. These models usually also capture the flow of objects in a process to represent data exchange between tasks.

Objects used in business process models are commonly standardized using reference models in data-intensive industries such as insurance, banking and healthcare. In general, reference models are valuable because they facilitate interoperability between industry partners and ensure fulfilment of legal regulations embodied in these models. Reference data models (e.g. from ACORD [1]) contain an industry vocabulary, where objects used in this industry are defined. Objects that undergo processing are usually associated with a set of states for representing their processing status at a given point in time.

In order to ensure that a business process manipulates object states as defined in a reference model, tasks in a business process model can be annotated with input and output states of an object. In addition, restrictions on object state transitions are usually required, when not all possible transitions are meaningful. Object life cycles [6,10,15,16,20] are a common means for explicitly modeling allowed state transitions of an object during its existence. In particular, reference object life cycles can be used to represent an established way of manipulating objects in a particular industry, e.g. IBM Insurance Application Architecture (IAA) [2].

G. Alonso, P. Dadam, and M. Rosemann (Eds.): BPM 2007, LNCS 4714, pp. 165–181, 2007.

Compliance with object life cycles ensures consistency within business processes of one organization and correct execution of business processes that span several organizations. As reference object life cycles often embody elements of policy, for example legal regulations for object processing, compliance demonstrates that policy requirements are satisfied.

One approach to achieving compliance of a business process with object life cycles is to check for possible compliance violations and then iteratively resolve them, which we proposed in [14]. However, this approach can lead to a lengthy resolution process. An alternative approach, proposed in this paper, is to use the reference object life cycles to generate an initial business process model that is compliant with these life cycles by construction. This initial process model can then be customized to the specific needs of an organization.

In this paper, we first introduce object life cycles and business process models in Sect.2. In Sect.3, we discuss the problem of compliance of business process models with object life cycles and establish a compliance notion. We then propose a technique for automatic generation of a compliant business process model from given object life cycles in Sect.4. In Sect.5, we discuss tool support and our initial validation of the approach using reference models in IAA. Finally, we describe related work in Sect.6 and conclude the paper in Sect.7.

2   Object Life Cycles and Business Process Models

An *object life cycle* [6,10,15,16,20] is a model that captures allowed states and state transitions for a particular *object type*. A non-deterministic finite state machine is a common means of modeling an object life cycle [6,16]:

Definition 1 (Object life cycle). *Given an object type o, its* object life cycle *$OLC_o = (S, s_\alpha, S_\Omega, \Sigma, \delta)$ consists of a finite set of* states *S, where $s_\alpha \in S$ is the* initial state *and $S_\Omega \subseteq S$ is the set of* final states; *a finite set of* events *Σ; a* transition function *$\delta : S \times \Sigma \to \mathcal{P}(S)$. Given $s_j \in \delta(s_i, e)$, we write $s_i \xrightarrow{e} s_j$.*

Figure 1 shows object life cycles for Claim and Payment object types.

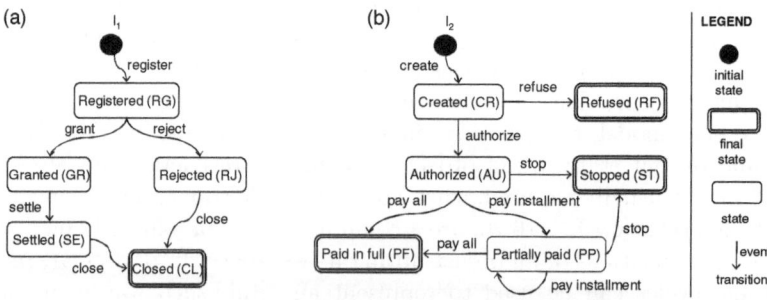

Fig. 1. Object life cycles: (a) Claim (b) Payment

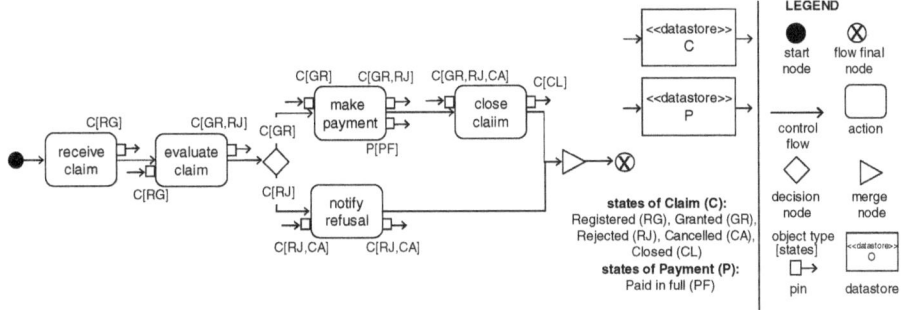

Fig. 2. Example business process model for Claim handling

According to the Claim life cycle, a claim is always created in state Registered, after which it can be either granted or rejected. Granted claims are settled and then closed, while Rejected claims are closed directly. The Payment life cycle shows that after a payment is created and authorized, it can either be paid in several installments or settled in full. When modeling an object life cycle, the initial state represents the state of the object before it is created and the final states indicate acceptable end points of the life cycle.

A business process model captures the coordination of individual tasks in a particular process and can additionally show the exchange of objects between these tasks. Figure 2 shows a process model for a simplified Claim handling process in the UML2 Activity Diagram (UML AD) notation [4]. In the beginning of this process, a claim is received and then an evaluation decision is made. If the claim is granted, a payment is made to the claimant and then the claim is closed. If the claim is rejected, the claimant is notified about the refusal.

As illustrated in the example, process tasks are modeled using *actions* and coordination of steps is done via *control flow* edges and *control nodes*, such as *decision* and *merge nodes*. Data inputs and outputs of actions are modeled with *input* and *output pins*. For example, the make payment action requires Claim (C for short) as input and produces Claim and Payment (P for short) as outputs.

For data exchange, we use *datastores* as intermediate object repositories, an approach supported by UML AD and also proposed by Reichert and Dadam [13]. A datastore for each object type is included in a process model and all output pins write objects to a datastore of their type, while input pins read objects from a datastore of their type. We omit explicit connections between pins and datastores here, as the object types already indicate their relationships.

Figure 2 also shows that object states can be associated with pins[1]. States of an input pin represent preconditions of an action with respect to the incoming object and similarly, states of an output pin are the postconditions. In the example, close claim accepts a Claim object in either state GR, RJ or CA and outputs this object in state CL. Note that we set branch conditions of the decision node to route control flow according to the state of the Claim object.

---

[1] In UML AD this is done using the *inState* attribute of a pin.

We use the following definition for a process model, which comprises model elements relevant for this paper:

Definition 2 (Process model). *A process model $P = (N, E, O, S, \beta, \mathcal{I}, \mathcal{O}, \mathcal{D})$ consists of*

- *a finite set N of nodes partitioned into sets:*
  - N_A *of actions,*
  - N_C *of control nodes partitioned into sets: N_D and N_M of decision and merge nodes, N_F and N_J of fork and join nodes, and N_S and N_{FF} of start and flow final nodes;*
  - N_O *of object nodes partitioned into sets: N_{IP} and N_{OP} of input and output pins, and N_{DS} of datastores;*
- *a relation $E : (N_A \cup N_C) \times (N_A \cup N_C)$ representing control flow;*
- *a finite set O of object types;*
- *a finite set S of object states, partitioned into sets of states for each object type, i.e. $S = S_{o_1} \cup \ldots \cup S_{o_n}$ if $O = \{o_1, \ldots, o_n\}$;*
- *a branch condition function $\beta : N_D \times N \times O \rightarrow \mathcal{P}(S)$;*
- *a family of functions $\mathcal{I} = \{instate_o : N_A \rightarrow \mathcal{P}(S_o)\}_{o \in O}$, where $instate_o(a)$ is the input state set of a for o;*
- *a family of functions $\mathcal{O} = \{outstate_o : N_A \rightarrow \mathcal{P}(S_o)\}_{o \in O}$, where $outstate_o(a)$ is the output state set of a for o;*
- *a family of functions $\mathcal{D} = \{dep_o : N_A \times S_o \rightarrow \mathcal{P}(S_o)\}_{o \in O}$, where $dep_o(a, s)$ is the dependency state set of a state $s \in outstate_o(a)$.*

All elements defined above have a visual representation used in Fig.2, except for *dependency state sets* introduced for expressing dependencies between input and output object states of an action. We can use the *dep*-function to capture that notify refusal does not change the state of Claim: dep_C(notify refusal, RJ) = {RJ} and dep_C(notify refusal, CA) = {CA}. If an output state of an action does not have a dependency on specific input states, i.e. any input state can give rise to this output state, the dependency state set can be left empty. For example, dep_C(close claim, CL) = $\emptyset$ means that close claim always outputs Claim in state CL, irrespective of Claim's input state.

3   Object Life Cycle Compliance

Object life cycles provide a means for modeling allowed transitions, initial and final states of an object. Compliance of states used in a business process with a reference data model, such as ACORD Life & Annuity Data Model [1], is straightforward to show by comparing the set of states used in the process with the set of states prescribed by the reference model. However, compliance of a business process with an object life cycle requires a more elaborate approach.

We introduce the notion of *object life cycle conformance* that requires a business process to induce only those object state transitions that are defined in a given reference object life cycle, to create objects in valid states with respect to the life cycle and to leave objects in valid states upon termination. Furthermore, policy requirements commonly imply that some or all predefined object states must be covered, i.e. some or all objects reach these states during process execution. We introduce the notion of *object life cycle coverage* to express requirements with respect to what transitions and states in a reference object life cycle must be covered by a business process. In the following, we provide definitions for the concepts of an object provider, an induced transition, first and last states, which are then used to formally define conformance and coverage.

Given a process model $P = (N, E, O, S, \beta, \mathcal{I}, \mathcal{O}, \mathcal{D})$, we define a *path* as a finite sequence $n_1, ..., n_k$ where $n_i \in N$ and $(n_i, n_{i+1}) \in E$ for $1 \leq i < k$. To determine state transitions that can be induced in a process model, we need to know the order in which actions update objects in datastores:

Definition 3 (Object provider). *Let a process model $P = (N, E, O, S, \beta, \mathcal{I}, \mathcal{O}, \mathcal{D})$, an object type $o \in O$, a state $s \in S_o$ and actions $a_1, a_2 \in N_A$ be given, such that $s \in outstate_o(a_1) \cap instate_o(a_2)$. Action a_1 is an object provider for a_2 with respect to o and s, written $a_1 \lhd_o^s a_2$, if there is a path $p = a_1, ..., a_2$ such that:*

- *there is no other action $a' \in N_A$ with an output pin of type o on path p, and*
- *for all decision nodes $d \in N_D$ on path p and for all nodes $n \in N$ on path p, $(d, n) \in E$ implies that $s \in \beta(d, n, o)$.*

Given an action a_2, $s \in instate_o(a_2)$ means that a_2 reads objects from a datastore of type o and accepts these objects in state s. Object providers for a_2 with respect to o and s are actions that can write o in state s to the datastore before a_2 reads it. In Fig.2, evaluate claim is an object provider for make payment and notify refusal with respect to Claim and states GR and RJ, respectively.

Definition 4 (Induced transition and effective output states). *Let a process model $P = (N, E, O, S, \beta, \mathcal{I}, \mathcal{O}, \mathcal{D})$ and an object type $o \in O$ be given. An induced transition of o in P is a triple (a, s_{src}, s_{tgt}), such that:*

- $a \in N_A$, $s_{src} \in instate_o(a)$ *and* $s_{tgt} \in outstate_o(a)$, *and*
- $dep_o(a, s_{tgt}) = \emptyset$ *or* $s_{src} \in dep_o(a, s_{tgt})$, *and*
- *there exists an action $a' \in N_A$, such that $a' \lhd_o^{s_{src}} a$ and $s_{src} \in outstate_o^{eff}(a')$, where $outstate_o^{eff} : N_A \to \mathcal{P}(S_o)$ defines effective output states of an action:*

$$outstate_o^{eff}(a') = \{s \in S_o \mid s \in outstate_o(a') \text{ and } (a' \text{ has no input pins of type } o \text{ or } (a', s', s) \text{ is an induced transition of } o \text{ in } P \text{ for some } s' \in S_o)\}.$$

Induced transitions of o in P identify all state transitions that can occur for objects of type o during execution of P. Given an induced transition (a, s_{src}, s_{tgt}) of o in P, s_{src} and s_{tgt} are elements of a's input and output state sets for o, respectively. Furthermore, s_{tgt} either has no dependencies on input states or s_{src} is an element of its dependency state set. Finally, P's execution must allow for o to be in state s_{src} at the time a is enabled, i.e. s_{src} must be an effective output state of some object provider a' for a with respect to o. Induced transitions can be computed for a given process model using data flow analysis techniques [11]. In Fig.2, (close claim, GR, CL) is an induced transition for Claim, but (close claim, CA, CL) is not, because CA is not an effective output state of make payment.

Definition 5 (First and last states). *Let a process model* $P = (N, E, O, S, \beta,$ $\mathcal{I}, \mathcal{O}, \mathcal{D})$ *and an object type* $o \in O$ *be given.*

- *A* first state *of* o *in* P *is a state* $s_{first} \in S_o$, *such that* $s_{first} \in outstate_o(a)$ *for some action* $a \in N_A$ *that has no input pins of type* o;
- *A* last state *of* o *in* P *is a state* $s_{last} \in S_o$, *such that there is an action* $a \in N_A$ *where* $s_{last} \in outstate_o^{\text{eff}}(a)$ *and there is a path* $p = a, ..., f$ *from* a *to a flow final node* $f \in N_{FF}$, *such that:*
  - *there is no other action* $a' \in N_A$ *with an output pin of type* o *on path* p,
  - *and for all decision nodes* $d \in N_D$ *on path* p *and for all nodes* $n \in N$ *on path* p, $(d, n) \in E$ *implies that* $s_{last} \in \beta(d, n, o)$.

In Fig.2, RG is the first state and CL and RJ are the last states of Claim in the claim handling process model. We are now equipped to provide formal definitions for object life cycle conformance and coverage.

Definition 6 (Object life cycle conformance). *Given a process model* $P =$ $(N, E, O, S, \beta, \mathcal{I}, \mathcal{O}, \mathcal{D})$ *and an object life cycle* $OLC_o = (S, s_\alpha, S_\Omega, \Sigma, \delta)$ *for object type* o, *we say that* P *satisfies* object life cycle conformance *with respect to* OLC_o *if the following conditions hold:*

- *for each induced transition* $t = (a, s_{src}, s_{tgt})$ *of* o *in* P, $s_{tgt} \in \delta(s_{src}, e)$ *for some* $e \in \Sigma$ (transition conformance),
- *for each first state* s_{first} *of* o *in* P, $s_{first} \in \delta(s_\alpha, e)$ *for some* $e \in \Sigma$ (first state conformance),
- *for each last state* s_{last} *of* o *in* P, $s_{last} \in S_\Omega$ (last state conformance).

The claim handling process model in Fig.2 satisfies first state conformance with respect to the reference object life cycle defined for Claim in Fig.1 (a), but does not satisfy transition and last state conformance. Transition conformance does not hold, because (make payment, GR, RJ) is an induced transition for Claim and (GR, RJ) is not defined in the object life cycle. Transition conformance violation can lead to various problems. For example, a customer who is informed that his claim has been granted has no doubt that it will be settled given the information in the reference life cycle. If the claim is rejected at a later stage, the customer can declare breach of contract. Last state conformance is not satisfied, because RJ is a last state of Claim in the process, but it is not a final state in the life cycle. Violation of last state conformance can lead to incorrect archiving of claims, given an application that only archives claims in state CL and considers all other claims to still be active.

Definition 7 (Object life cycle coverage). *Given a process model* $P =$ $(N, E, O, S, \beta, \mathcal{I}, \mathcal{O}, \mathcal{D})$ *and an object life cycle* $OLC_o = (S, s_\alpha, S_\Omega, \Sigma, \delta)$ *for object type* o, *we say that* P *satisfies* object life cycle coverage *with respect to* OLC_o *if the following conditions hold:*

- *for each* $s_{src} \in S \setminus \{s_\alpha\}$, $e \in \Sigma$ *and* $s_{tgt} \in \delta(s_{src}, e)$, *there is an induced transition* (a, s_{src}, s_{tgt}) *of* o *in* P *for some* $a \in N_A$ (transition coverage),

  – *for each $s \in \delta(s_\alpha, e)$ for some $e \in \Sigma$, s is a first state of o in P* (first state coverage),
  – *each final state $s_\Omega \in S_\Omega$ is a last state of o in P* (last state coverage).

The claim handling process model in Fig.2 satisfies first and last state coverage with respect to the Claim reference life cycle in Fig.1 (a), but does not satisfy transition coverage. Transitions GR $\xrightarrow{settle}$ SE and SE $\xrightarrow{close}$ CL are not covered in the process, even though a settlement action called make payment is captured in the process model. If other processes are enabled when the claim is in state SE or triggered when the claim changes its state to SE, correct overall execution of these processes would require that transitions GR $\xrightarrow{settle}$ SE and SE $\xrightarrow{close}$ CL are covered in the claim handling process.

   Our definition of coverage requires that some, but not necessarily all, objects in a process model go through a particular transition, first state or last state. For transition coverage, we do not specify that each transition in the object life cycle must be covered by exactly one induced transition in the process model. Variants of this coverage definition can be devised to suit different requirements.

4   Generation of a Business Process Model

In this section, we present our technique for generating a process model from one or more reference object life cycles. Given several object life cycles, points where they need to be synchronized must first be identified manually. The rest of the technique is fully automatic: composition of the object life cycles is computed and used to generate a process model.

4.1   Synchronization and Composition of Object Life Cycles

When compliance with more than one object life cycle is required, we first compute a composition of the given life cycles, which incorporates joint prescribed behavior of these objects. As processing of some objects requires synchronization, we need to identify transitions in the given object life cycles that should be triggered at the same time and result in both objects transiting to new states. Identifying synchronization ensures that invalid composite states cannot be reached in the composite object life cycle:

Definition 8 (Synchronization event). *Given two object life cycles $OLC_{o_1} = (S_1, s_{\alpha_1}, S_{\Omega_1}, \Sigma_1, \delta_1)$ and $OLC_{o_2} = (S_2, s_{\alpha_2}, S_{\Omega_2}, \Sigma_2, \delta_2)$, an event $e \in \Sigma_1 \cap \Sigma_2$ is called a* synchronization event.

Suppose that we wish to generate a new claim handling process model on the basis of the reference object life cycles for Claim and Payment in Fig.1. Since the payment should only be created if the claim is granted, we create a synchronization event called grant^C | create^P and use it to replace the grant and create events in the Claim and Payment object life cycles, respectively. Furthermore, a claim can be settled only once the full payment has been made and thus we introduce another synchronization event called settle^C | pay all^P to replace the settle and pay all events in the Claim and Payment life cycles.

Once synchronization events are introduced, composition of object life cycles is computed. We use the following definition for the composition of two object life cycles, which can be reapplied to compose any number of life cycles:

Definition 9 (Object life cycle composition). *Given two object life cycles* $OLC_{o_1} = (S_1, s_{\alpha_1}, S_{\Omega_1}, \Sigma_1, \delta_1)$ *and* $OLC_{o_2} = (S_2, s_{\alpha_2}, S_{\Omega_2}, \Sigma_2, \delta_2)$, *their object life cycle composition is* $OLC = (S_1 \times S_2, (s_{\alpha_1}, s_{\alpha_2}), S_{\Omega_1} \times S_{\Omega_2}, \Sigma_1 \cup \Sigma_2, \delta)$ *where:*

$$\delta((s_1, s_2), e) = \begin{cases} \delta_1(s_1, e) \times \delta_2(s_2, e) & \textit{if } e \in \Sigma_1 \cap \Sigma_2 \\ \delta_1(s_1, e) \times \{s_2\} & \textit{if } e \in \Sigma_1 \setminus \Sigma_2 \\ \{s_1\} \times \delta_2(s_2, e) & \textit{if } e \in \Sigma_2 \setminus \Sigma_1 \end{cases} \tag{1}$$

Figure 3 shows the composition of the Claim and Payment object life cycles after they were augmented with synchronization events. In the diagram, states and events are marked with superscripts C and P to reflect that they belong to Claim and Payment, respectively.

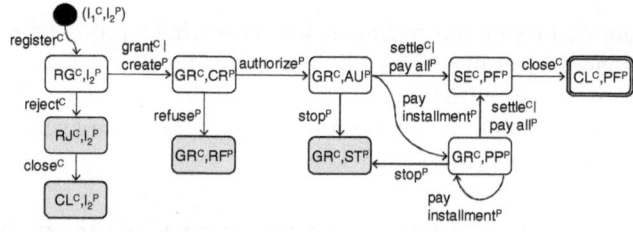

Fig. 3. Composition of the Claim and Payment object life cycles

Figure 3 shows only those states that are reachable from the composite initial state l_1^C, l_2^P. Two composite final states CL^C,RF^P and CL^C,ST^P are not reachable in the object life cycle composition and the states highlighted in gray do not lead to a composite final state. These are essentially deadlock states and it is arguable whether they should be used for the process model generation. For example, the transition trace register^C, reject^C, close^C seems valid and should be reflected in the generated process model, even though the final state of the Payment object is not reached. The trace register^C, grant^C | create^P, refuse^P also seems valid, although it may not be desirable that the Claim is still in state GR (Granted) even though the Payment has been refused. Such phenomena are typical if the composed object life cycles were created independently from each other, which may often be the case in practice. We use all the states reachable from the composite initial state for the generation of the process model. In a practical application however, it will be valuable to inform the user of the traces that do not lead to a final state and let him choose whether they should be included or not.

4.2 Process Model Generation

For generating a business process model from one object life cycle or a composition of several object life cycles, we propose a technique that comprises four steps: In step 1, the object life cycle (composition) is used to generate a set of actions for the process model. In step 2, the order in which these actions should appear in the process model is determined. In step 3, actions are combined into process fragments, where they are additionally connected to decision and merge nodes. Finally, the process fragments are connected to produce the resultant process model in step 4. The four steps are described in detail next.

In **step 1**, given an object life cycle $OLC = (S, s_\alpha, S_\Omega, \Sigma, \delta)$ that is a composition of object life cycles for object types $o_1, ...o_n$, we iterate over all its transitions $(s_i^{o_1}, ..., s_i^{o_n}) \xrightarrow{e} (s_j^{o_1}, ..., s_j^{o_n})$ and create a set of actions N_A. Each created action a_e matches one of the following *pin patterns (pp)* with respect to each object type o_k where $1 \le k \le n$: a_e has input and output pins of type o_k (*transition*), a_e has only an output pin of type o_k (*creation*) or a_e has no pins of type o_k (*no-transition*). Different transitions in OLC give rise to actions with different pin patterns, as described by the following generation algorithm:

for each transition $(s_i^{o_1}, ..., s_i^{o_n}) \xrightarrow{e} (s_j^{o_1}, ..., s_j^{o_n})$ in OLC
  for each o_k where $1 \le k \le n$
    if $(s_i^{o_k} \ne s_\alpha^{o_k}$ and $s_i^{o_k} \ne s_j^{o_k})$ then $pp_{o_k} = $ transition
    else if $(s_i^{o_k} = s_\alpha^{o_k}$ and $s_i^{o_k} \ne s_j^{o_k})$ then $pp_{o_k} = $ creation
    else if $(s_i^{o_k} = s_j^{o_k})$ then $pp_{o_k} = $ no-transition
  if (there exists action a_e in N_A that matches pin pattern $\{pp_{o_1}, ..., pp_{o_n}\}$)
    for each o_k where $1 \le k \le n$
      if $(pp_{o_k} == $ transition or $pp_{o_k} == $ creation$)$
        add $s_j^{o_k}$ to $outstate_{o_k}(a_e)$
      if $(pp_{o_k} == $ transition$)$
        add $s_i^{o_k}$ to $instate_{o_k}(a_e)$ and $s_i^{o_k}$ to $dep_{o_k}(a_e, s_j^{o_k})$
  else
    add new action a_e to N_A
    for each o_k where $1 \le k \le n$
      if $(pp_{o_k} == $ transition or $pp_{o_k} == $ creation$)$
        add an output pin of type o to a_e and add $s_j^{o_k}$ to $outstate_{o_k}(a_e)$
      if $(pp_{o_k} == $ transition$)$
        add an input pin of type o to a_e, add $s_i^{o_k}$ to $instate_{o_k}(a_e)$ and $s_i^{o_k}$ to $dep_{o_k}(a_e, s_j^{o_k})$

Figure 4 illustrates how an example transition in a composition of two object life cycles for object types o_1 and o_2 is processed by the generation algorithm.

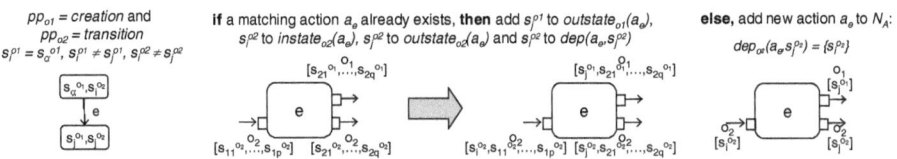

Fig. 4. Example action generation

Using the composition of Claim and Payment object life cycles (Fig.3), transition $grant^C \mid create^P$ from RG^C, I_2^P to GR^C, CR^P would generate an action $grant^C \mid create^P$ with input and output pins of type Claim and another output pin of type Payment.

Once the set of actions N_A is generated, we compute a relation on this set by examining the input and output state sets of the actions, in **step 2**:

Definition 10 (Object state relation). *Given an action $a_1 \in N_A$ with output pins of types $o_{11}, ..., o_{1k}$ and an action $a_2 \in N_A$ with input pins of types $o_{21}, ..., o_{2m}$, a_1 is a predecessor of a_2 in the* object state relation, *written $a_1 \prec_o a_2$, if and only if for all object types $o \in \{o_{11}, ..., o_{1k}\} \cap \{o_{21}, ..., o_{2m}\}$, $outstate_o(a_1) \cap instate_o(a_2) \neq \emptyset$.*

In **step 3**, we iterate over the actions in N_A and generate *process fragments* using the computed object state relation, as shown by **rules 3.1-3.4** in Fig.5 (process fragments are indicated with dashed-line rectangles).

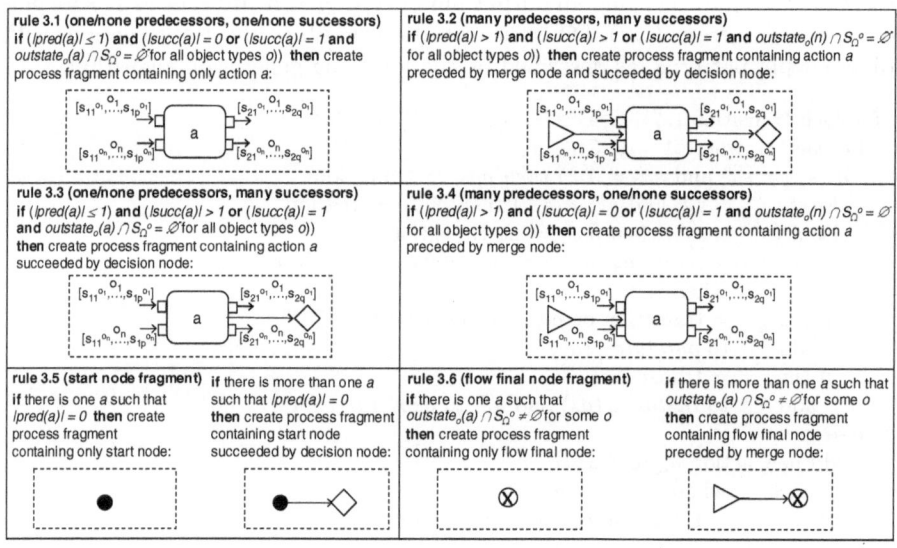

Fig. 5. Generating process fragments in **step 3**

For each action a, the numbers of its predecessors $|pred(a)|$ and successors $|succ(a)|$ in the object state relation are examined and based on these an appropriate process fragment is generated. If a has more than one predecessor, it is preceded by a merge node in the process fragment, so that in the final process model multiple control flows from the predecessor nodes can be merged into one control flow connected to a. If a has more than one successor, it is followed by a decision node in the process fragment. A decision node is also added to the process fragment when a has only one successor, but for at least one object type o some of the states in $outstate_o(a)$ are final states of o. In this case, the decision node will split control flow from a into two control flows, one leading to its successor node and the other to the flow final node. The conditions given for **rules 3.1-3.4** are mutually exclusive, which means that exactly one rule applies for each action. After the iteration over N_A, **rules 3.5 and 3.6** are applied to generate process fragments containing the start and flow final nodes.

In the final **step 4**, process fragments are connected according to the rules in Fig.6. Once again, we iterate over the actions in N_A and use the object state relation to determine how the generated fragments should be connected.

rule 4.1 (connect start fragment)	rule 4.2 (connect flow final fragment)	rule 4.3 (connect successor fragments)
if $|pred(a)| = 0$ **then** connect process fragments for start node and action a:	if $(|succ(a)| = 0)$ or $(outstate_o(a) \cap S_\Omega^o \neq \varnothing$ for some object type $o)$ **then** connect process fragments for action node a and flow final node:	if $|succ(a)| > 0$ **then for each** $a_s \in succ(a)$ connect process fragments for actions a and a_s
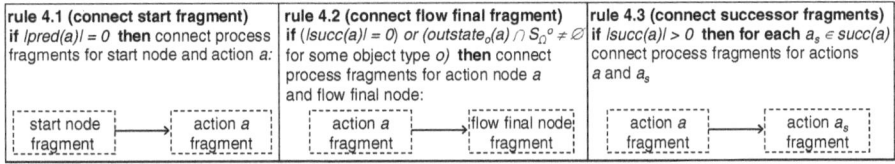		

Fig. 6. Connecting process fragments in **step 4**

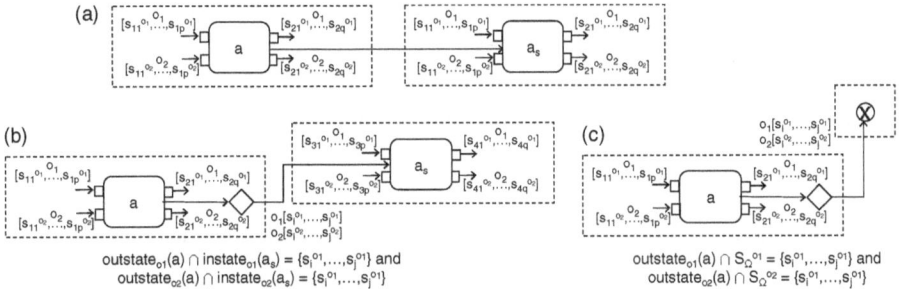

Fig. 7. Connection of process fragments

Connection of two process fragments is performed as follows. If the predecessor fragment contains no decision node, a new control flow is simply created to connect the last node of the predecessor fragment to the first node of the successor fragment. An example of such a connection is shown in Fig.7 (a). The connection is established in the same way if there is a decision node in the predecessor fragment, but an additional branch condition is added to the new control flow that connects the decision node to the first node of the successor fragment. Figure 7 (b) illustrates the connection of two action fragments, where the branch condition is set to $outstate_{o_1}(a) \cap instate_{o_1}(a_s)$ and $outstate_{o_2}(a) \cap instate_{o_2}(a_s)$. Figure 7 (c) shows that when action and flow final fragments are connected, the branch condition is set to $outstate_{o_1}(a) \cap S_\Omega^{o_1}$ and $outstate_{o_2}(a) \cap S_\Omega^{o_2}$. These conditions are necessary to ensure correct routing of control flow based on object state. At the end of **step 4**, a datastore for each object type is added to produce the final process model.

Figure 8 (a) shows the process model generated from the Claim object life cycle only. All object life cycle conformance and coverage conditions are

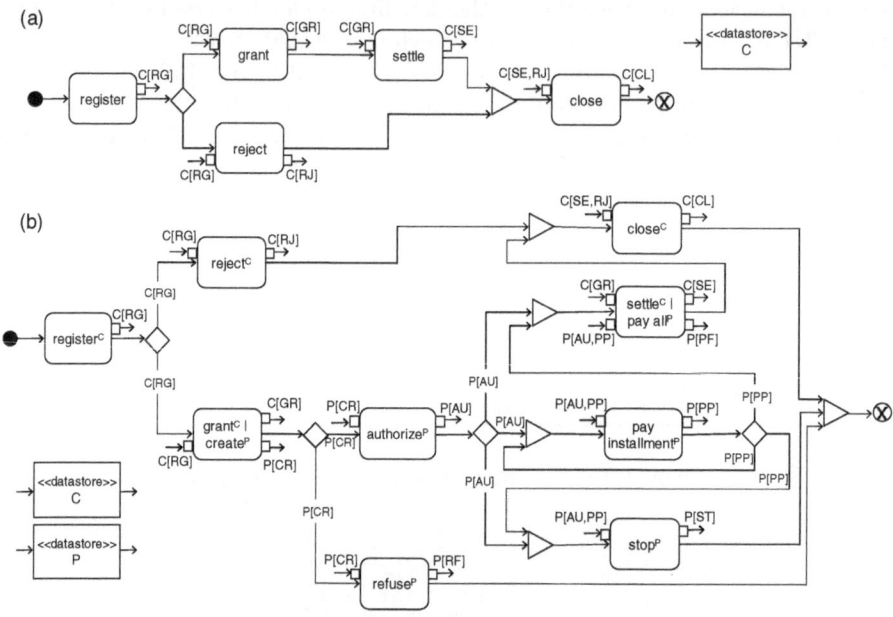

Fig. 8. Generated process models: (a) from Claim object life cycle (b) from both Claim and Payment object life cycles

satisfied when one life cycle is used for the generation, as shown in the following theorem.

Theorem 1 (Conformance and coverage). *A process model $P = (N, E, O, S, \beta, \mathcal{I}, \mathcal{O}, \mathcal{D})$ generated from an object life cycle $OLC_o = (S, s_\alpha, S_\Omega, \Sigma, \delta)$ for object type o satisfies conformance and coverage with respect to OLC_o (Definitions 6 and 7).*

Proof sketch: **Conformance:** Given any induced transition (a, s_1, s_2) of o in P, we know that $s_1 \in instate_o(a)$, $s_2 \in outstate_o(a)$ and $s_1 \in dep_{o_1}(a, s_2)$ for some $a \in N_A$. Since a has both an input and an output pin of type o, it matches the transition pin pattern and must have been generated from some transition $s_1 \xrightarrow{e} s_2$ in OLC_o. $\diamond$ Given any first state s of o in P, we know by definition that $s \in outstate_o(a)$ for some action a that does not have an input pin of type o. Action a matches the creation pin pattern and must have been generated from some $s_\alpha \xrightarrow{e} s$ in OLC_o. $\diamond$ Given any last state s of o in P, we know that $s \in outstate_o(a)$ for some action a that leads to a flow final node. Then a must have been connected to a flow final node process fragment with rule 4.2, which means $s \in S_\Omega$.

Lemma: For all actions $a \in N_A$ and object types $o \in O$, $s \in outstate_o(a)$ implies $s \in outstate_o^{\text{eff}}(a)$. *Proof by contradiction:* There exists an action a with $s \in outstate_o(a)$ and $s \notin outstate_o^{\text{eff}}(a)$. This means that a has an input pin of type o and (a, s_i, s) is not induced for all states $s_i \in instate_o(a)$. The first two conditions of Definition 4 hold by the generation step 1. This means that for all object providers a_j of a with respect to o and s_i, $s_i \notin outstate_o^{\text{eff}}(a_j)$ and hence each a_j has an input pin of type o. By construction, we know that there exists at least one such a_j. We can continue in this manner for the object providers of each a_j, which means that we never reach an action where o is created. This is a contradiction, as by construction an action that creates an object is always reachable from any action that changes its state.

Coverage: Given any $s_1 \in S \setminus \{s_\alpha\}$, $e \in \Sigma$ and $s_2 \in \delta(s_1, e)$, we know that $s_1 \in instate_o(a)$, $s_2 \in outstate_o(a)$ and $s_1 \in dep_o(a, s_2)$ for some action a from generation step 1. Since s_1 is not an initial state, it must be a target of some transition used to generate an action a_1 that is an object provider for a with respect to o and s_1 (rule 4.3). Since output states of all actions are their effective output states by the lemma, (a, s_1, s_2) is an induced transition of o in P. Therefore, transition coverage holds. $\diamond$ Given $s \in \delta(s_\alpha, e)$ for some $e \in \Sigma$, we know that s is a first state of o in P from step 1. $\diamond$ Given a final state $s_\Omega \in S_\Omega$, we know that s_Ω is also a last state of o in P by construction using rule 4.2.

Figure 8 (b) shows the process model generated from the composition of reference life cycles for Claim and Payment (Fig.3). This process model satisfies transition and first state conformance with respect to both object life cycles, which can be proven in a similar way as for the generation from one life cycle (Theorem 1). Last state conformance does not hold, because we used the object life cycle composition that contained states without outgoing transitions, which were not composite final states according to the definition. For instance, GR is a last state of Claim in the generated process model, but it is not a final state in the Claim object life cycle. In this example, the generated process model satisfies all coverage conditions with respect to the two life cycles, but this is not guaranteed by the generation. In general, different degrees of compliance can be achieved, depending on how object life cycles are synchronized and which parts of the composite life cycle are used for the generation. A formal proof of this is outside the scope of this paper.

A generated process model can be subsequently customized to the specific needs of an organization. Possible customization steps are parallelization of actions, addition of extra input pins to actions that read objects without changing their state and addition of supplementary actions. Subprocesses can also be factored out of the generated process model, such that each subprocess covers different parts of the original object life cycles. Our example demonstrates that the generation can produce process models with non-deterministic decision nodes (see Fig.8), in which case refinement of decision logic needs to be done as part of the customization. Checking object life cycle compliance after the customization phase is necessary, provided that the changes introduced during customization are not restricted. Alternatively, only compliance-preserving changes can be allowed during customization.

5   Tool Support

We have implemented a prototype as an extension to IBM WebSphere Business
Modeler [3], which offers several features for managing compliance of business
process models with object life cycles (see Fig.9). Currently supported features
include: object life cycle conformance and coverage checking, semi-automatic
resolution of selected compliance violations, extraction of object life cycles from
a process model and generation of a process model from several object life cycles.

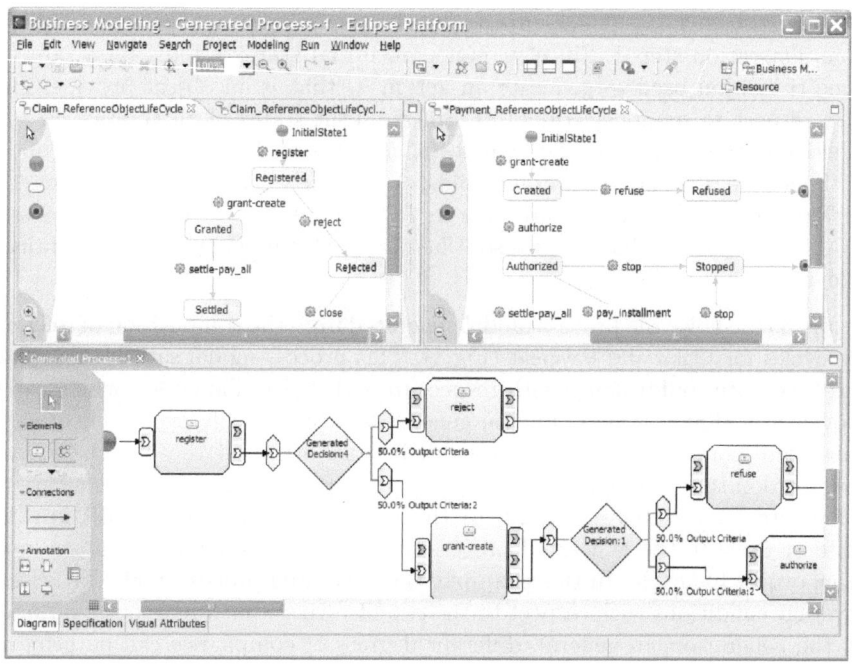

Fig. 9. Object life cycle compliance prototype in IBM WebSphere Business Modeler

As an initial validation, we applied our approach in the context of business
process models and object life cycles in IAA [2]. We focused on claim handling, a
key process in insurance industry, which is modeled as a composition of several
other processes in IAA. Many objects are exchanged between actions in this
process composition, some of which have reference object life cycles. By analyzing
the processes for object life cycle conformance, we were able to identify non-
conformant object manipulations in the process models that had to be adapted.
Coverage checking revealed a case where two objects of the same type played
different roles in the process model and covered different non-overlapping parts
of their reference object life cycle. In this case it was best to create two different
object life cycles by splitting the existing one. We have also shown the viability
of our generation technique in the context of IAA by constructing new process

models from selected object life cycles. As future work, we plan a more extensive case study to demonstrate measurable benefits of the generation.

6   Related Work

Object life cycles and in particular specialization of object life cycles have been the subject of intensive research in the object-oriented and database communities (e.g. [10,15,16,20]). In the context of business process modeling, Preuner and Schrefl [12] propose an approach for integration of several object life cycles into a business process, based on Petri nets. Each object life cycle represents a specific view on the behavior of the same object and the integrated business process is itself an object life cycle that captures the overall object behavior. Frank and Eder [7] propose incorporating different views on object behavior with state-chart integration. In contrast to these approaches, we integrate object life cycles for different objects to produce a process model that uses all of them and synchronizes their behavior. Other related work on integration of behavioral models includes synthesis of state machines from scenarios (e.g. [17]), where several scenario specifications are used to generate state machines for participating objects. In our approach, we take state machines as input for generating a process model.

Work on business process compliance includes research by van der Aalst et al [18] that addresses compliance in the context of process mining. Delta analysis is used to compare a reference process model with a process model constructed from event logs using process mining techniques [19]. We consider compliance of two given models that describe different aspects of a business process. Agrawal et al [5] study the problem of ensuring compliance with Sarbanes-Oxley (SOx). They present a solution architecture that consists of workflow modeling, active enforcement, workflow auditing and anomaly detection. Further work on process compliance includes an approach by Governatori et al [9], and Goedertier and Vanthienen [8]. Governatori et al check compliance of a business process with business contracts. Events arising from a business process are checked for compliance with contracts that are represented in the so-called Formal Contract Logic. Goedertier and Vanthienen represent timing constraints for activities in processes in temporal logic and then generate compliant process models from these constraints. The generated process model is not to be used for execution, but rather for comparison with existing processes to check whether an existing process is compliant. It is an interesting question for future work, whether and how object life cycle compliance can be integrated into a larger solution architecture that spans various compliance aspects.

7   Conclusions and Future Work

In this paper, we introduced object life cycle conformance and coverage notions for checking whether a business process model is compliant with reference object life cycles. We also presented a technique for generating a process model from one or more object life cycles. Our experiments with IAA have shown the viability of the approach for sizeable reference models. Overall, our solution can be seen as a contribution to bridging the gap between process and object modeling.

As future work, we will focus on further validation of the approach with a more extensive case study. We also intend to investigate how significantly the size of the generated process model is affected by an increase in the number of object life cycles taken as input. Support for iterative process model generation may be required to alleviate possible explosion in the size of the produced process model. Finally, we aim to develop support for compliance-preserving customization of generated process models.

Acknowledgement. We would like to thank Jana Koehler, Cesare Pautasso, Jussi Vanhatalo and Hagen Völzer for their valuable feedback on this paper.

References

1. ACORD Insurance Data Standards. http://www.acord.org
2. IBM Insurance Application Architecture. http://www-03.ibm.com/industries/financialservices/doc/content/solution/278918103.html
3. IBM WebSphere Business Modeler. http://www-306.ibm.com/software/integration/wbimodeler/
4. UML2.0 Superstructure, formal/05-07-04. OMG Document (2005)
5. Agrawal, R., Johnson, C., Kiernan, J., Leymann, F.: Taming Compliance with Sarbanes-Oxley Internal Controls Using Database Technology. In: Proceedings of the 22nd International Conference on Data Engineering (ICDE 2006), p. 92. IEEE Computer Society, Los Alamitos (2006)
6. Ebert, J., Engels, G.: Specialization of Object Life Cycle Definitions. Fachberichte Informatik 19/95, University of Koblenz-Landau (1997)
7. Frank, H., Eder, J.: Integration of Statecharts. In: Proceedings of the 3rd IFCIS International Conference on Cooperative Information Systems, pp. 364–372. IEEE Computer Society, Los Alamitos (1998)
8. Goedertier, S., Vanthienen, J.: Designing Compliant Business Processes with Obligations and Permissions. In: Eder, J., Dustdar, S. (eds.) Business Process Management Workshops. LNCS, vol. 4103, pp. 5–14. Springer, Heidelberg (2006)
9. Governatori, G., Milosevic, Z., Sadiq, S.: Compliance Checking between Business Processes and Business Contracts. In: Proceedings of the 10th IEEE Conference on Enterprise Distributed Object Computing, pp. 221–232. IEEE Computer Society Press, Los Alamitos (2006)
10. Kappel, G., Schrefl, M.: Object/Behavior Diagrams. In: Proceedings of the 7th International Conference on Data Engineering, pp. 530–539. IEEE Computer Society, Los Alamitos (1991)
11. Muchnick, S.: Advanced Compiler Design and Implementation. Morgan Kaufmann, San Francisco (1997)
12. Preuner, G., Schrefl, M.: Observation Consistent Integration of Views of Object Life-Cycles. In: Embury, S.M., Fiddian, N.J., Gray, W.A., Jones, A.C. (eds.) Advances in Databases. LNCS, vol. 1405, pp. 32–48. Springer, Heidelberg (1998)
13. Reichert, M., Dadam, P.: ADEPT$_{flex}$-Supporting Dynamic Changes of Workflows Without Losing Control. Journal of Intelligent Information Systems 10(2), 93–129 (1998)

14. Ryndina, K., Küster, J.M., Gall, H.: Consistency of Business Process Models and Object Life Cycles. In: Kühne, T. (ed.) Workshops and Symposia at MoDELS 2006. LNCS, vol. 4364, pp. 80–90. Springer, Heidelberg (2007)

15. Schrefl, M., Stumptner, M.: Behavior-Consistent Specialization of Object Life Cycles. ACM Transactions on Software Engineering and Methodology 11(1), 92–148 (2002)

16. Stumptner, M., Schrefl, M.: Behavior Consistent Inheritance in UML. In: Laender, A.H.F., Liddle, S.W., Storey, V.C. (eds.) Conceptual Modeling - ER 2000. LNCS, vol. 1920, pp. 527–542. Springer, Heidelberg (2000)

17. Uchitel, S., Kramer, J., Magee, J.: Synthesis of Behavioral Models from Scenarios. IEEE Transactions on Software Engineering 29(2), 99–115 (2003)

18. van der Aalst, W.M.P.: Business Alignment: Using Process Mining as a Tool for Delta Analysis and Conformance Testing. Requirements Engineering 10(3), 198–211 (2005)

19. van der Aalst, W.M.P., Weijters, T., Maruster, L.: Workflow Mining: Discovering Process Models from Event Logs. IEEE Transactions on Knowledge and Data Engineering 16(9), 1128–1142 (2004)

20. van der Aalst, W.M.P., Basten, T.: Identifying Commonalities and Differences in Object Life Cycles using Behavioral Inheritance. In: Colom, J.-M., Koutny, M. (eds.) ICATPN 2001. LNCS, vol. 2075, pp. 32–52. Springer, Heidelberg (2001)

Highly Dynamic Adaptation
in Process Management Systems
Through Execution Monitoring

Massimiliano de Leoni, Massimo Mecella, and Giuseppe De Giacomo

Dipartimento di Informatica e Sistemistica
SAPIENZA – Università di Roma
Via Ariosto 25, 00185 Roma, Italy
{deleoni,mecella,degiacomo}@dis.uniroma1.it

Abstract. Nowadays, process management systems can be used not only in classical business scenarios, but also in highly mobile and dynamic situations, e.g., in supporting operators during emergency management in order to coordinate their activities. In such challenging situations, processes should be adapted, in order to cope with anomalous situations, including connection anomalies and task faults. In this paper, we present a general approach, based on execution monitoring, which is *(i)* practical, by relying on well-established planning techniques, and *(ii)* does not require the definition of the adaptation strategy in the process itself (as most of the current approaches do). We prove the correctness and completeness of the approach.

1 Introduction

Nowadays, process management systems (PMSs, [1,2]) are widely used in many business scenarios, such as government agencies, insurances, banks, etc. Besides such scenarios, which present mainly static characteristics (i.e., deviations are not the rule, but the exception), PMSs can be used also in mobile and highly dynamic situations, such as in coordinating operators/devices/robots/sensors in emergency situations [3,4].

As an example, in [5] a project is presented in which PMSs are used within teams of emergency operators, in order to coordinate their activities. In such scenarios, the members of a team are equipped with PDAs and coordinated through a PMS residing on a leader device (usually a laptop); devices communicate among them through ad hoc networks, and in order to carry on the process, they need to be continually connected each other. But this is not simply guaranteed: the environment is highly dynamic, since nodes (i.e., devices and the related operators) move in the affected area to carry out assigned tasks; movements may cause possible disconnections and, so, unavailability of nodes. Therefore the process should be adapted. Adaptivity might simply consist in assigning the task in progress to another device, but collecting actual user requirements [6] shows that typical teams are formed by a few nodes (less than 10 units), and therefore frequently such reassignment is not feasible. Conversely, other kind of adaptivity can be envisioned, such as recovering somehow the disconnecting node through

G. Alonso, P. Dadam, and M. Rosemann (Eds.): BPM 2007, LNCS 4714, pp. 182–197, 2007.

specific tasks, e.g., when X is disconnecting, the PMS could assign the "follow X" task to another node so to guarantee the connection. This example shows that in such scenarios *(i)* the process is designed (and deployed on the PMS) as if everything would be fine during run-time, and *(ii)* it needs to be continuously adapted on the basis of rules that would be infeasible to foresee at design time.

The aim of this paper is to propose a general conceptual framework for the above issue, and to present a practical technique for solving it, which is based on planning in AI; moreover, we prove the correctness and completeness of the approach. In a PMS, process schemas are defined that describe the different aspects, i.e., tasks/activities, control and data flow, tasks assignment to services[1], etc. Every task gets associated a set of conditions which have to be true in order to perform the task. Conditions are defined on control and data flow (e.g., a previous task has to be finished, a variable needs to be assigned a specific range of values, etc.). This kind of conditions can be somehow considered as "internal": they are handled internally by the PMS and, thus, easily controllable. Another type of conditions exist, that is the "external" ones: they depend on the environment where process instances are carried on. These conditions are more difficult to keep under control and a continuous *monitoring* to detect discrepancies is required. Indeed we can distinguish between a *physical reality* and a *virtual reality* [7]; the physical reality is the actual values of conditions, whereas the virtual reality is the model of reality that PMS uses in making deliberations. A PMS builds the virtual reality by assuming the effects of tasks/actions fill expectations (i.e., they modify correctly conditions) and no exogenous events break out, which are capable to modify conditions.

When the PMS realizes that one or more events caused the two kinds of reality to deviate, there are three possibilities to deal with such a discrepancy:

1. Ignoring deviations – this is, of course, not feasible in general, since the new situation might be such that the PMS is no more able to carry out the process instance.
2. Anticipating all possible discrepancies – the idea is to include in the process schema the actions to cope with each of such failures. As we discuss in Section 7, most PMSs use this approach. For simple and mainly static processes, this is feasible and valuable; but, especially in mobile and highly dynamic scenarios, it is quite impossible to take into account all exception cases.
3. Devising a general recovery method able to handle any kind of exogenous events – this can be seen as a `try-catch` approach, used in some programming languages such as Java. The process is defined as if exogenous actions cannot occur, that is everything runs fine (the `try` block). Whenever the execution monitor (i.e., the module intended for execution monitoring) detects discrepancies leading the process instance not to be terminable, the control flow moves to the `catch` block. The `catch` block activates the general recovery method to modify the old process P in a process P' so that P' can terminate in the new environment and its goals are included in those of P.

---

[1] In this work, we abstract all possible actors a process can coordinate, i.e., human operators commonly interacting through worklists, software applications/components, etc. as *services* providing capabilities to be matched with the ones required by the tasks.

Here the challenge is to *automatically* synthesize P' during the execution itself, without specifying a-priori all the possible `catches`.

The contribution of this paper is *(i)* to introduce a general conceptual framework in accordance with the third approach previously described, and *(ii)* to present a practical technique, in the context of this framework, that is able to *automatically* cope with anomalies. We prove the correctness and completeness of such a technique, which is based on planning techniques in AI.

The rest of the paper is organized as follows: Section 2 introduces some preliminary notions, namely Situation Calculus and CONGOLOG, that are used as proper formalisms to reason about processes and exogenous events. Section 3 presents the general conceptual framework to address adaptivity in highly dynamic scenarios, and introduces a running example. Section 4 presents the proposed formalization of processes, and Section 5 deals with the adaptiveness. Section 6 presents the specific technique and proves its correctness and completeness. Related works are discussed in Section 7, and finally Section 8 concludes the paper.

2   Preliminaries

In this section we introduce the Situation Calculus, which we use to formalize the adaptiveness in PMSs. The Situation Calculus [8] is a second-order logic targeted specifically for representing a dynamically changing domain of interest (the world). All changes in the world are obtained as result of *actions*. A possible history of the actions is represented by a *situation*, which is a first-order term denoting the current situation of the world. The constant s_0 denotes the initial situation. A special binary function symbol $do(\alpha, s)$ denotes the next situation after performing the action α in the situation s. Action may be parameterized.

Properties that hold in a situation are called *fluents*. These are predicates taking a situation term as their last argument. Changes in fluents (resulting from executing actions) are specified through *successor state axioms*. In particular for each fluent F we have a successor state axioms as follows:

$$F(\overrightarrow{x}, do(\alpha, s)) \Leftrightarrow \Phi_F(\overrightarrow{x}, do(\alpha, s), s)$$

where $\Phi_F(\overrightarrow{x}, do(\alpha, s), s)$ is a formula with free variables $\overrightarrow{x}$, α is an action, and s is a situation. Besides successor state axioms, Situation Calculus theories are characterized by *action precondition axioms*, which specify whether a certain action is executable in a situation. Action precondition axioms have the form:

$$Poss(\alpha, s) \Leftrightarrow \Pi_\alpha(s)$$

where the formula $\Pi_\alpha(s)$ defines the conditions under which the action α may be performed in the situation s.

In order to control the executions of actions we make use of high level programs, expressed in Golog-like programming languages [9]. In particular we focus on CONGOLOG [10] which is equipped with primitives for expressing concurrency. The Table 1 summarizes the constructs of CONGOLOG used in this work. Basically, these constructs allow to define every well-structured process as defined in [11].

Table 1. CONGOLOG constructs

Construct	Meaning
a	A primitive action
$\phi?$	Wait while the ϕ condition is false
$(\delta_1; \delta_2)$	Sequence of two sub-programs δ_1 and δ_2
$proc\ P(\vec{v})\ \delta$	Invocation of a procedure passing a vector $\vec{v}$ of parameters
$if\ \phi\ then\ \delta_1\ else\ \delta_2$	Exclusive choice between δ_1 and δ_2 according to the condition ϕ
$while\ \phi\ do\ \delta$	Iterative invocation of δ
$(\delta_1 \parallel \delta_2)$	Concurrent execution

From the formal point of view, CONGOLOG programs are terms. The execution of CONGOLOG programs is expressed through a *transition semantic* based on single steps of execution. At each step a program executes an action and evolves to a new program which represents what remains to be executed of the original program. Formally two predicates are introduced to specify such a sematic:

- $Trans(\delta', s', \delta'', s'')$, given a program δ' and a situation s', returns *(i)* a new situation s'' resulting from executing a single step of δ', and *(ii)* δ'' which is the remaining program to be executed.
- $Final(\delta', s')$ returns true when the program δ' can be considered successfully completed in situation s'.

By using $Trans$ and $Final$ we can define a predicate $Do(\delta', s', s'')$ that represent successful complete executions of a program δ' in a situation s', where s'' is the situation at the end of the execution of δ'. Formally:

$$Do(\delta', s', s'') \Leftrightarrow \exists \delta''.Trans^*(\delta', s', \delta'', s'') \wedge Final(\delta'', s'')$$

where $Trans^*$ is the definition of the reflective and transitive closure of $Trans$.

3 General Framework

The general framework which we introduce in this paper is based on execution monitoring formally represented in Situation Calculus [12,7]. After each action, the PMS has to align the internal world representation (i.e., the virtual reality) with the external one (i.e., the physical reality), since they could differ due to unforeseen events.

When using CONGOLOG for process management, tasks are considered as predefined sequences of actions (see later) and processes as CONGOLOG programs.

Before a process starts to be executed, the PMS takes the initial context from the real environment as initial situation, together with the program (i.e. the process) δ_0 to be carried on. The initial situation s_0 is given by first-order logic predicates. For each execution step, the PMS, which has a complete knowledge of the internal world (i.e., its virtual reality), assigns a task to a service. The only

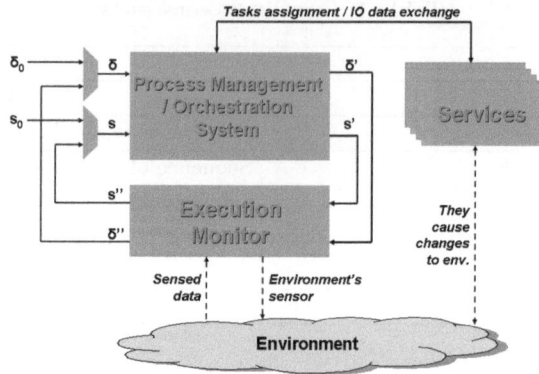

Fig. 1. Execution Monitoring

assignable tasks are those ones whose preconditions are fulfilled. A service can collect from the PMS the data which are required in order to execute the task. When a service finishes executing the task, it alerts the PMS of its completion.

The execution of the PMS can be interrupted by the monitor when a misalignment between the virtual and the physical reality is sensed. When this happens, the monitor adapts the program to deal with such a discrepancy.

Figure 1 illustrates such an execution monitoring. At each step, PMS advances the process δ in the situation s by executing an action, resulting in a new situation s' with the process δ' remaining to be executed. The state[2] is represented as first-order formulas that are defined on situations. The current state corresponds to the boolean values of these formulas evaluated on the current situation.

Both the situation s' and the process δ' are given as input to the monitor. It collects data from the environment through *sensors* (here *sensor* is any software or hardware component enabling to retrieve contextual information). If a discrepancy between the virtual reality as represented by s' and the physical reality is sensed, the monitor changes s' in s'' by internally simulating a sequence of actions that re-aligns the virtual and physical reality (i.e., those are not really executed). Notice that the process δ' may fail to be correctly executed (i.e., by assigning all tasks as required) in s''. If so, the monitor adapts the process by generating a new process δ'' that pursues at least each δ''s goal and is executable in s''. At this point, the PMS is resumed and the execution is continued from δ'' and s''.

We end this section by introducing our running example, stemming from the project described in [5,6].

Example 1. *A Mobile Ad hoc NETwork (MANET) is a P2P network of mobile nodes capable of communicating with each other without an underlying infrastructure. Nodes can communicate with their own neighbors (i.e., nodes in radio-*

---

[2] Here we refer as *state* both the tasks' state (e.g, performable, running, terminated, etc.) and the process' variables. The use of the latter variables are twofold: from the one hand, the routing is defined on them and, from the other hand, they allow to learn when a task may fire.

range) directly by wireless links. Non-neighbor nodes can communicate as well, by using other intermediate nodes as relays that forward packets toward destinations. The lack of a fixed infrastructure makes this kind of network suitable in all scenarios where it is needed to deploy quickly a network, but the presence of access points is not guaranteed, as in emergency management.

Coordination and data exchange requires MANET *nodes to be continually connected each other. But this is not guaranteed in a* MANET. *The environment is highly dynamic, since nodes move in the affected area to carry out assigned tasks. Movements may cause possible disconnections and, so, unavailability of nodes, and, consequently, unavailability of provided services. Therefore processes should be adapted, not simply by assigning tasks in progress to other services, but also considering possible recovery of the services.*

Figure 2 shows a possible scenario for information collecting after an earthquake: a team is sent to the affected area to evaluate the situation of three buildings. For each building, an actor compiles a questionnaire (by using a service, i.e., an application that it has got installed). Questionnaire compiling can be done everywhere: that is, movement is not required. Then, another actor/service has to be sent to the specific building to collect some pictures (this, conversely, requires movement). Finally, according to information in the questionnaire, a third actor/service evaluates quality and effectiveness of collected pictures. If pictures are of bad quality, the task of taking new pictures is scheduled again. Whenever these steps have been performed for the three buildings A, B and C, the collected data (questionnaires and pictures) are sent by GPRS or UMTS elsewhere. □

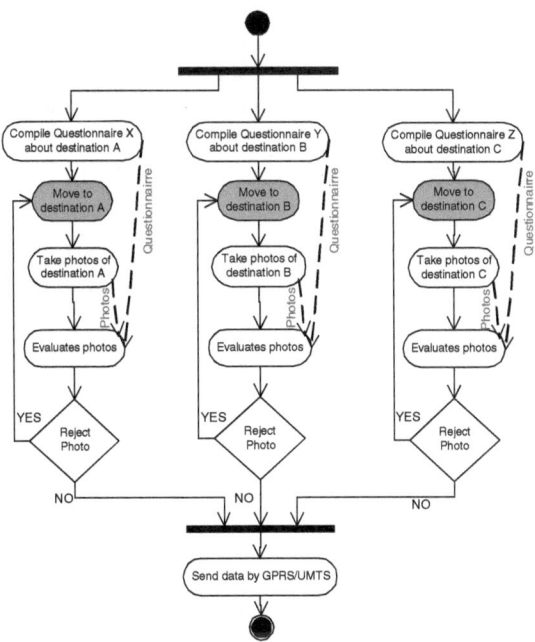

Fig. 2. A possible process to be carried on in disaster management scenarios

4   Formalization in Situation Calculus

Next we detail the general framework proposed above by using Situation Calculus and CONGOLOG. We use some domain-independent predicates to denote the various objects of interest in the framework:

- $service(a)$: a is a service
- $task(x)$: x is a task
- $capability(b)$: b is a capability
- $provide(a, b)$: the service a provides the capability b
- $require(x, b)$: the task x requires the capability b

Every task execution is the sequence of four actions: *(i)* the assignment of the task to a service, resulting in the service being not free anymore; *(ii)* the notification to the service to start executing the task. Then, the service carries out the tasks and, after finishing, *(iii)* the PMS stops the service, acknowledging the successful termination of its task. Finally, *(iv)* the PMS releases the service, which becomes free again. We formalize these four actions as follows (these are the only actions used in our formalization):

- $Assign(a, x)$: the task x is assigned to a service a
- $Start(a, x, p)$: the service a is notified to perform the task x on input p
- $Stop(a, x, q)$: the service a is stopped acknowledging the successful termination of x with output q
- $Release(a, x)$: the service a is released with respect to the task x

The terms p and q denote arbitrary sets of input/output, which depend on the specific task; if no input or output is needed, p and q are $\emptyset$.

For each specific domain, we have several fluents representing the properties of situations. Among them, we have the fluent $free(a, s)$, which is indeed domain-independent, that denotes the fact that the service a is free, i.e., no task has been assigned to it, in the situation s. The corresponding successor state axiom is as follows:

$$free(a, do(t, s)) \Leftrightarrow \\ \big(\forall x.t \neq Assign(a, x) \wedge free(a, s)\big) \vee \\ \big(\neg free(a, s) \wedge \exists x.t = Release(a, x)\big) \tag{1}$$

This says that a service a is considered free in the current situation if and only if a was free in the previous situation and no tasks have been just assigned to it, or a was not free and it has been just released.

In addition, we make use, in every specific domain, of a predicate $available(a, s)$ which denotes whether a service a is available in situation s for tasks assignment. However, $available$ is domain-dependent and, hence, requires to be defined specifically for every domain. Its definition must enforce the following condition:

$$\forall a \; s.available(a, s) \Rightarrow free(a, s) \tag{2}$$

Precondition axioms are also domain dependent and, hence, vary from case to case. However the following condition must be true:

$$\forall x, p, q \; Poss\big(Start(a, x, p), s\big) \Rightarrow available(a, s) \tag{3}$$

Knowing whether a service is available is very important for the PMS when it has to perform assignments. Indeed, a task x is assigned to the best service a which is available and provides every capability required by x. In order to model the best choice among available services, we introduced a special construct, named *pick*. The statement *pick* $a.[\phi(a)]$ δ chooses the best service a matching the condition $\phi(\cdot)$ on predicates and fluents applied in the current situation. This choice is performed with respect to a given (typically domain-dependent) metric. For instance, the *pick* might consider the queueing of tasks that are assigned to the members, as well as the execution of multiple parallel process instances sharing the same resources. Observe that such a choice is deterministic, even when there are more than one service matching the condition $\phi(\cdot)$. Then it instantiates δ with the chosen a and executes the first step of the resulting program. If no service matches the condition, the process δ stays blocked, until some other services make $\phi(a)$ true.

We illustrate such notions on our running example.

Example 1 (cont.). *We formalize the scenario in Example 1. We make use of the following domain-dependent fluents (for sake of brevity we focus on the most relevant ones):*

- *connected(a, b, s): which is true if in the situation s the services a and b are connected through multi-hop paths*
- *neigh(a, b, s): which is true if in the situation s the services a and b are in radio-range in the situation s*
- *at(a, p, s) it is true if in the situation s the service a is located at the coordinate $p = \langle p_x, p_y, p_z \rangle$ in the situation s.*

The successor state axioms for this domain are:

$$available(a, do(x, s)) \Leftrightarrow free(a, do(x, s)) \wedge connected(a, \textbf{Coord}, do(x, s))$$

$$connected(a_0, a_1, do(x, s)) \Leftrightarrow neigh(a_0, a_1, do(x, s)) \vee$$
$$\left(\exists a_2.service(a_2) \wedge neigh(a_0, a_2, do(x, s)) \wedge connected(a_2, a_1, do(x, s)) \right)$$

$$neigh(a_0, a_1, do(x, s)) \Leftrightarrow$$
$$at(a_0, p_0, do(x, s)) \wedge at(a_1, p_1, s) \wedge \parallel p_0 - p_1 \parallel < rrange$$

$$at(a, p, do(x, s)) \Leftrightarrow$$
$$\forall\, p, q.\ x \neq Stop(a, \textbf{Go}, p) \wedge at(a, p, s) \vee \ \forall\, q.\ x = Stop(a, \textbf{Go}, p)$$

The first successor state axiom is the one for available, *which states a service is available if it is connected to the coordinator device (denoted by* **Coord**) *and it is free. Notice that the condition 2 is fulfilled. The axiom for* connected *states two devices are connected if and only if they are neighbors (i.e., in radio-range) or there exists a path in the* MANET. *The successor state axiom* neigh *states how neighbors evolve: two nodes a and b are neighbors in situation s if and only if their distance $\parallel p_a - p_b \parallel$ is less than the radio-range. The successor state axiom for* at *states that the position p for a does not change until the assigned task* Go *is acknowledged to be finished.*

In the reality, in order to know the position returned by the Go *task, the PMS gets such an information from the service a (here not modelled). In case the node (hence the service) is getting disconnected, the monitor will get in and generate a* Stop *action which communicates the actual position, and a recovery is instructed in order to keep the connection (see later). Indeed, in such a scenario nodes need be continually connected to each other, as a disconnected node is out of the PMS's control [3].*

For sake of brevity we do not look at the precondition axioms, and instead we look directly at the CONGOLOG *program (implicitly assuming that such precondition axioms allow for all instructions in the program). The* CONGOLOG *program corresponding to Figure 2 is shown in Figure 3. The main program is the procedure* Process, *which executes in parallel on three threads the sub-procedure* EvalTake *and then assigns the task* SendByGPRS *to the proper service that is the one providing the capability to send data by means of GPRS (or similar).* ☐

5   Adaptation

Next we formalize how the monitor works. Intuitively, the monitor takes the current program δ' and the current situation s' from the PMS's virtual reality and, analyzing the physical reality by sensors, introduces fake actions in order to get a new situation s'' which aligns the virtual reality of the PMS with sensed information. Then, it analyzes whether δ' can still be executed in s'', and if not, it adapts δ' by generating a new correctly executable program δ''. Specifically, the monitor work can be abstractly defined as follows (we do not model how the situation s'' is generated from the sensed information):

$$
\begin{aligned}
Monitor(\delta', s', s'', \delta'') \Leftrightarrow & \\
\big(Relevant(\delta', s', s'') \wedge Recovery(\delta', s', s'', \delta'')\big) \vee & \qquad (4)\\
\big(\neg Relevant(\delta', s', s'') \wedge \delta'' = \delta'\big) &
\end{aligned}
$$

where: *(i)* $Relevant(\delta', s', s'')$ states whether the change from the situation s' into s'' is such that δ' cannot be correctly executed anymore; and *(ii)* $Recovery$ $(\delta', s', s'', \delta'')$ is intended to hold whenever the program δ', to be originally executed in the situation s', is adapted to δ'' in order to be executed in the situation s''.

Formally *Relevant* is defined as follows:

$$Relevant(\delta', s', s'') \Leftrightarrow \neg SameConfig(\delta', s', \delta', s'')$$

where $SameConfig(\delta', s', \delta'', s'')$ is true if executing δ' in s' is "equivalent" to executing δ'' in s'' (see later for further details).

In this general framework we do not give a definition for *SameConfig* $(\delta', s', \delta'', s'')$. However we consider any definition for *SameConfig* to be correct if it denotes a bisimulation [13]. Formally, for every $\delta', s', \delta'', s''$ holds:

1. $Final(\delta', s') \Leftrightarrow Final(\delta'', s')$
2. $\forall\, a, \delta'.Trans\big(\delta', s', \overline{\delta'}, do(a, s')\big) \Rightarrow$
   $\exists\, \overline{\delta''}.Trans\big(\delta'', s'', \overline{\delta'}, do(a, s'')\big) \wedge SameConfig\big(\overline{\delta'}, do(a, s), \overline{\delta''}, do(a, s'')\big)$

```
01 proc EvalTake(Location, Questionnaire, Photos)
02 pick a₀[actor(a₀) ∧ available(a₀) ∧ ∀b service(b) ∧ require(b, Compile) ⇒ provide(a₀, b)]
03          Assign(a₀, Compile);
04          Start(a₀, Compile, Location);
05          Stop(a₀, Compile, Questionnaire);
06          Release(a₀, Compile);
07 isOk := false;
08 while(isOk == false)
09          (pick a₁[actor(a₁) ∧ available(a₁) ∧ ∀b service(b) ∧ require(b, TakePhoto)
              ⇒ provide(a₁, b)]
10              Assign(a₁, TakePhoto);
11              Start(a₁, Go, Location);
12              Stop(a₁, Go, Location);
13              Start(a₁, TakePhoto, Location);
14              Stop(a₁, TakePhoto, Photos);
15              Release(a₁, TakePhoto); )
16          pick a₂[actor(a₂) ∧ available(a₂) ∧ ∀b service(b) ∧ require(b, Evaluate)
              ⇒ provide(a₂, b)]
17              Assign(a₂, Evaluate);
18              Start(a₁, Evaluate, [Location, Questionnaire, Photos]);
19              Stop(a₁, Evaluate, isOk);
20              Release(a₂, Evaluate); )
21 endproc
22
23 proc Process
24 (EvalTake(LocA, Qₐ, Fₐ) ∥
25 EvalTake(LocB, Q_b, F_b) ∥
26 EvalTake(LocC, Q_c, F_c));
27 pick a[actor(a)] ∧ available(a) ∧ ∀b service(b) ∧ require(b, SendByGPRS)
      ⇒ provide(a, b)?;
28          Assign(a, SendByGPRS);
29          Start(a, SendByGPRS, [Qₐ, Fₐ, Q_b, F_b, Q_c, F_c]);
30          Stop(a, SendByGPRS, nil);
31          Release(a, SendByGPRS);
32 endproc
```

Fig. 3. The CONGOLOG program of the process in Figure 2

3. $\forall\, a, \delta'. Trans(\delta'', s'', \overline{\delta'}, do(a, s'')) \Rightarrow$
$\exists\, \overline{\delta''}. Trans(\delta', s', \overline{\delta'}, do(a, s')) \wedge SameConfig(\overline{\delta''}, do(a, s''), \overline{\delta'}, do(a, s'))$

Intuitively, a predicate $SameConfig(\delta', s', \delta'', s'')$ is said to be correct if δ' and δ'' are terminable either both or none of them. Furthermore, for each action a performable by δ' in the situation s', δ'' in the situation s'' has to enable the performance of the same actions (and viceversa). Moreover, the resulting configurations $(\overline{\delta'}, do(a, s'))$ and $(\overline{\delta''}, do(a, s'))$ must still satisfy $SameConfig$.

The use of the bisimulation criteria to state when a predicate $SameConfig$ ($\cdots$) is correct, derives from the notion of equivalence introduced in [14]. When comparing the execution of two formally different business processes, the internal states of the processes may be ignored, because what really matters is the process behavior that can be observed. This view reflects the way a PMS works: indeed what is of interest is the set of tasks that the PMS offers to its environment, in response to the inputs that the environment provides.

Next we turn our attention to the procedure to adapt the process formalized by $Recovery(\delta, s, s', \delta')$. Formally is defined as follows:

$$Recovery(\delta', s', s'', \delta'') \Leftrightarrow$$
$$\exists \delta_a, \delta_b. \delta'' = \delta_a; \delta_b \wedge Deterministic(\delta_a) \wedge \qquad (5)$$
$$Do(\delta_a, s'', s_b) \wedge SameConfig(\delta', s', \delta_b, s_b)$$

$Recovery$ determines a process δ'' consisting of a $deterministic$ δ_a (i.e., a program not using the concurrency construct), and an arbitrary program δ_b. The aim of δ_a is to lead from the situation s'' in which adaptation is needed to a new situation s_b where $SameConfig(\delta', s', \delta_b, s_b)$ is true.

Notice that during the actual recovery phase δ_a we disallow for concurrency because we need full control on the execution of each service in order to get to a recovered state. Then the actual recovered program δ_b can again allow for concurrency.

6   Adaptation: A Specific Technique

In the previous sections we have provided a general description on how adaptation can be defined and performed. Here we choose a specific technique that is actually feasible in practice. Our main step is to adopt a specific definition for $SameConfig$, here denoted as SAMECONFIG, namely:

$$\text{SAMECONFIG}(\delta', s', \delta'', s'') \Leftrightarrow$$
$$SameState(s', s'') \wedge \delta' = \delta'' \qquad (6)$$

In other words, SAMECONFIG states that δ', s' and δ'', s'' are the same configuration if (i) all fluents have the same truth values in both s' and s'' ($SameState$)[3], and (ii) δ'' is actually δ'.

The following shows that SAMECONFIG is indeed correct.

Theorem 1. SAMECONFIG$(\delta', s', \delta'', s'')$ *is correct.*

Proof. We show that SAMECONFIG is a bisimulation. Indeed:

- Since $SameState(s', s'')$ requires all fluents to have the same values both in s' and s'', we have that $(Final(\delta, s') \Leftrightarrow Final(\delta, s''))$.

---

[3] Observe that $SameState$ can actually be defined as a first-order formula over the fluents, as the conjunction of $F(s') \Leftrightarrow F(s'')$ for each fluent F.

– Since $SameState(s', s'')$ requires all fluents to have the same values both in s' and s'', it follows that the PMS is allowed for the same process δ' to assign the same tasks both in s' and in s'' and moreover for each action a and situation s' and s'' s.t. $SameState(s', s'')$, we have that $SameState(do(a, s'), do(a, s''))$ hold. As a result, for each a and $\overline{\delta'}$ such that $Trans(\delta', s', \overline{\delta'}, do(a, s'))$ we have that $Trans(\delta', s'', \overline{\delta'}, do(a, s''))$ and SAMECONFIG$(\overline{\delta'}, do(a, s), \overline{\delta''}, do(a, s''))$. Similarly for the other direction.

Hence, the thesis holds. □

Next let us denote by $LinearProgram(\delta)$ a program constituted only by sequences of actions, and let us define RECOVERY as:

$$\begin{aligned} &\text{RECOVERY}(\delta', s', s'', \delta'') \Leftrightarrow \\ &\exists \delta_a, \delta_b.\delta'' = \delta_a; \delta_b \wedge LinearProgram(\delta_a) \wedge \\ &Do(\delta_a, s'', s_b) \wedge \text{SAMECONFIG}(\delta', s', \delta_b, s_b) \end{aligned} \tag{7}$$

Next theorem shows that we can adopt RECOVERY as a definition of *Recovery* without loss of generality.

Theorem 2. *For every process δ' and situations s' and s'', there exists a δ'' such that* RECOVERY$(\delta', s', s'', \delta'')$ *if and only if there exists a $\overline{\delta''}$ such that Recovery $(\delta', s', s'', \overline{\delta''})$, where in the latter we use* SAMECONFIG *as SameConfig.*

Proof. Observe that the only difference between the two definitions is that in one case we allow only for linear programs (i.e., sequences of actions) as δ_a, while in the second case also for deterministic ones, that may include also if-then-else, while, procedures, etc.

($\Rightarrow$) Trivial, as linear programs are deterministic programs.

($\Leftarrow$) Let us consider the recovery process $\overline{\delta''} = \delta_a; \delta_b$ where δ_a is an arbitrary deterministic program. Then by definition of *Recovery* there exists a (unique) situation s'' such that $Do(\delta_a, s', s'')$. Now consider that s'' as the form $s'' = do(a_n, do(a_{n-1}, \ldots, do(a_2, do(a_1, s')) \ldots))$. Let us consider the linear program $p = (a_1; a_2; \ldots; a_n)$. Obviously we have $Do(p, s', s'')$. Hence the process $\delta'' = p; \delta_b$ is a recovery process according to the definition of RECOVERY. □

The nice feature of RECOVERY is that it asks to search for a linear program that achieves a certain formula, namely $SameState(s', s'')$. That is we have reduced the synthesis of a recovery program to a classical Planning problem in AI [15]. As a result we can adopt a well-developed literature about planning for our aim. In particular, if the services and input and output parameters are finite, then the recovery can be reduced to *propositional* planning, which is known to be decidable in general (for which very well performing software tools exists).

Theorem 3. *Let assume a domain in which services and input and output parameters are finite. Then given a process δ' and situations s' and s'', it is decidable to compute a recovery process δ'' such that* RECOVERY$(\delta', s', s'', \delta'')$ *holds.*

Proof. In domains in which services and input and output parameters are finite, also actions and fluents instantiated with all possible parameters are finite. Hence we can phrase the domain as a propositional one and the thesis follows from decidability of propositional planning [15].   □

Example 1 (cont.). *In the running example, consider the case in which the process is between the lines 11 and 12 in the execution of the procedure invocation EvalTake(LocA, Q_A, F_A). Now, let us assume that the node a_1 is assigned the task* TakePhoto. *But it is moving to a location such that it is not connected to the coordinator anymore; the monitor sees that it is getting out of reach and generates a spurious (not inside the original process) action Stop(a_1, Go, RealPosition), where* RealPosition *is the actual position as sensed by the monitor. Since* RealPosition *is not* LocA, *adaptation is needed; the Monitor generates the recovery program $\delta_a; \delta_b$ where δ_b is the original one from line 11 and δ_a is as follows:*

$$Start(a\_3, Go, NewLocation);$$
$$Stop(a\_3, Go, NewLocation);$$
$$Start(a\_1, Go, LocA)$$

where NewLocation *is within the radio-range of* RealPosition[4].   □

7   Related Works

Adaptation in PMSs can be considered at two level: at the process schema or at the process instance level [16]. Process schema changes become necessary, for example, to adapt the PMS to optimized business processes or to new laws [17,18,19]. In particular, applications supporting long-running processes (e.g., handling of mortgage or medical treatments) and the process instances controlled by them are affected by such changes. As opposed to this, changes of single process instances (e.g., to insert, delete, or shift single process steps) often have to be carried out in an ad-hoc manner in order to deal with an exceptional situation, e.g., peer disconnection in mobile networks [3], or evolving process requirements [20].

Table 2 shows a comparison of PMSs approaches supporting changes. The columns show the adaptation features addressed by existing PMSs. The second column illustrates which softwares support adaptation at schema level. As we can see, all analyzed softwares support it. The other three columns show the support for adaptation of single instances. The "Pre-Planned" PMSs refer to those systems that enable to specify adaptation rules to handle a set of exceptional (but foreseen) events. Conversely, the "Ad-hoc" support means PMSs to be able to adapt when unforeseen events fire. Ad-hoc adaptation of a process instance can be performed by the responsible person who manually changes the structure or, automatically, by the PMS.

We note that there is no row having value "yes" in the column *Ad-hoc/Automatic*. That means that no considered approach allows users to manage

---

[4] Observe that if the positions are discretized, so as to become finite, this recovery can be achieved by a propositional planner.

Table 2. Comparison of process adaptation approaches present in literature

	Schema	Instance		
		Pre-planned/Automatic	Ad hoc	
			Manual	Automatic
Woflan	Yes	No	Yes	No
ADEPT	Yes	No	Yes	No
WASA$_2$	Yes	No	Yes	No
Chautauqua	Yes	No	Yes	No
TRAM	Yes	No	Yes	No
Breeze	Yes	No	Yes	No
MILANO	Yes	No	No	No
WIDE	Yes	Yes	No	No
AgentWork	Yes	Yes	No	No
DYNAMITE	Yes	Yes	No	No
EPOS	Yes	Yes	No	No
MQ Worflow	Yes	No	No	No
Staffware	Yes	No	No	No
InConcert	Yes	No	Yes	No
SER Process	Yes	No	Yes	No
FileNet	Yes	No	Yes	No
FLOWer	Yes	No	Yes	No

unforeseen exceptions in a fully automatic way. Actually, only few systems (AgentWork[21], DYNAMITE[22], EPOS[23] and WIDE[24]) support automated process instance changes, but only in pre-planned way.

The work [25] is one of the few coping with exogenous events in the field of the Web service composition. This work considers the issue of long term optimality of the adaptation but, anyway, it does not manage unforeseen events. Moreover, it does require the definition of the probability according to which each of such events fires.

We underline that our approach is not another way to capture expected exceptions. Other approaches rely on rules to define the behaviors when special events are triggered. Here we simply model (a subset of) the running environment and the actions' effects, without considering possible special exceptional events. We argue that in some cases modeling the environment, even in detail, is easier than modeling all possible exceptions.

8 Conclusion

In this paper, we have presented a general approach, based on execution monitoring, for automatic process adaptation in dynamic scenarios. Such an approach is (i) practical, by relying on well-established planning techniques, and (ii) does not require the definition of the adaptation strategy in the process itself (as most of the current approaches do). We have proved the correctness and completeness of the approach, and we have shown its applicability to a running example stemming from a real project. Future works include to actually develop the Adaptive Process Management System. This will be done by using the `IndiGolog` module developed by the Cognitive Robotics Group of the Toronto University.

Acknowledgements. This work has been supported by the European Commission through the project FP6-2005-IST-5-034749 WORKPAD.

References

1. Leymann, F., Roller, D.: Production Workflow: Concepts and Techniques. Prentice Hall PTR, Englewood Cliffs (1999)
2. van der Aalst, W., van Hee, K.: Workflow Management. Models, Methods, and Systems. MIT Press, Cambridge (2004)
3. de Leoni, M., Mecella, M., Russo, R.: A Bayesian Approach for Disconnection Management in Mobile Ad-hoc Networks. In: Proc. 4th International Workshop on Interdisciplinary Aspects of Coordination Applied to Pervasive Environments: Models and Applications (CoMA) (at WETICE 2007) (2007)
4. de Leoni, M., De Rosa, F., Mecella, M.: MOBIDIS: A Pervasive Architecture for Emergency Management. In: Proc. 4th International Workshop on Distributed and Mobile Collaboration (DMC 2006) (at WETICE 2006) (2006)
5. Catarci, T., De Rosa, F., de Leoni, M., Mecella, M., Angelaccio, M., Dustdar, S., Krek, A., Vetere, G., Zalis, Z.M., Gonzalvez, B., Iiritano, G.: WORKPAD: 2-Layered Peer-to-Peer for Emergency Management through Adaptive Processes. In: Proc. 2nd International Conference on Collaborative Computing: Networking, Applications and Worksharing (CollaborateCom 2006) (2006)
6. de Leoni, M., De Rosa, F., Marrella, A., Poggi, A., Krek, A., Manti, F.: Emergency Management: from User Requirements to a Flexible P2P Architecture. In: Proc. 4th International Conference on Information Systems for Crisis Response and Management (ISCRAM 2007) (2007)
7. De Giacomo, G., Reiter, R., Soutchanski, M.: Execution monitoring of high-level robot programs. In: KR, pp. 453–465 (1998)
8. Reiter, R.: Knowledge in Action: Logical Foundations for Specifying and Implementing Dynamical Systems. MIT Press, Cambridge (2001)
9. Levesque, H.J., Reiter, R., Lespérance, Y., Lin, F., Scherl, R.B.: Golog: A logic programming language for dynamic domains. J. Log. Program. 31, 59–83 (1997)
10. De Giacomo, G., Lespérance, Y., Levesque, H.J.: Congolog, a concurrent programming language based on the situation calculus. Artif. Intell. 121, 109–169 (2000)
11. Kiepuszewski, B., ter Hofstede, A.H.M., Bussler, C.: On structured workflow modelling. In: Wangler, B., Bergman, L.D. (eds.) CAiSE 2000. LNCS, vol. 1789, pp. 431–445. Springer, Heidelberg (2000)
12. Lesperance, Y., Ng, H.: Integrating planning into reactive high-level robot programs (2000)
13. Milner, R.: A Calculus of Communicating Systems. Springer, Heidelberg (1980)
14. Hidders, J., Dumas, M., van der Aalst, W.M.P., ter Hofstede, A., Verelst, J.: When are two workflows the same? In: CATS, pp. 3–11 (2005)
15. Ghallab, M., Nau, D., Traverso, P.: Automated Planning: Theory and Practice. Morgan Kaufmann, San Francisco (2004)
16. Weber, M., Illmann, T., Schmidt, A.: Webflow: Decentralized workflow management in the world wide web. In: Proc. of the International Conf. on Applied Informatics (AI'98) (1998)
17. Reichert, M., Rinderle, S., Dadam, P.: On the common support of workflow type and instance changes under correctness constraints. In: Meersman, R., Tari, Z., Schmidt, D.C. (eds.) CoopIS 2003, DOA 2003, and ODBASE 2003. LNCS, vol. 2888, Springer, Heidelberg (2003)
18. Rinderle, S., Reichert, M., Dadam, P.: Correctness criteria for dynamic changes in workflow systems - a survey. Data and Knowledge Engineering 50, 9–34 (2004)

19. van der Aalst, W., Basten, T.: Inheritance of Workflows: an approach to tackling problems related to change. In: Theoretical Computer Science, vol. 270, pp. 125–203. Elsevier Science Publishers, Amsterdam (2002)
20. Reichert, M., Dadam, P.: ADEPT$_{flex}$ supporting dynamic changes of workflows without losing control. Journal of Intelligent Information Systems 10, 93–129 (1998)
21. Müller, R., Greiner, U., Rahm, E.: AGENTWORK: A Workflow-System Supporting Rule-Based Workflow Adaptation. Data and Knowledge Engineering 51(2), 223–256 (2004)
22. Heimann, P., Joeris, G., Krapp, C., Westfechtel, B.: DYNAMITE: dynamic task nets for software process management. In: Proc. of the 18th International Conference Software Engineering (ICSE) Berlin, pp 331–341 (1996)
23. Liu, C., Conradi, R.: Automatic replanning of task networks for process model evolution. In: Proc. of the European Software Engineers Conference, Garmisch-Partenkirchen, Germany, pp. 434–450 (1993)
24. Ceri, S., Paul, S.G.: Wide: A distributed architecture for workflow management. In: 7th International Workshop on Research Issues in Data Engineering (RIDE) (1997)
25. Verma, K., Doshi, P., Gomadam, K., Miller, J., Sheth, A.: Optimal adaptation in web processes with coordination constraints. In: The IEEE International Conference on Web Services (ICWS'06), IEEE Computer Society Press, Los Alamitos (2006)

Version Management in the Business Process Change Context

Xiaohui Zhao and Chengfei Liu

Centre for Information Technology Research
Faculty of Information and Communication Technologies
Swinburne University of Technology
Melbourne, Australia
{xzhao,cliu}@ict.swin.edu.au

Abstract. The current business endures a fast changing environment, which drives organisations to continuously adapt their business processes to new conditions. In this background, the workflow version control plays an important role for the change management of business processes. To better handle the versions of evolving workflow process definitions, a new versioning method is introduced in this paper. To capture the dynamics of the workflow evolvement, we propose a novel version preserving directed graph model to represent the run time evolvement of a workflow process, and devise a series of modification operations to characterise workflow updating on the fly. The extraction of workflow versions from a version preserving graph is also discussed with two different extraction strategies. Particularly, our method allows the execution of multiple workflow instances of different versions within a single graph, and supports the evolvements initiated by temporary changes.

1 Introduction

Current varying market opportunities are commented as "Change has become the only certainty." [1] in nowadays business globalisation background. To stay efficient and effective in such a turbulent environment, organisations are required to adapt their structures and business processes to new conditions continuously [2, 3]. As a response, organisations are seeking for new facilitating technologies to manage their dynamic, expanding and changing business processes [4, 5].

Technically, this trend puts challenges to the issues such as business process updating, instance updating, version control etc. A frequently changing workflow process definition requires dynamic updating without suspending related running workflow instances. Further, a running workflow instance needs to keep up with the changed process definition by evolving to the latest version on the fly. In this scenario, some temporary and parallel changes may cause a lot of workflow variants which will result in various versions of workflow process definitions and their workflow instances. As such, some innovative version management mechanism is in great demand to harmonise the various versions of workflow processes and instances.

G. Alonso, P. Dadam, and M. Rosemann (Eds.): BPM 2007, LNCS 4714, pp. 198–213, 2007.

The previous work [6] done with other colleagues particularly focused on the handover of the running instances from an old workflow model to a new model, i.e., between only two versions. While, this paper concentrates on the version management in the context of multiple changes to business processes. A novel version preserving directed graph (VPG) model is proposed to represent the version evolution of a workflow process definition, and support the execution of workflow instances belonging to different versions within the same graph. A set of run time modification operations are developed for this VPG model, to support the dynamic updating to a workflow process definition. Two strategies for extracting a workflow process definition of a given version from a VPG are illustrated with formal algorithms, together with a performance analysis.

The remainder of this paper is organised as follows, Section 2 discusses the version issues in workflow process evolvements with a motivating example; a version preserving directed graph model is presented in Section 3, to support business process changes; strategies for dynamically extracting a workflow process definition of a given version are addressed in Section 4, together with a performance analysis on different strategies; Section 5 lists the work related to business process change management, and discusses the advantages of the proposed method; conclusion remarks and future work are given in Section 6.

2   Motivating Example

In this section, we use a production business process to demonstrate the process evolvement. The contextual scenario is that a factory owns several pipelines, and at the beginning, each pipeline follows the same workflow process shown in Figure 1 (a). Here, we see that the production process includes several activities: production scheduling, production using a work centre, i.e., work centre #1, quality checking and final packaging. To meet the soaring market demands, the factory may add a parallel work centre, for example work centre #2, to each pipeline for the purpose of increasing the production capability. In this case, the original workflow process upgrades to the one shown in Figure 1 (b).

As this workflow process is shared by multiple pipelines, the workflow process may have variants for different pipelines due to practical situations. For example, sometimes work centre #1 of a pipeline, say pipeline A, may come across a technical malfunction, and therefore has to be removed from the pipeline for maintenance. Here, we suppose that pipeline A attempts to keep the production output by fixing unqualified products at the absence of work centre #1. Therefore, the workflow process will evolve to the one shown in Figure 1 (c), accordingly.

While for other pipeline, for example pipeline B, its work centre #1 may also endure a temporary maintenance, yet it uses manual labour to replace its work centre #1. In this case, the workflow process will evolve to the one shown in Figure 1 (d). Afterwards, a technical upgrading to the work centre #2 of all pipelines may improve the product quality, and the products made by work centre #2 are thus not required to pass the quality checking. Due to the upgrading benefit, the workflow process for other pipelines, except pipeline A and B, will evolve from Figure 1 (b) to Figure 1 (e), whlist for pipeline B, the workflow process will evolve from Figure 1 (d) to Figure 1 (f). Further, when work centre #1 of pipeline *B* comes back from maintenance, the workflow process for this pipeline evolves to the one shown in Figure 1 (e), as well.

Besides parallel evolvements, a workflow process may possibly go back to a previous copy. For example, after the workflow process for pipeline *A* evolves to Figure 1 (c) and before the upgrading to work centre #2, the workflow process may be changed back to Figure 1 (b) if work centre comes back to work.

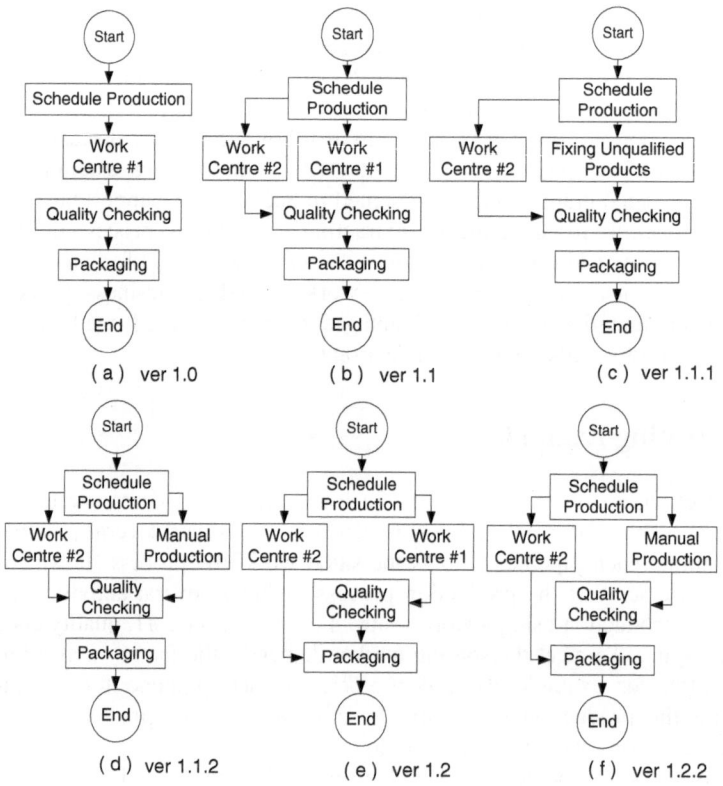

Fig. 1. Workflow process evolvement example

From this example, we see that a workflow process may not simply go along a linear evolvement. In fact, the actual evolvement is driven by many factors, such as unit replacement, technology shift, external changes, etc. Some of these factors, for example, unit replacement and external changes, may only cause temporary changes of a workflow process. While, some factors, such as technology shift etc., may cause permanent changes. Nevertheless, static workflow process definitions are not acceptable in such evolvement scenarios, and more supports for dynamic evolvement representation and description are highly needed. In such a business process change context, the workflow version is a direct indicator for the variants of an evolving workflow process, and therefore the representation and manipulation of workflow versions are of significant importance to assist business process changes. Here, we summarise the requirements for version supports as follows:

- Version representation. A version representation method is expected to clearly depict the evolvement relation and dependency between versions of a workflow process definition.
- Version transformation. A set of modification operations are expected to transform a workflow process definition from one version to another on the fly.
- Version compatibility. For a workflow process definition, this denotes the compatibility that allows the workflow instances of different versions to be executed at the same time.
- Version extraction. For a workflow process definition, this stands for the process of dynamically deducing a specific version from a mass of version information during the execution period. This feature particularly helps the version change of workflow instances.

The whole lifecycle of business process changes comprises identifying tasks and links to replace, updating workflow processes, updating running workflow instances, together with version control and extraction, etc. Some work in adaptive workflow [7-9] and workflow evolution [10, 11] already addressed the issues of instance updating and process validation. Yet, to our best knowledge, few efforts have been put on the workflow version control in workflow process updating. This paper mainly targets at the process updating and the process version control. A particular versioning method is proposed to represent workflow process version evolvement; and a version preserving directed graph model is established to support the dynamic modifications and transformations of workflow process versions, as well as version compatibility. Additionally, two version extraction strategies are discussed with performance analysis.

3 Version Control in Business Process Change Management

This section discusses the version evolvement of workflow process definitions. A versioning method is proposed for workflow process definitions, and a version preserving directed graph is used to represent the version evolvement of workflow process definitions.

3.1 Workflow Process Version Evolvement

Once a workflow process definition is changed, a new version will be assigned to indicate the changed workflow process definition at this stage. In this way, a workflow process definition may own several versions during its lifecycle.

Currently, there are few standards specifying the versions of workflow process definitions. Some workflow products [12, 13] simply use the incremental numbering system that is widely used in the software development area, for versioning workflow process definitions. In such a versioning system, different numbers denote different versions, and dots separate main versions and sub versions [14]. Though this numbering system can well represent the inheritance relation in software development, yet it fails to represent some sporadic changes of a workflow process, where the inheritance relation does not exist between versions.

In contrary to the software development, a workflow process definition may evolve along two axes, i.e., the process improvement and the temporary adaptation. The process improvement denotes the permanent evolvement of a workflow process definition driven by technology upgrading or strategy changes; while the temporary adaptation denotes the variation of the workflow process definition driven by unit replacements or other sporadic reasons.

Here, we propose a new versioning method to represent the evolvement of a workflow process definition along the above two axes.

A version of a workflow process definition is defined as a three-digit string separated by dots, $x.y.z$, where,

- the first digit x denotes the major version of the workflow process definition;
- the second digit y denotes the minor version of the workflow process definition;
- the third digit z denotes the temporary variation of a workflow process definition.

The first two digits represent the progress of the process improvement; while the last digit denotes the temporary variation of a workflow process definition.

Figure 2 illustrates the version evolvement of the workflow process definition example discussed in Section 2, along the two axes.

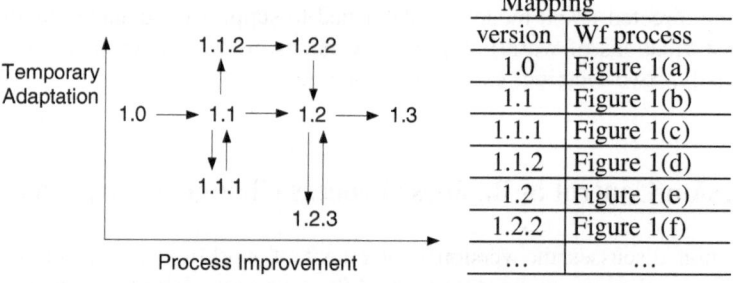

Mapping	
version	Wf process
1.0	Figure 1(a)
1.1	Figure 1(b)
1.1.1	Figure 1(c)
1.1.2	Figure 1(d)
1.2	Figure 1(e)
1.2.2	Figure 1(f)
...	...

Fig. 2. Workflow process evolvement figure

In Figure 2, the horizontal axis denotes the process improvement, and the vertical axis denotes the temporary adaptation. The mapping table illustrates the relation between versions and corresponding workflow process definitions. Here, we name the start version as the *base version* for all other versions. In Figure 1, version 1.0 is the base version. For version v, a version that contains a larger number for at least one of the first two digits and the other is no less than v's counterpart is called v's *subsequent version*. For examples, versions 1.2, 1.2.2 are subsequent versions of version 1.1.

In Figure 2, each arrow represents an evolvement from one version to another. For any version, there always exists a path leads from the base version to this version in this evolvement figure. Take version 1.2.2 as an example, the evolvement starts from base version, 1.0, to 1.1, then arrives to 1.1.2, and finally to 1.2.2. As discussed in the motivating example, a workflow process may have multiple evolvement branches. A good example is that from version 1.1, it has three possible evolvement branches, i.e., to version 1.2, to version 1.1.1 and to version 1.1.2. Choosing which route is dependant on the actual situation.

3.2 Version Preserving Directed Graph

Although a workflow process definition may change frequently, we need to minimise the effect to the execution of its workflow instances. Our primary intention is to keep the nodes and arcs of all the versions belonging to the same workflow process definition in a single graph. Figure 3 shows an example of such a graph according to the production workflow process discussed in the previous section. In this graph, each node represents a workflow task, and the versions of nodes and arcs are marked aside as labels.

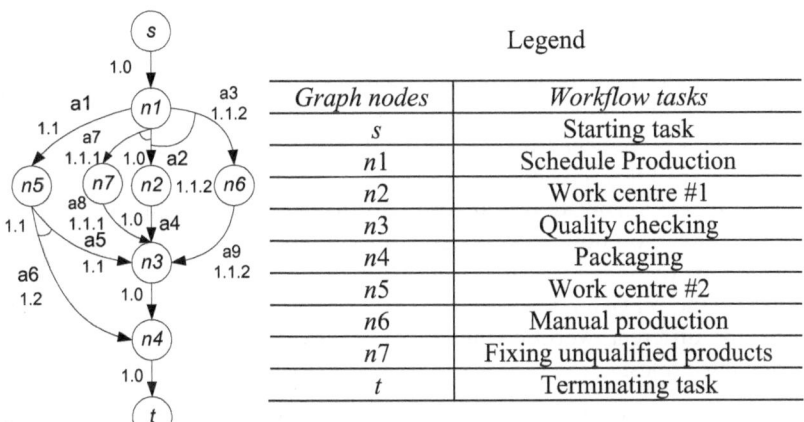

Graph nodes	Workflow tasks
s	Starting task
*n*1	Schedule Production
*n*2	Work centre #1
*n*3	Quality checking
*n*4	Packaging
*n*5	Work centre #2
*n*6	Manual production
*n*7	Fixing unqualified products
t	Terminating task

Fig. 3. An example of VPG

Obviously, there may exist exclusive branches between different versions. For example, from node *n*5 in Figure 3, a workflow instance of version 1.1 is only allowed to go through arc *a*5, yet a workflow instance of version 1.2 or 1.2.2 can only go through arc *a*6. In this situation, we call that arc *a*5 and arc *a*6 are in an exclusive relation.

In this methodology, we extend the conventional directed graph with enhancements for version control to model workflow process definitions in the business process change context. In particular, a version set, a version mapping and a binary relation are designed for the version preservation purpose. We name the extended graph as a *version preserving directed graph (VPG)*.

A VPG for a workflow process *p*, can be defined as a tuple ($\mathcal{N}$, $\mathcal{A}$, $\mathcal{V}$, f, $\mathcal{R}$), where,

– $\mathcal{N}$ is the set of nodes, where each node $v \in \mathcal{N}$ represents a workflow task of *p*. Additionally, there must exist one and only one starting node $s \in \mathcal{N}$ whose incoming degree is 0; and one and only one terminating node $t \in \mathcal{N}$ whose outgoing degree is 0. This means that a workflow process must have one and only one starting task, and one and only one terminating task;

- $\mathcal{A}$ is the set of arcs, where each arc $a \in \mathcal{A}$, represents a link connecting two workflow tasks of p;
- $\mathcal{V}$ is the set of version numbers, such as "1.1", "1.2", "1.2.2" etc.;
- $f: \mathcal{N} \cup \mathcal{A} \rightarrow \mathcal{V}$ is a mapping, which assigns proper version number to each node and arc in the graph;
- $\mathcal{R}$ is a binary relation $\{ (a1, a2) \mid a1, a2 \in \mathcal{A} \wedge a1$ and $a2$ are in the exclusive relation $\}$. With this binary relation, the exclusive relation between the arcs in a VPG can be easily represented. Note, here $\mathcal{R}$ only records the exclusive relation that are caused by versioning, not by business constraints.

In general, this graph keeps the version information in mapping f, stores the exclusive relation between arcs using relation $\mathcal{R}$, and represents the workflow structure with nodes and arcs.

Particularly, the VPG model tries to minimise the information to store, by dropping all deducible information. For example, arc $a6$ marked version 1.2 in Figure 3, represents the evolvement triggered by work centre #2's upgrading, which can be shared by the workflow processes of version 1.1.2 and version 1.1. Therefore, there is no need to create a new arc (exclusive to $a6$) from $n5$ to $n4$ with version 1.2.2. We will see that the workflow process definition of version 1.2.2 is deducible from the information for versions 1.0, 1.1, 1.2 and 1.1.2.

Based on the VPG for a specific workflow process, we can determine different versions for different workflow instances at any time during the execution, by following three rules:

Rule (1). Version v cannot include the arcs and nodes with v's subsequent versions.

Rule (2). The arcs and nodes with the version in the form of $x.y.z$ ($z \neq$ null) will not be included in the version in the form of $u.v.w$, where $w \neq z$.

For example, in Figure 3, $n1$, $a1$, $a5$ and $a7$ etc. are not includable in version 1.0, and $a6$ is not includable in version 1.1, because of Rule 1. $a7$, $a8$ and $n7$ are not includable in either version 1.1.2 or version 1.2.2, because of Rule 2.

Rule (3). The selection of an arc, with regards to the version in the form of $x.y.z$, from the set of arcs with an exclusive relation, is subject to the order of its version in the following priority list:

1. versions in the form of $x.y.z$;
2. versions in the form of $u.v.z$ ($u \neq x$ or $v \neq y$);
3. versions in the form of $x.y$;
4. versions in the form of $x.v$ ($v < y$, v is the closet to y);
5. versions in the form of $u.v$ ($u < x$, u is the closest to x, or v is the largest if u is the same).

The arcs with a version that is not listed in the priority list will not be considered.

For example, arcs a2, a3 and a7 are in an exclusive relation in Figure 3. For version 1.2.2, the selection priority is $a3>a2$, while $a7$ is not considered.

3.3 Run Time Operations

Obviously, it is unacceptable to suspend all running workflow instances for updating, thus all modifications are required to perform on the fly. Furthermore, such run time modifications are expected to be information preserved for previous versions. This is required to guarantee the consistency between workflow instances and the log information that is maintained by a workflow management system. The log records may have used the workflow process definition of previous versions, and the information about all these versions should be preserved. The loss of previous version information may disable the restoration of a workflow process back to a previous version after a temporary change.

In short, a run time modification operation should be *dynamic, information preserved* and *restorable*. In Table 1, we list the node modification operations, which satisfy all the three requirements.

Table 1. Node modification operations

Node modification operations			
Add a node		Remove a node	Replace a node
Sequential inserting	Parallel inserting		
$b \to \mathcal{N}$; create arc $a1= (n1, b)$, $a2=(b, n2)$; $a1 \to \mathcal{A}$; $a2 \to \mathcal{A}$; "1.1" $\to \mathcal{V}$; $(a1,$ "1.1") $\to f$; $(b,$ "1.1") $\to f$; $(a2,$ "1.1") $\to f$; $(a0, a1) \to \mathcal{R}$	$b \to \mathcal{N}$; create arc $a1=(n1, b)$, $a2=(b, n3)$; $a1 \to \mathcal{A}$; $a2 \to \mathcal{A}$; "1.1" $\to \mathcal{V}$; $(a1,$ "1.1") $\to f$; $(b,$ "1.1") $\to f$; $(a2,$ "1.1") $\to f$	create arc $a1=(n1, n3)$; $a1 \to \mathcal{A}$; "1.1" $\to \mathcal{V}$; $(a1,$ "1.1") $\to f$; $(a0, a1) \to \mathcal{R}$	$b \to \mathcal{N}$; create arc $a1= (n1, b)$, $a2=(b, n3)$; $a1 \to \mathcal{A}$; $a2 \to \mathcal{A}$; "1.1" $\to \mathcal{V}$; $(a1,$ "1.1") $\to f$; $(b,$ "1.1") $\to f$; $(a2,$ "1.1") $\to f$; $(a0, a1) \to \mathcal{R}$

In this table, each operation is illustrated by an example graph, where the boldfaced nodes or arcs denote the appended components of latest version, say 1.1 in this example, and an inclined angle between two arcs stands for the exclusive relation between these two arcs. Below each example graph, the corresponding codes are given for the modification operation.

Table 2 lists the arc modification operations.

In operation "remove an arc", as for the arc to remove, i.e., $a0$, its starting node, i.e., $n2$, must own more than one outgoing arc, to avoid a dead result node. In the example diagram, we see that $a0$ is first replaced by a new arc $a2$, and $a2$ in turn replaces an existing outgoing arc $a1$. Because $a2$ also links $n2$ to $n3$, it is equivalent to $a1$, but with different version. The result of this operation is equal to replace $a0$ with an existing arc.

Table 2. Arc modification operations

Arc modification operations		
Add an arc	*Replace an arc*	*Remove an arc*
create arc $a1$=$(n2, n3)$; $a1{\rightarrow}\mathcal{A}$; "1.1"${\rightarrow}\mathcal{V}$; $(a1,$ "1.1"$){\rightarrow}f$	*create arc* $a1$=$(n1, n4)$; $a1{\rightarrow}\mathcal{A}$; "1.1"${\rightarrow}\mathcal{V}$; $(a1,$ "1.1"$){\rightarrow}f$; $(a0, a1){\rightarrow}\mathcal{R}$	*create arc* $a1$=$(n2, n3)$; $A2{\rightarrow}\mathcal{A}$; "1.1"${\rightarrow}\mathcal{V}$; $(a1,$ "1.1"$){\rightarrow}f$; $(a0, a2){\rightarrow}\mathcal{R}$ $(a1, a2){\rightarrow}\mathcal{R}$

3.4 Updating a VPG

A VPG is updated without actual removal of any nodes or arcs, and it can preserve the information of previous versions in the same graph. There are two rules for updating a VPG with the discussed modification operations.

Rule (4) Horizontal evolvement. An evolvement from version $x.y1.z$ to version $x.y2.z$ ($y1 \neq y2$) is projected to an evolvement from version $x.y1$ to $x.y2$.

This rule means that all parallel horizontal evolvements can be represented by an evolvement along the process improvement axis, which indicates the permanent change to all parallel branch versions. This mechanism caters for the purpose of reusing versions.

Rule (5) Vertical evolvement. For two evolvements from version $x.y$ to $x.y.z$ and from $x1.y1$ to $x1.y1.z1$ ($z, z1 \neq$ null, $x \neq x1$ or $y \neq y1$), respectively, $z = z1$, if the two evolvements are caused by the same temporary change; otherwise $z \neq z1$.

This rule means that the third digit of a version identifies the reason for the evolvement along temporary adaptation axis.

Consider the production workflow process discussed in Section 2. The initial workflow process can be represented as a VPG shown in Figure 4 (a), where all nodes and arcs are marked as version 1.0. When the workflow process evolves to version 1.1 as an additional work centre is inserted, the VPG will be updated to Figure 4 (b) with an "insert a parallel task" operation. The inserted arcs and nodes, i.e., $a1$, $a5$ and $n5$, are marked with version 1.1, according to Rule 4. Following this, when the workflow process for a pipeline evolves to version 1.1.1 as task "work centre #1" is replaced by task "fixing unqualified products", the VPG will be updated to Figure 4 (c) with an "replace a task" operation. The added arcs and nodes, i.e., *a*7, *a*8 and *n*7, are marked with version 1.1.1. While, the workflow process for another pipeline may replace task "work centre #1" with "manual production", and therefore evolves to version 1.1.2 with the VPG shown in Figure 4 (d). The added arcs *a*3 and *a*9 and node *n*6 are marked with version 1.1.2. Thus, we see that these two versions are marked differently at digit *z*, because their evolvements are initiated by different temporary changes, according to Rule 5.

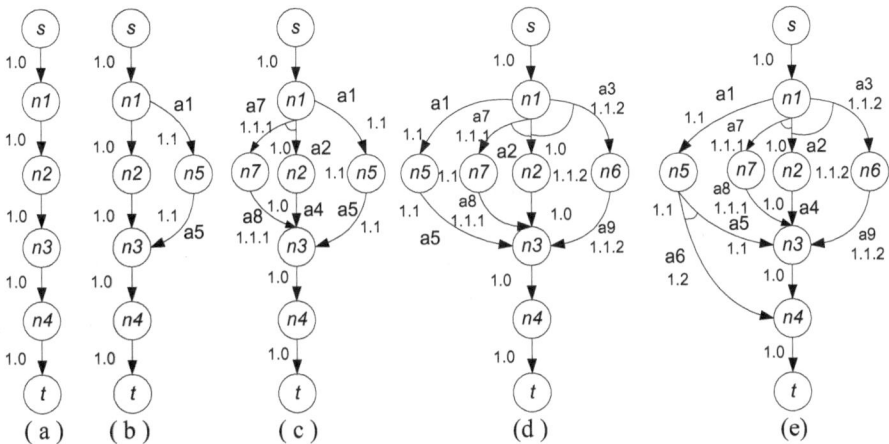

Fig. 4. VPG samples

When handling the evolvement to version 1.2.2, we need to note that arc *a*6 is added by a "replace an arc" operation, as shown in Figure 4 (e). According to Rule 4, *a*6 is marked with version 1.2 instead of 1.2.2. This denotes that the insertion of arc *a*6 represents a permanent change rather than a temporary change. Though there are no nodes or arcs marked with version 1.2.2 in Figure 4 (e), version 1.2.2 can be obtained by aggregating the arcs and nodes of version 1.2 and 1.1.2. In this way, the stored information can be maximally reused, and in turn, a better space efficiency is obtained.

As a VPG records the key changes during evolvements of a workflow process, its arcs and nodes cover all possible combinations of workflow evolvements. For example, we mentioned that version 1.2.2 can be deduced from the VPG, even version 1.2.2 does not appear in the VPG at all. This feature reflects the strong expression ability of the VPG, as it can deduce any version that exists in the real evolvement situation. In addition, a VPG can also deduce any version that is achievable during evolvements of it workflow process definition. For example, version 1.2.1 is achievable so it can also be deduced from the VPG in Figure 4 (e).

4 Runtime Version Management

A VPG contains the information of different versions of a workflow process definition. However, many workflow management operations, such as initiating workflow instances, reviewing workflow processes, etc., only refer to a workflow process definition of a specific version. This requires the capability of dynamically extracting a workflow process definition of a specific version from the changing VPG.

Basically, the extraction can be achieved with two different strategies, viz., backward assembling and top-down exploration. The following two sections are to discuss these two strategies, respectively.

4.1 Backward Assembling Strategy

The most direct strategy is to start with the nodes and arcs with the requested version, or the closest to the requested version if the requested one does not exist in the VPG. Then, it continues with searching and assembling the nodes and arcs with versions in the priority list discussed in Rule 3 of Section 3.2, in a descending order.

Before collecting the nodes and arcs of the next highest priority, we need to delete all arcs that are in an exclusive relation with any collected arc. This removal may result in some unreachable nodes, i.e., nodes with no incoming arcs. These unreachable nodes need to be deleted, and in turn, we need to remove those arcs connect to these nodes.

This collecting and removing process keeps running until all arcs or nodes with the versions on the priority list are handled. For example, suppose we extract a workflow process definition of version 1.2.2 from the VPG shown in Figure 4 (e). According to the priority sequence, version 1.1.2 holds the highest priority among all the versions contained in the VPG. Thus, we first collect all arcs and nodes with version 1.1.2, viz. arc $a3$, $a9$ and $n6$. Afterwards, we find that arcs $a7$ and $a2$ are in the exclusive relation with a collected arc $a3$, therefore $a2$ and $a7$ are removed from the VPG. Thereafter, nodes $n2$ and $n7$ are deleted as they become unreachable, and then arcs $a4$ and $a8$ are deleted too for the same reason. After that, arc $a6$ is collected, as version 1.2 holds the highest priority in the remaining VPG, while arc $a5$ is removed due to its exclusive relation with $a6$. The workflow process definition of version 1.2.2 will be obtained after we handle the nodes and arcs of the base version, i.e., version 1.0. Algorithm 1 formalises the extraction procedure under this strategy.

In this algorithm, Function $relatedArcs(\mathcal{G}, ASet)$ returns the set of arcs that are in an exclusive relation with the arcs in set $ASet$ in VPG $\mathcal{G}$; Function $in(\mathcal{G}, n)$ returns the in-degree of node n in VPG $\mathcal{G}$; Fucntion $outArcs(\mathcal{G}, n)$ returns a set of node n's outgoing arcs in VPG $\mathcal{G}$; Function $linkedNode(\mathcal{G}, a)$; returns the node that arc a links to in VPG $\mathcal{G}$; Function $highestVer(\mathcal{G}, v)$ returns the version with the currently highest priority in VPG $\mathcal{G}$ with version v.

Algorithm 1. Backward assembling

Input	$\mathcal{G}$	-	The VPG for a workflow process definition
	v	-	The requested version
Output	$\mathcal{G}'$	-	The graph for the workflow process definition of the requested version

1.	$ATarget = \varnothing$; $NTarget = \varnothing$;
2.	**add** the nodes and arcs of version $highestVer(\ \mathcal{G},\ v\ )$ **to** sets $NTemp$ and $ATemp$, respectively;
3.	$A = relatedArcs(\ \mathcal{G}, ATemp\ )$;
4.	**while** ($A \neq \varnothing$) **do**
5.	**pick** arc $a \in A$
6.	$n = linkedNode(\ \mathcal{G}, a\ )$;
7.	**if** $in(\ n\ ) = 1$ **then**
8.	$A = A \cup outArcs(\ n\ )$;
9.	**delete** n **from** $\mathcal{G}$;
10.	**end if**
11.	**delete** a **from** A **and** $\mathcal{G}$;
12.	**end while**
13.	$NTarget = NTarget \cup NTemp$;
14.	$ATarget = ATarget \cup ATemp$;
15.	**delete** the arcs and nodes in $ATemp$ and $NTemp$ **from** $\mathcal{G}$;
16.	$ATemp = \varnothing$; $NTemp = \varnothing$
17.	**if** $highestVer(\ \mathcal{G}, v\ )$ is not *null* **then goto** line 2;
18.	$\mathcal{G}' = (\ NTarget, ATarget\ )$;

This algorithm uses sets *NTemp* and *ATemp* to keep the newly collected nodes and arcs, respectively. Set *A* temporarily stores the arcs to be deleted from the VPG. After picking an arc *a* in set *A*, the algorithm will check whether *a* is the only incoming arc to its linked node *n*. If so, node *n* will be deleted with *a* from the VPG, and the outgoing arcs of *n* will be inserted to set *A* for future checking. The collected nodes and arcs will be inserted to the result graph by moving the elements in *NTemp* and *ATemp* to *NTarget* and *ATarget*, respectively.

4.2 Top-Down Exploration Strategy

Another strategy is to search for the requested version from the top of a VPG. For each outgoing arc, if it has a version in the priority list with regard to the requested version and is not in an exclusive relation with any other arcs, it will be collected. As to the arcs in an exclusive relation, we need to select one proper arc that owns the highest priority among the exclusively coupled peers. The arcs and nodes with a version that is not in the priority list will not be considered at all.

For example, suppose we also extract a workflow process definition of version 1.2.2 from the VPG shown in Figure 4 (e). The extraction process starts from the starting node *s*, and then comes to node *n1* which has four outgoing arcs, viz., *a1*, *a2*, *a3* and *a7*. Here, *a1* is not in an exclusive relation with other three arcs, and version

1.1 meets the fourth requirement of the priority with regard to version 1.2.2 (please refer to Rule 3). Thus, $a1$ will be first selected. As to the three exclusively coupled arcs, $a3$ with version 1.1.2 holds a higher priority than the other two peers, $a2$ with version 1.0 and $a7$ with version 1.1.1. Thus, only $a3$ is selected, while $a2$ and $a7$ are not considered. This process goes on as the trace flows along the collected arcs, and finally we can obtain the nodes and arcs for version 1.2.2 when the trace ends at the terminating node, t. Algorithm 2 formalises the extraction procedure under this strategy.

In this algorithm, Fucntion $outArcs(\mathcal{G}, n)$ returns a set of node n's outgoing arcs in VPG $\mathcal{G}$; Function $coulpedArcs(\mathcal{G}, n)$ returns a set of node n's outgoing arcs that are in the exclusive relation in VPG $\mathcal{G}$; Funcntion $pickPriorityArc(ASet, v)$ returns the arc with the highest priority with regard to version v among set $ASet$; Function $checkNodes(\mathcal{G}, a)$ returns the set of nodes that arc a links to in VPG $\mathcal{G}$.

Algorithm 2. Top-down exploration

Input	$\mathcal{G}$	-	The VPG for a workflow process definition
	v	-	The requested version
Output	$\mathcal{G}'$	-	The graph for the workflow process definition of the requested version

1.	$NTarget = \varnothing$; $ATarget = \varnothing$;
2.	$NTemp = \{ \mathcal{G}.s \}$;
3.	**while** ($NTemp \neq \varnothing$) **do**
4.	**for each** $n \in NTemp$
5.	$A = coulpedArcs(\mathcal{G}, n)$;
6.	$ATemp = outArcs(\mathcal{G}, n) - A$;
7.	$ATemp = ATemp \bigcup \{ pickPriorityArc(A, v) \}$;
8.	$NTarget = NTarget \bigcup \{ n \}$;
9.	**end for**
10.	$NTemp = \varnothing$;
11.	**for each** $a \in ATemp$
12.	$NTemp = NTemp \bigcup (checkNodes(\mathcal{G}, a) - NTarget)$;
13.	**end for**
14.	$ATarget = ATarget \bigcup ATemp$;
15.	**end while**
16.	$\mathcal{G}' = (NTarget, ATarget)$;

This algorithm starts searching from the starting node, s, and collects the includable nodes and arcs in sets $NTarget$ and $ATarget$. When the search arrives to the outgoing arcs of the collected nodes, the algorithm (line 4 to line 9) checks whether the arcs are collectable by referring to the priority sequence and the exclusive relation. The search moves on to the nodes to which are linked from the newly collected arcs, and checks whether these nodes have been collected before to reduce potential redundant processing. Finally, the search terminates when it arrives to node t.

4.3 Strategy Analysis

Under the backward assembling strategy, the algorithm needs to process most nodes and arcs. Whiling removing an arc that is in the exclusive relation with a collected arc, it may result in a chain reaction that may cause the linked node to be with no incoming arcs, and therefore the removal of this node and all its outgoing arcs. This process may cover a lot of nodes and arcs in the graph, no matter these nodes or arcs are really useful for the extraction or not. In fact, for version v, the arcs and nodes belonging to v's subsequent versions have nothing to do with the extraction of version v, because these arcs and nodes only serve for the evolvements occurred after version v. Additionally, the arcs and nodes belonging to v's parallel branch versions, offer no contributions, either. For example, the components for version 1.1.1 do not contribute to the extraction of version 1.1.2. However, the backward assembling strategy still processes the components of version 1.1.1 during the extraction of version 1.1.2.

In contrast, the top-down exploration strategy is more intelligent. When the top-down exploration strategy comes across a splitting structure, it leaves all irrelevant arcs untouched as long as they are not in the priority list with regard to the requested version. Thereby, this strategy pleasantly sidesteps the searching with irrelevant nodes or arcs, and in turn it outperforms the backward assembling strategy. As the version extraction is a frequent operation for a VPG, this improvement can lead to a considerable performance gain.

5 Related Work and Discussion

Workflow evolution is the most related to version management. Casati et al., [10] presented a workflow modification language (WFML) to support modifications of a workflow model. They also discussed the case evolution policies and devised three main policies to manage case evolution, viz., abort, flush and progressive. The proposed language contains declaration primitives and flow primitives for the changes of workflow variables and flow structures.

Work in adaptive workflows, addresses run time modifications for dynamic exception handling purpose. Hamadi and Benatallah [7] proposed a self-adaptive recovery net (SARN) to support workflow adaptability during unexpected failures. This net extends Petri net by deploying recovery tokens and recovery transitions to represent the dynamic adaptability of a workflow process, and a set of operations are used to modify the net structure.

In project ADEPT$_{flex}$ [15, 16], Rinderle, Reichert and Dadam did extensive studies on schema evolution in process management systems, which covered common workflow type and instance changes, as well as disjoint and overlapping process changes. Their work formally specified the change operations to both process schemas and workflow instances, as well as the related migration policies in handling potential conflicts.

In Sadiq et al.'s work on process constraints for flexible workflows [17], they proposed the concept of "pockets of flexibility" to allow ad hoc changes and/or building of workflows, for highly flexible processes.

Unfortunately, none of the above work mentions the versions of workflows. Therefore, they can hardly keep the trail about a series of evolutions and change-backs, or only support a kind of one-off modifications. The transformation between subsequent versions or sibling versions is not touched, let alone the compatibility of multiple workflow versions.

Kradolfer and Geppert [11] presented a framework for dynamic workflow schema evolution based on workflow type versioning and workflow migration. In their work, a version tree was proposed to represent the evolvement of a workflow schema, and to keep track of the resulting history. However, the version tree only provides primitive supports for version management. Typically, to re-assign a pervious version to a running workflow instance, this method has to perform a series of inverse modification operations to achieve that version along the version tree. Yet, in our VPG approach, the version re-assignment can be easily realised by switching to the requested version according to the VPG.

In summary, our VPG approach has the following appealing features for business process change management:

- Dynamic updating

The proposed version preserving directed graph allows dynamic modifications without suspending running workflow instances. The defined modification operations preserve all the information during the modification on the fly. We can extract a workflow process definition of any version at any time. This feature enhances the flexibility of workflow technology at process level.

- Multiple version compatibility

A VPG allows the co-existence of workflow instances of different versions in a single graph. With the help of its strong expressive ability, this VPG provides enough navigation information for a workflow engine to execute these workflow instances. This feature enhances the flexibility of workflow technology at instance level.

- Compact model

Compared with other work, a VPG is a lightweight graph model for representing workflow evolvements. With the defined modification operations and proposed rules, a VPG preserves all information for existing versions, and it can derive a meaningful version that may not explicitly appear in the graph.

6 Conclusion and Future Work

This paper addressed the version control of workflow process definition in the business process change context. A versioning method was designed to represent the workflow evolvement along the axes for both temporary changes and permanent improvements. A novel version preserving directed graph, together with a series of run time modification operations, were proposed to update a workflow process definition on the fly. Strategies on extracting a workflow process definition of a given version from the corresponding version preserving directed graph were also discussed. Our future work is to incorporate the handover policies with our version control method, and provide a comprehensive solution for workflow version control.

References

[1] Smith, H., Fingar, P.: Business Process Management - The Third Wave: Meghan-Kiffer Press (2003)

[2] van der Aalst, W.M.P., ter Hofstede, A.H.M., Weske, M.: Business Process Management: A Survey. In: Proceedings of International Conference on Business Process Management, pp. 1–12 (2003)

[3] Khoshafian, S.: Service Oriented Enterprise: Auerbach Publisher (2006)

[4] Kock, N.: System Analysis & Design Fundamentals - A Business Process Redesign Approach. Sage Publications, Inc., Thousand Oaks (2006)

[5] Zhao, X., Liu, C., Yang, Y., Sadiq, W.: Handling Instance Correspondence in Inter-Organisational Workflows. In: Proceedings of the 19th International Conference on Advanced Information Systems Engineering (CAiSE'07), Trondheim, Norway, pp. 51–65 (2007)

[6] Liu, C., Orlowska, M.E., Li, H.: Automating Handover in Dynamic Workflow Environments. In: Proceedings of 10th International Conference on Advanced Information Systems Engineering, Pisa, Italy, pp. 159–171 (1998)

[7] Hamadi, R., Benatallah, B.: Recovery Nets: Towards Self-Adaptive Workflow Systems. In: Proceedings of the 5th International Conference on Web Information Systems Engineering, Brisbane, Australia, pp. 439–453 (2004)

[8] Kammer, P.J., Bolcer, G.A., Taylor, R.N., Hitomi, A.S., Bergman, M.: Techniques for Supporting Dynamic and Adaptive Workflow. Computer Supported Cooperative Work 9, 269–292 (2000)

[9] Narendra, N.C.: Flexible Support and Management of Adaptive Workflow Processes. Information Systems Frontiers 6, 247–262 (2004)

[10] Casati, F., Ceri, S., Pernici, B., Pozzi, G.: Workflow Evolution. Data & Knowledge Engineering 24, 211–238 (1998)

[11] Kradolfer, M., Geppert, A.: Dynamic Workflow Schema Evolution Based on Workflow Type Versioning and Workflow Migration. In: Proceedings of International Conference on Cooperative Information Systems, Edinburgh, Scotland, pp.104–114 (1999)

[12] IBM: IBM WebSphere Business Integration Handbook (2005)

[13] SAP: SAP Business Workflow and WebFlow Documentation

[14] Conradi, R., Westfechtel, B.: Version Models for Software Configuration Management. ACM Computing Surveys 30(2), 232–282 (1998)

[15] Reichert, M., Dadam, P.: ADEPTflex -Supporting Dynamic Changes of Workflows without Losing Control. Journal of Intelligent Information Systems 10, 93–129 (1998)

[16] Rinderle, S., Reichert, M., Dadam, P.: Disjoint and Overlapping Process Changes: Challenges, Solutions, Applications. In: Proceedings of 12th International Conference on Cooperative Information Systems, Agia Napa, Cyprus, pp. 101–120 (2004)

[17] Sadiq, S.W., Orlowska, M.E., Sadiq, W.: Specification and Validation of Process Constraints for Flexible Workflows. Information System 30, 349–378 (2005)

BPEL^light

Jörg Nitzsche, Tammo van Lessen, Dimka Karastoyanova, and Frank Leymann

Institute of Architecture of Application Systems
University of Stuttgart
Universitaetsstrasse 38, 70569 Stuttgart, Germany
{joerg.nitzsche,tammo.van.lessen,dimka.karastoyanova,
frank.leymann}@iaas.uni-stuttgart.de
http://www.iaas.uni-stuttgart.de

Abstract. In this paper we present BPEL^light which decouples process logic from interface definitions. By extending BPEL 2.0 with a WSDL-less interaction model, BPEL^light allows to specify process models independent of Web service technology. Since its interaction model is based on plain message exchange, it is completely independent of any interface description language. This fosters flexibility and reusability of process models and enables modelling platform and component model independent business processes. The presented approach takes a significant step towards narrowing down the gap between business level and IT level by facilitating a more business-oriented modelling of executable processes.

Keywords: BPM, Workflow, BPEL, SOA, Web services, flexibility, reusability.

1 Introduction

Business Process Management (BPM) and the workflow technology [1,2] in particular has become a very successful area with heavy impact on industry and research. Process orientation has been discussed for many years but with the emergence of Web Services [3,4] (WS) which is the most popular implementation of a service oriented architecture [5,6] (SOA) workflow technology and BPM got established to a great extent. The separation of business process logic and separate implementation of business functions enables programming on a higher, i.e. business process oriented level [7]. A workflow comprises 3 dimensions: process logic ('what' is to be done), organization ('who' does it) and infrastructure ('which' tools are used). There are two major standards for business processes. The execution centric Business Process Execution Language [8] (BPEL) has currently been approved as an OASIS[1] standard and the modelling focussed Business Process Modelling Notation (BPMN) [9] is standardized by OMG[2]. BPEL is part of the WS standard stack and is therefore based on WSs in particular on the Web Service Description Language [10] (WSDL). The 'who' dimension is not supported yet and the 'which' dimension is simply based on WSs.

---

[1] http://www.oasis-open.org/
[2] http://www.omg.org/

G. Alonso, P. Dadam, and M. Rosemann (Eds.): BPM 2007, LNCS 4714, pp. 214–229, 2007.

In BPEL the 'what' and 'which' dimensions are strongly coupled since activities which are an aspect of the process logic ('what') directly refer to WSDL operations ('which'). This is a major drawback because it inhibits the reuse of processes or parts thereof in different contexts with different partners. Also this ties BPEL to WSDL for referring to activity implementations.

With BPEL^{light} we present an approach that gets over these deficiencies. First, we use BPEL's extensibility mechanisms to define a unified interaction model by introducing a new, single type of interaction activity resuming all interaction activities [3] currently defined by BPEL. Second, BPEL^{light} enables a strict decoupling of business logic and interface definitions (port types); as a result, interfaces in BPEL^{light} processes can be described via any interface definition languages (IDL, including WSDL). Without the fixed dependency on WSDL, BPEL^{light} can be used even in non-WS environments (*WSDL-less BPEL*). Especially, partner services even do not have to be described in terms of interface definitions at all: It is sufficient to describe how the process wants to interact with a partner in terms of a bilateral message exchange. Such a message exchange can be mapped to appropriate interfaces during deployment or even during runtime via proper tools and middleware. This results in a more business-like modelling style supported by BPEL^{light} and is a significant step towards narrowing down the gap between business level (e.g. BPMN) and IT level (BPEL).

Also, our approach fosters both, reusability and flexibility of processes. Since BPEL^{light} describes interactions in terms of message exchanges only, i.e. independent of interface definitions, processes or process fragments can be reused and bound to specific interfaces in any IDL. Binding may even happen during runtime, e.g. proper middleware can dynamically decide on an appropriate interface and corresponding implementation.

Our paper is structured as follows. Section 2 provides an overview of BPEL's interaction model. The subsequent section (3) introduces and discusses two different approaches of WSDL-less BPEL. In section 4 BPEL^{light} is presented. Section 5 shows how to realize BPEL's interaction semantics using BPEL^{light} in conjunction with WSDL. Section 6 discusses and summarizes the advantages of BPEL^{light} compared to conventional BPEL.

2   BPEL

BPEL is the de facto standard for specifying business processes in a WS world and has gained broad acceptance in industry and research. It enables both, the composition of WSs [3] and rendering the composition itself as WSs. Thus, BPEL provides a recursive aggregation model for WSs. Currently, extensions to BPEL are developed to support human interactions (BPEL4People [11]) and use of sub-processes (BPEL-SPE [12]). The composition of WSs can be specified as a flow between operations of WS. Therefore BPEL provides several so called *structured activities* that facilitate prescribing the control flow between the *interaction activities*. BPEL does not support explicit data flow; instead, data is stored in shared variables that are referenced and accessed by interaction activities and manipulation activities (e.g. <assign> activity). The control flow between activities can be structured either block-based by nesting structured activities like <sequence> (for sequential control flow), <flow> (for parallel control flow) and <if> (for conditional branches in the control flow) activities, or graph-based by defining <links> (i.e. directed edges) between activities in a <flow> activity; both styles can be used intermixed.

Since BPEL processes are intended to support robust applications, transactionality and fault handling are an integral part of BPEL and are defined by means of scopes, compensation handlers and fault handlers. Scopes represent units of works with compensation-based recovery semantics. Fault and compensation handlers are attached to a scope: fault handlers define how to proceed when faults occur, compensation handlers define how to compensate already completed activities in a custom manner.

WSs rendering process instances typically have state. Therefore it is important that messages can be sent to a particular process instance. This can be either achieved by using a standard BPEL mechanism called correlation sets, or by using WS-Addressing [13]. Correlation sets are based on pointing to key fields embedded in messages exchanged between the process instance and its partners.

In order to enable communication with other services or processes BPEL introduces the concept of a partner link type which is defined as an extension to WSDL. A partner link type binds two port types, namely a port type the process offers to a partner and a port type the process requires from the corresponding partner.

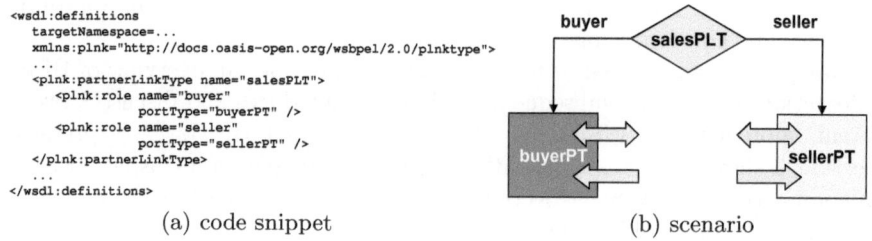

(a) code snippet   (b) scenario

Fig. 1. The WSDL extension <partnerLinkType>

Figure 1 shows an example of such a partner link type. It defines a channel (*salesPLT*) between two abstract business partners (roles) called *buyer* and *seller* through which the partners exchange messages; these roles are defined as port types, in the example *buyerPT* and *sellerPT*. In cases of a process synchronously interacting with a partner, such a channel is just unidirectional, i.e. the corresponding partner link type contains a single role. In order to establish a contract (i.e. an agreement between two partners which message channel to use), BPEL's partner links reference a partner link type and specify which role is taken by the process itself (myRole) and which role is taken by the partner (partnerRole).

The interaction activities [3] (`<receive>`, `<reply>`, `<invoke>`, `<pick>`) and the event handlers are used to define the actual message exchange corresponding to a partner link, i.e. data transmitted and style of communication (synchronous vs. asynchronous). For that purpose, interaction activities reference a partner link and a WSDL operation. Receiving activities (i.e. `<receive>` and `<pick>`) and the `<reply>` activity as well as the event handler reference an operation of the process's port type, whereas the `<invoke>` activity references an operation of the partner's port type. Note, that a synchronous invocation of a process is specified via a receiving activity and a matching reply activity.

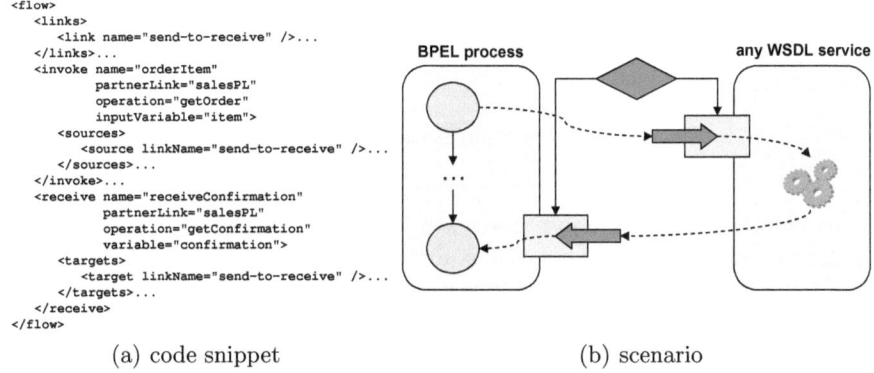

(a) code snippet   (b) scenario

Fig. 2. Asynchronous invocation of a WSDL service

Figure 2 illustrates the use of an `<invoke>` and a `<receive>` activity to model an asynchronous invocation of a partner via two one-way operations. The partner link used within this example references the partner link type given in Figure 1 and defines `myRole="buyer"` and `partnerRole="seller"`.

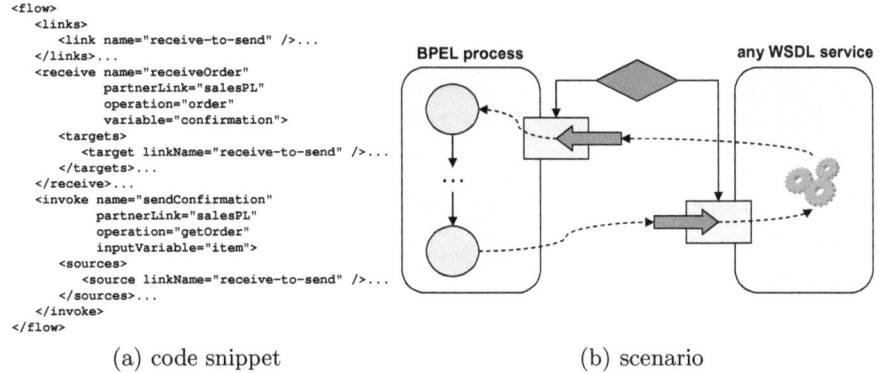

(a) code snippet   (b) scenario

Fig. 3. Asynchronous invocation of a BPEL process

An example of an asynchronous invocation of the process is shown in Figure 3. In this example the partner link type presented in Figure 1 is also used but the partner link defines myRole="seller" and partnerRole="buyer".

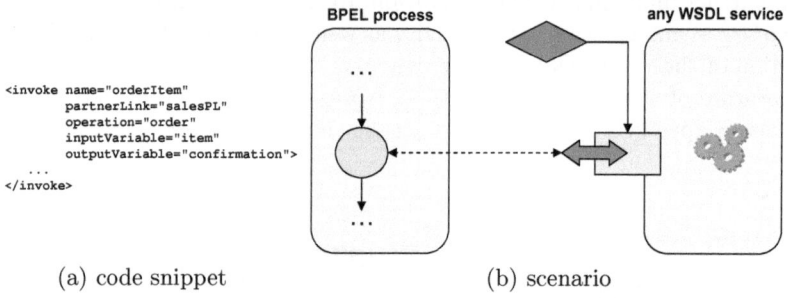

(a) code snippet   (b) scenario

Fig. 4. Synchronous invocation of a WSDL service

The simple synchronous use cases are illustrated in Figure 4 and Figure 5. The former shows how a synchronous invocation of a service can be modelled: The <invoke> activity of the process uses a request-response operation (*order*) provided by the partner service. In this case only the partner role of the *salesPL* is specified. The latter depicts a synchronous invocation of the process. It is realized by a <receive>-<reply> pair referencing the *order* operation the process offers. The partner link only specifies the myRole part of the partner link definition.

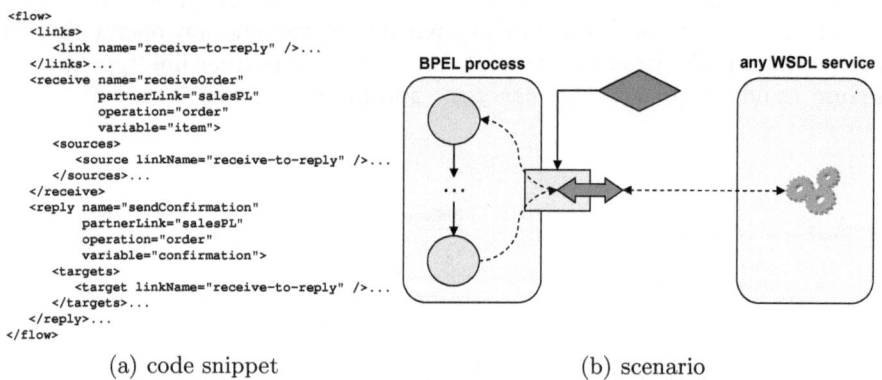

(a) code snippet   (b) scenario

Fig. 5. Synchronous invocation of a BPEL process

The <pick> activity and the <eventHandler> play a special role with respect to the WSDL dependency since they do not depend on WSDL itself but encapsulate elements which references a WSDL operation, the <onMessage> element and <onEvent> element respectively.

Both the interaction activities and the grouping mechanism that allows modelling complex message exchanges depend on WSDL. For this reason, reusability and flexibility of BPEL processes or parts of processes (process fragments) are very limited. In the next section we present two approaches that decouple process logic from the WSDL interfaces (or any other interface descriptions) and thus increase reusability and flexibility of the processes and process fragments.

3   The Notion of WSDL-Less BPEL

There are two major shortcomings of BPEL: limited reusability of (parts of) processes and lack of flexibility in terms of interfaces.

Hard-coding (partner) interfaces in the process logic limits reusability. Assume a process sends a message to a partner service, receives a response and dependent on this response different branches are taken in the subsequent flow. This combination of an interaction activity and a decision taken occurs very often in processes [14] and thus is a good candidate for reuse ("process fragment"). However, since such a fragment is bound to specific WSDL operations it cannot be reused in other scenarios where the same logic is required but the interaction is specified in terms of different WSDL operations and different WSDL port types.

The other downside of hard-coding interfaces in process logic is lack of flexibility. Only services that implement the predefined WSDL interface can be used during process execution, whereas services that provide the same functionality but implement a different interface are excluded from the service discovery procedure.

In addition, explicitly specifying partner interfaces in a process definition results in tight-coupling of the two dimensions of WS composition, namely process logic ('what') and activity implementations ('which'). For instance, modelling a two-way invoke enforces the use of exactly a WSDL request-response operation at the partner side. However, such a two-way message exchange pattern [15] could be realized by two one-way operations, increasing flexibility by weakening the assumption on the concrete type of WSDL operation to be used. Thus, it should be sufficient to model an activity with one outgoing message and one incoming message, and leaving the selection of the proper WSDL operation(s) and interaction style to the supporting middleware. In this case, the BPEL navigator must understand that the activity is only completed after a response message has been received. We argue that this drawback is eliminated by decoupling the 'what' and 'which' dimensions, and thus separate process logic and communication.

We identify two possible approaches for discarding the static specification of port types and operations in processes and thus improving process reusability and flexibility. These alternative approaches will be presented in the following sections.

3.1   Profile for Abstract BPEL

BPEL enables the definition of profiles for abstract processes. These profiles enable omitting information that is necessary for describing an executable BPEL process. The BPEL 2.0 specification identifies two use cases for abstract processes: (i) definition of the *observable behaviour* of a process, (ii) definition of process *templates*.

However, it is envisioned that there are other use cases for profiles of abstract processes. Thus, the BPEL specification defines a starting point for abstract profiles, the *Common Base* that defines the syntactic form to which all abstract processes have to conform. The Common Base defines that activities, expressions, attributes and from-specifications may be hidden by replacing them with opaque tokens. However, it does not define the semantics of an abstract process. The semantics have to be defined in a profile. Additionally, the profile defines more precisely which information may be omitted. The profile for observable behaviour for instance defines, that the interaction activities themselves and the attributes `partnerLink` and `operation` must not be opaque.

Following the generic approach of abstract profiles enables specifying a profile that allows omitting WSDL specific details and thereby increases reusability of process models. This approach is for instance used in [16] to define a language for choreographies using BPEL.

3.2   Extensions to Executable BPEL

BPEL is designed to be extensible. BPEL 1.1 [17] can be extended by defining new attributes and standard elements. However, in BPEL 1.1 the extensibility is limited since there is no way to introduce new activity types without violating the BPEL Schema and specification and losing BPEL compliance. In order to eliminate this drawback BPEL 2.0 [8] introduces the `<extensionActivity>` that is the designated extension point for new activity types. Additionally, BPEL 2.0 facilitates defining custom assign operations. In both specifications the extensions must not change the semantics of the BPEL language. The extensibility features of BPEL can be used to define new interaction activity types that do not reference WSDL interfaces. In particular this can be done using the `<extensionActivity>` mechanism. This implies that a new partner link definition (WSDL-less partner link) is necessary, which also does not refer to a WSDL definition. This way BPEL enables defining a WSDL-less interaction model by introducing new WSDL-less activity types and partner links.

3.3   Discussion

The approach of creating a profile for abstract BPEL allows omitting WSDL specific details during design time and thereby increasing reusability of abstract processes. However, when completing such an abstract process into an executable process the 'what' dimension and the 'which' dimension are coupled, and the BPEL process depends on WSDL again. For this reason, the approach using profiles for abstract BPEL results in design time flexibility only, improving the reusability of process definitions only during the modelling phase.

The WSDL-less interaction model defined using BPEL's extensibility mechanism provides for flexibility of process models at modelling time and at execution time. This results in reusable executable processes and process fragments. The flexibility of executable processes is further increased because WSDL interfaces of partners are no longer part of process models: Activities are bound during deployment or even as late as runtime to proper implementations. Obviously, this requires proper tooling and runtime support [18]. Moreover, interface definitions are not restricted to be specified in WSDL, but rather any other IDLs can be used.

Since our second approach is more powerful the rest of the paper is focussed on that. The extended BPEL language we introduce in the next section is a lightweight version of BPEL that can be applied for specifying business processes not only in WS-* environments. We call this language BPEL^{light}.

4   BPEL^{light}

BPEL^{light} is an extension of BPEL 2.0 [8], i.e. the existing semantics of the language remains unchanged, including variable handling and typing. It defines a new mechanism to describe the interaction between two partners without dependency on WSDL and therefore it decouples the two dimensions of BPEL processes, namely 'what' and 'which'. BPEL^{light} introduces new elements in a separate namespace[3] which represent a WSDL-less conversation between partners using WSDL-less interaction activities. We describe the BPEL^{light} interaction model and enhance and adapt the concept of uniquely identifiable partners to support stateful WSDL-less conversations.

4.1   The BPEL^{light} Interaction Model

We define the BPEL^{light} interaction model in terms of two elements, namely `<conversation>` and `<interactionActivity>`.

The `<conversation>` element plays the role of a WSDL-less partner link not referencing a partner link type. Thus it defines a contract between two partners independent of their WSDL port types, i.e. interfaces. The `<conversation>` element allows grouping of interaction activities and thus enables defining a complex message exchange between two partners. Hence the requirements to the partner service is not expressed using WSDL port types, but rather by the ability to send messages to and receive messages from a process during a conversation.

Similarly to the `<partnerLink>` which is defined in the `<partnerLinks>` section, every `<conversation>` is defined within a `<conversations>` element. The syntax is shown in Listing 1.

In order to decouple the interaction activities from the activity implementation dimension ('which') we define interaction activities that do not refer to WSDL interfaces. The interaction activities defined in BPEL (`<receive>`, `<reply>`, `<invoke>` and `<onMessage>` within a `<pick>`) cannot be used since the WSDL specific attributes `partnerLink` and `operation` are mandatory. These new interaction activities can model simple and complex message exchanges with a partner by referencing a `<conversation>` element.

---

[3] `xmlns:bl=http://iaas.uni-stuttgart.de/BPELlight/`

```
<bl:conversations>
    <bl:conversation name="NCName"/>+
</bl:conversations>
```

Listing 1. The `<conversation>` element

In BPEL[light] we utilize the `<extensionActivity>` mechanism to introduce a new activity type – the `<interactionActivity>` (see Listing 2). This activity type is capable of modelling all interaction activities defined in BPEL. Additionally, it can be configured to represent an activity that receives a message and is not completed before sending a response message.

```
<extensionActivity>
    <bl:interactionActivity name="NCName"
                            inputVariable="NCName"?
                            outputVariable="NCName"?
                            mode="in-out|out-in"?
                            conversation="NCName"
                            createInstance="yes|no"?
                            standard-attributes>
        standard-elements
    </bl:interactionActivity>
</extensionActivity>
```

Listing 2. BPEL[light]'s `<interactionActivity>`

The activity types that are covered by the `<interactionActivity>` are summarised in the following:

1. activities that only receive a message (like a BPEL `<receive>`)
2. activities that only send a message (like a BPEL `<invoke>` or `<reply>`)
3. activities that first send a message and then receive a message (like a BPEL synchronous/two-way `<invoke>`)
4. activities that first receive a message and then send a message

The BPEL[light] `<interactionActivity>` is comparable to a BPMN task. Similarly to BPEL[light], BPMN [9] does not define different task types but rather specifies one task and this task may have incoming and outgoing messages. However, BPMN is only a modelling notation, whereas BPEL[light] is executable.

Table 1 shows how the interaction activity has to be configured to model the different activity types listed above. Activities that receive a message must specify the output variable whereas activities that send a message must specify the input variable. Activities that send a message only must not define the output variable, and activities that only receive a message must not define the input variable. For these activities the value for the attribute "mode" is not evaluated. Activities that do both, receive and send a message, must specify the attribute mode. The value has to be set to in-out for activities that first receive a message and out-in for activities that first send a message. The default value for the attribute createInstance is no. Activities that start with a receiving message may specify this attribute, for the other activity types this attribute is not evaluated.

Table 1. Modelling different interaction activity types

	input variable	output variable	mode	create instance
Activity that only receives a message	MUST NOT	MUST		MAY
Activity that only sends a message	MUST	MUST NOT		
Activity that first receives and then sends a message	MUST	MUST	in-out	MAY
Activity that first sends and then receives a message	MUST	MUST	out-in	

In order to be aligned with BPEL we introduce a new <pick> activitiy with semantics similar to the pick activity in BPEL. This is required since the BPEL specification enforces to have at least one conventional <onMessage> element specified, whose dependency on WSDL breaks the idea of BPEL^{light}. Instead the new activity allows to specify WSDL-less <onMessage> elements that reference a conversation just as the interaction activity. Additionally and a new WSDL-less <onEvent> element for the <eventHandler> is defined.

To close the description of the BPEL^{light} interaction model Listing 3 illustrates how the sample BPEL process showed in Figure 2a is modelled using BPEL^{light}.

4.2 The Notion of Partners

BPEL 1.1 includes a <partner> element that groups a subset of partner links to identify a partner within a process. This way the <partner> element postulates that several partner links have to be established with one and the same business partner. Thus it specifies what capabilities (in terms of port types) a specific partner has to provide. In BPEL 2.0 the partner element has been removed.

In BPEL^{light} we introduces a new <partner> element that enables grouping the WSDL independent <conversation>s. Thus it can be defined that several conversations have to take place with one business partner. The new <partner> element, which is referring to a <conversation> instead of a partner link is illustrated in Listing 4. This is a way to impose constraints on a partner to support multiple conversations, i.e. message exchanges, and thereby multiple business goals. Assume a flight should be booked after the price for this particular flight has been checked. In this case it is required that both activity implementations are using the same partner to avoid checking the price at Lufthansa and then booking a British Airways flight. Since the granularity of these business goals and thereby the granularity of the conversations cannot be standardised the <partner> element is needed to support the explicit specification of different granules in a user-friendly manner.

```
<bl:conversations>
   <bl:conversation name="salesConv"/>...
</bl:conversations>...
<flow>
   <links>
      <link name="send-to-receive" />...
   </links>...
   <extensionActivity>
      <bl:interactionActivity name="orderItem"
                              conversation="salesConv"
                              inputVariable="item">
         <sources>
            <source linkName="send-to-receive"/>...
         </sources>...
      </bl:interactionActivity>
   </extensionActivity>
   <extensionActivity>
      <bl:interactionActivity name="receiveConfirmation"
                              conversation="salesConv"
                              outputVariable="confirmation">
         <targets>
            <target linkName="send-to-receive"/>...
         </targets>...
      </bl:interactionActivity>
   </extensionActivity>...
</flow>
```

Listing 3. Asynchronous invocation of a service using BPEL[light]

```
<bl:partners>?
   <bl:partner name="NCName"
               businessEntity="QName"?>+
      <bl:conversation name="NCName">+
   </bl:partner>
</bl:partners>
```

Listing 4. The <partner> element in BPEL[light]

In addition, the <partner> element may define the concrete partner instance that has to be used for a set of conversations. This is realized using the businessEntity attribute, which specifies the name of an organisation.

Consequently BPEL[light] comes with an extension to the <assign> activity that enables copying a partner identification into the <partner> element. Therefore the empty <to> specification is extended with a <partner> attribute that defines to which partner definition the partner instance information is copied. Note, that a partner can only be set if its corresponding conversations have not been established yet. This is similar to copying an endpoint reference to a partner link.

5 Using BPEL[light] in WS-* Environment

As already discussed, BPEL[light] decouples from WSDL. Since WS-* is the most popular service-based integration technology we show how BPEL[light] can be used to support WSs based compositions. Therefore when using BPEL[light] in a WS-* environment it emulates the interaction model of BPEL. This way BPEL[light] also provides a recursive aggregation model for WSs analogously to conventional BPEL, i.e. a BPEL^{light} process can expose its functionality as a WS and it can invoke conventional WSs.

Note that even though the communication semantics of BPEL can be emulated, the two dimensions are still decoupled since the mapping of the technology neutral interaction model of BPEL^{light} to WSDL is external, i.e. not within the process logic.

To enable interaction among WSDL-based services, a conversation serves the role of a partner link and is associated with a partner link type. The role of a partner service and the role the process itself takes are also specified. In addition to the association of the conversation to the partner link type, all interaction activities have to be mapped to WSDL operations.

The semantics of the BPEL interaction activities can be achieved using the following mappings: an interaction activity with both variables specified and mode="out-in" is mapped to a request-response type operation the partner provides, which is similar to a synchronous BPEL <invoke>. An interaction activity with the output variable specified, which corresponds to a BPEL <receive>, can be assigned to a one-way operation the process provides. However, it can also be assigned to a request-response operation the process provides. In this case there must be a successive interaction activity with the input variable specified that is also assigned to that particular operation. Together, these two activities provide the semantics of a synchronous <receive>-<reply> pair in BPEL. The interaction activity with only the input variable specified may also be assigned to a one-way operation the partner service provides, which corresponds to an asynchronous <invoke> in BPEL.

Additionally, an interaction activity with both variables specified and the attribute mode set to "in-out" can be assigned to a request-response operation provided by the the process. This scenario has no direct counterpart in BPEL (instead, a receive-reply pair is used).

The assignment of the activities to a communication infrastructure can be done (i) using an *assignment file* that is interpreted during deployment (ii) using WS-PolicyAttachment [19] or (iii) by delegating all communication issues to the underlying middleware, e.g. the ESB [20]. In this paper we focus only on the first approach.

The assignment of the process logic to WSDL operations via an assignment file is depicted in Listing 5. The <conversation> is associated with a partner link type and it is specified which role is taken by the partner service and which is taken by the process itself using the myRole and partnerRole attribute. This is similar to the association of a partner link to a partner link type. Additionally, the activities have to be mapped to corresponding WSDL operations using the operation attribute like in BPEL.

So far we have shown that BPEL^{light} can be used to express the communication semantics of BPEL. However, a consequence of this approach is again a tight coupling of the 'what' and 'which' dimensions since there is a direct dependency of the behaviour of the navigator and the kind of communication used: a

```
<assignmentFor process="QName">
    <conversation name="NCName"
                  partnerLinkType="QName"
                  myRole="NCName"
                  partnerRole="NCName" />*
    <activity name="NCName"
              operation="NCName" />*
</assignmentFor>
```

Listing 5. Assignment file

blocking activity implies a synchronous request-response operation. However, there is an alternative and maybe even more promising approach of applying WSDL to BPEL[light]. The idea is not to map the activities directly to operations but rather map the input- and output variable to an operation. This way a blocking interaction activity that first sends and then receives a message can for instance be mapped to two one-way operations, one provided by the partner service and one by the process.

Since the consequences of this approach have to be investigated in depth we consider it future work.

6   Discussion and Assessment

BPEL[light] decouples process logic and interface definitions. Interfaces are defined separately and bound to activities in processes separate from BPEL[light]. Moreover interfaces can be specified in any IDL.

BPEL[light] eases modelling of business processes. By separating interfaces and process logic the amount of IT artefacts a process modeller must understand is reduced. It is sufficient to describe how the process wants to interact with a partner. This behaviour can be mapped separately during deployment or at runtime by proper middleware to an interface of a partner. Figure 6 illustrates how BPEL[light] improves the business process modelling lifecycle: The grey parts indicate the artefacts a process modeller needs to know. On the top of the figure the situation with traditional BPEL is shown whereas in the bottom it is depicted that BPEL[light] frees the modeller from IT specific details.

BPEL[light] decouples activity definitions from component models. Different IDLs can be mixed and matched within one and the same process model. Based on the concept of assignment files, proper middleware can be configured that allows to bridge to the hosting environment of the corresponding components.

BPEL[light] increases reusability and flexibility of process models. One and the same piece of process logic can be bound to completely different interfaces dependent on the set of interfaces available in a target environment.

BPEL[light] eases mapping of BPMN to an execution environment. By supporting the specification of message exchange patterns directly, BPEL[light] removes the impedance mismatch of message orientation and interface orientation which causes problems in mapping BPMN to conventional BPEL.

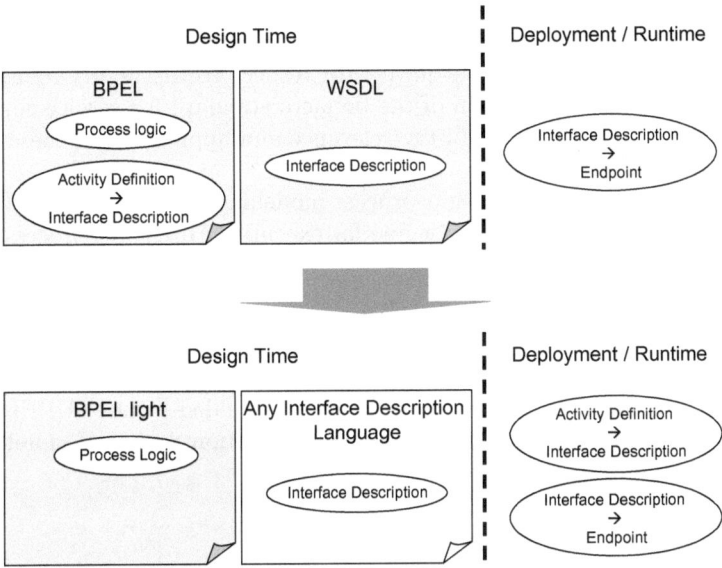

Fig. 6. Modelling with BPEL^{light} and BPEL: Improvements

BPEL^{light} eases the construction of matching partner processes, e.g. in chore-ographies. It is straightforward to construct to a given activity the matching dual activity in a partner process: the requested activity can be found by simply mirroring the conversation.

7   Conclusion

The work in this paper strives improving the flexibility and reusability of process-based compositions especially in service-oriented environments. We presented a language for composition, called BPEL^{light}, that facilitates decoupling of the two dimensions of process compositions - business logic ('what') and the activity im-plementations ('which'). The advantage of BPEL^{light} over conventional BPEL is that it allows to specify process models independent of WS technology; in fact it is independent of any other interface technology used to implement activities. As a result, BPEL^{light} improves both, reusability and flexibility of process models.

Reusability of process definitions is improved since the process definitions can be used with different service technologies while the business logic remains un-changed. In addition, a mixture of service technologies may be utilized when a process model is executed. Moreover, any BPEL^{light} process definition can be used to generate partner interfaces automatically based on information about message exchange patterns defined in BPEL^{light}. This is enabled by the inherent symmetry of the message exchange patterns of interacting partners. BPEL^{light} improves the flexibility of process definitions because both deployment time configuration and run time discovery and binding to appropriate interfaces is enabled. In our view, the process language introduced in this paper is an adequate answer to the needs businesses have with respect to reusability and flexibility of processes. It is an extension of the de facto standard for service composition (BPEL) and therefore the industry relevance and application of these language extensions is not hampered.

Currently we are developing a process modelling tool with native BPEL^{light} extension support. Building an engine for executing BPEL^{light} processes is part of our future work.

Acknowledgments

The work published in this article was partially funded by the SUPER project[4] under the EU 6th Framework Programme Information Society Technologies Objective (contract no. FP6-026850).

References

1. Leymann, F., Roller, D.: Production workflow. Prentice-Hall, Englewood Cliffs (2000)
2. van der Aalst, W., van Hee, K.: Workflow management. MIT Press, Cambridge (2002)
3. Weerawarana, S., Curbera, F., Leymann, F., Storey, T., Ferguson, D.F.: Web Services Platform Architecture: SOAP, WSDL, WS-Policy, WS-Addressing, WS-BPEL, WS-Reliable Messaging and More. Prentice Hall PTR, Upper Saddle River, NJ, USA (2005)
4. Alonso, G., Casati, F., Kuno, H., Machiraju, V.: Web Services: Concepts, Architectures and Applications. Springer, Heidelberg (2004)
5. Burbeck, S.: The Tao of e-business services. IBM Corporation (2000)
6. Krafzig, D., Banke, K., Slama, D.: Enterprise SOA: Service-Oriented Architecture Best Practices (The Coad Series). Prentice Hall PTR, Upper Saddle River, NJ, USA (2004)
7. Leymann, F., Roller, D.: Workflow-based applications. IBM Systems Journal 36(1), 102–123 (1997)
8. Alves, A., Arkin, A., Askary, S., Barreto, C., Bloch, B., Curbera, F., Ford, M., Goland, Y., Guízar, A., Kartha, N., Liu, C.K., Khalaf, R., König, D., Marin, M., Mehta, V., Thatte, S., van der Rijn, D., Yendluri, P., Yiu, A.: Web Services Business Process Execution Language Version 2.0. Committee specification, OASIS Web Services Business Process Execution Language (WSBPEL) TC (January 2007)
9. White, S.: Business Process Modeling Notation (BPMN) Version 1.0. Object Management Group/Business Process Management Initiative, BPMN.org (2004)
10. Christensen, E., Curbera, F., Meredith, G., Weerawarana, S.: Web Services Description Language (WSDL) 1.1 (2001)
11. Kloppmann, M., Koenig, D., Leymann, F., Pfau, G., Rickayzen, A., von Riegen, C., Schmidt, P., Trickovic, I.: WS-BPEL Extension for People – BPEL4People. Joint white paper, IBM and SAP (July 2005)

[4] http://www.ip-super.org/

12. Kloppmann, M., Konig, D., Leymann, F., Pfau, G., Rickayzen, A., von Riegen, C., Schmidt, P., Trickovic, I.: WS-BPEL Extension for Sub-processes – BPEL-SPE. Joint white paper, IBM and SAP (2005)
13. Box, D., Curbera, F., et al.: Web Services Addressing (WS-Addressing). W3C Member Submission (August 2004)
14. van der Aalst, W., ter Hofstede, A., Kiepuszewski, B., Barros, A.: Workflow Patterns. Distributed and Parallel Databases 14(1), 5–51 (2003)
15. Barros, A., Dumas, M., ter Hofstede, A.: Service interaction patterns: Towards a reference framework for service-based business process interconnection. Technical Report FIT-TR-2005-02, Faculty of Information Technology, Queensland University of Technology, Brisbane, Australia (March 2005)
16. Decker, G., Kopp, O., Leymann, F., Weske, M.: BPEL4Chor: Extending BPEL for modeling choreographies. In: ICWS 2007. IEEE Computer Society Press, Los Alamitos (2007)
17. Andrews, T., Curbera, F., Dholakia, H., Goland, Y., Klein, J., Leymann, F., Liu, K., Roller, D., Smith, D., Thatte, S., Trickovic, I., Weerawarana, S.: Business Process Execution Language for Web Services (BPEL) 1.1 (2003), http://www.ibm.com/developerworks/library/specification/ws-bpel/
18. Karastoyanova, D., van Lessen, T., Nitzsche, J., Wetzstein, B., Wutke, D., Leymann, F.: Semantic Service Bus: Architecture and Implementation of a Next Generation Middleware. In: 2nd International Workshop on Services Engineering (SEIW), Istanbul, Turkey (April 2007)
19. Bajaj, S., Box, D., Chappell, D., Curbera, F., Daniels, G., Hallam-Baker, P., Hondo, M., Kaler, C., Malhotra, A., Maruyama, H., et al.: Web Services Policy Attachment (WS-PolicyAttachment). W3C Member Submission (April 2006)
20. Chappell, D.A.: Enterprise Service Bus. O'Reilly (2004)

An Enactment-Engine Based on Use-Cases

Avner Ottensooser and Alan Fekete

School of Information Technologies, University of Sydney, Australia
{avner,fekete}@it.usyd.edu.au

Abstract. We show how one can control a workflow enactment engine based on the information which is available in written use cases (as produced by requirements elicitation). We give details of how different aspects of the engine can be configured, including the process definition, workflow participant profiles, user interface, audit data, *etc.* These techniques have been carried out in an industrial setting, with considerable success. Our methods are applicable to engines for business process management, web service orchestration, and traditional workflow.

1 Introduction

The automation of enterprise activity has been a major trend in recent decades, and a key enabler for this trend is the widespread adoption of engines that allow the computational management of processes. These engines were much studied in the 1990s under the term "workflow management", and later a wider horizon has been represented as "business process" execution engines; most recently there has been much attention given to "orchestration for composite web services" which involves the same ideas in the context of business-to-business integration. In this paper we will speak of workflow, but the ideas apply equally in all these settings.

A key feature of any enactment engine is a format for defining the processes that will be executed. Many proprietary languages have been used in commercial products, standards have been proposed, and many more research papers have been written. The most widespread approaches have their roots in a graph or network models, and can be formalised with Petri Nets or similar representations. For example, some vendors of industrial workflow engines, such as IBM and TIBCO, deploy dialects of the UML activity diagram to configure their workflow engines. Other proposals have been based on event-condition-action rules. All these approaches, however much they differ in details, depend on a workflow configuration officer producing a model or definition of each process in a special format, for the purpose of controlling the execution in the enactment engine.

In this paper, we propose a different approach. Rather than asking the workflow configuration officer to model the business processes in a special format, we make use of a well-accepted format for eliciting system requirements: the written use cases [3], which are commonly produced during the requirements gathering stages of projects. We conjecture that the use cases contain the information needed to configure the enactment engine. A great advantage of our approach

G. Alonso, P. Dadam, and M. Rosemann (Eds.): BPM 2007, LNCS 4714, pp. 230–245, 2007.

is the reduction in effort by the workflow configuration officers, who can re-use artifacts business analysts usually generate, instead of undertaking a separate step to analyse and model the business processes. As well, there is good evidence that use cases are an effective means for communicating with domain experts. Use cases seem to scale well, in contrast to say UML Activity Diagrams which become very crowded on realistic domains.

Here is a brief overview of our approach from the point of view of its users; much more detail is given in section 3. With use cases on hand, the workflow administrator creates routing sheets, each describing several action steps which should be performed as a group. When a work item arrives, the first workflow participant to touch the work item begins by cataloguing the work item, and then pilots[1] the work item's flow through the organisation, by linking routing sheets with the work item. Following this, each activity is done by a workflow participant, who continues to perform activities according to the routing sheets, until eventually an activity is found that the participant can't deal with, at which point the work item is passed to another participant. As each activity is executed, the participant acknowledges this to the system. From time to time the workflow system records audit data describing the work item's attributes and progress.

The techniques discussed in this paper have been exploited in commercial practise by the first author at BT Financial Group, an Australian financial services enterprise that is now a subsidiary of Westpac Banking Corporation. BT Financial Group developed a unique Workflow Enactment Engine, whose details were configured as described above. This engine was configured manually from the use cases by business analysts, and the engine ran on top of a conventional workflow engine. One can also imagine similar ideas used in other settings, for example, the configuration might be generated automatically (with suitable natural language processing), or the enactment could be done using a standard relational dbms.

In Section 2, we summarise related work, introduce the terminology, and describe in detail the components of workflow engines. In Section 3, we explain how each configuration component is inferred from the written use cases. Section 3.6 presents some enhancements on the basic idea of use-case-based configuration. Section 4 describes our larger research agenda and its progress to date. In section 5 we conclude with a report on our experience at BT Financial Group, and our reflections on this.

2   Background, Use Cases and Workflow

Here we point to some of the most closely relevant or seminal work. There is of course far more published on both use cases and workflow management than we can cite; more citations can be found in expositions such as [16] and [26]. We then describe the key ideas we build on, as a way of fixing the terminology used in this paper.

---

[1] We use the word as in a maritime pilot, who helps a ship follow the correct path.

2.1   Previous Related Work

This paper stands on the shoulders of two research communities: Requirements Engineering within Software Engineering research, and Workflow (later called Business Process Management) within Databases and Information Systems. In one of the few researches we found that bridges the two communities, Lee *et al* show that use cases can be transformed into Petri Nets [15].

Use cases were proposed by Jacobson [13] and a diagramming notation for them was included within the UML standard in 1997. The use case technique, arguably one of the best and most widely employed requirement gathering techniques in the industry, is accepted by both IT professionals and business managers [16, Page 297] [4]. Of the 28 dialects of use cases Hurlbut surveyed [12] we adopted the written one described by Cockburn [3]. There are various guidelines for expressing requirements in use cases [5]. Use cases have been found to be effective for generating test suites [7], and for generating security policies [9].

Since the 1990s, the Workflow community researched many different approaches to defining and enacting business processes, and many research prototypes and commercial products have embodied these. The community has an industry body, the Workflow Management Coalition [28], which provided a reference model [11] and terminology [29] which we adopted. There is also a rich pattern library [30, 21] which we use elsewhere to evaluate our method [19].

By far the most popular category of process definition languages uses a visual presentation based on a graph, which connects activities in the order they must be carried out, with connectors representing decision branches, parallel forks, merges *etc.* For example, the UML activity diagram has become widespread for informal modelling, and it is also accepted as an input notation in some engines [22]. The underlying theory for all these graph-based approaches can be expressed in terms of Petri Nets, and some proposals have even adopted variants of the Petri Net directly as a notation. Van der Aalst summarised and evaluated the research [24, 25]. Particular virtues of Petri Nets include their support for automated analysis [1], such as checking for deadlocks [8]. Another class of workflow description languages is based on Event Condition Action rules [6]. A recent example, focusing on service oriented systems, is [17]. Casati *et al* [2] show how to convert graph-based definitions to rules, and provide models for the relational structures we have used to store descriptions within our engine. Non-functional properties such as performance and cost have also been studied [18].

2.2   Use Case

The use case model is an illustrative, incremental requirements elicitation tool that uses *Actors* and *Use Cases*. *Actors* illustrate what exists outside the system and interacts with it. An Actor may be a person in a role (eg Customer), or it may be an external system (eg a credit rating agency) or even a device. *Use Cases* describe what the system is supposed to do. A use-case illustrates what is (or will be) in the system by following a specific, yet complete, flow in the system [13, Section 6.4]. According to Cockburn [3], each use cases describes, in a controlled

```
Use case name: Apply to invest money in a fund

Main success scenario:

1. The mail room scans the application form to the imaging system.   Order = 1
2. The data entry person keys the deposit to the system.            Order = 2 ! Parallel to 2a
3. The system sends transaction confirmation to the investor.       Order = 6
4. The process ends.                                                Order = 7

Extensions:

2a. The application is for more than AU$1,000,000                              ! AND-Split
    2a1. The Senior Data Entry Person also keys the deposit.        Order = 2 ! Parallel to 2
    2a2. The system reconciles the two data entries.               Order = 3 ! AND-Join
    2a2. The flow continues at line 3

    2a2a. The reconciliation failed                                           ! OR-Split
          2a2a1. The system sends the two data entries to the      Order = 4
                 senior data entry.
          2a2a2. Senior data entry corrects the data in the system Order = 5
          2a2a3. The flow continues at line 3

2b. The form arrived unsigned.                                                ! OR-Split
    2b1. The Data Entry Person calls the Investor, requesting
         a signed form.                                            Order = 2
    2b2. The current process ends (the signed application
         will restart the process).                               Order = 3
```

Fig. 1. The sample business process used in our paper expressed as a written use case

natural language (English phrases), the interactions between users who wish to achieve a goal and a system, and thus it functions as a contract for the behaviour of the system in meeting the goal. A written use case mentions: (1) Actors such as humans or systems who interact with the system. (2) What must be true in the system for the interactions to be feasible. (3) A main success scenario (happy day scenario) and alternative scenarios, that indicate how the interaction with the system occurs when every thing goes well. And (4) extensions which indicate an abnormal, incorrect, or otherwise unusual situation. *E.g.*, in (Figure 1), the success scenario is steps 1 to 4, while 2b is an extension which is applied when an investor forgot to sign a form.

When we wish to change the system's behaviour, we remodel the appropriate *Actor* and *Use Case*. With the changed *Use Case Model* in hand, we change other models (object, analysis, design , implementation and testing). When we design systems this way the system model will be *Use Case Driven* [13, Section 6.4.2]. In this paper we show how one can configure an enactment engine directly from the written use-case. The following use case is the example we use throughout this paper, it follows the written use-case as described in [3] except that we add an extra attribute "Order" to each step. The order is closely related to the step number, but it allows for indication of when steps can be done independently.

2.3 Workflow

Workflow is the automation of a business process, in whole or part, during which information and work lists are passed from one participant to another for action, according to a set of procedural rules [29, Page 8].

In early times, computer applications were designed to fully support several business transaction types. Administrators invoked applications once all required information was at hand, and processed transactions from start to end, each in a single iteration. In the 70s image management emerged, creating queues in front of administrators who pulled work from the queues and processed the work sequentially. Today, the processing of business transactions is spanning multiple systems, by multiple specialised organisational role bearers, as data drips into the organisation(s). This style of business processing is supported by workflow engines. A *Workflow Engine* is a generic software system driven by explicit process design to enact and manage operational business process [21]. A *Workflow Management System* defines, creates and manages the execution of workflow through the use of software, running on one or more workflow engines, which is able to interpret the process definition, interact with workflow participants and, where required, invoke the use of IT tools and applications [29, Page 9].

Here we describe, using figure 2, the data the workflow administrator gathers, when configuring the enactment-engine which we have used in BT Financial Group. In section 3 we describe an algorithm we used to infer this data from written use cases which were produced during requirements elicitation. In section 4 we outline further research, in which we will explore the wider relevance of this approach.

Our data model is shown in figure 2. At its core resides the business transaction routing sheet. Like the routing documentation used in production floors to describe the production processes an order has to pass, the business transaction routing sheet explains the activities that have to be executed as a group to fulfil part of the use case.

A business transaction routing sheet has one or more activities [29, Page 12]. To each activity one organisational role is assigned [29, Page 54], and an attribute named "order". As will be described later, the "order" attribute is instrumental in handling parallel work.

Each routing sheet has an attribute named "observation" that the workflow engine uses to build a menu from which the pilot links routing sheets with work items. Each activity has an attribute named "instruction" which the workflow engine uses to prompt the workflow participant to execute the activity.

The details of the workflow participants [29, Page 17] are stored in a table, and another table describes the proficiency of workflow participants in various roles. These two tables together are the workflow participant profile, and one may be right to assume that the profile is populated by human resources.

The last data element is created at run time. We named it "run time construct". At its core resides the work item [29, Page 18]. The work item is logically linked to one or more routing sheets. Physically we link it to all the activities that constitute these routing sheets. At run time, the workflow engine groups one or more activities into a worklist [29, Page 19] and dispatches this to a workflow participant. A "worklist" is the atomic unit of work dispatched to workflow participants (indeed the activities that combine to form a worklist may come from different work items or even different business processes).

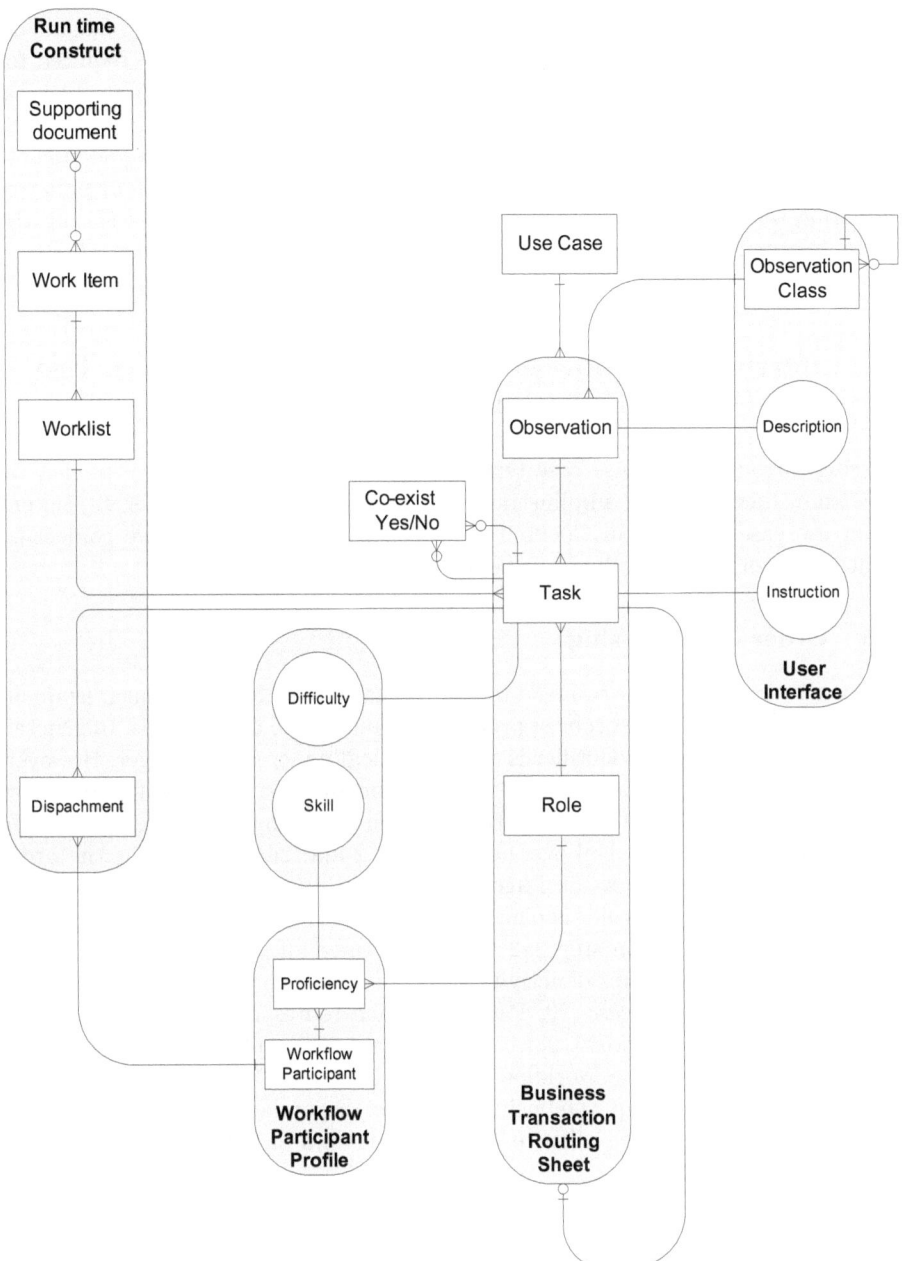

Fig. 2. Use Case Oriented Data Flow Engine — Data Model

A work item is associated with supporting documents. In older times, when imaging systems were promoted as workflow engines, one supporting document was equivalent to one work item; a 1 : 1 ratio. Nowadays, any ratio is acceptable. 0 : 1 ratio exists when a work item is not initiated by a document, *e.g.* periodic review. n : 1 ratio exists when several documents are required for a work item to complete. 1 : n ratio exists when one document initiates several work items, *e.g.* when employer sends the details of several pension payments in one spreadsheet. We even observed $m : n$. The nature of supporting documents evolved as well, from paper to XML. Here we made an exception to our policy of adhering to the Workflow Management Coalition Terminology by selecting the term "Supporting Document" over the coalition's "Workflow Relevant Data" [29, Page 45].

3   Inferring Workflow Engine's Configuration from Use Cases — An Algorithm

Having introduced the use case terminology and the workflow data model, we now show how workflow administrators in BT Financial Group infer its content from use cases written in Cockburn's notation [3]. In section 4 we conjecture that the algorithm described can be followed in general.

3.1   Order of Processing

The only change we had to make to the use case dialect of Cockburn, as documented [3], is to add the order of processing identifier to action steps. In general, the order of processing identifier is a monotonically increasing integer. However, if the order of some action steps is of no importance, or the action steps follow an AND-Split [29, Page 30], then these action steps share an order processing identifier. *E.g.* in figure 1 above, action steps 2 and 2a1 share '2' as the order of processing. AND-Joins [29, Page 31] are described by an action step whose order of processing identifier is bigger than that of the parallel action steps. *E.g.* in Figure 1 above, action step 2a2 with '4' as order of processing, joins steps 2 and 2a1. If several streams of activity start, then the streams are represented by sub-use cases (Sub Process [29, Page 27]), each represented by a single action step. In our technical report [19] we offer use-case descriptions for all 43 workflow patterns identified by the Workflow Patterns Initiative [30].

In BT Financial Group, the business specific, dispatcher related data elements were: value date, product, client pressure, value, and distribution channel.

3.2   Inferring the Process Definition

A process is described by a set of individual business transactions routing sheets. In our example (Figure 3), four individual business transactions routing sheets are configured. The main success scenario, each alternate flow and each extension are all the observation elements in individual business transactions routing sheet. Each group of action steps that follows them is the reoccurring activity element.

To infer the role, and the activity, from the use-case step, is easy because the use case structure clearly defines who does what. According to Cockburn

```
Business-Transactions Routing Sheet 1

    Observation     = Small Application ! (Or default flow)

        Activity    = Scan the application form
            Role    = mail room
           Order    = 1

        Activity    = Key into the system
            Role    = Data Entry Person
           Order    = 2

        Activity    = Send transaction confirmation
            Role    = The system
           Order    = 6




Business-Transactions Routing Sheet 2

    Observation     = Application Bigger than AU$1,000,000.00

        Activity    = Key into the system
            Role    = Senior Data Entry Person
           Order    = 2

        Activity    = Reconcile the two data entries
            Role    = The system ! Automated process
           Order    = 3 ! If order was 1, the dispatcher would be
                          ! able to dispatch the two Activities in parallel,
                          ! something that may be sensible.




Business-Transactions Routing Sheet 3

    Observation     = Application with a missing signature

        Activity    = Call the investor requesting a signature.
            Role    = Senior Data Entry Person
           Order    = 99 ! any number will do as this is a fatal error.




Business-Transactions Routing Sheet 4

    Observation     = The reconciliation failed

        Activity    = Send the two data entries to the senior data entry.
            Role    = System
           Order    = 4

        Activity    = Correct the data
            Role    = Senior Data Entry Person
           Order    = 5
```

Fig. 3. The routing sheets for our sample business process (Figure 1)

[3, page 90] the action step structure should be absolutely simple, as shown in Figure 4. The role for the activity is the grammatical subject in the step, and the activity is given by the verb and any grammatical direct or indirect objects.

```
Subject... Verb... direct object... prepositional phrase.

The data entry person ... keys ... the deposit ... to the system.
```

Fig. 4. The syntax of an action step

3.3   Inferring the User Interface Specification

In this section we articulate the basic constructs needed to apply the use case notation to the configuration of a workflow engine's run time user interface. At run time, workflow participants request the next work item (GetNext). The dispatcher, a component of workflow engines, matches the workflow participant's roles and skills with the work in the queues and assigns a work item to the workflow participant. The workflow participant then:

Catalogue –   When a work item arrives, the first workflow participant to touch the work item catalogues the work item by assigning to the work item attributes such as the business process which the work item must follow, the customer identifier (in BT Financial Group, that is the point where new customers are keyed into the systems), as well as business specific dispatcher related information. To catalogue work items, BT Financial Group uses a key combining the customer's identifier, the business line and the transaction type. Supporting-Documents are catalogued in BT Financial Group using monotonically increasing, non contiguous integers, with a check digit concatenated. An XML document is usually catalogued by a computer programme.

Pilot –   As in a maritime pilot, pilots describe the route the work item will pass through the organisation by linking routing sheets to work items using a classified menu of observations (more on the classification structure in section 3.6). At this stage work items can be spawned or merged, and supporting documents, that arrived previously, can be attached to the work item. A pilot can be a computer programme or a human. At every stage in the life cycle of the work item, a workflow participant may further refine the piloting of the work item.

Execute –   The pilot may execute the work, or leave it to a specialised workflow participant. At this stage the workflow participant requests the next work item (Get Next) and the workflow engine dispatches a work item, the cataloguing attributes that was previously assigned, the supporting document(s) and, according to the observations the pilot had prescribed, a list of activities the processor is expected to perform. The workflow participant then performs the appropriate activity on the work item (in Figure 1, key it to the mainframe, verify it, or contact the customer).

Acknowledge –   Following the execution of each activity the workflow participant flags it as "Done", and other activities as "Diarised" or "Should not be done", until all Activities are completed. Following the acknowledgement, the workflow participant may either request the next work item or terminate the session.

3.4   Inferring the Audit Data Terminology

In BT Financial Group, the Workflow-Engine uses event-driven asynchronous messages to communicate with an external reporting engine by sending instances of the following three message classes:

Work Item Message – Sent when a work item is created, spawned, re-catalogued, terminated, or, merged into anther work item. Records a time stamp and the cataloguing information (described in section 3.3 above). Used to monitor adherence to external Service Level Agreements.

Observation Message – Sent when an Activity is assigned to a work item. Records properties of a work item. Used for quality assurance (*e.g* in Figure 1, how often do investors forget to sign application forms).

Worklist Message – Sent when a Worklist is queued, starts, ends, or diarised. Records who performed the activity and how fast. Used to monitor adherence to internal service level agreements.

3.5   Inferring the Content of the Dispatching Queue

The dispatcher watches two lists: (1) available workflow participants with roles and skills; and (2) piloted activities, with roles, difficulty and other configurable dispatching parameters. These two lists are used to implement dispatching patterns that are only limited by the imagination.

Thus, in this section we have demonstrated how the content of the data model can be inferred from use cases.

3.6   Extensions

This section describes further refinements to Cockburn's use case notation [3], which we have found to be useful.

Skills and Difficulty – To increase the granularity of the dispatching of Activities to Role bearers, difficulty was assigned to activities and Skill was assigned to Role bearers. The dispatcher is configured to assign Worklists to Role bearers who are sufficiently skilled to handle the most difficult Activity in the Worklist.

Activity co-existence – To increase piloting quality (see section 3.3 above), the Workflow configuration officer may articulate whether certain activities may co-exist with other activities.

Observation Menu – To ease the task of locating observations, a category based tree structure was implemented.

3.7   Implementation of the Use Case Model on Off the Shelf Workflow Engine

While the ideas expressed above can be implemented on a relational database, users may find it beneficial to implement the model on top of commercial Workflow Engine, as happened in BT Financial Group where FileNET software was

used. In that case it is recommended to connect all workflow participants to each
other and to direct the flow using the dispatcher described above. In that case,
the system should be configured as having only three queues.

Unpiloted Work – As its name suggests, that queue will hold all work items
that are not catalogued. As cataloguing all incoming document may be a
priority, this queue may have higher priority than the Work in progress
queue.

Work in progress – The queue from which the dispatcher allocates work items
to workflow participants.

Completed work – The storage of work that ended.

4   Further Research

We presented an approach which we have applied in one, albeit complex, environment within BT Financial Group. At this point we offer two conjectures.

Conjecture 1. *Use cases written in the Cockburn format [3], with order assigned to action steps, provide sufficient information to describe the workflow in
any reasonable system.*

Conjecture 2. *A workflow which is given as a written use-case avoids many of
the errors that can arise with general graph-based notations: it has an end, has
only reachable nodes, and has no dead ends.*

We plan to explore the validity of the conjectures through several research activities. For the first conjecture, we will start by showing that written use-cases can
deal with many of the workflow situations already known. In particular, we have
followed the methodology deployed by Russell *et al* for evaluating the richness
of UML2.0 activity diagrams [22]; we have shown how to give written use-case
descriptions for the standard workflow patterns. Our analysis is in [19]. The second conjecture will be explored by following the research of Lee *et al* [15], and
looking at the properties of Petri Net equivalents to use case descriptions.

5   Experience, Evaluation, Discussion and Conclusion

5.1   Experience Gained at BT Financial Group

Starting in 2002, a group at BT Financial Services, managed by the first author,
operated a Workflow Management System, supported by a specially-written enactment engine. This system was based on the principles presented in this paper.
In BT Financial Group we found that:

– In April 2007, 368 Business-Process were controlled by the system. Each
business process had on average 26 possible activities. At that point in time,

on a typical day, about 600 administrators were logged in. On average day in April 2007, approximately 10,000 business process instances which were supported by 12,000 images were executed. The number of audit rows generated daily was about 300,000. The administrators were located in three Australian states and in India.

- Use cases became the primary tool for the workflow configuration officers. These officers' productivity was so high that in 2006 Westpac Life, a sister company which is in the life insurance business, migrated its entire processes into BT Financial Group's Workflow-Engine within five weeks.
- Analysis of the audits data collected was instrumental for the identification, quantitative justification, and subsequent quantitative evaluation, of Six-Sigma process improvements programmes.
- Line managers, with general accounting skills, feel comfortable to add, maintain, or remove activities.
- In BT Financial Group, worklists are created whenever a processor requests the next worklist. The approach where administrators requests a work item (get next) and the dispatcher assigns them the most appropriate one, rather then letting administrators "Cherry Pick" work items, increases the management control.
- When BT Financial Group placed skilled personnel as pilots, quality was built from the beginning at the price of overloading experts with mundane activities. When BT Financial Group placed unskilled processors at the beginning, work often arrived to the skilled personnel none the less, but for the wrong reason — repair.
- Some business areas encouraged pilots to pilot and perform the prescribed activity in a single session. Other business areas discouraged this.
- Some business areas tried to complete the piloting early in the morning and process in the rest of the day. Other business lines piloted and processed throughout the day.
- BT Financial group experimented with the following dispatcher patterns:
  - FIFO
  - The hardest job one can do in descending age order.
  - The oldest un–piloted work, then the oldest and the hardest work item a Workflow Participant may perform, from the oldest day.
  - Business related consideration such as priority for redemptions over deposits and of cash transactions over manged fund transactions.
- The large majority of business processes did not have any scope for within-instance parallelism.
- Unfortunately we found that the routing sheet observation attribute was too often identical to the instruction attribute of the activity.

5.2 Limitations

We identified several issues where the use case notation is less satisfactory than other workflow description notations. We discuss these in turn.

Use cases can be *ambiguous* as they use natural language. This seems to be an evident trade-off against the ease of communication with business experts. To overcome the natural language ambiguities, Cox *et al.* [4, 5] show how to improve the quality of use cases with checklists driven reviews. As Törner *et al* suggests [23], it is possible to increase the Correctness, Consistency, Completeness, Readability and level of detail as well as to avoid ambiguity.

There is little direct support for *analysing flaws* in use case descriptions, compared to Petri Net methods which allow automated detection of deadlocks possibility, unreachable nodes and uncontrolled process termination. However, as Lee *et al* [15] have shown, use cases can be considered as a set of interacting and concurrently executing threads, and that use cases can be transformed into a Constraint-Based Modular Petri Nets based formalism [25]. Once converted into Petri-Nets we can (1) identify inconsistent dependency specifications among Activities; (2) test for workflow safety, *i.e.* test whether the Workflow terminates in an acceptable state; (3) for a given starting time, test whether it is feasible to execute a Workflow with the specified temporal constraints [1] ; (4) test the Workflow for possibility of deadlocks [8].

Use case descriptions generally lead to sequential execution, or at best *low levels of parallelism* within each business process instance.

While the use case notation had these limitations, the overall impact on the company was very positive. In the next subsection we reflect on the ways our approach was beneficial.

5.3 Value Proposition

The value proposition of our approach to Workflow-Engine configuration is that it:

- Reduces the amount of effort required to configure workflow engines, by reusing the organisation's investment in use cases. As use cases are ubiquitous in today's business analysis arena, one would expect that the workflow configuration officers would have use cases available before the Workflow configuration commences.
- Audit data and the user interface are maintained as part and parcel of the process definition reducing development effort.
- Allows the two flexibilities that Heinl *et al* [10] required from a Workflow-Engine, namely:
  Flexibility by Selection – the processor has the freedom to choose between different execution paths if necessary.
  Flexibility by Adaptation – it is possible to change the Workflow definition at run-time by adding, removing or altering Business-Transaction Routing Sheets.
- Written use cases provide descriptions which can be understood by various stake holders in a straightforward manner. Cox *et al* suggest that end-users

do understand well written use cases [4]. We have not found corresponding research that suggests that end-users can understand and review Workflow annotated by Petri-Nets, and our experience, together with the discussion in [22], suggests that complex UML2.0 Activity Diagrams are beyond end-users' reach when modelling resource-related or organisational aspects of business process. This approach to workflow has allowed workflow activities to be performed by a wider range of employees. In particular, it is not necessary for participants to understand workflow notations like graphs or activity diagrams; the written use-case can be followed by all employees.

- Our approach enables pilots who are unfamiliar with the underlying routing to make complex routing decisions by concentrating on observations rather then activities.

References

[1] Adam, N.R., Atluri, V., Huang, W.: Modeling and Analysis of Workflows Using Petri Nets. Journal of Intelligent Information Systems 10, 131–158 (1998)

[2] Casati, F., Ceri, S., Pernici, B., Pozzi, G.: Deriving Active Rules for Workflow Enactment. In: Thoma, H., Wagner, R.R. (eds.) DEXA 1996. LNCS, vol. 1134, pp. 94–115. Springer, Heidelberg (1996)

[3] Cockburn, A.: Writing effective use cases. Addison-Wesley, London (1999)

[4] Cox, K., Aurum, A., Jeffery, R.: An Experiment in Inspecting the Quality of use case Descriptions. Journal of Research and Practice in Information Technology 36(4), 211–229 (2004)

[5] Cox, K., Phalp, K., Shepperd, M.: Comparing use case Writing Guidelines. In: Proc. Workshop on Requirements Engineering: Foundation of Software Quality (REFSQ'01), pp. 101–112 (2001)

[6] Dayal, U., Hsu, M., Ladin, R.: Organizing Long- Running Activities with Triggers and Transactions. In: Proc ACM International Conference on Management of Data (SIGMOD'90), pp. 204–214 (1990)

[7] de Figueiredo, A.L.L., Andrade, W.L., Machado, P.D.L.: Generating Interaction Test Cases for Mobile Phone Systems from use case Specifications. ACM SIGSOFT Software Engineering Notes 31(6), 1 (November 2006)

[8] Ezpeleta, J., Colom, J.M., Martinez, J.: A Petri net based deadlock prevention policy for flexible manufacturing systems. IEEE Trans on Robotics and Automation 11(2), 173–184 (1995)

[9] Fernandez, E.B., Hawkins, J.C.: Determining role rights from use cases. In: Proc ACM Workshop on Role-Based Access Control (RBAC '97), pp. 121–125 (1997), DOI= http://doi.acm.org/10.1145/266741.266767

[10] Heinl, P., Horn, S., Jablonski, S., Neeb, J., Stein, K., Teschke, M.: A comprehensive approach to flexibility in Workflow management systems. In: Proceedings of the international Joint Conference on Work Activities Coordination and Collaboration (WACC'99) pp. 79–88. (1999), DOI= http://doi.acm.org/10.1145/295665.295675

[11] Hollingsworth, D.: The Workflow Reference Model. Document Number TC00-1003 of the Workflow Management Coalition, Document Status - Issue 1.1 (January 19, 1995)

[12] Hurlbut, R.: A Survey of Approaches for Describing and Formalizing use cases. Technical Report 97– 03, Department of Computer Science, Illinois Institute of Technology, USA. (1997), Found at
http://www.iit.edu/~rhurlbut/xpt-tr-97-03.html

[13] Jacobson, I.: Object-Oriented Software Engineering. Addison-Wesley, London (1992)

[14] Kim, J., Spraragen, M., Gil, Y.: An intelligent assistant for interactive Workflow composition. In: Proc International Conference on Intelligent User interfaces (IUI'04), pp. 125–131 (2004), DOI=
http://doi.acm.org/10.1145/964442.964466

[15] Lee, W.J., Cha, S.D., Kwon, Y.R.: Integration and analysis of use cases using modular Petri nets in requirements Engineering. IEEE Transactions on Software Engineering 24(12), 1115–1130 (1998)

[16] Leffingwell, D., Widring, D.: Managing Software Requirements: A use case Approach, 2nd edn. Addison-Wesley, London (2003)

[17] Nepal, S., Fekete, A., Greenfield, P., Jang, J., Kuo, D., Shi, T.A: Service-oriented Workflow Language for Robust Interacting Applications. In: Proc International Conference on Cooperative Information Systems (CoopIS'05), pp. 40–58 (2005)

[18] O'Sullivan, J., Edmond, D., ter Hofstede, A.: What's in a Service? Distrib. Parallel Databases 12, 117–133 (2002)

[19] Ottensooser, A., Fekete, A.: Workflow Patterns Represented in Use-Cases, Technical Report Number 611, School of Information Technologies, University of Sydney

[20] Russell, N., ter Hofstede, A.H., Edmond, D., van der Aalst, W.M.P.: Workflow Resource Patterns. BETA Working Paper Series, WP 127, Eindhoven University of Technology, Eindhoven (2004), http://fp.tm.tue.nl/beta/

[21] Russell, N., van der Aalst, W.M.P., ter Hofstede, A.H., Edmond, D.: Workflow Resource Patterns: Identification, Representation and Tool Support. In: Pastor, Ó., Falcão e Cunha, J. (eds.) CAiSE 2005. LNCS, vol. 3520, pp. 216–232. Springer, Heidelberg (2005)

[22] Russell, N., van der Aalst, W.M.P., ter Hofstede, A.H., Wohed, P.: On the suitability of UML 2.0 activity diagrams for business process modelling. In: Gruska, J. (ed.) Mathematical Foundations of Computer Science 1977. LNCS, vol. 53, pp. 95–104. Springer, Heidelberg (1977)

[23] Törner, F., Ivarsson, M., Pettersson, F., Öhman, P.: Defects in automotive use cases. In: Proc ACM/IEEE international Symposium on Empirical Software Engineering (ISESE'06), pp. 115–123 (2006), DOI=
http://doi.acm.org/10.1145/1159733.1159753

[24] van der Aalst, W.M.P.: Three Good Reasons for Using a Petri-net-based Workflow Management System. In: Proc International Working Conference on Information and Process Integration in Enterprises (IPIC'96), pp. 179–201 (1996)

[25] van der Aalst, W.M.P.: The Application of Petri Nets to Workflow Management. Journal of Circuits, Systems, and Computers 8(1), 21–66 (1998)

[26] van der Aalst, W.M.P., Van Hee, K.: Workflow Management: Models, Methods and Systems. MIT Press, Cambridge (2002)

[27] van der Aalst, W.M., Barros, A.P., ter Hofstede, A.H., Kiepuszewski, B.: Advanced Workflow Patterns. In: Scheuermann, P., Etzion, O. (eds.) CoopIS 2000. LNCS, vol. 1901, pp. 18–29. Springer, Heidelberg (2000)

[28] The Workflow Management Coalition can be found, at http://www.wfmc.org/

[29] Workflow Management Coalition. Terminology and glossary. Technical Report WFMC-TC-1011, Workflow Management Coalition (February 1999)

[30] The Workflow Patterns initiative is a joint effort of Eindhoven University of Technology (led by Professor Wil van der Aalst) and Queensland University of Technology (led by Associate Professor Arthur ter Hofstede). The publications of the Workflow Patterns Initiative can be found at
http://www.Workflowpatterns.com/

Requirements-Driven Design and Configuration Management of Business Processes

Alexei Lapouchnian[1], Yijun Yu[2], and John Mylopoulos[1]

[1] Department of Computer Science, University of Toronto,
Toronto, ON M5S 3G4, Canada
{alexei,jm}@cs.toronto.edu
[2] Computing Department, The Open University,
Milton Keynes, MK7 6AA, U.K.
y.yu@open.ac.uk

Abstract. The success of a business process (BP) depends on whether it meets its business goal as well as non-functional requirements associated with it. BP specifications frequently need to accommodate changing business priorities, varying client preferences, etc. However, since business process goals and preferences are rarely captured explicitly in the dominant BP modeling approaches, adapting business processes proves difficult. We propose a systematic requirements-driven approach for BP design and configuration management that uses requirements goal models to capture alternative process configurations and provides the ability to tailor deployed processes to changing business priorities or customer preferences (i.e., non-functional constraints) by configuring their corresponding goal models at the goal level. A set of design time and runtime tools for configuring business processes implemented using WS-BPEL is provided, allowing to easily change the behaviour of deployed BP instances at a high level, based on business priorities and stakeholder preferences.

1 Introduction

At present, process orientation is a dominant paradigm for businesses. There are many definitions of what a business process is, but in general a BP is seen as a collection of activities that achieves some business *purpose* or *objective* aiming to create value for customers. So, business processes specify ways to achieve business *goals*. Thus, it seems to be natural for business process modeling methods to include facilities for modeling these goals. However, relatively few approaches explicitly capture, refine and analyze business goals (e.g., [9, 6]). Most leading BP modeling approaches capture processes at a workflow level, in terms of activities, flows, etc. (e.g., [20]).

Due to the need to accommodate changing business priorities as well as business cases with varying characteristics (e.g., customers with different preferences), business process specifications need to be flexible as well as capable of being configured and reconfigured appropriately. Currently, techniques as diverse as business rules and late modeling are used for changing BPs. However, these approaches are usually quite low-level and the possible configurations are not explicitly evaluated with respect to

G. Alonso, P. Dadam, and M. Rosemann (Eds.): BPM 2007, LNCS 4714, pp. 246–261, 2007.

business goals and priorities. Thus, it is hard to select process alternatives with desired non-functional characteristics. Additionally, most of these methods require extensive knowledge of the process and, possibly, the modeling notation to be effectively applied thus making it difficult for non-technical users to configure BPs.

To alleviate the above difficulties, we are proposing a systematic business requirements-driven method for configuration of *high-variability* business processes at a high level, in terms of business priorities. In our approach, we start by employing goal models to capture and refine business goals as well as to explore and analyze the variability (the various ways these goals can be attained) in the business domain. Quality attributes such as customer satisfaction serve as the selection criteria for choosing among BP alternatives induced by the goal models. These high-variability goal models are then used in a semi-automatic variability-preserving transformation to generate customizable executable business processes (in our case study we use the Business Process Execution Language (BPEL) [16]). Through the preserved traceability links to goal models, the executable processes can be configured based on qualitative preferences of stakeholders. Automated analysis of the models is used at design time or at runtime to identify process alternatives that best match these preferences. A GUI tool for capturing user preferences and a prototype runtime infrastructure are also provided.

The rest of this paper is structured as follows. Section 2 provides some background on goal models, and on how they can be used for software configuration and to capture and analyze variability. Section 3 describes our approach in detail. Discussion and future work section follows, while Section 5 concludes the paper.

2   Goal Models and Preferences

In this section, we introduce goal models and the relevant work on using them for software configuration.

A major breakthrough of the past decade in (software) Requirements Engineering is the development of a framework for capturing and analyzing stakeholder intentions to generate functional and non-functional (quality) requirements – Goal-Oriented RE (GORE) [2, 3]. The main concept in GORE is the *goal*. For example, a stakeholder goal for a library information system may be Fulfill Every Book Request. This goal may be decomposed in different ways. One might consist of ensuring book availability by limiting the borrowing period and also by notifying users who requested a book that the book is available. This decomposition may lead (through intermediate steps) to functional requirements such as Remind Borrower and Notify User. A different decomposition of the initial goal, however, may involve buying a book whenever a request cannot be fulfilled[1]. Obviously, there are in general many ways to fulfill a goal. Analyzing the space of alternatives makes the process of generating functional and quality requirements more systematic in the sense that the designer is exploring an *explicitly represented* space of alternatives. It also makes it more rational in that the designer can point to an explicit evaluation of these alternatives in terms of stakeholder criteria to justify his choice. An authoritative account of GORE can be found in [21].

---

[1] This is not, however, a very practical alternative.

At the very heart of this new phase of Software Engineering are goal models that represent stakeholder intentions and their refinements using formally defined relationships. Functional goals are modeled in terms of hard goals (or simply goals, when there is no ambiguity). For example, Supply Customer and Fulfill Every Book Request are functional goals that are either fulfilled (satisfied) or not fulfilled (denied). Other stakeholder goals are qualitative and are hard to define formally. For instance, Customer Satisfaction and Have a Productive Meeting are qualitative goals and they are modeled in terms of *softgoals*. A softgoal by its very nature doesn't have a clear-cut criterion for its fulfillment, and may be fully or partially satisfied or denied. Softgoals can be *satisficed* – met to an acceptable degree.

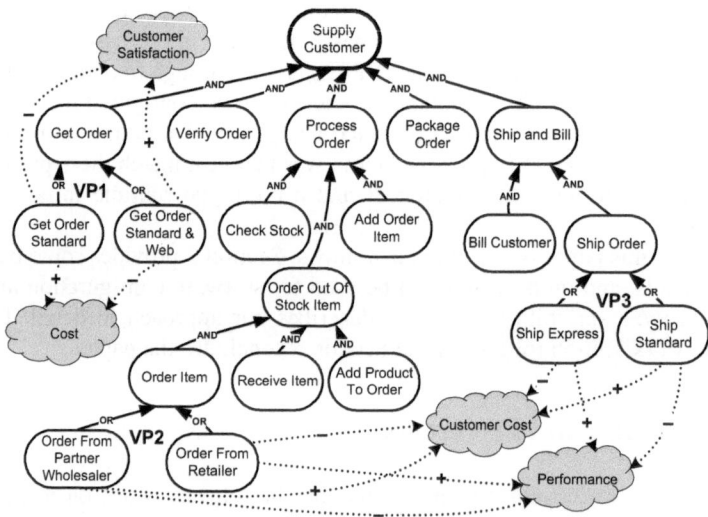

Fig. 1. A goal model showing interdependencies among goals and qualities

Goals and/or softgoals may be related through AND/OR relationships that have the obvious semantics that the AND-decomposed subgoals must all be attained for their parent goal to be achieved and at least one OR-decomposed subgoal needs to be achieved for achieving its parent goal. In addition, goals/softgoals can be related to softgoals through help (+), hurt (–), make (++), or break (--) relationships (represented with the dotted line arrows in Fig. 1). These *contribution links* allow us to *qualitatively* specify that there is evidence that certain goals/softgoals contribute positively or negatively to the satisficing of softgoals. Then, a softgoal is satisficed if there is sufficient positive and little negative evidence for this claim. This simple language is sufficient for modeling and analyzing goals during early requirements, covering both functional and quality requirements, which in this framework are treated as first-class citizens.

To illustrate what goal models are, let us look at a distribution company selling goods to customers. We will use this example throughout the remainder of the paper to demonstrate our approach. The company gets its products from wholesalers and sells the goods to customers (see Fig. 1). It does not have any retail stores, so it receives orders though phone, fax, and, possibly, a web site and ships products using a shipping company. The top-level goal here is Supply Customer, which is AND-decomposed into a number of goals including Get Order, Process Order, and Ship and Bill [order]. Some of the subgoals have alternative solutions. For example, to ship an order, one can achieve either the Ship Express goal or the Ship Standard goal.

Quality attributes are represented as softgoals (cloudy shapes in the figure). In our example, the four top-level desired qualities are Customer Satisfaction, [Minimize distributor] Cost, [Minimize] Customer Cost, and Performance. Clearly, express shipping is fast, but expensive, thus it helps the softgoal Performance while hurting Customer Cost. Similarly, providing a web site for order submission (Get Order Standard & Web) may be more expensive for the distributor (thus the negative link to Cost), but contributes positively to Customer Satisfaction. As shown in Fig. 1, such partial contributions are explicitly expressed in the goal model. In all, the goal model in Fig. 1 shows eight alternative ways for fulfilling the goal Supply Customer. It is easy to verify that generally the number of alternatives represented by a typical goal model depends exponentially on the number of OR decompositions (labelled as variation points "VP1" through "VP3" in Fig. 1) present in the goal model (assuming a "normalized" goal model where AND and OR decompositions are interleaved). As such, goal models make it possible to capture during requirements analysis – in stake-holder-oriented terms – all the different ways of fulfilling top-level goals. A systematic approach for thoroughly analyzing the variability in the problem domain with the help of high-variability goal models is discussed in [14]. The paper proposes a taxonomy of *variability concerns* as well as the method for making sure these concerns are properly addressed during the goal model elicitation process. Now, if one were designing a flexible, customizable implementation for a process, it would make sense to ensure that the implementation is designed to accommodate most or all ways of fulfilling top-level goals (i.e., delivering the desired functionality), rather than just some.

Another feature of goal models is that alternatives can be ranked with respect to the qualities modeled in the figure by comparing their overall contributions to respective softgoals. So, the model of Fig. 1 represents a space of alternative behaviours that can lead to the fulfillment of top-level business goals, and also captures how these alternatives stack up with respect to qualities desired by stakeholders.

Goal Model Enrichments. While the goal models as described above are a useful tool in requirements elicitation and analysis, they lack precision and the level of detail for a more thorough analysis of the problem domain that is required for the subsequent design phases. For example, it might be important to model data/resource dependencies and the precedence constraints among subgoals in the problem domain. Similarly, specifying inputs and outputs for the subgoals in the goal model (i.e., what information and/or resources are required for the attainment of each goal and what resources and/or information are produced when the goal is achieved) is necessary for deriving precise system requirements. In general, a variety of enrichments can be used with goal models. The choice for enrichments depends on the types of analyses or model transformations that one would like to carry out on goal models.

We use textual *annotations* to add the necessary details to goal models. Most of the annotations specify the details of control flow among the subgoals. For example, the sequence annotation (";") can be added to AND goal decomposition to indicate that all the subgoals are to be achieved in sequence from left to right. Sequence annotations are useful to model data dependencies or precedence constraints among subgoals. The absence of any dependency among subgoals in an AND decomposition can be indicated by the concurrency ("||") annotation. Conditional annotations can also be added to specify that certain goals are to be achieved only under some specific circumstances. Lapouchnian and Lespérance [10] discuss various annotations, including loops, interrupts, etc.

It is important to note that the above-mentioned annotations capture properties of the problem domain in more detail and are not used to capture design choices, so they are requirements-level annotations.

Reasoning with Goal Models. While goal models are used for modeling and communicating requirements, we are also interested in the automated analysis of these models. To this end, Sebastiani et al. [18] devised a sound and complete goal satisfaction label propagation algorithm that given a goal model with a number of alternative ways to satisfy its goals and a number of softgoals, can be used to find the alternative that achieves the chosen subset of goals in the model while best addressing these quality constraints (in order of their priority).

Goal Model-based Customization and Configuration. There has been interest in applying goal models in practice to configure and customize complex software systems. In [4], goal models were used in the context of "personal software" (e.g., an email system) specifically to capture alternative ways of achieving user goals as a basis for creating highly customizable systems that can be fine-tuned for each particular user. The Goals-Skills-Preferences approach for ranking alternatives is also proposed in [4]. The approach takes into consideration the user's preferences (the desired quality attributes) as well as the user's physical and mental *skills* to find the best option for achieving the user's goals. This is done by comparing the skills profile of the user to the skills requirements of various system configuration choices. For example, for the user who has difficulty using the computer keyboard, the configurator system will reject the alternatives that require typing in favour of voice input.

Goal models can also be used for configuring complex software systems based on high-level user goals and quality concerns. Liaskos et al. [13] propose a systematic way of eliciting goal models that appropriately explain the intentions behind existing systems. In [23], Yu et al. show how goal models can be used to automatically configure relevant aspects of a complex system without accessing its source code.

3 The Approach

In this section, we describe our technique for business process modeling and configuration. It is requirements-driven and is motivated by the lack of support in most current BP modeling approaches for high-level, intentional configuration of business processes. The approach involves the modeling and analysis (using quality criteria) of alternative ways of achieving business goals with subsequent generation of executable business processes that preserve the variability captured at a goal level. The assumption behind this approach is that in the business domain where it is applied, the characteristics of business cases demand tailored business process variants. Below, we briefly outline the steps of the process and highlight the responsibilities of various actors while the subsequent sections describe the process in detail:

Table 1. Overview of the process steps

	Responsible Role	Description	Artefact Produced
1	Business Analyst (BA), Business Users	Capture and refine the goals of the business process with emphasis on variability	High-Variability (HV) Goal Model
2	BA, Requirements Engineer	Enrich the model with control flow and I/O annotations	Annotated HV Goal Model
3	BA	Analyze BP alternatives, remove infeasible ones	Annotated HV Goal Model
4	Automated	Generate High-Variability BPEL specification from HV Goal Model	Initial HV BPEL process
5	BPEL/Integration Developer	Complete the HV BPEL process, select partner Web Services, deploy process	Executable HV BPEL process
6	Business Users	Select prioritizations among available quality criteria	BP Preferences, Configured Goal Model
7	Automated	Select the best BP configuration matching user preferences	BP Configuration
8	Automated	Create BP instance with the selected configuration, execute it	Configured BPEL process

3.1 Business Process Design with Goal Models

Using goals for business process modeling is not a new idea. A number of different goal modeling notations have been used for this [6, 9]. In addition, requirements goal models have shown to be a convenient notation for the elicitation, modeling, and analysis of variability in the context of software development, configuration, and customization [13, 23]. In our approach, we use high-variability goal models to capture *why* a business process is needed – its purpose or goal – and the many different ways *how* this goal can be attained. Business process alternatives implied by the models are then evaluated with respect to their quality (non-functional) attributes.

We continue to use the Supply Customer process from Fig. 1 in this section. We have added some more details to it in Fig. 2 (note that the annotations are described in Section 3.2). To model a BP in our approach we first identify its business goal (e.g., Supply Customer). This goal becomes the root of the goal model. It is then refined using AND/OR decompositions until the resultant subgoals can be delegated to either human actors or software services.

Let us walk through the Supply Customer process once again. First, customer orders are received either through phone, fax, or the web. After verifying an order, the distributor processes the order by checking if it has all the ordered goods in stock. If so, each product is added to the order. If some item is not in stock, it is ordered from either a wholesaler or a retailer. Ordering out of stock goods through the usual channel from a wholesaler is cheaper (positive contribution to Customer Cost), but requires more time (negative contribution to Performance), while ordering the goods from a nearby retailer to complete the order has the opposite contributions to these softgoals. After an order is packaged, it is shipped (using either the express or the standard shipping method) while the customer is sent a bill.

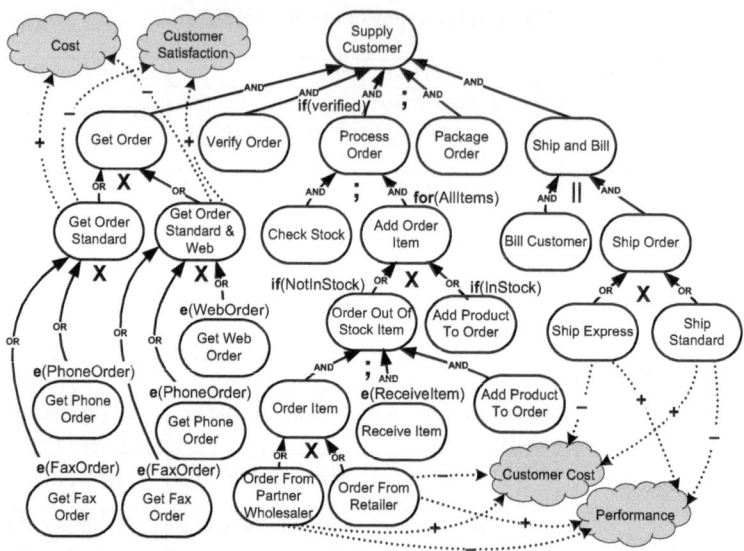

Fig. 2. A goal model for the "Supply Customer" business process

We are placing a special emphasis on business process variability since explicitly representing the space of alternatives using goal models allows for a systematic analysis and comparison of the various ways of achieving high-level business goals (i.e., the various BP alternatives). Whenever there is a number of different ways to achieve some business goal, the modeler uses OR decompositions to capture that fact. Some of these alternatives contribute differently to the non-functional business concerns such as Customer Satisfaction, [Minimize] Cost, etc. represented as softgoals in the model. We describe how these quality criteria are used in selecting the appropriate process configurations in Section 3.3.

3.2   Enriching Goal Models for BP Modeling

Since we are interested in the automated execution of business processes, we need to capture more information about BPs than the basic goal models allow. A few annotations are introduced for this purpose. Note that the annotations presented here are not required to be formal. We use the following control flow annotations when employing goal models to represent business processes:

- Parallel ("||") and sequence (";") annotations can be used with AND-decomposed goals to specify whether or not their subgoals are to be achieved in a temporal order. For example, billing customers and shipping goods is done concurrently in the process.
- By default, in goal models, OR decompositions are inclusive. Exclusive OR decompositions are marked with the "X" annotation. All of the OR decompositions in our example in Fig. 2 are exclusive.

- Conditions ("if(condition)") indicate the necessary conditions for achieving subgoals. For example, in Fig. 2 the goal Order Out Of Stock Product is achieved only if the item is not already in stock.
- Loops ("while(condition)" or "for(setOfItems)"). For instance, the goal Add Order Item must be achieved for all items in the order.
- Event handlers or interrupts ("e(Event)"). In Fig. 2, the arrival of customer orders through fax, phone, or web is modeled by the events (e.g., e(PhoneOrder)) that trigger the achievement of the appropriate goals.

In addition to the above annotations, modeling of input/output parameters of goals is also important for BP modeling. Identifying inputs and outputs during the analysis of a business domain helps in determining resource requirements for achieving goals as well as for the sequencing of the goals. The types of inputs and outputs can also be specified. While optional, the input/output types can be used to generate detailed specifications for messages and service interfaces in a BP implementation. For example, Fig. 3 shows a parameterized fragment of the Supply Customer goal model. The parameters are specified inside goal nodes and the output parameters are identified with the star ("*") symbol. Deliberating about which resources/data are required for the attainment of a goal and which are produced when the goal is achieved can frequently help to identify important process details that are easy to miss otherwise. For instance, Fig. 3 adds the subgoal Pick Order Bin, which picks a location where ordered items are physically stored before being packaged.

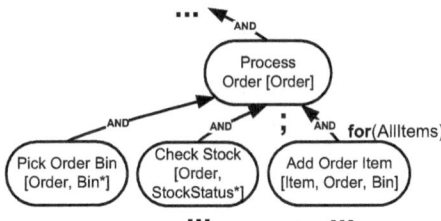

Fig. 3. Adding goal parameters

3.3 Specifying Goal Model Configurations

In goal models, there exist OR decompositions where the selection of alternatives is driven by data or events. For example, in Fig. 2 the OR decomposition of the goal Get Order Standard is event-driven as the choice depends on the way the customer submits an order. Similarly, the choice for achieving the Add Order Item goal depends on whether the item is in stock. However, there are other OR decompositions with alternatives, whose selection is not dependent on data/events. We call them *preference-driven* OR decompositions, or variation points (the data-/event-driven OR decomposition are not considered VPs as they cannot be used to configure processes). In the example in Fig. 2, these variation points are: Get Order, Order Item, and Ship Order. From the point of view of the functionality of a business process, the achievement of any of the alternative subgoals of these VPs is exactly the same. The difference is in the way these choices contribute to the quality attributes of the process. These VPs play a central role in our business process configuration approach as they allow the selection of the best way to meet quality constraints of the stakeholders while delivering the required functionality of business processes. Thus, softgoals act as (possibly *conflicting*, as seen in our example) selection criteria for choosing the right BP alternative based on the priorities (among softgoals) of process owners, customers, etc.

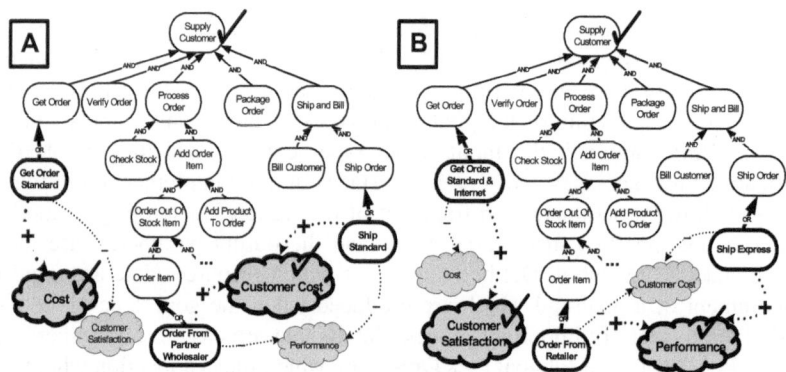

Fig. 4. Two alternative goal model configurations

To illustrate the above discussion, Fig. 4 shows two alternative configurations of the process Supply Customer. These configurations are the result of applying the top-down goal reasoning algorithm of [18] to the model in Fig. 2. The checkmarks indicate the highlighted (soft)goals, whose achievement we are interested in – the input to the algorithm (another input is the relative ranking of the softgoals, which we assume to be the same here). The first configuration (Fig. 4A) is where the Cost of running the process for the distributor and Customer Cost are the top priorities. The highlighted VP decisions contribute positively to the selected softgoals. This configuration includes, for instance, Ship Standard as it is cheaper. If, however, Customer Satisfaction and process Performance are the top priorities, then the configuration changes to the one in Fig. 4B. Thus, high-variability goal models provide a high-level view of processes with the ability to (automatically) generate BP configurations based on preferences of stakeholders expressed as prioritizations among quality criteria. These features greatly simplify the task of configuring business processes by non-technical users as these individuals can configure processes in terms of user-oriented abstract qualitative notions such as customer satisfaction, etc.

It is easy to notice that in our example, the goal model can be configured by multiple stakeholders, both from the point of view of the process owner (the distributor) by prioritizing among the Cost and the Customer Satisfaction softgoals and from the point of view of the customer by prioritizing among Customer Cost and Performance. This allows the stakeholder that owns the process to partially configure it based on that stakeholder's own preferences (i.e., the *binding* some of the variation points) while leaving other VPs unbound for the customers, partners, etc.

Note that the alternatives deemed not acceptable by the process owner (e.g., due to being too costly) can be removed from goal models, thus reducing the BP variability before the generation of executable BP models.

3.4 Generating Flexible Executable Business Processes

As we have just shown, goal models can be a useful tool for high-level configuration of business processes based on stakeholder prioritization among quality criteria. The above techniques can be used to develop, analyze, and configure BP models at design time. However, we would also like to be able to use the high-variability goal models as a starting point for the development of executable business processes that preserve the variability found in the source goal models as well as for configuring these BPs though the appropriate traceability links.

To this end, we have devised a method for using goal models to assist with the development and configuration of high-variability (flexible) BPEL processes. Unlike some workflow-level notations such as BPMN [20], our goal modeling notation is highly structured, with goals organized in refinement hierarchies. This makes it possible to generate BPEL processes (albeit lacking some low-level details) that are easily readable by humans and are structured after the respective goal models. The BPEL code generation is *semi-automatic* and the generated code, while not immediately executable and thus needing to be completed (mainly due to the fact that we do not require conditions in annotations to be formalized), nevertheless provides valuable help in producing an executable BP based on the source goal model. The code is to be further developed by integration developers, who will also be selecting/designing Web services to be used by the process.

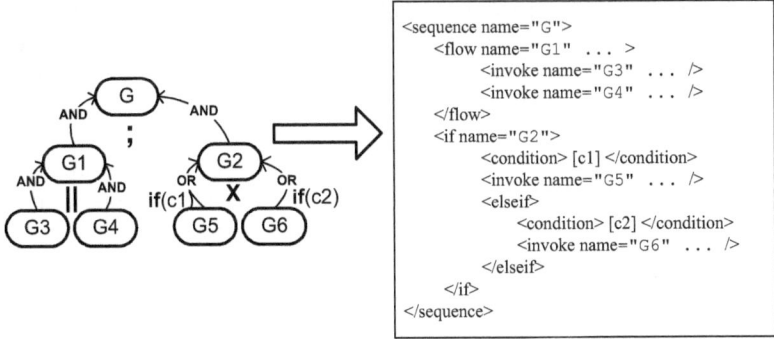

Fig. 5. Example of WS-BPEL 2.0 code generation

Since BPEL is a workflow-level language, only activities that are executed by human actors or software systems (Web services) are represented in BPEL specifications. On the other hand, using goal models, we start modeling from abstract high-level goals and refine them into goals that can be assigned to humans or software. Thus, leaf-level goals correspond to the actual work that is done within a BP, while higher-level ones provide the rationale for why this work has to be done and how it relates to the ultimate purpose of a process. Thus, non-leaf goals do not create basic

BPEL activities, but since they are used to group lower-level goals based on their decomposition types (AND/OR) and control flow annotations, they help in generating the corresponding BPEL control flow constructs. We start BPEL generation from the root goal and recursively traverse the goal tree until we reach leaf goals.

We now present some of the goal model to BPEL 1.1 or 2.0[2] mappings through the example in Fig. 5, which shows a generic annotated goal model fragment. The root goal G has a sequential AND refinement, so it corresponds to the `sequence` operator in BPEL. G1 has a parallel AND refinement, so it maps to the `flow` construct. G2 has a data-driven XOR refinement (note the annotations), so it generates the `if-elseif` (BPEL 2.0) or the `switch` (BPEL 1.1) operator. Note that the conditions c1 and c2, which are informal descriptions in the goal model, will be replaced with the appropriate conditions by a BPEL developer. The leaf goals correspond to Web service invocations. This is how enriched goal models are used to generate the overall structure of a BPEL process.

While we abstract from some of the low-level BPEL details such as correlations, with the information captured in the annotated goal models, we also generate the following aspects of BPEL/WSDL specifications (we do not show the complete mapping due to the lack of space):

- We do an initial setup by defining the appropriate interface (`portType`), etc. for the process. A special `portType` for invoking the process and providing it with the (initial) configuration is also defined.
- An event-driven OR decomposition (e.g., **Get Order Standard** in Fig. 2) maps into the `pick` activity with each alternative subgoal corresponding to an `on-Message` event. Since each such event must match an operation exposed by the process, an operation with the name of each subgoal is added to the `portType` of the process. A message type for the received event is also added to the process interface. A BPEL developer must define the message as the event annotations specified at the requirements level usually lack the required message details. The activities that are executed for each `onMessage` event are the BPEL mappings of the subtrees rooted at the subgoals in the decomposition.
- A conditional/loop annotation for a goal G is mapped to the appropriate BPEL construct (e.g., `if-elseif` or `switch, while`, etc.) with the activity to be executed being the result of mapping the goal model subtree rooted at G into BPEL. The formal conditions currently have to be specified manually.
- Leaf-level goals map into Web service invocations. The information in the goal model helps in defining the interface for the Web services invoked by the BP. We define appropriate WSDL messages based on input/output parameters of these goals. If data types are omitted from the goal model, they have to be supplied by a developer.
- Softgoals are used as the evaluation criteria in the configuration process and thus do not map into the resulting BPEL specification.

The main idea behind the generation of high-variability BPEL processes is the preservation of BP variability captured in goal models. As we have shown above, data- and

---

[2] While in our case study we generated BPEL 1.1 processes, WS-BPEL 2.0 [16] allows for simpler, more natural mapping from annotated goal models.

event-driven variability is directly preserved through the appropriate mapping to BPEL. Additionally, we need to preserve the preference-driven VPs in the executable BPs since they are the main vehicle for process configuration based on stakeholder preferences. In our approach, for each preference-driven VP we generate a BPEL switch construct (or if-elseif if using BPEL 2.0) where each case (branch) corresponds to an alternative subgoal (e.g., Ship Order in Fig. 2 will produce the cases for Ship Express and Ship Standard). The condition in each case checks to see if the case is the current choice for the VP by comparing the name of the alternative subgoal it corresponds to (e.g., "Ship Express") to the string extracted from the current BP configuration (see the next section for details), thus ensuring the correct branch is taken. The activities executed in each case are automatically generated and represent the BPEL mapping of the alternative subgoals of the VP. A VP also gets a name from the corresponding goal node (we assume that VP names are unique).

Fig. 6 shows our Eclipse-based goal modeling and analysis tool OpenOME [17] being used to design business processes with both the goal model (right pane) and the BPEL (left pane) visualizations.

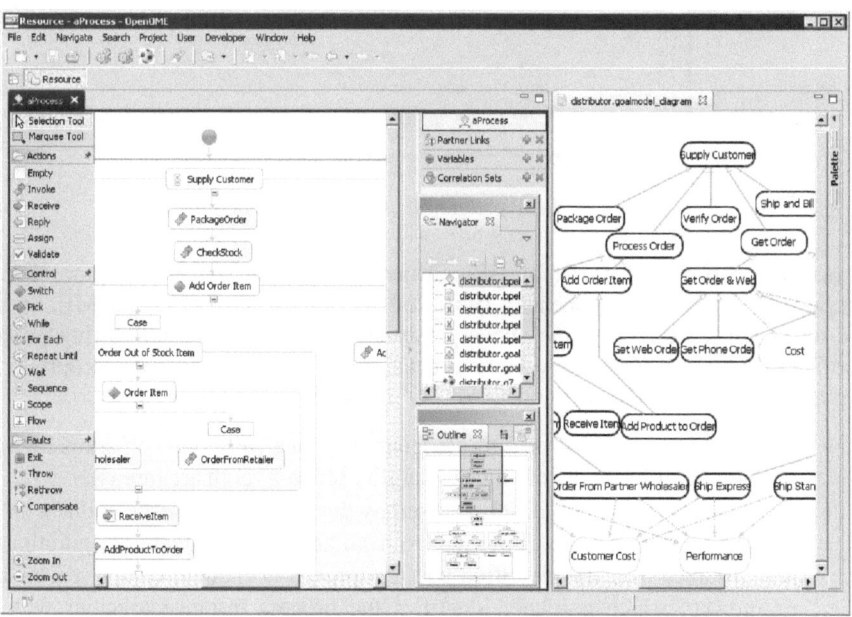

Fig. 6. OpenOME being used to design a business process

3.5   Quality-Based Business Process Configuration

Once a High-Variability BPEL process is fully developed and deployed, its instances can be configured by users through the prioritization among its associated quality criteria. This task has two elements. First, we elicit user preferences and generate the corresponding process configuration. Second, an instance of a BP has to be provided with this configuration. Let us look at these two subtasks in more detail.

There are several ways to specify user preferences in our approach. First, users can use OpenOME to specify which softgoals they want satisficed in a process and run a top-down analysis algorithm (similar to what we did in Fig. 4). The result will be a particular BP configuration that best suits the user. Another possibility is to use the GUI tool (see Fig. 7) that simplifies the task even more by only exposing quality attributes of a process and by allowing users to specify the partial ordering of the attributes in terms of their importance (Rank) as well as their expected satisficing level (with convenient sliders). Multiple profiles can be created for a particular BP model – for varying market conditions, customers, etc. Behind the scenes, a preference profile is converted into a goal model configuration (using the same goal reasoning algorithm of [18]). The tool can then create instances of processes with the desired configuration.

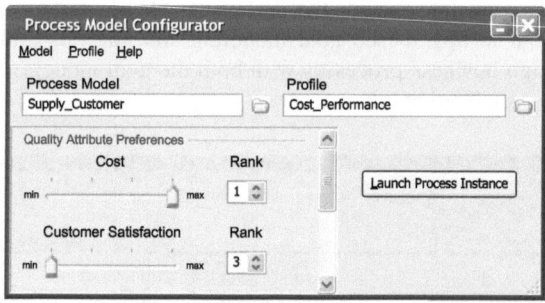

Fig. 7. BP preference configuration tool

Another part of our prototype BP configuration toolset is the Configurator Web service. This service implements a subset of the functionality of OpenOME, mainly the top-down reasoning engine and a persistent knowledge base for storing process configurations. It is designed to communicate these configurations to appropriate BP instances at runtime. The main operations of the service are as follows:

- `registerProcess` is used to associate a unique `processID` parameter with the endpoint of a deployed high-variability process (both are inputs).
- `launchProcessInstance` is be used by the GUI tool to create and run an instance of a process. Inputs are `processID` and a goal model configuration. A new instance of a BP identified by `processID` is created. It is given an `instanceID`, which uniquely identifies the process instance together with its configuration so that it is possible to evolve BP configurations independently. The configuration is stored in a knowledge base. The configuration and the `instanceID` are communicated to the BP instance.
- `getConfiguration`, which can be used by process instances to get their configurations from the Configurator Web service. The input is an `instanceID` and the output is the current configuration for that process instance. This operation can be used to get an updated configuration for a process instance.

The configuration provided to process instances is a list of variation points and the name of the selected subgoal in each of them. Below is an example:

```
<FullConfig>
        <VPConfig>
                <VP> ShipOrder </VP>
                <Selection> ShipStandard </Selection>
        </VPConfig>
        ...
</FullConfig>
```

Then, XPath [22] queries are used to extract the configuration. For example, the query `/FullConfig/VPConfig[VP="ShipOrder"]/Selection` extracts the configuration for the variation point `ShipOrder`. The result is matched with the appropriate case in the switch construct corresponding to the variation point as described in the previous section. Thus, the executing process becomes configured according to the user preferences specified in terms of priorities among quality criteria associated with the business process.

4 Discussion and Future Work

Most popular BP modeling approaches such as BPMN [20] or EPCs [8] are work-flow-level notations. They do not allow the analysis of process alternatives in terms of high-level quality attributes or business goals and thus do not provide traceability of BP alternatives to requirements. There are, however, BP modeling approaches that explicitly capture and refine business goals (e.g., [6, 9]). Unlike our approach, these notations do not model process variability or the effect of alternatives on quality attributes. While some research has focused on variability in business process models [19], our approach centers on capturing and analyzing variability at the requirements level. Similarly, research on configurable BPEL processes (e.g., [5]) so far mostly concentrated on low-level configurability that may not be visible to process users.

A number of approaches based on the Tropos framework [1] applied ideas from requirements engineering and agent-oriented software engineering to BPEL process design [7] and SOA architecture design [12]. Both these approaches give heuristics on creating BPEL processes based on requirements models, but fall short from providing semi-automatic generation procedures. Likewise, BP variability is not explored. Nevertheless, we believe that agent-oriented modeling techniques of Tropos are useful for BP modeling and analysis and are currently working on integrating them into our approach. Similarly, we are looking at supporting context-based softgoal prioritization where the preferences change depending on the characteristics of business cases. For instance, in our Supply Customer example, the process owner may want to set Customer Satisfaction to be the top priority for high-valued customers.

We are collaborating with a large BPM software vendor to use our method with their workflow-level BP modeling and analysis notation and tools, thus allowing a more gradual development of BPs first with goal models, then with a workflow-level notation, and finally with BPEL while preserving the traceability among the notations, specifically, among the variation points.

This approach is part of a larger effort for developing requirements-driven adaptive business processes. To this end, we are working on implementing the support for the dynamic reconfiguration of high-variability processes based on changing requirements, stakeholder preferences and data captured by a BP monitoring environment. In terms of the approach presented here, dynamic process adaptation requires changes in the way BP configurations are updated and propagated to process instances. For example, one technique, which is currently implemented, is to push the updated configuration to the process instance through a special callback operation.

The drawbacks of the approach presented here include the need to explicitly model and analyze process alternatives as well as the fact that the qualitative analysis of alternatives may be too imprecise and subjective. We are working on integrating quantitative analysis of alternatives into our approach [11]. One of the elements of this addition to the method is a more precise specification of process alternatives' contributions to softgoals. Similarly, the softgoals themselves can be *opertionalized* into measurable quantities. Another extension that we are working on is the introduction of hard constraints that will play a role similar to the role of skills in [4] – helping to remove process alternatives that are incompatible with the characteristics of the process participants. We are also developing better tool support for this approach and working on improving the infrastructure and the generation of BPEL code as well as on supporting the modeling and analysis of BP exceptions.

5 Conclusion

We have presented an approach for requirements-driven design and configuration of business processes. Requirements goal models are used to capture and refine business goals with the emphasis on identifying alternative ways of attaining them while (possibly conflicting) quality constraints are used to analyze and select appropriate process alternatives. Goal model annotations for capturing process-relevant details are also introduced. Then, given an annotated high-variability goal model, a variability-preserving procedure generates a well-structured high-variability WS-BPEL specification (with programmers needing to fill in details of data handling, to define conditions and some other aspects of the process), which can be configured given high-level user preferences. A prototype system for preference profile specification and BP configuration is discussed.

The benefits of the approach include the fact that BPs can be automatically configured in terms of criteria accessible to non-technical users, thus greatly simplifying process configuration. The method helps in transitioning from business requirements analysis to BP design and implementation by allowing to gradually increase the level of detail in process models and by providing a semi-automated variability- and structure-preserving procedure for generation of executable business processes. The approach is also helping to maintain the processes' traceability to requirements.

References

1. Castro, J., Kolp, M., Mylopoulos, J.: Towards Requirements-Driven Information Systems Engineering: The Tropos Project. Information Systems 27(6), 365–389 (2002)
2. Dardenne, A., van Lamsweerde, A., Fickas, S.: Goal-Directed Requirements Acquisition. Science of Computer Programming 20, 3–50 (1993)
3. Chung, L., Nixon, B., Yu, E., Mylopoulos, J.: Non-Functional Requirements in Software Engineering. Kluwer, Dordrecht (2000)

4. Hui, B., Liaskos, S., Mylopoulos, J.: Requirements Analysis for Customizable Software: Goals-Skills-Preferences Framework. In: Proc. International Requirements Engineering Conference (RE'03), Monterrey, CA (September 2003)
5. Karastoyanova, D., Leymann, F., Buchmann, A.: An approach to Parameterizing Web Service Flows. In: Proc. International Conference on Service-Oriented Computing 2005, Amsterdam, The Netherlands (December 2005)
6. Kavakli, V., Loucopoulos, P.: Goal-Driven Business Process Analysis Application in Electricity Deregulation. Information Systems 24(3), 187–207 (1999)
7. Kazhamiakin, R., Pistore, M., Roveri, M.: A Framework for Integrating Business Processes and Business Requirements. In: Proc. EDOC 2004, Monterey, USA (2004)
8. Keller, G., Nuttgens, M., Scheer, A.W.: Semantische Prozessmodellierung auf der Grundlage Ereignisgesteuerter Prozessketten (EPK). Technical Report 89, Institut fur Wirtschaftsinformatik Saarbrucken, Saarbrucken, Germany (in German) (1992)
9. Kueng, P., Kawalek, P.: Goal-Based Business Process Models: Creation and Evaluation. Business Process Management Journal 3(1), 17–38 (1997)
10. Lapouchnian, A., Lespérance, Y.: Modeling Mental States in Agent-Oriented Requirements Engineering. In: Dubois, E., Pohl, K. (eds.) CAiSE 2006. LNCS, vol. 4001, pp. 480–494. Springer, Heidelberg (2006)
11. Lapouchnian, A., Yu, Y., Liaskos, S., Mylopoulos, J.: Requirements-Driven Design of Autonomic Application Software. In: Proc. International Conference on Computer Science and Software Engineering CASCON 2006, Toronto, Canada (October 16-19, 2006)
12. Lau, D., Mylopoulos, J.: Designing Web Services with Tropos. In: Proc. International Conference on Web Services (ICWS'04), San Diego, CA, USA (2004)
13. Liaskos, S., Lapouchnian, A., Wang, Y., Yu, Y., Easterbrook, S.: Configuring Common Personal Software: a Requirements-Driven Approach. In: Proc. International Requirements Engineering Conference (RE'05), Paris, France (August 29 - September 2, 2005)
14. Liaskos, S., Lapouchnian, A., Yu, Y., Yu, E., Mylopoulos, J.: On Goal-based Variability Acquisition and Analysis. In: Proc. International Requirements Engineering Conference (RE'06), Minneapolis, USA (September 11-15, 2006)
15. Mylopoulos, J., Chung, L., Nixon, B.: Representing and Using Non-functional Requirements: a Process-oriented Approach. IEEE Transactions on Software Engineering 18(6), 483–497 (1992)
16. OASIS: Web Services Business Process Execution Language Version 2.0 Primer (Draft) (2007), Available at www.oasis-open.org/committees/documents.php?wg_abbrev=wsbpel
17. OpenOME: (2007), Available at www.cs.toronto.edu/km/openome/
18. Sebastiani, R., Giorgini, P., Mylopoulos, J.: Simple and minimum-cost satisfiability for goal models. In: Persson, A., Stirna, J. (eds.) CAiSE 2004. LNCS, vol. 3084, Springer, Heidelberg (2004)
19. Schnieders, A., Puhlmann, F.: Variability Mechanisms in E-Business Process Families. In: Proc. International Conference on Business Information Systems (BIS 2006), Klagenfurt, Austria (2006)
20. White, S.: Business Process Modeling Notation (BPMN) Version 1.0. Business Process Management Initiative, BPMI.org (May 2004)
21. van Lamsweerde, A.: Requirements Engineering in the Year 00: A Research Perspective. In: Proc. International Conference on Software Engineering (ICSE'00), Limerick, Ireland (June 2000)
22. World Wide Web Consortium: XML Path Language (XPath) 2.0 Recommendation (2007), Available at www.w3.org/TR/2007/REC-xpath20-20070123/
23. Yu, Y., Lapouchnian, A., Liaskos, S., Mylopoulos, J.: Requirements-Driven Configuration of Software Systems. In: Proc. WCRE 2005 Workshop on Reverse Engineering to Requirements (RETR'05), Pittsburgh, PA, USA (November 7, 2005)

SAP WebFlow Made Configurable: Unifying Workflow Templates into a Configurable Model

Florian Gottschalk, Wil M.P. van der Aalst, and Monique H. Jansen-Vullers

Eindhoven University of Technology,
P.O. Box 513, 5600 MB Eindhoven, The Netherlands
{f.gottschalk,w.m.p.v.d.aalst,m.h.jansen-vullers}@tue.nl

Abstract. To facilitate the implementation of workflows, enterprise and workflow system vendors typically provide workflow templates for their software. Each of these templates depicts a variant of how the software supports a certain business process, allowing the user to save the effort of creating models and links to system components from scratch by selecting and activating the appropriate template. A combination of the strengths from different templates is however only achievable by manually adapting the templates which is cumbersome. We therefore suggest in this paper to combine different workflow templates into a single configurable workflow template. Using the workflow modeling language of SAP's WebFlow engine, we show how such a configurable workflow modeling language can be created by identifying the configurable elements in the original language. Requirements imposed on configurations inhibit invalid configurations. Based on a default configuration such configurable templates can be used as easy as the traditional templates. The suggested approach is also applicable to other workflow modeling languages.

Keywords: Process Configuration, Reference Model, Workflow Template.

1 Introduction

A workflow engine facilitates the execution of business processes by guiding and monitoring the process while "running through the company". Whenever needed it assigns tasks to the responsible individuals, provides all relevant information, and takes action in case tasks are not performed in time [10].

To execute a workflow in a workflow engine, it must be specified in the engine's workflow modeling language which is quasi an extended business process modeling language (like Event-driven Process Chains (EPCs) [9] or BPMN [17]). Besides depicting the process, it allows for the integration of the process model with other systems like enterprise systems, office software, or intranet portals.

The effort to establish this integration is typically high. When modeling a workflow, it is not only required to ensure the correct control flow, but also the data flow between the different steps and components must be "programmed"

G. Alonso, P. Dadam, and M. Rosemann (Eds.): BPM 2007, LNCS 4714, pp. 262–270, 2007.
© Springer-Verlag Berlin Heidelberg 2007

and assignment rules for resources must be set up. Thus, the re-use of workflow models promises huge costs savings when implementing workflows in similar system environments. This holds especially for enterprise systems, which due to the system structure already imply the set-up of processes in quite specific ways.

The biggest enterprise system vendor worldwide is SAP with more than 100,000 installations [14]. SAP's workflow engine is called WebFlow. It is delivered together with each of their enterprise system installations since the R/3 Release 3.0. Together with the engine, SAP also delivers hundreds of simple, predefined workflow templates for all areas of the system – from logistics to personal time or compensation management [10]. Thus, the template repository can be regarded as a reference model of common workflows in SAP's enterprise system. The templates, which typically fit comfortably on one A4 page, can easily be activated in the SAP system. Without a local workflow designer having ever spent a significant amount of time on the workflow definition, they are then triggered automatically whenever their execution is required. Often SAP users are therefore working on the predefined workflows without even knowing it.

For many business processes the repository includes several workflow templates, each suggesting a different implementation of the particular process. For example, a dedicated workflow template exists not only for the approval of a travel request, but also for the automatic approval of a travel request, the approval of a travel plan, and both the approval and the automatic approval of a trip. All these templates are of course similar. To decide on the appropriate template, each template is documented in SAP's online help system, typically also combined with an EPC of the process [13]. However, there is no information available that highlights the differences between the templates. Instead, the workflow designer has to familiarize herself with each workflow template, compare them manually, and find the small differences. If a certain degree of inconsistency exists in the documentation of the templates (as for example in the EPCs documenting the templates for supporting the approval of a travel request and the automatic approval of a travel request where it is unclear if "Create travel request" and "Enter travel request" actually depict the same task [13]), this comparison requires even more efforts. Further on, the workflow designer might come up with the conclusion that a combination of two templates is the optimal solution as each template has its strength at a different point. As such a template is not available she can then only manually adapt the weak point of one of the templates to match the not selected one here as close as possible.

To help the workflow designers in getting the optimal workflow template we propose in the following to combine the different workflow template variants into a single template using an extension to the workflow modeling language making it a configurable language. Using SAP's workflow modeling language and the travel approval process example, we will show how this configuration extension allows the workflow designer to select or eliminate the relevant or irrelevant template parts in the integrated model. Instead of searching for the possibilities in various, similar templates, the designer can thus focus on the workflow requirements.

An extended description of the approach is available as an internal report [7].

2   Configurable Workflow Models in SAP

In almost all graphical process modeling languages the routing of cases through the model is determined by the triggering of tasks, functions, steps or any other type of performed action as well as by the release of cases after the actions' completion. We call each possibility to trigger an action an *input port* of the action and each way an action can trigger subsequent paths an *output port* of the action. When integrating several workflow variants into one workflow model, ports are thus the elements of the integrated workflow where we can apply the two general applicable configuration methodologies of blocking and hiding which we identified in our previous research [6].

Actions, ports, and their configuration in SAP WebFlow. SAP WebFlow is mainly based on so-called *steps* and *events* which are organized in a block structure (see Figure 1 for the before-mentioned travel approval process which is accessible in SAP as workflow WS20000050). Steps represent either routing constructs or system functionalities. In the simplest case a single step as, e.g., an activity, forms a block. However, whenever a step causes the branching of the control-flow (as, e.g., a fork, a condition, or a user-decision) the branching of the control flow is matched by exactly one corresponding join and all elements

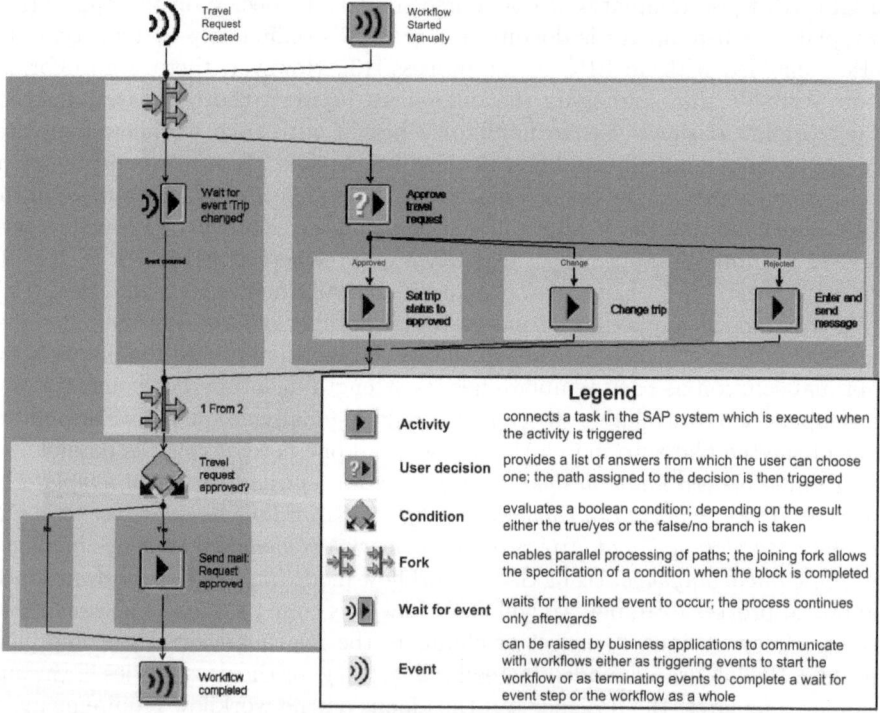

Fig. 1. SAP's workflow template for travel approval processes (WS20000050)

until (and including) the join belong to the branching step's block. The elements in each of the branches represent then sub-blocks of the branching block. For example, in Figure 1 the block of the fork is highlighted in light grey. It contains two sub-blocks for the two branches. The block of the user-decision *Approve travel request* branches again in three sub-blocks for the particular activities.

Thus, each block can be seen as an action. Basically, each block contains just one unique input path and one unique output path which are the ports of the action. The largest block is the complete workflow itself. It is the only block which can be triggered in multiple ways as it can be triggered not only manually but also by (various) events which are linked to the workflow block (see top of Figure 1). In addition, events can be linked to a workflow block or a *wait for event* step to terminate them. Thus, each of these links connecting events to the workflow block can also be seen as a port. As they have some different characteristics from a block's in- and output ports, we call them *event ports*.

The linkage between steps or events and workflows includes also the linkage of the data in the data containers of the step or event and the workflow. This linkage enables starting workflows or steps with the right parameters, e.g. to select responsible resources or correct documents. We will skip such implementation details here, but not without repeating that this modeling and customizing effort is far more time-consuming than the pure creation of a process model. These efforts therefore motivate the development of a configurable SAP WebFlow.

To configure a workflow model, we can use the configuration methodologies of blocking and hiding [6] at the ports of actions. If a port of an action is *blocked*, the action cannot be triggered. Thus, the process will never continue after the action or reach any subsequent action. If an action's port is *hidden*, the action's performance is not observable, i.e. it is skipped and consumes neither time nor resources. But the process flow continues afterwards and subsequent actions will be performed. If an action in a workflow model is neither blocked nor hidden, then we say it is *enabled*, which refers to its normal execution. This concept can be applied to the input ports of blocks in SAP WebFlow in a straightforward manner. If the input port of a block is enabled, cases can normally enter and be executed in the block. If the input port is hidden, a case entering the block is directly forwarded to the unique exit port of the block, quasi bypassing all the content of the block. If the input port is blocked, the case cannot enter the block at all and needs to continue via other alternative branches.

Common soundness criteria for workflow models require that cases must always have a chance to complete a workflow. Thus, a block's input port can only be blocked if an alternatively executable branch exists which leads to the workflow's completion. For example, instead of the *Change trip* step, the *Set trip status to approved* or the *Enter and send message* steps can be executed. It is however impossible to block the input port at the *Travel request approved?* step as no alternative routing exists here. In the case of this particular fork step, it is possible to block one of the two sub-blocks, but only because the join requires just one of the two branches to complete. If the condition at the join would have been "2 From 2" a blocking of one of the sub-blocks would have made it impossible to later satisfy this condition and thus caused a deadlock. There-fore, when configuring the sub-blocks of a fork, the condition at the joining fork determines the maximal amount of sub-blocks that can be blocked.

Each case entering a block must be able to leave the block via its unique output port. Thus, this port can only be blocked if the block's input port is blocked. However, if the input port is blocked no tokens can arrive at the output port, i.e. the configuration has no influence on the process. Hiding of an output port is not feasible either because the path to the next block does not contain any action that can be skipped. We can therefore consider the output port configuration as practically irrelevant in SAP WebFlow.

In SAP WebFlow an event only triggers a workflow if the link between the event and the workflow is activated. SAP WebFlow already supports the deacti-vation of such a link, quasi corresponding to the blocking of the particular event port. Although a triggering event port is an inflow port, hiding of such a port is quite useless because it would basically mean skipping the whole workflow block without performing any step. Terminating event ports for wait-for-event steps are output ports. Even though terminating events are externally triggered, they basically enforce the removal of the case from the particular block. Thus, the functionality of SAP to activate or deactivate such linkages already provides exactly the required functionality to configure event ports.

In Figure 2 we combined the workflow template from Figure 1 with SAP's tem-plate for the automatic approval of travel requests (WS12500021). By blocking the *change trip* step the corresponding block is quasi removed from the workflow. By hiding of the *Travel request approved?* step, also the sub-block of mailing the request's approval is skipped. All other blocks are enabled. Although the two process templates were integrated, the result of this configuration corresponds exactly to the template for the automatic approval of travel requests. By block-ing the sub-block of the *Criteria for Automatic Approval* step's *Automatically Approve Travel Request* outcome and instead enabling the *Change trip* and the *Travel request approved?* blocks, we would get the workflow from Figure 1.

Restricting the configuration opportunities. Not all such combinations are feasible in practice. We already mentioned the requirement that a workflow always has to have the opportunity to complete. In addition, there are always a lot of semantic requirements. For example, it is well possible to block or en-able the *Wait for event 'Changed'* step's block. However, hiding it prevents the workflow from working correctly as it causes a direct forwarding of cases to the joining fork whose condition would immediately be satisfied. The other branch would get superfluous and cancelled before any decision on the approval can be made.

Using logical expressions to denote such requirements, we could for exam-ple write `configuration("Enter and send short message")=ENABLED` to de-pict that the particular block must be enabled or `configuration("Wait for event 'changed'")!=HIDDEN` for the requirement that the block cannot be hidden. Such atomic logical expressions can then be combined, e.g., to formu-late a requirement that if the *Change trip* block is blocked then the *Travel*

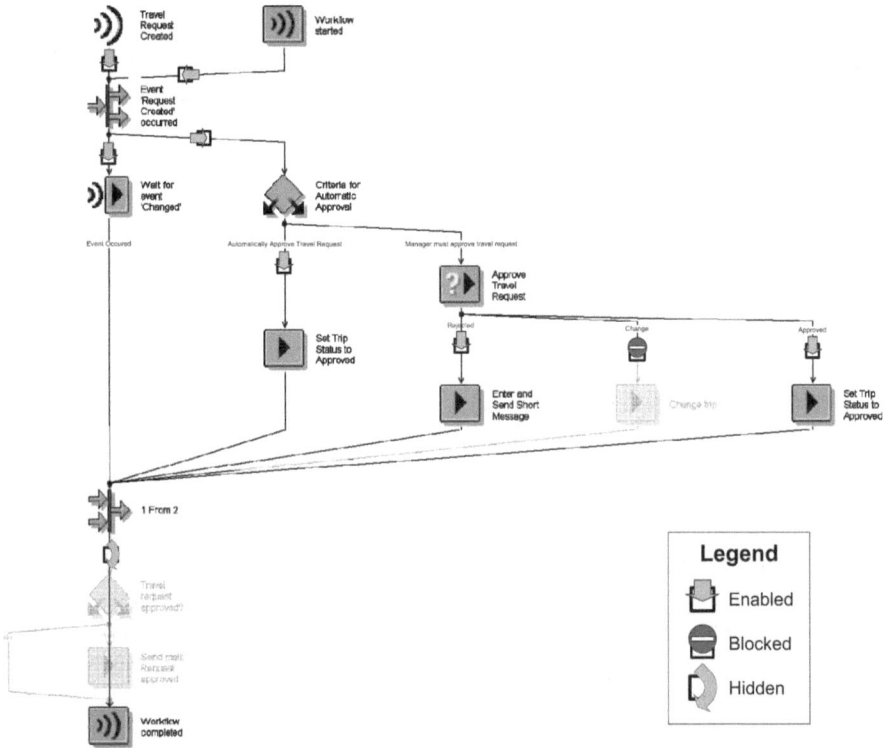

Fig. 2. The combined workflow template of SAP's travel approval and automatic travel approval templates, configured as the automatic approval workflow

request approved? must be hidden (`configuration("Change trip")=BLOCKED => configuration("Travel request approved?")=HIDDEN`).

To test if a configuration fulfills all requirements, the requirements can be combined using `AND` operators. By determining blocks which can change their configuration values without breaking these requirements, a tool that regularly re-evaluates the configuration opportunities could even highlight those workflow blocks which are not bound to their current value and thus really configurable.

Plug and Play. The current SAP WebFlow templates allow for an easy integration of the predefined workflow templates into a running SAP system by just assigning the relevant resources to the steps and activating the triggering events. To enable such an easy activation also for configurable workflow templates, each workflow template has to have a default configuration that satisfies the specified requirements. For example, the configuration of Figure 2 representing the automatic approval template could be the default configuration for the combined travel approval workflow template. When activating the triggering event, the workflow corresponding to this configuration would automatically be enabled. However, if it is for example desired, that the manager is also able to ask for a change of the travel request, it is sufficient to assign the responsible resource to the *Change* step and activate the currently blocked port. Without any modeling effort the new configuration of the workflow template can be used.

3   Related Work

The workflow templates of SAP's WebFlow engine depict suggestions how to execute the particular processes in SAP. Thus, as the conceptual *SAP reference model* [4] they are reference models for processes in SAP, but on an executable level. Motivated by the "Design by Reuse" paradigm, reference models simplify the process model design by providing repositories of generally valid and potentially relevant models to accelerate the modeling process [5].

To be applicable in a particular context (e.g., a specific enterprise), a generally valid reference model must be adjusted to individual needs. To enable the adaptation of reference models by means of configuration, several variants of the process must be integrated. Extensions to conceptual process modeling languages allowing for such integrations are suggested by Becker et al. [3], Rosemann and van der Aalst [12], and Soffer et al. [15]. Although the potential efficiency benefits of using configurable process models during enterprise system implementations are highlighted by all the authors, the suggested usage of their approaches remains on the conceptual level.

The idea of providing configurable workflow models as suggested here implies to have different variants of the process in different contexts. Of course, the required workflow configuration can change over time which then requires the transfer of running workflow instances to the new configuration. Systems tackling these problems are also called configurable, re-configurable or adaptive workflow systems (e.g., in [8,16]), but typically neglect the preceding aspect of how the change of the workflow model can be supported.

4   Conclusions and Outlook

Based on the block-structured workflow notation of SAP's WebFlow engine, which comes with a huge set of pre-defined workflow templates, we showed the advantages of integrating several workflow templates into a single workflow model from which workflow variants can be derived by means of configuration. To make a workflow modeling language configurable the elements representing *actions* and their *ports* which route the cases through the actions must be identified. Representing runtime alternatives, ports can be *enabled* to allow the action's execution, be *hidden* to skip the particular action, or be *blocked* to prevent any flow of cases via the action. *Requirements* on the configuration ensure the configuration's applicability on the workflow. A *default configuration* enables the usage of a configurable workflow template even without any configuration effort and serves as the starting point for any configuration. All that is needed to use such configurable models in SAP WebFlow is an implementation of the user interface for performing configuration decisions, a tool checking the requirements, and a transformation of the configurable model into the configured model.

In future research, we have to show that our ideas are also applicable to non-block-structured workflow modeling languages. For this purpose, we are currently applying these ideas onto YAWL, an open-source workflow system supporting far more patterns than SAP WebFlow [1,2]. To provide further assistance for the configuration of workflow models, we aim at integrating the idea of configurable workflow modeling languages into a configuration framework enabling the use of advanced decision-making tools for performing the configuration [11], and a synchronized configuration between workflows and other software applications.

References

1. van der Aalst, W.M.P., ter Hofstede, A.H.M.: YAWL: Yet Another Workflow Language. Information Systems 30(4), 245–275 (2005)
2. van der Aalst, W.M.P., ter Hofstede, A.H.M., Kiepuszewski, B., Barros, A.P.: Workflow Patterns. Distributed and Parallel Databases 14(1), 5–51 (2003)
3. Becker, J., Delfmann, P., Dreiling, A., Knackstedt, R., Kuropka, D.: Configurative Process Modeling – Outlining an Approach to increased Business Process Model Usability. In: Proceedings of the 15th IRMA IC, New Orleans (2004)
4. Curran, T., Keller, G., Ladd, A.: SAP R/3 Business Blueprint: Understanding the Business Process Reference Model, Upper Saddle River. Prentice Hall, Englewood Cliffs (1998)
5. Fettke, P., Loos, P.: Classification of Reference Models – a Methodology and its Application. Information Systems and e-Business Management 1(1), 35–53 (2003)
6. Gottschalk, F., van der Aalst, W.M.P., Jansen-Vullers, M.H.: Configurable Process Models – A Foundational Approach. In: Becker, J., Delfmann, P. (eds.) Reference Modeling. Efficient Information Systems Design Through Reuse of Information Models, pp. 59–78. Springer, Heidelberg (2007)
7. Gottschalk, F., van der Aalst, W.M.P., Jansen-Vullers, M.H.: SAP WebFlow Made Configurable: Unifying Workflow Templates into a Configurable Model. Beta Working Paper 221, Eindhoven University of Technology, The Netherlands (2007)
8. Han, Y., Schaaf, T., Pang, H.: A Framework for Configurable Workflow Systems. In: Proceedings of the 31st International Conference on Technology of Object-Oriented Language and Systems, Los Alamitos, pp. 218–224 (1999)
9. Keller, G., Nüttgens, M., Scheer, A.W.: Semantische Prozeßmodellierung auf der Grundlage Ereignisgesteuerter Prozeßketten (EPK). Veröffentlichungen des Instituts für Wirtschaftsinformatik, Heft 89 (in German), Saarbrücken (1992)
10. Rickayzen, A., Dart, J., Brennecke, C., Schneider, M.: Practical Workflow for SAP – Effective Business Processes using SAP's WebFlow Engine. Galileo Press (2002)
11. La Rosa, M., Lux, J., Seidel, S., Dumas, M., ter Hofstede, A.H.M.: Questionnaire-driven Configuration of Reference Process Models. In: Proceedings of the 19th CAiSE, Trondheim, Norway, pp. 424–438 (2007)
12. Rosemann, M., van der Aalst, W.M.P.: A Configurable Reference Modelling Language. Information Systems 32(1), 1–23 (2007)
13. SAP AG. SAP Library – Workflow Scenarios in Travel Management (FI-TV) (2006), http://help.sap.com/saphelp_erp2005vp/helpdata/en/d5/202038541ec006e10000009b38f8cf/frameset.htm

14. SAP AG. SAP History: From Start-Up Software Vendor to Global Market Leader (April 2007), http://www.sap.com/company/history.epx
15. Soffer, P., Golany, B., Dori, D.: ERP modeling: a comprehensive approach. Information Systems 28(6), 673–690 (2003)
16. Tam, S., Lee, W.B., Chung, W.W.C., Nam, E.L.Y.: Design of a re-configurable workflow system for rapid product development. Business Process Management Journal 9(1), 33–45 (2003)
17. White, S.A., et al.: Business Process Modeling Notation (BPMN), Version 1.0 (2004)

Behavioral Constraints for Services

Niels Lohmann[1,*], Peter Massuthe[1], and Karsten Wolf[2]

[1] Humboldt-Universität zu Berlin, Institut für Informatik,
Unter den Linden 6, 10099 Berlin, Germany
{nlohmann,massuthe}@informatik.hu-berlin.de
[2] Universität Rostock, Institut für Informatik,
18051 Rostock, Germany
karsten.wolf@informatik.uni-rostock.de

Abstract. In service-oriented architectures (SOA), deadlock-free interaction of services is an important correctness criterion. To support service discovery in an SOA, *operating guidelines* serve as a structure to characterize all deadlock-freely interacting partners of a services. In practice, however, there are *intended* and *unintended* deadlock-freely interacting partners of a service. In this paper, we provide a formal approach to express intended and unintended behavior as *behavioral constraints*. With such a constraint, unintended partners can be "filtered" yielding a customized operating guideline. Customized operating guidelines can be applied to validate a service and for service discovery.

Keywords: Business process modeling and analysis, Formal models in business process management, Process verification and validation, Petri nets, Operating guidelines, Constraints.

1   Introduction

Services are an emerging paradigm of interorganizational cooperation. They basically encapsulate self-contained functionalities that interact through a well-defined interface. A service can typically not be executed in isolation — services are designed for being invoked by other services or for invoking other services themselves. *Service-oriented architectures* (SOA) [1] provide a general framework for service interaction. Thereby, three roles of services are distinguished. A *service provider* publishes information about his service to a public repository. A *service broker* manages the repository and allows a *service requester* (also called client) to find an adequate published service. Then, the provider and the requester may bind their services and start interaction.

In [2,3] we introduced the notion of an *operating guideline* (*OG*) of a service as an artifact to be published by a provider. The operating guideline OG_{Prov} of a service *Prov* characterizes all requester services *Req* that interact deadlock-freely with *Prov*. Operating guidelines therefore enable the broker to return only those published services *Prov* to a querying *Req* such that their interaction

---

* Funded by the BMBF project "Tools4BPEL".

G. Alonso, P. Dadam, and M. Rosemann (Eds.): BPM 2007, LNCS 4714, pp. 271–287, 2007.
© Springer-Verlag Berlin Heidelberg 2007

is guaranteed to be deadlock-free. Additionally, an operating guideline is an operational description and can therefore be used to *generate* a deadlock-free interacting service *Req*.

In practice, there are *intended* and *unintended* clients for a service. For example, an online shop is intendedly designed for selling goods to its customers. After an update of its functionality, it might introduce the possibility to abort the ordering at any time. The *OG* of such a shop would now also characterize customers that abort after the first, second, etc. step of the ordering process. These interactions with aborting partners are deadlock-free. However, the owner of the shop is interested whether it is still possible to actually purchase goods in his shop.

On the other hand, a service broker might classify provider services as intended or unintended. For example, he may want to assure certain features, like payment with certain credit cards only. Finally, a client requesting for a travel agency might want to exclude going by train and thus is only interested in flights. Even more involved, he could prefer arranged communication such that certain actions occur in a given order (first hotel reservation, then flight booking, for instance).

In this paper we study *behavioral constraints* (constraints for short) that have to be satisfied in addition to deadlock freedom. We provide a formal approach for steering the communication with *Prov* into a desired direction and extend operating guidelines to *customized* operating guidelines. A customized *OG* of *Prov* characterizes all those services *Req* that communicate deadlock-freely with *Prov* satisfying a given constraint.

We identified four scenarios involving behavioral constraints.

1. *Validation.* Before publishing, the designer of a service *Prov* wants to check whether a certain feature of *Prov* can be used.
2. *Restriction.* A specialized repository might require a certain constraint to be fulfilled by published services. To add a service *Prov* to this repository, its behavior might have to be restricted to satisfy the constraint.
3. *Selection.* For a service *Req*, the broker is queried for a matching provider service *Prov* satisfying a given constraint.
4. *Construction.* A requester does not have a service yet, but expresses desired features as a constraint. The broker returns all operating guidelines providing these features. With this operational description, the requester service can then be constructed.

In the first two scenarios, the operational description — in this paper given as a Petri net — of *Prov* itself is available. This has the advantage that constraints are not restricted to communication actions but may involve internal behavior of the service. This way, a service can, for instance, be customized to legal requirements (publish, for example, an operating guideline where only those partners are characterized, for which the internal action "add added value tax" has been executed). In contrast, in the last two scenarios, a customized operating guideline is computed from a given general operating guideline of *Prov*, without having access to an operational description of *Prov* itself.

In this paper, we propose solutions for all four scenarios. That is, we show how to compute customized operating guidelines (a) from a given operational description of *Prov* itself, or (b) from a given general operating guideline.

It is worth being mentioned that our approach is fully residing on the behavioral (protocol) level. That is, we abstract from semantic as well as nonfunctional issues. Our approach is not meant to be a competitor to those approaches but rather a complement. In fact, a proper treatment of semantic discrepancies between services is a prerequisite of our approach, but does not replace the necessity to send and receive messages in a suitable order. Policies and nonfunctional criteria can be integrated into our approach as far as they can be reduced to behavioral constraints. They are, however, not the focus of this paper. We chose deadlock freedom as the principle notion of "correct interaction". There are certainly other correctness criteria which make sense (for instance, additional absence of livelocks) but our setting is certainly the most simple one and part of any other reasonable concept of correctness. Thus, our setting can be seen as an intermediate step towards more sophisticated settings.

The rest of this paper is organized as follows. In Sect. 2, we set up the formal basis for our approach and introduce an online shop as running example throughout the paper. Section 3 is devoted to implement constraints into the operational description of a service. Our solutions to compute a customized operating guideline from a general one are presented in Sect. 4. We conclude with a presentation of related work in Sect. 5 and a discussion of future work in Sect. 6.

2   A Formal Approach to SOA

Our algorithms are based on open workflow nets (oWFNs) [4] and descriptions of their behavior (service automata [2]). Suitability of oWFNs for modeling services has been proven through an implemented translation from the industrial service description language WS-BPEL [5] into oWFNs [6]. Service automata form the basis of our concept of an operating guideline. The presentation of our constructions on this formal level simplifies the constructions and makes our approach independent of the evolution of real-world service description languages. As our approach is to a large extend computer-aided, the formalisms can, however, be hidden in real applications of our methods.

2.1   Open Workflow Nets

Open workflow nets (oWFNs) are a special class of Petri nets. They generalize the classical workflow nets [7] by introducing an interface for asynchronous message passing. oWFNs provide a simple but formal foundation to model services and their interaction.

We assume the usual definition of (place/transition) Petri nets. An *open workflow net* is a Petri net $N = [P, T, F]$, together with an *interface* $P_i \cup P_o$ such that $P_i, P_o \subseteq P$, $P_i \cap P_o = \emptyset$, and for all transitions $t \in T$: $p \in P_i$ (resp. $p \in P_o$) implies $(t, p) \notin F$ (resp. $(p, t) \notin F$); a distinguished marking m_0, called the *initial marking*; and a distinguished set Ω of *final markings*. P_i (resp. P_o) is called the set of *input* (resp. *output*) places.

We require that the initial or a final marking neither marks input nor output places. We further require that final markings do not enable a transition. A nonfinal marking that does not enable a transition is called *deadlock*.

Throughout this paper, consider an online shop as running example. An open workflow net N_{shop} modeling this online shop is depicted in Fig. 1. The only final marking is [final]; that is, only place final is marked. Though the online shop is a small toy example, it allows to demonstrate the results of this paper.

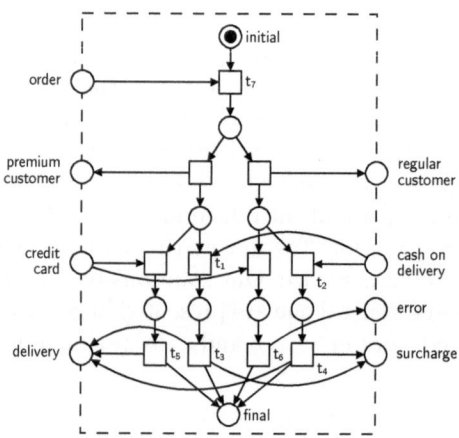

Fig. 1. An oWFN N_{shop} modeling an online shop. It initially receives an **order** from a customer. Depending on the previous orders, the customer is classified as **premium** or **regular customer**. Premium customers can pay with **credit card** or **cash on delivery**, whereas regular customers can only pay **cash on delivery**: If a regular customer tries to pay with **credit card**, the online shop will respond with an **error** message. Otherwise, a **delivery** notification — and in case of **cash on delivery** payment a **surcharge** notification — is sent.

Open workflow nets — like common Petri nets — allow for diverse analysis methods of computer-aided verification. The explicit modeling of the interface further allows to analyze the communicational behavior of a service [6,8].

The interaction of services is modeled by the composition of the corresponding oWFN models. For composing two oWFNs M and N, we require that M and N share interface places only. The composed oWFN $M \oplus N$ can then be constructed by merging joint places and merging the initial and final markings. All interface places of M and N become internal to $M \oplus N$.

For a given oWFN *Prov* of a service provider we are particularly interested in the set of oWFNs *Req* of service requesters, such that $Req \oplus Prov$ is deadlock-free. Each such *Req* is called a *strategy* for *Prov*. We write $Strat(Prov)$ to denote the set of strategies for *Prov*. The term strategy originates from a control-theoretic point of view (see [9,10], for instance): We may see *Req* as a controller for *Prov* imposing deadlock freedom of $Req \oplus Prov$.

As an example, consider a client of our online shop firstly placing an order and then receiving either premium customer or regular customer. In any case, he pays cash on delivery and then receives the surcharge notice and the delivery. Obviously, the described client is a strategy for N_{shop}.

In this paper, we restrict ourselves to oWFNs with bounded state space. That is, we require the oWFNs M, N, and $M \oplus N$ to have finitely many reachable markings.

2.2   Service Automata

In the following, we recall the concepts of *service automata* and *operating guidelines*, which were introduced in [2] and generalized in [3]. Operating guidelines are well-suited to characterize the set of all services *Req* for which $Req \oplus Prov$ is deadlock-free. Since absence of deadlocks is a behavioral property, two oWFNs which have the same behavior but are structurally different have the same strategies. Thus, we may refrain from structural aspects and consider the behavior of oWFNs only. Service automata serve as our behavioral model.

A *service automaton* $A = [Q, I, O, \delta, q_0, \Omega]$ consists of a set Q of states; a set I of input channels; a set O of output channels, such that $I \cap O = \emptyset$; a nondeterministic transition relation $\delta \subseteq Q \times (I \cup O \cup \{\tau\}) \times Q$; an initial state $q_0 \in Q$; and a set of final states $\Omega \subseteq Q$ such that $q \in \Omega$ and $(q, x, q') \in \delta$ implies $x \in I$. A service automaton is finite if its set of states is finite.

As an example, the service automaton modeling the described client of the online shop is depicted in Fig 2.

Fig. 2. An automaton describing a strategy for the online shop. The client first sends an order message to the shop, then either receives the regular customer or the premium customer message. In either case he decides for cash on delivery, receives the surcharge note, and finally waits until he receives his delivery. As a convention, we label a transition sending (resp. receiving) a message x with !x (resp. ?x).

The translation of an oWFN into its corresponding service automaton is straightforward [3]. Thereby, we consider the *inner* of the oWFN, easily constructed by removing the interface places and their adjacent arcs, and compute its reachability graph. Transitions of the oWFN that are connected to interface places correspond to transition labels of the service automaton. Similarly, a service automaton can be retranslated into its corresponding oWFN model, using the existing approach of region theory [11], for instance.

The composition of two service automata is the service automaton $A \oplus B$ where the shared interface channels become internal. To reflect our proposed model of asynchronous communication, a state of $A \oplus B$ is a triple of a state of A, a state of B, and a multiset of currently pending messages (see [3] for details). The notions of deadlocks and strategies can be canonically extended from oWFNs to service automata.

2.3 Operating Guidelines

Given a service automaton A, consider now a function Φ that maps every state q of A to a Boolean formula $\Phi(q)$. Let the propositions of $\Phi(q)$ be labels of transitions that leave q in A. Φ is then called *annotation* to A. An *annotated automaton* is denoted by A^{Φ}. We use annotated automata to represent sets of automata. Therefore, we need the concept of *compliance* defined in Def. 1.

Let A and B be two service automata. Then, $R_{(A,B)} \subseteq Q_A \times Q_B$, the *matching relation of A and B*, is inductively defined as follows: $(q_{0_A}, q_{0_B}) \in R_{(A,B)}$. If $(q_A, q_B) \in R_{(A,B)}$, $(q_A, x, q'_A) \in \delta_A$ and $(q_B, x, q'_B) \in \delta_B$, then $(q'_A, q'_B) \in R_{(A,B)}$. Let furthermore β_{q_A} denote an assignment at state q_A of A that assigns *true* to all propositions x for which there exists a transition $(q_A, x, q'_A) \in \delta_A$ and *false* to all other propositions.

Definition 1 (Compliance). *Let A be a service automaton, let B^{Φ} be an annotated service automaton and let $R_{(A,B)}$ and β be as described above. Then, A complies to B^{Φ} iff for every state $q_A \in Q_A$:*
- *there exists a state $q_B \in Q_B$ with $(q_A, q_B) \in R$, and*
- *for every state $q_B \in R(q_A)$ holds: β_{q_A} satisfies the formula $\Phi(q_B)$.*

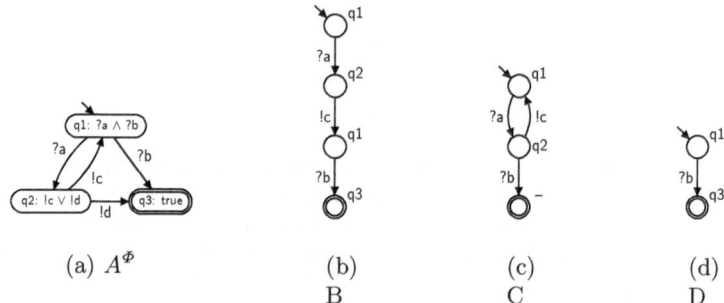

(a) A^{Φ} (b)   (c)   (d)
                       B   C   D

Fig. 3. (a) An annotated service automaton A^{Φ}. The annotation $\Phi(q)$ is depicted inside a state. (b)–(d) Three service automata B, C, and D. A state q of A^{Φ} attached to a state s of B, C, or D represents the element (q, s) in the corresponding matching with A^{Φ}. Since the final state of C has no matching state in A, C does not comply to A^{Φ}. D does not comply to A^{Φ}, because it violates the annotation $\Phi(\text{q1})$ in D's initial state.

Let $Comply(B^\Phi)$ denote the set of all service automata that are compliant to B^Φ. This way, the annotated automaton B^Φ characterizes the set $Comply(B^\Phi)$ of service automata.

As an example, Fig. 3(a) shows an annotated service automaton A^Φ. The service automaton B from Fig. 3(b) complies to A^Φ whereas the automata C and D (cf. Fig. 3(c) and 3(d)) do not comply to A^Φ.

Finally, the operating guideline OG_{Prov} of a service $Prov$ is a special annotated service automaton that represents the set $Strat(Prov)$ of strategies for $Prov$.

Definition 2 (Operating guideline). *Let A be a service automaton. An annotated service automaton B^Φ with $Comply(B^\Phi) = Strat(A)$ is called* operating guideline *of A, denoted OG_A.*

In [3], we presented an algorithm to compute operating guidelines for finite-state service automata. If there is no single strategy for a service $Prov$, then OG_{Prov} is empty. In that case, $Prov$ is obviously ill-designed and has to be corrected. In [6], we demonstrated that even very small changes of a service $Prov$ can have crucial effects on the set of strategies for $Prov$. The calculation of operating guidelines is implemented in the tool Fiona[1], giving the designer of services the possibility to detect and repair errors, that would have been hard or impossible to find manually.

As an example, Fig. 4 depicts the operating guideline for our online shop. Obviously, there are some interleavings in which an error message is received by the client (?e). These interleavings describe deadlock-free interactions though cannot be regarded as successful interactions by the owner of the online shop. Constraints can help to, for example, exclude this unwanted behavior.

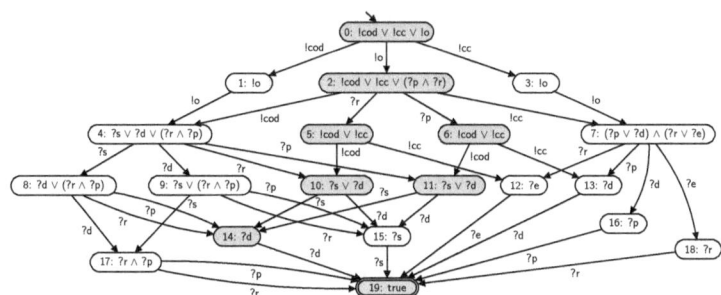

Fig. 4. The operating guideline OG_{shop} of the online shop. For reasons of space we abbreviated message names by its first letter (!o means !order, for instance). !cod abbreviates !cash on delivery, !cc means !credit card. It is easy to see that the client of Fig. 2 complies to OG_{shop}. The matching involves the highlighted states of OG_{shop}.

We propose to use operating guidelines as an artifact generated by the owner of a provider service $Prov$ to be published to the service broker. The broker can

---

[1] Available at http://www.informatik.hu-berlin.de/top/tools4bpel

then check whether or not a given requester service *Req* will have deadlocks with *Prov* even before actually plugging them together.

In Sect. 4, we will use the operating guideline for *Prov* to characterize all requester services for which their composition with *Prov* satisfies a given constraint, thus realizing the third and the fourth scenario from the introduction.

3   Adding Constraints to Open Workflow Nets

As stated in the introduction, we aim at putting constraints on the *behavior* of two oWFNs *Prov* and *Req* in their interaction. Therefore we consider the notion of a *run* of an oWFN N: A run of N is a transition sequence $t_0 \dots t_n$ starting in the initial marking of N and ending in a final marking of N.

We distinguish two effects of constraints: *exclusion* of unwanted behavior and *enforcement* of desired behavior. Using oWFN service models, these effects can be expressed by sets of transitions that are either not permitted to fire, or that are required to fire.

A service *Prov* in isolation usually deadlocks (e. g., the shop in Fig. 1 deadlocks in its initial state). Hence, investigating *Prov* in isolation does not make sense in general. Instead, we consider the composition of *Req* and *Prov*, and check whether this composition satisfies the given constraint. This leads to the following definition of exclude and enforce.

Definition 3 (Exclude, enforce). *Let Req and Prov be two oWFNs and let t be a transition of Prov. $Req \oplus Prov$ excludes t iff no run of $Req \oplus Prov$ contains t. $Req \oplus Prov$ enforces t iff every run of $Req \oplus Prov$ contains t.*

Definition 3 can be canonically extended to *sets* of excluded or enforced transitions. As an example, the composition of the online shop and the client described above excludes the transitions t_5 and t_6, because it has no run where the client sends a credit card message. Furthermore, this composition enforces transition t_7, because in every run an order is sent by the client.

When two services *Req* and *Prov* are given, the exclusion or enforcement of transitions can be checked with the help of the runs of $Req \oplus Prov$. Therefore, standard model checking techniques could be used. However — coming back to the scenarios described in the introduction — when a service provider wants to validate his service *Prov*, there is no fixed partner service *Req*. Hence, we follow a different approach: We suggest to change the oWFN *Prov* according to a given constraint in such a way that the set $Strat(Prov')$ of the resulting oWFN $Prov'$ will be exactly the set of requester services *Req* for which the composition of *Req* and the original oWFN *Prov* satisfies the constraint.

To formulate constraints, we propose *constraint oWFNs*. A constraint oWFN is an oWFN with an empty interface whose transitions are labeled with transitions of the oWFN to be constrained.

Definition 4 (Constraint oWFN). *Let N be an oWFN. Let N' be an oWFN with $P_{i_{N'}} = P_{o_{N'}} = \emptyset$ such that $P_N \cap P_{N'} = \emptyset$ and $T_N \cap T_{N'} = \emptyset$. Let L be a labeling function $L : T_{N'} \to 2^{T_N}$. Then $C = [N', L]$ is a constraint oWFN for N.*

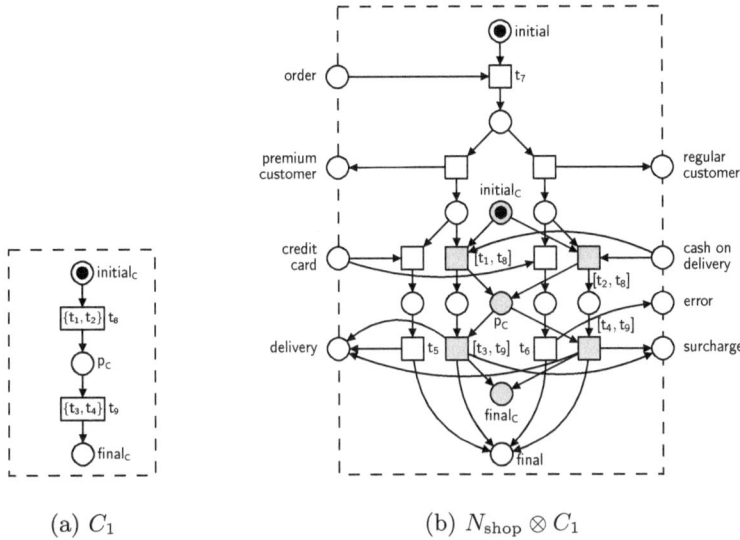

(a) C_1 (b) $N_{\text{shop}} \otimes C_1$

Fig. 5. (a) The constraint oWFN C_1 for the online shop of Fig. 1. As a convention, the labels of the labeling function L are written inside a transition. (b) The product of the online shop and C_1. Gray nodes highlight the changes of the original oWFN.

Constraint oWFNs are a general means to describe constraints: The exclusion and enforcement of transitions can also be expressed by constraint oWFNs.

Figure 5(a) depicts a constraint oWFN, C_1, for the online shop N_{shop} of Fig. 1. The transitions are labeled with sets of transitions of N_{shop}. Intuitively, C_1 is satisfied if the online shop receives a cash on delivery message (i. e., t_1 or t_2 fires) and then sends a surcharge message (i. e., t_3 or t_4 fires). C_1 is an example for constraining the *order* of transitions and therefore cannot be expressed by exclude/enforce constraints as defined in Def. 3.

To implement a constraint in an oWFN, we construct the product of the respective constraint oWFN and the oWFN to be constrained. Intuitively, labeled transitions of the constraint oWFN are merged (i. e., "synchronized") with the transitions of the considered oWFN. So, the product reaches a final marking if both the constraint and the considered oWFN reach a final marking. Define $L(T) = \bigcup_{t \in T} L(t)$ to be the set of all transitions used as a label.

Definition 5 (Product of oWFN and constraint oWFN). *Let N be an oWFN and let $C = [N', L]$ be a constraint oWFN for N. The product of N and C is the oWFN $N \otimes C = [P, P_i, P_o, T, F, m_0, \Omega]$, defined as follows:*

- *$P = P_{N \oplus N'}$, $P_i = P_{i_N}$, $P_o = P_{o_N}$,*
- *$T = (T_N \setminus L(T_{N'})) \cup \{(t, t') \mid t' \in T_{N'}, t \in L(t')\} \cup \{t' \in T_{N'} \mid L(t') = \emptyset\}$,*

$$- F = F_N \setminus ((P_N \times L(T_{N'})) \cup (L(T_{N'}) \times P_N))$$
$$\cup \{[(t,t'),p] \mid t' \in T_{N'}, t \in L(t'), p \in t^\bullet \cup t'^\bullet\}$$
$$\cup \{[p,(t,t')] \mid t' \in T_{N'}, t \in L(t'), p \in {}^\bullet t \cup {}^\bullet t'\},$$
$$- m_0 = m_{0_N} \oplus m_{0_{N''}},$$
$$- \Omega = \Omega_{N \oplus N'}.$$

The product of the online shop of Fig. 1 and the constraint oWFN C_1 of Fig. 5(a) is depicted in Fig. 5(b). The marking [final, final$_c$] is the only final marking of the product. Only when composed to a requester who chooses cash on delivery and then receives the surcharge note, the product can reach this marking.

To check whether an oWFN N satisfies a constraint oWFN $C = [N', L]$, the runs of N and N' have to be considered. A run σ' of N' induces an ordered labeled transition sequence. Each label consists of a set of transitions of N. Thus, σ' describes which transitions of N have to be fired in which order. However, σ' might contain unlabeled transitions, and a run σ of N might contain transitions that are not used as a label in N'. Let $\sigma'_{|L}$ be the transition sequence σ' without all transitions with an empty label. Similarly, let $\sigma_{|L}$ be the transition sequence σ without all transitions that are not used as labels.

Definition 6 (Equivalence, satisfaction). *Let N be an oWFN an $C = [N', L]$ a constraint oWFN for N. Let σ and σ' be a run of N and N', respectively. σ and σ' are equivalent iff $\sigma_{|L} = t_1 \ldots t_n$ and $t_i \in L(t'_i)$ for all $1 \leq i \leq n$. N satisfies the constraint oWFN C, denoted $N \models C$, iff for every run of N there exists an equivalent run of N'.*

We now can link the satisfaction of a constraint with the product:

Theorem 1. *Let Prov and Req be two oWFNs and $C = [N, L]$ a constraint oWFN for Prov.*

Then, Req is a strategy for Prov $\otimes$ C iff Req is a strategy for Prov and Req $\oplus$ Prov $\models$ C.

Proof (sketch)
($\rightarrow$) Every run of $Req \oplus (Prov \otimes C)$ can be "replayed" by $Req \oplus Prov$. This run satisfies C — if not, C would deadlock in $Req \oplus (Prov \otimes C)$, contradicting the assumption that Req is a strategy for $Prov \otimes C$.

($\leftarrow$) As $Req \oplus Prov \models C$, there exists a sub-run of C for every run of $Req \oplus Prov$. From a run of $Req \oplus Prov$ and its sub-run of C, a run of $Req \oplus (Prov \otimes C)$ can be derived. $\square$

Theorem 1 underlines the connection between the product of an oWFN with a constraint oWFN and the runs satisfying a constraint. This connection justifies more efficient solutions for the first two scenarios described in Sect. 1. In the first scenario, a service provider wants to validate his service *Prov*. In particular, he wants to make sure that for all strategies *Req* for *Prov* the composition *Req⊕Prov* satisfies certain constraints, for example that payments will be made, or no errors occur. We suggest to describe the constraint as a constraint oWFN C. Then,

Theorem 1 allows to analyze the product of *Prov* and *C*, *Prov* $\otimes$ *C*, instead of *Prov*. The operating guideline of *Prov* $\otimes$ *C* characterizes all strategies *Req* for *Prov* such that *Req* $\oplus$ *Prov* satisfies *C*. The benefit of this approach is that instead of calculating all strategies *Req* and checking whether *Req* $\oplus$ *Prov* satisfies the constraint *C*, it is possible to characterize *all* *C*-satisfying strategies *Req*. In addition, the latter calculation usually has the same complexity as calculating all strategies for *Prov*.

Similarly, the problem of the second scenario, the publication of a provider service in special repositories, can be solved. We assume that the constraints that have to be satisfied by a provider service to be published in a special repository — for example, the required acceptance of credit cards — are published by the service broker. We again suggest to describe these constraints as a constraint oWFN *C*. The service provider can now calculate the operating guideline $OG_{Prov \otimes C}$ of the product of his service *Prov* and the constraint *C*. Theorem 1 states that this operating guideline characterizes all strategies *Req* for *Prov* such that *Req* $\oplus$ *Prov* satisfies the constraint *C*. If the set of these strategies is not empty, the service provider can publish $OG_{Prov \otimes C}$ in the service repository.

The service *Prov*, however, can remain unchanged. This is an advantage as — instead of adjusting, re-implementing, and maintaining several "versions" of *Prov* for each repository and constraint — only a single service *Prov* has to be deployed. From this service the customized operating guidelines are constructed and published. If, for example, *Prov* supports credit card payment and cash on delivery, then only the strategies using credit card payments would be published to the repository mentioned above. Though there exist strategies *Req* for *Prov* using cash on delivery, those requesters would not match with the published operating guideline.

To conclude this section, we return to the exclude/enforce constraints defined in Def. 3. As mentioned earlier, they can be expressed as constraint oWFNs.

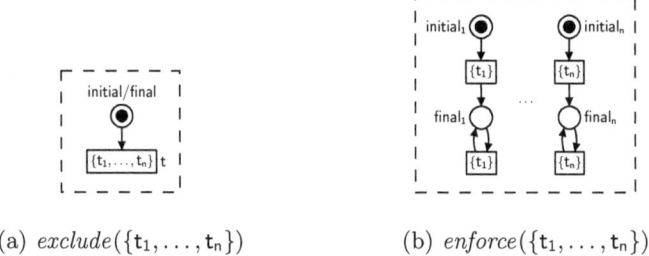

(a) $exclude(\{t_1, \ldots, t_n\})$ (b) $enforce(\{t_1, \ldots, t_n\})$

Fig. 6. In the constraint oWFN to exclude a set of transitions (a), the initial and final marking coincide. Thus, the final marking of the composition becomes unreachable when transition t fires. The constraint oWFN to enforce a set of transitions (b) consists of n similar nets. Each net consists of two labeled transitions to ensure that the enforced transition may fire arbitrarily often. To enforce every of the n transitions to fire at least once, the final marking is $[final_1, \ldots, final_n]$.

The canonic constraint oWFNs expressing the exclusion and enforcement of transitions are depicted in Fig. 6(a) and Fig. 6(b), respectively.

To enforce a certain communication event (the sending of the delivery notification by the online shop, for example), however, a constraint oWFN like the one in Fig. 6(b) cannot be used: enforcing, for instance, *all* three transitions sending delivery (t_3, t_4, and t_5) would require *each* of the transitions to fire in every run of $Req \oplus N_{shop}$ for a client Req. This is not possible as at most one delivery message is sent. Still, the constraint can be expressed by a constraint oWFN similar to C_1 (cf. Fig. 5(a)) with the set $\{t_3, t_4, t_5\}$ used in a label, meaning one of these transition has to fire.

4   Customized Operating Guidelines

The last section was devoted to implementing constraints at build time. We changed the service by building the product of the oWFN model of the service and the constraint oWFN describing the required behavioral restrictions. The presented solutions can be used to validate a given provider service or to publish the service in special repositories.

In a service-oriented approach, however, we also want to be able to dynamically bind provider and requester services *Prov* and *Req* at runtime without the need to change an already published *Prov*. Thus, the question arises whether it is still possible to satisfy a given constraint after publishing the service *Prov*. In this section, we extend our operating guideline approach to this regard. We show that it is possible to describe a constraint as an annotated automaton C^{Ψ}, called *constraint automaton*, and apply it by building the product of C^{Ψ} and the operating guideline OG_{Prov}. The resulting *customized* operating guideline guideline $C^{\Psi} \otimes OG_{Prov}$ will describe the set of all requester services *Req* such that $Req \oplus Prov$ satisfies the constraint.

An advantage of this setting is that we do not need the original oWFN model of *Prov*. A drawback, however, is that for the same reason we are not able to enforce, exclude, or order concrete transitions of the oWFN any more. C^{Ψ} may only constrain send or receive actions as such. For example, if two or more transitions send a message a, then a C^{Ψ} excluding a means that all the original transitions are excluded.

Definition 7 (Constraint automaton). *Let OG_{Prov} be an operating guideline with input channels I_{OG} and output channels O_{OG}. Let $C = [Q, I, O, \delta, q_0, \Omega]$ be a service automaton such that $I \subseteq I_{OG}$ and $O \subseteq O_{OG}$ and let Ψ be an annotation to C. Then, C^{Ψ} is a constraint automaton for OG_{Prov}.*

The product $A^{\Phi} \otimes B^{\Psi}$ of two annotated automata A^{Φ} and B^{Ψ} can be constructed as follows. The states of $A^{\Phi} \otimes B^{\Psi}$ are pairs (q_A, q_B) of states $q_A \in Q_A$ and $q_B \in Q_B$. The initial state is the pair (q_{0_A}, q_{0_B}). A state (q_A, q_B) is a final state of $A^{\Phi} \otimes B^{\Psi}$ iff q_A and q_B are final states of A and B, respectively. There is a transition $((q_A, q_B), x, (q'_A, q'_B))$ in $A^{\Phi} \otimes B^{\Psi}$ iff there are transitions (q_A, x, q'_A) in A *and* (q_B, x, q'_B) in B. The interface of the product is defined as

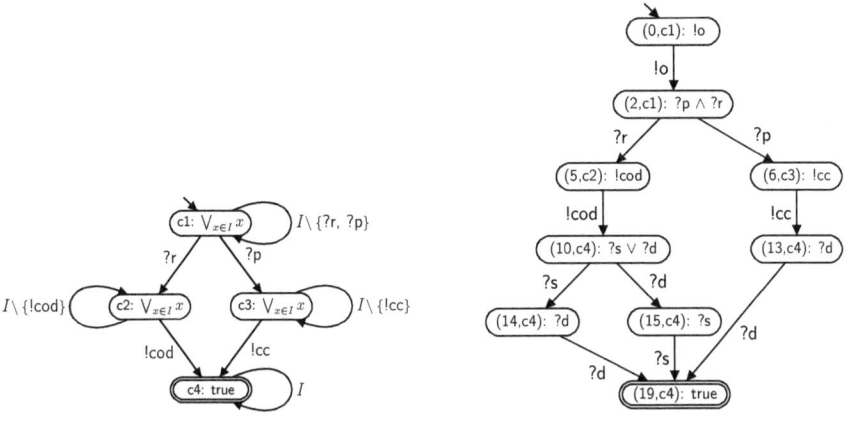

(a) A constraint automaton C^Ψ.   (b) The product $OG_{\text{shop}} \otimes C^\Psi$.

Fig. 7. (a) A constraint automaton for OG_{shop} of Fig. 4. A transition labeled with a set means a transition for each element. $I = \{!o, !cc, !cod, ?r, ?p, ?s, ?e, ?d\}$ is the set of all messages that can be sent to or received by the online shop. (b) The product $OG_{\text{shop}} \otimes C^\Psi$. The annotations were simplified for reasons of better readability.

$I_{A^\Phi \otimes B^\Psi} = I_A \cap I_B$ and $O_{A^\Phi \otimes B^\Psi} = O_A \cap O_B$. The annotation of a state (q_A, q_B) is the conjunction of the annotations of q_A and q_B.

As an example, a constraint automaton C^Ψ for OG_{shop} of Fig. 4 is depicted in Fig. 7(a). It assures that premium customers pay with credit card and regular customers pay cash on delivery. Thereby, we exclude the error message and avoid a surcharge where possible. The product of OG_{shop} with C^Ψ is depicted in Fig. 7(b). It can easily be seen that every requester service that complies to $OG_{\text{shop}} \otimes C^\Psi$ sends !cc after receiving ?p and therefore avoids the surcharge. A regular customer (message ?r) sends !cod, avoiding an error message. Hence, the interaction of the original online shop with a service requester complying to the new OG satisfies the constraint.

The following theorem justifies the construction.

Theorem 2. *Let OG_{Prov} be an operating guideline and let C^Ψ be a constraint automaton for OG_{Prov}.*

Then, $Req \in Comply(OG_{Prov} \otimes C^\Psi)$ iff $Req \in Comply(OG_{Prov})$ and $R \in Comply(C^\Psi)$.

Proof (sketch). Let OG_{Prov} be equal to A^Φ.

($\rightarrow$) $Req \in Comply(A^\Phi \otimes C^\Psi)$ means that Req matches with $A^\Phi \otimes C^\Psi$ structurally (first item of Def. 1) and each state of Req fulfills the annotation of the matching state(s) of $A^\Phi \otimes C^\Psi$ (second item of Def. 1). Let q_{Req} be an arbitrary state of Req. Then, if $(q_{Req}, (q_A, q_C)) \in R_{(Req, A^\Phi \otimes C^\Psi)}$, then $(q_{Req}, q_A) \in R_{(Req, A^\Phi)}$ and $(q_{Req}, q_C) \in R_{(Req, C^\Psi)}$. Hence, Req matches with A and Req matches with C. By assumption, each assignment $\beta_{q_{Req}}$ fulfills the annotation

$\Phi(q_A) \wedge \Psi(q_C)$ for each $(q_A, q_C) \in R_{(Req, A^\Phi \otimes C^\Psi)}$. Hence, $\beta_{q_{Req}}$ fulfills $\Phi(q_A)$ and $\beta_{q_{Req}}$ fulfills $\Psi(q_C)$.

($\leftarrow$) By assumption, Req's states match with the states of A and of C. Let q_A and q_C be the corresponding states in $R_{(Req,A)}(q_A)$ and $R_{(Req,C)}(q_A)$, respectively. Then, the state (q_A, q_C) is in $A^\Phi \otimes C^\Psi$ and $(q_{Req}, (q_A, q_C)) \in R_{(Req, A^\Phi \otimes C^\Psi)}$. Hence, Req matches with $A^\Phi \otimes C^\Psi$. Finally, since the assignment $\beta_{q_{Req}}$ fulfills the annotation $\Phi(q_A)$ and the annotation $\Psi(q_C)$ of matching states in A or C, $\beta_{q_{Req}}$ fulfills their conjunction as well. □

With the result of Theorem 2 we are able to come back to the last two scenarios described in the introduction. As already seen in our example, in these scenarios the constraint is modeled as a constraint automaton C^Ψ. C^Ψ characterizes the set of accepted behaviors and can be formulated without knowing the structure of the OG needed later on. Only the interface (i. e., the set of input and output channels of the corresponding service automaton) must be known.

In the third scenario, the (general) operating guidelines of all provider services are already published in the repository and a requester Req queries for a matching service $Prov$ under a given constraint C^Ψ. Theorem 2 allows that the broker computes the customized operating guideline of a provider first and then matches Req with the customized OG. That way, the consideration of constraints refines the "find" operation of SOAs: Instead of finding *any* provider service $Prov$ such that the composition with a requester service Req is deadlock-free, only the subset of providers $Prov$ for which $Req \oplus Prov$ satisfies the constraint is returned. To speed up the matching, the two steps of building the product and matching Req with the product can easily be interleaved. Additionally, the broker could prepare customized OGs for often-used constraints.

In the fourth scenario, the requester service Req is yet to be constructed. Therefore, the desired features of Req are described as a constraint automaton. For example, consider a requester who wants to book a flight paying with credit card. If these features are expressed as a constraint automaton C^Ψ, it can be sent to the broker who returns all operating guidelines of provider services $Prov$ offering these features (i. e., where the product of OG_{Prov} with C^Ψ is not empty). From this operational descriptions, the service Req can easily be constructed.

(a) *enforce*(a)　　　　　　　　　　　　　　(b) *exclude*(a)

Fig. 8. The constraint automata for enforcing or excluding a communication action a

To conclude this section, we depict generic constraint automata for enforcing or excluding a communication action a in Fig. 8. The broker could apply such constraint automata and store customized *OG*s enforcing or excluding the most common typical communication actions (as payments, errors, etc.) in addition to the general *OG* version of the provider services.

5   Related Work

There is a lot of research being done to enforce constraints in services. The originality of this paper lies in the application of constraints to the communication between a requester and a provider service. Furthermore, the presented model of constraints allows us to refine "find" operation in SOAs.

The idea to constrain the behavior of a system by composing it with an automaton is also used in the area of model checking. When a component of a distributed system is analyzed in isolation, it might reach states that are unreachable in the original (composed) system. To avoid these states, [12] introduce an *interface specification* which is composed to the considered component and mimics the interface behavior of the original system. In [13], *cut states* are added to the interface specification which are not allowed to be reached in the composition. These states are similar states with *false* annotation in Fig. 8(b).

In [14], services are described with a logic, allowing the enforcement of constraints by logical composition of a service specification with a constraint specification. Similarly, several protocol operators, including an intersection operator are introduced in [15]. Though these approaches consider synchronous communication, they are similar to our product definition of Sect. 3.

An approach to describe services and desired (functional or nonfunctional) requirements by *symbolic labeled transition systems* is proposed in [16]. An algorithm then selects services such that their composition fulfils the given requirements. However, the requirements have to be quite specific; that is, the behavior of the desired service have to be specified in detail. In our presented approach, the desired behavior can be described by a constraint instead of a specific workflow. However, the discovery of a composition of services to satisfy the required constraint is subject of future work. Another approach is presented in [17], where a *target service* is specified which is then constructed by composing available services. Again, this approach bases on synchronous communication.

6   Conclusion

We presented algorithms for the calculation of customized operating guidelines from different inputs. Computing a customized *OG* from a general one is useful for scenarios where a requester wants to explore specific features of a service that is published through its (general) operating guideline. Computing a customized *OG* from the service description itself may be useful for registration in specialized repositories as well as for validation purposes.

We implemented all results of this paper in our analysis tool Fiona. Fiona's main functionality is to compute the *OG* of a service from the oWFN description of that service. Suitability of oWFNs for modeling services has been proven through an implemented translation from the industrial service description language WS-BPEL [5] into oWFNs [6]. Additionally, Fiona can (1) apply a constraint given as a constraint oWFN C to N and calculate the OG of the product $N \otimes C$ and (2) read an OG and apply a constraint automaton C^Ψ to the OG to compute the customized OG. First case studies with real-life WS-BPEL processes show that both approaches have the same complexity.

In ongoing work, we are further exploring the validation scenario. In case that a service turns out not to have partners, we are trying to produce convincing diagnosis information to visualize *why* a constraint cannot be satisfied. In addition, we work on an extension of the set of requirements that can be used for customizing an operating guideline. For instance, we explore the possibility of replacing the finite automata used in this paper with Büchi automata, thus being able to handle arbitrary requirements given in linear time temporal logic.

References

1. Gottschalk, K.: Web Services Architecture Overview. IBM whitepaper, IBM developerWorks (2000), `http://ibm.com/developerWorks/web/library/w-ovr`
2. Massuthe, P., Schmidt, K.: Operating Guidelines – An Automata-Theoretic Foundation for the Service-Oriented Architecture. In: Cai, K.Y., Ohnishi, A., Lau, M. (eds.) Proceedings of the Fifth International Conference on Quality Software (QSIC 2005), Melbourne, Australia, pp. 452–457. IEEE Computer Society, Los Alamitos (2005)
3. Lohmann, N., Massuthe, P., Wolf, K.: Operating Guidelines for Finite-State Services. In: Kleijn, J., Yakovlev, A. (eds.) 28th International Conference on Applications and Theory of Petri Nets and Other Models of Concurrency, ICATPN 2007, Siedlce, Poland. LNCS, vol. 4546, Springer, Heidelberg (2007)
4. Massuthe, P., Reisig, W., Schmidt, K.: An Operating Guideline Approach to the SOA. Annals of Mathematics, Computing & Teleinformatics 1(3), 35–43 (2005)
5. Alves, A., et al.: Web Services Business Process Execution Language Version 2.0. Committee Specification, Organization for the Advancement of Structured Information Standards (OASIS) (2007)
6. Lohmann, N., Massuthe, P., Stahl, C., Weinberg, D.: Analyzing Interacting BPEL Processes. In: Dustdar, S., Fiadeiro, J.L., Sheth, A. (eds.) BPM 2006. LNCS, vol. 4102, pp. 17–32. Springer, Heidelberg (2006)
7. Aalst, W.M.P.v.d.: The application of Petri nets to workflow management. Journal of Circuits, Systems and Computers 8(1), 21–66 (1998)
8. Lohmann, N., Massuthe, P., Stahl, C., Weinberg, D.: Analyzing Interacting WS-BPEL Processes Using Flexible Model Generation. In: Dustdar, S., Fiadeiro, J.L., Sheth, A. (eds.) BPM 2006. LNCS, vol. 4102, Springer, Heidelberg (2006)
9. Cassandras, C., Lafortune, S.: Introduction to Discrete Event Systems. Kluwer Academic Publishers, Dordrecht (1999)
10. Ramadge, P., Wonham, W.: Supervisory control of a class of discrete event processes. SIAM J. Control Optim. 25(1), 206–230 (1987)
11. Badouel, E., Darondeau, P.: Theory of Regions. In: Reisig, W., Rozenberg, G. (eds.) Lectures on Petri Nets I: Basic Models. LNCS, vol. 1491, pp. 529–586. Springer, Heidelberg (1998)

12. Graf, S., Steffen, B.: Compositional Minimization of Finite State Systems. In: Clarke, E., Kurshan, R.P. (eds.) CAV 1990. LNCS, vol. 531, pp. 186–196. Springer, Heidelberg (1991)

13. Valmari, A.: Composition and Abstraction. In: Cassez, F., Jard, C., Rozoy, B., Dermot, M. (eds.) MOVEP 2000. LNCS, vol. 2067, pp. 58–98. Springer, Heidelberg (2001)

14. Davulcu, H., Kifer, M., Ramakrishnan, I.V.: CTR-S: a logic for specifying contracts in semantic web services. In: Feldman, S.I., Uretsky, M., Najork, M., Wills, C.E. (eds.) Proceedings of the 13th international conference on World Wide Web, WWW 2004, pp. 144–153. ACM, New York (2004)

15. Benatallah, B., Casati, F., Toumani, F.: Representing, analysing and managing web service protocols. Data Knowl. Eng. 58(3), 327–357 (2006)

16. Pathak, J., Basu, S., Honavar, V.: Modeling Web Services by Iterative Reformulation of Functional and Non-functional Requirements. In: Dan, A., Lamersdorf, W. (eds.) ICSOC 2006. LNCS, vol. 4294, pp. 314–326. Springer, Heidelberg (2006)

17. Berardi, D., Calvanese, D., Giacomo, G.D., Mecella, M.: Composition of Services with Nondeterministic Observable Behavior. In: Benatallah, B., Casati, F., Traverso, P. (eds.) ICSOC 2005. LNCS, vol. 3826, pp. 520–526. Springer, Heidelberg (2005)

Towards Formal Analysis of
Artifact-Centric Business Process Models

Kamal Bhattacharya[1], Cagdas Gerede[2,*], Richard Hull[3,*],
Rong Liu[1], and Jianwen Su[2,*]

[1] IBM T.J. Watson Research Center
[2] University of California at Santa Barbara
[3] Bell Labs, Alcatel-Lucent

Abstract. Business process (BP) modeling is a building block for design and management of business processes. Two fundamental aspects of BP modeling are: a formal framework that well integrates both *control flow* and *data*, and a set of tools to assist all phases of a BP life cycle. This paper is an initial attempt to address both aspects of BP modeling. We view our investigation as a precursor to the development of a framework and tools that enable automated construction of processes, along the lines of techniques developed around OWL-S and Semantic Web Services.

Over the last decade, an *artifact-centric* approach of coupling control and data emerged in the practice of BP design. It focuses on the "moving" data as they are manipulated throughout a process. In this paper, we formulate a formal model for artifact-centric business processes and develop complexity results concerning static analysis of three problems of immediate practical concerns, which focus on the ability to complete an execution, existence of an execution "deadend", and redundancy. We show that the problems are undecidable in general, but under various restrictions they are decidable but complete in PSPACE, CO-NP, and NP; and in some cases decidable in linear time.

1 Introduction

In recent years, competitive business environment has forced companies to be operationally innovative in order to outperform their competitors [8]. This challenge requires business process models not only to ensure work to be done as desired but also to enable operational innovations. In general, a process model describes activities conducted in order to achieve business goals, informational structure of a business, and organizational resources. Workflows, as a typical process modeling approach, often emphasize the sequencing of activities (i.e., control flows), but ignore the informational perspective or treat it only within the context of single activities. Without a complete view of the informational context, business actors often focus on what should be done instead of what can be done, hindering operational innovations [8,1].

The goal of this paper is to develop and investigate a new modeling framework centered around "business artifacts". Business artifacts (or simply artifacts) are the information entities that capture process goals and allow for evaluating how thoroughly these

---

* Supported in part by NSF grants IIS-0415195 and CNS-0613998.

G. Alonso, P. Dadam, and M. Rosemann (Eds.): BPM 2007, LNCS 4714, pp. 288–304, 2007.

goals are achieved. Business "services" (or tasks) act on artifacts and then modify artifacts based on business rules. A fundamental thesis of this paper is that business services are typically less frequently changed; a technical challenge is to properly "chain" the services together or "evolve" the current workflow of the services to adapt for new business requirements. In our framework, "business rules" are used to assemble the services together; they are specified in declarative languages and are easy to modify. A process model thus consists of business artifacts, services, and rules. Based on this framework, we study properties of process models that concern both information perspective and control flows. In particular, we develop complexity results on the following problems: Can an artifact be successfully processed? Does a dead-end path exist in a process? Are there redundant data in artifacts or redundant services?

This paper makes the following contributions.

1. The development of a formal artifact-based business model and a declarative semantics based on the use of business rules which can be created and modified separately from the artifacts.
2. A preliminary set of technical results concerning statically analysing the semantics of a specified artifact-based business process model. The results range from
   (a) undecidability for the general case,
   (b) PSPACE-complete when no new artifacts are created during the execution,
   (c) intractable (co-NP-complete or NP-complete) under various restrictions including "monotonic" services, and
   (d) linear time under more limited restrictions.

Organization: §2 provides a motivating example for business artifacts and modeling. A formal artifact-centric process model is introduced in §3. In §4, we present technical results on static analysis of process models specified in our framework. §5 discusses related work. §6 concludes this paper with a brief discussion on future work.

2   A Motivating Example

Consider an IT service provider aimed to provide IT services to an enterprise comprising a large number of geographically distributed "small sites". Provided services include IT provisioning, installation, and maintenance as well as general support. Typical examples for small sites are individual hotels part of a larger chain or fast food restaurants that are part of a franchise. The service provider typically signs a contract with the franchise corporation, which determines the service level agreements for each order of a given IT service. For example, a hotel corporation might sign a contract with a service provider that allows the provider to execute any kind of IT systems related services at individual hotel sites. The service provider receives a service request from a hotel site and creates an order. Fig. 1 illustrates the high level business process for a particular corporation. Typically, after initiating the accounting (e.g. performing a credit check and filing the invoice) a schedule for executing the requested services will be planned (e.g. performing an update on all cash registers in the hotel and an upgrade of the main reservation terminals). Insufficient funds may lead to a termination of the order (before the schedule is created). After the corporation approves the install for the hotel site, the IT services can execute the planned schedule and complete the order.

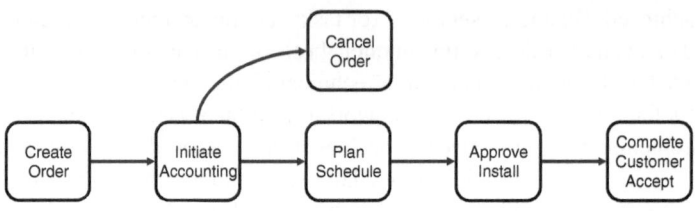

Fig. 1. An IT Service Provider's Process Model

The high-level process model describes the sequence of activities executed by the service provider to reach the business goal of completing the IT services delivery. Each task in the process model describes business intent. In our context it is convenient to consider each task as a service which requires an input, produces an output, may have pre-conditions and have an effect on an external system. (This is similar in spirit to semantic web services, e.g., [5,14].) In recent years, some of the authors have investigated a different approach to modeling business operations. The artifact-centered approach has been documented in various papers [4,18,13,7], and has been applied in various both internal and external IBM client engagements. The key idea is to shift the focus of business modeling from the actions taken to the entities that are acted upon. These entities (business artifacts or simply artifacts), such as an Order, a Request, a Plan, or an Invoice are information entities used by enterprises to keep track of their business operations. Not every information entity in a business is a business artifact. The focus for artifact-centric modeling is on business entities that (a) are records used to store information pertinent to a given business context, (b) have a distinct life-cycle from creation to completion, and (c) have a unique identifier that allows identification of an artifact across the enterprise. Business artifacts are an abstraction to focus businesses on not just any information but on the core information entities that are most significant from a perspective of accountability. The artifact is an information record that allows for measuring whether or not the business is on track to achieve their business goals. See [4,18,13] for more information on the methodology to identify business artifacts.

In the previous example, the key business artifact is the Order. The Order stores different aspects such as the date created, the result of the credit check, planned execution date, etc. The Order exists in different states or stages such as Pending Order, Planning, Live Order and Completed. The services interact with the artifacts by (a) instantiating an artifact instance, (b) updating (the contents of) an artifact, and (c) triggering state transitions on artifacts. We require that each service will at least update one or many business artifacts, or change the state of at least one artifact. The reasoning behind the update requirement is the intent to model for accountability. Fig. 2 illustrates the artifact-centric modeling approach using the service delivery example.

The Create Order service creates an instance of the Order artifact, updates the artifact (update dateCreated) and triggers the transition from Pending Order into Planning. The Initiate Accounting service interacts with the Invoice artifact, which captures information pertinent to accounting. The result of this interaction is (typically) a validation of a sufficient credit. Business rules are used to either cancel the order or instantiate the Plan Schedule service. The Initiate Accounting will update the Order artifact with the

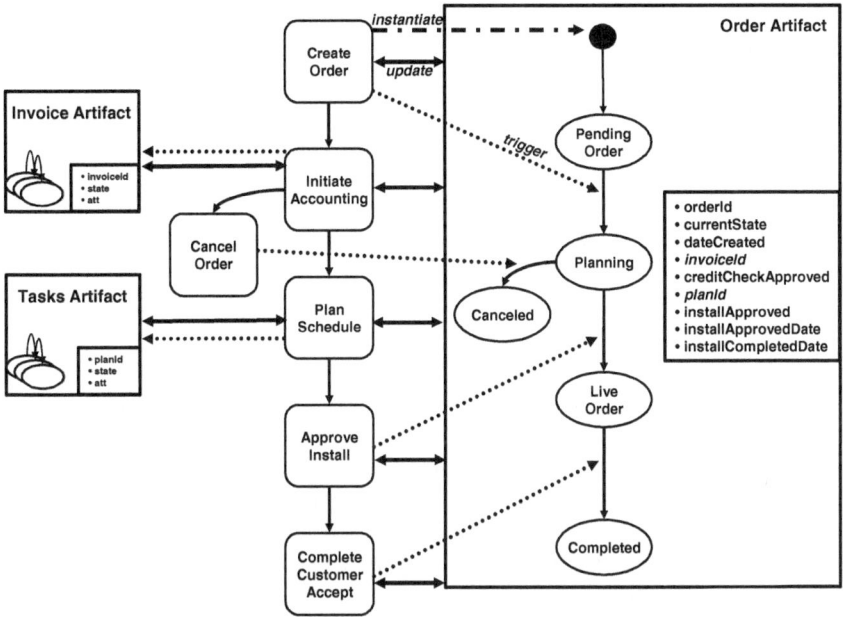

Fig. 2. An artifact-based view of the same workflow

appropriate decision (update creditCheckApproved with either true or false). The Plan Schedule service will create an execution plan by interaction with the Tasks artifact. Neither the Initiate Accounting service nor the Plan Schedule services trigger a state transition but both update the Order artifact.

The three artifacts shown in Fig. 2 are related to each other. The information content of the Order artifact references both the Invoice artifact and the Tasks artifact. This implies traceability of Tasks and Invoices from an Order artifact. There are different models for artifact relationships. In the context of this paper we omit details about the different models, but assume for simplicity that each artifact in the given business context is associated to other artifacts in the same business context.

The abstraction of artifacts and services that act upon artifacts facilitate customization of services flows. In an engagement scenario, identifying artifacts of a business precedes the definition of the services flows that will execute the operations on artifacts. The sequence of services can be exchanged unless some constraints prevent it, e.g., because of a data dependency between services. To illustrate customization, suppose that for Hotel Corporation A the contract between the service provider and A requires to perform a credit check before the plan execution as the contract requires each hotel site to provide their own budget for maintenance services. For Hotel Corporation B, which centrally budgets maintenance, planning the execution schedule is the only action required, hence, Initiate Accounting can be skipped altogether as accounting is covered in the overall contract. Finally, for Hotel Corporation C may be charged by the service provider on a per-site and per-service level. Thus, Corporation C expects a quote before each transaction, and the schedule is planned prior to accounting. We believe that the challenges one typically encounters for building systems that allow for on-demand customization can be overcome with a shift of focus from an activity (or verb)-centric to an artifact (or noun)-centric perspective.

Recent articles [4,18,13] on artifact-centric modeling describe various techniques and experiences to support business transformation through the design of artifact-based operation models, and some [18,13] lay out how to graphically represent business operations using artifacts. The artifact-centric approach has been applied in various client engagements at IBM and has been used both for business analysis and business-driven development engagements. Our goal in this paper is to define a more generic formal model that provides us with the tools to reason about some very practical problems encountered in real world engagements.

In order to help lay the groundwork for the formal study of the artifact-based approach to business processes, we study three fundamental issues in this paper.

Issue 1: As with any other business process modeling technique, artifact-centric operation models can get quite complex, especially when a large number of artifacts are involved to describe a business scenario. In this case it is helpful to perform a reachability analysis to support the needs of both business and solution architects. A reachability analysis will allow to determine if an artifact is processed properly through its life-cylce from creation to completion.

Issue 2: An artifact can reach a valid state, which is a dead-end, i.e. a final state which is not the completed state. Most of the times, these dead-end paths exist by design, as e.g. in Figure 2 where the canceled state is introduced by design. Techniques to detect non-intended dead-end situations are valuable especially if one can provide guidance how to resolve the situation.

Issue 3: Any process modeling engagement is iterative. The artifact-based approach can be a valuable tool in business transformation, because it allows a business to make the key data in their processes visible. In practice, however, there is a tendency to keep all of the data used by the legacy processes in the artificats as they are designed. This however may lead to the design of services that act upon on potentially redundant data. In this case it is useful to have tools that reason about the pre-design of the business artifact, to reduce redundancy and to re-organize the services flows to remove unnecessary attributes and tasks/services.

3   Formal Model for Artifact-Centric Business Processes

In this section we introduce the formal model for business processes. The key notions include, artifacts, schemas, services, and business rules. These are brought together by the notion of "artifact system".

3.1   Artifacts and Schemas

To begin with, we assume the existence of the following pairwise disjoint countably infinite sets: $\mathcal{T}_p$ of *primitive types*, $\mathcal{C}$ of *(artifact) classes (names)*, $\mathcal{A}$ of *attributes (names)*, STATES of artifact *states*, and ID_C of *(artifact) identifiers* for each class $C \in \mathcal{C}$. A *type* is an element in the union $\mathcal{T} = \mathcal{T}_p \cup \mathcal{C}$.

The *domain* of each type t in $\mathcal{T}$, denoted as $\textsc{dom}(t)$, is defined as follows: (1) if $t \in \mathcal{T}_p$ is a primitive type, the domain $\textsc{dom}(t)$ is some known set of *values* (integers, strings, etc.); (2) if $t \in \mathcal{C}$ is an artifact type, $\textsc{dom}(t) = \textsc{id}_t$.

Definition. An *(artifact) class* is a tuple $(C, \boldsymbol{A}, \tau, Q, s, F)$ where $C \in \mathcal{C}$ is a class name, $\boldsymbol{A} \subseteq \mathcal{A}$ is a finite set of attributes, $\tau : \boldsymbol{A} \to \mathcal{T}$ is a total mapping, $Q \subseteq \textsc{states}$ is a finite set of states, and $s \in Q, F \subseteq Q$ are *initial, final* states (resp.).

An *artifact (object)* of class $(C, \boldsymbol{A}, \tau, Q, s, F)$ is a triple (o, μ, q) where $o \in \textsc{id}_C$ is an identifier, μ is a partial mapping that assigns each attribute A in $\boldsymbol{A}$ an element in its domain $\textsc{dom}(\tau(A))$, and $q \in Q$ is the current state. An artifact object (o, μ, q) is *initial* if $q = s$ (initial state) and μ is undefined for every attribute, and *final* if $q \in F$.

ARTIFACT CLASS ORDER		AN ORDER OBJECT
STATES:	ATTRIBUTES:	ID: *id927461*
PendingOrder (initial)	invoice: Invoice	STATE: *LiveOrder*
Planning	task: Task	ATTRIBUTES:
Canceled	dateCreated : String	invoice: *id1317231*
LiveOrder	crediCheckApproved : bool	task: *id540343*
Completed (final)	currentCredit: int	dateCreated: *"2 April 2007"*
. . .	installAprroved: bool	creditCheckApproved: *true*
	. . .	currentCredit: *undefined*
		installApproved: *undefined*
		. . .

Fig. 3. Order Artifact and an Order Object

Example 3.1. Fig. 3 illustrates the Order artifact class from the example of Section 2, along with an object of this class. As defined by that class, an order has a record of important business information such as the date the order is created, and has references to the related artifacts such as Invoice and Task. The class description also contains possible states an order can be in such as "Pending Order". An artifact of the Order class has three parts: "ID" maps to a unique identifier for the artifact; "STATE" maps to one of the states defined by the Order class; and each attribute maps to either *undefined* or a value in the domain of the attribute's type. ∎

When the context is clear, we may denote an artifact class $(C, \boldsymbol{A}, \tau, Q, s, F)$ simply as $(C, \boldsymbol{A})$, or even C. A class C_2 is *referenced by* another class C_1 if an attribute of C_1 has type C_2. Similarly, an identifier o is *referenced in* an artifact $\boldsymbol{o}$ if o occurs as an attribute value of $\boldsymbol{o}$.

An artifact o' *extends* another artifact o if (1) they have the same identifier and (2) the partial mapping of o' extends that of o' (i.e. if an attribute is defined in o, then it is also defined in o' and has the same value as in o).

Note that an artifact may have some of its attributes undefined.

Definition. A *schema* is a finite set Γ of artifact classes with distinct names such that every class referenced in Γ also occurs in Γ.

Without loss of generality, we assume that classes in a schema have pairwise disjoint sets of states. Note that distinct classes have disjoint sets of identifiers.

Let S be a set of artifacts of classes in a schema Γ. S is *valid* if artifacts in S have distinct identifiers; S is *complete* if every identifier of type C referenced in an artifact in S is an identifier of another artifact in S.

Definition. Let Γ be a schema. An *instance* of Γ is a mapping I that assigns each class C in Γ a finite, valid, and complete set of artifacts of class C. Let $inst(\Gamma)$ denote the set of all instances of Γ. An instance $I \in inst(\Gamma)$ is *initial, final* (resp.) if every artifact in I is initial, final (resp.).

Notation. Let J be a collection of artifacts and o an identifier of an artifact in J. We denote by $J(o)$ the artifact $o = (o, \mu, s)$ in J; and by $J(o).A$ or $o.A$ the value $\mu(A)$, where A is an attribute of o.

Example 3.2. Consider a schema consists of 3 artifacts: Order, Task, and Invoice, as in Section 2. An instance I of this schema is $I(Order) = \{o_1, o_2\}$, $I(Task) = \{o_3\}$, $I(Invoice) = \{o_4\}$, where o_1 is an order artifact illustrated in Fig. 3 such that "o_1.task" holds the ID of o_3, and "o_1.invoice" holds the ID of o_4; whereas, "o_2.task" and "o_2.invoice" are undefined.   ∎

3.2 Services and Their Semantics

We now proceed to modeling "services". These are essentially existing software modules used to act on artifacts, and serve as the components from which business models are assembled. We assume the existence of pairwise disjoint countably infinite sets of variables for classes in $\mathcal{C}$. A variable of type $C \in \mathcal{C}$ may hold an identifier in ID_C.

Definition. The set of *(typed) terms over* a schema Γ includes the following.
 – Variables of a class C in Γ, and
 – $x.A$, where x is a term of some class C (in Γ) and A an attribute in C. (Note that $x.A$ has the same type as A.)

Roughly, a "service" is described by input variables, a precondition, and conditional effect. This can be viewed as a variation on the spirit of OWL-S [5,14], where services have input, output, precondition, and conditional effects. In the case of OWL-S, the precondition and effects may refer to the inputs and outputs, and also to some underlying "real world". In our context, the artifacts correspond to the OWL-S "real world", and the conditional effects typically write new values into the artifacts (or change their state) – it is for this reason that we don't explicitly specify the outputs of services. The preconditions and conditional effects are defined using logical formula characterizing properties of the artifacts before and after the service execution. In the present paper, we focus on the static analysis of artifacts and their associated processing flow, and thus do not model repositories explicitly. Reference [7] presents a model that models and studies the artifact repositories in a much more refined manner.

   We now define the notions of "atoms" and "conditions", which are used to specify the preconditions and conditional effects..

Definition. An *atom over* a schema Γ is one of the following:
1. $t_1 = t_2$, where t_1, t_2 are terms of class C in Γ,
2. DEFINED(t, A), where t is a term of class C and A an attribute in C,
3. NEW(t, A), where t is a term of class C and A an artifact typed attribute in C, and
4. $s(t)$ (a *state* atom), where t is a term of class C and s a state of C.

A *negated atom* is of form "$\neg c$" where c is an atom. A *condition over* Γ is a conjunction of atoms and negated atoms. A condition is *stateless* if it contains no state atoms.

Let I be an instance of a schema Γ. An *assignment (resp. for I)* is a mapping from variables to IDs (resp. occurring in I) such that a variable of class C is mapped to an ID in ID_C. Under a given instance I and a given assignment ν for I, all variables are assigned (identifiers of) artifacts, the *truth value* of a condition is defined naturally (details omitted) with the following exceptions: (1) DEFINED(t, A) is true if the attribute A of the artifact t has a value, and (2) NEW(t, A) is true if the attribute A of the artifact t holds an identifier not in I. If ν is an assignment for an instance I, we denote by $I \models \varphi[\nu]$ if under the assignment ν, the artifacts in I satisfies a condition φ. Let $\mathbb{V}$ denote the set of all assignments.

Following the spirit of OWL-S, we provide a mechanism to specify the "effect" of executing a service. In our case, the effect will be described in terms of how it impacts whether artifact attributes become defined or undefined, and whether new artifacts are created. We follow the spirit of OWL-S in allowing non-determinism in the model – execution of a service might result in one of several possible effects – this corresponds to the intuition that our model is fairly abstract, and does not encompass many relevant details about the underlying artifacts.

Let V be a set of variables of classes in a schema Γ. A *(conditional) effect* over V is a finite set $E = \{\psi_1, \ldots, \psi_q\}$ of stateless conditions over V. In this context we call each ψ_p a *potential effect* of E. Intuitively, if a service s with conditional effect E is applied to an instance I, then the resulting instance will satisfy ψ_p for some $p \in [1..q]$. We also incorporate a condition based on the notion of circumscription [19] to capture the intuition that "nothing is changed in the input instance except things required to satisfy ψ_p". (This contrasts with the approach taken by OWL-S, in which the effect portion of a conditional effect is interpreted using the conventional logic semantics rather than one based on circumscription.)

We can now describe services and their semantics. We assume the existence of a disjoint infinite set $\mathbb{S}$ of *service names*.

Definition. A *service* over a schema Γ is tuple (n, V_r, V_w, P, E), where $n \in \mathbb{S}$ is a service name, V_r, V_w finite sets of variables of classes in Γ, P a stateless condition over V that does not contain NEW, and E a conditional effect.

Intuitively, V_r, V_w are artifacts to be read, modified (resp.) by a service. (These may overlap). Note, however, that if $v \in V_r$, then terms such as $v.A.B$ can be used, for some artifact-valued attribute A, to read attribute values associated with artifacts lying

SERVICE *UpdateCredit*	SERVICE *PlanSchedule*
WRITE: $\{x: \text{Order}\}$	WRITE: $\{x: \text{Order}\}$
READ: $\{y: \text{CreditReport}\}$	READ: $\{x: \text{Order}, s: \text{Supplier}, c: \text{Site}\}$
PRE: $\neg$DEFINED$(x, \text{creditCheckApproved})$	PRE: $\neg$DEFINED$(x.\text{task})$
$\quad \wedge \neg$DEFINED$(x, \text{currentCredit})$	EFFECTS:
EFFECTS:	$\quad$ – NEW$(x, \text{task}) \wedge$
$\quad$ – DEFINED$(x, \text{creditCheckApproved})$	$\quad\quad$ DEFINED$(x.\text{task}, \text{expectedStartDate}) \wedge$
$\quad$ – DEFINED$(x, \text{creditCheckApproved})$	$\quad\quad$ DEFINED$(x.\text{task}, \text{expectedEndDate}) \wedge$
$\quad \wedge$ DEFINED$(x, \text{currentCredit})$	$\quad\quad$ DEFINED$(x.\text{task}, \text{supplier}) \wedge$
	$\quad\quad$ DEFINED$(x.\text{task}, \text{site}) \wedge$
	$\quad\quad x.\text{task.supplier} = s \wedge x.\text{task.site} = c$

Fig. 4. Example Services

outside of the image of V_r under an assignment ν. The analogous observation holds for V_w. It is possible to prevent this through syntactic restrictions.

Example 3.3. Fig. 4 illustrates two services. Service UpdateCredit updates an order's credit information according to the credit report. In some cases, when the credit check is approved, the credit amount is not known at the time of the update; in those cases, only the credit check approved field is defined. This is modeled with two possible effects. Service PlanSchedule creates a task for an order and defines attributes of the task such as expectedStartDate and supplier.   ∎

Definition. Let $\sigma = (n, V_r, V_w, P, E)$ be a service over a schema Γ. The (*circumscribed*) *semantics* of σ is a set $[\![\sigma]\!] \subseteq \mathbb{V} \times inst(\Gamma) \times inst(\Gamma)$ such that for each $I \in inst(\Gamma)$ and assignment ν for I over $V_r \cup V_w$,

(1) There is at least one J with $(\nu, I, J) \in [\![\sigma]\!]$ iff $I \models P[\nu]$ (i.e., I satisfies the precondition P under assignment ν), and
(2) If $(\nu, I, J) \in [\![\sigma]\!]$ then there is some potential effect $\psi \in E$ for which there exist sets K_{prev} and K_{new} of artifacts over schema Γ having disjoint sets of distinct artifact IDs such that:
   (a) $J = K_{prev} \cup K_{new}$ is an instance of Γ.
   (b) The collections of artifacts in I and in K_{prev} have the same set of identifiers. (This implies that ν is an assignment for K_{prev}.)
   (c) For each artifact ID o occuring in I, the artifact class and state of o in K_{prev} is identical to the artifact class and state of o in I.
   (d) For each atom in ψ of form NEW(t, A) there is a distinct artifact ID o in K_{new}, such that $\nu(t.A) = o$. Further, each artifact ID o in K_{new} corresponds to some atom of form NEW(t, A) occurring in ψ.
   (e) For each artifact $o \in$ ID$_C$ in K_{new}, o is in the start state for C.
   (f) ("Satisfaction") $J \models \psi[\nu]$.
   (g) ("Circumscription") Suppose that $o \in$ ID$_C$ occurs in J, and let A be an attribute of C. Suppose that $o \neq t[\nu]$ for any term t which occurs in an atom of ψ that has any of the following forms:
      (i) $t.A = t'.B$ or $t'.B = t.A$ for some attribute B;
      (ii) DEFINED(t, A) occuring in ψ;
      (iii) NEW(t, A)
      Then we have the following
      (α) If o occurs in I, then $o.A$ is defined in J iff $o.A$ is defined in I.
      (β) If o occurs in K_{new}, then $o.A$ is undefined in J.

Intuitively, the set K_{prev} in the above definition captures the way that existing artifacts in I are changed by potential effect ψ, and the set K_{new} corresponds to new artifacts that are created by ψ. The circumscription condition ensures that if $(\nu, I, J) \in [\![\sigma]\!]$, then an attribute value is changed in J only if this is required in order to satisfy ψ.

Concrete business services will assign specific values for attributes, or might invalidate an existing value, with the result of making it undefined again. In our abstract model, we focus only on whether the service gives a defined value to an attribute, or makes the attribute undefined again. It is useful to consider services that are "monotonic", by which is meant that each attribute can be written at most once (and not reassigned nor moved back to the undefined condition). Artifact schemas with monotonic services enjoy certain decidability and complexity properties. Further, in many real situations the underlying business artifacts are in fact monotonic, due to the need for historical logging. (Typically, some attributes of the artifact schemas in those situations are set- or list-valued, so that multiple "draft" values for an attribute can be assigned before a final value is committed to. An analysis of the impact of including such value types in the model is beyond the scope of the current paper.)

Definition. Let I and J be instances of an artifact schema Γ. Then J *extends* I if for each artifact ID o in I, o occurs in J and $J(o)$ extends $I(o)$.

Definition. A service σ is *monotonic* if J extends I for each $(\nu, I, J) \in [\![\sigma]\!]$.

For the technical development, it is useful to work with services which affect just one attribute value.

Definition. The service $\sigma = (n, V_r, V_w, P, E)$ is *atomic* if it is monotonic, $V_w = \{x\}$ is a singleton set, and for each $(\nu, I, J) \in [\![\sigma]\!]$, I and J differ only in the following ways:

(a) For at most one artifact ID o and one attribute A of o, $I(o).A$ is undefined and $J(o).A$ is defined.
(b) If in (a) the type of A is artifact class C, then J has one artifact ID that I does not, namely $J(o).A$.
(c) The set of artifact IDs in I is contained in the set of artifact IDs in J.

The service σ is *scalar atomic* if the attribute changed is of a primitive type in $\mathcal{T}_p$.

3.3 Business Rules

Based on an artifact schema and a set of available services, a business model is then formulated by "business rules". Roughly, business rules can specify what services are to be excuted on which artifacts and when.

Technically, we assume some fixed enumeration of all variables. If σ is a service, we will use the notation $\sigma(x_1, ..., x_\ell; y_1, ..., y_k)$ to mean that $x_1, ..., x_\ell$ is an enumeration of variables in the modify set and $y_1, ..., y_k$ an enumeration of read only variables (i.e., in the read set but not the modify set).

Definition. Given a schema Γ and a set of services S, a *business rule* is an expression with one of the following two forms:

- "**if** φ **invoke** $\sigma(x_1, ..., x_\ell; y_1, ..., y_k)$", or
- "**if** φ **change state to** ψ".

If PendingOrder(x) $\wedge$ DEFINED(x, creditCheckApproved) **invoke** InitiateAccounting(x;)
If DEFINED(x.task.expectedStartDate) $\wedge$ DEFINED(x.task.expectedEndDate)
    $\wedge$ DEFINED(x, installApproved)
    change state to LiveOrder(x) $\wedge$ PendingTask(x.task)

Fig. 5. Example Business Rules

where φ is a condition over variables $x_1, ..., x_\ell, y_1, ..., y_k$ ($\ell, k \geqslant 0$), σ a service in S such that $x_1, ..., x_\ell$ are all artifact variables to be modified and $y_1, ..., y_k$ are all read only variables of σ, and ψ a condition consisting of only positive state atoms over $x_1, ..., x_\ell$.

Example 3.4. Fig. 5 illustrates two business rules. The first rule says if an order is in *PendingOrder* state and the credit check is approved, then the service *InitiateAccounting* is invoked. The second rule says if for an order, the expected start date and the expected end date of the associated task are defined, and the installation is approved, then the order moves to *LiveOrder* state, while the associated task moves to *PendingTask* state. ∎

We now briefly describe the semantics of business rules. For two given instances I, J of a schema Γ, and a given assignment $\nu \in \mathbb{V}$, a business rule r, we say I *derives* J *using r and ν*, denoted as $I \overset{r,\nu}{\to} J$, if one of the following holds.

- $I \models \varphi[\nu]$ and $(\nu, I, J) \in [\![\sigma]\!]$, if r is the rule "**if** φ **invoke** $\sigma(x_1, ..., x_\ell; y_1, ..., y_k)$".
- $I \models \varphi[\nu]$ and J is identical to I except that each $J(\nu(x_i))$ has the state according to ψ, if r is the rule "**if** φ **change state to** ψ".

3.4   Artifact Systems and Their Semantics

Definition. An *artifact system* is a triple $W = (\Gamma, S, R)$ where Γ is a schema, S is a family of services over Γ, and R is a family of business rules with respect to Γ and S.

In the next section, we shall also include, as a fourth component, a set C of constraints; in these cases we shall indicate the class of constraints from which C is drawn.

We now sketch the semantics of artifact systems, and define the notion focused path for an artifact, which will be the basis for much of the technical investigation.

Definition. Let $W = (\Gamma, S, R)$ be an artifact system and C a class in Γ. A *path* in W is a finite sequence $\pi = I_0, I_1, ..., I_n$ of instances of Γ. The path is *valid* if

(i) For each $j \in [1..n]$, I_j is the result of applying one business rule r of R to I_{j-1}, i.e., $I_{j-1} \overset{r,\nu}{\to} I_i$ for some assignment $\nu \in \mathbb{V}$.

For an artifact ID o, the path π is *o-relevant* if

(ii) $n \geqslant 1$,
(iii) o does not occur in I_0, and
(iv) o does occur in I_1.

(Intuitively, this means that artifact ID o is created in the transition from I_0 to I_1.) If the path is o-relevant, then it is *o-successful* if $I_n(o)$ is in a final state. It is *o-dead-end* if o is not in a final state for C and there is no sequence $I_{n+1}, ..., I_m$ such that $I_0, I_1, ..., I_n, I_{n+1}, ..., I_m$ is a valid, o-successful path. Finally, a valid path $I_0, I_1, ..., I_n$ is *o-focused* if it is o-relevant and

(v) o does occur in I_j for each $j \in [1..n]$
(vi) for each $j \in [2..n]$, we have $I_j(o) \neq I_{j-1}(o)$ (i.e., o has changed state or some attribute value of o has changed).
(vii) for each $j \in [2..n]$, and for each $o' \neq o$, we have $I_j(o') = I_{j-1}(o')$ (i.e., o' does not change state and no attribute value of o' has changed).

We close this section by introducing a formalism that characterizes "redundant attributes". For an attribute A of a class C, let $\rho_A(C)$ represent the class identical to C but without A. For a schema Γ, let $\rho_{C.A}(\Gamma)$ be the schema $(\Gamma - \{C\}) \cup \{\rho_A(C)\}$. If S is a set of services, let $S_{C.A}$ be the set $\{\sigma \mid \sigma \in S \text{ and } \sigma \text{ references } A \text{ of } C\}$. Similarly, for a set R of business rules, let $R_{C.A}$ be the set $\{r \mid r \in R \text{ and } r \text{ references } C.A, \text{ or } r \text{ invokes a service in } S_{C.A} \}$. Let $W = (\Gamma, S, R)$ be an artifact system. Define $\rho_{C.A}(W)$ as the artifact system $(\rho_{C.A}(\Gamma), S - S_{C.A}, R - R_{C.A})$. Intuitively, $\rho_{C.A}(W)$ is an artifact system similar to W but with attribute A of class C completely removed. This removal operation $\rho_{A.C}$ is natually extended to instances, and to paths. For the latter, if the result of $\rho_{A.C}$ on a consecutive block of instances in the path yield identical instances, then all but one of the indentical instances are removed in the resulting path.

Definition. For an identifier o of class C, we say an attribute A of a class C is *redundant on* an [o-focused and] o-successful path π in W if $\rho_{C.A}(\pi)$ is an [o-focused and] o-successful path in $\rho_{C.A}(W)$. An attribute A of a class C is *redundant in W* [for C-focused paths] if A is redundant on every [o-focused and] o-successful path in W.

4 Technical Results

The artifact model can provide the backbone for the automated construction of workflow schemas, or more specifically the automated construction of artifact schemas. This section studies complexity characterizations for some basic decision problems about schemas. The problems are chosen based on our interest in testing whether automatically generated schemas satisfy key reachability and minimality properties. (We omit the proofs of the technical results here; details can be found in [3].)

We now provide formal counterparts to the intuitive decision problems introduced in Section 2. Each of these is of fundamental importance when constructing artifact-based workflows (either manually or automatically). Suppose that $W = (\Gamma, S, R)$ is an artifact system (possibly with constraints), and C is an artifact class in Γ.

Q1: (*Successful completion for C.*) Is there an ID$_C$ o and a valid, o-successful path in W?

Q2: (*Dead-end path for C.*) Is there a ID$_C$ o and a valid, o-dead-end path in W? Given W with dead-end paths, is there a way to construct an artifact system W' which (a) is "equivalent" to W (according to a definition given below) and (b) has no dead-end paths for C?

Q3: (*Attribute redundancy for C*). Is an attribute A of C redundant in W?

Intuitively, **Q1** focuses on whether class C in W is "satisfiable". The existence of at least one successful completion for C is a minimum test on whether W is well-formed.

Q2 is based on a more refined notion of well-formedness. Suppose that W does have a valid, dead-end, o-focused path. This suggests that an execution of the workflow can reach a point in which the artifact o cannot be further extended to completion. In other words, the workflow would need to perform a "roll-back" for this artifact. To avoid this undesirable situation, it might be possible to construct a new artifact system W' from W which supports all of the same successful paths as W, but which has no dead-end paths. (This might be achieved, for example, by adding constraints to W, which for any successful, non-dead-end path $I_0, ..., I_j$, prevent moves into an instance I_{j+1} for which $I_0, ..., I_j, I_{j+1}$ is valid but dead-end. See Theorem 4.5 below.)

Q3 can be used to assist in optimizing an artifact system. If W has a redundant attribute, then this attribute, all business rules and services referring to this attribute can be removed from W which reduces the complexity of the design specification.

We first note that all three questions are undecidable for general artifact systems.

Theorem 4.1. Let $W = (\Gamma, S, R)$ be an artifact system. Then each of **Q1, Q2**, and **Q3** for class C is undecidable. When W does not contain predicate NEW, **Q1, Q2**, and **Q3** are in PSPACE, and furthermore, they are complete in PSPACE for o-focused paths.

We now look at some restricted forms of artifact systems for which the questions are either tractible or NP-complete.

To obtain various decidability results, we focus hereafter on artifact systems that are monotonic. Also, to simplify the discussion, we assume that all artifact systems under consideration are atomic.

Our first result yields tractable decidability for **Q1**, using a slight variation on the conditions used elsewhere in the paper. Recall that an atom over schema Γ may have the form $s(t)$ where t is an artifact term of some class C and s is a state of C in Γ.

Definition. A *previous-or-current-state* atom has the form $[prev\_curr]s(t)$. Let ν be a variable assignment and $I_0, I_1, ..., I_n$ a $\nu(t)$-relevant path. Then $[prev\_curr]s(t)$ is true under ν for I_n in the context of $I_0, I_1, ..., I_n$ if $I_j(\nu(t))$ is in state s for some $j \in [1..n]$, (i.e., if $\nu(t)$ is in state s in I_n, or was in state s in some preceding instance of the path).

Theorem 4.2. Let $W = (\Gamma, S, R)$ be a monotonic artifact system. Assume that

(i) Each service S in S is *deterministic*, i.e., it has exactly one conditional effect, whose antecedant is "true".

(ii) The pre-condition for each service is positive (i.e., no negated atoms), has no atoms of the form $s(t)$ for a state s, but may have atoms of the form $[prev\_curr]s(t)$.

(iii) The antecedant of each rule in R is positive, has no atoms of the form $s(t)$ for a state s, but may have atoms of the form $[prev\_curr]s(t)$.

Let A be an attribute of a class C in Γ, and o a ID$_C$. Then there are linear-time algorithms to decide the following.

(a) For an attribute A of C, whether there is an o-focused, o-successful path $I_0, \ldots, I_n$ in W such that $I_n(o).A$ is defined.

(b) Whether there is an o-focused, o-successful path $I_0, \ldots, I_n$ in W.

Our next result shows that slight relaxation of most of the conditions in the above theorem yields NP-completeness for **Q1**.

Theorem 4.3. Let $W = (\Gamma, S, R)$ be a monotonic artifact system. In connection with monotonic, o-successful paths (which have no artifact invention but which are not required to be o-focused), Question **Q1** is NP-complete for the following cases. (Here conditions (i) through (iii) refer to the conditions of Theorem 4.2

(a) Conditions (ii), (iii) are satisfied by W but condition (i) is not. Furthermore, each service can be applied at most once to a given artifact.

(b) Conditions (i), (ii), (iii) are satisfied by W, except that negation is permitted in the pre-conditions of services.

(c) Conditions (i), (ii), (iii) are satisfied by W, except that negation is permitted in the antecedents of business rules.
(d) Instead of using previous-or-current-state atoms the rule pre-conditions and condional effect antecedants may use atoms of the form $s(t)$. All other conditions of Theorem 4.2 apply.

These are all NP-hard even in the case of o-focused paths.

While the various decision problems just mentioned are all NP-complete in the worst case, we expect that heuristics can be developed to decide these problems in commonly arising cases.

In an artifact system $W = (\Gamma, \mathbf{S}, \mathbf{R})$, the business rules $\mathbf{R}$ provide the mechanism for a workflow execution to "make forward progress". In some cases it may also be convenient to specify constraints on the execution, which can succinctly prevent certain rules from executing. A simple form of constraint is now introduced.

Definition. Let Γ be an artifact schema and C an artifact class in Γ. The *undefined-att-state-blocking* constraint for a set $\mathbf{A} = A_1, \ldots, A_n$ of attributes for C and state s for C is the expression $\neg\text{DEFINED} A_1 \land \ldots \land \neg\text{DEFINED} A_n \rightarrow$ *block* **change state to** s. A short-hand for this is $\text{UNDEFINED} A \rightarrow$ *block* s.

We extend the notion of artifact system to include such constraints.

Definition. An artifact system (*with undefined-att-state-blocking constraints*) is a 4-tuple $W = (\Gamma, \mathbf{S}, \mathbf{R}, \mathbf{C})$ where $(\Gamma, \mathbf{S}, \mathbf{R})$ is an artifact system as defined before and $\mathbf{C}$ is a family of undefined-att-state-blocking constraints over Γ. Each path $\pi = I_0, \ldots, I_n$ for $W' = (\Gamma, \mathbf{S}, \mathbf{R})$ is also a path for W. This path is *valid* for W if it is valid for W' and for each $j \in [1..n]$ and each constraint $\text{UNDEFINED} A \rightarrow$ *block* s in $\mathbf{C}$, if the transition from I_j to I_{j+1} includes moving an artifact o into class s, then $I_j(o).A$ is defined for some $A \in \mathbf{A}$.

As it turns out, a system with blocking constraints can be replaced by an "equivalent" system without constraints. but there may be an exponential blow-up in the size of the system.

Definition. Let $W = (\Gamma, \mathbf{S}, \mathbf{R}, \mathbf{C})$ and $W' = (\Gamma', \mathbf{S}', \mathbf{R}', \mathbf{C}')$ be two artifact systems. Then W and W' have the *same basis* if $\Gamma = \Gamma'$. In this case, W and W' are *path-wise equivalent* if the set of W-valid paths is equivalent to the set of W'-valid paths. W and W' are *functionally equivalent* over artifact class C if the set of o-successful paths for W is equal to the set of o-successful paths for W'. They are *functionally equivalent for C-focused paths* for artifact class C if for each $o \in \text{ID}_C$, the set of o-focused, o-successful paths for W is equal to the set of o-focused, o-successful paths for W'.

(Obviously, if W and W' are path-wise equivalent, then they are functionally equivalent for each class C.)

Theorem 4.4. Let $W = (\Gamma, \mathbf{S}, \mathbf{R}, \mathbf{C})$ be a monotonic artifact system and C an artifact class in Γ. Then it is Π_2^P-complete whether there is a dead-end path for C in W. This remains true under the various restrictions described in the statement of Theorem 4.3.

We now provide a construction that can be used to eliminate dead-end paths.

Theorem 4.5. Let $W = (\Gamma, \mathbf{S}, \mathbf{R}, \mathbf{C})$ be a monotonic artifact system and C an artifact class in Γ, and C a class in Γ. Then there is an artifact system $W' = (\Gamma, \mathbf{S}, \mathbf{R}, \mathbf{C} \cup \mathbf{C}')$, with C' a family of undefined-att-state-blocking constraints, which is functionally equivalent for C-focused paths to W, and for each $o \in \text{ID}_C$, W' has no o-focused dead-end paths. Further, the size of W' is no greater than exponential in the size of W.

A similar result can be obtained that starts with an artifact system with no constraints, and produces a functionally equivalent artifact system with no constraints and no dead-end paths.

Turning to **Q3**, we show that this problem is decidable under the same restrictions.

Theorem 4.6. Let (Γ, S, R) be an artifact system. Deciding whether an attribute A of a class $C \in \Gamma$ is redundant is coNP-complete for all cases (a, b, c, d) of Theorem 4.3.

Finally, we briefly outline an extension of the positive results.

Definition. Let Γ be a schema and I, J two instances of Γ. J *link-extends* I, $I \leqslant_L J$, if for each class C, each ID_C o, and each attribute A of C whose type is artifact ID, (1) there is an artifact in I with ID o implies that there an artifact in J with ID o, and (2) $J(o).A = I(o).A$.

Definition. Let $W = (\Gamma, S, R)$ be an artifact system, and $k \geqslant 0$. A path $I_0, I_1, ..., I_n$ is a *k-fixed-link structure* if (1) for each $j \in [0..k]$, I_j has at most k artifacts for each class, and (2) for each $j \in [1..n]$, $I_{j-1} \leqslant_L I_j$.

Paths for the Order artifact of Section 2 have 4-fixed-link structure.

Theorem 4.7. For all k, Theorems 4.2-4.3, 4.5-4.6 hold for k-fixed-link structure paths.

5   Related Work

The concept of business artifacts was introduced in [18,11] and further studied in [17,4,13,7]. [18] introduces the concept of business artifacts and the business modeling of artifact lifecycles, while [11] provides a programming model for adaptive documents, a concept finally merged with that of business artifacts. A further development of the programming model of business artifacts can be found in [17]. In [4], the authors lay out the methodology in the context of Model Driven Business Transformation and describes the positive feedback received in real-world engagements. [13] presents nine patterns emerging in artifact-centric process models and develops a computational model based on Petri Nets. [7] uses a different model and develops static analysis techniques for artifact-centric model properties such as arrival, persistence, and uniqueness.

Many tools and techniques were proposed for the development of business process models using workflows (e.g., [10,16,12]). These approaches have followed a process-centric approach focused on the control and coordination of tasks [6]. The importance of a data-centric view of processes is also advocated in [2] and [9]. In [2], the authors encourage an "object view" of scientific workflows where the data generated and used is the central focus; while [9] investigates "attribute-centric" workflows where attributes and modules have states. [15] proposes a mixed approach which can express both control and data flow. Compared to these approaches, our work favors a data-centric view.

Another thread of related work is the new paradigm of workflow research which concerns both control flows and data flows. The Product-driven case handling approach

[1] addresses many concerns of traditional workflows especially with respect to the treatment of process context or data. Wang and Kumar [23] proposed document-driven workflow systems where data dependencies, in addition to control flows, are introduced into process design in order to make more efficient process design. In their framework, business tasks are defined using input and output documents as well as other constraints, like business rules and policies, imposed on the documents. In comparison, our artifact-centric model re-organizes documents into structured business artifacts, which significantly reduces complexity of modeling data-control flow interactions.

Process verification has been studied extensively in the workflow community, with activity sequencing in Petri nets [22], in graphs [20], data dependencies [21]. (See [7] for additional references.)

6   Conclusions

The artifact-based approach uses key business data, in the form of "artifacts", as the driving force in the design of business processes. It enables a separation of data management concerns from process flow concerns, and can support rich flexibility in the creation and evolution of business processes. In particular, the artifact-based approach holds the promise of enabling automatic creation of new business processes from existing ones, or from initial specifications of the artifacts and basic services for operating on them. This paper lays the foundation for a formal study of the artifact-based approach and its use as the basis for automated workflow creation.

The focus of this paper is on basic decision problems, related to reachability, avoiding dead-ends, and redundancy. While providing key insights, extensions and refinements of these results will be useful, that take into account actual data values, and structural properties of the artifacts and their state diagrams. More broadly, we are interested to develop tools and techniques for automatic construction of business processes, in the spirit of the Semantic Web Services community.

References

1. Aalst, W.M.P., Weske, M., Grünbauer, D.: Case handling: a new paradigm for business process support. Data and Knowledge Engineering 53, 129–162 (2005)
2. Ailamaki, A., Ioannidis, Y., Livny, M.: Scientific workflow management by database management. In: Proc. Int. Conf. on Statistical and Scientific Database Management (1998)
3. Bhattacharya, K., Gerede, C., Hull, R., Liu, R., Su, J.: Towards formal analysis of artifact-centric business process models (full paper) (in preparation, 2007)
4. Bhattacharya, K., Guttman, R., Lymann, K., Heath III, F.F., Kumaran, S., Nandi, P., Wu, F., Athma, P., Freiberg, C., Johannsen, L., Staudt, A.: A model-driven approach to industrializing discovery processes in pharmaceutical research. IBM Sys. J. 44(1), 145–162 (2005)
5. OWL Services Coalition. OWL-S: Semantic markup for web services (November 2003)
6. Georgakopoulos, D., Hornick, M., Sheth, A.: An overview of workflow management: From process modeling to workflow automation infrastructure. Distributed and Parallel Databases 3(2), 119–154 (1995)
7. Gerede, C.E., Bhattacharya, K., Su, J.: Static analysis of business artifact-centric operational models. In: IEEE Int. Conf. on Service-Oriented Computing and Applications (2007)

8. Hammer, M.: Deep change: How operational innovation can transform your company. Havard Business Review, pp. 84–93 (April 2004)
9. Hull, R., Llirbat, F., Simon, E., Su, J., Dong, G., Kumar, B., Zhou, G.: Declarative workflows that support easy modification and dynamic browsing. In: Proc. Int. Joint Conf. on Work Activities Coordination and Collaboration (1999)
10. Jackson, M., Twaddle, G.: Business Process Implementation Building Workflow Systems. Addison-Wesley, ACM Press Books, Boston (1997)
11. Kumaran, S., Nandi, P., Heath, T., Bhaskaran, K., Das, R.: ADoc-oriented programming. In: Symposium on Applications and the Internet (SAINT), pp. 334–343 (2003)
12. Leymann, F., Roller, D.: Business process management with flowmark. In: Proc. of COMP-CON (1994)
13. Liu, R., Bhattacharya, K., Wu, F.Y.: Modeling business contexture and behavior using business artifacts. In: CAiSE. LNCS, vol. 4495, Springer, Heidelberg (2007)
14. McIlraith, S.A., Son, T.C., Zeng, H.: Semantic web services. In: IEEE Intelligent Systems (March/April 2001)
15. Medeiros, C., Vossen, G., Weske, M.: Wasa: a workflow-based architecture to support scientific database applications. In: Revell, N., Tjoa, A.M. (eds.) DEXA 1995. LNCS, vol. 978, Springer, Heidelberg (1995)
16. Morrison, J.P.: Flow-Based Programming. Van Nostrand ReinHold, New York (1994)
17. Nandi, P., Kumaran, S.: Adaptive business objects – a new component model for business integration. In: Proc. Int. Conf. on Enterprise Information Systems, pp. 179–188 (2005)
18. Nigam, A., Caswell, N.S.: Business artifacts: An approach to operational specification. IBM Sys. J. 42(3), 428–445 (2003)
19. Reiter, R.: A logic for default reasoning. Artificial Intelligence 13, 81–132 (1980)
20. Sadiq, W., Orlowska, M.E.: Analyzing process models using graph reduction techniques. Inf. Syst. 25(2), 117–134 (2000)
21. Sun, S.X., Nunamaker, J.F., Zhao, J.L., Sheng, O.R.L.: Formulating the data-flow perspective for business process management. Info. Systems Research 17(4), 374–391 (2006)
22. van der Aalst, W.M.P.: The application of Petri nets to workflow management. J. of Circuits, Systems and Computers 8(1) (1998)
23. Wang, J., Kumar, A.: A framework for document-driven workflow systems. In: Business Process Management, pp. 285–301 (2005)

Local Enforceability in Interaction Petri Nets

Gero Decker and Mathias Weske

Hasso-Plattner-Institute, University of Potsdam, Germany
{gero.decker,mathias.weske}@hpi.uni-potsdam.de

Abstract. In scenarios where a set of independent business partners engage in complex conversations, global interaction models are a means to specify the allowed interaction behavior from a global perspective. In these models atomic interactions serve as basic building blocks and behavioral dependencies are defined between them. Global interaction models might not be *locally enforceable*, i.e. they specify constraints that cannot be enforced during execution without additional synchronization interactions. As this property has only been defined textually so far, this paper presents a formal definition. For doing so, this paper introduces interaction Petri nets, a Petri net extension for representing global interaction models. Algorithms for deriving the behavioral interface for each partner and for enforceability checking are provided.

1 Introduction

In business-to-business collaboration scenarios different partners interact with each other in order to reach a common goal. Different means of interaction are possible such as exchanging faxes or phone calls. However, as more and more interaction is carried out through electronic messages, e.g. through web service invocations, there is a high need for establishing precise interaction specifications so that interoperability between the different partners' systems is guaranteed.

Choreographies are a means to describe interaction behavior from a global perspective. They enlist the allowed message exchanges as well as the control and data flow constraints between them. Once all partners have agreed on a choreography, the individual specifications for each partner (the behavioral interfaces) can be derived which in turn serve as starting point for adapting existing implementations and configurations or for implementing new services [7].

We can generally distinguish between two different styles for modeling choreographies. On the one hand we find *interaction modeling* languages where interactions are the basic building blocks and control and data flow dependencies are defined between them. In these models a certain atomicity of the message exchanges is assumed and only later on this atomicity is replaced by more detailed handling of asynchronism and exception handling. The Web Services Choreography Description Language (WS-CDL [11]) and Let's Dance [19] are examples for interaction modeling languages. On the other hand we find languages where message send and message receipt actions are the basic building blocks. Different actions are connected through control and data flow and corresponding send

G. Alonso, P. Dadam, and M. Rosemann (Eds.): BPM 2007, LNCS 4714, pp. 305–319, 2007.

and receive actions are connected through message flow. We call this second kind of choreography models *stitched behavioral interfaces*. The Business Process Modeling Notation (BPMN [1]) and basic Message Sequence Charts (MSC [10]) are examples for the second category. Also the Business Process Execution Language (BPEL [2]) falls into that category although it disqualifies as choreography language as it only shows the communication behavior of an individual process.

In contrast to stitched behavioral interfaces, where control flow is defined within the individual partners, certain anomalies are possible in choreography models when describing the control flow from a global point of view. Imagine a setting where partners C and D can only exchange a message after A has sent a message to B. Here, it is unclear how C knows when the message exchange between A and B has occurred. Only the introduction of additional synchronization messages could help to enforce the specified control flow. However, as a choreography should enlist all allowed interactions, it is unacceptable to leave the choreography unenforceable. All necessary interactions have to be factored into the model before it is used as specification for the collaboration.

Petri nets [17] are a popular formalism for describing the control flow aspects of processes. However, in the field of choreography modeling, Petri nets have only been used for modeling stitched behavioral interfaces. Therefore, this paper introduces interaction modeling using Petri nets.

The remainder of this paper is structured as follows. Section 2 introduces interaction Petri nets, before an algorithm for generating behavioral interfaces is introduced in section 3. Section 4 provides formal definitions for realizability and local enforceability of choreographies and section 5 presents algorithms for checking these properties. Section 6 reports on related work and section 7 concludes.

2   Interaction Petri Nets

This section introduces *interaction Petri nets*, a formal language to describe global interaction models based on classical place transition nets. Such nets consist of places and transitions that are connected through a flow relation. Places can contain tokens, which in turn are needed to enable transitions. Once a transition fires, tokens are consumed and produced. That way tokens flow through the net. In the Business Process Management world, Petri nets are used to describe business processes and workflows [17]. Here, transitions are interpreted as activities that are carried out by an actor. Workflow nets are a popular class of Petri nets, where there is exactly one input and one output place and every transition is on a path from the input to the output place.

In the case of interaction Petri nets, transitions are interpreted as interactions, i.e. message exchanges between two partners. These interactions are atomic in the sense that the send and receive actions are not decoupled but rather happen at the same time. An interaction Petri net specifies a set of valid conversations, i.e. sequences of message exchanges. The following two subsections will present the formal model for interaction Petri nets and conversations.

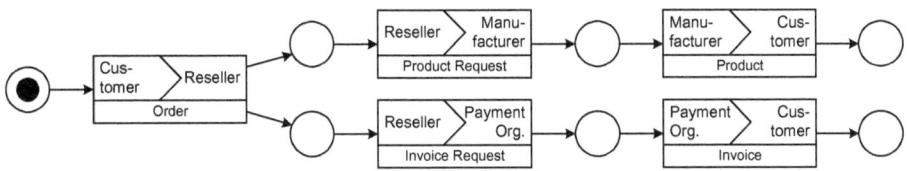

Fig. 1. Sample interaction Petri net

Figure 1 depicts a sample interaction Petri net. The visual representation of the interactions is inspired by the choreography language Let's Dance [19]: The upper left corner indicates the sending role, the upper right corner the receiving role and the bottom label the message type. In this example four partners engage in a conversation. A customer sends an order to a reseller, who then sends a product request to the manufacturer and an invoice request to the payment organization. Finally, the customer receives the product as well as the invoice.

2.1 Formal Model

In the remainder we will distinguish between *interaction models* and *interaction model occurrences*, where an interaction model is a triple of sender role, receiver role and message type. As several messages of the same type might be exchanged between the same sender and receiver in a conversation, we allow several occurrences of the same interaction model within an interaction Petri net.

Definition 1 (Interaction Petri net). *An interaction Petri net IPN is a tuple IPN = (P, T, F, R, s, r, MT, t, M_0) where*

- *P is a set of places,*
- *T is a set of transitions (interaction model occurrences),*
- *F ⊆ (P × T) ∪ (T × P) is a flow relation connecting places with interaction model occurrences,*
- *R is a set of roles,*
- *s, r : T → R are functions assigning the sender and the receiver role to an interaction model occurrence,*
- *MT is a set of message types,*
- *t : T → MT is a function assigning a message type to an interaction model occurrence and*
- *M_0 : P → ℕ is the initial marking.*

The set of interaction models IM for an interaction Petri net is defined as $IM :=$ $\{im \in R \times R \times MT \mid \exists t \in T \ (im = (s(t), r(t), t(t))\}$. We introduce the auxiliary functions $roles : T \to \wp(R)$ where $roles(t) := \{s(t), r(t)\}$ and $in, out : T \to \wp(P)$ where $in(t) := \{p \in P \mid (p, t) \in F\}$ and $out(t) := \{p \in P \mid (t, p) \in F\}$.

We denote the marking of an interaction Petri net using functions $M : P \to \mathbb{N}$. If an interaction model occurrence t is enabled in marking M, i.e. it can fire, and actual firing results in marking M', we write $M \xrightarrow{t} M'$. A marking M' is said to be reachable from marking M if there is a (potentially empty) sequence of interaction model occurrences that lead from M to M', which we denote as $M \xrightarrow{*} M'$. We call a marking M a final marking, if there is no interaction model occurrence enabled in M. More details on execution semantics of Petri nets and reachability can be found in [17].

2.2   Conversations and Conformance

Choreographies can be interpreted in two ways:

1. **Interaction obligations.** Imagine an interaction Petri net with two inter-action model occurrences arranged in a sequence where first an actor of role A sends a message $m1$ to B before B sends a message $m2$ back to A (depicted in Figure 2). When interpreting this choreography as interaction obligations, B must eventually send a message $m2$ back to A after having received a message $m1$ from A. A conversation that does not include a message exchange from B back to A would therefore not *conform* to the choreography.

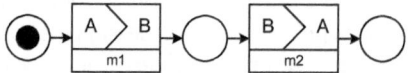

Fig. 2. Choreographies: obligations vs. constraints

2. **Interaction constraints.** When interpreting the interaction Petri net in Figure 2 as collection of interaction constraints, we would formulate that B can only send a message $m2$ back to A after it has received a message $m1$ from A. In this case a conversation only consisting of a message exchange from A to B would *weakly conform* to the choreography. Even an empty conversation would weakly conform to the choreography as none of the constraints is violated.

For defining conformance and weak conformance we introduce the following formal framework:

- I is a set of interaction instances,
- A is a set of actors,
- $s_I, r_I : I \to A$ are functions linking an interaction instance to the sending and receiving actors and
- $t_I : I \to MT$ is a function linking an interaction instance to a message type.

Definition 2 (Weak Conformance). *Let a conversation c be a sequence of interaction instances* $i_1, \ldots, i_n$. *Then c weakly conforms to an interaction Petri net IPN and a partial function map* : $R \to A$ *if and only if there exist markings* $M_1, \ldots, M_n$ *and interaction model occurrences* $t_1, \ldots, t_n$ *such that for all* $j = 1, \ldots, n$:

$$M_{j-1} \xrightarrow{t_j} M_j \ \wedge \ s_I(i_j) = map(s(t_j)) \wedge r_I(i_j) = map(r(t_j)) \wedge t_I(i_j) = t(t_j)$$

The fact that *map* is a partial function relating actors and roles implies that there is at most one actor playing a particular role in a conversation. However, one actor can also play different roles and there can be conversations where there is no actor playing a particular role. For the latter case imagine e.g. a procurement scenario where the seller sometimes carries out liability checks with a financial institute before actually delivering the goods. As the liability checks are optional, a financial institute does not necessarily appear in the conversation.

Definition 3 (Conformance). *A conversation c conforms to an interaction Petri net IPN and a partial function map* : $R \to A$ *if and only if c weakly conforms to* (IPN, map) *and marking* M_n *is a final marking.*

3   Generation of Behavioral Interfaces

An interaction Petri net can be used for modeling two distinct viewpoints in choreography design: (i) a choreography and (ii) a behavioral interface of a role r_i. In the latter case that particular role r_i must be involved in every interaction model occurrence, i.e. $\forall t \in T \ [r_i \in roles(t)]$.

```
 1: procedure reduceIPN(IPN = (P, T, F, R, s, r, MT, t, M_0), r_i)
 2: while t ∈ T (r_i ∉ roles(t))
 3:     if ¬∃t_2 ∈ T (in(t) ∩ in(t_2) ≠ ∅ ∧ t_2 ≠ t)
 4:         for each (p_1, p_2) ∈ in(t) × out(t)
 5:             p_new := new(), P := P ∪ {p_new}
 6:             M_0(p_new) := M_0(p_1) + M_0(p_2)
 7:             F := F ∪ {(t_2, p_new) | (p_1 ∈ out(t_2) ∨ p_2 ∈ out(t_2)) ∧ t_2 ≠ t}
 8:                  ∪ {(p_new, t_2) | p_2 ∈ in(t_2))}
 9:         P := P \ (in(t) ∪ out(t))
10:     else
11:         for each t_2 ∈ T (out(t) ∩ in(t_2) ≠ ∅ ∧ t_2 ≠ t)
12:             t_new := new(), T := T ∪ {t_new}
13:             s(t_new) := s(t_2), r(t_new) := r(t_2), t(t_new) := t(t_2)
14:             F := F ∪ ((in(t) ∪ (in(t_2) \ out(t))) × {t_new})
15:                  ∪ ({t_new} × ((out(t) \ in(t_2)) ∪ out(t_2))
16:     T := T \ {t}, F := F ∩ (P × T ∪ T × P)
17: return (P, T, F, R, s, r, MT, t, M_0)
```

Fig. 3. Algorithm for generating the behavioral interface of role r_i

In a top-down choreography design process first the choreography is designed and agreed upon before behavioral interfaces are generated for all participants. A behavioral interface then serves as specification for the individual participant. If a participant already has a process implementation in place it must be checked whether it needs to be adapted to conform to the specification. If no process implementation is in place, the behavioral interface can serve as skeleton that needs to be refined. An overview of conformance relations between process specifications and implementations and typical refinements of specifications towards a complete implementation can be found in [6].

Figure 3 shows the algorithm for generating the behavioral interface of a role r_i out of a choreography. The basic idea is to identify all transitions (interaction model occurrences) where r_i is not involved and to then reduce the net accordingly. Simply marking these transitions as τ-transitions and leaving them in the net is not an option as choices might be possible between τ-transitions and other transitions. Imagine a choreography where role A can choose to either send a message to B or C where in the latter case C would then interact with B. From the perspective of B the interaction between A and C is not visible. Therefore, B only knows which path was taken as soon as a message of either A or C arrives. Figure 4 depicts this scenario.

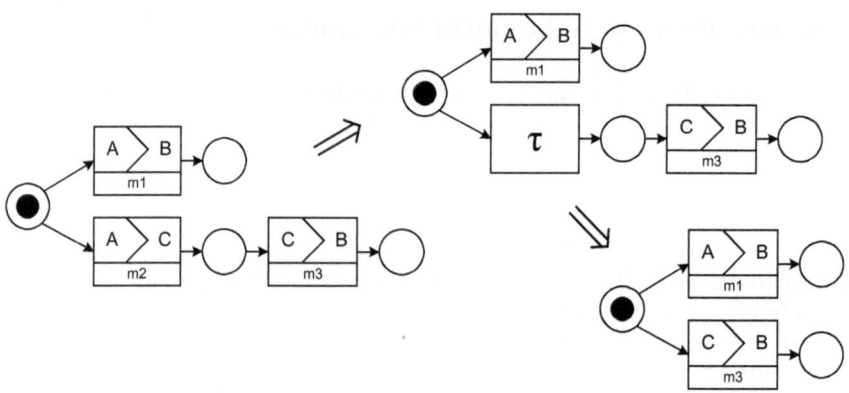

Fig. 4. τ-transitions need to be removed

We introduce two reduction rules. (i) The first can be found in lines 4-9 of Figure 3 and applies to those transitions t that do not share input places with other transitions. New places and flow relationships are introduced for connecting the preceding transitions with the succeeding transitions. Afterward, t and all places connected to it are removed (line 16). Figure 5 illustrates this rule.

(ii) The second rule covers those cases where t shares input places with other transitions (lines 11-15). Here, either one of these alternative transitions or one of the transitions succeeding t execute. If there are transitions t_2 succeeding t in parallel, then sequentialization has to be applied to the transitions t_2. This is

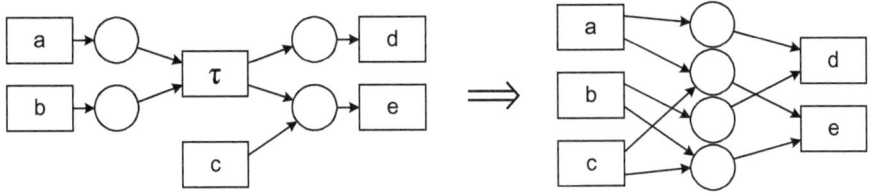

Fig. 5. Reduction rule (i)

achieved through the duplication of these transitions as illustrated in Figure 6. In contrast to the first rule no new places are created and none need to be removed. However, if there is no parallelism following t, the algorithm still duplicates transitions. This often leads to nets, where the transitions originally succeeding t are not reachable any longer. These transitions can easily be detected and removed for readability. Further optimization of the resulting nets would include the removal of redundant places and transitions.

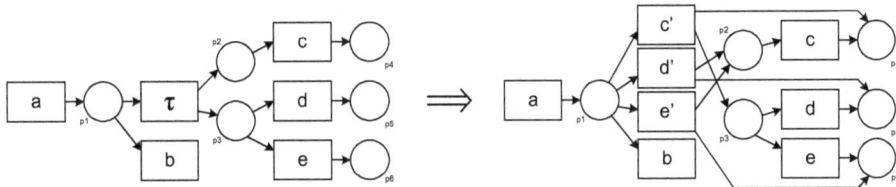

Fig. 6. Reduction rule (ii)

Actually, rule (i) could be skipped and rule (ii) could be applied to all cases. However, as rule (ii) flattens parallelism through the duplication of transitions, applying rule (i) where possible typically results in smaller nets.

The behavioral interface generated by the algorithm for role r_i exactly captures the choreography as seen by r_i. Therefore, it realizes a projection of a choreography IPN for role r_i. We denote this as $\pi_{r_i}(IPN)$.

4   Properties of Choreographies

This section will formally define the two properties *realizability* and *local enforceability* for interaction Petri nets. Both properties are essential for choreographies with more than two roles.

4.1   Realizability

Realizability is a well-known property in the space of software engineering. It is investigated whether a choreography can be implemented in a set of interacting processes in such a way that their composition exactly shows the specified

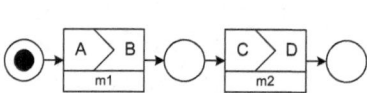

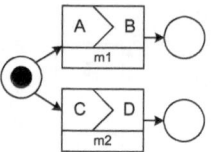

Fig. 7. Unrealizable sequence   **Fig. 8.** Unrealizable choice

message exchange behavior [8]. The choreography is given in the form of a finite state machine in the referenced paper.

The realizability criterion can also be applied to interaction Petri nets. Figures 7 and 8 show two examples of unrealizable choreographies. In Figure 7 we see the problem that C and D cannot know if a message exchange between A and B has already occurred or not. When deriving the behavioral interfaces for the four roles using our algorithm from section 3, we would loose the control flow relationship between the two transitions. In Figure 8 we find a similar problem: This time the two message exchanges exclude each other. A and B cannot know whether the other message exchange has already happened between C and D and vice versa.

When bringing realizability to interaction Petri nets, we need to introduce the auxiliary function $JOIN$ that composes a set of behavioral interfaces $bi_1, \ldots, bi_n$, where $bi_i = (P_i, T_i, F_i, R_i, s_i, r_i, MT_i, t_i, M_{0i})$, into a choreography $chor$. The definition is shown in Figure 9. We assume $\bigcap_{i=1}^{n} P_i = \emptyset$.

1: **procedure JOIN** $(bi_1, \ldots, bi_n)$
2: $P := \bigcup_{i=1}^{n} P_i$
3: $M_0 := \bigcup_{i=1}^{n} M_{0i}$
4: $R := \bigcup_{i=1}^{n} R_i$
5: $MT := \bigcup_{i=1}^{n} MT_i$
6: **for each** $u, v : \exists i, j \in 1, \ldots, n \ (i < j \land u \in T_i \land v \in T_j$
7: $\qquad \land (s_i(u), r_i(u), t_i(u)) = (s_j(v), r_j(v), t_j(v))$
8: $\qquad t_{new} := new(), T := T \cup \{t\}$
9: $\qquad s(t_{new}) := s_i(u), r(t_{new}) := r_i(u), t(t_{new}) := t_i(u)$
10: $\qquad F := F \cup ((in(u) \cup in(v)) \times \{t_{new}\}) \cup (\{t_{new}\} \times (out(u) \cup out(v)))$
11: **return** $(P, T, F, R, s, r, MT, t, M_0)$

Fig. 9. $JOIN$ function for composing behavioral interfaces

Definition 4 (Realizability). *An interaction Petri net Chor is realizable if and only if there exists a set of behavioral interfaces $bi_1, \ldots, bi_n$ such that their composition $JOIN(bi_1, \ldots, bi_n)$ is branching bi-simulation related to Chor.*

Branching bi-simulation was introduced by van Glabbeek and Weijland in [18] and defines a semantic equivalence relation on process models. It respects the branching structure of the models. Van der Aalst and Basten have shown in [14] how branching bi-simulation can be applied to labeled Petri nets. Interaction Petri nets can be seen as special kind of labeled Petri nets where the label is composed of sender role, receiver role and message type.

4.2 Local Enforceability

The example in Figure 10 is not realizable, either. However, this time we can create corresponding behavioral interfaces the composition of which only produces traces (conversations) that conform to the choreography. Figure 11 illustrates that the interactions involving B / C and C / D are arranged in a sequence in the behavioral interface bi_C.

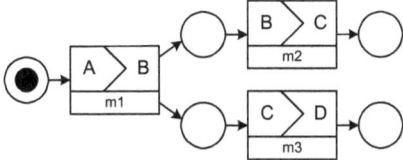

Fig. 10. Unrealizable but locally enforceable choreography

We see that realizability is very restrictive as it demands that *all* conversations produced by the choreography must also be produced by the composition of the behavioral interfaces. Therefore, realizability would not allow an additional control flow dependency as it can be found in bi_C.

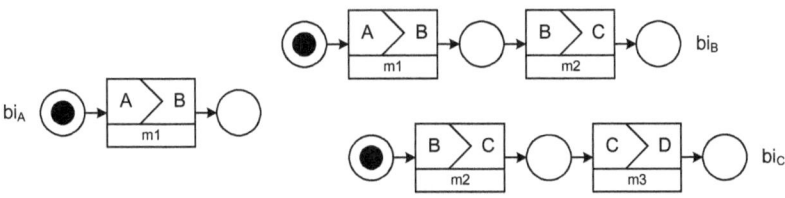

Fig. 11. Behavioral interfaces introducing an additional constraint

Choreographies are typically treated as collection of obligations in the sense that termination of conversations as specified in the choreography is required. We resort to the notion of local enforceability as initially presented in [20] for checking choreographies. There, a locally enforceable choreography is textually defined as follows: "The global model can be mapped into local ones in such a way that the resulting local models satisfy the following two conditions: (i) they contain only interactions described in the global model; and (ii) they are able to collectively enforce all the constraints expressed in the global model."

In the remainder of this section we are going to introduce a formal definition for local enforceability. As the textual definition leaves some ambiguities, e.g. concerning the question whether all or at least some interactions in the choreography must be reachable in the behavioral interfaces and whether local models are required that actually reach a conversation end as specified in the choreography. In order to eliminate these ambiguities we also take the enforceability checking algorithm into account that was also introduced in [20].

As it is demanded that all constraints are enforced in the global model, we disallow message exchanges in a marking of the composition of the behavioral interfaces that are not allowed in the corresponding markings of the choreography. This can be checked using simulation techniques as presented in [18]. The choreography must simulate all behavior possible in the composition of the behavioral interfaces. This enables the introduction of additional constraints as shown in Figure 11. However, a drawback of simulation techniques is that proper termination is not checked. A choreography consisting of a sequence of four interaction model occurrences would of course be simulation-related to a composition of behavioral interfaces where only the first two interaction model occurrences appear. This is not desired and we therefore introduce the additional condition that a final marking has to be reached in the choreography every time a final marking is reached in the composition of the behavioral interfaces. We call such an extended simulation relation *termination similarity*.

Definition 5 (Local Enforceability). *An interaction Petri net Chor* $= (P_C,$ $T_C,$ $F_C,$ $R_C,$ $s_C,$ $r_C,$ $MT_C,$ $t_C,$ $M_{0C})$ *where all interaction model occurrences are reachable is* locally enforceable *if and only if there exists a set of behavioral interfaces* $bi_1, \ldots, bi_n$ *such that their composition* $BI = JOIN(bi_1, \ldots, bi_n) =$ $(P_B,$ $T_B,$ $F_B,$ $R_B,$ $s_B,$ $r_B,$ $MT_B,$ $t_B,$ $M_{0B})$ *fulfills the following three criteria:*

1. *the set of interaction models is equal for Chor and BI, i.e.* $IM_C = IM_B$,
2. *for every interaction model there is at least one reachable interaction model occurrence in BI, i.e.* $\forall im \in IM_C \; [\exists u \in T_B, M, M' \; (im = (s_B(u), r_B(u),$ $t_B(u)) \wedge M_{0B} \stackrel{*}{\to} M \wedge M \stackrel{u}{\to} M')]$, *and*
3. *Chor termination simulates BI, i.e.* $BI \leq_{ts} Chor$.

Definition 6 (Termination Similarity). *Two interaction Petri nets* $IPN_1 =$ $(P_1,$ $T_1,$ $F_1,$ $R_1,$ $s_1,$ $r_1,$ $MT_1,$ $t_1,$ $M_{01})$ *and* $IPN_2 = (P_2,$ $T_2,$ $F_2,$ $R_2,$ $s_2,$ $r_2,$ $MT_2,$ $t_2,$ $M_{02})$ *are* termination similar, *denoted* $IPN_1 \leq_{ts} IPN_2$, *if and only if there exists a relation R between the markings of* IPN_1 *and* IPN_2 *such that:*

1. $M_{01} \; R \; M_{02}$,
2. $M_1 \; R \; M_2 \wedge M_1 \stackrel{u}{\to} M_1' \;\Rightarrow\; \exists v \in T_2, M_2' \; (M_2 \stackrel{v}{\to} M_2' \wedge M_1' \; R \; M_2' \wedge$ $(s_1(u), r_1(u), t_1(u)) = (s_2(v), r_2(v), t_2(v)))$ *and*
3. $M_1 \; R \; M_2 \wedge \neg \exists u \in T_1 \; (M_1 \stackrel{u}{\to} M_1') \;\Rightarrow\; \neg \exists v \in T_2, M_2' \; (M_2 \stackrel{v}{\to} M_2')$.

It is obvious that all realizable choreographies are also locally enforceable, i.e. the set of realizable choreographies is a subset of the set of locally enforceable choreographies.

5   Detection Algorithms

This section will show how choreographies can be checked for the properties introduced in the previous section.

Detection of Realizability. The algorithm for generating behavioral interfaces from section 3 can be used for checking realizability. For each role involved in a choreography the corresponding behavioral interface is generated. These behavioral interfaces are composed using the *JOIN* function. The result is compared with the original choreography using branching bi-simulation.

$$JOIN(\pi_{r_1}(IPN), \ldots, \pi_{r_n}(IPN)) \sim_b IPN$$

Detection of Local Enforceability. Figure 12 presents the algorithm for checking local enforceability. It is restricted to interaction Petri nets that are bounded, i.e. for every place there is a maximum number of tokens. This restriction leads to the fact that the number of reachable markings is finite. The algorithm is recursively defined and runs through all reachable markings of the interaction Petri net. The basic idea is to identify the two different sources of unenforceability always caused by pairs of transitions u, v not sharing a common role: (i) u disables v or (ii) u enables v. The first case cannot be solved by adding synchronization interactions or adding further control flow dependencies. Lines 9 and 10 detect this case.

The second case, where a transition u enables v and u and v do not share a common role, can be resolved in the following manner: The execution of v is always delayed until another transition w fires that shares a common role with v. This delay is realized through *blocked* in the algorithm. If a transition is blocked in a marking M we do not investigate the case that it fires. If a transition v that is not enabled in marking M becomes enabled in marking M' and $M \xrightarrow{u} M'$ then it is added to the set *blocked* (line 12). A transition can be unblocked as soon as a transition fires that shares a role with v (line 11).

Sometimes there is no chance of reaching the end of a conversation without unblocking a transition. This indicates that an unenforceable control flow dependency is present. *wasReached* indicates which interaction models have already been reached while traversing the reachable markings. In order to support cyclic Petri nets, we have to keep track of which markings have already been visited. This is realized through *visited*. *visited_cancel* contains all those markings where transitions are enabled but all of them are either blocked or lead to other markings in *visited_cancel*. As different paths might lead to the same marking but with different blocking history, we allow to visit a marking several times – once per blocking configuration. As the number of blocking configurations and the number of markings are finite we can conclude that the algorithm always terminates. In the worst case there are $2^{|T|}|\mathcal{M}|$ combinations to be checked, where $\mathcal{M}$ is the set of all reachable markings. However, for most choreography examples we have verified, the computational complexity of the algorithm is close to linear to $|\mathcal{M}|$.

```
 1: procedure checkEnforceability (IPN)
 2:
 3:     procedure recursivelyCheck (M, blocked)
 4:     if (M, blocked) ∈ visited
 5:         return true
 6:     visited := visited ∪ {(M, blocked)}
 7:     completed := false
 8:     for each u ∈ T, M' : M →ᵘ M' ∧ u ∉ blocked
 9:         if ∃v ∈ enabled(M) \ enabled(M') (roles(u) ∩ roles(v) = ∅)
10:             return false
11:         blocked' := (blocked \ {v ∈ T | roles(u) ∩ roles(v) ≠ ∅}) ∪
12:             {v ∈ enabled(M') \ enabled(M) | roles(u) ∩ roles(v) = ∅}
13:         if ¬ recursivelyCheck (M', blocked')
14:             return false
15:         if (M', blocked') ∉ visited_cancel
16:             wasReached := wasReached ∪ {(s(u), r(u), t(u))}
17:             completed := true
18:     if ¬completed ∧ enabled(M) ≠ ∅
19:         visited_cancel := visited_cancel ∪ {(M, blocked)}
20:     return true
21:
22: visited := ∅, visited_cancel := ∅, wasReached := ∅
23: return ( recursivelyCheck (M₀, ∅) ∧ wasReached = IM )
```

Fig. 12. Algorithm for detecting locally unenforceable choreographies

The auxiliary function *enabled* is used throughout the algorithm, linking a set of transitions to a marking M in the following way: $enabled(M) = \{u \in T \mid \exists M' (M \xrightarrow{u} M')\}$.

6   Related Work

Endpoint-oriented formalisms for describing interacting systems are more common than formalisms following the interaction-centric paradigm. In the field of software engineering it is very common to describe interacting components using communicating finite state machines (FSM). However, problems of state explosion in the case of bounded message queues and undecidability for unbounded message queues has motivated the use of conversation models. Here, the control flow between the interactions is seen from the global perspective in the sense that all send events are related in one FSM. It has been reported that for an important subclass of communicating FSMs there is a conversation model where the described interaction behavior is equivalent to behavior of the interconnected FSMs. This synchronizability is introduced in [9]. Realizability of conversation models is studied in [8].

Most work on choreography modeling using Petri nets uses the stitched behavioral interfaces approach, e.g. [16,7]. Behavioral interfaces can be represented

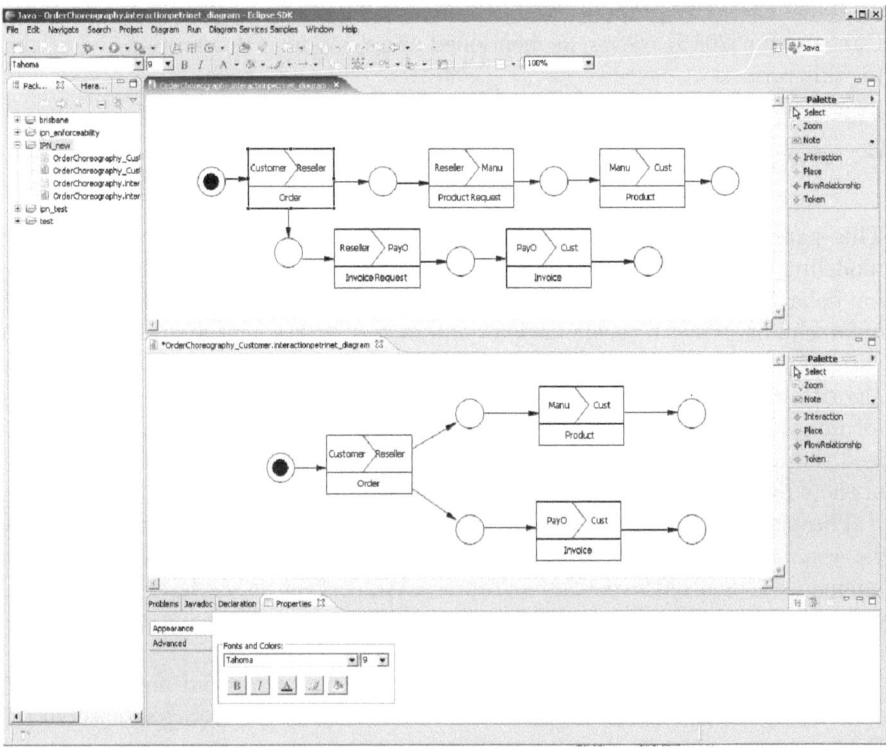

Fig. 13. Screenshot of the graphical editor for interaction Petri nets

using workflow modules, a subclass of Petri nets where a distinction is made between internal, input and output places [12]. Input and output places represent inbound and outbound message queues for communication with the environment. Different workflow modules are stitched together for carrying out compatibility checking.

π-calculus is a popular endpoint-centric process algebra especially suited for describing interacting processes [13]. There has been work on process algebras for interaction modeling. The work presented in [5] was driven by the Web Service Choreography Description Language (WS-CDL [11]). Another global calculus is presented in [4].

The different interpretations of choreographies regarding obligations and constraints are introduced in [3]. DecSerFlow [15] is a graphical notation for describing constraints in processes. The constructs introduced in the language translate into linear temporal logic expressions. Let's Dance [19] is a graphical choreography language that incorporates both notions of obligations and constraints. Constructs like for each repetitions rather express obligations, whereas also constructs for inhibition, a useful means for expressing constraints, are also part of the language. The property of local enforceability was only reported for Let's Dance so far [20]. However, as mentioned above, no formal definition is available for this property.

7 Conclusion

This paper has presented interaction Petri nets, an extension for interaction modeling based on Petri nets along with an algorithm for deriving corresponding behavioral interfaces. Furthermore, the two properties realizability and local enforceability have been defined for interaction Petri nets and algorithms for checking choreographies have been introduced. We have validated the proposed algorithms through implementation. Our GMF[1]-based tool is a graphical editor for interaction Petri nets. Generated behavioral interfaces can be neatly visualized thanks to automatic layouting functionality. Figure 13 shows a screenshot of the editor.

Throughout this paper, message exchanges were assumed to be atomic, i.e. we assumed synchronous communication. As a next step we will consider the impact of asynchronism on choreographies. What effect does it have if the derived behavioral interfaces are distributed to the different partners and executed with asynchronous communication?

In future work we are going to investigate mappings from higher level interaction modeling languages such as WS-CDL and Let's Dance to interaction Petri nets.

Acknowledgments. We would like to thank Marlon Dumas for his valuable input on this topic.

References

1. Business Process Modeling Notation (BPMN) Specification, Final Adopted Specification. Technical report, Object Management Group (OMG) (February 2006), http://www.bpmn.org/
2. Andrews, T., Curbera, F., Dholakia, H., Goland, Y., Klein, J., Leymann, F., Liu, K., Roller, D., Smith, D., Thatte, S., Trickovic, I., Weerawarana, S.: Business Process Execution Language for Web Services, version 1.1. Technical report, OASIS (May 2003),
   http://www-106.ibm.com/developerworks/webservices/library/ws-bpel
3. Baldoni, M., Baroglio, C., Martelli, A., Patti, V.: A priori conformance verification for guaranteeing interoperability in open environments. In: Dan, A., Lamersdorf, W. (eds.) ICSOC 2006. LNCS, vol. 4294, pp. 339–351. Springer, Heidelberg (2006)
4. Busi, N., Gorrieri, R., Guidi, C., Lucchi, R., Zavattaro, G.: Choreography and Orchestration: A Synergic Approach for System Design. In: Benatallah, B., Casati, F., Traverso, P. (eds.) ICSOC 2005. LNCS, vol. 3826, Springer, Heidelberg (2005)

---

[1] See http://www.eclipse.org/gmf/

5. Carbone, M., Honda, K., Yoshida, N.: Structured communication-centred programming for web services. In: Proceedings 16th European Symposium on Programming (ESOP) as part of the European Joint Conferences on Software Theory and Practice (ETAPS), Braga, Portugal (March 2007)
6. Decker, G., Weske, M.: Behavioral Consistency for B2B Process Integration. In: Krogstie, J., Opdahl, A.L., Sindre, G. (eds.) CAiSE 2007. LNCS, vol. 4495. Springer, Heidelberg (2007)
7. Dijkman, R., Dumas, M.: Service-oriented Design: A Multi-viewpoint Approach. International Journal of Cooperative Information Systems 13(4), 337–368 (2004)
8. Fu, X., Bultan, T., Su, J.: Conversation protocols: A formalism for specification and analysis of reactive electronic services. Theoretical Computer Science 328(1-2), 19–37 (2004)
9. Fu, X., Bultan, T., Su, J.: Synchronizability of conversations among web services. IEEE Trans. Softw. Eng. 31(12), 1042–1055 (2005)
10. ITU-T. Message sequence chart. Recommendation Z.120, ITU-T (2000)
11. Kavantzas, N., Burdett, D., Ritzinger, G., Lafon, Y.: Web Services Choreography Description Language Version 1.0, W3C Candidate Recommendation. Technical report (November 2005), http://www.w3.org/TR/ws-cdl-10
12. Martens, A.: Analyzing Web Service based Business Processes. In: Cerioli, M. (ed.) FASE 2005. LNCS, vol. 3442, Springer, Heidelberg (2005)
13. Milner, R., Parrow, J., Walker, D.: A Calculus of Mobile Processes. Information and Computation 100, 1–40 (1992)
14. van der Aalst, W.M.P., Basten, T.: Inheritance of workflows: an approach to tackling problems related to change. Theor. Comput. Sci. 270(1-2), 125–203, January
15. van der Aalst, W.M.P., Pesic, M.: Decserflow: Towards a truly declarative service flow language. In: Bravetti, M., Núñez, M., Zavattaro, G. (eds.) WS-FM 2006. LNCS, vol. 4184, pp. 1–23. Springer, Heidelberg (2006)
16. van der Aalst, W.M.P., Weske, M.: The P2P Approach to Interorganizational Workflows. In: Dittrich, K.R., Geppert, A., Norrie, M.C. (eds.) CAiSE 2001. LNCS, vol. 2068, pp. 140–156. Springer, Heidelberg (2001)
17. van der Aalst, W.v.d., van Hee, K.v. (eds.): Workflow Management: Models, Methods, and Systems (Cooperative Information Systems). The MIT Press, Cambridge (2002)
18. van Glabbeek, R.J., Weijland, W.P.: Branching time and abstraction in bisimulation semantics. J. ACM 43(3), 555–600 (1996)
19. Zaha, J.M., Barros, A., Dumas, M., ter Hofstede, A.: A Language for Service Behavior Modeling. In: Meersman, R., Tari, Z. (eds.) CoopIS 2006. LNCS, vol. 4276, Springer, Heidelberg (2006)
20. Zaha, J.M., Dumas, M., ter Hofstede, A., Barros, A., Decker, G.: Service Interaction Modeling: Bridging Global and Local Views. In: Proceedings 10th IEEE International EDOC Conference (EDOC 2006), Hong Kong (October 2006)

Modelling with History-Dependent Petri Nets

Kees van Hee, Alexander Serebrenik, Natalia Sidorova,
Marc Voorhoeve, and Jan Martijn van der Werf

Department of Mathematics and Computer Science
Eindhoven University of Technology
P.O. Box 513, 5600 MB Eindhoven, The Netherlands
{k.m.v.hee, a.serebrenik, n.sidorova,
m.voorhoeve, j.m.e.m.v.d.werf}@tue.nl

Abstract. Most information systems that are driven by process models
(e.g., workflow management systems) record events in event logs, also
known as transaction logs or audit trails. We consider processes that not
only keep track of their history in a log, but also make decisions based
on this log. Extending our previous work on history-dependent Petri
nets we propose and evaluate a methodology for modelling processes by
such nets and show how history-dependent nets can combine modelling
comfort with analysability.

1 Introduction and a Motivating Example

Modern enterprise information systems commonly record information on the
ongoing processes as series of events, known as *logs*. Such information might be
useful to ensure quality of the processes or of the software, or might even form a
legal conformance requirement. Moreover, numerous business processes involve
decision making based on previously observed events. For instance, medication
should not be ministered if an allergic reaction to a similar medication has been
observed in the past.

In classical Petri nets, commonly used to model business processes, the enabling of a transition depends only on the availability of tokens in the input
places of the transition. In our previous work we introduced *history-dependent
nets* extending the classical model by recording the history of the process and
evaluating transition guards with respect to the history [6]. One of the major advantages of history-dependent nets consists in separating the process information
from additional constraints imposed to guarantee certain desirable properties of
the design. Therefore, the resulting nets are more readable. To illustrate this
point consider the following well-known example.

Example 1. The model [5,7] consists of a circular unidirectional railway track of
seven sections and two trains *a* and *b*. Safety requires that two adjacent sections
are never occupied by more than one train. Intuitively, we would like to model
the railway track as a set of seven places corresponding to sections, and seven

G. Alonso, P. Dadam, and M. Rosemann (Eds.): BPM 2007, LNCS 4714, pp. 320–327, 2007.

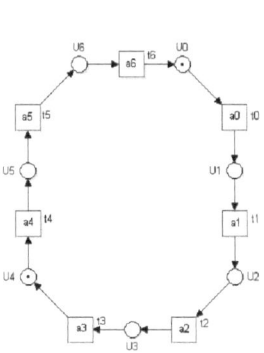

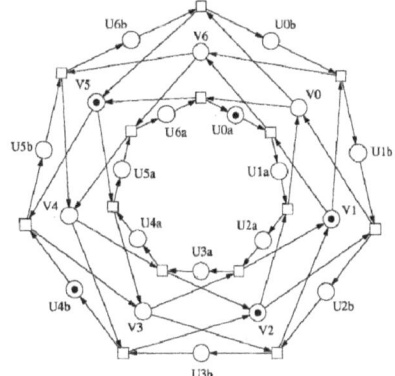

(a) As a history-dependent net

(b) As a classical Petri net [5]

Fig. 1. Simple railway example

transitions corresponding to movements of a train from one section to another. Trains themselves are then represented by tokens (see Figure 1(a)).

Being a classical Petri net, this model, however, does not respect the safety requirement stated. Figure 1(b) presents the original solution as proposed in [5]. For $i = 0, \ldots, 6$ and $z = a, b$, U_{iz} means that section i is occupied by train z, and V_i means that the sections i and $(i+1) \ mod \ 7$ are vacant. Observe that the sole purpose of U_{ib} and V_i is to impose the safety restrictions. We believe that understanding such a model and designing it is a difficult task for a layman.

To ease the modeling task, we use *guards* stating that the transition following U_i fires if U_i has exactly one token, while $U_{(i+1) \ mod \ 7}$ and $U_{(i+2) \ mod \ 7}$ are empty. It should be noted that U_i has exactly one token if and only if the initial number of tokens at U_i together with the number of firings of the preceding transition exceeds by one the number of firings of the subsequent transition. Similarly, U_i is empty if and only if the initial number of tokens at U_i together with the number of firings of the preceding transition is equal to the number of firings of the subsequent transition. Hence, the guards can be constructed by using the information stored in the history, which is the sequence of firings till the current moment together with the initial marking.

Unlike the original solution, our approach allows to separate the process information (trains move along the sections of a circular rail) from the mechanism used to impose the safety requirements (additional transitions and places in Figure 1(b)).

Clearly, the same history-dependent Petri net can be modelled in many different ways. As one extreme, one can consider expressing all dependencies by means of places and transitions. This approach is illustrated by an overly-complex Petri net on Figure 1(b). As another extreme, one can put the entire information

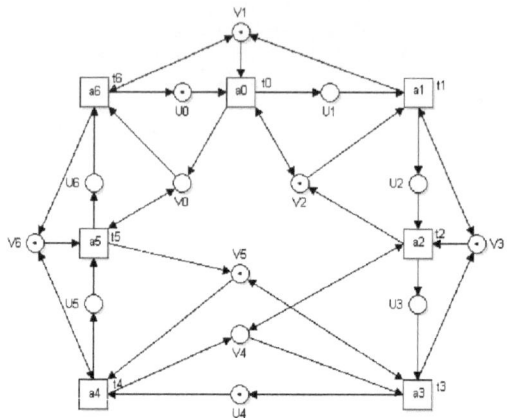

Fig. 2. Railway example: eliminating the guards

in transition guards, i.e., opt for a history-dependent net with just one place, connected to all transitions. We refer to such net as so-called *"flower" net*. Such a net without transition guards can execute transitions in any order and with history-based guards we can restrict this behavior the way we like. The best solution, in our view, is between both extremes: the basic process steps are expressed in the structure of the net, while additional constraints on the execution are imposed by transition guards.

An important aspect of history-dependent nets is the language for expressing transition guards. We developed a language that is powerful enough to express inhibitor arcs, which means that we have a Turing-complete formalism. We considered two subsets of this language, namely the counting formulae and the next-free LTL and showed that by restricting the language to these subsets we can automatically transform history-dependent nets into classical Petri nets (in some cases with inhibitor arcs). Figure 2 shows the net obtained by translating the history-dependent Petri net from Figure 1(a). These nets have more places and transitions than corresponding history-dependent nets and therefore more difficult to read, but they allow for classical analysis methods and for model checking.

In this paper we consider *global history*, which means that any transition may have a guard based on the total history of the net. Access to global history is realistic in many situations, for instance in health care, where all care providers have access to an electronic patient record, or in highly integrated supply chains. The focus of this paper is on the methodology of using history-dependent nets for modelling and analysis of business processes.

The remainder of the paper is organized as follows. In section 2 we describe the methodology for modeling and analysis of history-based nets. In Section 3 we discuss a example from juridical practice. Finally, we review the related work and conclude the paper.

2 Methodology

In this section we describe our approach to modeling with history-dependent nets. We present two different methodologies applicable depending on the project intake: modelling from scratch or re-engineering a data-centered model. A modeling methodology should be seen as a set of guidelines rather than a rigid algorithm.

2.1 Modelling from Scratch

In this subsection we assume that modelling is done from scratch, i.e. a new information system is to be developed. The *first* step in modeling consists in determining the *stages* in the life cycle of the *objects* that play a role in the system. For instance, in Example 1 the objects are trains and the stages are railway tracks. In a hospital care model the objects are patients and the stages can be "blood sample being analysed" or "on medication". Observe that in this case, an object (patient) can be in different stages at the same time: the patient can be X-rayed and at the same time a blood sample can be tested. In general, non-experts should be able to understand what are the objects and what are the stages. In Petri nets the objects are represented by tokens while the stages are modelled as places. It should be noted that *a direct attempt* to model the process as a Petri net will typically result in places representing both process stages and artificial mechanisms needed to express such constructs as choice.

The *second* step aims at the events that cause the change from one stage to another. In Petri nets these events are modeled as transitions. For example, in the patient care process the transition from the X-ray stage to the examination stage may be taken only if the blood test stage has been completed. Upon completing this step one usually has a process model that allows too much behavior, so many occurrence sequences allowed in the model are disallowed in practice.

So the *third step* consists in *restricting* the behaviour of the model constructed so far by means of guards on the existing transitions. These guards dependent solely on events happened in the past, i.e., transition firings, event occurrence time and data involved. For instance, the choice of a medication can depend on an evolution of blood pressure as observed in recent measurements. To ensure correctness of the specified behaviour we often have *global constraints*, such as in the railway case where it is forbidden that two trains are in places with a distance smaller than two. Based on these global constraints the model designer should formulate history-dependent guards restricting firings of individual transitions.

Finally, the *fourth step* aims at assessing correctness of the model, e.g., checking whether the constraints are implied by the guards. To this end we make use of the transformations to classical (inhibitor) Petri nets.

2.2 Modelling from an Existing Data-Centered Model

The four steps of the methodology described in Section 2.1 are not applicable if the development starts from a legacy information system. A legacy information

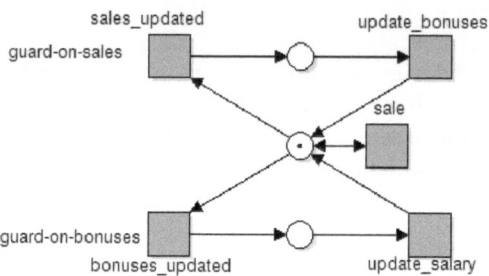

Fig. 3. Active rules as a history-dependent net

system is typically database-centered. Process information is expressed by means of *active rules* [9] that should ensure global constraints [3]. Unfortunately, it is a commonly recognised fact that implicit relations between the rules and unpredictable (non-deterministic) behaviour can jeopardise maintainability of a system. Therefore, we propose an alternative approach, deriving a history based net from an active database.

The *first* step consists in listing all possible basic actions. To illustrate our approach we consider two rules: (1) if the updated sales figure exceed ten units, the bonus of the salesperson is increased; (2) if a salesperson has obtained three bonuses, her salary is increased. In this particular case we have only one basic action, namely, *sell*. We construct the flower net using these basic actions.

The *second* step is constructing a *windmill net* based on the place of the previously constructed flower net. Every vane represents a rule, i.e., consists of a linear Petri net formed by an event and a series of actions (Figure 3). Condition acts as a part of a guard of the transition representing the triggering event. Observe, however, that every event can be handled only once. Therefore, the guard needs to count a number of occurrences of the corresponding action *after* the transition represented by the last action of the rule has been fired for the last time. Therefore, *guard-on-sales* is $\#_{\succ last(update\_bonuses)}\{sale\} > 10$. The guard corresponding to the second rule can be written in a similar way.

3   Example: The "Supply Chain" of Criminal Justice

To illustrate the advantages of history-dependent nets we consider a simplified example of a process of criminal justice. In this process four parties are involved. They form a so-called "supply chain". The participating parties are the police department, the prosecutor's office, the court house and the prison.

At the first stage a person is called "free" and is presumed innocent. If the person is suspected of committing a crime, the police department will try to arrest the suspect, charge him with the crime and either let him go free (with some restrictions like taking his passport), if the suspect is not dangerous and there is no escape risk, or put him in custody, otherwise. Next, the prosecutor's office interrogates the suspect and the witnesses, and, upon the results of the

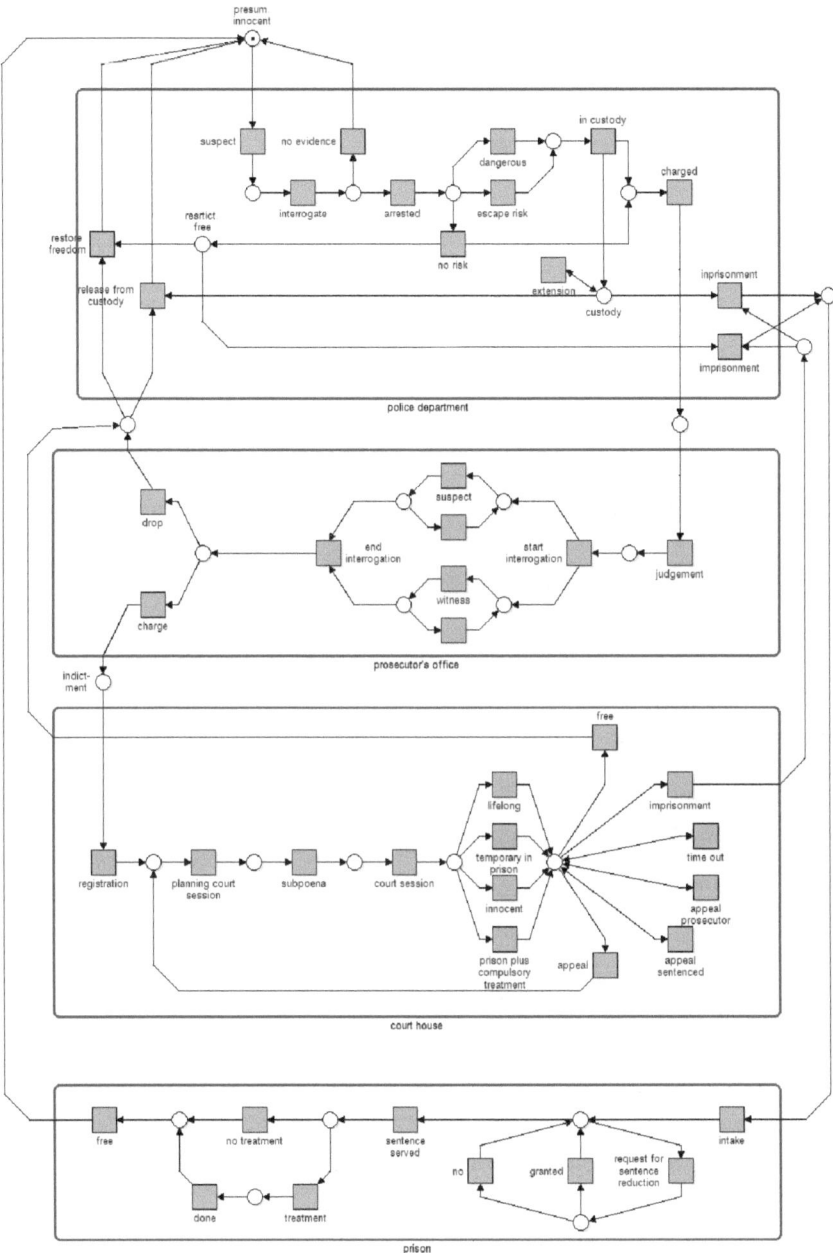

Fig. 4. Criminal justice

interrogation, decides either to drop the charges (in which case the suspect is either released from the custody or his freedom is restored) or to proceed with the charges leading to an indictment.

The process of the court house involves deciding whether the suspect is guilty and what kind of punishment should be carried out. Depending on the court's decision, the suspect or his attorney can decide to submit an appeal. In this case the process is repeated. If the suspect has been convicted and no appeal has been submitted, he is imprisoned. During his stay at the prison the convict can apply for a sentence reduction. Depending on the court decision, the person might need to undergo a special treatment upon servicing the sentence. If no such treatment is needed or the treatment has been done, the person is freed and the entire process restarts.

Similarly to Example 1 we make a clear separation between the four basic parts of the process presented in Figure 4 and additional constraints existing between the steps of each part and between the parts. To model these and similar constraints we use the guards, which are expressions over the history. The following table illustrates a number of constraints and their formalisation as formulae of our history logic [6]. (Note that $\lambda(e)$ denotes the label of event e from the history log.)

Constraint	Transition	Guard
Both the prosecutor and the sentenced may submit an appeal once after the first court session and once after the second court session. Appeal should be submitted before the time out.	appeal	$\#_{\succ last(\{registration\})}\{court\ session\} \leq 2$ $\wedge \forall_{\succ last(\{court\ session\})} u :$ $\neg(\lambda(u) \in \{time\ out, appeal\})$ $\wedge \exists_{\succ last(\{court\ session\})} v :$ $\lambda(v) \in \{appeal\ sentenced,$ $appeal\ persecutor\}$
A prisoner may apply only three times for reduction of punishment and if the application is granted once, no further requests are allowed. If a lifelong sentence has been proclaimed no requests are possible.	request for sentence reduction	$\#_{\succ last(\{court\ session\})}\{lifelong\} = 0$ $\wedge\#_{\succ last(\{court\ session\})}\{request$ $for\ sentence\ reduction\} \leq 2$ $\wedge\#_{\succ last(\{court\ session\})}\{granted\} = 0$
If somebody has a lifelong sentence the *sentence served* transition may not fire.	sentence served	$\#_{\succ last(\{court\ session\})}\{lifelong\} = 0$

4   Conclusions and Related Work

In this paper we have presented a modelling methodology based on history-dependent nets. We have seen that history-dependent nets improve the modelling comfort by allowing a clear separation between the graphically represented process information on the one hand, and the logically represented information on the additional constraints on the other. Moreover, in many practical cases history-dependent nets can be automatically translated to bisimilar classical Petri nets, which accounts for their analysability and verifiability.

Histories and related notions such as event systems [10] and pomsets [4,2] have been used in the past to provide causality-preserving semantics for Petri nets. Baldan *et al.* [1] use two different notions of history. Unlike our approach, none of these works aims at restricting the firings by means of history-dependent guards. *History-dependent automata* [8] extend states and transitions of an automaton with sets of local names: each transition can refer to the names associated to its source state but can also generate new names which can then appear in the destination state. This notion of history implies that one cannot refer to firings of other transitions but by means of shared names. We believe that the ability to express dependencies on previous firings explicitly is the principal advantage of our approach.

References

1. Baldan, P., Busi, N., Corradini, A., Pinna, G.M.: Domain and event structure semantics for Petri nets with read and inhibitor arcs. Theoretical Computer Science 323(1-3), 129–189 (2004)
2. Best, E., Devillers, R.R.: Sequential and concurrent behaviour in petri net theory. Theoretical Computer Science 55(1), 87–136 (1987)
3. Ceri, S., Widom, J.: Deriving production rules for constraint maintainance. In: 16th International Conference on Very Large Data Bases, August 13-16, 1990, Brisbane, Queensland, Australia, pp. 566–577 (1990)
4. Goltz, U., Reisig, W.: The non-sequential behavior of Petri nets. Information and Control 57(2/3), 125–147 (1983)
5. Hartmann, J.G.: Predicate/transition nets. In: Advances in Petri Nets, pp. 207–247 (1986)
6. van Hee, K.M., Serebrenik, A., Sidorova, N., van der Aalst, W.M.P.: History-dependent Petri nets. In: Kleijn, J., Yakovlev, A. (eds.) ICATPN 2007, Springer, Heidelberg (2007)
7. Junttila, T.A.: New canonical representative marking algorithms for place/transition-nets. In: Cortadella, J., Reisig, W. (eds.) ICATPN 2004. LNCS, vol. 3099, pp. 258–277. Springer, Heidelberg (2004)
8. Montanari, U., Pistore, M.: History-dependent automata: An introduction. In: SFM, pp. 1–28 (2005)
9. Widom, J., Ceri, S. (eds.): Active Database Systems: Triggers and Rules For Advanced Database Processing. Morgan Kaufmann, San Francisco (1996)
10. Winskel, G.: Event structures. In: Brauer, W., Reisig, W., Rozenberg, G. (eds.) Advances in Petri Nets. LNCS, vol. 255, pp. 325–392. Springer, Heidelberg (1987)

Fuzzy Mining – Adaptive Process Simplification Based on Multi-perspective Metrics

Christian W. Günther and Wil M.P. van der Aalst

Eindhoven University of Technology
P.O. Box 513, NL-5600 MB, Eindhoven, The Netherlands
{c.w.gunther, w.m.p.v.d.aalst}@tue.nl

Abstract. Process Mining is a technique for extracting process models from execution logs. This is particularly useful in situations where people have an idealized view of reality. Real-life processes turn out to be less structured than people tend to believe. Unfortunately, traditional process mining approaches have problems dealing with unstructured processes. The discovered models are often "spaghetti-like", showing all details without distinguishing what is important and what is not. This paper proposes a new process mining approach to overcome this problem. The approach is configurable and allows for different faithfully simplified views of a particular process. To do this, the concept of a roadmap is used as a metaphor. Just like different roadmaps provide suitable abstractions of reality, process models should provide meaningful abstractions of operational processes encountered in domains ranging from healthcare and logistics to web services and public administration.

1 Introduction

Business processes, whether defined and prescribed or implicit and ad-hoc, drive and support most of the functions and services in enterprises and administrative bodies of today's world. For describing such processes, modeling them as graphs has proven to be a useful and intuitive tool. While modeling is well-established in process design, it is complicated to do for monitoring and documentation purposes. However, especially for monitoring, process models are valuable artifacts, because they allow us to communicate complex knowledge in intuitive, compact, and high-level form.

Process mining is a line of research which attempts to extract such abstract, compact representations of processes from their logs, i.e. execution histories [1,2,3,5,6,7,10,14]. The α-algorithm, for example, can create a Petri net process model from an execution log [2]. In the last years, a number of process mining approaches have been developed, which address the various *perspectives* of a process (e.g., control flow, social network), and use various techniques to generalize from the log (e.g., genetic algorithms, theory of regions [12,4]). Applied to explicitly designed, well-structured, and rigidly enforced processes, these techniques are able to deliver an impressive set of information, yet their purpose is somewhat limited to verifying the compliant execution. However, most processes in real life have not been purposefully designed and optimized, but have evolved over time or are not even explicitly defined. In such situations, the application of process mining is far more interesting, as it is not limited to re-discovering what we already know, but it can be used to *unveil previously hidden knowledge*.

G. Alonso, P. Dadam, and M. Rosemann (Eds.): BPM 2007, LNCS 4714, pp. 328–343, 2007.
© Springer-Verlag Berlin Heidelberg 2007

Over the last couple of years we obtained much experience in applying the tried-and-tested set of mining algorithms to real-life processes. Existing algorithms tend to perform well on structured processes, but often fail to provide insightful models for less structured processes. The phrase "spaghetti models" is often used to refer to the results of such efforts. The problem is not that existing techniques produce incorrect results. In fact, some of the more robust process mining techniques guarantee that the resulting model is "correct" in the sense that reality fits into the model. The problem is that the resulting model shows all details without providing a suitable abstraction. This is comparable to looking at the map of a country where all cities and towns are represented by identical nodes and all roads are depicted in the same manner. The resulting map is correct, but not very suitable. Therefore, the concept of a roadmap is used as a metaphor to visualize the resulting models. Based on an analysis of the log, the importance of activities and relations among activities are taken into account. Activities and their relations can be clustered or removed depending on their role in the process. Moreover, certain aspects can be emphasized graphically just like a roadmap emphasizes highways and large cities over dirt roads and small towns. As will be demonstrated in this paper, the roadmap metaphor allows for meaningful process models.

In this paper we analyze the problems traditional mining algorithms have with less-structured processes (Section 2), and use the metaphor of maps to derive a novel, more appropriate approach from these lessons (Section 3). We abandon the idea of performing process mining confined to one perspective only, and propose a multi-perspective set of log-based process metrics (Section 4). Based on these, we have developed a flexible approach for *Fuzzy Mining*, i.e. adaptively simplifying mined process models (Section 5).

2   Less-Structured Processes – The Infamous Spaghetti Affair

The fundamental idea of process mining is both simple and persuasive: There is a process which is unknown to us, but we can follow the traces of its behavior, i.e. we have access to enactment logs. Feeding those into a process mining technique will yield an aggregate description of that observed behavior, e.g. in form of a process model.

In the beginning of process mining research, mostly artificially generated logs were used to develop and verify mining algorithms. Then, also logs from real-life workflow management systems, e.g. Staffware, could be successfully mined with these techniques. Early mining algorithms had high requirements towards the qualities of log files, e.g. they were supposed to be complete and limited to events of interest. Yet, most of the resulting problems could be easily remedied with more data, filtering the log and tuning the algorithm to better cope with problematic data.

While these successes were certainly convincing, most real-life processes are not executed within rigid, inflexible workflow management systems and the like, which enforce correct, predictive behavior. It is the inherent inflexibility of these systems which drove the majority of process owners (i.e., organizations having the need to support processes) to choose more flexible or ad-hoc solutions. Concepts like Adaptive Workflow or Case Handling either allow users to change the process at runtime, or define processes in a somewhat more "loose" manner which does not strictly define a specific path of execution. Yet the most popular solutions for supporting processes do not enforce any defined behavior at all, but merely offer functionality like sharing data and passing messages between users and resources. Examples for these systems are ERP (Enterprise Resource Planning) and CSCW (Computer-Supported Cooperative Work) systems, custom-built solutions, or plain E-Mail.

It is obvious that *executing a process within such less restrictive environments will lead to more diverse and less-structured behavior.* This abundance of observed behavior, however, unveiled a fundamental weakness in most of the early process mining algorithms. When these are used to mine logs from less-structured processes, the result is usually just as unstructured and hard to understand. These "spaghetti" process models do not provide any meaningful abstraction from the event logs themselves, and are therefore useless to process analysts. It is important to note that these "spaghetti" models are not incorrect. The problem is that *the processes themselves* are really "spaghetti-like", i.e., the model is an accurate reflection of reality.

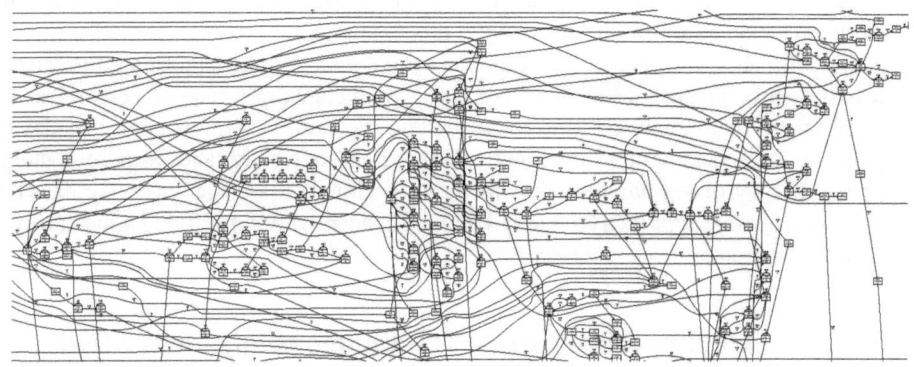

Fig. 1. Excerpt of a typical "Spaghetti" process model (ca. 20% of complete model)

An example of such a "spaghetti" model is given in Figure 1. It is noteworthy that this figure shows only a small excerpt (ca. 20%) of a highly unstructured process model. It has been mined from machine test logs using the Heuristics Miner, one of the traditional process mining techniques which is most resilient towards noise in logs [14]. Although this result is rather useful, certainly in comparison with other early process mining techniques, it is plain to see that deriving helpful information from it is not easy.

Event classes found in the log are interpreted as activity nodes in the process model. Their sheer amount makes it difficult to focus on the interesting parts of the process. The abundance of arcs in the model, which constitute the actual "spaghetti", introduce an even greater challenge for interpretation. Separating cause from effect, or the general direction in which the process is executed, is not possible because virtually every node is transitively connected to any other node in both directions. This mirrors the crux of flexibility in process execution – when people are free to execute anything in any given order they will usually make use of such feature, which renders monitoring business activities an essentially infeasible task.

We argue that the fault for these problems lies neither with less-structured processes, nor with process mining itself. Rather, it is the result of a number of, mostly implicit, assumptions which process mining has historically made, both with respect to the event logs under consideration, and regarding the processes which have generated them. While being perfectly sound in structured, controlled environments, *these assumptions do not hold in less-structured, real-life environments*, and thus ultimately make traditional process mining fail there.

Assumption 1: **All logs are reliable and trustworthy.** Any event type found in the log is assumed to have a corresponding logical activity in the process. However, activities in real-life processes may raise a random number of seemingly unrelated events. Activities may also go unrecorded, while other events do not correspond to any activity at all.

The assumption that logs are well-formed and homogeneous is also often not true. For example, a process found in the log is assumed to correspond to one logical entity. In less-structured environments, however, there are often a number of "tacit" process types which are executed, and thus logged, under the same name.

Also, the idea that all events are raised on the same level of abstraction, and are thus equally important, is not true in real-life settings. Events on different levels are "flattened" into the same event log, while there is also a high amount of informational events (e.g., debug messages from the system) which need to be disregarded.

Assumption 2: **There exists an exact process which is reflected in the logs.** This assumption implies that there is the one perfect solution out there, which needs to be found. Consequently, the mining result should model the process *completely*, *accurately*, and *precisely*. However, as stated before, spaghetti models are not necessarily incorrect – the models look like spaghetti, because they precisely describe every detail of the less-structured behavior found in the log. A more high-level solution, which is able to abstract from details, would thus be preferable.

Traditional mining algorithms have also been confined to a single *perspective* (e.g., control flow, data), as such isolated view is supposed to yield higher precision. However, perspectives are interacting in less-structured processes, e.g. the data flow may complement the control flow, and thus also needs to be taken into account.

In general, the assumption of a perfect solution is not well-suited for real-life application. Reality often differs significantly from theory, in ways that had not been anticipated. Consequently, useful tools for practical application must be *explorative*, i.e. support the analyst to tweak results and thus capitalize on their knowledge.

We have conducted process mining case studies in organizations like Philips Medical Systems, UWV, Rijkswaterstaat, the Catharina Hospital Eindhoven and the AMC hospital Amsterdam, and the Dutch municipalities of Alkmaar and Heusden. Our experiences in these case studies have shown the above assumptions to be violated in all ways imaginable. Therefore, to make process mining a useful tool in practical, less-structured settings, these assumptions need to be discarded. The next section introduces the main concept of our mining approach, which takes these lessons into account.

3 An Adaptive Approach for Process Simplification

Process mining techniques which are suitable for less-structured environments need to be able to provide a high-level view on the process, abstracting from undesired details. The field of cartography has always been faced with a quite similar challenge, namely to simplify highly complex and unstructured topologies. Activities in a process can be related to locations in a topology (e.g. towns or road crossings) and precedence relations to traffic connections between them (e.g., railways or motorways).

Fig. 2. Example of a road map

When one takes a closer look at maps (such as the example in Figure 2), the solution cartography has come up with to simplify and present complex topologies, one can derive a number of valuable concepts from them.

Aggregation: To limit the number of information items displayed, maps often show *coherent clusters of low-level detail information* in an aggregated manner. One example are cities in road maps, where particular houses and streets are combined within the city's transitive closure (e.g., the city of Eindhoven in Figure 2).

Abstraction: Lower-level information which is *insignificant in the chosen context* is simply omitted from the visualization. Examples are bicycle paths, which are of no interest in a motorist's map.

Emphasis: More significant information is *highlighted* by visual means such as *color*, *contrast*, *saturation*, and *size*. For example, maps emphasize more important roads by displaying them as thicker, more colorful and contrasting lines (e.g., motorway "E25" in Figure 2).

Customization: There is no one single map for the world. Maps are specialized on a defined *local context*, have a specific *level of detail* (city maps vs highway maps), and a dedicated *purpose* (interregional travel vs alpine hiking).

These concepts are universal, well-understood, and established. In this paper we explore how they can be used to simplify and properly visualize complex, less-structured processes. To do that, we need to develop appropriate decision criteria on which to base the simplification and visualization of process models. We have identified two fundamental *metrics* which can support such decisions: (1) *significance* and (2) *correlation*.

Significance, which can be determined both for event classes (i.e., activities) and binary precedence relations over them (i.e., edges), measures the *relative importance* of behavior. As such, it specifies the level of interest we have in events, or their occurring after one another. One example for measuring significance is by frequency, i.e. events or precedence relations which are observed more frequently are deemed more significant.

Correlation on the other hand is only relevant for precedence relations over events. It measures *how closely related* two events following one another are. Examples for measuring correlation include determining the overlap of data attributes associated to two events following one another, or comparing the similarity of their event names. More closely correlated events are assumed to share a large amount of their data, or have their similarity expressed in their recorded names (e.g. "check_customer_application" and "approve_customer_application").

Based on these two metrics, which have been defined specially for this purpose, we can sketch our approach for process simplification as follows.

– *Highly significant* behavior is *preserved*, i.e. contained in the simplified model.
– *Less significant* but *highly correlated* behavior is *aggregated*, i.e. hidden in clusters within the simplified model.
– *Less significant* and *lowly correlated* behavior is *abstracted from*, i.e. removed from the simplified model.

This approach can greatly reduce and focus the displayed behavior, by employing the concepts of aggregation and abstraction. Based on such simplified model, we can employ the concept of *emphasis*, by highlighting more significant behavior.

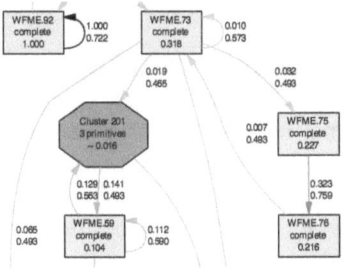

Fig. 3. Excerpt of a simplified and decorated process model

Figure 3 shows an excerpt from a simplified process model, which has been created using our approach. Bright square nodes represent significant activities, the darker octagonal node is an aggregated cluster of three less-significant activities. All nodes are labeled with their respective significance, with clusters displaying the mean significance of their elements. The brightness of edges between nodes emphasizes their significance, i.e. more significant relations are darker. Edges are also labeled with their respective significance and correlation values. By either removing or hiding less significant information, this visualization enables the user to focus on the most interesting behavior in the process.

Yet, the question of what constitutes "interesting" behavior can have a number of answers, based on the process, the purpose of analysis, or the desired level of abstraction. In order to yield the most appropriate result, significance and correlation measures need to be configurable. We have thus developed a set of metrics, which can each measure significance or correlation based on different perspectives (e.g., control flow or data) of the process. By influencing the "mix" of these metrics and the simplification procedure itself, the user can *customize* the produced results to a large degree.

The following section introduces some of the metrics we have developed for significance and correlation in more detail.

4   Log-Based Process Metrics

Significance and correlation, as introduced in the previous section, are suitable concepts for describing the importance of behavior in a process in a compact manner. However, because they represent very generalized, condensed metrics, it is important to measure them in an *appropriate* manner. Taking into account the wide variety of processes, analysis questions and objectives, and levels of abstraction, it is necessary to make this measurement *adaptable* to such parameters.

Our approach is based on a configurable and extensible framework for measuring significance and correlation. The design of this framework is introduced in the next subsection, followed by detailed introductions to the three primary types of metrics: unary significance, binary significance, and binary correlation.

4.1   Metrics Framework

An important property of our measurement framework is that for each of the three primary types of metrics (unary significance, binary significance, and binary correlation) different implementations may be used. A metric may either be measured directly from the log (*log-based metric*), or it may be based on measurements of other, log-based metrics (*derivative metric*).

When the log contains a large number of undesired events, which occur in between desired ones, actual causal dependencies between the desired event classes may go unrecorded. To counter this, our approach also measures *long-term relations*, i.e. when the sequence A, B, C is found in the log, we will not only record the relations $A \rightarrow B$ and $B \rightarrow C$, but also the *length-2-relationship* $A \rightarrow C$. We allow measuring relationships of arbitrary length, while the measured value will be *attenuated*, i.e. decreased, with increasing length of relationship.

4.2   Unary Significance Metrics

Unary significance describes the relative importance of an event class, which will be represented as a node in the process model. As our approach is based on removing less significant behavior, and as removing a node implies removing all of its connected arcs, unary significance is the primary driver of simplification.

One metric for unary significance is *frequency significance*, i.e. the more often a certain event class was observed in the log, the more significant it is. Frequency is a log-based metric, and is in fact the most intuitive of all metrics. Traditional process mining techniques are built solely on the principle of measuring frequency, and it remains an important foundation of our approach. However, real-life logs often contain a large number of events which are in fact not very significant, e.g. an event which describes saving the process state after every five activities. In such situations, frequency plays a diminished role and can rather distort results.

Another, derivate metric for unary significance is *routing significance*. The idea behind routing significance is that points, at which the process either forks (i.e., split nodes) or synchronizes (i.e., join nodes), are interesting in that they substantially define the structure of a process. The higher the number and significance of predecessors for a node (i.e., its incoming arcs) differs from the number and significance of its successors (i.e., outgoing arcs), the more important that node is for *routing* in the process. Routing significance is important as *amplifier metric*, i.e. it helps separating important routing nodes (whose significance it increases) from those less important.

4.3   Binary Significance Metrics

Binary significance describes the relative importance of a precedence relation between two event classes, i.e. an edge in the process model. Its purpose is to amplify and to isolate the observed behavior which is supposed to be of the greatest interest. In our simplification approach, it primarily influences the selection of edges which will be included in the simplified process model.

Like for unary significance, the log-based *frequency significance* metric is also the most important implementation for binary significance. The more often two event classes are observed after one another, the more significant their precedence relation.

The *distance significance* metric is a derivative implementation of binary significance. The more the significance of a relation differs from its source and target nodes' significances, the less its distance significance value. The rationale behind this metric is, that globally important relations are also always the most important relations for their endpoints. Distance significance locally amplifies crucial key relations between event classes, and weakens already insignificant relations. Thereby, it can clarify ambiguous situations in edge abstraction, where many relations "compete" over being included in the simplified process model. Especially in very unstructured execution logs, this metric is an indispensible tool for isolating behavior of interest.

4.4   Binary Correlation Metrics

Binary correlation measures the distance of events in a precedence relation, i.e. how closely related two events following one another are. Distance, in the process domain, can be equated to the magnitude of context change between two activity executions. Subsequently occurring activities which have a more similar context (e.g., which are executed by the same person or in a short timeframe) are thus evaluated to be higher correlated. Binary correlation is the main driver of the decision between *aggregation or abstraction* of less-significant behavior.

Proximity correlation evaluates event classes, which occur shortly after one another, as highly correlated. This is important for identifying clusters of events which correspond to one logical activity, as these are commonly executed within a short timeframe.

Another feature of such clusters of events occurring within the realm of one higher-level activity is, that they are executed by the same person. *Originator correlation* between event classes is determined from the names of the persons, which have triggered two subsequent events. The more similar these names, the higher correlated the respective event classes. In real applications, user names often include job titles or function identifiers (e.g."sales_John" and "sales_Paul"). Therefore, this metric implementation is a valuable tool also for unveiling implicit correlation between events.

Endpoint correlation is quite similar, however, instead of resources it compares the *activity names* of subsequent events. More similar names will be interpreted as higher correlation. This is important for low-level logs including a large amount of less significant events which are closely related. Most of the time, events which reflect similar tasks also are given similar names (e.g., "open_valve13" and "close_valve13"), and this metric can unveil these implicit dependencies.

In most logs, events also include additional attributes, containing snapshots from the *data perspective* of the process (e.g., the value of an insurance claim). In such cases, the *selection of attributes* logged for each event can be interpreted as its context. Thus, the *data type correlation* metric evaluates event classes, where subsequent events share a large amount of data types (i.e., attribute keys), as highly correlated. *Data value correlation* is more specific, in that it also takes the values of these common attributes into account. In that, it uses relative similarity, i.e. small changes of an attribute value will compromise correlation less than a completely different value.

Currently, all implementations for binary correlation in our approach are log-based. The next section introduces our approach for adaptive simplification and visualization of complex process models, which is based on the aggregated measurements of all metric implementations which have been introduced in this section.

5   Adaptive Graph Simplification

Most process mining techniques follow an *interpretative* approach, i.e. they attempt to map behavior found in the log to typical process design patterns (e.g., whether a split node has AND- or XOR-semantics). Our approach, in contrast, focuses on high-level mapping of behavior found in the log, while not attempting to discover such patterns. Thus, creating the initial (non-simplified) process model is straightforward: All event classes found in the log are translated to activity nodes, whose importance is expressed by unary significance. For every observed precedence relation between event classes, a corresponding directed edge is added to the process model. This edge is described by the binary significance and correlation of the ordering relation it represents.

Subsequently, we apply three *transformation methods* to the process model, which will successively simplify specific aspects of it. The first two phases, *conflict resolution* and *edge filtering*, remove edges (i.e., precedence relations) between activity nodes, while the final *aggregation and abstraction* phase removes and/or clusters less-significant nodes. Removing edges from the model first is important – due to the less-structured nature of real-life processes and our measurement of long-term relationships, the initial model contains *deceptive* ordering relations, which do not correspond to valid behavior and need to be discarded. The following sections provide details about the three phases of our simplification approach, given in the order in which they are applied to the initial model.

5.1 Conflict Resolution in Binary Relations

Whenever two nodes in the initial process model are connected by edges in both directions, they are defined to be *in conflict*. Depending on their specific properties, conflicts may represent one of three possible situations in the process:

- *Length-2-loop:* Two activities A and B constitute a loop in the process model, i.e. after executing A and B in sequence, one may return to A and start over. In this case, the conflicting ordering relations between these activities are explicitly allowed in the original process, and thus need to be preserved.
- *Exception:* The process orders $A \rightarrow B$ in sequence, however, during real-life execution the exceptional case of $B \rightarrow A$ also occurs. Most of the time, the "normal" behavior is clearly more significant. In such cases, the "weaker" relation needs to be discarded to focus on the main behavior.
- *Concurrency:* A and B can be executed in any order (i.e., they are on two distinct, parallel paths), the log will most likely record both possible cases, i.e. $A \rightarrow B$ and $B \rightarrow A$, which will create a conflict. In this case, both conflicting ordering relations need to be removed from the process model.

Conflict resolution attempts to classify each conflict as one of these three cases, and then resolves it accordingly. For that, it first determines the *relative significance* of both conflicting relations.

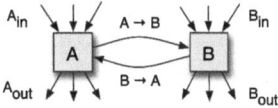

Fig. 4. Evaluating the relative significance of conflicting relations

Figure 4 shows an example of two activities A and B in conflict. The relative significance for an edge $A \rightarrow B$ can be determined as follows.

Definition 1 (Relative significance). *Let $\mathcal{N}$ be the set of nodes in a process model, and let $sig : \mathcal{N} \times \mathcal{N} \rightarrow \mathbb{R}_0^+$ be a relation that assigns to each pair of nodes $A, B \in \mathcal{N}$ the significance of a precedence relation over them. $rel : \mathcal{N} \times \mathcal{N} \rightarrow \mathbb{R}_0^+$ is a relation which assigns to each pair of nodes $A, B \in \mathbb{N}$ the* relative importance *of their ordering relation:* $rel(A, B) = \frac{1}{2} \cdot \frac{sig(A,B)}{\sum_{X \in \mathcal{N}} sig(A,X)} + \frac{1}{2} \cdot \frac{sig(A,B)}{\sum_{X \in \mathcal{N}} sig(X,B)}$.

Every ordering relation $A \to B$ has a set of *competing relations* $Comp_{AB} = A_{out} \cup B_{in}$. This set of competing relations is composed of A_{out}, i.e. all edges starting from A, and of B_{in}, i.e. all edges pointing to B (cf. Figure 4). Note that this set also contains the reference relation itself, i.e. more specifically: $B_{in} \cap A_{out} = \{A \to B\}$. By dividing the significance of an ordering relation $A \to B$ with the sum of all its competing relations' significances, we get the importance of this relation in its *local context*.

If the relative significance of both conflicting relations, $rel(A, B)$ and $rel(B, A)$ exceeds a specified *preserve threshold* value, this signifies that A and B are apparently forming a *length-2-loop*, which is their most significant behavior in the process. Thus, in this case, both $A \to B$ and $B \to A$ will be preserved.

In case at least one conflicting relation's relative significance is below this threshold, the *offset* between both relations' relative significances is determined, i.e. $ofs(A, B) = |rel(A, B) - rel(B, A)|$. The larger this offset value, the more the relative significances of both conflicting relations differ, i.e. one of them is clearly more important. Thus, if the offset value exceeds a specified *ratio threshold*, we assume that the relatively less significant relation is in fact an *exception* and remove it from the process model.

Otherwise, i.e. if at least one of the relations has a relative significance below the *preserve threshold* and their offset is smaller than the *ratio threshold*, this signifies that both $A \to B$ and $B \to A$ are relations which are of no greater importance for both their source and target activities. This low, yet balanced relative significance of conflicting relations hints at A and B being executed *concurrently*, i.e. in two separate threads of the process. Consequently, both edges are removed from the process model, as they do not correspond to factual ordering relations.

5.2 Edge Filtering

Although conflict resolution removes a number of edges from the process model, the model still contains a large amount of precedence relations. To infer further structure from this model, it is necessary to remove most of these remaining edges by *edge filtering*, which isolates the most important behavior. The obvious solution is to remove the globally least significant edges, leaving only highly significant behavior. However, this approach yields sub-optimal results, as it is prone to create small, disparate clusters of highly frequent behavior. Also, in the subsequent *aggregation* step, highly correlated relations play an important part in connecting clusters, even if they are not very significant.

Therefore, our *edge filtering* approach evaluates each edge $A \to B$ by its *utility* $util(A, B)$, a weighed sum of its significance and correlation. A configurable *utility ratio* $ur \in [0, 1]$ determines the weight, such that $util(A, B) = ur \cdot sig(A, B) + (1 - ur) \cdot cor(A, B)$. A larger value for ur will preserve more significant edges, while a smaller value will favor highly correlated edges.

Figure 5 shows an example for processing the incoming arcs of a node A. Using a utility ratio of 0.5, i.e. taking significance and correlation equally into account, the utility value is calculated, which ranges from 0.4 to 1.0 in this example.

Filtering edges is performed on a local basis, i.e. for each node in the process model, the algorithm preserves its incoming and outgoing edges with the highest utility value. The decision of which edges get preserved is configured by the *edge cutoff* parameter

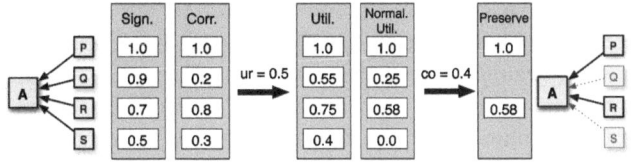

Fig. 5. Filtering the set of incoming edges for a node A

$co \in [0, 1]$. For every node N, the utility values for each incoming edge $X \rightarrow N$ are normalized to $[0, 1]$, so that the weakest edge is assigned 0 and the strongest one 1. All edges whose normalized utility value exceeds co are added to the preserved set. In the example in Figure 5, only two of the original edges, are preserved, using a edge cutoff value of 0.4: $P \rightarrow A$ (with normalized utility of 1.0) and $R \rightarrow A$ (norm. utility of 0.56). The outgoing edges are processed in the same manner for each node.

The *edge cutoff* parameter determines the aggressiveness of the algorithm, i.e. the higher its value, the more likely the algorithm is to remove edges. In very unstructured processes, where precedence relations are likely to have a balanced significance, it is often useful to use a lower utility ratio, such that correlation will be taken more into account and resolve such ambiguous situations. On top of that, a high edge cutoff will act as an amplifier, helping to distinguish the most important edges.

Note that our edge filtering approach starts from an empty set of precedence relations, i.e. all edges are removed by default. Only if an edge is selected locally for at least one node, it will be preserved. This approach keeps the process model connected, while clarifying ambiguous situations. Whether an edge is preserved depends on its utility for describing the behavior of the activities it connects – and not on global comparisons with other parts of the model, which it does not even interact with.

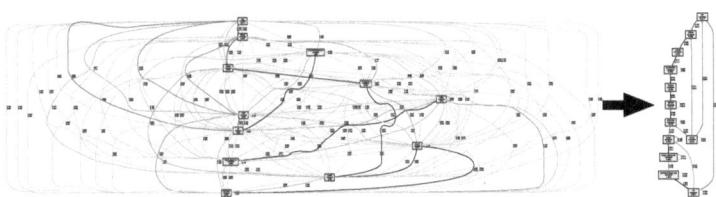

Fig. 6. Example of a process model before (left) and after (right) edge filtering

Figure 6 shows the effect of edge filtering applied to a small, but very unstructured process. The number of nodes remains the same, while removing an appropriate subset of edges clearly brings structure to the previously chaotic process model.

5.3   Node Aggregation and Abstraction

While removing edges brings structure to the process model, the most effective tool for simplification is removing nodes. It enables the analyst to focus on an interesting subset of activities. Our approach preserves highly correlated groups of less-significant nodes as aggregated clusters, while removing isolated, less-significant nodes. Removing nodes is based on the *node cutoff* parameter. Every node whose unary significance is below this threshold becomes a *victim*, i.e. it will either be aggregated or abstracted from. The first phase of our algorithm builds initial clusters of less-significant behavior as follows.

– For each victim, find the most highly correlated neighbor (i.e., connected node)
– If this neighbor is a cluster node, add the victim to this cluster.
– Otherwise, create a new cluster node, and add the victim as its first element.

Whenever a node is added to a cluster, the cluster will "inherit" the ordering relations of that node, i.e. its incoming and outgoing arcs, while the actual node will be hidden. The second phase is *merging* the clusters, which is necessary as most clusters will, at this stage, only consist of one single victim. The following routine is performed to aggregate larger clusters and decrease their number.

– For each cluster, check whether all predecessors or all successors are also clusters.
– If all predecessor nodes are clusters as well, merge with the most highly correlated one and move on to the next cluster.
– If all successors are clusters as well, merge with the most highly correlated one.
– Otherwise, i.e. if both the cluster's pre- and postset contain regular nodes, the cluster is left untouched.

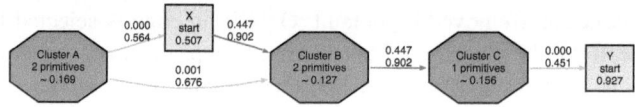

Fig. 7. Excerpt of a clustered model after the first aggregation phase

It is important that clusters will only be merged, if the "victim" has only clusters in his pre- or postset. Figure 7 shows an example of a process model after the first phase of clustering. Cluster A cannot merge with cluster B, as they are also both connected to node X. Otherwise, X would be connected to the merged cluster in both directions, making the model less informative. However, clusters B and C can merge, as B's postset consists only of C. This simplification of the model does not lessen the amount of information, and is thus valid.

The last phase, which constitutes the *abstraction*, removes *isolated* and *singular* clusters. Isolated clusters are detached parts of the process, which are less significant and highly correlated, and which have thus been folded into one single, isolated cluster node. It is obvious that such detached nodes do not contribute to the process model, which is why they are simply removed. Singular clusters consist only of one, single activity node. Thus, they represent less-significant behavior which is not highly correlated to adjacent behavior. Singular clusters are undesired, because they do not simplify the model. Therefore, they are removed from the model, while their most significant precedence relations are transitively preserved (i.e., their predecessors are artificially connected to their successors, if such edge does not already exist in the model).

6   Implementation and Application

We have implemented our approach as the Fuzzy Miner plugin for the ProM framework [8]. All metrics introduced in Section 4 have been implemented, and can be configured by the user. Figure 8 shows the result view of the Fuzzy Miner, with the simplified graph view on the left, and a configuration pane for simplification parameters on the right. Alternative views allow the user to inspect and verify measurements for all metrics, which helps to tune these metrics to the log.

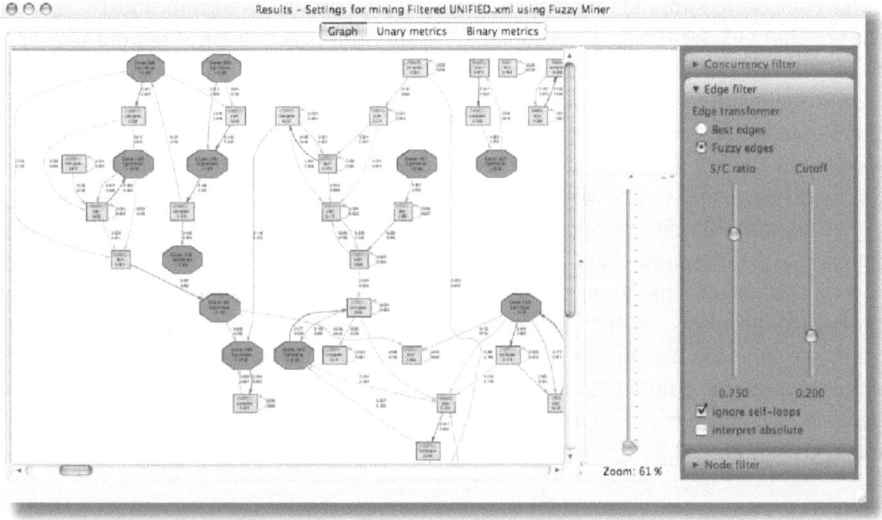

Fig. 8. Screenshot of the Fuzzy Miner, applied to the very large and unstructured log also used for mining the model in Figure 1

Note that this approach is the result of valuable lessons learnt from a great number of case studies with real-life logs. As such, both the applied metrics and the simplification algorithm have been optimized using large amounts actual, less-structured data. While it is difficult to validate the approach formally, the Fuzzy Miner has already become one of the most useful tools in case study applications.

For example, Figure 8 shows the result of applying the Fuzzy Miner to a large test log of manufacturing machines (155.296 events in 16 cases, 826 event classes). The approach has been shown to scale well and is of linear complexity. Deriving all metrics from the mentioned log was performed in less than ten seconds, while simplifying the resulting model took less than two seconds on a 1.8 GHz dual-core machine. While this model has been created from the raw logs, Figure 1 has been mined with the Heuristics Miner, after applying log filters [14]. It is obvious that the Fuzzy Miner is able to clean up a large amount of confusing behavior, and to infer and extract structure from what is chaotic. We have successfully used the Fuzzy Miner on various machinery test and usage logs, development process logs, hospital patient treatment logs, logs from case handling systems and web servers, among others. These are notoriously flexible and unstructured environments, and we hold our approach to be one of the most useful tools for analyzing them so far.

7 Related Work

While parting with some characteristics of traditional process mining techniques, such as absolute precision and describing the complete behavior, it is obvious that the approach described in this paper is based on previous work in this domain, most specifically control-flow mining algorithms [2,14,7]. The mining algorithm most related to Fuzzy Mining is the Heuristics Miner, which also employs heuristics to limit the set of precedence relations included in the model [14]. Our approach also incorporates concepts from log filtering, i.e. removing less significant events from the logs [8]. However, the foundation on multi-perspective metrics, i.e. looking at all aspects of the process at once, its interactive and explorative nature, and the integrated simplification algorithm clearly distinguishes Fuzzy Mining from all previous process mining techniques.

The adaptive simplification approach presented in Section 5 uses concepts from the domains of data clustering and graph clustering. Data clustering attempts to find related subsets of attributes, based on a binary distance metric inferred upon them [11]. Graph clustering algorithms, on the other hand, are based on analyzing structural properties of graphs, from which they derive partitioning strategies [13,9]. Our approach, however, is based on a unique combination of analyzing the *significance* and *correlation* of graph elements, which are based on a wide set of process perspectives. It integrates abstraction and aggregation, and is also more specialized towards the process domain.

8 Discussion and Future Work

We have described the problems traditional process mining techniques face when applied to large, less-structured processes, as often found in practice. Subsequently, we have analyzed the causes for these problems, which lie in a mismatch between fundamental assumptions of traditional process mining, and the characteristics of real-life processes. Based on this analysis, we have developed an adaptive simplification and visualization technique for process models, which is based on two novel metrics, *significance* and *correlation*. We have described a framework for deriving these metrics from an enactment log, which can be adjusted to particular situations and analysis questions.

While the fine-grained configurability of the algorithm and its metrics makes our approach universally applicable, it is also one of its weaknesses, as finding the "right" parameter settings can sometimes be time-consuming. Thus, our next steps will concentrate on deriving higher-level parameters and sensible default settings, while preserving the full range of parameters for advanced users. Further work will concentrate on extending the set of metric implementations and improving the simplification algorithm.

It is our belief that process mining, in order to become more meaningful, and to become applicable in a wider array of practical settings, needs to address the problems it has with unstructured processes. We have shown that the traditional desire to model the *complete* behavior of a process in a *precise* manner conflicts with the original goal, i.e. to provide the user with *understandable, high-level information*. The success of process mining will depend on whether it is able to balance these conflicting goals sensibly. Fuzzy Mining is a first step in that direction.

Acknowledgements. This research is supported by the Technology Foundation STW, applied science division of NWO and the technology programme of the Dutch Ministry of Economic Affairs.

References

1. van der Aalst, W.M.P., van Dongen, B.F., Herbst, J., Maruster, L., Schimm, G., Weijters, A.J.M.M.: Workflow Mining: A Survey of Issues and Approaches. Data and Knowledge Engineering 47(2), 237–267 (2003)
2. van der Aalst, W.M.P., Weijters, A.J.M.M., Maruster, L.: Workflow Mining: Discovering Process Models from Event Logs. IEEE Transactions on Knowledge and Data Engineering 16(9), 1128–1142 (2004)
3. Agrawal, R., Gunopulos, D., Leymann, F.: Mining Process Models from Workflow Logs. In: Sixth International Conference on Extending Database Technology, pp. 469–483 (1998)
4. Badouel, E., Bernardinello, L., Darondeau, P.: The Synthesis Problem for Elementary Net Systems is NP-complete. Theoretical Computer Science 186(1-2), 107–134 (1997)
5. Cook, J.E., Wolf, A.L.: Discovering Models of Software Processes from Event-Based Data. ACM Transactions on Software Engineering and Methodology 7(3), 215–249 (1998)
6. Datta, A.: Automating the Discovery of As-Is Business Process Models: Probabilistic and Algorithmic Approaches. Information Systems Research 9(3), 275–301 (1998)
7. van Dongen, B.F., van der Aalst, W.M.P.: Multi-Phase Process Mining: Building Instance Graphs. In: Atzeni, P., Chu, W., Lu, H., Zhou, S., Ling, T.-W. (eds.) ER 2004. LNCS, vol. 3288, pp. 362–376. Springer, Heidelberg (2004)
8. van Dongen, B.F., de Medeiros, A.K.A., Verbeek, H.M.W., Weijters, A.J.M.M., van der Aalst, W.M.P.: The ProM framework: A New Era in Process Mining Tool Support. In: Ciardo, G., Darondeau, P. (eds.) ICATPN 2005. LNCS, vol. 3536, pp. 444–454. Springer, Heidelberg (2005)
9. van Dongen, S.: Graph Clustering by Flow Simulation. PhD thesis, University of Utrecht (2000)
10. Herbst, J.: A Machine Learning Approach to Workflow Management. In: López de Mántaras, R., Plaza, E. (eds.) ECML 2000. LNCS (LNAI), vol. 1810, pp. 183–194. Springer, Heidelberg (2000)
11. Jain, A.K., Murty, M.N., Flynn, P.J.: Data clustering: A review. ACM Computing Surveys 31(3), 264–323 (1999)
12. de Medeiros, A.K.A., Weijters, A.J.M.M., van der Aalst, W.M.P.: Genetic Process Mining: A Basic Approach and its Challenges. In: Bussler, C., Haller, A. (eds.) BPM 2005. LNCS, vol. 3812, pp. 203–215. Springer, Heidelberg (2006)
13. Pothen, A., Simon, H.D., Liou, K.: Partitioning sparse matrics with eigenvectors of graphs. SIAM J. Matrix Anal. Appl. 11(3), 430–452 (1990)
14. Weijters, A.J.M.M., van der Aalst, W.M.P.: Rediscovering Workflow Models from Event-Based Data using Little Thumb. Integrated Computer-Aided Engineering 10(2), 151–162 (2003)

Inducing Declarative Logic-Based Models from Labeled Traces

Evelina Lamma[1], Paola Mello[2], Marco Montali[2],
Fabrizio Riguzzi[1], and Sergio Storari[1]

[1] ENDIF – Università di Ferrara
Via Saragat, 1 – 44100 – Ferrara, Italy
{evelina.lamma, sergio.storari, fabrizio.riguzzi}@unife.it
[2] DEIS – Università di Bologna
viale Risorgimento, 2 – 40136 – Bologna, Italy
{pmello, mmontali}@deis.unibo.it

Abstract. In this work we propose an approach for the automatic discovery of logic-based models starting from a set of process execution traces. The approach is based on a modified Inductive Logic Programming algorithm, capable of learning a set of declarative rules.

The advantage of using a declarative description is twofold. First, the process is represented in an intuitive and easily readable way; second, a family of proof procedures associated to the chosen language can be used to support the monitoring and management of processes (conformance testing, properties verification and interoperability checking, in particular).

The approach consists in first learning integrity constraints expressed as logical formulas and then translating them into a declarative graphical language named DecSerFlow.

We demonstrate the viability of the approach by applying it to a real dataset from a health case process and to an artificial dataset from an e-commerce protocol.

Topics: Process mining, Process verification and validation, Logic Programming, DecSerFlow, Careflow.

1 Introduction

In recent years, many different proposals have been developed for mining process models from execution traces (e.g. [1,18,9]). All these approaches aim at discovering complex and procedural process models, and differ by the common structural patterns they are able to mine. While recognizing the extreme importance of such approaches, we advocate the necessity of discovering also declarative logic-based knowledge, in the form of process fragments or business rules/policies, from execution traces.

By following this approach, we do not mine a complete process model, but rather discover a set of common declarative patterns and constraints. Being

G. Alonso, P. Dadam, and M. Rosemann (Eds.): BPM 2007, LNCS 4714, pp. 344–359, 2007.

declarative, this information captures what is the high-level process behavior without expressing how it is procedurally executed, hence giving a concise and easily interpretable feedback to the business manager. The importance of adopting a declarative approach rather than an imperative one to model service flows and, more generally, business processes, has been recently pointed out in very interesting and promising works and proposals, such as ConDec [16] and DecSerFlow [17].

In this work we propose an approach for the automatic discovery of rule-based declarative models starting from a set of process execution traces, previously labeled as compliant or not. Learning a process model from both compliant and non compliant traces is not commonly considered in the literature on process mining but it is interesting in a variety of cases: for example, a bank may divide its transactions into fraudulent and normal ones and may desire to learn a model that is able to discriminate the two. In general, an organization may have two or more sets of process executions and may want to understand in what sense they differ.

As the target language, we choose $\mathcal{S}$CIFF [4,3], a declarative language based on computational logic and abductive logic programming in particular, which was originally developed for the specification and verification of global interaction protocols. $\mathcal{S}$CIFF models interaction patterns as forward rules which state what is expected to be performed when a given condition, expressed in terms of already performed activities, holds.

An important advantage of adopting a logic programming representation is that it is possible to exploit the techniques developed in the field of Inductive Logic Programming (ILP for short) [12] for learning models from examples and background knowledge; in fact, the system ICL [8] has been adapted to the problem of learning $\mathcal{S}$CIFF constraints [11].

There are two reasons for using a $\mathcal{S}$CIFF description. First, the process is represented in an intuitive and easily readable way; second, a family of proof procedures associated to $\mathcal{S}$CIFF can be used to support the monitoring and management of processes [2] (conformance testing, properties verification and interoperability checking in particular).

Moreover, we present an approach for translating the learned $\mathcal{S}$CIFF description into a DecSerFlow/ConDec model. We call the resulting system DecMiner.

We demonstrate the viability of the approach by applying it to a real dataset from a health care process and to an artificial dataset from an e-commerce protocol.

The paper is organized as follows. Section 2 briefly introduces the $\mathcal{S}$CIFF framework. Section 3 is devoted to presenting preliminaries on ILP, on the ICL algorithm and on how it can be used to learn $\mathcal{S}$CIFF constraints. Section 4 introduces the basic concepts of DecSerFlow and shows how the learned $\mathcal{S}$CIFF constraints can be interpreted as a DecSerFlow model. Section 5 describes the experiments performed for validating the approach. Section 6 presents related works and, finally, Section 7 concludes the paper and presents directions for future work.

2   An Overview of the SCIFF Framework

The $\mathcal{S}$CIFF framework [4,3] was originally developed for the specification and verification of agent interaction protocols within open and heterogeneous societies. The framework is based on abduction, a reasoning paradigm which allows to formulate hypotheses (called *abducibles*) accounting for observations. In most abductive frameworks, *integrity constraints* are imposed over possible hypotheses in order to prevent inconsistent explanations. $\mathcal{S}$CIFF considers a set of interacting peers as an open society, formalizing interaction protocols by means of a set of global rules which constrain the external and observable behaviour of participants (for this reason, global rules are called Social Integrity Constraints).

To represent that an event ev happened (i.e., an atomic activity has been executed) at a certain time T, $\mathcal{S}$CIFF uses the symbol $\mathbf{H}(ev, T)$, where ev is a term and T is a variable. Hence, an execution trace is modeled as a set of happened events. For example, we could formalize that *bob* has performed activity a at time 5 as follows: $\mathbf{H}(a(bob), 5)$. Furthermore, $\mathcal{S}$CIFF introduces the concept of expectation, which plays a key role when defining global interaction protocols, choreographies, and more in general event-driven process. It is quite natural, in fact, to think of a process in terms of rules of the form: "if A happened, then B is expected to happen". Positive (resp. negative) expectations are denoted by $\mathbf{E}(ev, T)$ (resp. $\mathbf{EN}(ev, T)$), meaning that ev is expected (resp. not expected) to happen at time T. To satisfy a positive (resp. negative) expectation an execution trace must contain (resp. not contain) a matching happened event.

Social Integrity Constraints (ICs for short) are forward rules of the form $body \rightarrow head$, where *body* can contain literals and happened events, and *head* contains a disjunction of conjunctions of expectations and literals.

In this paper, we consider a syntax of ICs that is a subset of the one in [4,3]. In this simplified syntax, a Social Integrity Constraint, C, is a logical formula of the form

$$Body \rightarrow DisjE_1 \vee \ldots \vee DisjE_n \vee DisjEN_1 \vee \ldots \vee DisjEN_m \qquad (1)$$

We will use $Body(C)$ to indicate $Body$ and $Head(C)$ to indicate $DisjE_1 \vee \ldots \vee DisjE_n \vee DisjEN_1 \vee \ldots \vee DisjEN_m$. $Body$ is of the form $b_1 \wedge \ldots \wedge b_l$ where the b_i are literals. Some of the literals may be of the form $\mathbf{H}(ev, T)$ meaning that event ev has happened at time T.

$DisjE_j$ is a formula of the form $\mathbf{E}(ev, T) \wedge d_1 \wedge \ldots \wedge d_k$ where ev is an event and d_i are literals. All the formulas $DisjE_j$ in $Head(C)$ will be called *positive disjuncts*.

$DisjEN_j$ is a formula of the form $\mathbf{EN}(ev, T) \wedge d_1 \wedge \ldots \wedge d_k$ where ev is an event and d_i are literals. All the formulas $DisjEN_j$ in $Head(C)$ will be called *negative disjuncts*.

The literals b_i and d_i refer to predicates defined in a $\mathcal{S}$CIFF knowledge base. Variables in common to $Body(C)$ and $Head(C)$ are universally quantified ($\forall$) with scope the whole IC. Variables occurring only in $DisjE_j$ literals are existentially quantified ($\exists$) with scope the $DisjE_j$ literal itself. Variables occurring only in $DisjEN_j$ literals are universally quantified ($\forall$) with scope the $DisjEN_j$ literal itself. An example of an IC is

$$\mathbf{H}(a(bob), T) \wedge T < 10$$
$$\rightarrow \mathbf{E}(b(alice), T1) \wedge T < T1 \vee \qquad (2)$$
$$\mathbf{EN}(c(mary), T1) \wedge T < T1 \wedge T1 < T + 10$$

The interpretation of an IC is the following: if there exists a substitution of variables such that the body is true in an interpretation representing a trace, then one of the disjuncts in the head must be true. A disjunct of the form $DisjE$ means that we expect event ev to happen with T and its variables satisfying $d_1 \wedge \ldots \wedge d_k$. Therefore $DisjE$ is true if there exist a substitution of variables occurring in $DisjE$ such that ev is present in the trace.

A disjunct of the form $DisjEN$ means that we expect event ev not to happen with T and its variables satisfying $d_1 \wedge \ldots \wedge d_k$. Therefore $DisjEN$ is true if for all substitutions of variables occurring in $DisjEN$ and not appearing in $Body$ either ev does not happen or, if it happens, its properties violate $d_1 \wedge \ldots \wedge d_k$.

The meaning of the IC (2) is the following: if bob has executed action a at a time $T < 10$, then we expect $alice$ to execute action b at some time $T1$ later than T ($\exists T1$) or we expect that $mary$ does not execute action c at any time $T1$ ($\forall T1$) within 9 time units after T.

3   Learning Models

This work starts from the idea that there is a similarity between learning a $\mathcal{S}$CIFF theory, composed by a set of Social Integrity Constraints, and learning a clausal theory as described in the learning from interpretation setting of Inductive Logic Programming [12]. In fact, as a $\mathcal{S}$CIFF theory, a clausal theory can be used to classify a set of atoms (i.e. an interpretation) by returning positive unless there is at least one clause that is false in the interpretation.

A clause C is a formula in the form $b_1 \wedge \cdots \wedge b_n \rightarrow h_1 \vee \cdots \vee h_m$ where b_i are logical literals and h_i are logical atoms. A formula is ground if it does not contain variables. An interpretation is a set of ground atoms. Let us define $head(C) = \{h_1, \ldots, h_m\}$ and $body(C) = \{b_1, \ldots, b_n\}$. Sometimes we will interpret clause C as the set of literals $\{h_1, \ldots, h_m, \neg b_1, \ldots, \neg b_n\}$.

The clause C is true in an interpretation I iff, for all the substitutions θ grounding C, $(I \models body(C)\theta) \rightarrow (head(C)\theta \cap I \neq \emptyset)$. Otherwise, it is false.

Sometimes we may be given a background knowledge B with which we can enlarge each interpretation I by considering, instead of simply I, the interpretation given by $M(B \cup I)$ where M stands for a model, such as Clark's completion [7]. By using a background knowledge we are able to encode each interpretation parsimoniously, by storing separately the rules that are not specific to a single interpretation but are true for every interpretation.

The learning from interpretation setting of ILP is concerned with the following problem:

Given

- a space of possible clausal theories $\mathcal{H}$;
- a set P of positive interpretations;
- a set N of negative interpretations;
- a definite clause background theory B.

Find a clausal theory $H \in \mathcal{H}$ such that;

- for all $p \in P$, H is true in the interpretation $M(B \cup p)$;
- for all $n \in N$, H is false in the interpretation $M(B \cup n)$.

Given a disjunctive clause C (theory H) we say that C (H) *covers* the interpretation I iff C (H) is true in $M(B \cup I)$. We say that C (H) *rules out* an interpretation I iff C (H) does not cover I.

An algorithm that solves the above problem is ICL [8]. It performs a covering loop (function Learn, Figure 1) in which negative interpretations are progressively ruled out and removed from the set N. At each iteration of the loop a new clause is added to the theory. Each clause rules out some negative interpretations. The loop ends when N is empty or when no clause is found.

---

function Learn(P, N, B)
initialize $H := \emptyset$
do
    $C :=$ FindBestClause(P, N, B)
    if best clause $C \neq \emptyset$ then
        add C to H
        remove from N all interpretations that are false for C
while $C \neq \emptyset$ and N is not empty
return H

function FindBestClause(P, N, B)
initialize $Beam := \{false \leftarrow true\}$
initialize $BestClause := \emptyset$
while $Beam$ is not empty do
    initialize $NewBeam := \emptyset$
    for each clause C in $Beam$ do
        for each refinement Ref of C do
            if Ref is better than $BestClause$ then $BestClause := Ref$
            if Ref is not to be pruned then
                add Ref to $NewBeam$
                if size of $NewBeam > MaxBeamSize$ then
                    remove worst clause from $NewBeam$
    $Beam := NewBeam$
return $BestClause$

Fig. 1. ICL learning algorithm

The clause to be added in every iteration of the covering loop is returned by the procedure FindBestClause (Figure 1). It looks for a clause by using beam search with $p(\ominus|\overline{C})$ as a heuristic function, where $p(\ominus|\overline{C})$ is the probability that an example interpretation is classified as negative given that it is ruled out by the clause C. This heuristic is computed as the number of ruled out negative interpretations over the total number of ruled out interpretations (positive and negative). Thus we look for clauses that cover as many positive interpretations as possible and rule out as many negative interpretations as possible. The search starts from the clause $false \leftarrow true$ that rules out all the negative interpretations but also all the positive ones and gradually refines that clause in order to make it more general.

The generality order that is used is the θ-subsumption order: C is more general than D (written $C \geq D$) if there exist a substitution θ such that $D\theta \subseteq C$. If $C \geq D$ then the set of interpretation where C is true is a superset of those where D is true. The same is true if $D \subseteq C$. Thus the clauses in the beam can be gradually refined by adding literals to the body and atoms to the head. For example, let us consider the following clauses:

$C = accept(X) \vee refusal(X) \leftarrow invitation(X)$
$D = accept(X) \vee refusal(X) \leftarrow true$
$E = accept(X) \leftarrow invitation(X)$

Then C is more general than D and E, while D and E are not comparable.

The aim of FindBestClause is to discover a clause that covers all (or most of) the positive interpretations while still ruling out some negative interpretations.

The literals that can possibly be added to a clause are specified in the *language bias*, a collection of statements in an ad hoc language that prescribe which refinements have to be considered. Two languages are possible for ICL: dlab and rmode (see [10] for details). Given a language bias which prescribes that the body literals must be chosen among $\{invitation(X), paptest(X)\}$ and that the head disjuncts must be chosen among $\{accept(X), refusal(X)\}$, an example of refinements sequence performed by FindBestClause is the following:

$false \leftarrow true$
$accept(X) \leftarrow true$
$accept(X) \leftarrow invitation(X)$
$accept(X) \vee refusal(X) \leftarrow invitation(X)$

The refinements of clauses in the beam can also be pruned: a refinement is pruned if it cannot produce a value of the heuristic function higher than that of the best clause (the best refinement that can be obtained is a clause that covers all the positive examples and rules out the same negative examples as the original clause).

When a new clause is returned by FindBestClause it is added to the current theory. The negative interpretations that are ruled out by the clause are ruled out as well by the updated theory, so they can be removed from N.

3.1   Application of ICL to Integrity Constraint Learning

An approach to applying ICL for learning ICs is described in [11]. Each IC is seen as a clause that must be true in all the positive interpretations (compliant execution traces) and false in some negative interpretation (non compliant execution traces). The theory composed of all the ICs must be such that all the ICs are true when considering a compliant trace and at least one IC is false when considering a non compliant one.

In order to apply ICL, a generality order and a refinement operator for ICs must be defined. The generality order is the following: an IC C is more general than an IC D (written $C \geq D$) if there exists a substitution θ for the variables of $body(D)$ such that $body(D)\theta \subseteq body(C)$ and, for each disjunct d in the head of D:

- if d is positive, then there exist a positive disjunct c in the head of C such that $d\theta \supseteq c$
- if d is negative, then there exist a negative disjunct c in the head of C such that $d\theta \subseteq c$

For example, the IC
$$\mathbf{H}(invitation, T) \wedge \mathbf{H}(accept, T3) \rightarrow \mathbf{E}(papTest, T1) \wedge T1 > T \; \vee$$
$$\mathbf{E}(refusal, T2) \wedge T2 > T$$
is more general than
$$\mathbf{H}(invitation, T) \wedge \mathbf{H}(accept, T3) \rightarrow \mathbf{E}(papTest, T1) \wedge T1 > T$$
which in turn is more general than
$$\mathbf{H}(invitation, T) \rightarrow \mathbf{E}(papTest, T1) \wedge T1 > T$$
Moreover
$$\mathbf{H}(invitation, T) \rightarrow \mathbf{E}(papTest, T1) \vee \mathbf{E}(refusal, T2)$$
is more general than
$$\mathbf{H}(invitation, T) \rightarrow \mathbf{E}(papTest, T1) \vee \mathbf{E}(refusal, T2) \wedge T2 > T$$
and
$$\mathbf{H}(sendPapTestResult(neg), T) \rightarrow \mathbf{EN}(papTest, T1) \wedge T1 > T$$
is more general than
$$\mathbf{H}(sendPapTestResult(neg), T) \rightarrow \mathbf{EN}(papTest, T1)$$

A refinement operator can be obtained in the following way: given an IC C, obtain a refinement D by:

- adding a literal to the body;
- adding a disjunct to the head;
- removing a literal from a positive disjunct in the head;
- adding a literal to a negative disjunct in the head.

The language bias specifies which literals can be added to the body, which disjuncts can be added to the head and which literals can be added or removed from head disjuncts.

When adding a disjunct to the head, the refinement operator behaves differently depending on the sign of the disjunct:

- in the case of a positive disjunct, the disjunct formed by the **E** literal plus all the literals in the language bias for the disjunct is added;
- in the case of a negative disjunct, only the **EN** literal is added.

Given an IC C, the refinement operator returns a set of ICs $\rho(C)$ that contains the ICs obtained by applying in all possible ways one of the above mentioned operations. Every IC of $\rho(C)$ is more general than C.

4   From $\mathcal{S}$CIFF Integrity Constraints to DecSerFlow

The meaning of the learned $\mathcal{S}$CIFF Integrity Constraints is very close to the one of various DecSerFlow relation formulas [17]. We therefore tackled the problem of translating a DecSerFlow model into a set of ICs and vice-versa, with the aim of integrating the advantages of both approaches:

- DecSerFlow represents a process model in a declarative and user-friendly graphical notation;
- $\mathcal{S}$CIFF Integrity Constraints are declarative intuitive rules easy to read by humans;
- DecSerFlow has a mapping to LTL and hence could be used to perform monitoring functionalities or to directly enact the model;
- the $\mathcal{S}$CIFF framework associates to the $\mathcal{S}$CIFF language a family of proof procedures capable of performing conformance testing, properties verification and interoperability checking.

DecSerFlow is briefly described in Section 4.1 giving an intuition about the translation from a DecSerFlow model to the $\mathcal{S}$CIFF formalism as addressed in [6]. We then describe in Section 4.2 how we can learn DecSerFlow constraints from labeled traces.

4.1   DecSerFlow: A Brief Recap

DecSerFlow is a graphical language that adopts a declarative style of modeling: the user does not specify possible process flows but only a set of constraints (namely policies or business rules) among activities. For a detailed description of the language and its mapping to Linear Temporal Logic, see [17].

To illustrate the advantages of declarative modeling, the authors consider the problem of specifying that two different activities should not be executed together (i.e. it is possible to execute the first or the latter activity multiple times, but the two activities exclude each other). A procedural language is not able to directly represent the requirement and must explicitly represent all the possible executions (see Figure 2), leading to some problems:

- the process becomes over-specified;
- the modeler must introduce decision points to handle the possible executions, but it is not clear how and when these decisions should be evaluated.

procedural language   DecSerFlow

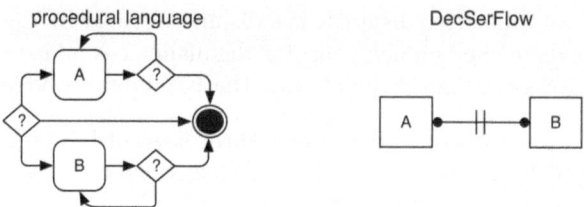

Fig. 2. Procedural vs. declarative approach when modeling the not coexistence between two activities

Instead, by using a declarative language such as DecSerFlow, forbidding the coexistence of two activities A and B may be expressed by a special edge between the two nodes representing A and B. This will be translated into the simple LTL formula: $\neg(\Diamond A \wedge \Diamond B)$.

As shown in Figure 2, the basic intuitive concepts of DecSerFlow are: *activities*, atomic units of work; *constraints among activities*, to model policies/business rules and constrain their execution.

Constraints are given as relationships between two (or more) activities. Each constraint is then expressed as an LTL formula, hence the name "formulas" to indicate DecSerFlow relationships.

DecSerFlow core relationships are grouped into three families:

- *existence formulas*, unary relationships used to constrain the cardinality of activities
- *relation formulas*, which define (positive) relationships and dependencies between two (or more) activities;
- *negation formulas*, the negated version of relation formulas (as in $\mathcal{S}$CIFF, DecSerFlow follows an open approach i.e. the model should express not only what has to be done but also what is forbidden).

The intended meaning of DecSerFlow formulas can be expressed by using $\mathcal{S}$CIFF. In [6], the authors propose a translation by mapping atomic DecSerFlow activities to $\mathcal{S}$CIFF events and formulas to corresponding integrity constraints.

For example, let us consider the *succession* formula among two whatsoever activities A and B: it states that every execution of A should be *followed* by the execution of B and each B should be *preceded* by A, i.e. that B is *response* of A and, in turn, A is *precedence* of B. This formula could be translated as follows. First, the succession between activities is mapped to the response and precedence formulas, as described above; the response and precedence formulas are then both formalized by using a specific integrity constraint. In particular, the response formula between A and B is mapped to

$$\mathbf{H}(A, T_A) \rightarrow \mathbf{E}(B, T_B) \wedge T_B > T_A. \tag{3}$$

while the precedence formula between B and A is mapped to

$$\mathbf{H}(B, T_B) \rightarrow \mathbf{E}(A, T_A) \wedge T_A < T_B. \tag{4}$$

4.2   Learning DecSerFlow Models

In order to learn DecSerFlow models, we first learn $\mathcal{S}$CIFF ICs and then manually translate them into DecSerFlow constraints using the equivalences discussed in the previous section. We call the system implementing this approach DecMiner.

We decided to use $\mathcal{S}$CIFF as intermediate language instead of LTL because it can handle times and data in an explicit and quantitative way, exploiting Constraint Logic Programming to define temporal and data-related constraints. This is useful to deal with many processes as, for example, the Screening and NetBill ones described in details in Section 5. Moreover it allows to think about how to extend DecSerFlow to explicitly consider time and data. However, at the moment, $\mathcal{S}$CIFF does not support model enactment and we are working on an extension of the $\mathcal{S}$CIFF proof procedure capable of dealing with it.

To ease the translation, we provide ICL with a language bias ensuring that the learned ICs can be translated into DecSerFlow.

Thus the language bias takes the form of a set of templates that are couples (BS, HS): BS is a set that contains the literals that can be added to the body and HS is a set that contains the disjuncts that can be added to the head. Each element of HB is a couple $(Sign, Literals)$ where $Sign$ is either + for a positive disjunct or - for a negative disjunct, and $Literals$ contains the literals that can appear in the disjunct. We will have a set of templates for each DecSerFlow constraint, where each template in the set is an application of the constraint to a set of activities.

5   Experiments

The experiments have been performed over a real dataset and an artificial dataset. The real dataset regards a health care process while the artificial dataset regards an e-commerce protocol.

5.1   Cervical Cancer Screening Careflow and Log

As a case study for exploiting the potentialities of our approach we choose the process of cervical cancer screening [5] proposed by the sanitary organization of the Emilia Romagna region of Italy. Cervical cancer is a disease in which malignant (cancer) cells form in the tissues of the cervix of the uterus. The screening program proposes several tests in order to early detect and treat cervical cancer. It is usually composed by five phases: Screening planning; Invitation management; First level test with pap-test; Second level test with colposcopy, and eventually biopsy. The process is composed by 16 activities.

To perform our experiments we collected 157 traces from a database of an Italian cervical cancer screening center. All the 157 traces have been analyzed by a domain expert and labeled as compliant or non compliant with respect to the cervical cancer screening protocol adopted by the screening center. The traces classified as compliant were 55 over 157.

Each event trace was then adapted to the format required by the ICL algorithm, transforming each trace into an interpretation. For this preliminary study, we considered only the performed activities (without taking into account originators and other parameters, except from the posted examinations results); furthermore, we use sequence numbers rather than actual execution times.

An example of an interpretation is the following:

```
begin(model(m1)).
H(invitation,1).
H(refusal,2).
end(model(m1)).
```

5.2   NetBill

NetBill is a security and transaction protocol optimized for the selling and delivery of low-priced information goods, such as software or journal articles, across the Internet. The protocols involves three parties: the customer, the merchant and the NetBill server. It is composed of two phases: negotiation and transaction. In the negotiation phase, the customer requests a price for a good from the merchant, the merchant propose a price for the good and the customer can accept the offer, refuse it or make another request to the merchant, thus initiating a new negotiation. The transaction phase starts if the customer accepts the offer: the merchant delivers the good to the customer encrypted with key K; the customer creates an electronic purchase order (EPO) that is countersigned by the merchant that add also the value of K and send the EPO to the NetBill server; the NetBill server checks the EPO and if customer's account contains enough funds it transfers the price to the merchant's account and sends a signed receipt that includes the value K to the merchant; the merchant records the receipt and forwards it to the customer (who can then decrypt her encrypted goods).

The NetBill protocol is represented using 19 ICs [13]. One of them is

$$
\begin{aligned}
\mathbf{H}&(request(C, M, good(G, Q), Nneg, Trq)) \wedge \\
\mathbf{H}&(present(M, C, good(G, Q), Nneg, Tp)) \wedge Trq \leq Tp \\
\rightarrow & \mathbf{E}(accept(C, M, good(G, Q)), Ta) \wedge Tp \leq Ta \vee \\
& \mathbf{E}(refuse(C, M, good(G, Q)), Trf) \wedge Tp \leq Trf \vee \\
& \mathbf{E}(request(C, M, good(G, Qrql), Nnegl), Trql) \wedge Tp \leq Trql
\end{aligned} \tag{5}
$$

This IC states that if there has been a *request* from the customer to the merchant and the merchant has answered with the same price, then the customer should either *accept* the offer, *refuse* the offer or start a new negotiation with a *request*.

The traces have been generated randomly in two stages: first the negotiation phase is generated and then the transaction phase. In the negotiation phase, we add to the end of the trace a *request* or *present* message with its arguments randomly generated with two possible values for Q (quote). The length of the negotiation phase is selected randomly between 2 and 5. After the completion of the negotiation phase, either an *accept* or a *refuse* message is added to the trace and the transaction phase is entered with probability 4/5, otherwise the trace is closed. In the transaction phase, the messages *deliver*, *epo*, *epo_and_key*, *receipt* and *receipt_client* are added to the trace. With probability 1/4 a message from the whole trace is then removed. Once a trace has been generated, it is classified with the ICs of the correct model and assigned to the set of compliant or non compliant traces depending on the result of the test. The process is repeated until 2000 compliant traces and 2000 non compliant traces have been generated.

5.3   Results

Five experiments have been performed for the screening and the NetBill processes. For the screening process, five folds cross validation was used, i.e., the dataset was divided into 5 sets and in each experiment 4 were used for training and the remaining for testing. For NetBill, the training and testing set were generated with the procedure sketched above with different seeds for the random function for each experiments.

DecMiner, the α-algorithm [19] and the Multi-Phase Mining approach [20] have been applied in each experiment. The α-algorithm is one of the first process mining algorithms and it induces Petri nets. The Multi-Phase (MP) mining algorithm can be used to construct an Event-driven Process Chain (EPC) that can be also translated in a Petri net. We used the implementation of these algorithms available in the ProM suite [14]. Since the α-algorithm and the Multi-Phase miner take as input a single set of traces, we have provided them with compliant traces only.

Table 1. Results of the experiments

Experiment	DecMiner	α algorithm	MP algorithm
Screening	97.44%	96.15%	94.89%
NetBill	96.11%	66.81%	60.52%

The average accuracy of each algorithm is reported in Table 1. The accuracy is defined as the number of compliant traces that are correctly classified as compliant by the learned model plus the number of non compliant traces that are correctly classified as not compliant by the learned model divided by the total number of traces. Compliance of an execution trace with respect to a learned Petri net has been evaluated by using the *Conformance checker* ProM plug-in.

The average time taken by DecMiner are 2 minutes for Screening and 6.5 hours for NetBill on a Athlon XP64 1.80 GHz machine. The average times taken by the α-algorithm and the MP miner are under one minute for both datasets.

5.4   Mapping the Learned ICs to DecSerFlow

In order to illustrate the behavior of the approach for inducing DecSerFlow constraints, we report in this Section the ICs learned from the screening dataset together with their translation into DecSerFlow constraints.

Running DecMiner on the screening dataset, we obtained the following ICs:

$$true$$
$$\rightarrow \mathbf{E}(examExecution(papTest), A) \ \vee \ \mathbf{E}(refusal, B) \qquad (IC_1)$$

(IC_1) states that there must be a pap test execution or a refusal.

$$\mathbf{H}(resultPosting(positive, papTest), A)$$
$$\rightarrow \mathbf{E}(examExecution(colposcopy), B) \qquad (IC_2)$$

(IC_2) states that if there is a positive pap test then there must be also a colposcopy.

$$\mathbf{H}(examExecution(papTest), A)$$
$$\rightarrow \mathbf{E}(invitation, B) \wedge prec(B, A) \qquad (IC_3)$$

(IC_3) states that a pap-test execution must be immediately preceeded by an invitation.

$$\mathbf{H}(resultPosting(doubtful, colposcopy), A)$$
$$\rightarrow \mathbf{E}(examExecution(biopsy, B) \wedge less(A, B) \qquad (IC_4)$$

(IC_4) states that a biopsy should be executed after a doubtful colposcopy.

The predicates $less(A, B)$ and $prec(A, B)$ are defined in the background knowledge as follows:

$$less(A, B) \leftarrow A < B - 1.$$
$$prec(A, B) \leftarrow A \ is \ B - 1.$$

The ICs have been mapped into DecSerFlow constraints in the following way:

- IC_1 is translated into a mutual substitution constraint between *examExecution(papTest)* and *refusal*.
- IC_2 is translated into a responded presence constraint between *resultPosting(positive,papTest)* and *examExecution(colposcopy)*.
- IC_3 is translated into a chain precedence constraint between *invitation* and *examExecution(papTest)* meaning that *examExecution(papTest)* must be immediately preceded by *invitation*.
- IC_4 is translated into a response constraint between *resultPosting(doubtful, colposcopy)* and *examExecution(biopsy)*.

The resulting DecSerFlow model is shown in Figure 3.

In the future we plan to automate this translation process. This will require an appropriate tuning of the language bias in order to learn constraints very close to the form of the template constraints used in [6].

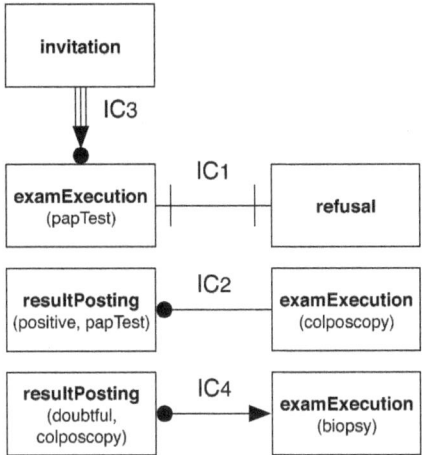

Fig. 3. The DecSerFlow representation of the ICs learned from the event log

6   Related Works

[1] introduced the idea of applying process mining to workflow management. The authors propose an approach for inducing a process representation in the form of a directed graph encoding the precedence relationships.

[19] presents the α-algorithm for inducing Petri nets from data and identifies for which class of models the approach is guaranteed to work. The α-algorithm is based on the discovery of binary relations in the log, such as the follows relation.

In [20] the authors describe an algorithm which derives causal dependencies between activities and use them for constructing instance graphs, presented in terms of Event-driven Process Chains (EPCs).

[9] is a recent work where a process model is induced in the form of a disjunction of special graphs called workflow schemes.

We differ from all of these works in three respects. First, we learn from compliant and non compliant traces, rather than from compliant traces only. Second, we use a representation that is declarative rather than procedural as Petri nets are, without sacrificing expressivity. For example, the $\mathcal{S}$CIFF language supports conjunction of happened events in the body, to model complex triggering conditions, as well as disjunctive expectations in the head. Third, our language is able to model and reason upon data, by exploiting either the underlying Constraints Solver or the Prolog inference engine.

In [15] the authors use an extension of the Event Calculus (EC) of Kowalski and Sergot to declaratively model event based requirements specifications. The choice of EC is motivated by both practical and formal needs, that are shared by our approach. In particular, in contrast to pure state-transition representations, both the EC and $\mathcal{S}$CIFF representations include an explicit time structure and are very close to most event-based specifications. Moreover they allows us to use the same logical foundation for verification at both design time and runtime [2].

In this paper, however, our emphasis is about the learning of the model, instead of the verification issue. We deal with time by using suitable CLP constraints on finite domains, while they use a temporal formalism based on Event Calculus.

We are aware that the temporal framework we use is less expressive than EC, but we think that it is enough powerful for our goals and is a good trade off between expressiveness and efficiency.

7   Conclusions

In this work we presented the result of our research activity aimed at proposing a methodology for analyzing a log containing several traces labeled as compliant or not compliant. From them we learn a $\mathcal{S}$CIFF theory, containing a minimal set of constraints able to accurately classify a new trace.

The proposed methodology is based on Inductive Logic Programming and, in particular, on the ICL algorithm. Such an algorithm is adapted to the problem of learning integrity constraints in the $\mathcal{S}$CIFF language. By considering not only compliant traces, but also non compliant ones, our approach is able to learn a model which expresses not only what should be done, but also what is forbidden.

Furthermore, the learned $\mathcal{S}$CIFF formulas can be translated into DecSerFlow constraints. We called the resulting system DecMiner.

In order to test the proposed methodology, we performed a number of experiments on two dataset: a cervical cancer screening log and an e-commerce log. The accuracy of DecMiner was compared with the one of the α-algorithm. Moreover, the ICs learned from the screening dataset are shown together with their translation into DecSerFlow.

In the future, we plan to make the translation from the $\mathcal{S}$CIFF formalism into the DecSerFlow one automatic. Moreover, we plan to consider explicitly activity originators and the actual execution time of each event (for example represented as the number of days from the 1st of January 1970) in order to learn constraints which involve also deadlines. Finally, we will investigate the effect of noise on DecMiner, by studying the effect of misclassified examples.

Acknowledgments. This work has been partially supported by NOEMALIFE under the "SPRING" regional PRRITT project, by the PRIN 2005 project "Specification and verification of agent interaction protocols" and by the FIRB project "TOCAI.IT".

References

1. Agrawal, R., Gunopulos, D., Leymann, F.: Mining process models from workflow logs. In: Schek, H.-J., Saltor, F., Ramos, I., Alonso, G. (eds.) EDBT 1998. LNCS, vol. 1377, pp. 469–483. Springer, Heidelberg (1998)
2. Alberti, M., Chesani, F., Gavanelli, M., Lamma, E., Mello, P., Montali, M., Storari, S., Torroni, P.: Computational logic for run-time verification of web services choreographies: Exploiting the ocs-si tool. In: Bravetti, M., Núñez, M., Zavattaro, G. (eds.) WS-FM 2006. LNCS, vol. 4184, pp. 58–72. Springer, Heidelberg (2006)

3. Alberti, M., Chesani, F., Gavanelli, M., Lamma, E., Mello, P., Torroni, P.: Verifiable agent interaction in abductive logic programming: the SCIFF framework. ACM Transactions on Computational Logics (accepted for publication, 2007)
4. Alberti, M., Gavanelli, M., Lamma, E., Mello, P., Torroni, P.: An abductive interpretation for open societies. In: Cappelli, A., Turini, F. (eds.) AI*IA 2003. LNCS, vol. 2829, Springer, Heidelberg (2003)
5. Cervical cancer screening web site: Available at: http://www.cancer.gov/cancertopics/pdq/screening/cervical/healthprofessional
6. Chesani, F., Mello, P., Montali, M., Storari, S.: Towards a decserflow declarative semantics based on computational logic. Technical Report DEIS-LIA-07-002, DEIS, Bologna, Italy (2007)
7. Clark, K.L.: Negation as failure. In: Logic and Databases, Plenum Press, New York (1978)
8. De Raedt, L., Van Laer, W.: Inductive constraint logic. In: Zeugmann, T., Shinohara, T., Jantke, K.P. (eds.) ALT 1995. LNCS, vol. 997, Springer, Heidelberg (1995)
9. Greco, G., Guzzo, A., Pontieri, L., Saccá, D.: Discovering expressive process models by clustering log traces. IEEE Trans. Knowl. Data Eng. 18(8), 1010–1027 (2006)
10. ICL manual: Available at: http://www.cs.kuleuven.be/~ml/ACE/Doc/ACEuser.pdf
11. Lamma, E., Mello, P., Riguzzi, F., Storari, S.: Applying inductive logic programming to process mining. In: ILP 2007, Springer, Heidelberg (2007)
12. Muggleton, S., De Raedt, L.: Inductive logic programming: Theory and methods. Journal of Logic Programming 19/20, 629–679 (1994)
13. SCIFF specification of the netbill protocol: Available at: http://edu59.deis.unibo.it:8079/SOCSProtocolsRepository/jsp/protocol.jsp?id=8
14. Prom framework: Available at: http://is.tm.tue.nl/~cgunther/dev/prom/
15. Rouached, M., Perrin, O., Godart, C.: Towards formal verification of web service composition. In: Dustdar, S., Fiadeiro, J.L., Sheth, A. (eds.) BPM 2006. LNCS, vol. 4102, pp. 257–273. Springer, Heidelberg (2006)
16. van der Aalst, W.M.P., Pesic, M.: A declarative approach for flexible business processes management. In: Eder, J., Dustdar, S. (eds.) Business Process Management Workshops. LNCS, vol. 4103, pp. 169–180. Springer, Heidelberg (2006)
17. van der Aalst, W.M.P., Pesic, M.: DecSerFlow: Towards a truly declarative service flow language. In: Bravetti, M., Núñez, M., Zavattaro, G. (eds.) WS-FM 2006. LNCS, vol. 4184, pp. 1–23. Springer, Heidelberg (2006)
18. van der Aalst, W.M.P., van Dongen, B.F., Herbst, J., Maruster, L., Schimm, G., Weijters, A.J.M.M.: Workflow mining: A survey of issues and approaches. Data Knowl. Eng. 47(2), 237–267 (2003)
19. van der Aalst, W.M.P., Weijters, T., Maruster, L.: Workflow mining: Discovering process models from event logs. IEEE Trans. Knowl. Data Eng. 16(9), 1128–1142 (2004)
20. van Dongen, B.F., van der Aalst, W.M.P.: Multi-phase process mining: Building instance graphs. In: Atzeni, P., Chu, W., Lu, H., Zhou, S., Ling, T.-W. (eds.) ER 2004. LNCS, vol. 3288, pp. 362–376. Springer, Heidelberg (2004)

Approaching Process Mining with Sequence Clustering: Experiments and Findings

Diogo Ferreira[1,3], Marielba Zacarias[2,3], Miguel Malheiros[3], and Pedro Ferreira[3]

[1] IST – Technical University of Lisbon, Taguspark, Portugal
[2] Universidade do Algarve, ADEEC-FCT, Faro, Portugal
[3] Organizational Engineering Center, INOV, Lisbon, Portugal
diogo.ferreira@ist.utl.pt, mzacaria@ualg.pt,
{miguel.malheiros, pedro.romeu}@gmail.com

Abstract. Sequence clustering is a technique of bioinformatics that is used to discover the properties of sequences by grouping them into clusters and assigning each sequence to one of those clusters. In business process mining, the goal is also to extract sequence behaviour from an event log but the problem is often simplified by assuming that each event is already known to belong to a given process and process instance. In this paper, we describe two experiments where this information is not available. One is based on a real-world case study of observing a software development team for three weeks. The other is based on simulation and shows that it is possible to recover the original behaviour in a fully automated way. In both experiments, sequence clustering plays a central role.

Keywords: Process Mining, Sequence Clustering, Task Identification, Process Discovery, Workflow Logs.

1 Introduction

In bioinformatics, sequence clustering algorithms have been used to automatically group large protein datasets into different families [12,13], to search for protein sequences that are homologous to a given sequence [17], and to map or align a given DNA sequence to an entire genome [20], to cite only some of the most common applications. In all of these applications, sequence clustering becomes a valuable tool to gain insight into otherwise seemingly senseless sequences of data.

A similar kind of challenge arises in process mining, where the goal is to extract meaningful task sequences from an event log, usually resorting to special-purpose algorithms that can recover the original workflow that produced the log [1].

The idea of applying sequence clustering to process mining comes at a time when process mining is still heavily dependent on the assumption that the event log contains "sufficient" information [4], i.e., that each event in the log is clearly associated with a specific activity and case (process instance) [1]. This comes as a major disadvantage since (1) the classes of information systems that are able to generate such logs are restricted to process-aware systems, and (2) it becomes impossible to apply and benefit from process mining in scenarios where the log data is not available in that form.

G. Alonso, P. Dadam, and M. Rosemann (Eds.): BPM 2007, LNCS 4714, pp. 360–374, 2007.

A sequence clustering approach can alleviate these requirements by grouping similar sequences and identifying typical ones without the need to provide any input information about the business logic. Of course, the results will bear a degree of uncertainty, whereas process mining approaches typically aim at finding exact models. Still, sequence clustering can provide valuable insight into the kind of sequences that are being executed.

The paper is structured as follows: section 2 provides an overview of process mining approaches, and section 3 presents the sequence clustering algorithm. Then sections 4 and 5 describe two different experiments and report on the problems encountered and the results obtained.

2 Process Mining Approaches

In general, all process mining approaches take an event log as input and as a starting point for the discovery of underlying processes. The event log (also called process trace or audit trail) is list of records resulting from the execution of some process. For the log to be "minable", each record usually contains information about the activity that was executed, the process instance that it belongs to, and the time of execution. The requirements on the log, i.e. the kind of information it should contain, varies according to the process mining algorithm being used.

In fact, it is the choice of mining algorithms that often leads to different process mining approaches. Some of the algorithms used for process mining include:

- *the α-algorithm* [4] – an algorithm that is able to re-create the Petri-net workflow from the ordering relations found in the even log. For the algorithm to work, the log must contain the process instance identifier (*case id*) and it must be rather complete in the sense that all ordering relations should be present in the log.
- *inference methods* [8] – a set of three different algorithms used to infer a finite state machine (FSM) from an event log, where the log is regarded as a simple sequence of symbols. The three algorithms represent different levels of compromise between accuracy and robustness to noise. The MARKOV algorithm, inspired by Markov models, seems to be the most promising. The algorithm works by building up an event graph as the result of considering Markov chains with increasing order. In the last step, the graph is converted to a FSM, which represents the process that was found.
- *directed acyclic graphs* [5] – an algorithm that is able to generate a dependency graph from a workflow system log. The log must contain a relatively high number of executions of the same process so that the dependency graph for that process can be completely built. Originally, the algorithm was proposed to support the adoption of workflow systems rather than actually pursuing process mining.
- *inductive workflow acquisition* [16] – an approach in which the goal is to find a hidden markov model (HMM) that best represents the structure of the original process. The HMM can be found by either top-down or bottom-up refinement of an initial HMM structure; these are known as model splitting and model merging algorithms, respectively. The initial HMM structure is built directly from the log, which is regarded as a simple sequence of symbols. Reported results suggest that model splitting is faster and more accurate than model merging.

- *hierarchical clustering* [14] – an algorithm that, given a large set of execution traces of a single process, separates them into clusters and finds the dependency graph separately for each cluster. The clusters of workflow traces are organized into a tree, hence the concept of model hierarchy. After the workflow models for the different clusters have been found, a bottom-up pass through the tree generalizes them into a single one.
- *genetic algorithm* [2] – an algorithm in which several candidate solutions are evaluated by a fitness function that determines how consistent each solution is with the log. Every solution is represented by a causal matrix, i.e. a map of the input and output dependencies for each activity. Candidate solutions are generated by selection, crossover and mutation as in typical genetic algorithms. The search space is the set of all possible solutions with different combinations of the activities that appear in the event log. The log should contain a relatively high number of execution traces.
- *instance graphs* [10] – an approach that aims at portraying graphical representations of process execution, especially using Event-driven Process Chains (EPCs). For each execution trace found in the log, an instance graph is obtained for that process instance. In order to identify possible parallelism, each instance graph is constructed using the dependencies found in the entire log. Several instance graphs can then be aggregated in order to obtain the overall model for that log [11].

In general, as far as input data is concerned, all these algorithms require an event log that contains several, if not a very large number, of execution traces of the same process instance. (An exception is the RNET algorithm used in [8] which can receive a single trace as training input, but the results can vary widely depending on that given input sequence.) Because the log usually contains the traces of multiple instances, it is also required to have labelling field – usually called the *case id* [1] – which specifies the process instance for every recorded event.

Another requirement on the content of the event log is that, for algorithms such as [4] and [10], which rely on finding causal relations in the log, task *A* can be considered the cause of task *B* only if *B* follows *A* but *A* never follows *B* in the log. Exceptional behaviour, errors or special conditions that would make *A* appear after *B* could ruin the results. These conditions are referred to as *noise*; algorithms that are able to withstand noise are said to be robust to noise [3]. Most algorithms can become robust to noise by discarding causal relations with probability below a given threshold; this threshold is usually one of the algorithm parameters.

The problem with these requirements is that they may be difficult to apply in many potential scenarios for process mining. For example, in some applications the *case id* may be unavailable if the log is just an unclassified stream of recorded events. In other applications, it may be useful to clearly identify and distinguish normal behaviour from exceptional one, without ruling out small variations simply as noise. These issues suggest that other kind of algorithms could provide valuable insight into the original behaviour that produced the log. If there is no *case id* available, and there is an unpredictable amount of ad-hoc behaviour, then an algorithm that allows us to sort out and understand that behaviour could be the first step before actually mining those processes. Sequence clustering algorithms are a good candidate for this job.

3 Sequence Clustering

Sequence clustering is a collection of methods that aim at partitioning a number of sequences into meaningful clusters or groups of similar sequences. The development of such methods has been an active field of research especially in connection with challenges in bioinformatics [7]. Here we will present the basic principles by referring to a simple sequence clustering algorithm based on first-order Markov chains [6].

In this algorithm, each cluster is associated with a first-order Markov chain, where the current state depends only on the previous state. The probability that an observed sequence belongs to a given cluster is in effect the probability that the observed sequence was produced by the Markov chain associated with that cluster. For a sequence $x = \{x_0, x_1, x_2,...,x_{L-1}\}$ of length L this can be expressed simply as:

$$p(x \mid c_k) = p(x_0, c_k) \cdot \prod_{i=1}^{i=L-1} p(x_i \mid x_{i-1}, c_k) \tag{1}$$

where $p(x_0, c_k)$ is the probability of x_0 occurring as the first state in the Markov chain associated with cluster c_k and $p(x_i|x_{i-1}, c_k)$ is the transition probability of state x_{i-1} to state x_i in that same Markov chain. Given the way to compute $p(x|c_k)$, the sequence clustering algorithm can be implemented as an extension to the well-known Expectation-Maximization (EM) algorithm [9]. The steps are:

1. Initialize the model parameters $p(x_0, c_k)$ and $p(x_i|x_{i-1}, c_k)$ randomly, i.e. for each cluster the state transition probabilities of the associated Markov chain are initialized at random.
2. Using the current model parameters, assign each sequence to each cluster with a probability given by equation (1).
3. Use the results of step 2 to re-estimate the model parameters, i.e. recalculate the state transition probabilities of each Markov chain based on the sequences that belong to that cluster.
4. Repeat steps 2 and 3 until the mixture model converges.

This sequence clustering algorithm has been implemented in Microsoft SQL Server 2005® [19] and is readily available for use either programmatically via an OLE DB for Data Mining interface [18] or via a user-friendly interface in Microsoft Visual Studio 2005®.

In either case, the algorithm must be provided with two input tables: a *case table* and a *nested table*. The case table contains one record for each sequence; it conveys the number of sequences in the input data set together with some descriptive information about each sequence. The nested table contains the steps for all sequences, where each step is numbered and labelled. The number is the order of occurrence within the sequence, and the label is a descriptive attribute that denotes the state in a Markov chain. The case and nested tables share a one-to-many relationship: each sequence in the case table is associated with several steps in the nested table. The connecting attribute, which is application-specific, serves as key in the case table and as sequence scope delimiter in the nested table.

For the sake of clarity, let us consider a simple example. Suppose the members of a given family have different ways of zapping through TV channels according to

364   D. Ferreira et al.

their own interests. Let us assume that each member always finds the TV switched off, and after turning it on, goes through a set of channels before turning it off again. Every time it is turned on, the TV generates a new session identifier (*session id*) and records both session-related information as well as the sequence of channel changes. Figure 1 shows the case and nested tables for this scenario. The session identifier is both the key to the case table and the sequence scope delimiter for the nested table. The case table contains descriptive, non-sequence attributes about each session, whereas the nested table contains the steps for each sequence, both numbered and labelled.

sessionid	timeofday
1234	2007-04-09 19:41:00
1235	2007-04-09 21:15:00
1236	2007-04-10 18:56:00
1237	2007-04-10 20:38:00
1238	2007-04-10 21:25:00
1239	2007-04-11 19:06:00
1240	2007-04-11 20:23:00

sessionid	channel	numchange
1234	Music	1
1234	Music	2
1234	Movies	3
1234	Movies	4
1235	News	1
1235	Sports	2
1235	News	3

(a)   (b)

Fig. 1. Case (a) and nested (b) tables for the simple TV usage scenario

It can be seen from this simple example that the input data to be provided to the sequence clustering algorithm already has a form of *case id*, which is the session identifier. Pre-processing techniques will have to be used to assign this *case id* if it is not available in the first place. We will look at this problem ahead in the context of two different experiments. What is interesting to note here is the kind of results that the sequence clustering algorithm is able to produce. Figure 2 shows four of the clusters that the algorithm was able to identify from a given set of 24 sequences for the simple TV usage scenario. Each cluster has a different Markov chain that is able to generate the sequences assigned to that cluster. This effectively captures the dominant behaviour of similar sequences.

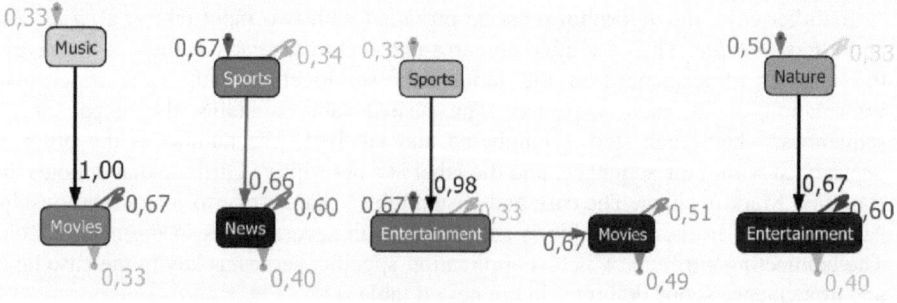

Fig. 2. The Markov chains in four of the clusters obtained for the simple TV usage scenario

The number of clusters to be found can be set manually or automatically by letting the algorithm perform a heuristic to determine the number of clusters for the given data. This is usually very useful to use as an initial guess before trying to run the algorithm with different parameters.

To produce the results shown in figure 2 the algorithm performed a number of iterations, where each iteration comprises two steps: the *expectation step* and the *maximization step*. In the expectation step the algorithm assigns each sequence x to the cluster c_k that gives the highest membership probability $p(x|c_k)$ according to equation (1). Once this step is complete, the algorithm has a provisional estimate of which sequences belong to which cluster. In the maximization step the algorithm re-computes the transition probabilities $p(x_i|x_{i-1},c_k)$ for each cluster c_k based on the sequences that belong to that cluster. After the maximization step, the next expectation step will produce different results from the previous iteration, since $p(x|c_k)$ will now be computed with the updated values of $p(x_i|x_{i-1},c_k)$. The algorithm converges when there is no change in the values of these model parameters.

4   Experiment #1: Mining Human Activity Observations

The first experiment is taken from a research project that aims at discovering recurrent action patterns from action repositories [25]. This experiment was motivated by the difficulties encountered in the manual extraction of action patterns for log sizes of a few hundred actions. Thus, the aim was to test the ability of the sequence clustering algorithm to support manual identification of recurrent action sequences from action logs, where no information of the sequence associated with each individual action was available. Rather than finding Markov chains, the goal here was to evaluate the soundness of the sequence clusters provided by the algorithm.

The experimental data represents the actions of a software development team comprising four software developers and a project leader [24]. The team develops web applications and performs systems analysis, design, programming, test and maintenance activities. The action log was collected within an observation period of three weeks, during which the team members performed tasks on the following applications: (1) *Suppliers*, (2) *Claims*, (3) *Customer Correspondence* (called *Mail application*), (4) *Evictions* and (5) *Marketing Campaigns*. The team leader performed both system development and project management tasks.

Team observation was carried out by its own members by registering their actions and interactions in chronological order[1]. Both computer- and non-computer-supported actions and interactions were registered, each by means of a summarizing sentence. These sentences were first parsed using grammatical rules to separate the subject and predicate (verb and its complements). Synonym verbs were replaced by a single verb to avoid inconsistencies. Each action and interaction description was augmented with a set of application, information and human resources involved. The results were further structured as described in [23] into an event table as shown in figure 3. The data collected over three weeks led to a table with 534 entries.

---

[1] For details on the modeling concepts of action, interaction and context please refer to [21].

#	Day	Actor Send.	Rec.	Action. Interacc.	Description	Tools	Information	Human competencies
8	6-01	Catarina		SOLVE	automatic table update problem	Sql Server, message management application	Sql Server and message management application documentation	programming & debugging skills
9	6-01	Catarina	Mariana	PROPOSE	solution to automatic table update problem			
10	6-01	Mariana	Catarina	ACCEPT	solution to automatic table update problem			

Fig. 3. Examples of structured actions and interactions collected during observation [22]

By identifying the action contexts of each actor [23] it was possible to group events that belong to the same or to intimately related tasks. This grouping into contexts can be done manually or, in case of large data sets, applying a clustering algorithm can provide a good starting point [22]. For the team leader alone, 12 different action contexts have been identified. Given the chronological order of events within each personal context and the interactions that took place between actors, it was possible to determine the sequences of events that took place across actors. This led to a number of rather long sequences, which were then broken down into shorter, scope-delimited tasks. About 140 tasks were found.

A brief analysis these task sequences revealed two issues. The first was that some of these tasks were not actually sequences, but just arbitrary repetitions of the same action. For example, all team members had at least one task in which they repeated the action "program" from 2 to 20 times. Therefore, consecutive repeating steps within each sequence were eliminated, and sequences ending up with just one single step were discarded. Figure 4 shows the total number of occurrences of each action, both before and after repeating steps were eliminated.

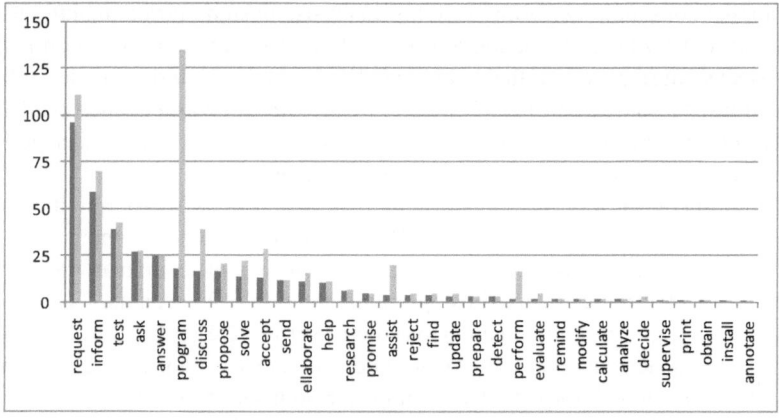

Fig. 4. Total number of occurrences for each action, both before (light column) and after (dark column) eliminating repeating steps, ordered by decreasing number of the latter

The second issue was that the relatively high number of different actions led to a set of very dissimilar sequences, despite the fact that most of them shared a limited set of common actions. For example, most tasks involve some form of "request", whereas the action "annotate" happened only once in the entire study. This suggests that the emphasis should be put on highly recurrent actions, which provide the skeleton for most sequences. The least recurrent actions (in the tail of figure 4) represent ad-hoc variations that provide no real insight into the structure of tasks. The last pre-processing stage was therefore to decide on a threshold for the number of occurrences; only actions above that threshold were allowed to remain in the sequences.

Once these pre-processing stages were complete, it was straightforward to build the case and nested tables for the sequence clustering algorithm. In order to present a complete result set, here we will use a relatively high threshold of 20 minimum occurrences. This means that only the first five actions in figure 4 will be allowed. As a consequence, the sequences will also be rather short. Figure 5 shows the results of applying the algorithm to the input sequences. The sequences have been grouped into five clusters.

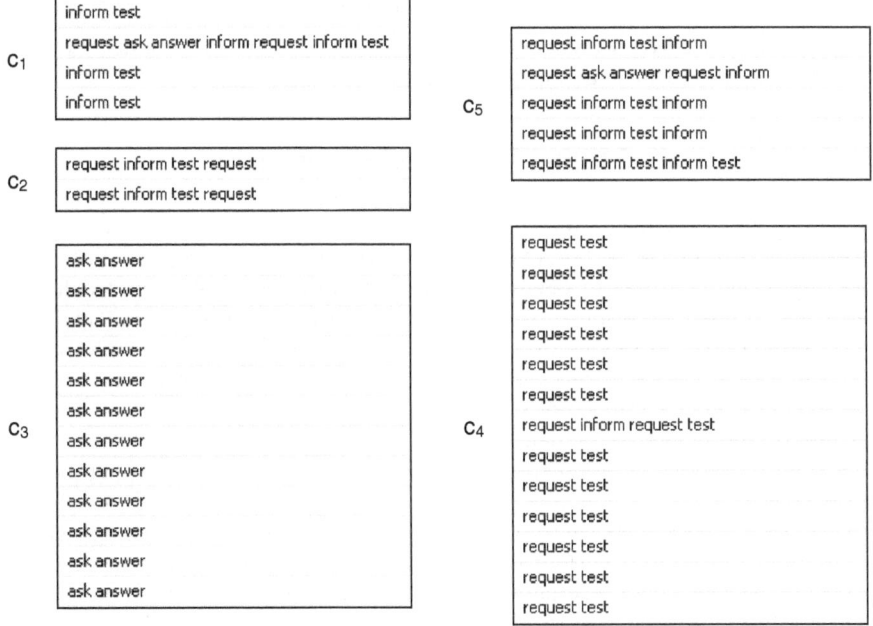

Fig. 5. Results of applying the sequence clustering algorithm to a set of input sequences restricted to five different actions only

It is arguable whether some sequences should have ended up in a particular cluster. Both cluster c_1 and cluster c_4 contain one sequence that would make as much sense if it had shown up in another cluster. The key issue here is that similar sequences actually ended up in the same cluster, and that each cluster has its own distinctive features.

Since the goal was to determine the effectiveness of the algorithm in obtaining meaningful clusters, evaluating the clustering results in this case requires knowledge of the problem domain. In terms of the particular business context, and despite the fact that the set of actions is so limited, it is still possible to draw meaningful conclusions from the results in figure 5:

- The sequences inform-test (cluster c_1) and request-test (cluster c_4) concern software integration tests. Team members confirmed that integration tests are performed either upon explicit request or when the project leader is informed of the result of previous tests. Clusters c_1 and c_4 capture these two scenarios. The sequence inform-test actually comprises the states analyze-inform-test, but the action "analyze" was not recorded since it is usually performed by an individual that was not observed in this study.
- The sequences request-inform-test-request (cluster c_2) and request-inform–test-inform (cluster c_5) concern software publishing activities. These sequences have an additional state – request-publish-inform-test-request and request-publish-inform-test-inform – but the action "publish" is also performed by an unobserved member. In all these cases, it is remarkable the algorithm was able to distinguish these activities even though such a key action was missing.
- The sequence ask-answer (cluster c_3) occurs in several kinds of tasks, but mostly in connection with team members helping each other.

5   Experiment #2: Mining Database System Traces

In the previous experiment, the application of sequence clustering was just the final phase after several weeks of collecting and pre-processing data. In this second experiment, the goal was to devise a scenario in which all these steps would be as automated as possible. Inspired by the bank experiment, we developed an application to perform simple operations over a fictitious banking database. Examples of such operations are: creating a checking account, creating a savings account, creating a loan, paying a loan, etc. Each of these operations comprises several database queries that insert, select, update or delete records in several tables. Operations requiring transactional control were implemented inside stored procedures, so as not to clutter the log.

Creating a checking account for a new customer involves the following steps: (1) create a new customer, (2) create a new account at the branch, (3) save the account as a checking account with a certain withdrawal limit, (4) associate the customer as a depositor of the account, and (5) associate an employee as account manager for that customer. In terms of SQL, this operation would look like:

```
INSERT INTO Customer VALUES (85045,'John Hayes','North Street','Southampton')
INSERT INTO Account VALUES (34220,705,'Downtown')
INSERT INTO Checking_Account VALUES (34220, 207)
INSERT INTO Depositor VALUES (85045,34220)
INSERT INTO Cust_Banker VALUES (85045,6,'account manager')
```

The steps may be performed in this or in a slight different order. In total, there are four variations for this sequence.

Creating a savings account takes different steps: (1) choose a checking account belonging to the customer, (2) create a new account at the branch, (3) save the account as a savings account with a certain interest rate, (4) associate the customer as a depositor of the account, and (5) transfer the initial funds from the checking account to the newly created savings account. There are two variations for this sequence; the steps in the order just described correspond to the following queries:

```
SELECT a.account_number, a.balance
   FROM Depositor AS d, Account AS a, Checking_Account AS c
   WHERE a.account_number = d.account_number
     AND c.account_number = a.account_number AND d.customer_id = 17214
INSERT INTO Account VALUES (74652,0,'Downtown')
INSERT INTO Savings_Account VALUES (74652, 3.5)
INSERT INTO Depositor VALUES (17214,74652)
EXEC INTERNAL_ACCOUNT_TRANSFER 7583,74652,189
```

In this experiment, a simulator generates a large amount of these and other operations. The queries from different operations are sent to the database system randomly interleaved, in order to simulate the concurrent execution of both different and similar operations. As the operations are being performed, they are captured as a trace using the SQL Server Profiler, a tool for monitoring the SQL Server Database Engine and capturing data about each event. Figure 6 illustrates how the data is captured with the Profiler. There is no *case id* or any other information that explicitly indicates that an event belongs to a certain sequence. As it stands, the trace is just an unclassified stream of events.

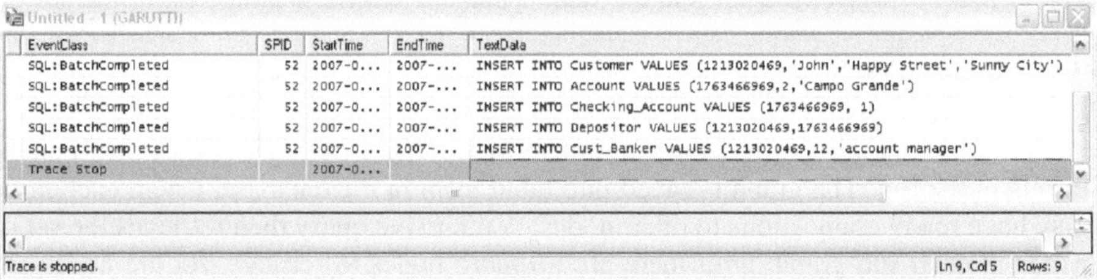

Fig. 6. A database system trace as captured by the SQL Server Profiler. The data can be saved to a file or to a database table as it is being captured.

The second stage of this experiment is supported by the SequenceBuilder module, a software component that pre-processes the trace in order to create the case and nested tables for sequence clustering. However, the algorithm requires a set of independent sequences grouped by a *case id* and sorted by a sequential number (as shown earlier in figure 1). This means that SequenceBuilder must figure out where each sequence begins and ends, and find the events that belong to the sequence. The database trace contains profile information – such as date, username, client application, connection identifier, etc. – that could provide an indication of whether two events are related or not. But this information is not enough to find an accurate set of sequences. In [15] the authors make use of similar event logs, but the *case id* is given for each event. For the log shown in figure 6 some kind of reliable method for sequence identification had to be found.

The chosen method was to analyze the content of each query in order to determine whether it used the same objects of other queries or not. By retrieving the parameter values of each query, two queries that are close together in the log and use the same customer id, for example, are very likely to belong to the same sequence. And even if they do not share the same parameters, but a third query uses both of their parameter values, then all the three queries are likely to belong to the same sequence. This led to the idea of computing the graph of relations between queries in the trace: events connected directly or indirectly through other nodes belong to the same sequence; the islands in the graph correspond to different sequences. Figure 7 shows the connecting graphs for the queries described earlier.

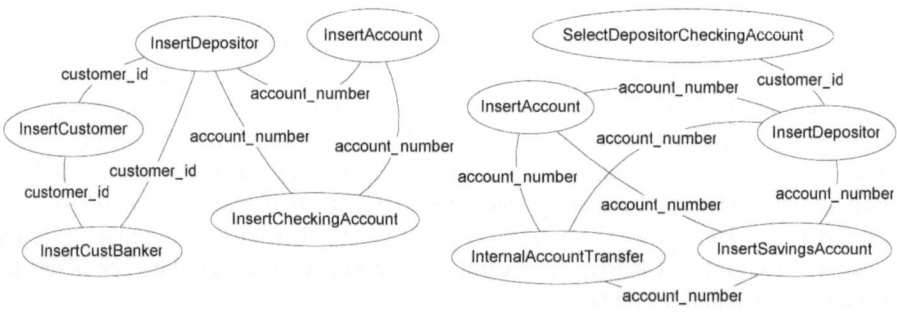

Fig. 7. Links between the queries in the bank operations described earlier. Each link has the name of the parameter whose value is equal in the two queries. Separate sub-graphs correspond to different sequences.

The whole graph can be computed at most in $O(N^2)$ by comparing every pair of events in the log. The graph is saved into table form in the database, where each node may have many connections to other nodes. A recursive query then retrieves the set of nodes in each sub-graph, until there are no more nodes to retrieve. As the nodes are being retrieved, they are sorted by the chronological order in which they originally appeared in the trace. The incoming nodes are assigned a sequential number and saved to a nested table, with a different *case id* for each sequence. The case table is then generated by retrieving the set of all distinct *case ids*.

This simple method works well in all cases except one: when the same object – be it the customer, account, loan, etc. – shows up in another instance of the same or different sequence. This may happen because the same customer opens more than one savings account, because the customer sends payment for a previously created loan, etc. The problem is illustrated in figure 8, where there should be three sequences but there are only two since a link is established to a later sequence that refers to the same object. If these long, unintended sequences are left in the input data, they will ruin the sequence clustering results since the algorithm will try to find some way to fit these sequences in by generating Markov chains that are able to produce them.

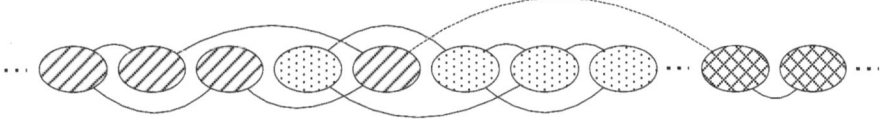

Fig. 8. When running through the log, links may be established between events that actually belong to different sequences

Fortunately, this phenomenon can be detected using a simple heuristic based on the average length of links between events. A link whose length is noticeably higher than the average length of all links is likely to be a spurious connection rather than a meaningful relationship between two events. Suppose, for example, that links with length over two times the average are rejected. In the example shown in figure 8, the average length is $(18+ x)/11$ where x is the length of the dashed link. We reject the dashed link if $x \geq 2*(18+ x)/11$ which gives $x \geq 4$ which is obviously appropriate in this example, where the maximum length of "true" links is 3. Of course, these decisions are all but trivial, since the "false" links could actually provide insight into higher-level patterns of behaviour, although this possibility in not being pursued at the time of writing.

Figure 9 shows five of the eight clusters found for a database trace with about 100 sequences. The first three clusters – c_2, c_4 and c_7 – are three of the four variations of creating a checking account; clusters c_5 and c_6 represent the two variations of creating a savings account. The remaining clusters had similar results for other kinds of operations dealing with loans. The algorithm was able to clearly distinguish all operations and their variations, and put each sequence in a separate cluster. As a result, the Markov chains turned into deterministic graphs, since all transitions probabilities equal 100%.

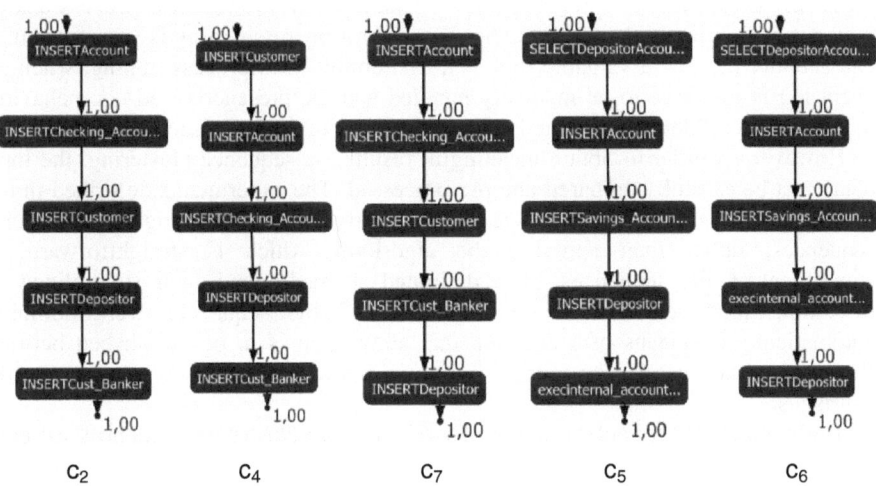

Fig. 9. Markov chains associated with five of the eight clusters found in the bank example

In terms of similarity between the sequences, the algorithm was able to find that clusters c_2, c_4, and c_7 are very similar, and the same happens with clusters c_5 and c_6. Figure 10 shows the cluster diagram for the same results, where the shading of lines that connect two clusters represents the strength of the similarity between those clusters, and the shade of each cluster represents its population. From the diagram it becomes apparent that there is a cluster c_8 which is similar to clusters c_2, c_4, and c_7. Indeed, cluster c_8 contains the fourth variation of creating a checking account. It corresponds to the steps of cluster c_4 being executed in the order $(1) \rightarrow (5) \rightarrow (2) \rightarrow (3) \rightarrow (4)$.

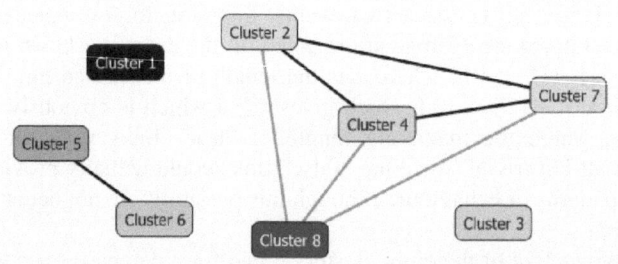

Fig. 10. Cluster diagram for the results obtained in the bank example

6 Conclusion

Sequence clustering is a powerful technique to sort out different behaviours and to provide insight into the underlying structure of those behaviours. This insight is especially useful when approaching new scenarios, that the business process analyst may not be familiar with, or where the potential for process mining is yet uncertain. It can actually become a valuable tool as a first approach to process mining, when the event log is too large to be manually handled and the presence of ad-hoc behaviour makes it impossible for automated processing by more deterministic algorithms.

However, in order to obtain meaningful results via sequence clustering, the input data must be carefully prepared and pre-processed. The experiments described in this paper show that the challenge is actually in identifying and compiling the set of input sequences, rather than applying the algorithm, which is straightforward. In experiment #1 the sequences were delimited manually and then streamlined by discarding infrequent actions. In experiment #2 the sequences were delimited automatically by means of a criterion that allowed links to be established between events. In both cases, the *case id* was assigned based on application-specific heuristics.

These experiments confirm the ability of sequence clustering to identify different tasks and to discover their composition in terms of elemental steps. In future work, further sequence analysis over these clusters is expected to provide insight into behaviour at the process level.

References

1. van der Aalst, W.: Workflow mining: A survey of issues and approaches. Data & Knowledge Engineering 47, 237–267 (2003)
2. van der Aalst, W., Medeiros, A., Weijters, A.: Genetic Process Mining. In: Ciardo, G., Darondeau, P. (eds.) ICATPN 2005. LNCS, vol. 3536, pp. 48–69. Springer, Heidelberg (2005)
3. van der Aalst, W., Weijters, A.: Process Mining: A Research Agenda. Computers in Industry 53(3), 231–244 (2004)
4. van der Aalst, W., Weijters, T., Maruster, L.: Workflow Mining: Discovering Process Models from Event Logs. IEEE Transactions on Knowledge and Data Engineering 16(9), 1128–1142 (2004)
5. Agrawal, R., Gunopulos, D., Leymann, F.: Mining Process Models from Workflow Logs. In: Schek, H.-J., Saltor, F., Ramos, I., Alonso, G. (eds.) EDBT 1998. LNCS, vol. 1377, pp. 469–483. Springer, Heidelberg (1998)
6. Cadez, I., Heckerman, D., Meek, C., Smyth, P., White, S.: Model-Based Clustering and Visualization of Navigation Patterns on a Web Site. Data Mining and Knowledge Discovery 7(4), 399–424 (2003)
7. Chen, Y., Reilly, K., Sprague, A., Guan, Z.: SEQOPTICS: a protein sequence clustering system. BMC Bioinformatics 7(suppl 4), 10 (2006)
8. Cook, J., Wolf, A.: Automating process discovery through event-data analysis. In: Proceedings of the 17th International Conference on Software Engineering, pp. 73–82. ACM Press, New York (1995)
9. Dempster, A., Laird, N., Rubin, D.: Maximum Likelihood from Incomplete Data via the EM Algorithm. Journal of the Royal Statistical Society, Series B 39(1), 1–38 (1977)
10. van Dongen, B., van der Aalst, W.: Multi-Phase Process Mining: Building Instance Graphs. In: Atzeni, P., Chu, W., Lu, H., Zhou, S., Ling, T.-W. (eds.) ER 2004. LNCS, vol. 3288, pp. 362–376. Springer, Heidelberg (2004)
11. van Dongen, B., van der Aalst, W.: Multi-Phase Mining: Aggregating Instances Graphs into EPCs and Petri Nets. In: Proceedings of the Second International Workshop on Applications of Petri Nets to Coordination, Workflow and Business Process Management, pp. 35–58 (2005)
12. Enright, A., van Dongen, S., Ouzounis, C.: An efficient algorithm for large-scale detection of protein families. Nucleic Acids Research 30(7), 1575–1584 (2002)
13. Enright, A., Ouzounis, C.: GeneRAGE: a robust algorithm for sequence clustering and domain detection. Bioinformatics 16(5), 451–457 (2000)
14. Greco, G., Guzzo, A., Pontieri, L.: Mining Hierarchies of Models: From Abstract Views to Concrete Specifications. In: van der Aalst, W.M.P., Benatallah, B., Casati, F., Curbera, F. (eds.) BPM 2005. LNCS, vol. 3649, pp. 32–47. Springer, Heidelberg (2005)
15. Günther, C., van der Aalst, W.: Mining Activity Clusters from Low-Level Event Logs, BETA Working Paper Series, WP 165, Eindhoven University of Technology, Eindhoven (2006)
16. Herbst, J., Karagiannis, D.: Integrating Machine Learning and Workflow Management to Support Acquisition and Adaptation of Workflow Models. In: Proceedings of the 9th International Workshop on Database and Expert Systems Applications, pp. 745–752 (1998)
17. Li, W., Jaroszewski, L., Godzik, A.: Sequence clustering strategies improve remote homology recognitions while reducing search times. Protein Engineering 15(8), 643–649 (2002)

18. Microsoft Corporation: OLE DB for Data Mining Specification, Version 1.0 (July 2000)
19. Tang, Z., MacLennan, J.: Data Mining with SQL Server 2005. Wiley, Chichester (2005)
20. Wu, T., Watanabe, C.: GMAP: a genomic mapping and alignment program for mRNA and EST sequences. Bioinformatics 21(9), 1859–1875 (2005)
21. Zacarias, M., Caetano, A., Pinto, H., Tribolet, J.: Modeling Contexts for Business Process Oriented Knowledge Support. In: Workshop on Knowledge Management for Distributed Agile Processes: Models, Techniques, and Infrastructure (April 2005)
22. Zacarias, M., Gomes, R., Coimbra, J., Pinto, H., Tribolet, J.: Discovering Personal Action Contexts with SQL Server Integration and Analysis Services. In: Proceedings of the 2nd International Conference on Innovative Views of .NET Technologies (October 2006)
23. Zacarias, M., Marques, A., Pinto, H., Tribolet, J.: Enhancing Collaboration Services with Business Context Models. In: International Workshop on Cooperative Systems and Context, 5th International and Interdisciplinary Conference on Modeling and Using Context (July 2005)
24. Zacarias, M., Pinto, H., Tribolet, J.: A Context-based Approach to Discover Multitasking Behavior at Work. In: Proceedings of the 5th International Workshop on Task Models and Diagrams for User Interface Design (October 2006)
25. Zacarias, M., Pinto, H., Tribolet, J.: Reverse-engineering of Personal and Inter-personal Work Practices: A Context-Based Approach. In: International Workshop on Role of Contextualization in Human Tasks: Enriching Actors (CHUT-07) held in conjunction with CONTEXT 07, Denmark (August 2007)

Process Mining Based on Regions of Languages

Robin Bergenthum, Jörg Desel, Robert Lorenz, and Sebastian Mauser

Department of Applied Computer Science,
Catholic University of Eichstätt-Ingolstadt
{firstname.lastname}@ku-eichstaett.de

Abstract. In this paper we give an overview, how to apply region based methods for the synthesis of Petri nets from languages to process mining.

The research domain of process mining aims at constructing a process model from an event log, such that the process model can reproduce the log, and does not allow for much more behaviour than shown in the log. We here consider Petri nets to represent process models. Event logs can be interpreted as finite languages. Region based synthesis methods can be used to construct a Petri net from a language generating the minimal net behaviour including the given language. Therefore, it seems natural to apply such methods in the process mining domain. There are several different region based methods in literature yielding different Petri nets. We adapt these methods to the process mining domain and compare them concerning efficiency and usefulness of the resulting Petri net.

1 Introduction

Often, business information systems log all performed activities together with the respective cases the activities belong to in so called event logs. These event logs can be used to identify the actual workflows of the system. In particular, they can be used to generate a workflow definition which matches the actual flow of work. The generation of a workflow definition from event logs is known as *process mining*. Application of process mining and underlying algorithms gained increasing attention in the last years, see e.g. [18] and [17]. There are a number of process mining tools, mostly implemented in the ProM framework [13].

The formal problem of generating a system model from a description of its behaviour is often referred to as synthesis problem. Workflows are often defined in terms of Petri nets [16]. Synthesis of Petri nets is studied since the 1980s [8,9]. Algorithms for Petri net synthesis have often been applied in hardware design [5]. Obviously, process mining and Petri net synthesis are closely related problems. Mining aims at a system model which has at least the behaviour given by the log and does not allow for much more behaviour. In the optimal case the system has minimal additional behaviour. The goal is to find such a system which is not too complex, i.e., small in terms of its number of components. This is necessary, because practitioners in industry are interested in controllable and interpretable reference models. Apparently, sometimes a trade-off between the size of the model and the additional behaviour has to be found.

G. Alonso, P. Dadam, and M. Rosemann (Eds.): BPM 2007, LNCS 4714, pp. 375–383, 2007.

One of the main differences in Petri net synthesis is that one is interested in a Petri net representing exactly the specified behaviour. Petri net synthesis was originally assuming a behavioural description in terms of transition systems. For a transition system, sets of nodes called *regions* can be identified. Each region refers to a place of the synthesized net. Analogous approaches in the context of process mining are presented in [19,15]. Since process mining usually does not start with a transition system, i.e., a state based description of behaviour, but rather with a set of sequences, i.e., a language based description of behaviour, the original synthesis algorithms are not immediately applicable. In [19,15] artificial states are introduced into the log in order to generate a transition system. Then synthesis algorithms transforming the state-based model into a Petri net, that exactly mimics the behaviour of the transition system, are applied. The problem is that these algorithms include reproduction of the state structure of the transition system, although the artificial states of the transition system are not specified in the log. In many cases this leads to a bias of the process mining result. However, there also exist research results on algorithmic Petri net synthesis from languages [6,1,2,10]. In these approaches, regions are defined on languages. It seems natural to directly use these approaches for process mining, because logs can directly be interpreted as languages. The aim of this paper is to adjust such language based synthesis algorithms to solve the process mining problem. This approach is very well suited for process mining, because wether or not the synthesized net exactly represents the given language, it always reproduces the language (given by an event log).

We present and compare methods for process mining adapted from language based synthesis and give a complete overview of the applicability of regions of languages to the process mining problem. Finally, we provide a bridge from the more theoretical considerations of this paper to practically useful algorithms. The process mining algorithms discussed in this paper are completely based on formal methods of Petri net theory guaranteeing reliable results. By contrast, most existing process mining approaches are partly based on heuristic methods, although they borrow techniques from formally developed research areas such as machine learning and grammatical inference [18,12], neural networks and statistics [18,4], or Petri net algorithms [7,19,15].

We omitted formal definitions, lemmas, theorems and proofs in this short paper. These are provided by the technical report [3]. In [3] the interested reader can also find more detailed explanations and pseudo code of the developed algorithms.

2   Application of Regions of Languages to Process Mining

First we introduce the process mining problem and show how the classical language based theory of regions [6,1] can be adapted to solve this problem. Process mining aims at the construction of a process model from an *event log* which is able to reproduce the behaviour (the process) of the log, and does not allow for much more behaviour than shown in the log. The following example log σ will serve as a running example. Since we focus on the control flow of activities (their ordering), we abstract from some additional log information such as originators of events and time stamps of events. The control flow, i.e. the behaviour, of the event log is given by a prefix-closed finite language over the alphabet of activities, the so called *process language* $L(\sigma)$.

> **event log (activity,case):**
> (a,1) (b,1) (a,2) (b,1) (a,3) (d,3) (a,4) (c,2) (d,2) (e,1) (c,3) (b,4) (e,3) (e,2) (b,4) (e,4)
> **process language:**
> a ab abb *abbe* ac acd *acde* ad adc *adce*

Figure 1 shows a *marked place/transition-net (p/t-net)* (N, m_0) having exactly the process language $L(\sigma)$ as its *language of occurrence sequences* $L(N, m_0)$. That means this Petri net model is a process model describing the process given by the event log σ.

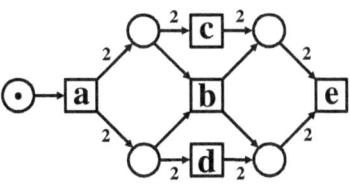

Fig. 1. Petri net model fulfilling $L(N, m_0) = L(\sigma)$

The process model in the ideal case serves as a reference model interpretable by practitioners. Therefore the model should be as small as possible. As we will show, there is a trade-off between the size of the constructed model and the degree of the match of the behaviour generated by the model and the log. In this paper we formalize process models as Petri nets and consider the following *process mining problem*:

Given: An event log σ. **Searched:** A preferably small finite marked p/t-net (N, m_0) such that **(1)** $L(\sigma) \subseteq L(N, m_0)$ and **(2)** $L(N, m_0) \setminus L(\sigma)$ is small.

In the following we will consider a fixed process language $L(\sigma)$ given by an event log σ with set of activities T. An adequate method to solve the process mining problem w.r.t. $L(\sigma)$ is applying synthesis algorithms using regions of languages: The set of transitions of the searched net (N, m_0) is given by the set of characters T used in $L(\sigma)$. The behaviour of this net is restricted by adding places. Every place is defined by its initial marking and the weights of the arcs connecting them to each transition $t \in T$. In order to guarantee (1), i.e. to reproduce the log, only places are added, which do not prohibit sequences of $L(\sigma)$. Such places are called *feasible (w.r.t. $L(\sigma)$)*. The more feasible places we add the smaller is the set $L(N, m_0) \setminus L(\sigma)$. Adding *all* feasible places minimizes $L(N, m_0) \setminus L(\sigma)$ (preserving (1)). That means the resulting net – called the *saturated feasible net* – is an optimal solution for the process mining problem concerning (1) and (2). But it is not small, even not finite. Here the trade-off between the size of the constructed net and (2) comes into play: The more feasible places we add the better (2) is reached, but the bigger becomes the constructed net. The central question is which feasible places should be added. Two procedures are candidates to solve this problem: There are two basic algorithmic approaches throughout the literature to synthesize a finite net (N, m_0) from a finite language. The crucial idea in these approaches is to define feasible places structurally on the level of the given language: Every feasible place is defined by a so called *region* of the language. A region is simply a $(2|T| + 1)$-tuple of natural numbers which represents the initial marking of a place and the number of tokens each transition consumes respectively produces in that place, satisfying some property which ensures that no occurrence sequence of the given (process) language $L(\sigma)$ is prohibited by this place. The set of regions can be characterized as the set of non-negative integral solutions of a homogenous linear inequation system $\mathbf{A}_{L(\sigma)} \cdot \mathbf{r} \geq \mathbf{0}$ (with integer coefficients) having $|L(\sigma)|$ rows. Both approaches use linear programming techniques and convex geometry to calculate a certain adequate finite set of solutions of this system. In the following we adjust both procedures to the considered process mining problem and discuss their applicability and their results in this context.

The first strategy to add a certain finite set of feasible places, used in [10], computes a so called *finite basis* of the set of all feasible places (any feasible place is a non-negative linear combination of the basis). Adding all basis places leads to a finite representation of the saturated feasible net. Consequently, this approach leads to an optimal solution of the process mining problem concerning (2). The set of regions is given by the integer points of a pointed *polyhedral cone* [14]. The finite set of rays of the cone leads to a (minimal) basis of the set of regions and thus defines a finite basis of the set of feasible places [3,14]. It can be effectively computed from $\mathbf{A}_{L(\sigma)}$ (see for example [11]). The time complexity of the computation essentially depends on the number k of basis regions which is bounded by $k \leqslant \binom{|L(\sigma)|+2|T|+1}{2|T|+1}$. That means, in the worst case the time complexity is exponential in $|L(\sigma)|$, whereas in most practical examples the number of basis solutions is reasonable. The calculated finite set of basis places usually still includes so called redundant places, which can be omitted from the net without changing its language of occurrence sequences. Some of these redundant places can easily be identified [3]. These are finally deleted from the constructed net. The resulting process mining algorithm, called method 1 in the following, is shown in [3].

For the event log of the running example, method 1 computes 55 basis places (corresponding to rays). 15 of these places are directly deleted as easily identifiable redundant places. Many of the 40 places of the resulting net are still redundant. It is possible to calculate a minimal subset of places generating the same language of occurrence sequences. This would lead to the net shown in Figure 1 with only five key places. But this is extremely inefficient. Thus, more efficient heuristic approaches to delete redundant places are of interest. The practical applicability of the algorithm could be drastically improved with such heuristics. In the considered example, most of the redundant places are so called loop places. If we delete all loop places from the constructed net with 40 places, there remain the five places shown in Figure 1 plus the eight redundant places shown in Figure 2. In this case this procedure did not change the behaviour of the net.

In this example the process language is exactly reproduced by the constructed net. Usually this is not the case. For example omitting the word *acde* (but not its prefixes) from the process language, the inequation system is not changed. Therefore the net constructed from this changed language with method 1 coincides with the above example. This net has the additional occurrence sequence *adce* not belonging to the changed process language. Since the net calculated by method 1 is the best approximation to the given language, the changed process language (given by a log) has to be completed in this way to be describable as a p/t-net.

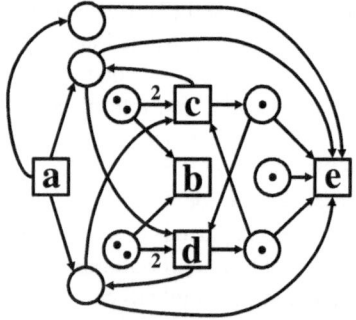

Fig. 2. Redundant places computed with method 1

The main advantage of method 1 is the optimality w.r.t. (2). The resulting process model may be seen as a natural completion of the given probably incomplete log file. Problematic is that the algorithm in some cases may be inefficient in time and space consumption. Moreover, the resulting net may be relatively big.

The second strategy to synthesize a finite net, used e.g. in [1,2], is to add such feasible places to the constructed net, which *separate* specified behaviour from non-specified behaviour. That means for each $w \in L(\sigma)$ and each $t \in T$ such that $wt \notin L(\sigma)$, one searches for a feasible place p_{wt}, which prohibits wt. Such wt is called *wrong continuation* (also called faulty word in [1]) and such places are called *separating feasible places*. If there is such a separating feasible place, it is added to the net. The number of wrong continuations is bounded by $|L(\sigma)| \cdot |T|$. Thus the set containing one separating feasible place for each wrong continuation, for which such place exists, is finite. The net resulting from adding such a set of places yields a good solution for the process mining problem: If the process language of the log can exactly be generated by a p/t-net, the constructed net is such a net. Consequently, in this case (2) is optimized. In general (2) is not necessarily optimized, since it is possible that even if there is no feasible place prohibiting wt, there might be one prohibiting wtt' – but such places are not added. However, in most practical cases this does not happen [3].

In order to compute a separating feasible place which prohibits a wrong continuation wt, one defines so called *separating regions* defining such places. These are defined by one additional (strict) inequation ensuring that wt is prohibited. Thus a separating region r w.r.t. a wrong continuation wt can be calculated (if it exists) as a non-negative integer solution of a homogenous linear inequation system with integer coefficients of the form $\mathbf{A}_{L(\sigma)} \cdot \mathbf{r} \geq \mathbf{0}, \mathbf{b}_{wt} \cdot \mathbf{r} < \mathbf{0}$. The matrix $\mathbf{A}_{L(\sigma)}$ is defined as before. If there exists no non-negative integer solution of this system, there exists no separating region w.r.t. wt and thus no separating feasible place prohibiting wt. If there exists a non-negative integer solution of the system, any such a solution defines a separating feasible place prohibiting wt.

There are several linear programming solver to decide the solvability of such a system and to calculate a solution if it is solvable. The choice of a concrete solver is a parameter of the process mining algorithm, that can be used to improve the results or the runtime. Since the considered system is homogenous, we can apply solvers searching for rational solutions. In order to decide if there is a non-negative rational solution and to find such a solution in the positive case, the ellipsoid method by Khachiyan [14] can be used. The runtime of this algorithm is polynomial in the size of the inequation system. Since there are at most $|L(\sigma)| \cdot |T|$ wrong continuations, the time complexity for computing the final net is polynomial in the size of the input event log σ. Although the method of Khachiyan yields an algorithm to solve the process mining problem in polynomial time, usually a better choice is the classical Simplex algorithm or variants of the Simplex algorithm [20]. While the Simplex algorithm is exponential in the worst case, probabilistic and experimental results [14] show that the Simplex algorithm has a significant faster average runtime than the algorithm of Khachiyan. The standard procedure to calculate a starting edge with the Simplex algorithm is a natural approach to decide, if there is a non-negative integer solution of the linear inequation system and to find such solution in the positive case. But it makes also sense to use the whole

Simplex method including a linear objective function. The choice of a reasonable objective function for the Simplex solver is a parameter of the algorithm to improve the results, e.g. a function minimizing the arc weights and the initial markings of the separating feasible places. Moreover, there are several variants of the Simplex algorithm that can improve the runtime of the mining algorithm [20]. For example the inequation systems for the wrong continuations only differ in the last inequation $\mathbf{b}_{wt} \cdot \mathbf{r} < \mathbf{0}$. This enables the efficient application of incremental Simplex methods.

Independently from the choice of the solver, certain separating feasible places may separate more than one wrong continuation. For not yet considered wrong continuations, that are prohibited by feasible places already added to the constructed net, we do not have to calculate a separating feasible place. Therefore we choose a certain ordering of the wrong continuations. We first add a separating feasible place for the first wrong continuation (if such place exists). Then we only add a separating feasible place for the second wrong continuation, if it is not prohibited by an already added feasible places, and so on. This way we achieve, that in the resulting net, various wrong continuations are prohibited by the same separating feasible place. The chosen ordering of the wrong continuations can be used as a parameter to positively adjust the algorithm. In particular, given a fixed solver, there always exists an ordering of the wrong continuations, such that the net has no redundant places. But in general the net may still include redundant places. Again easily identifiable redundant places are finally deleted from the computed net. The resulting process mining algorithm, called method 2, is shown in [3].

To calculate a net from the log of the running example with method 2, we consider the length- plus-lexicographic order of the 45 wrong continuations: b, c, d, e, aa, ae, aba, abc, abd, abe, ... To compute a separating feasible place for a given wrong continuation, we use the standard Simplex algorithm. We choose an objective function (for the Simplex algorithm) that minimizes all arc weights outgoing from the constructed place as well as the initial marking. Figure 3 shows the places resulting from the first five wrong continuations b, c, d, e and aa. In Figures we annotate the constructed separating feasible places with the wrong continuation, for which the place was calculated. The next wrong continuation ae leads the ae-place in Figure 4. Then aba is already prohibited by the aa-place and thus no additional place is computed. The next three wrong continuations abc, abd and abe lead to the respective separating feasible places in Figure 4. Then all remaining 35 wrong continuations are prohibited by one of the already

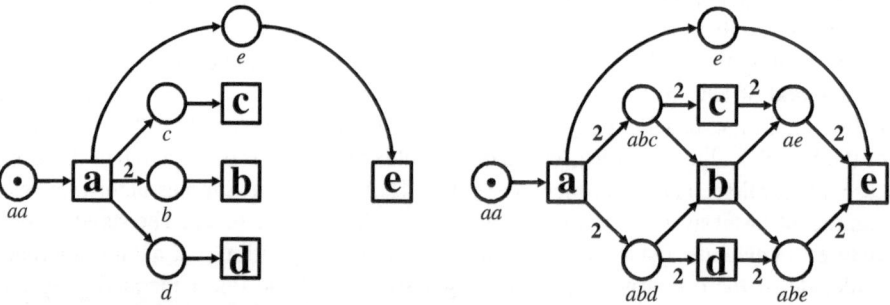

Fig. 3. First places computed with method 2   **Fig. 4.** Final net constructed with method 2

calculated nine feasible places. The b-, c-, and d-place from Figure 3 are finally deleted in Figure 4 as easily identifiable redundant places. Consequently the net in Figure 4 with six places results from Method 2 (only the e-place is still redundant).

The main advantage of method 2 is that the number of added places is bounded by $|L(\sigma)| \cdot |T|$ and that in most practical cases it is a lot smaller. Usually the resulting net is small and concise. The calculation of the net is efficient. There exists a polynomial time algorithm. Problematic is, that a good solution regarding (2) is not guaranteed, i.e. there may be intricate examples leading to a bad solution of the process mining problem. In [3] we show an example, where the constructed net is not optimal regarding (2), but this example was really hard to find. Therefore, in most cases the net should be an optimal solution. Moreover if the constructed net is not optimal, the respective example in [3] indicates that it is usually still a good solution of the process mining problem. Altogether the process model resulting from method 2 is a reasonable completion of the given probably incomplete log file. Although optimality regarding (2) is not guaranteed, the distinct advantages of method 2 concerning the runtime and the size of the calculated net altogether argue for method 2. But method 1 can still lead to valuable results, in particular if combined with some heuristics to decrease the number of places of the constructed net. Mainly, algorithms deleting redundant places are of interest.

3   Conclusion

The presented methods only considered p/t-nets as process models. To complete the outline of applying language based Petri net synthesis to process mining, we discuss alternative Petri net classes in this paragraph. In the example using method 1, we proposed to omit loops to simplify the constructed net. Leaving loops from p/t-nets in general, leads to the simpler class of pure nets. The process mining approach can analogously be developed for this net class. The inequation systems get simpler, in particular the number of variables is halved. Therefore the process mining approach gets more efficient for pure nets, but the modelling power is restricted in contrast to p/t-nets. Typical workflow Petri nets often have unweighted arcs. To construct such nets from a log with the presented methods, one simply has to add additional inequations ensuring arc weights smaller or equal than one. A problem is that the resulting systems are inhomogeneous. Method 1 is not applicable in this case (adaptions are still possible). Method 2 is still useable, but the linear programming techniques to find separating feasible places become less efficient [14]. A popular net class with unweighted arcs are elementary nets. In elementary nets the number of tokens in a place is bounded by one. This leads to additional inhomogeneous inequations ensuring this property. Note that the total number of possible places is finite in the case of elementary nets. Thus also the set of feasible places is finite leading to improvements of method 1. So far our considerations were based on the regions definition in [6,1]. There exists one further synthesis approach based on regions of languages [10], which we discuss and compare in [3].

The big advantage of the presented process mining approaches based on regions of languages is that they lead to reliable results. Other process mining algorithms are often more or less heuristic and their applicability is shown only with experimental results. We showed theoretical results that justify that the presented methods lead to a good or even optimal solution regarding (2), while (1) is guaranteed. A problem of the algorithms may be the required time and space consumption as well as the size of the resulting nets. The presented algorithms can be seen as a basis, that can be improved in several directions. Method 2 for computing separating feasible places is flexible w.r.t. the used solver and the chosen ordering of the wrong continuations. Varying the solver could improve time and space consumption, heuristics for fixing an appropriate ordering of the wrong continuations could lead to smaller nets. Both methods could be improved by additional approaches to find redundant places yielding smaller nets. For example, in this paper we used a simple special objective function in the simplex algorithm to rule out some redundant places. To develop such approaches, experimental results and thus an implementation of the algorithms is necessary.

References

1. Badouel, E., Bernardinello, L., Darondeau, P.: Polynomial algorithms for the synthesis of bounded nets. In: Mosses, P.D., Schwartzbach, M.I., Nielsen, M. (eds.) CAAP 1995, FASE 1995, and TAPSOFT 1995. LNCS, vol. 915, pp. 364–378. Springer, Heidelberg (1995)
2. Badouel, E., Darondeau, P.: Theory of regions. In: Reisig, W., Rozenberg, G. (eds.) Lectures on Petri Nets I: Basic Models. LNCS, vol. 1491, pp. 529–586. Springer, Heidelberg (1998)
3. Bergenthum, R., Desel, J., Lorenz, R., Mauser, S.: Technical report: Process mining based on regions of languages (2007), http://www.informatik.ku-eichstaett.de/mitarbeiter/lorenz/techreports/bpm2007.pdf
4. Cook, J.E., Wolf, A.L.: Discovering models of software processes from event-based data. ACM Trans. Softw. Eng. Methodol. 7(3), 215–249 (1998)
5. Cortadella, J., Kishinevsky, M., Kondratyev, A., Lavagno, L., Yakovlev, A.: Petrify: A tool for manipulating concurrent specifications and synthesis of asynchronous controllers. IEICE Trans. of Informations and Systems E80-D(3), 315–325 (1997)
6. Darondeau, P.: Deriving unbounded petri nets from formal languages. In: Sangiorgi, D., de Simone, R. (eds.) CONCUR 1998. LNCS, vol. 1466, pp. 533–548. Springer, Heidelberg (1998)
7. de Medeiros, A.K.A., van der Aalst, W.M.P., Weijters, A.J.M.M.: Workflow mining: Current status and future directions. In: Meersman, R., Tari, Z., Schmidt, D.C. (eds.) CoopIS 2003, DOA 2003, and ODBASE 2003. LNCS, vol. 2888, pp. 389–406. Springer, Heidelberg (2003)
8. Ehrenfeucht, A., Rozenberg, G.: Partial (set) 2-structures. part i: Basic notions and the representation problem. Acta Inf. 27(4), 315–342 (1989)
9. Ehrenfeucht, A., Rozenberg, G.: Partial (set) 2-structures. part ii: State spaces of concurrent systems. Acta Inf. 27(4), 343–368 (1989)
10. Lorenz, R., Bergenthum, R., Mauser, S., Desel, J.: Synthesis of petri nets from finite partial languages. In: Proceedings of ACSD 2007 (2007)
11. Motzkin, T.: Beiträge zur Theorie der linearen Ungleichungen. PhD thesis, Jerusalem (1936)
12. Parekh, R., Honavar, V.: Automata induction, grammar inference, and language acquisition. In: Dale, R., Moisl, H., Somers, H. (eds.) Handbook of Natural Language Processing, Marcel Dekker, New York (2000)
13. Process mining group eindhoven technical university: Prom-homepage, http://is.tm.tue.nl/cgunther/dev/prom/
14. Schrijver, A.: Theory of Linear and Integer Programming. Wiley, Chichester (1986)
15. van der Aalst, W., Rubin, V., van Dongen, B., Kindler, E., Guenther, C.: Process mining: A two-step approach using transition systems and regions. Technical Report BPM Center Report BPM-06-30, Department of Technology Management, Eindhoven University of Technology (2006)

16. van der Aalst, W., van Hee, K.: Workflow Management: Models, Methods, and Systems. MIT Press, Cambridge, Massachsetts (2002)
17. van der Aalst, W., Weijters, A., Verbeek, H.W., et al.: Process mining: research tools application, http://www.processmining.org
18. van der Aalst, W.M.P., van Dongen, B.F., Herbst, J., Maruster, L., Schimm, G., Weijters, A.J.M.M.: Workflow mining: A survey of issues and approaches. Data Knowl. Eng. 47(2), 237–267 (2003)
19. van Dongen, B., Busi, N., Pinna, G., van der Aalst, W.: An iterative algorithm for applying the theory of regions in process mining. Technical Report Beta rapport 195, Department of Technology Management, Eindhoven University of Technology (2007)
20. Vanderbei, R.J.: Linear Programming: Foundations and Extensions. Kluwer Academic Publishers, Dordrecht (1996)

Extending Representational Analysis: BPMN User and Developer Perspectives

Jan Recker[1], Marta Indulska[2], and Peter Green[2]

[1] School of Information Systems, Queensland University of Technology,
Brisbane, Australia
j.recker@qut.edu.au
[2] UQ Business School, The University of Queensland,
Brisbane, Australia
{m.indulska, p.green}@business.uq.edu.au

Abstract. Over the last years, significant academic progress has been made in the area of representational analyses that use ontology as a benchmark for evaluations and comparisons of modeling techniques. This paper proposes a research model to guide representational analysis projects, which extends existing procedural models by incorporating different stakeholder perspectives. The paper demonstrates the application of this model for the purpose of analyzing the Business Process Modeling Notation (BPMN), a recent and popular candidate for a new process modeling industry standard. A brief overview of the underlying research model characterizes the different steps in such a research project, while the BPMN analysis project emphasizes the importance of validating with users the propositions obtained via the analysis and communicating those to the technique developers in order to increase the impact of evaluation research to Information Systems practice.

Keywords: BPMN, representational analysis, Bunge-Wand-Weber model, ontology.

1 Introduction

Over the recent decades, a large number of process modeling techniques have been developed, creating a situation in which users have vast choice but limited means for evaluating or comparing the techniques. The Business Process Modeling Notation (BPMN) [1] is the most recent addition to the growing list of process modeling choices. The lack of means for evaluation of such techniques alongside the still increasing number of techniques is creating an imminent demand for a shift of academic resources committed to the development of new and further extensions of existing modeling techniques to the critical evaluation and comparison of the already available set of modeling techniques [2]. This move is a pre-requisite for an evolving research discipline that builds on the existing body of knowledge, has an awareness for the remaining open challenges, and is guided by a methodological procedure in its future research efforts [3, 4].

G. Alonso, P. Dadam, and M. Rosemann (Eds.): BPM 2007, LNCS 4714, pp. 384–399, 2007.

While there is unfortunately no one single framework that facilitates a comprehensive analysis of all facets of a process modeling technique, such as its expressive power, the consistency and correctness of its meta model, the perceived intuitiveness of its notation, and the available tool support, reasonably mature research has emerged over the years with a focus on the *representational capabilities* of process modeling techniques. It is referred to as *representational analysis*, e.g., [5].

Representational analysis uses models of representation, such as the Bunge-Wand-Weber representation model [4, 6, 7], as a benchmark for the evaluation of the representational capabilities of a process modeling technique. While the underlying Bunge-Wand-Weber representation model has over the years obtained a significant level of maturity and dissemination as a theory in the IS discipline [8], the process of applying this model as part of a representational analysis is less specified. It was only recently that more advanced procedural models have been proposed [9] that guide researchers through the process of using the representation model for the critical evaluation of a selected modeling technique. While these procedural models have been shown to increase the overall rigor of representational analyses [10], a comprehensive research model putting the principles of representational analysis in an overall context that comprises *relevant stakeholder perspectives* as well as *ultimate dependant variables* of interest has been missing so far.

Accordingly, the *aim of this paper* is two-fold. First, it is to present a research model for comprehensive representational analyses *including* empirical evidence. Second, it is to report on the progress of applying this model to the case of the Business Process Modeling Notation (BPMN) [1], in particular reporting on the developer feedback to our communicated analysis outcomes. The development of the research model is motivated by the lack of guidance for researchers who use a representational theory for the purposes of analysis. In many cases the analysis ends with reporting the theoretical propositions, without ever validating those with users, let alone developers, of the analyzed technique – hence not making an impact on the technique itself. The application of the presented model shows how both developers and users may be able to pinpoint and scrutinize representational shortcomings of a technique specification in order to derive a more sophisticated, revised technique, which in turn ultimately has consequences on a real-world phenomenon of interest, *viz.*, conceptual models of higher quality.

We proceed by first presenting a brief introduction to BPMN, the BWW model - which forms the basis of our analysis - and a review of related work on analyses of process modeling techniques. Next we provide an overview of the general research model. We then discuss the application of this model in the case of analyzing BPMN. We pay particular attention to the empirical part of this analysis, and report on the outcomes of user and developer responses. We conclude with limitations of the study and future research directions.

2 Background and Related Work

2.1 The Business Process Modeling Notation

BPMN [1] is a recently proposed process modeling technique, the development of which has been based on the revision of other notations including UML, IDEF, ebXML, RosettaNet, LOVeM and EPCs. The development of BPMN stemmed from the demand for a graphical notation that complements the BPEL4WS standard for executable business processes. The specification document differentiates the BPMN constructs into a set of core graphical elements and an extended specialized set. For the purpose of this research we investigated both sets. The complete BPMN specification defines thirty-eight distinct language constructs plus attributes, grouped into four basic categories of elements, *viz., Flow Objects, Connecting Objects, Swimlanes* and *Artefacts. Flow Objects*, such as events, activities and gateways, are the most basic elements used to create Business Process Diagrams (BPDs). *Connecting Objects* are used to inter-connect *Flow Objects* through different types of arrows. *Swimlanes* are used to group activities into separate categories for different functional capabilities or responsibilities (*e.g.*, different roles or organizational departments). *Artefacts* may be added to a diagram where deemed appropriate in order to display further related information such as processed data or other comments. For more information on BPMN refer to [1].

2.2 The BWW Representation Model

In the process of requirements engineering for Information Systems Analysis and Design, various stakeholders are confronted with the need to represent the requirements in a conceptual form. Often, however, they do not possess an underlying conceptual structure on which to base such models [11]. This deficit motivated research for a theoretical foundation for conceptual modeling. A promising theory emerged from the observation that, in their essence, computerized Information Systems are representations of real world systems. Real world systems, in turn, can be explained and described using ontology – the study of the nature of the world and attempt to organize and describe what exists in reality, in terms of the properties of, the structure of, and the interactions between real- world things [12]. Wand and Weber [6, 7] suggest that the theory of ontology can be used to help define and build models of information systems that contain the necessary representations of real world constructs, including their properties and interactions. They developed and refined a set of models based on an ontology defined by [12] for the evaluation of modeling techniques and the scripts prepared using such techniques. The BWW *representation model* is one of three theoretical models defined by Wand and Weber [6] and its application to Information Systems foundations has been referred to by a number of researchers [8]. Its key constructs can be grouped into four clusters: things including properties and types of things; states assumed by things; events and transformations occurring on things; and systems structured around things. For a complete description of the BWW constructs please refer to, for example, [4].

2.3 Analysis of Process Modeling Techniques

Limited research efforts have been made to compare process modeling techniques based on an established theoretical model. Söderström *et al.* [13] for example, compare process modeling techniques based on a framework of some core concepts in the area of process modeling. Van der Aalst *et al.* [14] report on the use of a set of workflow patterns for the comparison of process modeling techniques. Furthermore, some authors have proposed more or less comprehensive lists of correctness criteria such as soundness, e.g., [15].

This work has in common that it is of pure theoretical nature and of limited dissemination in IS research practice overall. The BWW representation model, on the other hand, has been used in over thirty-five research projects for the evaluation of different modeling techniques (see [16] for an overview), including data models, object-oriented models, use case models and reference models. Its main premises have also in a number of empirical studies, e.g., [17-19] been shown to affect various aspects of quality in conceptual modeling. It also has a strong track record in the area of process modeling with contributions coming from many international researchers. In this section, we briefly summarize BWW-related studies that involved the analysis of a process modeling technique by means of a representational model. Keen and Lakos [20] determined essential rules for a process modeling scheme by evaluating six process modeling techniques. Their evaluation was based on the BWW representation model. Among the modeling techniques evaluated were ANSI flowcharts, Data Flow Diagrams and IDEF3. From the analysis, the authors concluded that, in general, the BWW model facilitates the interpretation and comparison of process modeling techniques. Yet, the authors did not empirically verify their findings on the features of process modeling schemes. Green and Rosemann [21] analyzed the EPC notation with the help of the BWW model. Their findings have been empirically validated through interviews and surveys [22]. Confirmed shortcomings were found in the EPC notation with regard to the representation of real world objects and business rules, and in the thorough demarcation of systems. Green et al. [23] compared different modeling standards for enterprise system interoperability, including BPEL4WS v1.1, BPML v1.0, WSCI v1.0, and ebXML v1.1. The study found that ebXML provides a wider range of language constructs for specification requirements than the other techniques. At the present point in time, this analysis too, has not yet been empirically validated. Overall, most of the research conducted lacks, at the time of writing, empirical verification of the theoretical findings, let alone communication of these to the technique developers in an effort to impact the revision of the technique.

Overcoming this shortcoming of previous analyses, our foremost research objective was to conduct a comprehensive study on BPMN that included the empirical testing of our findings *and* further also included the communication of these to the developers.

Research relating directly to the evaluation of the Business Process Modeling Notation is still limited as BPMN is a very recent modeling technique. Wahl and Sindre [24] report on an analytical evaluation of BPMN using the Semiotic Quality Framework [25]. They conclude that BPMN particularly excels in terms of comprehensibility appropriateness due to its construct specializations and type aggregations, and is well-suited generally for the domain of business process modeling. Interestingly, they also see the need for, and potential of, a representational analysis. Similarly, Nysetvold and Krogstie [26] compared BPMN to UML Activity Diagrams and EEML in a case study based on the same framework, finding that BPMN achieves the highest score in all categories except for domain appropriateness. Finally, based on the workflow patterns framework [14], Wohed et al. [27] evaluated BPMN as to its capability to express a series of control flow, data and resource patterns. They found that BPMN supports the majority of the control flow patterns, nearly half of the data patterns and a few resource patterns. The outcomes of their study align with most of our findings, *e.g.*, the lack of means in BPMN for representing states assumed by things or the unclear specification of the constructs Lane and Pool (see Table 1).

3   A Research Model for Representational Analyses

While a number of existing models of representation can be used as part of our proposed model, the use of the BWW representation model in studies on the representational capabilities of modeling techniques can be justified on at least three premises. First, unlike other modeling theories based on ontology, the BWW model has been derived with the IS discipline in mind. Second, the BWW model officiates as an upper ontology, and thus its foundational character and comprehensive scope allows for wide applicability. Third, there is an established track record and demonstrated usefulness of representational analyses of modeling techniques using the BWW representation model. As indicated above, over thirty-five research projects have used this model for the evaluation of different modeling techniques [8].

The process of using a representational theory, such as the BWW representation model, as a benchmark for the evaluation of the representational capabilities of a modeling technique forms the core of the research method of *representational analysis*. During this analysis, the constructs of the representation model (e.g., thing, transformation) are compared with the language constructs of the modeling technique (e.g. event, actor). The basic assumption is that any deviation from a 1-1 relationship between the corresponding constructs in the representation model and the modeling technique leads to a situation of representational deficiency in the use of the technique potentially causing confusion to the end users. Such cases are classified as theoretical, *i.e.*, potential, representational shortcomings. These undesirable situations can be further categorized into four types, as shown in Fig. 1.

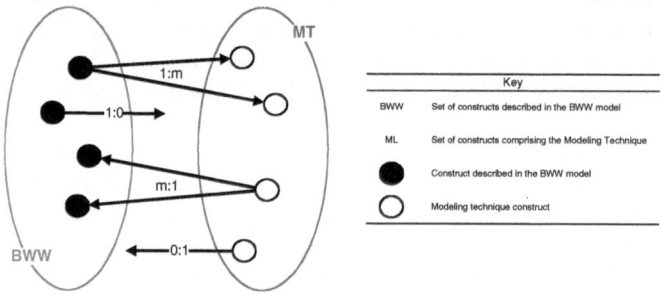

Fig. 1. Types of Potential Representational Deficiencies [4]

- *construct overload* exists where a construct in the modeling technique maps to two or more representation model constructs (m:1 relationship),
- *construct redundancy* exists where one construct in the representation model is mapped to two or more constructs in the modeling technique (1:m relationship),

- *construct excess* exists where at least one construct in the modeling technique does not map to any construct in the representation model (0:1 relationship), and
- *construct deficit* exists where at least one construct in the representation model does not map to any construct in the modeling technique (1:0 relationship).

Based on these four types of deficiencies, it is possible to predict the capabilities of a process modeling technique for providing *complete* and *clear* representations of the domain being modeled [4]. In particular, if construct deficit is not present in a modeling technique then the technique is regarded as *ontologically complete*. In turn, the *ontological clarity* of a modeling technique can be measured by the degrees of construct overload, construct redundancy, and construct excess. However, at this stage of the research progress, these representational issues are of a theoretical nature. The findings denote *potential* issues for developers and users working with the modeling technique in question. Most of the existing research so far has exclusively focused on this step within the research model, however, the identified potential issues require further empirical testing.

Empirically testing the identified representational issues requires access to sources of evidence. In most cases, this will mean interviews and occasionally focus groups, or experiments, with business analysts or students as practitioner proxies. Surveys as a way of collecting related data are another option, but often researchers struggle to identify the required number of participants for such a study. In our experience, predominantly semi-structured interviews have been used as an empirical research method in the process of representational analysis, with either business analysts [10, 28] or experienced coursework students [22] as participants.

The design of such interviews should follow a defined protocol that explores the significance of the identified issues [10, 28] (see Fig. 2). As Fig. 2 indicates, five different levels of severity of an issue can be differentiated, with level V representing a most critical issue. Follow-up questions would explore how the interview partner addresses this problem. We predict that if the problem is seen to be critical then users will create new symbols, modify existing symbols or use an additional tool. Hence, the follow-up questions aim to verify this prediction, and in general allow for extended reasoning and exploration of further factors that may have remained invisible from the theoretical analysis.

Gathered responses can be further codified based on collected demographic data in order to identify exogenous variables that moderate the effect of perceived criticality of representational deficiencies. Further investigations into possible correlations will provide insights into the extent to which a perceived problem corresponds with moderating variables. For instance, previous research has shown that besides *years of experience* [28] and the *role* [29] of the *person* who uses the modeling technique, the *purpose of modeling* [28] is a primary contextual factor impacting the perceived criticality of the identified issue.

Overall, the subset of theoretical representational issues that is evaluated as critical in light of the empirical data becomes the set of empirically tested representational shortcomings, and thus potentially form an important input for further revisions and improvements of existing process modeling techniques. In this phase, it would be important to communicate the research outcomes back to the developers of the modeling technique or tool providers. Without such communication, there is little chance of the validated issues ever being considered and incorporated by the

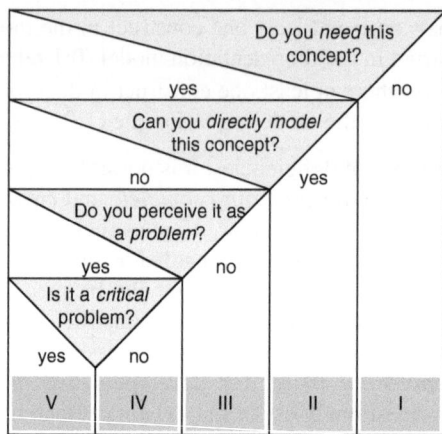

Fig. 2. User Questionnaire Structure and Response Classification

technique developers. Thus, there is little chance of following the overall guideline of developing research outcomes in order to improve existing practices [30]. In fact, it is observable generally that research assessment usually stops when weaknesses in the theory or the developed artifact have been identified rather than incorporated in revisions [31]. In order to counteract this trend we argue that taking into account a developer perspective in this type of research can strengthen not only the practitioner impact of research but also contribute to the overall objective of this research, *viz.*, improving the quality of process modeling practice.

Fig. 3 summarizes the phases of this type of research project and indicates the ultimate dependant variable of interest – the *quality of the model produced*. In this context it has to be noted that while the level of dissemination of studies based on the BWW model is very substantial and the resulting findings are proven to be of relevance, there remains a need for representational analysis studies to transcend beyond the level of grammar capabilities. To that end, Gemino and Wand [18] investigated the effect of a representational proposition related to the Entity-Relationship grammar regarding the use of optional versus mandatory properties on the complexity of understanding the resulting model. Aside from this example, however, several researchers, most notably Wand and Weber [2] themselves, note that there is a paucity of research exploring the impact that representational deficiencies of modeling grammars have on further dependant variables, such as the effectiveness and efficiency of the grammar for modeling practice, the user acceptance of the grammar, or the quality of the model produced. We address the latter and argue that one dependant variable of interest that can be studied using the principles of representational analyses is the quality of the model produced, following the argumentations in [32] that an improvement in a modeling technique will contribute ultimately to the success of the overall process modeling effort.

Fig. 3 also shows how we have followed a Kuhnian approach to scientific method in our work. According to Kuhn [33], scientific method is the process by which scientists, collectively and over time, endeavor to construct an accurate (that is, reliable, consistent and non-arbitrary) representation of real-world phenomena. As noted, ultimately, the real-world phenomenon that we are interested in is the *quality* of model produced. The items through which we measure quality include, *inter alia*, completeness, level of ambiguity, and level of understandability. Our underlying assumption is that, if the modeling technique(s) used to produce the models is representationally incomplete and/or representationally ambiguous, then, *ceteris paribus*, the models produced using those techniques will suffer the same problems. Finally, if suggestions to improve the modeling capacity of the technique are made based on the empirically confirmed measures, resultant models produced using the revised modeling technique can be assessed in terms of their improved quality. Indeed, this aspect of the research program leads us to an exciting phase whereby we hope to be able to test the improved conceptual model quality resulting from revisions to the modeling technique provided by the results of our representational analysis of the original modeling technique. Hence, in our work with the Business Process Modeling Notation (BPMN), we contacted the development team in order to prepare for this type of study. The outcome of the contact with BPMN's developers is discussed in the following section.

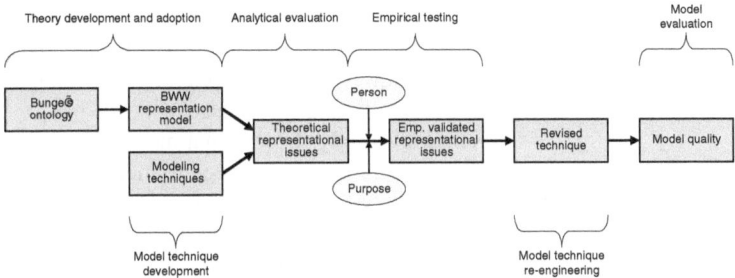

Fig. 3. Research Model for Representational Analyses

4   BPMN Analysis and Feedback

4.1   The User Perspective

In preparation for this study, we completed a representational analysis of the emerging process modeling standard BPMN [1]. The representational analysis was performed according to a methodology proposed by Rosemann *et al.* [9], to guarantee objectivity of the analysis. Following the established methodology, first we performed a representation mapping between the language constructs in BPMN against the constructs specified in the BWW representation model. This allowed us to identify situations of construct deficit, redundancy, overload and excess. Following this step, nine propositions were derived based on the existence of these four situations of representational deficiency. In [10] we describe the proposition-building in more detail. The propositions were consequently tested via two series of interviews, with the interview protocol format following the suggested design as discussed earlier. In total, we interviewed nineteen BPMN users from six Australian organizations. The users ranged in terms of process modeling experience and role in process modeling initiatives while the organizations varied in terms of industry sector and purpose of the process modeling initiative. A summary of the two series of interview results is presented in Table 1, while in-depth discussions of the conduct and findings of the analysis and the related empirical tests can be found in [10].

Table 1. BWW-based BPMN Propositions and Summary of User Responses

Proposition		Description
Construct deficit		
P1	Modeling business rules	The analysis predicts that modelers using BPMN will have problems capturing business rules of a given situation because BPMN lacks capabilities to depict aspects and concepts of states. Our empirical research confirmed this proposition: 75% of interviewees having a need to model business rules said they were unable to do so with BPMN. Some workarounds include narrative descriptions of business rules, spreadsheets, and even UML state diagrams.
P2	Modeling the History of State Changes	The analysis predicts that modelers using BPMN will have problems capturing the history of state changes of important entities (*e.g.,* an application that traversed the states 'received', and 'processed'). Our empirical study showed that most of the interviewed BPMN users do not have a need to model this concept. If, they do, they find that workarounds such as additional diagrams are sufficient for overcoming the deficiency. In particular, the study found that mostly modelers from a technical background had a need for modeling the history of state changes.
P3	Modeling Process Structure and Scope	The analysis predicts that modelers using BPMN will have problems capturing process structure and scope (*e.g.,* for structuring process models into constituent models). Our empirical research showed that 71% of BPMN users indicated that they lacked direct modeling capabilities in BPMN and some commented that having an explicit way of modeling would be "nice".
Construct redundancy		
P4	Modeling Real-world Objects	The analysis predicts that modelers using BPMN will have problems modeling real-world objects (*e.g.,* an organizational department, a document). This problem is in particular predicted to arise from unclear specifications of the Lane and Pool constructs, and so modelers would get confused as to which one to use to model a real-world object. Our empirical study found that while most users did not find this to be a critical problem some more experienced users pointed out that it would probably be problematic if

		BPMN was used without additional tool support, *i.e.*, in isolation.
P5	Modeling Transformations	The analysis predicts that modelers using BPMN will encounter confusion when representing transformations due to the multiplicity of available BPMN constructs (*e.g.*, sub-process, task, transaction).
		Our empirical study showed that 94% of BPMN users do not experience problems in representing transformations. However, some needed workarounds in order to allow for further differentiation, e.g., color coding for distinguishing automated from manual tasks. Also, our results indicate that without established organizational modeling methodologies and guidelines confusion would manifest more severely.
P6	Modeling Events	The analysis predicts that modelers using BPMN will encounter confusion when modeling events due to the multiplicity of available BPMN constructs (*e.g.*, message, timer).
		Our empirical study found that the majority of BPMN users are in fact pleased with the differentiation of events provided. Interestingly, however, we found that core set users encountered difficulties due to a lack of differentiation of events.

Construct excess

P7	Using Excess constructs	The analysis predicts that modelers using BPMN will avoid some BPMN constructs (*e.g.*, text annotation, group) in order to limit confusion when interpreting the model.
		Empirical study showed that some BPMN constructs are indeed being avoided (*e.g.*, off-page connector, multiple instances) by most of the interviewed modelers.

Construct overload

P8	Using the Lane construct	The analysis predicts that modelers using BPMN will encounter confusion as to the usage of the Lane construct, in particular, which concept exactly is modeled by a Lane (*e.g.*, an organizational entity, a role).
		Empirical study clearly confirms this proposition. More than 50% of the BPMN users use the Lane construct for two or more purposes (*e.g.*, roles, organizational units, business areas).
P9	Using the Pool construct	The analysis predicts that modelers using BPMN will encounter confusion as to the usage of the Pool construct, in particular, which concept exactly is modeled by a Pool (*e.g.*, an organizational entity, an external entity).
		Empirical study clearly confirms this proposition. More than 60% of the BPMN users use the Pool construct for two or more purposes (*e.g.*, external organizational units, internal business areas, scoping).

4.2 The Developer Perspective

While the validation of the theoretical propositions is necessary in differentiating potential shortcomings of a technique from those shortcomings that are actually experienced as such by users in practice, it is also important to then communicate these validated results so that they can make a difference and improve existing practice. This next step is particularly important in emerging modeling techniques when there is a "window of opportunity" to impact the technique before its wider uptake, which is the case of BPMN and the related ongoing standardization process. Ultimately, the research findings need to be communicated to the people that have the authority to change and improve the technique in question. To that end, we interviewed the lead designer of BPMN to communicate and elicit feedback on our findings. Again, in order to apply rigor to this type of study, we developed an interview protocol with a predefined response classification scheme (see Fig. 4).

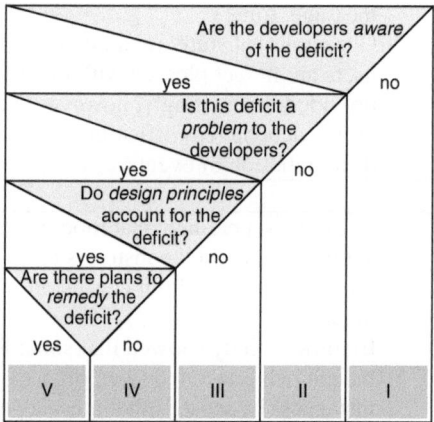

Fig. 4. Developer Interview Structure and Response Classification

First, we were interested whether our identified deficiencies of BPMN have at all been identified as such by the developers and, if so, whether they denote problems that would be identified as critical to a revision of BPMN. Follow-up questions sought to explore whether potential underlying design principles that were applied to the development of BPMN could be identified as potential sources for some of the deficiencies, and if so, whether there are plans to re-visit these principles based on our findings. Table 2 summarizes the responses per proposition, and a brief discussion of developer feedback follows. Only responses classified as type III, IV, and V are indicated in Table 2. These classifications correspond with the users experiencing a problem with the specification or the developer identifying the issue as a problem.

Table 2. Comparison of User and Developer Responses per Proposition

Deficiency type	Proposition	User Responses			Developer Responses		
		III	**IV**	**V**	**III**	**IV**	**V**
Construct deficit	P1	4 21%	5 26%	0 0%			✓
	P2	5 26%	1 5%	0 0%			
	P3	6 32%	3 16%	3 16%			
	P4	5 26%	1 5%	1 5%		✓	
Construct redundancy	P5	0 0%	0 0%	1 5%			✓
	P6	1 5%	3 16%	1 5%		✓	
Construct excess (average)	P7	2.47	1.58	6.32			
Construct overload	P8	9 48%	1 5%	0 0%		✓	
	P9	5 26%	3 16%	1 0%			✓

In regards to construct deficit, the developer voiced strong support for enhancing BPMN's capability to model business rules. In the earlier phase of the project, this particular issue was found to affect 75% of the interviewed users who had a need to modeling business rules and was hence a supported proposition. The developer stated that this is an aspect of BPMN on which they expect to improve in the future. Weaknesses related to BPMN's inability to model the history of state changes, as well as its inability to model process structure and scope, were of less consequence. In relation to modeling the history of state changes, the developer commented that this was something that they understood a need for and made possible via allowing the users to have different property values for a particular object, which would allow the indication of state. The low relevance of an explicit way to model a history of state changes was also found to be supported in the user interviews, with only one respondent naming it as a minor problem. The developer commented on the lack of BPMN's ability to model the structure and scope of processes by stating that this is a feature that should be provided by a modeling tool rather than the technique. Our empirical findings align with this comment as it seems that, with respect to this particular deficiency, users indeed rely on complementary support in form of modeling tool features as was envisaged by the developers. Yet, we also found support that users would appreciate more process structure support within BPMN.

While the user perspective resulted in at most partial support for the construct redundancy propositions, these propositions were more strongly supported by the developer, with all three seen as some type of shortcoming in BPMN. In particular, the developer indicated that standardizing the transformation constructs was on the agenda for a future revision of BPMN. The gathered user responses, however, indicated that the provided differentiation of constructs, though theoretically classified as redundant, was in fact perceived as helpful for communicating dedicated instances of transformations. Our identified issues of modeling real-world objects as well as events were recognized in discussion as potentially confusing to BPMN users, but no revision of BPMN constructs was planned based on this, which in turn concurs with the limited level of support we found for this proposition from user interviews. With regards to proposition six, the developer commented that the confusion may stem from a lack of a detailed "BPMN primer" for users, and hence including that in the specification might alleviate the suggested problem, which was seen as a minor or major issue for over 20% of the interviewed BPMN users.

The developer classified the construct excess proposition as being due to different users with differing purposes. They commented that it was unlikely that any BPMN constructs were going to be removed completely in the future. More likely, there would be a classification of constructs for different types of users. This, however, does not seem supported by our user investigation as we found that different user groups (core set users versus full set users) do not significantly differ in their perception of most proposed excess constructs [10].

The construct overload propositions were also supported by the developer, with an indication that there are plans for a significant revision related to proposition nine. While this work is very early at this stage, the developer indicated that the confusion may stem from different purposes of modeling (e.g., process choreography versus orchestration). In terms of the usage of the BPMN Lane construct (proposition eight), the developer indicated that this construct was meant to be flexible, thus we observe that this deficit in fact stems from a dedicated design principle. However, the developer also conceded that there should be use of additional graphical representations that differentiate the purposes for which a Lane is used in a business process diagram, based on our findings that the principle of construct flexibility was mostly perceived as causing confusion when building or interpreting a model.

While the users and developer responses are aligned in some cases, there is also disparity. For example, proposition two and three have some level of user support, while the developer classified both as not being an issue. Differences like this one may stem from the lack of communication between user and developer communities, or from a lack of shared understanding of the purposes of modeling. It is therefore important to follow-up with a comprehensive report to the developers so that they gain an understanding of (a) the context within which issues arise, and (b) who in fact is using BPMN and for what purposes.

Overall, developer feedback was positive and, in over sixty percent of cases, acknowledged some/all aspects of the proposed shortcoming. Thirty-three percent of the shortcomings identified through our study were indicated to be likely to be considered at future BPMN developer work meetings.

5   Conclusion

In this paper we presented a comprehensive research model to consistently guide the process of representational analysis and further *extended* it to create an impact on the technique under analysis. We then demonstrate the application of this model in our work with the analysis of the Business Process Modeling Notation, in particular, communicating the analysis results to BPMN developers and reporting on the results herein.

While this research provides valuable insights into capabilities of BPMN and its perceived shortcomings from different stakeholder perspectives, it has limitations. Most notably, in the first step of our theoretical analysis, we only identified issues in light of the BWW model. While a focus on representational capabilities has been found to be useful in studies on modeling techniques [8], without any doubt, further criteria such as BPMN's perceived usefulness, its support for workflow concepts and technologies or its intuitiveness, have to be considered for a more comprehensive analysis of BPMN. Second, due to limited resource availability we were only able to discuss our research with one designer of BPMN. However, we contacted the head of the working group who we can assume to answer with a considerably high level of response validity as well as to have authority to communicate our findings, and thus, to actually make an impact to the technique's further development.

The next step in our research is to examine whether the improvement suggestions we recommended based on our validated propositions stemming from the representational analysis of BPMN will (a) be incorporated in the currently ongoing revision of the BPMN technique, and (b) whether these revisions in fact have an impact on our dependant variable of interest, *i.e.*, whether they increase, *ceteris paribus*, the quality of the process model produced. A second related stream of research could also investigate whether the weaknesses experienced with BPMN are solved by other process modeling techniques or if they are shared.

Acknowledgements

We would like to thank the BPMN.org development team, in particular Dr. Stephen A. White, for sharing with us insights into the BPMN development processes. We also would like to thank our colleague Dr. Michael Rosemann for his stimulating input into this paper.

References

1. BPMI.org, OMG: Business Process Modeling Notation Specification. Final Adopted Specification. Object Management Group (2006), available at http://www.bpmn.org
2. Wand, Y., Weber, R.: Research Commentary: Information Systems and Conceptual Modeling - A Research Agenda. Information Systems Research 13, 363–376 (2002)
3. Keen, P.G.W.: MIS Research: Reference Disciplines and a Cumulative Tradition. In: McLean, E.R. (ed.) Proceedings of the 1st International Conference on Information Systems, pp. 9–18. ACM Press, Philadelphia, Pennsylvania (1980)
4. Weber, R.: Ontological Foundations of Information Systems. Coopers & Lybrand and the Accounting Association of Australia and New Zealand, Melbourne, Australia (1997)
5. Rosemann, M., Green, P., Indulska, M., Recker, J.: Using Ontology for the Representational Analysis of Process Modeling Techniques. International Journal of Business Process Integration and Management (in press) (forthcoming)

6. Wand, Y., Weber, R.: On the Deep Structure of Information Systems. Information Systems Journal 5, 203–223 (1995)
7. Wand, Y., Weber, R.: On the Ontological Expressiveness of Information Systems Analysis and Design Grammars. Journal of Information Systems 3, 217–237 (1993)
8. Green, P., Rosemann, M.: Applying Ontologies to Business and Systems Modeling Techniques and Perspectives: Lessons Learned. Journal of Database Management 15, 105–117 (2004)
9. Rosemann, M., Green, P., Indulska, M.: A Reference Methodology for Conducting Ontological Analyses. In: Atzeni, P., Chu, W., Lu, H., Zhou, S., Ling, T.-W. (eds.) ER 2004. LNCS, vol. 3288, pp. 110–121. Springer, Heidelberg (2004)
10. Recker, J., Indulska, M., Rosemann, M., Green, P.: How Good is BPMN Really? Insights from Theory and Practice. In: Ljungberg, J., Andersson, M. (eds.) Proceedings of the 14th European Conference on Information Systems. Goeteborg, Sweden (2006)
11. Floyd, C.: A Comparative Evaluation of System Development Methods. In: Olle, T.W., Sol, H.G., Verrijn-Stuart, A.A. (eds.) Information System Design Methodologies: Improving the Practice. North-Holland, Amsterdam, The Netherlands, pp. 19–54 (1986)
12. Bunge, M.A.: Treatise on Basic Philosophy Ontology I - The Furniture of the World, vol. 3. Kluwer Academic Publishers, Dordrecht, The Netherlands (1977)
13. Söderström, E., Andersson, B., Johannesson, P., Perjons, E., Wangler, B.: Towards a Framework For Comparing Process Modelling Languages. In: Pidduck, A.B., Mylopoulos, J., Woo, C.C., Ozsu, M.T. (eds.) CAiSE 2002. LNCS, vol. 2348, pp. 600–611. Springer, Heidelberg (2002)
14. van der Aalst, W.M.P., ter Hofstede, A.H.M., Kiepuszewski, B., Barros, A.P.: Workflow Patterns. Distributed and Parallel Databases 14, 5–51 (2003)
15. Verbeek, H.M.V., van der Aalst, W.M.P., ter Hofstede, A.H.M.: Verifying Workflows with Cancellation Regions and OR-joins: An Approach Based on Relaxed Soundness and Invariants. The Computer Journal 50, 294–314 (2007)
16. Green, P., Rosemann, M., Indulska, M.: Ontological Evaluation of Enterprise Systems Interoperability Using ebXML. IEEE Transactions on Knowledge and Data Engineering 17, 713–725 (2005)
17. Bodart, F., Patel, A., Sim, M., Weber, R.: Should Optional Properties Be Used in Conceptual Modelling? A Theory and Three Empirical Tests. Information Systems Research 12, 384–405 (2001)
18. Gemino, A., Wand, Y.: Complexity and Clarity in Conceptual Modeling: Comparison of Mandatory and Optional Properties. Data & Knowledge Engineering 55, 301–326 (2005)
19. Bowen, P.L., O'Farrell, R.A., Rohde, F.: Analysis of Competing Data Structures: Does Ontological Clarity Produce Better End User Query Performance. Journal of the Association for Information Systems 7, 514–544 (2006)
20. Keen, C.D., Lakos, C.: Analysis of the Design Constructs Required in Process Modelling. In: Purvis, M. (ed.) Proceedings of the International Conference on Software Engineering: Education and Practice, pp. 434–441. IEEE Computer Society, Dunedin, Ireland (1996)
21. Green, P., Rosemann, M.: Integrated Process Modeling. An Ontological Evaluation. Information Systems 25, 73–87 (2000)
22. Green, P., Rosemann, M.: Ontological Analysis of Integrated Process Models: Testing Hypotheses. The Australian Journal of Information Systems 9, 30–38 (2001)
23. Green, P., Rosemann, M., Indulska, M., Manning, C.: Candidate Interoperability Standards: An Ontological Overlap Analysis. Data & Knowledge Engineering 62, 274–291 (2007)

24. Wahl, T., Sindre, G.: An Analytical Evaluation of BPMN Using a Semiotic Quality Framework. In: Siau, K. (ed.) Advanced Topics in Database Research, vol. 5, pp. 102–113. Idea Group, Hershey, Pennsylvania (2006)
25. Krogstie, J., Sindre, G., Jørgensen, H.D.: Process Models Representing Knowledge for Action: a Revised Quality Framework. European Journal of Information Systems 15, 91–102 (2006)
26. Nysetvold, A.G., Krogstie, J.: Assessing Business Process Modeling Languages Using a Generic Quality Framework. In: Siau, K. (ed.) Advanced Topics in Database Research, vol. 5, pp. 79–93. Idea Group, Hershey, Pennsylvania (2006)
27. Wohed, P., van der Aalst, W.M.P., Dumas, M., ter Hofstede, A.H.M., Russell, N.: On the Suitability of BPMN for Business Process Modelling. In: Dustdar, S., Fiadeiro, J.L., Sheth, A. (eds.) BPM 2006. LNCS, vol. 4102, pp. 161–176. Springer, Heidelberg (2006)
28. Davies, I., Rosemann, M., Green, P.: Exploring Proposed Ontological Issues of ARIS with Different Categories of Modellers. In: Proceedings of the 15th Australasian Conference on Information Systems. Australian Computer Society, Hobart, Australia (2004)
29. Green, P., Rosemann, M.: Perceived Ontological Weaknesses of Process Modelling Techniques: Further Evidence. In: Wrycza, S. (ed.) Proceedings of the 10th European Conference on Information Systems. Association for Information Systems, Gdansk, Poland, pp. 312–321 (2002)
30. Benbasat, I., Zmud, R.W.: Empirical Research in Information Systems. The Practice of Relevance. MIS Quarterly 23, 3–16 (1999)
31. Hevner, A.R., March, S.T., Park, J., Ram, S.: Design Science in Information Systems Research. MIS Quarterly 28, 75–105 (2004)
32. Bandara, W., Gable, G.G., Rosemann, M.: Factors and Measures of Business Process Modelling: Model Building Through a Multiple Case Study. European Journal of Information Systems 14, 347–360 (2005)
33. Kuhn, T.S.: The Structure of Scientific Revolutions. Chicago University Press, Chicago, Illinois (1962)

Semantic Analysis of Flow Patterns in Business Process Modeling

Pnina Soffer[1], Yair Wand[2], and Maya Kaner[3]

[1] University of Haifa, Carmel Mountain 31905, Haifa 31905, Israel
[2] Sauder School of Business, The University of British Columbia, Vancouver, Canada
[3] Ort Braude College, Karmiel 21982, Israel
spnina@is.haifa.ac.il, yair.wand@ubc.ca, kmaya@braude.ac.il

Abstract. Control flow elements are important in process models. Such elements usually appear in graphic models as splits and joins of activity sequences. Workflow patterns reflect possible executions of different configurations of splits and joins. However, despite the importance of process flow control and workflow patterns, no way exists yet to assure that a particular set of patterns is complete and non-redundant. We use an ontologically-based model of business processes to analyze the control configurations that can exist in a process model. A process is modeled in terms of state changes of the domain in which the process occurs. The state changes are controlled by laws which model the actions allowed in the domain. This model is notation-independent and enables incorporating goals into process analysis. We use the model to suggest classification of control configurations and identify configurations that assure the enacted process can always reach its goal.

1 Introduction

The possible flows in business process execution are determined by points where parallel or alternative process paths might be taken, or where such paths merge. This paper aims at systematically analyzing, defining, and distinguishing the different types of phenomena that are described by splitting and merging in business processes. The motivation for this work is threefold.

First, while splitting and merging structures in process modeling languages are frequently well-defined formally (e.g., [1][6]), they often do not convey a well-defined ontological meaning [8]. Second, splitting and merging structures are major sources of logical errors in process models (e.g., deadlocks and lack of synchronization [2][7][9]). Third, the available notation for splitting and merging is usually not expressive enough for representing and distinguishing the different cases of possible process behaviors. Usually, AND and XOR constructs are available, sometimes an OR too (e.g., EPC [10]). In a few cases (e.g., BPMN) there are specific constructs that can express more complicated behavioral patterns, a variety of which are depicted by workflow patterns [3]. In addition, split and merge of the same logical type typically have the same graphical notation. However, while this may provide for

G. Alonso, P. Dadam, and M. Rosemann (Eds.): BPM 2007, LNCS 4714, pp. 400–407, 2007.
© Springer-Verlag Berlin Heidelberg 2007

easy visual representation, in essence, splitting and joining stand for different real-world situations. Hence, this is a case of construct overload [13]. We believe this situation can lead to modeling errors. Hence, a clear distinction of the different situations represented by splitting and merging elements is expected to assist process designers in producing logically correct models.

In this paper we suggest real-world semantics to splitting and merging in process models, and a framework to enable a systematic analysis of splitting and merging configurations. Our analysis is based on the Generic Process Model (GPM). GPM is a notation-independent framework for analyzing business processes based on Bunge's ontology [4][5] and its adaptation to information systems [13][14].

2   The Generic Process Model (GPM)

This section provides an informal and brief presentation of the ontological state-based view of a process, which we employ for our analysis. The focus of analysis is a *domain*, which is a part of the world. A domain is represented by a set of *state variables*, each depicting the value of a relevant property of the domain at a given time. A successful process is a sequence of *unstable states* of the domain, leading to a *stable state*, which reflects the process *goal*. An unstable state is a state that must change due to actions within the domain (an *internal event*) while a stable state is a state that does not change unless forced to by action of the environment (an *external event*). Internal events are governed by *transformation (transition) laws* that define the allowed (or necessary) state transitions (events).

In these terms, the task of the process designer is to define the transition law (and ways to enact it) so that the process can accomplish its goal. The goal is a set of stable states on which the process must terminate. The law is specified as mappings between sets of states and is often defined formally by predicates over the state variables used to model the properties of the domain. The process goal may also be formalized in terms of predicates that specify situations that should be achieved by the process.

Process models usually include the concept of activity (a function, a task). The state, events and laws view of a process can be used to define activities. Consider a domain as comprising *sub-domains*, each represented by a subset of the domain state variables. The state changes of sub-domains are termed the *projections* of the domain's behavior on the sub-domains. A sub-domain is said to behave *independently* if its state changes are independent of the states of other sub-domains. We then say that the domain law projects a (well-defined) law on the sub-domain.

We view an activity as a change of a sub-domain from an unstable state to a stable state with respect to its (projected) law. As an independent sub-domain changes its state to a stable one, it is possible some other independent sub-domains will become unstable and will begin transforming. Thus, an activity can lead to other activities. As long as the process is active, at least one other sub-domain is still in an unstable state.

Since a process goal can be represented explicitly, the state-based supports an analysis of goal reachability. A process whose design ensures its goal will always be achieved under a given set events external to the domain (but affecting it) is termed valid [11][12]. Our analysis is intended to support the design of valid processes.

3 Modeling and Configuring Splits and Joins

3.1 Model Assumptions

First, we assume the designer defines the law to achieve the process' goal. Hence, we consider only valid process models, i.e. those that ensure goal reachability. Our analysis depends on the observation that for such models as long as the enacted process has not reached its goal, at least one sub-domain is unstable or may become unstable as a result of a time-related event.

Second, we assume that the granularity level of the model is defined in a manner that supports the business needs. In particular, a repeated activity (e.g. processing several replications of the same product) can be viewed as one activity. Hence, we do not address a flow of multiple instances in our model.

Third, our model does not incorporate durations or resources availability. Activities are enacted immediately when they are enabled.

Finally, for simplicity we only consider a binary splitting. The model can be readily extended to address cases of more than two sub-domains.

3.2 Characterizing Parameters of the Model

Under our basic assumptions we identify five parameters to characterize all splitting and merging situations. Using the requirement that the process should reach its goal, the combinations of possible values of these parameters will determine the set of acceptable combinations of splitting and merging configurations.

Parameter 1: Domain Decomposability
Splitting and merging can relate to one of two basic situations. First, a set of states achieved at a certain point in the process may be partitioned into two or more subsets and the next transformation is defined differently for each subset. Such partitioning might occur because the law at this state becomes "sensitive" to a certain state variable. Consider, for example, a process where a standard product is manufactured, and then packaged according to each customer's requirements. Until production is completed, the customer is not considered (even though this information may be known). At the completion point, the "customer" state variable determines which packaging action will be performed. This situation is clearly an XOR split, since the domain may take exactly one of the packaging paths available.

Second, there may be a point in the process, where the domain can be decomposed into two or more independently behaving sub-domains. In such cases, for the process to continue, at least one sub-domain must be unstable. Several possibilities exist. First, several sub-domains are always in unstable states, and will change concurrently (AND split). Second, any number of sub-domains (but at least one) can be unstable (OR split). Third, exactly one sub-domain should be in an unstable state and proceed to change (XOR split). In the process discussed above, once products are ready, two independent concurrently transforming sub-domains exist: one where shipment to the customer is arranged and one where products are transferred into the warehouse.

Our first characterizing parameter identifies whether the process domain is decomposable or not. The following four parameters apply only to decomposition-related splitting and merging.

Parameter 2: The Number of Paths

For a decomposable process domain three possibilities exist:

1. Both sub-domains are in an unstable state, thus they will transform in parallel. In this case the process has *only one path* (no selection decision is made). The "splitting" is merely a result of the decomposition. This situation is typically described by "AND" splitting elements in process models.
2. Depending on some state variable(s) value(s), exactly one sub-domain can be in an unstable state. Hence, an exclusive choice between *two possible paths* is made. This situation is typically described by "XOR" in process models.
3. Depending on some state variable(s) value(s), at least one or both sub-domains can be in an unstable state. The process has *three possible paths*: (1) one sub-domain is active, (2) the other is active, and (3) both are active.

Parameter 3: Past Awareness at the Merge

In standard process design, the merge condition reflects the type of preceding split. This entails an implicit assumption that the merge decision is "aware" of the process "history". However, this cannot be taken for granted. We therefore incorporate a three-valued parameter to reflect the information available at the merge point.

1. No awareness – nothing is known about the preceding split. In other words, the view at the merge is purely *local*. We note this possibility is not of much interest, since usually the process designer is aware of the process structure.
2. Topology awareness – the type of split that precedes the merge is available at the merge point. This information can be considered available to the designer and hence incorporated in the law governing the behavior at the merge point.
3. Enactment awareness – this means that when the process is executed it is known at the merge point what happened at the preceding split. Specifically, for a two- or three- path split, it is known which path was actually chosen.

Parameter 4: Entry Condition into the Merge Sub-domain

The merge sub-domain is the sub-domain whose instability is affected by state variables of the two sub-domains. Several possibilities exist, but not all of them ensure a valid process. For example, each of the preceding sub-domains might activate the merge sub-domain, but not when both complete at the same time. It can be shown that only three cases exist for a valid process model:

1. Each branch is sufficient: stability (completion of action) of each preceding sub-domain causes instability of the merge sub-domain, independent of whether one or both sub-domains were activated.
2. Each branch is necessary and both together are sufficient: Only when both sub-domains reach stability (complete their activities) the merge sub-domain will become unstable. This is a *synchronizing merge*.

3. A specific branch is necessary and sufficient: stability of a specific one of the preceding sub-domains is necessary and sufficient for instability of the merge sub-domain. This is an *asymmetric synchronization*, where the merge can be activated by one sub-domain, or synchronize the two sub-domains, depending on which one has completed first.

Parameter 5: Process Goal Requirement

When two sub-domains become active at the split point, it may be sufficient that only one of them completes for activating the merge sub-domain, thus continuing the process. However, even if the process continues, it is possible that the goal depends on state variables that have to be set by actions in the other sub-domain. For example, one branch, necessary for the process to continue, deals with obtaining components for assembling a product. However, the process goal also includes securing means to deliver the product and this requires actions in the other sub-domain. Hence, we distinguish between two cases:

1. The process goal does not require that <u>both</u> sub-domains complete their activities. Of course, one must still complete for the process to continue.
2. The process goal is dependent on the completion of both sub-domains.

Table 1. Valid and invalid design possibilities

Past awareness	Split type	Merge entry condition		
		Each branch sufficient	Both necessary & together sufficient	Specific one sufficient
No awareness	One path (AND)	Always possible	it is not known a split happened	it is not known a split happened
	Two paths (XOR)	The only available option	it is not known two options exist	it is not known two options exist
	Three paths (OR)	The only available option	it is not known three options exist	it is not known three options exist
Topology awareness	One path (AND)	Always possible	It is known both branches must activate	It is known both branches must activate
	Two path (XOR)	Always possible	Only one branch activates	It is known one branch activated – not which one
	Three path (OR)	Always possible	It is not known if two branches activated	It is not known which branch activated
Enactment awareness	One path (AND)	Always possible	Same as for topology awareness	Same as for topology awareness
	Two path (XOR)	Always possible	Only one branch activates	whichever branch taken should suffice
	Three path (OR)	Always possible	If known that both branches active – condition on both possible(*)	If known that both branches active – condition on each possible(*)

(*) The designer can specify conditions related to both branches, but should also allow for activating the merge domain on each branch if only one is activated.

Table 2. Pattern composition (NA– "not applicable".)

No. of sub-domains	Number of paths	Past awareness	Merge entry condition	Goal requirement	Description	Example
1	2	NA	NA	NA	Single domain exclusive choice	Quality inspection determines whether a product is good and can be supplied (path 1) or needs rework (path 2). Merge after rework.
2	1	All values	One sufficient	Requires one domain	Concurrency with competition	An urgent loan is requested from two banks (each bank request is a domain). The first one to approve the loan is chosen.
2	1	Topology / enactment	One sufficient	Requires both	Concurrency with First-in-first-out (FIFO) merge	Sales data (domain1) and production data (domain 2) are collected for a periodical report, whose preparation starts once the first type of data arrives, but requires both to end.
2	1	Topology / enactment	Both necessary	Requires both	Concurrency with synchronization	When an order is received, the customer's credit (domain 1) and the availability of products (domain 2) are checked. After both complete, the order may be accepted.
2	1	Topology / enactment	Specific one sufficient	Requires one domain	Concurrency with asymmetric synch. / competition	When considering an architectural design, a professional drawing may be prepared (domain1); until it is ready, a draft may be made for demonstration purposes (domain 2). When the drawing is ready the draft is discarded and the process may proceed.
2	1	Topology / enactment	Specific one sufficient	Requires both	Concurrency with asymmetric synch. / FIFO	Information about product requirements (domain 1) and production resources (domain 2) is needed for production planning, which can start when product requirements are known, even if the resources are not known yet. When resource information arrives planning can complete.
2	2	All values	Either one sufficient	Requires one domain	Two domain exclusive choice	A product can be manufactured (domain 1) or outsourced (domain 2). Goal includes having product.
2	3	All values	One sufficient	Requires one domain	Multi-choice with competition	A message can be sent by mail (domain 1) or by fax (domain 2). If it is sent by both, the first one that arrives is addressed, and the other one is discarded.
2	3	Enactment	One sufficient	Requires both	Multi-choice with First-in-first-out (FIFO) merge	A person makes a claim to the insurance company after a car accident regarding car injury or physical injury (or both). Each claim (domain) is processed separately, and when its processing is completed the person is paid.
2	3	Enactment	Both necessary	Requires both	Multi-choice with synchronization	Planning a trip may involve flight booking (domain 1) and hotel reservation (domain 2). If both are performed, they have to be completed before the trip can take place.
2	3	Enactment	Specific one sufficient	Requires one domain	Multi-choice with asymmetric synch. / competition	A new employee receives salary only after his details are recorded in the information system (domain1). Before that, the company may make a cash advance (domain 2), not needed if salary is paid on time.
2	3	Enactment	Specific one sufficient	Requires both	Multi-choice with asymmetric synchronization / FIFO	Planning a trip may involve flight booking (domain 1) and hotel reservation (domain 2). Trip can begin before all hotels are reserved, but not before flight is booked. Some hotels can still be booked during the trip.

3.3 Combining Parameter Values

The combinations of the above parameters provide possible split and merge configurations. Analysis of these configurations can identify those that will always progress and those that may fail to progress in certain situations, thus preventing a process from reaching its goal. The latter should not be used in valid process models.

Table 1 presents the possible combinations of parameters 2-4. Combinations allowing goal reachability are marked by clear boxes. Combinations that do not guarantee process success are marked by shaded boxes. For example, a two-path split (XOR) leading to a merge where both branches are necessary cannot progress to the process goal, and is hence not a valid configuration.

Table 2 enumerates all possible valid combinations of the five parameters. In some cases, as indicated in the table, different values of the same parameters support the same behavior (e.g., when one sub-domain is sufficient for activating the merge, all valid values of past awareness may be considered equivalent). To illustrate the derivation of Table 2, consider, for example, lines 2 and 3. Line 2 refers to the case where the process continues when one branch completes, regardless of whether a second branch even exists. Hence, the goal should be reachable based on any of the branches completing. On the other hand, in line 3 it is known two branches were activated. Hence the process goal can depend on both.

4   Conclusion

Attempts to distinguish different types and behaviors represented by splitting and merging elements in process models were made in the past. The most comprehensive one is probably the workflow pattern initiative [3]. Workflow patterns address, in addition to flow structures, workflow management system functionality (e.g., cancellation). Some of our patterns are included in the control flow patterns, while others are not. Specifically, we distinguish between single-domain and two-domain XOR, and identify asymmetric synchronization, where synchronization may or may not be required, depending on the branch which completes first.

This paper adds to extant analysis in several ways. First, it anchors splitting and merging elements in an ontological theory, thus suggesting a real-world interpretation of process control elements. Second, it provides a framework for systematic identification of splitting and merging configurations. The framework is based on an explicitly specified set of assumptions and parameters. It can be shown that under this set the identified set of patterns is complete, if a process model is required to assure that the process can always reach its goal.

The framework thus forms a basis for further systematic analysis that can be achieved by relaxing these assumptions. Such analysis can yield a broader set of patterns, whose completeness with respect to its set of underlying assumptions can be analyzed. Third, the identified patterns include cases which have not been indicated and discussed so far. Finally, we identify patterns that provide for goal reachability of the designed process, thus suggesting a way to support the task of process designers.

Future research should investigate the applicability of the identified patterns as a benchmark for evaluating and developing process modeling languages and as guidance to the actual practice of process design. We believe that incorporating the view suggested in this paper into the practice of modeling (through, e.g., modeling rules) may lead to an improved quality of designed processes.

Acknowledgement. This work was supported in part by a grant to one of the authors from the Natural Sciences and Engineering Research Council of Canada.

References

[1]   van der Aalst, W.M.P.: The Application of Petri-nets to Workflow Management. Journal of Circuits, Systems and Computers 8(1), 21–66 (1998)

[2]   van der Aalst, W.M.P., Hirnschall, A., Verbeek, H.M.W.: An Alternative Way to Analyze Workflow Graphs. In: Pidduck, A.B., Mylopoulos, J., Woo, C.C., Ozsu, M.T. (eds.) CAiSE 2002. LNCS, vol. 2348, pp. 535–552. Springer, Heidelberg (2002)

[3]   van der Aalst, W.M.P., ter Hofstede, A.H.M., Kiepuszewski, B., Barros, A.P.: Workflow Patterns. Distributed and Parallel Databases 14(1), 5–51 (2003)

[4]   Bunge, M.: Treatise on Basic Philosophy: Ontology I: The Furniture of the World, vol. 3, Reidel, Boston (1977)

[5]   Bunge, M.: Treatise on Basic Philosophy: Ontology II: A World of Systems, vol. 4, Reidel, Boston (1979)

[6]   Kiepuszewski, B., ter Hofstede, A.H.M., van der Aalst, W.M.P.: Fundamentals of control flow in workflows. Acta Informatica 39(3), 143–209 (2003)

[7]   Kindler, E.: On the Semantics of EPCs: A Framework for Resolving the Vicious Circle. In: Desel, J., Pernici, B., Weske, M. (eds.) BPM 2004. LNCS, vol. 3080, pp. 82–97. Springer, Heidelberg (2004)

[8]   Rosemann, M., Recker, J., Indulska, M., Green, P.: A Study of the Evolution of the Representational Capabilities of Process Modeling Grammars. In: Dubois, E., Pohl, K. (eds.) CAiSE 2006. LNCS, vol. 4001, pp. 447–461. Springer, Heidelberg (2006)

[9]   Sadiq, W., Orlowska, M.E.: On Correctness Issues in Conceptual Modeling of Workflows. In: Proceedings of the 5th European Conference on Information Systems, Cork, Ireland, pp. 943–964 (1997)

[10] Scheer, A.W.: ARIS-Business Process Modeling. Springer, Berlin (1998)

[11] Soffer, P., Wand, Y.: Goal-driven Analysis of Process Model Validity. In: Persson, A., Stirna, J. (eds.) CAiSE 2004. LNCS, vol. 3084, pp. 521–535. Springer, Heidelberg (2004)

[12] Soffer, P., Wand, Y.: Goal-Driven Multi-Process Analysis, Journal of the Association of Information Systems (forthcoming, 2007)

[13] Wand, Y., Weber, R.: On the Ontological Expressiveness of Information Systems Analysis and Design Grammars. Journal of Information Systems 3, 217–237 (1993)

[14] Wand, Y., Weber, R.: Towards a Theory of Deep Structure of Information Systems. Journal of Information Systems 5(3), 203–223 (1995)

Towards CIM to PIM Transformation: From Secure Business Processes Defined in BPMN to Use-Cases

Alfonso Rodríguez[1], Eduardo Fernández-Medina[2], and Mario Piattini[2]

[1] Departamento de Auditoría e Informática
Universidad del Bio Bio
Chillán, Chile
alfonso@ubiobio.cl
[2] ALARCOS Research Group, Information Systems and Technologies Department,
UCLM-Indra Research and Development Institute,
University of Castilla-La Mancha
Ciudad Real, Spain
{Eduardo.FdezMedina,Mario.Piattini}@uclm.es

Abstract. The software community is currently paying attention to model transformation. The MDA approach is particularly orientated towards solving the problems of time, cost and quality associated with software creation. Enterprises are, moreover, aware of the importance that business processes and security have in relation to their competitive position and performance. In our previous work, we have proposed a BPMN extension which can be used to define security requirement in business process specifications. A Secure Business Process description is that of computation independent models in an MDA context. In this paper we propose a CIM to PIM transformation composed of QVT rules. Various UML use cases, which will be part of an information system, are obtained from the secure business process description.

Keywords: MDA, Business Processes, Security Requirement, BPMN, QVT.

1 Introduction

In recent years, enterprise performance has been linked to the capability that each enterprise has to adapt itself to the changes that arise in the business market. In this context, Business Processes (BP) have become valuable resources in the maintenance of competitiveness.

Furthermore, economic globalization, along with the intensive use of communication and information technologies, have given rise to the situation of enterprises not only expanding their businesses but also increasing their vulnerability. As a consequence of this, and with the increase in the number of attacks on systems, it is highly probable that sooner or later an intrusion may be successful.

Although the importance of business process security is widely accepted, the business analyst perspective in relation to security has hardly been dealt with until now. In the majority of cases, the identification of security requirements has been somewhat confused. In general, there has been a tendency to identify functional

G. Alonso, P. Dadam, and M. Rosemann (Eds.): BPM 2007, LNCS 4714, pp. 408–415, 2007.

security requirements. This type of requirements varies according to the type of application, whilst the security requirements do not vary at a high level of abstraction [6]. In previous work [18] we introduced security representation into business processes. To do so, we extended the BPMN-BPD (Business Process Modeling Notation - Business Process Diagram) [3]. A BPSec extension was created which allowed us to capture those security requirements which had been expressed by the business analyst. Such a specification gave origin to a Secure Business Process (SBP).

Moreover, software engineering is currently greatly influenced by MDA, a new paradigm that claims to work at a model and metamodel level. The MDA approach is composed of the following perspectives: the computation independent viewpoint (CIM, Computation Independent Model), the platform independent viewpoint (PIM, Platform Independent Model) and the platform specific viewpoint (PSM, Platform Specific Model) [14]. Since these models represent a different abstraction of the same system, an integration/transformation mechanism is required to establish *how* to move from one level to another. The OMG proposal for a transformation language is QVT (Query/View/Transformation) [17].

In this paper, we demonstrate how a set of UML Use Cases [15] which are considered to be a PIM can be obtained from the specification of an SBP, which is considered to be a CIM. The transformations have been described as a set of QVT rules, checklists and refinement rules. Both the description of the SBP and the use cases can be used in the software development process. We have chosen to use the UP (Unified Process) [9].

The structure of the remainder of the paper is as follows: in Section 2, we shall summarize our proposal and related work. In Section 3 we shall present the main issues concerned with security requirement specification in business processes. In Section 4, we shall describe the way in which use cases can be obtained. Finally, in Section 5, we shall put forward an example and in Section 6 our conclusions will be drawn.

2 Our Proposal and Related Work

A business process which has been constructed by a business analyst is useful in the business environment and can also be used in the software construction process. A BP description contains important system requirements (a starting point for all development processes in modern software). In this work, we have paid special attention to the attainment of more concrete models derived from the BP specification which are, in particular, related to the security requirements specification in BP.

The basic aspects of our proposal are shown in Figure 1. The first column (on the left) shows three types of models which conform to the MDA. In the last column we can see the UP disciplines. The central part shows our proposal and the artifacts which are derived from its application. The SBP specification is made by using the BPMN-BPD and BPSec extension. The transformation is made by using QVT rules, checklists and refinement rules (in dark grey). If Figure 1 is observed horizontally it will be noted that an SBP description corresponds with a CIM model and can be used as a complement to the *Business Modeling* discipline of the UP. In addition, the Use Cases, which form a part of a PIM model, will complement the *Requirement* and *Analysis & Design* disciplines.

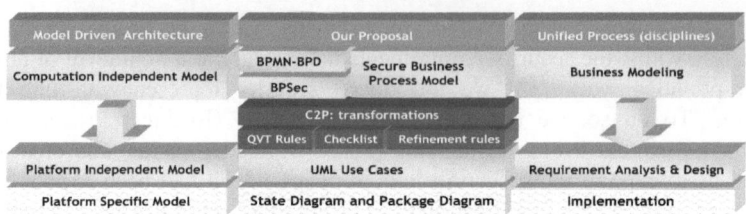

Fig. 1. An overview of our proposal

In related works we found that use cases (or misuse cases) [1, 5, 10, 16, 20], have been used to capture security requirements. However, unlike our proposal, they are not directly derived from BPMN-BPD security specifications.

In related works to the attainment of use cases from BP specifications, we have discovered that in [19], the possibility of obtaining use cases from a BP specification made with BPMN is suggested, and in [11], the automatic attainment of UML artifacts from a BP description that was made using BPMN is proposed. The authors extend the BPMN to add information about the sequence and the input and output flows. This allows them to apply rules from which use cases, state diagrams, sequence and collaboration are achieved. In [21], a transformation which was made from a business process described with UML 2.0 Activity Diagrams to use cases is stated and finally, in [4], use cases are obtained from business process models that are not represented by activity diagrams. Our proposal differs to the above works in that: (i) the business process specification includes security requirements, (ii) we have used the QVT for the specification of the transformations, and (iii) we have related the resulting artifacts to a software development process.

3   Security in Business Process

The works which are related to the specification of security requirements in business processes [2, 7, 8, 13] all coincide in the idea that it is necessary to capture the point of view of the business expert with regard to security, and to include these specifications within the software development process.

At present, security requirements are easy for business analysts to identify because: (i) business process representation has improved in BPMN, (ii) the security requirement tends to have the same basic kinds of valuable and potentially vulnerable assets [6], and (iii) empirical studies show that it is common at the business process level for customers and end users to be able to express their security needs [12].

Consequently, we have approached the problem of including security requirements in business processes by extending the BPMN-BPD. The proposed extension, which we have called BPSec, considers the graphical representation of security requirements; a non-limited list, taken from the taxonomy proposed in [6].

In our proposal we have used a padlock (see Figure 2a), standard *de facto*, to represent security requirements. The same symbol, the padlock, but with a twisted corner (see Figure 2b) is used to represent a Security Requirement with Audit Register. The set of security requirements are shown in Figure 2.

Fig. 2. Icons to represent security requirements in BPSec

4   Rules and Checklists to Obtain Use Cases from an SBP Model

A business process, built by a business analyst, is also very useful in a software construction process since it can be used to obtain numerous kinds of system requirements. Use cases and security use cases are derived from the SBP specification using BPMN-BPD by applying a set of QVT rules, checklists and refinement rules.

The QVT rules are orientated towards identifying actors and related use cases from Pools, Lanes, Groups, Activities, and security requirement specifications. In Table 1, rules expressed in textual QVT are described.

Table 1. Mapping between BPMN-BPD and Use Case elements

```
transformation BusinessProcessDiagram2UseCaseDiagram
   top relation R1   // from Pool to Actor
   {
      checkonly domain bpmn_BusinessprocessDiagram p:Pool {name=n}
      enforce domain uml_UseCaseDiagram a:Actor{name=n}
      where { ap.containedNode → forAll(cn:Activity|R4(cn)) }
   }
   top relation R2   // from Lane to Actor
   {
      checkonly domain bpmn_BusinessprocessDiagram l:Lane {name=n}
      enforce domain uml_UseCaseDiagram a:Actor{name=n}
      where { ap.containedNode → forAll(cn:Activity|R4(cn)) }
   }
   top relation R3   // from Group to Actor
   {
      checkonly domain bpmn_BusinessProcessDiagram g:Group {name=n}
      enforce domain uml_UseCaseDiagram a:Actor {name=n}
      where { ap.containedNode → forAll(cn:Activity|R4(cn)) }
   }
   relation R4 // from Activities to UseCase
   {
      checkonly domain bpmn_BusinessProcessDiagram ac:Activity {name=n, inPartition=ap}
      enforce domain uml_UseCaseDiagram uc:UseCase {name=n, subject= ACTORS: Set(Actor)};
      where { ACTORS→including (a:Actor{name=ap.name}) }
   }
transformation BPSec2UseCaseDiagram
   top relation R5   // from Security Requirement to subject
   {
      checkonly domain bpsec_BPSec sr:SecurityRequirement {requirementtype=n}
       enforce domain uml_UseCaseDiagram c:Clasifier {name=n}
   }
   top relation R6   // from Security Requirement to subject
   {
      checkonly domain bpsec_BPSec sr:SecurityRequirement
      enforce domain uml_UseCaseDiagram a:Actor {name="Security Staff"}
   }
```

A set of checklists has been created through which to obtain the security related use cases. Each checklist contains a set of generic tasks that must be applied to a specific SBP specification. A selection of these checklists is shown in Table 2.

Table 2. Checklist through which to obtain security use cases

Access Control
«Preconditions»   Secure Role, and Permissions over the objects in the secure role scope
«Postconditions» Secure role validated to access to resources, Permissions over the validated objects, and Audit Register (optional)
– Assign secure role to the partition, region or action

– Validate the secure role (this task is complemented with misuse cases described in [5]). This task is divided into:
  • Identify the secure role. This implies recognizing roles before starting the interaction
  • Authenticate the secure role: This task implies the verification of the role identity before starting the interaction
  • Authorize the secure role. This implies assigning privileges to roles that were duly authenticated

– Verify permissions over the objects in the role secure field. This implies a review of the permissions granted to the objects that are within the field of access control specification
– If audit register has been specified, then the information related to the security role, the security permissions and the objects in the access control specification field must be stored
Privacy
«Preconditions»   Secure Role
«Postconditions» Audit Register (optional)
– Assign a secure role (if anonymity was specified, then the role is generic and expires together with the session)

– Validate the role. This task is divided into:
  • Identify the secure role. This implies recognizing the role before starting the interaction
  • Authenticate the secure role. This task implies verifying the role identity before starting the interaction
  • Authorize the secure role. This implies assigning privileges to the role that was duly authenticated

– Verify revelation permissions (anonymity and confidentiality)
– Verify storage permissions (anonymity only)
– Verify audit register specification
– If audit register has been specified, then the information related to the security role must be stored

Finally, the refinement rules (see Table 3) are focused upon enriching the specifications obtained through the application of the QVT rules and checklists.

Table 3. Use case Refinement Rules (RR)

Rule	Description
RR1	Subject name (not related to security specification) is obtained from the business process name
RR2	Subject name for security requirement must be complemented with the name of the BPMN-BPD element
RR3	Group Name is obtained by linking the Pool or Lane names in which Group is contained
RR4	Main Actor corresponds to the Pool, Lane or Group name in which Start Event is present
RR5	Actor Generalization is obtained from Pool and Lane
RR6	Redundant specifications must be eliminated

5   Example

Our illustrative example (see Figure 3) describes a typical business process for the admission of patients to a health-care institution. In this case, the business analyst has identified the Pools: "Patient", "Administration Area" (divided into "Accounting" and "Admission" lanes), and "Medical Area" (divided into "Medical Evaluation" and "Examination" lanes).

The business analyst has specified «Privacy» (anonymity) for the "Patient" Pool, with the aim of preventing the disclosure of sensitive information about Patients. S/he has specified «Nonrepudiation» for the Message Flow that goes from the "Fill out Admission Request" activity to the "Review Admission Request" activity with the aim of avoiding the denial of the "Admission Request" reception. And finally, «AccessControl» has been defined in a Pool called "Administration Area". A «SecurityRole» can be derived from this specification. All objects in a Pool region must be considered for permission specification. Access control specification has been complemented with Audit Register requirement. This implies that information about the security role and security permissions must be registered.

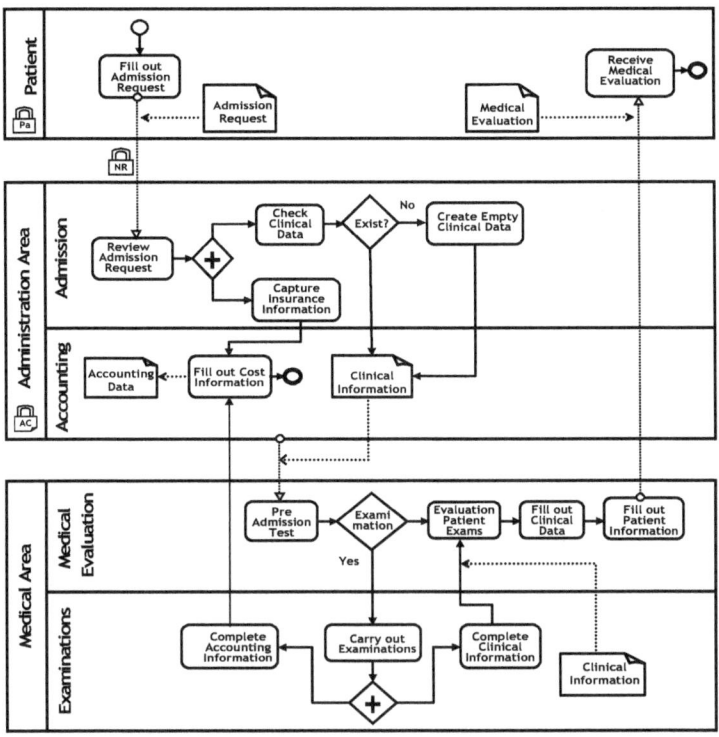

Fig. 3. Patient Admission to a Medical Institution

In Table 4 both the results of the application of the transformations defined with QVT and the application of the refinement rules are described.

Table 4. QVT and refinement rules applied to Patient Admission Business Process

Rule	Use Case element
R1	Actors: Patient, Administration Area, and Medical Area
R2	Actors: Admission, Accounting, Medical Evaluation and Examinations
R3	Actor: ⋯
R4	Use Case: Fill out Admission Request, Receive Medical Evaluation, Review Admission Request, Capture Insurance Information, Check Clinical Data, Create Empty Clinical Data, Fill out Cost Information, Pre-Admission Test, Evaluate Patient Examinations, Fill out Clinical Data, Fill out Patient Information, Complete Accounting Information, Carry out Examinations, and Complete Clinical information
R5	Subjects: Privacy, Non Repudiation, and Access Control
R6	Actor: Security Staff
RR1	Subject: Patient Admission
RR2	Subjects: Privacy in Patient, Non Repudiation in Admission Request, and Access Control in Administration Area
RR3	Actor: ⋯
RR4	Main Actor: Patient
RR5	Actor: Administration Area (Admission and Accounting) and Medical Area (Medical Evaluation and Exams)
RR6	Use cases: Review Admission Request, Capture Insurance Information, Check Clinical Data, Create Empty Clinical Data, and Fill out Cost Information can be excluded from the subject "Access Control in Administration Area"

In Figure 4, some use cases derived from the SBP for the admission of patients are graphically shown. The general use case is shown on the left-hand side and two use cases derived from security requirement specification (Privacy and Non Repudiation) are shown on the right-hand side.

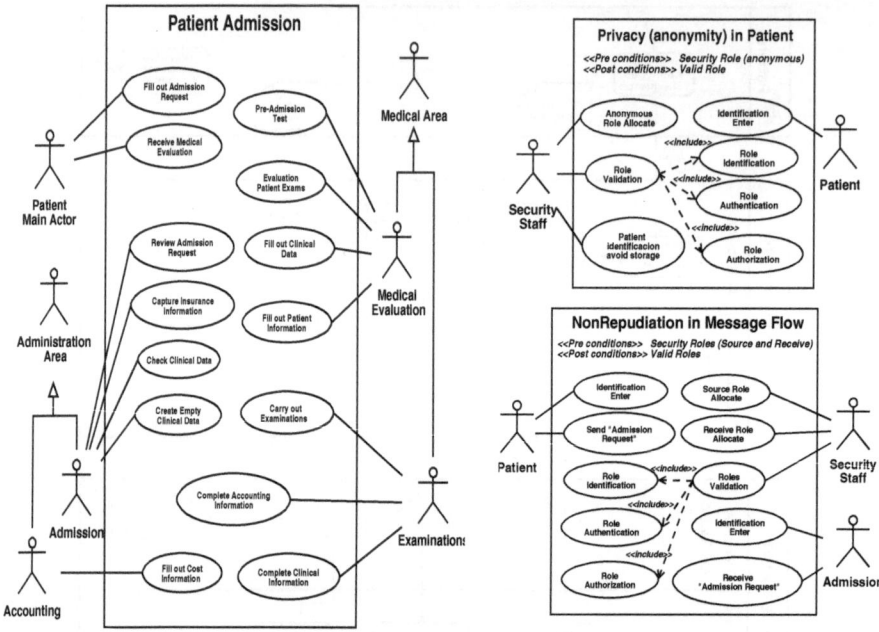

Fig. 4. Patient Admission, Privacy, and Non Repudiation use cases specification

6 Conclusion

One means by which to confront the problem of security consists of incorporating it into the business process specifications at an early stage. At this level, it is possible to capture security requirements which take the business analysts' viewpoint into account. In previous works, we have proposed a BPSec extension through which it is possible to specify security requirements at a high level of abstraction. Nevertheless, it is necessary to enable these specifications to form part of more concrete solutions. With this purpose in mind, we have used the MDA focus and QVT rules to specify the rules which allow us to pass from CIM to PIM. The result has been a set of UML Use Cases which have been obtained from the SBP specification described with BPMN-BPD.

Ongoing work is orientated towards enriching transformations in order to make it possible to obtain more complete models of use cases. Furthermore, in our future work we intend to optimize the prototype that we have created to carry out the transformations.

Acknowledgments. This research is part of the following projects: DIMENSIONS (PBC-05-012-1), and MISTICO (PBC06-0082) both partiality supported by the FEDER and the "Consejería de Ciencia y Tecnología de la Junta de Comunidades de Castilla-La Mancha", Spain, COMPETISOFT (506PI287), granted by CYTED and ESFINGE (TIN2006-15175-C05-05/) granted by the "Dirección General de Investigación del Ministerio de Ciencia y Tecnología", Spain.

References

1. Alexander, I.F.: Misuse Cases: Use Cases with Hostile Intent, IEEE Software. IEEE Software 20(1), 58–66 (2003)
2. Backes, M., Pfitzmann, B., Waider, M.: Security in Business Process Engineering. In: van der Aalst, W.M.P., ter Hofstede, A.H.M., Weske, M. (eds.) BPM 2003. LNCS, vol. 2678, pp. 168–183. Springer, Heidelberg (2003)
3. BPMN: Business Process Modeling Notation Specification, OMG Final Adopted Specification, dtc/06-02-01 (2006), In http://www.bpmn.org/Documents/ OMG%20Final%20-Adopted%20BPMN%201-0%20Spec%2006-02-01.pdf
4. Dijkman, R.M., Joosten, S.M.M.: An Algorithm to Derive Use Cases from Business Processes. In: 6th International Conference on Software Engineering and Applications (SEA). Boston, USA, pp. 679–684 (2002)
5. Firesmith, D.: Security Use Case. Journal of Object Technology 2(3), 53–64 (2003)
6. Firesmith, D.: Specifying Reusable Security Requirements. Journal of Object Technology 3(1), 61–75 (2004)
7. Herrmann, G., Pernul, G.: Viewing Business Process Security from Different Perspectives. In: 11th International Bled Electronic Commerce Conference. Slovenia, pp. 89–103 (1998)
8. Herrmann, P., Herrmann, G.: Security requirement analysis of business processes. Electronic Commerce Research 6(3-4), 305–335 (2006)
9. Jacobson, I., Booch, G., Rumbaugh, J.: The Unified Software Development Process, p. 463 (1999)
10. Jürjens, J.: Using UMLsec and goal trees for secure systems development. In: Nyberg, K., Heys, H.M. (eds.) SAC 2002. LNCS, vol. 2595, pp. 1026–1030. Springer, Heidelberg (2003)
11. Liew, P., Kontogiannis, P., Tong, T.: A Framework for Business Model Driven Development. In: 12 International Workshop on Software Technology and Engineering Practice (STEP), pp. 47–56 (2004)
12. Lopez, J., Montenegro, J.A., Vivas, J.L., Okamoto, E., Dawson, E.: Specification and design of advanced authentication and authorization services. Computer Standards & Interfaces 27(5), 467–478 (2005)
13. Maña, A., Montenegro, J.A., Rudolph, C., Vivas, J.L.: A business process-driven approach to security engineering. In: Mařík, V., Štěpánková, O., Retschitzegger, W. (eds.) DEXA 2003. LNCS, vol. 2736, pp. 477–481. Springer, Heidelberg (2003)
14. Object Management Group: MDA Guide Version 1.0.1 (2003), In http://www.omg.org/docs/omg/03-06-01.pdf
15. Object Management Group: Unified Modeling Language: Superstructure, version 2.0, formal/05-07-04 (2005), In http://www.omg.org/docs/formal/05-07-04.pdf
16. Popp, G., Jürjens, J., Wimmel, G., Breu, R.: Security-Critical System Development with Extended Use Cases. In: 10th Asia-Pacific Software Engineering Conference (APSEC). Chiang Mai, Thailand, pp. 478–487 (2003)
17. QVT: Meta Object Facility (MOF) 2.0 Query/View/Transformation Specification, OMG Adopted Specification ptc/05-11-01, p. 204 (2005)
18. Rodríguez, A., Fernández-Medina, E., Piattini, M.: A BPMN Extension for the Modeling of Security Requirements in Business Processes. IEICE Transactions on Information and Systems E90-D(4), 745–752 (2007)
19. Rungworawut, W., Senivongse, T.: A Guideline to Mapping Business Processes to UML Class Diagrams. WSEAS Trans. on Computers 4(11), 1526–1533 (2005)
20. Sindre, G., Opdahl, A.: Capturing Security Requirements through Misuse Cases, Norsk informatikkonferanse (NIK). Trondheim, Norway, pp. 219–230 (2001)
21. Štolfa, S., Vondrák, I.: A Description of Business Process Modeling as a Tool for Definition of Requirements Specification. In: Systems Integration 12th Annual International Conference. Prague, Czech Republic, pp. 463–469 (2004)

Author Index

Lecture Notes in Computer Science

Sublibrary 3: Information Systems and Application, incl. Internet/Web and HCI

For information about Vols. 1–4282
please contact your bookseller or Springer